Financial Markets and Financial Crises

A National Bureau
of Economic Research
Project Report

Financial Markets and Financial Crises

Edited by R. Glenn Hubbard

The University of Chicago Press

Chicago and London

R. Glenn Hubbard is professor of economics and finance at the Graduate School of Business at Columbia University, and a research associate of the National Bureau of Economic Research.

The University of Chicago Press, Chicago 60637
The University of Chicago Press, Ltd., London

Printed in the United States of America
00 99 98 97 96 95 94 93 92 91 5 4 3 2 1

Library of Congress Cataloging-in-Publication Data

Financial markets and financial crises / edited by R. Glenn Hubbard.
p. cm. —(A National Bureau of Economic Research project report)
"These papers were presented at the NBER conference . . . held in Key Biscayne, Florida, March 23–24, 1990"—
Includes indexes.
ISBN 0-226-35588-8 (alk. paper)
1. Finance—United States—History—Congresses. 2. Financial institutions—United States—History—Congresses. 3. Depressions—History—Congresses. 4. Panics (Finance)—Congresses. 5. Financial crises. I. Hubbard, R. Glenn. II. National Bureau of Economic Research. III. Series.
HG181.F6434 1991
338.5′42—dc20 91-8730
CIP

♾The paper used in this publication meets the minimum requirements of the American National Standard for Information Sciences—Permanence of Paper for Printed Library Materials, ANSI Z39.48–1984.

Relation of the Directors to the Work and Publications of the National Bureau of Economic Research

1. The object of the National Bureau of Economic Research is to ascertain and to present to the public important economic facts and their interpretation in a scientific and impartial manner. The Board of Directors is charged with the responsibility of ensuring that the work of the National Bureau is carried on in strict conformity with this object.

2. The President of the National Bureau shall submit to the Board of Directors, or to its Executive Committee, for their formal adoption all specific proposals for research to be instituted.

3. No research report shall be published by the National Bureau until the President has sent each member of the Board a notice that a manuscript is recommended for publication and that in the President's opinion it is suitable for publication in accordance with the principles of the National Bureau. Such notification will include an abstract or summary of the manuscript's content and a response form for use by those Directors who desire a copy of the manuscript for review. Each manuscript shall contain a summary drawing attention to the nature and treatment of the problem studied, the character of the data and their utilization in the report, and the main conclusions reached.

4. For each manuscript so submitted, a special committee of the Directors (including Directors Emeriti) shall be appointed by majority agreement of the President and Vice Presidents (or by the Executive Committee in case of inability to decide on the part of the President and Vice Presidents), consisting of the three Directors selected as nearly as may be one from each general division of the Board. The names of the special manuscript committee shall be stated to each Director when notice of the proposed publication is submitted to him. It shall be the duty of each member of the special manuscript committee to read the manuscript. If each member of the manuscript committee signifies his approval within thirty days of the transmittal of the manuscript, the report may be published. If at the end of that period any member of the manuscript committee withholds his approval, the President shall then notify each member of the Board, requesting approval or disapproval of publication, and thirty days additional shall be granted for this purpose. The manuscript shall then not be published unless at least a majority of the entire Board who shall have voted on the proposal within the time fixed for the receipt of votes shall have approved.

5. No manuscript may be published, though approved by each member of the special manuscript committee, until forty-five days have elapsed from the transmittal of the report in manuscript form. The interval is allowed for the receipt of any memorandum of dissent or reservation, together with a brief statement of his reasons, that any member may wish to express; and such memorandum of dissent or reservation shall be published with the manuscript if he so desires. Publication does not, however, imply that each member of the Board has read the manuscript, or that either members of the Board in general or the special committee have passed on its validity in every detail.

6. Publications of the National Bureau issued for informational purposes concerning the work of the Bureau and its staff, or issued to inform the public of activities of Bureau staff, and volumes issued as a result of various conferences involving the National Bureau shall contain a specific disclaimer noting that such publication has not passed through the normal review procedures required in this resolution. The Executive Committee of the Board is charged with review of all such publications from time to time to ensure that they do not take on the character of formal research reports of the National Bureau, requiring formal Board approval.

7. Unless otherwise determined by the Board or exempted by the terms of paragraph 6, a copy of this resolution shall be printed in each National Bureau publication.

(Resolution adopted October 25, 1926, as revised through September 30, 1974)

Contents

Acknowledgments

These papers were presented at the NBER conference, "Financial Markets and Financial Crisis," held in Key Biscayne, Florida, March 23–24, 1990. The research represents the culmination of efforts in one stage of the NBER's project on reducing the risk of financial crisis. I am grateful to Martin Feldstein for advice and support in the design of the program. Financial support was generously provided by the Ford Foundation, the Lilly Endowment, and the Seaver Institute. Kirsten Foss Davis and Ilana Hardesty ensured the smooth functioning of the conference with their customary spirit and efficiency. Finally, I would like to thank Mark Fitz-Patrick at the NBER and Julie McCarthy at the University of Chicago Press for their editorial guidance.

R. Glenn Hubbard
New York, New York

Introduction

R. Glenn Hubbard

Concern over financial crises is nothing new. Indeed, the operation of financial markets and institutions has often been reshaped in the wake of financial crises or panics—for example, the founding of the Federal Reserve System following financial panics in the late nineteenth and early twentieth centuries, or the regulation of U.S. banking in the aftermath of widespread bank failures in the early 1930s. While public policy has been focused largely on regulation and financial market developments, (at least) two deeper questions remain.

First, what does one mean by "financial crisis"? The old adage that "you would know one when you see it" provides an insufficient framework for analysis beyond deduction from case studies. The papers in this volume reflect a different framework for thinking about financial crises as episodes of breakdowns in financial trade. "Financial trade" refers to the way in which financial contracts, institutions, and markets channel funds from ultimate savers to ultimate investors in the economy, allocate risk, and provide information about and incentives for borrowers' performance. To the extent that actual episodes of panic or crisis are rare or unpredictable, economic research can focus discussion by analyzing why observed financial contracts, markets, and institutions exist. This microeconomic approach facilitates examination of the dynamic response of financial trade to economic disturbances.

Second, can or do financial crises affect the real economy in an important way? It is this query which has attracted the interest of macroeconomists. An emphasis on disruptions in financial trade has figured prominently in the examination of the economic effects of historical crises. Macroeconomic concerns extend to contemporary issues as well—for example, problems in financial institutions exposed to LDC debt and risky domestic corporate debt.

R. Glenn Hubbard is professor of economics and finance at the Graduate School of Business at Columbia University, and a research associate of the National Bureau of Economic Research.

Potential topics for analysis of these questions about financial crises as breakdowns in financial trade extend beyond the scope of any one collection of papers. In this volume, contributors address aspects of four themes:

1. ways in which problems in contracting in financial markets can magnify economic disturbances;
2. use of historical episodes of financial panics to discriminate among alternative hypotheses of the economic role of financial institutions;
3. constraints on public policy posed by (perceived or actual) fragility of financial markets or institutions; and
4. case studies of problems in one contemporary crisis, the sharp contraction of the U.S. savings and loan industry in the 1980s.

Financial Factors and Economic Activity

Microeconomic analyses of breakdowns in financial trade have relied on models of financial contracting under asymmetric information.[1] When borrowers have private information about their investment opportunities or about the way in which they allocate the funds contributed by outside investors, finance contracts not only allocate risk among investing parties but also serve to align the interests of insiders with those of suppliers of capital. In other words, financial arrangements will be structures to mitigate "agency costs." Movements in the stakes of insiders (internal finance) or in the availability of finance from outsiders specializing in information gathering and monitoring (e.g., banks) can have real effects—that is, on the level and variability of firms' investment, employment, or production.[2] To the extent that these movements are common across firms (owing, for example, to cyclical fluctuations in firms' internal funds or to "credit crunches"), magnification of effects of economic disturbances is possible.

Mark Gertler, Anil Kashyap, and I pursue one aspect of this line of thinking to obtain an indicator of financial trouble. We motivate a financial propagation mechanism by providing a rationale for why the agency costs of external finance may fluctuate countercyclically. Countercyclical movements in the wedge between the costs of external and internal finance in turn introduce a kind of "accelerator" effect, magnifying investment and output fluctuations. A key implication of these theories is that the spread between risky and safe interest rates should move inversely with investment and output. This implication is of particular interest, since recent work on postwar U.S. data has emphasized the role of interest rate differentials between risky and safe debt in forecasting real GNP (Stock and Watson 1989); increases in the spread are associated with subsequent downturns in GNP growth.

Gertler, Kashyap, and I stress an interpretation in which the widening of the spread is associated with increasing agency costs of external finance. In addition to being compatible with the time-series evidence, the theory also provides a formal underpinning for studies of financial crisis which have emphasized sharp increases in the spread as precursors to financially induced disruptions in real activity. In our model, changes in the interest rate spread predict future movements in investment and output. We present an example using the Euler equation corresponding to firms' intertemporal decisions about investment. Situations are identified where, owing to agency problems, the basic Euler equation for investment is violated. Shifts in interest rate differentials help predict investment in these periods. We present corroborating evidence for U.S. producers' durable equipment investment over portions of the postwar period.

Returning to microeconomic models of financial contracts and financial crisis, one potential "leading indicator" of financial crisis is a sharp reduction in the net worth of borrowers in the economy. A clear example of such an adverse shock is a debt deflation. If debt contracts are written in nominal terms, then the real values of both the principal obligation and the debt-service burden rise in response to a general deflation in prices. The significant deflation of the late 1920s and early 1930s is a well-known case, with international transmission facilitated by countries' adherence to the gold standard.

While the connection between gold standard linkages and international deflation is intuitive, the link between deflation (a nominal disturbance) and depression (a protracted decline in real activity) is not. It is this connection which is explored in the paper by Ben Bernanke and Harold James. Bernanke and James review some channels suggested by previous research—movements in interest rates or real wages—but focus their attention on a breakdown in financial trade, the disruptive effect of deflation on the financial system. They consider two mechanisms: (i) debt-deflation shocks to firms' net worth and (ii) the failure of banks with nominal demandable liabilities and troubled loan assets. These mechanisms extend previous research by Bernanke (1983) and Bernanke and Gertler (1990) on links between the financial system and the real economy.

Bernanke and James analyze the connection between deflation and depression by exploiting cross-sectional variation across twenty-four countries during the interwar period. Their goal is to assess differences (e.g., in output growth) between countries experiencing banking crises and those that did not, or between countries remaining on the international gold standard and those that did not. For each country, they use historical studies to classify periods of financial crisis and find that periods of financial crisis have a significant role in explaining the connection between declining prices and declining output. That is, by exploiting cross-sectional variation in institutions or historical development, it can be shown that countries for which deflationary shocks precipitated financial panics had significantly worse declines in economic activity than countries in which the financial system was more stable. The authors argue that much of the residual impact of deflation on output growth (that part not explained by financial crises) could be accounted for by debt-deflation effects on borrowers' net worth.[3] The Bernanke-James paper provides a careful example of the effects of the efficiency of financial trade on economic growth.

Information Problems and the Origins of Financial Panics

Considering financial panics or crises as breakdowns in financial trade, one can attempt to classify such events methodically.[4] Studying the behavior of financial markets during such periods is likely to be helpful in distinguishing among alternative economic explanations of events. Understanding the microeconomic foundations of observed disruptions in financial trade in turn provides guidance for analyses of central bank policy and regulation.

In his paper, Frederic S. Mishkin characterizes empirical regularities of historical financial crises in the United States. Going from the Panic of 1857 to the stock market crash of October 1987, he documents the breakdown in financial trading mechanisms in each episode. He finds that the onset of many panics follows the failure of a major financial institution; that panics are accompanied by rises in the spreads between risky and safe interest rates; and the most severe financial crises are associated with severe economic contractions.

Mishkin uses these regularities to distinguish between "monetarist" and "information" views of financial crises. The former view, associated most notably with Friedman and Schwartz (1963), stresses the importance of banking panics, since such episodes precipitate contractions in the supply of money and subsequent declines in economic activity. The alternative view stresses the microeconomic models of financial trade mentioned above. It emphasizes the importance of adverse selection and moral hazard problems during periods of unanticipated negative shocks to borrowers' net worth. The two views are actually complementary, as the "information" approach can provide a transmission mechanism for effects of declining money growth on economic activity during panics. Nonetheless, Mishkin argues that the information approach additionally contributes to our understanding of the dynamics of crises by accounting for timing patterns in the data which are otherwise difficult to explain.

Much of the concern to explain banking panics stems from the fact that their occurrence has been used to guide and rationalize government intervention in the banking industry. Empirical work has demonstrated the importance of institutional features (branch-banking regulation or arrangements for bank cooperation) for explaining the probability and resolution of bank panics. Charles W. Calomiris and Gary Gorton review recent theoretical and empirical work on the origins of banking panics. They stress that asymmetric information in financial markets amplifies effects of adverse economic news and problems of diversification of bank assets with unit banking in the United States.

Are banking panics the byproduct of random shocks to money demand under unit banking or the result of a combination of adverse news about bank assets and uncertainty about losses of unit banks because of asymmetric information? Recent theoretical work has focused on problems in bank liabilities and explains deposit-insurance contracts as being motivated by the problems of random-withdrawal shocks facing banks (from idiosyncratic liquidity requirements of depositors).[5] Since banks hold illiquid loans, large unanticipated withdrawals could lead to failures. Calomiris and Gorton present evidence against a narrow interpretation of this view, using case studies of historical banking panics.

This line of inquiry is important. While the introduction of deposit insurance in the United States virtually eliminated the prospect of banking panics, it has not done so without cost, as the recent troubles of the savings and loan industry illustrate. Motivating bank panics using asymmetric information problems surrounding bank assets leads instead to more consideration of the role of a central bank as a "lender of last resort." The summary of the issues in the paper makes clear the need for additional theoretical and empirical research on the role of banks in the provision of credit.

Maintaining Financial Stability: Limits on Public Policy

That the mechanisms of financial trade (the organization of financial markets and institutions) are affected by public policy is clear. It may also be the case, however, that concern over the stability of financial institutions or markets constrains monetary policy. Three such possibilities are elaborated in this volume, addressing (i) U.S. monetary policy between World War II and 1951; (ii) the current "corporate debt crisis;" and (iii) the question of whether foreign investors will remain willing to accumulate U.S. liabilities.

Barry Eichengreen and Peter M. Garber analyze U.S. monetary and financial policy from World War II until the famous Treasury–Federal Reserve Accord of 1951. During this period, government interest rates were stabilized at 2.5 percent (or lower), despite swings in the annual inflation rate from 25 percent to −3 percent. These pronounced fluctuations in ex post real interest rates did not undermine the stability of financial institutions; indeed, there were only five bank suspensions between 1945 and 1951. The authors demonstrate that the juxtaposition of periods of rapid inflation and deflation with stable nominal interest rates is a corollary of the Federal Reserve's implicit policy of maintaining a target zone for the price level.

Eichengreen and Garber show how a credible price-level target-zone regime decoupled inflationary expectations and stabilized nominal interest rates. They also argue that the Federal Reserve adhered to this target-zone regime because of perceived threats to financial stability. In the aftermath of the Second World War, higher interest rates were thought to pose a threat to the stability of a U.S. commercial banking system heavily invested in U.S. government bonds. Only when the banks' exposure to bond-market risk had been reduced was policy reoriented toward other targets.

Another set of policy concerns is related to the question of whether nonfinancial corporate leverage is "too high." Benjamin Friedman (1988) and others have raised the question of whether high leverage on the part of business firms may weaken the resolve of the Federal Reserve to fight inflation in the future, because of fears of large numbers of corporate bankruptcies. Aggregate data for the United States paint a clear picture for the 1980s of significant increases in net equity requirements and issuance of debt securities (see, e.g., Gertler and Hubbard 1990). This pattern is reflected in data for individual nonfinancial firms as well (Bernanke and Campbell 1988).

Mark J. Warshawsky extends the previous work of Bernanke and Campbell on micro data. While Bernanke and Campbell used data on a sample of firms followed by COMPUSTAT from 1969 through 1986, Warshawsky extends the sample through 1988, and expands it to include small corporations and corporations that have disappeared over the years owing to mergers, private buyouts, and bankruptcy. He also reports an additional measure of financial stability—the median bond rating of issuing firms.

Warshawsky's findings strengthen many of the conclusions reached by Bernanke and Campbell. Current values of the ratio of interest expense to cash flow are at or near the highs reached in 1982 and 1988. Small corporations tend to have higher ratios, and hence weaker financial conditions, than large corporations. The median bond rating declined from about A in 1978 to BBB in 1988. He concludes that, judged by the criterion of simulated interest expense exceeding simulated cash flow, as much as 27 percent of corporations in the sample—corresponding to more than 6 percent of total corporate assets in the sample—would be placed in severe financial distress in a future recession. Finally, Warshawsky notes that recent costly defaults by large issuers of junk bonds cast doubt on the claim that contemporary debt contracts are sufficiently renegotiable to ward off financial distress or default in the wake of an adverse shock to firms' ability to service debt.

The past several years have witnessed mounting concern over the sensitivity of U.S. financial markets and institutions to disturbances abroad or to sharp unanticipated movements in the foreign exchange value of the dollar. Such concerns are typically expressed in one of two ways. First, in the U.S. external position sustainable? If not, what will be the likely process of financial adjustment? Second, what would be the effects of a sudden loss of confidence by foreign investors in the United States? Would there be a "financial crisis"?

The sustainability of the U.S. external position hinges of course, on the willingness of international investors to add U.S. liabilities to their portfolios. In their paper for the volume, Bankim Chadha and Steven Symansky argue that investors are not likely to allow a large buildup of such claims. They model the effects of foreign investors imposing a sustainable foreign asset ratio on the United States by positing the existence of a premium on dollar assets when the foreign asset position is expected to deviate from this level. The process presents an example of a self-correcting mechanism for attaining external balance.

Chadha and Symansky try to obtain quantitative estimates using the MULTIMOD model of the International Monetary Fund. Simulations show that the premiums required may be modest for "correcting" potentially large movements in net foreign asset positions. However, the costs of such an imposed adjustment can be substantial in terms of lost output. Moreover, in the absence of a fiscal correction, this imposed external adjustment is likely to worsen the fiscal situation, thus increasing the costs of adjustment in terms of private consumption, investment, and future output.

Looking Ahead with the Savings and Loan Crisis: A Case Study

The collapse of large segments of the U.S. savings and loan industry during the 1980s has intermittently raised the specter of crisis. The debacle is certainly not over; many forecasts project the expenditure of hundreds of billions of dollars during the 1990s to make good on deposit-insurance liabilities incurred by failing institutions. Understanding the dynamics of the thrift crisis is important both for consideration of microeconomic models of institutional contractual design and for the evaluation of potential future troubles in the commercial banking industry.

At one level, the root of savings and loan problems is clear. Lacking an underlying economic rationale for the particular financial contracts they wrote (short-term deposits financing long-term fixed-rate mortgages), savings and loans were always vulnerable to interest rate risk. The combination in the early 1980s of financial deregulation and higher interest rates reduced, and in many cases eliminated, the economic net worth of the institutions. Since regulatory accounting conventions allowed low-net-worth institutions to continue operating, questions of excessive risk-taking owing to potential moral hazard problems arise. Other explanations for the extent of crisis include insufficient diversification on the part of thrifts and fraud. The three papers which constitute the savings and loan case study in this volume are prospective and address questions of whether thrifts remain vulnerable to interest rate risk; how derivative securities might be used to hedge interest rate risk; and the relative importance of such factors as "bad luck" and "excessive risk-taking" in explaining operating performance over time for a sample of thrifts.

The current deposit-insurance crisis in the savings industry is generally viewed as the result of sharply rising interest rates which effectively reduced to zero the net worth of thrifts funding fixed-rate loans with short-term deposits, and thrifts responding by taking even greater risks. Patric H. Hendershott and James D. Shilling ask how vulnerable thrift institutions remain to an interest-rate experience similar to that (over the 1977–86 period) which triggered the current crisis. They find that thrifts are even more vulnerable now than they were in 1977. The dollar volume of mortgages funded by short-term deposits is greater now than it was then and thrifts have also put over $325 billion of adjustable-rate loans with rate caps on their balance sheets. A sharp rise in interest rates (e.g., the one-year Treasury rate rose by 9 percentage points between 1977 and 1981) would cause significant losses on these loans, as well as on the fixed-rate loans. If thrifts were both well capitalized and profitable, their basic capital and earnings would be sufficient to cover such losses. However, Hendershott and Shilling estimate that, under the current conditions in the savings and loan industry, taxpayers would lose between $50 billion and $125 billion; this loss would be magnified, of course, if the institutions again assumed greater risk in their loan portfolio.

Savings and loan institutions can mitigate their exposure to interest rate risk by holding assets with flexible rates, in particular, adjustable-rate mortgages (ARMs). However, caps on ARMs still subject the originator to potentially severe interest-rate risk. Eduardo S. Schwartz and Walter N. Torous develop a two-factor model to value ARMs which takes into account their essential institutional features.[6] The valuation model also incorporates borrowers' prepayment behavior by specifying their conditional probability of prepaying as a function of the mortgage's age and prevailing interest rate conditions. The authors use their framework to value lifetime and periodic cap options, as well as to compute the sensitivities of the caps to changes in the mortgage's features.

Schwartz and Torous present two ways for thrifts to deal with residual interest rate risk. First an ARM-originating thrift can use dynamic hedging techniques. These techniques allow the originator to minimize the resulting interest rate risk by taking offsetting positions in other interest-sensitive charges for such as bonds or bond futures. Second, the ARM originator can purchase "lifetime cap insurance." Schwartz and Torous derive the fair fee to charge for such insurance, that is, the premium in equilibrium that the originating thrift should pay to transfer the interest rate risk arising from the adjustable-rate mortgage's lifetime cap.

Assessing the role played by moral hazard factors—the effect of diminished net worth on risk-taking—in the savings and loan crisis is difficult. Calculations based on averages from aggregate data may be misleading. George J. Benston, Mike Carhill, and Brian Olasov analyze micro data on individual thrifts in their paper. They consider seven (not necessarily mutually exclusive) hypotheses that purport to explain why some savings and loan institutions failed and others survived during the 1980s. The authors use information drawn from 517 thrifts operating continuously from 1984 through 1988, and for 62 thrifts that ceased independent operations during this period. The data are derived from regulatory financial statements filed by institutions in the southeast (fourth) district. The authors develop an algorithm for calculating the market value of the institutions' assets, so as to facilitate an assessment of economic net worth (as opposed to accounting net worth under regulatory standards).

Interest rate increases in the early and middle 1980s rendered many thrifts economically insolvent—though they continued to operate under existing regulation—even with interest rates subsequently declining somewhat. At year-end 1984, the market values of continuously operating savings and loan institutions in the Benston-Carhill-Olasov sample were 72 percent lower on average than their recorded book values. In their tabulations of the data, the authors find some evidence of greater risk-taking by institutions with low net worth—that is, evidence of increases in portfolio riskiness and loan losses conditional on negative economic net worth.

Lessons

Financial contracts, markets, and institutions constitute important trading mechanisms in the operation of the real economy. Disruptions in the efficient operation of these mechanisms draw attention both to their organization and to potential adverse economic effects. Understanding microeconomic foundations of financial trade and its breakdowns will be important for studies of episodes of interest. Much work remains to be done in careful case studies and exploration of micro data to shed light on competing models of financial crises.

Notes

1. For reviews of theoretical and empirical research in this area, see Gertler (1988), Fazzari, Hubbard, and Petersen (1988), and Hubbard (1990).
2. See, for example, Fazzari, Hubbard, and Petersen (1988), Gertler and Hubbard (1988), and Hubbard and Kashyap (1990).
3. This is akin to the accelerator mechanism stressed by Gertler, Hubbard, and Kashyap (in this volume).
4. Such an approach has long been employed by economic historians. See, for example, the early work of Sprague (1910).
5. See, most notably, Diamond and Dybvig (1983) and the literature that followed.
6. The two factors are taken to be the instantaneous riskless rate of interest and the continuously compounded yield on a default-free consol bond.

References

Bernanke, Ben. 1983. Non-monetary effects of the financial crisis in the propagation of the Great Depression. *American Economic Review* 73 (June): 257–76.

Bernanke, Ben, and John Y. Campbell. 1988. Is there a corporate debt crisis? *Brookings Papers on Economic Activity,* no. 1: 83–125.

Bernanke, Ben, and Mark Gertler. 1990. Financial fragility and economic performance. *Quarterly Journal of Economics* 105 (February): 87–114.

Diamond, Douglas, and Phillip Dybvig. 1983. Bank runs, liquidity, and deposit insurance. *Journal of Political Economy* 91 (June): 401–19.

Fazzari, Steven M., R. Glenn Hubbard, and Bruce C. Petersen. 1988. Financing constraints and corporate investment. *Brookings Papers on Economic Activity,* no. 1: 141–95.

Friedman, Benjamin M. 1988. *Day of reckoning*. New York: Random House.

Friedman, Milton, and Anna J. Schwartz. 1963. *A monetary history of the United States, 1867–1960*. Princeton, NJ: Princeton University Press.

Gertler, Mark. 1988. Financial structure and aggregate economic activity. *Journal of Money, Credit, and Banking* 20, pt. 2 (August): 559–88.

Gertler, Mark, and R. Glenn Hubbard. 1988. Financial factors in business fluctuations. In *Financial market volatility.* Kansas City, Mo: Federal Reserve Bank of Kansas City.

———. 1990. Taxation, corporate capital structure, and financial distress. In *Tax policy and the economy,* vol. 4, ed. L. H. Summers. Cambridge, Mass.: MIT Press.

Hubbard, R. Glenn. 1990. Introduction. In *Asymmetric information, corporate finance, and investment,* ed. R. G. Hubbard. Chicago: University of Chicago Press.

Hubbard, R. Glenn, and Anil Kashyap. 1990. Internal net worth and the investment process: An application to U.S. agriculture. NBER Working paper no. 3339. Cambridge, Mass.: National Bureau of Economic Research.

Sprague, O. M. W. 1910. *History of crises under the national banking system.* National Monetary Commission. 61st Cong., 2d sess. U.S. Senate Doc. 538.

Stock, James H., and Mark W. Watson. 1989. New indexes of coincident and leading economic indicators. In *NBER Macroeconomics Annual 1989,* ed. O. J. Blanchard and S. Fischer. Cambridge, Mass.: MIT Press.

1 Interest Rate Spreads, Credit Constraints, and Investment Fluctuations: An Empirical Investigation

Mark Gertler, R. Glenn Hubbard, and Anil Kashyap

Recent time-series work in macroeconomics has emphasized the role of the interest rate spread between risky and safe debt in forecasting real GNP. Stock and Watson (1989) and Friedman and Kuttner (1989) demonstrate that this interest differential has greater predictive power for output than money, interest rates, or any other financial variable. Increases in the spread are associated with subsequent downturns in GNP growth. While this analysis is limited to postwar data, similar results apply to the prewar period.[1]

Though the statistical relation between the spread and output appears robust, relatively little effort has been devoted to providing a sound structural interpretation of the evidence. It is clear that, under any story, movements in the spread reflect changes in "payoff" or "default" risk, broadly defined.[2] Nonetheless, the question emerges as to what are the sources of shifts in this payoff risk. In this paper, we argue that the countercyclical pattern in the spread may in part be symptomatic of a financial element in the business-cycle propagation mechanism. Our reasoning draws heavily on some recent theoretical work that links informational problems in capital markets at the micro level with fluctuations in aggregate economic activity. We also provide some

Mark Gertler is professor of economics at New York University and a research associate of the National Bureau of Economic Research. R. Glenn Hubbard is professor of economics and finance at the Graduate School of Business at Columbia University, and a research associate of the National Bureau of Economic Research. Anil Kashyap is assistant professor of business economics at the Graduate School of Business at the University of Chicago.

The authors thank Eugene Wan for excellent research assistance; Flint Brayton, Eileen Mauskopf, and David Reifschneider for comments and advice about data; and, for helpful suggestions, Benjamin Friedman, Gary Gorton, Bruce Greenwald, Frederic Mishkin, James Stock, Stephen Zeldes, conference participants, and participants in seminars at the Federal Reserve Bank of New York, the University of Pennsylvania, and the 1990 NBER Summer Institute. The conclusions expressed in this paper do not necessarily reflect the opinions of the Board of Governors of the Federal Reserve System or its staff.

supporting econometric evidence, extending methods used recently to test for the impact of credit-market imperfections on investment.

The theoretical literature to which we allude motivates a financial propagation mechanism by providing a rationale for why the agency costs of external finance may fluctuate countercyclically. Countercyclical movements in the wedge between external and internal finance, in turn, introduce a kind of "accelerator" effect on investment, ultimately magnifying investment and output fluctuations.[3] As Calomiris and Hubbard (1990) note, an associated implication of these theories is that the spread between risky and safe interest rates should move inversely with investment and output. The basic idea is that the widening of the spread is associated with, among other things, increased agency costs of external finance. In addition to being compatible with the time-series evidence, these theories also provide some formal underpinnings for the earlier work on financial crisis, which emphasized sharp increases in the spread as the precursors to financially induced disruptions in real activity.

An alternative to our story is that cyclical shifts in payoff risk are independent of financial factors. Defaults, for example, may be driven purely by technological factors. The spread is then useful as a "leading indicator" simply because it contains information about future technological disturbances, and not because there is any meaningful respect in which financial structure interacts with real activity. Indeed, this is a popular interpretation of the Stock-Watson results. While this explanation has some intuitive appeal, the underlying theory is incomplete. In the absence of any kind of imperfection in capital markets, the pattern of financial payoffs from borrowers to lenders is indeterminate (since the Modigliani-Miller theorem applies). In particular, since leverage ratios are indeterminate, there need be no particular connection between interest rate spreads and output fluctuations, as we demonstrate later.

In any event, a test of the competing theories is available. If the spread is simply an "information" variable and does not in any way reflect credit-market imperfections, then the data should not cause one to reject the neoclassical model of investment under perfect capital markets. If the story we offer is true—that is, movements in the spread reflect, at least in part, underlying movements in agency costs of external finance—then the null model should not hold. Further, an alternative model which relates firms' marginal cost of finance to agency factors should fit the data, where the movements in the interest rate spread can serve as a proxy for unobserved movements in agency costs.

We proceed in two steps. In section 1.1, we develop a simple model of investment and financial contracting under asymmetric information in which the link between interest differentials and the agency costs of external finance is made precise, and in which changes in the (endogenous) interest rate spread predict future movements in investment and output. We produce an example within the context of the Euler equation corresponding to firms' intertemporal decisions about investment. Situations are identified where, due to agency problems, the basic Euler equation for investment is violated. Shifts in interest rate differentials help predict investment in these periods. By necessity, the theoretical model is highly stylized and, therefore, cannot be matched directly to data. However, we estimate a model that loosely incorporates the key features of the simple stylized model. The estimation results are presented in section 1.2. Section 1.3 concludes.

1.1 Interest Differentials and Fluctuations Under Asymmetric Information

To illustrate how the empirical link between the spread and output fluctuations may, at least in part, reflect a financial mechanism, we present a simple model of investment finance under asymmetric information. We demonstrate first that in the benchmark case of symmetric information, there is no particular connection between financial variables (including the spread) and real variables; that is, the Modigliani-Miller theorem applies. A standard Euler equation for investment emerges. Under asymmetric information, however, a determinate pattern emerges. Firms' financial positions become relevant to the investment decision; investment moves inversely with firms' internal net worth. One manifestation of this relation is that changes in the spread help predict investment, even after controlling for changes in investment opportunities. In particular, an additional term emerges in the Euler equation, reflecting the impact of credit-market imperfections; this term covaries with the interest rate spread.

The model is a variant of Gertler and Hubbard (1988) and Gertler and Rogoff (1990). There are two periods, zero and one. In period zero, an entrepreneur (i.e., the firm) has access to a production technology which yields a random quantity of output in period one, taking capital as input. Investment I is done in period zero and entails convex adjustment costs $A(I)$, where $A(\cdot)$ is twice continuously differentiable with $A(0) = 0, A' > 0$ and $A'' > 0$. Capital K available for use as input in period one is given by

$$K = I + (1 - \delta)K_0, \tag{1}$$

where δ is the depreciation rate and K_0 is the period zero capital stock, which we take as given.

The mean level of output increases at a diminishing rate in the level of capital used as input. In particular, output y obeys the following two-point distribution:[4]

$$y = \begin{cases} Y \text{ with probability } P(K) \\ 0 \text{ with probability } 1 - P(K) \end{cases} \tag{2}$$

where $P(K)$ is increasing, strictly concave, and twice continuously differentiable, with $P(0) = 0$ and $P(\infty) = 1$. That is, more capital raises the probability of obtaining a high level of output, and the marginal gain is diminishing.

The entrepreneur/firm has initial resources W_0 ("internal net worth"). We interpret W_0 broadly here to include current cash, known collateralizable future resources, or valued relationships with lenders specializing in information gathering and monitoring (such as commercial banks). To invest more than W_0, the balance B must be borrowed using risky (noncollateralized) external finance.[5] To do so, the firm issues a state-contingent security which pays lenders L^g in the event of a good outcome and L^b in the event of a bad outcome. Given that R is the alternative gross riskless return available to lenders, and given that lenders are risk-neutral, the payments on the security must satisfy

$$P(K)L^g + (1 - P(K))L^b \geqq RB, \tag{3}$$

with

$$B \geqq I - W_0. \tag{4}$$

The pattern of payments offered by the security must also satisfy the following feasibility conditions, corresponding to limited liability (given that W_0 is already invested):

$$L^g \leq Y, \quad L^b \leq 0. \tag{5}$$

The firm maximizes expected terminal wealth $E(W_1)$. Given that the entrepreneur may invest in his project or lend at the market rate R, $E(W_1)$ is given by

$$\begin{aligned} E(W_1) = {} & P(K)Y - [P(K)L^g + (1 - P(K))L^b] \\ & + R(W_0 + B - I) - A(I). \end{aligned} \tag{6}$$

The first two terms in equation (6) are expected net project earnings; the third is the return from holding the safe asset; and the fourth is the adjustment cost of investing.

The outcome under symmetric information is simple to characterize. The firm invests in productive capital to the point at which expected marginal profitability of investment equals the gross riskless return plus the marginal cost of investing. That is, the first-best value of investment I^* is given by

$$P'(K^*)Y = R + A'(I^*), \tag{7}$$

where $K^* = I^* + (1 - \delta)K_0$. Equation (7) is a conventional Euler equation for capital accumulation.

It is also important to note that the pattern of contractual payments is indeterminate in this case. Any set of payoffs which satisfies the expected-return constraint (6) is acceptable. Because information is symmetric, there is no interdependence between financial structure and real economic decisions. As a consequence, there is no relation between the spread and investment in this case, after controlling for the variables that appear in equation (7).

To motivate a meaningful role for financial structure, we introduce a classic incentive problem, one described originally by Berle and Means (1932) as the basic motive for divergence of interests between ownership and management.[6] In particular, we assume lenders cannot observe the disposition of investment funds. That is, while outside lenders observe firms' initial resources W_0 and total borrowing B, the borrower has private information about how he allocates investment funds. For simplicity, we assume he can divert the funds to the safe asset and reap the benefits from this activity himself.

On the other hand, outside lenders may observe output. Under asymmetric information, therefore, contracts can be conditioned only on realized output y and not on investment I. Given the output-contingent payoffs (L^g, L^b) specified by the contract, the borrower will choose I to maximize expected final wealth, given by equation (6). This involves equating his expected marginal gain from investing with the opportunity cost of secretly diverting funds to a safe asset:

$$P'(K)[Y - (L^g - L^b)] = R + A'(I). \tag{8}$$

So long as L^g differs from L^b, investment I will differ from its first-best optimum value I^*, as may be seen by comparing (7) and (8). The problem is that the borrower's marginal gain from investing depends not only on the marginal gain in expected output but on the change in his expected obligation to lenders as well. In designing the contract, lenders take into account the borrower's decision rule, as given by (8).

Note that the larger is the spread between L^g and L^b, the larger is the gap between I and the first-best level, I^*. One way to obtain the first best would be to make L^b large enough that the contract would be truly "sum certain," so that $L^g = L^b = R(I^* - W_0)$. This optimum is not feasible when $W_0 < I^*$, because of the limited liability condition in equation (5) (recall that the project yields nothing in the bad state).

Consider the case for which borrowing is required ($W_0 < I^*$). The solution to the contracting problem is fairly intuitive. The contract pays lenders nothing in the bad state, so that the limited liability condition (5) is binding for L^b. (More generally, the contract always pays lenders the maximum feasible amount in the bad state.) This arrangement minimizes the spread between L^g and L^b, thereby minimizing the gap between I^* and I. Similarly, equation (4) is binding; under the incentive-compatible arrangement, the firm borrows only to finance investment and does not allocate funds to the riskless asset. Borrowing more than is required to finance investment I would raise the gap between L^g and L^b.

Given that $L^b = 0$ and $B = I - W_0$, the following two relations jointly determine I and L^g:

$$YP'(K) = R + A'(I) + L^g P'(K) \tag{9}$$

$$L^g = R(I - W_0)/P(K), \tag{10}$$

where $K = I + (1 - \delta)K_0$ from equation (1).

Equation (9) is obtained from the incentive condition (8) and is a downward-sloping locus in (I, L^g) space. The curve slopes downward since higher values of L^g lower the firm's expected marginal gain from investment and therefore must be offset by reduced investment. Equation (10) is obtained from the condition that the security must offer a competitive return (from eq. [3]) and is upward sloping in (I,L^g). The positive relation emerges because higher investment requires greater borrowing and because L^b cannot adjust, since the limited liability constraint is binding.

Whenever $W_0 < I^*$, investment I will be less than the first-best level, I^*. Increases in internal net worth raise investment by lowering L^g, thereby relaxing the impact of the incentive constraint on investment.

The spread S between the firm's marginal cost of finance and the riskless rate is given by

$$S = \frac{L^g}{B} - R$$

(11)
$$= \frac{L^g}{I - W_0} - R$$

$$= R\left(\frac{1}{P(K)} - 1\right)$$

When the incentive constraint is binding, the spread is always positive. Further, a rise in W_0 increases K, and therefore reduces S. That is, $\partial K/\partial W_0 > 0$, implying $\partial S/\partial W_0 < 0$.

If the only shocks in the economy were to firms' net worth (W_0), then there will be an inverse relation between *changes* in the spread (ΔS) and the level of investment $(\Delta K = I)$. In this case, movements in the spread contain information about movements in net worth.[7] Of course, in actual data, this relation is a correlation. Shocks to the level or distribution of the marginal product of capital will also shift the spread (given some level of net worth). To carry the simple Euler equation in (8) to data, it will be necessary in the estimation procedure to control for such shifts, as we describe in section 1.2.2 below.

It is worth emphasizing that shocks to internal net worth W_0 can be broadly interpreted here—for example, reductions in collateralizable resources (Gertler and Hubbard 1988), increases in debt-service burdens (Calomiris, Hubbard, and Stock 1986; Gertler and Hubbard 1991), or disruptions in ("bank") credit markets in which problems of asymmetric information are less severe (Bernanke 1983; Calomiris and Hubbard 1989). In each case the transmission mechanism is that movements in the "spread" correspond to shocks to internal net worth, owing to the impact of movements in net worth on the agency costs of external finance.

1.2 Empirical Evidence of U.S. GNP Growth and Investment

1.2.1 Interest Rate Spreads, GNP growth, and Investment: Reduced-Form Evidence

For our empirical work, we examine short-term spreads. One reason for preferring short-term measures to the alternative long-term Baa–Treasury bond spread is that the Baa-Treasury spread data are not stationary over our period (with a significant increase in the average value of the spread during the 1980s, relative to the 1950s, 1960s, and 1970s). We focus on the short-term interest rate differential corresponding to the spread between six-month commercial paper and Treasury bill rates. The spread is plotted in figure 1.1. The short-term spread is positive in all periods, of course, averaging 61 basis points. Following the intuition noted in the previous section, we will focus our attention on changes in the spread, which can be pronounced (as in 1970, 1974, and 1982, for example).

We begin our empirical analysis by corroborating the predictive power of the interest rate spread for output growth (measured by the growth rate of real GNP). As a simple reduced-form test, we regressed the quarterly GNP growth rate on a constant, on four lags of the GNP growth rate, and on four lagged values of the spread or changes in the spread. Given lags and consideration of the thickness of the market, the quarterly data cover the period from 1964 to 1989. We can reject at the 1.9×10^{-6} level the hypothesis that the spread coefficients are zero; approximately the same level of rejection holds for the change in the interest rate spread. The coefficient estimates suggest a negative effect of the spread on GNP growth.

Following the model in the previous section, our primary interest lies in

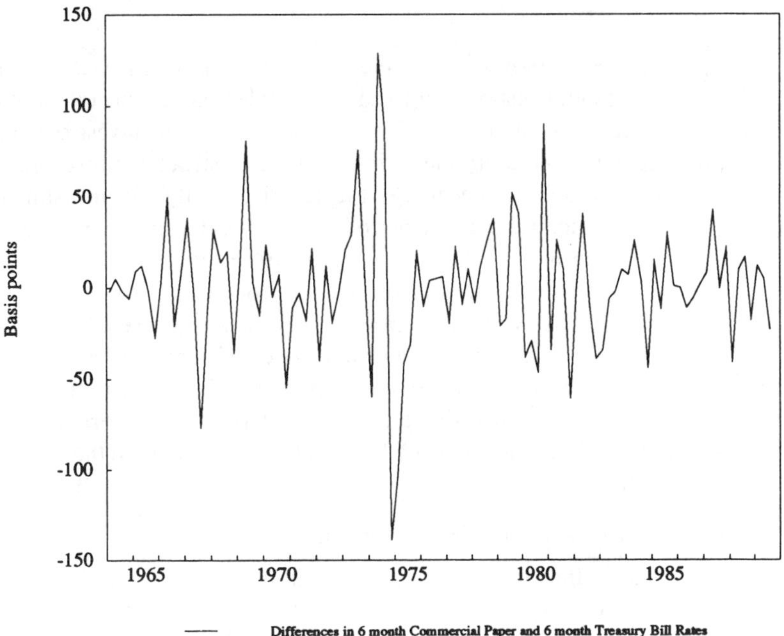

Fig. 1.1 Short-term commercial paper–Treasury bill interest rate differentials

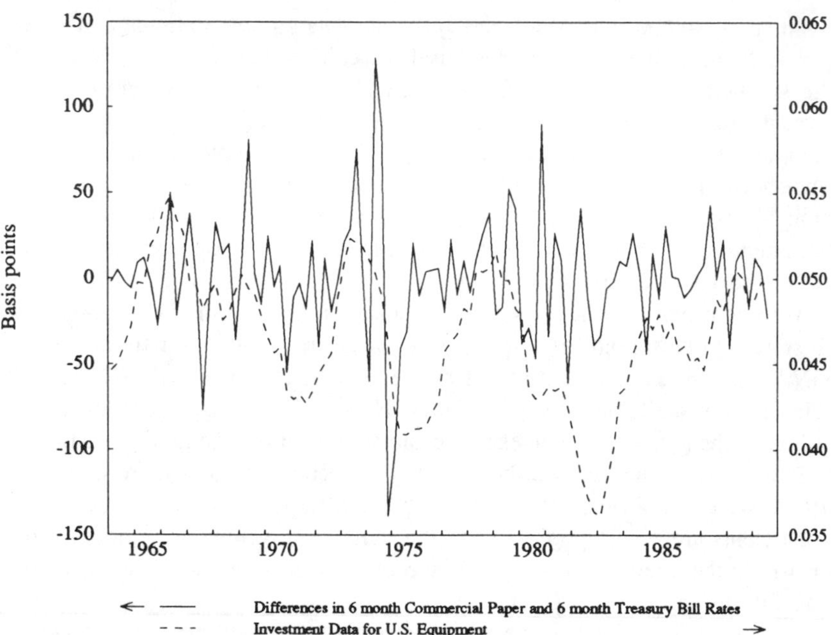

Fig. 1.2 Investment rate and the short-term interest rate differential

examining the effects of movements in the spread on investment. Data on real gross private domestic investment in fixed, nonresidential producers' durable equipment are plotted in figure 1.2. We selected equipment investment because of the greater variation in the series (relative to structures investment) during our sample period, and because of the negative trend in the investment-to-capital ratio for structures over the period. Repeating the simple time-series tests done for GNP growth for investment, we can reject at the 0.0014 level the hypothesis that the spread coefficients are zero (or at the 0.10 level for the change in the spread). As with GNP growth, there is a negative effect of the spread on the rate of investment. These results are consistent with the findings in Stock and Watson (1989) of the predictive power of the interest rate differential for real activity. To investigate these correlations more formally, we outline below an econometric approach to modeling investment in the spirit of the model of section 1.1.

1.2.2 Econometric Approach for Investment

There are serious difficulties in econometric implementation of investment models, even without considerations of capital market imperfections. One conventional approach stresses the role of "marginal q," the increase in firm value from additions to the capital stock. It is well known that by specifying a functional form for adjustment costs, one can solve for an investment function relating the rate of investment to q (see, for example, Hayashi 1982 and Summers 1981). The problems with this approach are three. First, its empirical success in explaining the variation in investment (in aggregate data or micro data) has not been overwhelming. Second, empirical proxies for "marginal q"—typically "average q"—are likely to be inadequate, owing to imperfect competition in the product market, non-constant returns to scale in production, or imperfect capital markets. Finally, the q model may be an inappropriate vehicle given our interest in asymmetric information, as expectations reflected in prices quoted on centralized securities markets will not in general reflect insiders' valuations of future investment projects.[8]

Our stylized model of section 1.1 suggests an Euler equation for investment with adjustment costs, modified to include a term that reflects credit-market imperfections (see eq. [8]). Since this model is not directly estimable, we follow the approach outlined in Hubbard and Kashyap (1990) to examine the effects on investment of proxies for movements in internal net worth. Specifically, we develop an empirical Euler equation for investment that incorporates the possibility that financial constraints are important. As in section 1.1, violations of a null ("perfect capital markets") Euler equation should be in the direction of an alternative model in which variations in net worth affect the marginal cost of outside finance, holding constant investment opportunities. We argue, expanding upon the model in section 1.1, that movements in the interest rate differential are good proxies for these shifts in net worth. This approach builds upon the related approach of Zeldes (1988) in testing for liquidity constraints on consumption.

While the discussion in section 1.1 applies to "investment" broadly, we present evidence below for effects of interest differentials (as proxies for internal net worth) on fixed investment using annual time-series data for producers' durable equipment investment in the United States. The specific framework within which we operate is derived under the assumption that risk-neutral firms maximize the present discounted value (V) of profits (Π) from investment, where

$$V_0 = E_0 \sum_{t=1}^{\infty} \beta_t \Pi_t, \qquad (12)$$

where β_t is the discount factor at time t. The maximization takes place subject to the following constraints:

1. *Capital Accumulation:* $K_t = (1 - \delta)K_{t-1} + I_t$, where I and K represent investment and the end-of-period capital stock, respectively, and where δ is the (assumed constant) rate of depreciation.

2. *Profits:* Profits are the residual after taxes, payments to variable factors,

investment (and adjustment costs), and debt service. Finance is composed of internal equity and debt.[9]

Let:

N = vector of variable factors of production;
w = vector of variable factor prices;
B = value of net debt outstanding (one-period loans);
i = interest rate on loans;
p^I = effective price of capital goods at time t (incorporating tax considerations);
$F(K_{t-1},N_t)$ = revenue function ($F'_K > 0$, $F''_K < 0$); and
$A(K_{t-1},I_t)$ = costs of adjusting the capital stock.

Then,

$$\Pi_t = F(K_{t-1},N_t) - w_tN_t - A(I_t,K_{t-1}) - i_{t-1}B_{t-1} + B_t - B_{t-1} - p_t^I I_t. \tag{13}$$

All prices and values are expressed relative to the general output price deflator (i.e., so that real profits are maximized).

3. *Transversality Condition:* So that firms cannot borrow an infinite amount to distribute, we require that

$$\lim_{T\to\infty} \sum_{t=0}^{T-1} \beta_t B_T = 0, \quad \forall_t.$$

The recent tradition in the q-theory literature is to assume that marginal and average q are equal, and to obtain an estimating equation. Instead of following this route, we choose to eliminate the shadow value of capital from the first-order condition for the choice of the capital stock, and work with the dynamic equation for investment, as in Hubbard and Kashyap (1990). That is, the first-order condition for the choice of the capital stock (from maximizing [12], subject to the constraints mentioned above) is given by

$$\beta_{t+1}E_t\{F_{Kt} - A_K(K_t,I_{t+1}) + (1 - \delta)\,[A_I(K_t,I_{t+1}) + p^I{}_{t+1}]\} - A_I(K_{t-1},I_t) - p^I{}_t = 0. \tag{14}$$

To obtain an equation for investment, it is necessary to parameterize the adjustment cost function A. We let[10]

$$A(K_{t-1},I_t) = [\alpha_0((I_t / K_{t-1}) - \mu) + (\alpha_1 / 2)((I_t / K_{t-1}) - \mu)^2]K_{t-1}, \tag{15}$$

where μ is the average (normal) investment rate. Now,

$$A_{It} = \alpha_0 + \alpha_1\,(I_t / K_{t-1} - \mu), \tag{16}$$

and

$$A_{Kt} = -(\alpha_1 / 2)(I_{t+1} / K_t)^2 - \mu(\alpha_0 - \alpha_1\mu / 2). \tag{17}$$

Substituting (16) and (17) into (14) yields the Euler equation:

$$(18)\quad \begin{aligned} &\beta_{t+1}E_tF_{Kt} + \beta_{t+1}E_t\{(\alpha_1 / 2)(I_{t+1} / K_t)^2 + \mu (\alpha_0 - \alpha_1\mu / 2)\} \\ &- \alpha_0 - \alpha_1 (I_t / K_{t-1} - \mu) - p_t^I \\ &+ \beta_{t+1} (1 - \delta)E_t\{\alpha_0 + \alpha_1 (I_{t+1} / K_t - \mu) + p_{t+1}^I\} = 0. \end{aligned}$$

We assume that expectations are rational and allow for an expectational error η, where $E_t(\eta_{t+1}) = 0$ and $E_t(\eta_{t+1}^2) = \sigma_\eta^2$. Hence we obtain:

$$(19)\quad \begin{aligned} &\beta_{t+1}E_tF_{Kt} + \beta_{t+1}E_t\{(\alpha_1 / 2)(I_{t+1} / K_t)^2 + \mu (\alpha_0 - \alpha_1\mu / 2)\} \\ &- \alpha_0 - \alpha_1(I_t/K_{t-1} - \mu) - p_t^I \\ &+ \beta_{t+1} (1 - \delta) E_t\{\alpha_0 + \alpha_1 (I_{t+1} / K_t - \mu) + p_{t+1}^I\} = \eta_{t+1}. \end{aligned}$$

The model in (19) is a nonlinear equation in I/K and can be estimated to identify α_1.

We incorporate financial factors by adding a constraint on the use of debt finance by firms. In particular, we assume that the outstanding debt B must be less than a debt ceiling B^*. The ceiling, while possibly unobservable to the econometrician, depends on measures of collateralizable net worth. That is, movements in the value of firms' net worth will affect firms' ability to finance investment, holding constant actual investment opportunities.[11] If we let ω be the Lagrange multiplier associated with the constraint that $B \leqq B^*$, the first order condition for borrowing (from the maximization of [12]) is now

$$(20)\quad 1 - \beta_{t+1}(1 + i_t) - \omega_t = 0,$$

so that when ω is nonzero, $\beta_{t+1} = (1 - \omega_t)/(1 + i_t)$. We can now rewrite equation (19) as:

$$(21)\quad \begin{aligned} &\{\alpha_0[\beta_{t+1}(1 - \delta) (1 - \omega_t) - 1 + \mu] + \alpha_1\mu[(1 - \mu) / 2]\} \\ &+ \beta_{t+1}[F_{Kt} + (\alpha_1 / 2)(I_{t+1} / K_t)^2 + \alpha_1(1 - \delta) (I_{t+1} / K_t) \\ &+ (1 - \delta)p_{t+1}^I] - \alpha_1(I_t / K_{t-1}) - p_t^I \\ &= \eta_{t+1} + \omega_t\beta_{t+1}[F_{Kt} + (\alpha_1 / 2)(I_{t+1} / K_t)^2 \\ &+ \alpha_1(1 - \delta)(I_{t+1} / K_t) + (1 - \delta)p_{t+1}^I]. \end{aligned}$$

During periods in which the constraint is binding, $\omega > 0$, and the error term contains the additional expression in (21).

Two issues arise in the estimation of (21). First, there is an obvious simultaneity problem because of the presence of other endogenous variables along with I/K. This necessitates the use of instrumental variables. The exact set of instruments used is discussed below. Second, comparison of equations (19) and (21) reveals the significance of financial constraints for the model to be estimated. When ω is zero, the standard "perfect capital markets" model is a good approximation. When $\omega > 0$, however, financial constraints affect investment spending. Ideally, we would like to have data on "internal net worth" to specify a relationship between ω and observable variables. We argued in the section 1.1 that changes in the interest rate spreads can serve as proxies for unobserved effects of net worth on investment. Hence, following equation (11), we let

$$\omega_t = \gamma_1 + \gamma_2 \Delta S_{t-1}, \tag{22}$$

where S represents the interest rate spread. Again, in the empirical results reported below, we employ as a proxy the difference between yields on six-month commercial paper and Treasury bills.

Our approach follows the intuition from the previous section. We first estimate the null model corresponding to equation (19) over our sample period. Second, we estimate the alternative model corresponding to (21), with the additional interaction terms incorporating the role of the interest rate spread.[12]

1.2.3 The Data

The data used in estimating the Euler equations for equipment investment are standard macroeconomic time-series that are available from several sources. From the terms in equation (19), the discount factor β is constructed using one of two proxies for the ex ante real rate of interest. First, we define the real rate as the difference between the average market yield on U.S. Treasury securities at a one-year constant maturity and the average expectation of the one-year-ahead change in the consumer price index. Expectations data are taken from the survey on inflation expectations conducted by the Survey Research Center of the University of Michigan.[13] Second, as a risky interest rate alternative, we use the Moody's Baa Bond rate minus the expected inflation proxy suggested in Gordon and Veitch (1986).

We use a series on the average product of capital to proxy for the marginal product of capital. The two variables will be proportional when the technology is constant returns to scale and factors are paid competitively. While the assumption that the ratio of price to marginal cost is unity is questionable, the alternative approach of using separate data for output and cost and estimating a markup is even more difficult at this level of aggregation. The difficulty arises primarily because, when using the National Income and Product Accounts, it is not possible to separate completely the returns to different factors.[14] Thus, we use the sum of pre-tax corporate profits (with capital consumption and inventory valuation adjustment) and net interest as the return to capital. In particular, the ratio of this sum to the beginning-of-period capital stock is our average product-of-capital measure.

As noted earlier, our investment data pertain to real gross private domestic investment in fixed, nonresidential producers' durable equipment. The corresponding capital-stock series is constructed by a perpetual inventory calculation starting in 1950 using an assumed (annual) rate of depreciation of 0.137 (the estimated rate obtained by Auerbach and Hines 1987). The initial value of the series for the capital stock is taken from the Bureau of Economic Analysis.

The price variable appearing in equation (19) is the tax-corrected price of investment goods (relative to the output price). The price deflators used in constructing this ratio are the implicit price deflator for gross private domestic investment in fixed, nonresidential producers' durable equipment and the implicit GNP deflator.

1.2.4 Evidence for Investment

Before outlining the results, we should stress two features of our estimation procedures. First, since we use interest rate data (nominal interest rates and measures of expected inflation) in constructing the discount factor β, shifts in interest rates are already accounted for, and cannot explain a correlation between the change in the interest rate spread and the investment residuals from equation (19). Second, we estimate using an instrumental variables procedure and exclude the current observed change in the spread from the instrument list. This is important, since using contemporaneous data on the change in the spread would not allow us to distinguish our hypothesis from a competing model in which contemporaneous movements in the spread reflect contemporaneous technology shocks not accounted for in our approach.

We present our results from estimating the structural model for investment in tables 1.1 and 1.2. The data are quarterly, covering the period from 1964 through 1989. First, we estimate the null model in equation (19) for producers' durable equipment. Second, we estimate the alternative model incorporating (21); that is, we allow the multiplier on the credit constraint to depend on a constant and lagged change in the spread.

Results from estimating (19) and (21) by generalized methods of movements are presented in table 1.1. Instruments for the endogenous variables include a constant and four lagged values of each of the following: I/K, $(I/K)^2$, the ratio of profits to capital, the commercial paper–Treasury bill interest rate spread, and the change in the log of the S&P 500 stock index, as well as a single lag of the discount factor and the current and lagged values of the tax-adjusted relative price of equipment investment goods. The two columns shown for each model correspond to the two ex ante real rate proxies used in constructing β—the "riskless" and "risky" alternatives, respectively. Overidentifying restrictions associated with the null model are soundly rejected at the 2 percent and 7 percent levels, respectively.

As noted in the second set of columns in table 1.1, the alternative model—in which the change in the interest rate spread affects the value of the Lagrange multiplier associated with the financial constraint—can be rejected only at the 10 or 11 percent level. The adjustment cost coefficient remains precisely estimated, and the estimate of the (transformed) share of equipment capital does not change much.[15] The coefficient on the (lagged) change in the interest rate spread, which measures the marginal impact on the Lagrange multiplier, is positive and precisely estimated. Taken literally, the implied effect is very large; a 10-basis-point increase in the spread would be equivalent to lowering

Table 1.1 **Euler Equation Estimates for U.S. Equipment Investment (1964–89), Including Interest Rate Spread Effects**

Parameter	Coefficient Estimates			
	Null Model		Alternative Model	
Constant	−1.04	−1.07	−.933	−1.02
	(.160)	(.168)	(.188)	(.167)
Constant (time-varying β)	1.03	1.08	.921	1.04
	(.164)	(.175)	(.191)	(.172)
Quadratic adjustment cost factor (α_1)	4.18	3.21	2.08	1.90
	(.864)	(.949)	(1.19)	(1.15)
Equipment share	.045	.103	.044	.113
	(.015)	(.036)	(.027)	(.046)
γ_2 (lagged change in spread)	—	—	.0054	.004
			(.002)	(.002)
Shift in constant due to time-varying credit-constraint multiplier (lagged change in spread)	—	—	−.0045	−.004
			(.0015)	(.002)
χ^2—Orthogonality test	34.4	29.9	25.5	25.9
(p value)	(.024)	(.072)	(.112)	(.102)

Note: The models are estimated using generalized method of moments. For the "null" and "alternative" models, the two columns refer to measures of β constructed from one-year Treasury and Baa bond rates, respectively. Instrumental variables include a constant and four lagged values each of I/K, $(I/K)^2$, the ratio of profits to capital, the commercial paper–Treasury bill interest rate spread, and the change in the log of the S&P 500 stock index, as well as a single lag of the discount factor and the current and lagged values of the tax-adjusted relative price of equipment investment goods. Heteroscedasticity-consistent standard errors are reported in parentheses.

the (quarterly) discount factor β from an average of about 0.99 to about 0.94, significantly increasing the (implied annual) discount rate. Given that information about future payoff risk is already in the level of the interest rate, such a shift is difficult to explain without information-related capital-market frictions.

We considered the possibility, however, that potential misspecification of the underlying null model could lead to a spurious correlation between the residuals (from [19]) and any forward-looking variable. To explore this case, we tried two other "leading indicator" variables suggested by Stock and Watson (1989), the percentage changes in "housing starts" and "manufacturers' unfilled orders" instead of the change in the spread. Those results are reported in table 1.2 using the "risky" discount factor; results using the risk-free rate in constructing β were virtually identical.

The first column for each variable represents results from estimating the null model in equation (19), adding the leading indicator variable to the instrument list. In both cases, the overidentifying restrictions associated with the model are rejected by the data; the coefficient estimates resemble closely those reported for similar cases in table 1.1. Allowing a separate effect of the lagged percentage change in housing starts or manufacturers' unfilled orders does not change this result. Rejection levels actually increase, and the signs on the coefficients on both variables are counterintuitive from the perspective of an omitted-leading-indicators explanation, although these coefficients are imprecisely estimated.

Finally, we add both the (lagged) change in the interest rate spread and the percentage change in the alternative "leading indicator" variables. Those results are reported in table 1.3 (using the risky rate alternative in constructing β). In both cases, the coefficient on the change in the spread is positive, precisely estimated, and approximately the same size as the estimate in table 1.1. The coefficients on either of the alternative leading indicator measures (housing starts and manufacturers' unfilled orders) are of the wrong sign and are very imprecisely estimated. The factors leading to the acceptance of the overidentifying restrictions for the alternative model are associated only with the interest rate spread variable and not with alternative "leading indicator" measures.

Table 1.2 **Euler Equation Estimates for U.S. Equipment Investment (1964–89), Including Alternative "Leading Indicator" Variable Effects**

	Coefficient Estimates			
	Null Model		Alternative Model	
Parameter	H	UO	H	UO
Constant	−1.03	−.987	−1.00	−1.02
	(.158)	(.150)	(.163)	(.179)
Constant (time-varying β)	1.02	.978	.990	1.02
	(.163)	(.155)	(.167)	(.187)
Quadratic adjustment cost factor (α_1)	4.10	3.92	4.38	3.51
	(.855)	(.859)	(.913)	(1.01)
Equipment share	.059	.055	.046	.044
	(.020)	(.020)	(.021)	(.063)
γ_2 (lagged percentage change in leading indicator variable)	—	—	.152	.254
			(.130)	(1.34)
Shift in constant due to time-varying credit-constraint multiplier (lagged percentage change in leading indicator)	—	—	−.137	−.388
			(.115)	(1.14)
χ^2—Orthogonality test	35.8	37.0	36.1	49.1
(p value)	(.057)	(.043)	(.030)	(.0008)

Note: The models are estimated using generalized method of moments. In all cases, β is constructed from the Baa bond rate and our measure of expected inflation. Instrumental variables include a constant and four lagged values each of I/K, $(I/K)^2$, the ratio of profits to capital, the percentage change in the "leading indicator" variable, and the change in the log of the S&P 500 stock index, as well as a single lag of the discount factor and the current and lagged values of the tax-adjusted relative price of equipment investment goods. The two leading indicator variables are denoted by "H" (housing starts) and "UO" (manufacturers' unfilled orders). Heteroscedasticity-consistent standard errors are reported in parentheses.

Table 1.3 **Euler Equation Estimates for U.S. Equipment Investment (1964–89), Including Interest Rate Spread and "Leading Indicator" Effects**

Parameter	Coefficient Estimates for Alternative Model: H	Coefficient Estimates for Alternative Model: UO
Constant	−1.01	−.974
	(.182)	(.183)
Constant (time-varying β)	1.00	.963
	(.19)	(.193)
Quadratic adjustment cost factor (α_1)	2.77	2.34
	(1.24)	(1.13)
Equipment share	.055	.034
	(.026)	(.050)
γ_2 (lagged change in spread)	.0034	.0048
	(.0014)	(.0018)
Shift in constant due to time-varying credit-constraint multiplier (lagged change in spread)	−.0029	−.0038
	(.0011)	(.0013)
γ_2 (lagged percentage change in leading indicator variable)	.218	.043
	(.190)	(1.13)
Shift constant due to time-varying credit-constraint multiplier (lagged percentage change in leading indicator variable)	−.182	−.056
	(.154)	(.911)
χ^2—Orthogonality test	27.2	29.4
(p value)	(.129)	(.080)

Note: The models are estimated using generalized method of moments. In both cases, β is constructed from the Baa bond rate and our measure of expected inflation. Instrumental variables include a constant and four lagged values each of I/K, $(I/K)^2$, the ratio of profits to capital, the percentage change in the "leading indicator" variable, and the change in the log of the S&P 500 stock index, as well as a single lag of the discount factor and the current and lagged values of the tax-adjusted relative price of equipment investment goods. The two leading indicator variables are denoted by "H" (housing starts) and "UO" (manufacturers' unfilled orders). Heteroscedasticity-consistent standard errors are reported in parentheses.

1.3 Conclusion and Implications

In this paper, we have presented a simple framework that incorporates a role for "interest spreads" in models of investment fluctuations. Our empirical work suggests that links between changes in interest rate spreads and investment are consistent with models emphasizing (i) how movements in agency costs of external finance can amplify investment fluctuations and, relatedly, (ii) how changes in the interest spread may signal movements in these agency costs. Because we worked with aggregate time-series data, the usual caveats apply. The results suggest, however, that fluctuations in agency costs (induced in large part by changes in firms' net worth) significantly affect the timing of investment. In addition, the findings shed light on the significance of widening interest rate spreads for predicting output declines in postwar time-series (Stock and Watson 1989), as well as during earlier periods of financial crises (Bernanke 1983; Calomiris and Hubbard 1989).

That the predictive power of short-term interest differentials likely reflects more than simple technological risk has also been argued recently by Bernanke (1990). Bernanke finds further that the commercial paper–Treasury bill spread measures the stance of monetary policy; specifically, he notes that the spread is related to traditional indicators of monetary policy (e.g., the Federal funds rate). An explanation, consistent with our analysis, is that contractionary monetary policy shrinks commercial bank lending, forcing marginal (high-agency-cost) firms to raise funds through the commercial paper market (e.g., see Kashyap, Stein, and Wilcox 1991). As well, in part, an increase in the riskless rate of interest (resulting from a tightening of monetary policy) lowers the value of firms' collateralizable net worth, increasing agency costs of external finance. That is, the effect on investment and output of a change in the riskless rate associated with contractionary monetary policy is magnified through the information-related channel we have stressed. While more careful research on these transmission mechanisms is needed, we believe that our approach and that taken by Bernanke are complementary.

A logical extension of our approach would be to study panel data and exploit predictions about cross-sectional differences in firm behavior. For example, as Calomiris and Hubbard (1990) note, the "perfect markets" neoclassical model of investment should work for firms unlikely to face financial constraints. Movements in the interest spread should be relevant to the investment behavior of those firms likely to be constrained. Presuming it is possible to divide the sample appropriately, it would be interesting to investigate this hypothesis with panel data.[16]

Notes

1. The associations with financial crisis of widening interest rate differentials among securities of different quality was stressed early on by Sprague (1910), who studied financial panics during the National Banking Period in the United States. During panic episodes, rates changed to risky borrowers rose dramatically relative to rates on safe securities. Historical accounts generally link financial crises to subsequent fluctuations (see, e.g., Bagehot 1873; Sprague 1910; and Mitchell 1913), though the precise channels are not always clear. Mishkin (in this volume) has documented the historical association of a widening differential between risky and safe rates and subsequent recessions.

Calomiris and Hubbard (1989) use models based on links between interest differentials and subsequent output fluctuations under asymmetric information in the period just prior to the founding of the Federal Reserve system. They construct a set of instruments to approximate the difference between the low-risk cost of capital under symmetric information and the actual cost of borrowed funds. Using a structural VAR model, they find that shocks to risk differentials had a positive effect on business failures and negative effects on bank loans and output. This focus on interest differentials parallels the seminal study by Bernanke (1983) of financial factors in the propagation mechanism of the economic downturn of the early 1930s. Focusing on the breakdown of the banking system, Bernanke notes that the pool of borrowers in loan markets (some of which would have been serviced by banks) was of lower quality in the 1930s, raising the differential between risky and safe interest rates. The differential between Baa corporate bond yields and the yields on U.S. government bonds was a strong explainer of current and future output growth.

2. A possible exception to this argument is that taxes and regulatory frictions may lead to shifts in safe rates and thereby widen the spread (for a discussion, see Cook and Lawler 1983).

3. See, for example, Keeton (1979), Stiglitz and Weiss (1981), Greenwald, Stiglitz, and Weiss (1984), Myers and Majluf (1984), Williamson (1987), Bernanke and Gertler (1990), Calomiris and Hubbard (1990), and the survey in Gertler (1988). Countercyclical movements in agency costs may be explained by procyclical movements in borrowers' net worth. See Hoshi, Kashyap, and Scharfstein (1991b) for evidence on the real costs (in terms of reduced investment and sales) of financial distress.

4. The use of zero in the bad-state outcome and the two-state description of the production realization are not crucial for the qualitative results that follow.

5. Strictly speaking, we are treating W_0 as "internal funds," so that $I - W_0$ is the amount borrowed. The real equilibrium is unaffected if W_0 is instead "collateralizable resources."

6. See also Jensen and Meckling (1976), Jensen (1986), and Gertler and Hubbard (1991).

7. Strictly speaking, in the example we present, the capital stock K contains as much information about internal net worth as does S (see eq. [9]). This is only because we have treated W_0 as "internal funds" to minimize algebra. If W_0 instead represented "collateralizable resources," S would reflect some information about W_0 not contained in K.

8. In micro-data studies in this area, "q" has been used as a reduced-form control for investment opportunities, so that some included measure of inside finance (arguably) does not substitute for expected future profits (see Fazzari, Hubbard, and Petersen 1988; and Hoshi, Kashyap, and Scharfstein 1991a).

9. We do not mean to suggest that equity finance is irrelevant at the margin in actual data. However, the inclusion of equity finance adds little to the basic setup for testing the effects of internal net worth on investment spending.

10. This formulation assumes convex adjustment costs. In addition, those costs are decreasing in the size of the capital stock.

11. This specification of a "finance constraint" is not particularly restrictive. If firms faced an upward-sloping debt-supply schedule, so that $i_t = i(B_{t-1} - B^*)$, where $i' > 0$, then $\beta_{t+1} = (1 - i'_t)/(1 + i_t)$.

12. Here we are building on recent Euler equation tests of effects of financial constraints on investment (see, e.g., Hubbard and Kashyap 1990; Whited 1990; Gilchrist 1989; and Himmelberg 1989). For an earlier treatment, see Bernstein and Nadiri (1986).

13. Using the (one-year-ahead) ex ante real rate calculated by Huizinga and Mishkin (1986) produced qualitatively similar results.

14. For example, proprietors' income relative to capital has declined markedly over the last forty years. If one excludes proprietors' income from variable costs, then the difference between output and cost (relative to capital) likewise has a downward trend.

Unfortunately, it is not possible to identify the portion of proprietors' income that represents labor input. Therefore, it is not possible to make a simple adjustment to produce a reliable series on variable costs.

15. The estimate is that of the share of equipment capital in total capital.

16. Work by Hubbard, Kashyap, and Whited (1991) directly pursues this approach. Other recent empirical studies have emphasized shifts in the distribution of net worth across firms (see Bernanke and Campbell 1988; Bernanke, Campbell, and Whited 1990; and Warshawsky, in this volume).

References

Auerbach, Alan J., and James R. Hines, Jr. 1987. Anticipated tax changes and the timing of investment. In *The Effects of Taxation on Capital Accumulation*, ed. M. Feldstein. Chicago: University of Chicago Press.

Bagehot, Walter. 1873. *Lombard Street*. London: Henry S. King.

Berle, Adolph, and Gardiner Means. 1932. *The Modern Corporation and Private Property*. New York: Macmillan.

Bernanke, Ben. 1983. Non-monetary effects of the financial crisis in the propagation of the Great Depression. *American Economic Review* 73 (June): 257–76.

———. 1990. On the predictive power of interest rates and interest rate spreads. Mimeograph, Princeton University.

Bernanke, Ben, and John Y. Campbell. 1988. Is there a corporate debt crisis? *Brookings Papers on Economic Activity*, no. 1: 83–125.

Bernanke, Ben, John Y. Campbell, and Toni Whited. 1990. U.S. corporate leverage: Developments in 1987 and 1988. *Brookings Papers on Economic Activity*, no. 1: 255–86.

Bernanke, Ben, and Mark Gertler. 1990. Financial fragility and economic performance. *Quarterly Journal of Economics* 105 (February): 87–114.

Bernstein, Jeffrey I., and M. Ishaq Nadiri. 1986. Financing and investment in plant and equipment and research and development. In *Prices, Competition, and Equilibrium*, ed. M. H. Peston and R. E. Quandt. New York: Philip Alan Publishers.

Calomiris, Charles W., and R. Glenn Hubbard. 1989. Price flexibility, credit availability, and economic fluctuations: Evidence from the United States, 1894–1909. *Quarterly Journal of Economics* 104 (August): 429–52.

———. 1990. Firm heterogeneity, internal finance, and credit rationing. *Economic Journal* 100 (March): 90–104.

Calomiris, Charles W., R. Glenn Hubbard, and James H. Stock. 1986. The farm debt crisis and public policy. *Brookings Paper on Economic Activity*, no. 2: 441–79.

Cook, Timothy Q., and Thomas A. Lawler. 1983. The behavior of the spread between Treasury bills and private money market rates since 1978. Federal Reserve Bank of Richmond, *Economic Review* 69 (November-December): 3–15.

Fazzari, Steven M., R. Glenn Hubbard, and Bruce C. Petersen. 1988. Financing constraints and corporate investment. *Brookings Papers on Economic Activity*, no. 1: 141–95.

Friedman, Benjamin M., and Kenneth N. Kuttner. 1989. Money, income, and prices after the 1980s. Working Paper no. 2852. Cambridge, Mass.: National Bureau of Economic Research.

Gertler, Mark. 1988. Financial structure and aggregate economic activity. *Journal of Money, Credit, and Banking* 20, pt. 2 (August): 559–88.

Gertler, Mark, and R. Glenn Hubbard. 1988. Financial factors in business fluctuations. In *Financial Market Volatility.* Kansas City, MO: Federal Reserve Bank of Kansas City.

———. 1991. Corporate overindebtedness and macroeconomic risk. Mimeograph, Columbia University.

Gertler, Mark, and Kenneth Rogoff. 1990. North-South lending and endogenous domestic capital market inefficiencies. *Journal of Monetary Economics* 26 (October): 245–66.

Gilchrist, Simon. 1989. An empirical analysis of corporate investment and financing hierarchies using firm level panel data. Mimeograph, University of Wisconsin.

Gordon, Robert J., and John M. Veitch. 1986. Fixed investment in the American business cycle, 1919–83. In *The American Business Cycle: Continuity and Change,* ed. R. J. Gordon. Chicago: University of Chicago Press.

Greenwald, Bruce C., Joseph E. Stiglitz, and Andrew Weiss. 1984. Information imperfections in the capital market and macroeconomic fluctuations. *American Economic Review* 74 (May): 194–99.

Hayashi, Fumio. 1982. Tobin's marginal *q* and average *q:* A neoclassical interpretation. *Econometrica* 50 (January): 213–24.

Himmelberg, Charles P. 1989. A dynamic analysis of dividend and investment behavior under borrowing constraints. Mimeograph, Northwestern University.

Hoshi, Takeo, Anil Kashyap, and David Scharfstein. 1991a. Corporate capital structure, liquidity, and investment: Evidence from Japanese industrial groups. *Quarterly Journal of Economics* 106 (February): 33–60.

———. 1991b. The role of banks in reducing the costs of financial distress in Japan. *Journal of Financial Economics,* in press.

Hubbard, R. Glenn, and Anil Kashyap. 1990. Internal net worth and the investment process: An application to U.S. agriculture. Working Paper no. 3339. Cambridge, Mass.: National Bureau of Economic Research.

Hubbard, R. Glenn, Anil Kashyap, and Toni M. Whited. 1991. Internal finance and firm level investment. Mimeograph, Columbia University.

Huizinga, John, and Frederic S. Mishkin. 1986. Monetary policy regime shifts and the unusual behavior of real interest rates. In *The National Bureau Method, International Capital Mobility, and Other Essays.* Carnegie-Rochester Conference Series on Public Policy, vol. 24, ed. K. Brunner and A. Meltzer. Amsterdam: North Holland.

Jensen, Michael C. 1986. Agency costs of free cash flow, corporate finance, and takeovers. *American Economic Review* 76 (May): 323–29.

Jensen, Michael C., and William Meckling. 1976. Theory of the firm: Managerial behavior, agency costs, and ownership structure. *Journal of Financial Economics* 3 (October): 305–60.

Kashyap, Anil, Jeremy Stein, and David Wilcox. 1991. Monetary policy and credit conditions: Evidence from the composition of external finance. Mimeograph, Board of Governors of the Federal Reserve System.

Keeton, William. 1979. *Equilibrium Credit Rationing.* New York: Garland Press.

Kindleberger, Charles P. 1978. *Manias, Panics, and Crashes: A History of Financial Crises.* New York: Basic Books.

Mitchell, Wesley C. 1913. *Business Cycles.* Berkeley: University of California Press.

Myers, Stewart C., and Nicholas S. Majluf. 1984. Corporate financing and investment decisions when firms have information that investors do not have. *Journal of Financial Economics* 13 (June): 187–221.

Sprague, O. M. W. 1910. *History of Crises Under the National Banking System.* National Monetary Commission. 61st Cong., 2d sess. U.S. Senate Doc. 538.

Stiglitz, Joseph E., and Andrew Weiss. 1981. Credit rationing in markets with imperfect information. *American Economic Review* 71 (June): 393–410.

Stock, James H., and Mark W. Watson. 1989. New indexes of coincident and leading economic indicators. In *NBER Macroeconomics Annual 1989*, ed. O. J. Blanchard and S. Fischer. Cambridge, Mass.: MIT Press.

Summers, Lawrence H. 1981. Taxation and corporate investment: A q-theory approach. *Brookings Papers on Economic Activity*, no 1: 67–127.

Whited, Toni M. 1990. Debt, liquidity constraints, and corporate investment: Evidence from panel data. Working Paper no. 114. Division of Research and Statistics, Board of Governors of the Federal Reserve System.

Williamson, Stephen D. 1987. Financial intermediation, business failures, and real business cycles. *Journal of Political Economy* 115 (December): 1196–1216.

Zeldes, Stephen P. 1988. Consumption and liquidity constraints: An empirical investigation. *Journal of Political Economy* 95 (December): 1196–1216.

2 The Gold Standard, Deflation, and Financial Crisis in the Great Depression: An International Comparison

Ben Bernanke and Harold James

2.1 Introduction

Recent research on the causes of the Great Depression has laid much of the blame for that catastrophe on the doorstep of the international gold standard. In his new book, Temin (1989) argues that structural flaws of the interwar gold standard, in conjunction with policy responses dictated by the gold standard's "rules of the game," made an international monetary contraction and deflation almost inevitable. Eichengreen and Sachs (1985) have presented evidence that countries which abandoned the gold standard and the associated contractionary monetary policies recovered from the Depression more quickly than countries that remained on gold. Research by Hamilton (1987, 1988) supports the propositions that contractionary monetary policies in France and the United States initiated the Great Slide, and that the defense of gold standard parities added to the deflationary pressure.[1]

The gold standard–based explanation of the Depression (which we will elaborate in section 2.2) is in most respects compelling. The length and depth of the deflation during the late 1920s and early 1930s strongly suggest a monetary origin, and the close correspondence (across both space and time) between deflation and nations' adherence to the gold standard shows the power of that system to transmit contractionary monetary shocks. There is also a high correlation in the data between deflation (falling prices) and depression (falling output), as the previous authors have noted and as we will demonstrate again below.

Ben Bernanke is professor of economics and public affairs at Princeton University and a research associate of the National Bureau of Economic Research. Harold James is assistant professor of history at Princeton University.

The authors thank David Fernandez, Mark Griffiths, and Holger Wolf for invaluable research assistance. Support was provided by the National Bureau of Economic Research and the National Science Foundation.

If the argument as it has been made so far has a weak link, however, it is probably the explanation of how the deflation induced by the malfunctioning gold standard caused depression; that is, what was the source of this massive monetary non-neutrality?[2] The goal of our paper is to try to understand better the mechanisms by which deflation may have induced depression in the 1930s. We consider several channels suggested by earlier work, in particular effects operating through real wages and through interest rates. Our focus, however, is on a channel of transmission that has been largely ignored by the recent gold standard literature; namely, the disruptive effect of deflation on the financial system.

Deflation (and the constraints on central bank policy imposed by the gold standard) was an important cause of banking panics, which occurred in a number of countries in the early 1930s. As discussed for the case of the United States by Bernanke (1983), to the extent that bank panics interfere with normal flows of credit, they may affect the performance of the real economy; indeed, it is possible that economic performance may be affected even without major panics, if the banking system is sufficiently weakened. Because severe banking panics are the form of financial crisis most easily identified empirically, we will focus on their effects in this paper. However, we do not want to lose sight of a second potential effect of falling prices on the financial sector, which is "debt deflation" (Fisher 1933; Bernanke 1983; Bernanke and Gertler 1990). By increasing the real value of nominal debts and promoting insolvency of borrowers, deflation creates an environment of financial distress in which the incentives of borrowers are distorted and in which it is difficult to extend new credit. Again, this provides a means by which falling prices can have real effects.

To examine these links between deflation and depression, we take a comparative approach (as did Eichengreen and Sachs). Using an annual data set covering twenty-four countries, we try to measure (for example) the differences between countries on and off the gold standard, or between countries experiencing banking panics and those that did not. A weakness of our approach is that, lacking objective indicators of the seriousness of financial problems, we are forced to rely on dummy variables to indicate periods of crisis. Despite this problem, we generally do find an important role for financial crises—particularly banking panics—in explaining the link between falling prices and falling output. Countries in which, for institutional or historical reasons, deflation led to panics or other severe banking problems had significantly worse depressions than countries in which banking was more stable. In addition, there may have been a feedback loop through which banking panics, particularly those in the United States, intensified the severity of the worldwide deflation. Because of data problems, we do not provide direct evidence of the debt-deflation mechanism; however, we do find that much of the apparent impact of deflation on output is unaccounted for by the mechanisms we explicitly consider, leaving open the possibility that debt deflation was important.

The rest of the paper is organized as follows. Section 2.2 briefly recapitulates the basic case against the interwar gold standard, showing it to have been a source of deflation and depression, and provides some new evidence consistent with this view. Section 2.3 takes a preliminary look at some mechanisms by which deflation may have been transmitted to depression. In section 2.4, we provide an overview of the financial crises that occurred during the interwar period. Section 2.5 presents and discusses our main empirical results on the effects of financial crisis in the 1930s, and section 2.6 concludes.

2.2 The Gold Standard and Deflation

In this section we discuss, and provide some new evidence for, the claim that a mismanaged interwar gold standard was responsible for the worldwide deflation of the late 1920s and early 1930s.

The gold standard—generally viewed at the time as an essential source of the relative prosperity of the late nineteenth and early twentieth centuries—was suspended at the outbreak of World War I. Wartime suspension of the gold standard was not in itself unusual; indeed, Bordo and Kydland (1990) have argued that wartime suspension, followed by a return to gold at prewar parities as soon as possible, should be considered part of the gold standard's normal operation. Bordo and Kydland pointed out that a reputation for returning to gold at the prewar parity, and thus at something close to the prewar price level, would have made it easier for a government to sell nominal bonds and would have increased attainable seignorage. A credible commitment to the gold standard thus would have had the effect of allowing war spending to be financed at a lower total cost.

Possibly for these reputational reasons, and certainly because of widespread unhappiness with the chaotic monetary and financial conditions that followed the war (there were hyperinflations in central Europe and more moderate but still serious inflations elsewhere), the desire to return to gold in the early 1920s was strong. Of much concern however was the perception that there was not enough gold available to satisfy world money demands without deflation. The 1922 Economic and Monetary Conference at Genoa addressed this issue by recommending the adoption of a gold exchange standard, in which convertible foreign exchange reserves (principally dollars and pounds) as well as gold would be used to back national money supplies, thus "economizing" on gold. Although "key currencies" had been used as reserves before the war, the Genoa recommendations led to a more widespread and officially sanctioned use of this practice (Lindert 1969; Eichengreen 1987).

During the 1920s the vast majority of the major countries succeeded in returning to gold. (The first column of table 2.1 gives the dates of return for the countries in our data set.) Britain returned at the prewar parity in 1925, despite Keynes's argument that at the old parity the pound would be overvalued. By the end of 1925, out of a list of 48 currencies given by the League of Nations (1926), 28 had been pegged to gold. France returned to gold gradually, following the Poincaré stabilization, although at a new parity widely believed to undervalue the franc. By the end of 1928, except for China and a few small countries on the silver standard, only Spain, Portugal, Rumania, and Japan had not been brought back into the gold standard system. Rumania went back on gold in 1929, Portugal did so in practice also in 1929 (although not officially until 1931), and Japan in December 1930. In the same month the Bank for International Settlements gave Spain a stabilization loan, but the operation was frustrated by a revolution in April 1931, carried out by republicans who, as one of the most attractive features of their program, opposed the foreign stabilization credits. Spain thus did not join the otherwise nearly universal membership of the gold standard club.

The classical gold standard of the prewar period functioned reasonably smoothly and without a major convertibility crisis for more than thirty years. In contrast, the interwar gold standard, established between 1925 and 1928, had substantially broken down by 1931 and disappeared by 1936. An extensive literature has analyzed the differences between the classical and interwar gold standards. This literature has focused, with varying degrees of emphasis, both on fundamental economic problems that complicated trade and monetary adjustment in the interwar period and on technical problems of the interwar gold standard itself.

In terms of "fundamentals," Temin (1989) has emphasized the effects of the Great War, arguing that, ultimately, the war itself was the shock that initiated the Depression. The legacy of the war included—besides physical destruction, which was relatively quickly repaired—new political borders drawn apparently without economic rationale; substantial overcapacity in some sectors (such as agriculture and heavy industry) and undercapacity in others, relative to long-run equilibrium; and reparations claims and international war debts that generated fiscal burdens and fiscal uncertainty. Some writers (notably Charles Kindleberger) have also pointed to the fact that the prewar gold standards was a hegemonic system, with Great Britain the unquestioned center. In contrast, in the interwar period the relative decline of Britain, the inexperience and insularity of the new potential hegemon (the United States), and ineffective cooperation among central banks left no one able to take responsibility for the system as a whole.

The technical problems of the interwar gold standard included the following three:

1. *The asymmetry between surplus and deficit countries in the required monetary response to gold flows.* Temin suggests, correctly we believe, that this was the most important structural flaw of the gold standard. In theory, under the "rules of the game," central banks of countries experiencing gold

Table 2.1 Dates of Changes in Gold Standard Policies

Country	Return to Gold	Suspension of Gold Standard	Foreign Exchange Control	Devaluation
Australia	April 1925	December 1929	—	March 1930
Austria	April 1925	April 1933	October 1931	September 1931
Belgium	October 1926	—	—	March 1935
Canada	July 1926	October 1931	—	September 1931
Czechoslovakia	April 1926	—	September 1931	February 1934
Denmark	January 1927	September 1931	November 1931	September 1931
Estonia	January 1928	June 1933	November 1931	June 1933
Finland	January 1926	October 1931	—	October 1931
France	August 1926–June 1928	—	—	October 1936
Germany	September 1924	—	July 1931	—
Greece	May 1928	April 1932	September 1931	April 1932
Hungary	April 1925	—	July 1931	—
Italy	December 1927	—	May 1934	October 1936
Japan	December 1930	December 1931	July 1932	December 1931
Latvia	August 1922	—	October 1931	—
Netherlands	April 1925	—	—	October 1936
Norway	May 1928	September 1931	—	September 1931
New Zealand	April 1925	September 1931	—	April 1930
Poland	October 1927	—	April 1936	October 1936
Rumania	March 1927–February 1929	—	May 1932	—
Sweden	April 1924	September 1931	—	September 1931
Spain	—	—	May 1931	—
United Kingdom	May 1925	September 1931	—	September 1931
United States	June 1919	March 1933	March 1933	April 1933

Source: League of Nations, *Yearbook,* various dates; and miscellaneous supplementary sources.

inflows were supposed to assist the price-specie flow mechanism by expanding domestic money supplies and inflating, while deficit countries were supposed to reduce money supplies and deflate. In practice, the need to avoid a complete loss of reserves and an end to convertibility forced deficit countries to comply with this rule; but, in contrast, no sanction prevented surplus countries from sterilizing gold inflows and accumulating reserves indefinitely, if domestic objectives made that desirable. Thus there was a potential deflationary bias in the gold standard's operation.

This asymmetry between surplus and deficit countries also existed in the prewar period, but with the important difference that the prewar gold standard centered around the operations of the Bank of England. The Bank of England of course had to hold enough gold to ensure convertibility, but as a profit-making institution it also had a strong incentive not to hold large stocks of barren gold (as opposed to interest-paying assets). Thus the Bank managed the gold standard (with the assistance of other central banks) so as to avoid both sustained inflows and sustained outflows of gold; and, indeed, it helped ensure continuous convertibility with a surprisingly low level of gold reserves. In contrast, the two major gold surplus countries of the interwar period, the United States and France, had central banks with little or no incentive to avoid accumulation of gold.

The deflationary bias of the asymmetry in required adjustments was magnified by statutory fractional reserve requirements imposed on many central banks, especially the new central banks, after the war. While Britain, Norway, Finland, and Sweden had a fiduciary issue—a fixed note supply backed only by domestic government securities, above which 100% gold backing was required—most countries required instead that minimum gold holdings equal a fixed fraction (usually close to the Federal Reserve's 40%) of central bank liabilities. These rules had two potentially harmful effects.

First, just as required "reserves" for modern commercial banks are not really available for use as true reserves, a large portion of central bank gold holdings were immobilized by the reserve requirements and could not be used to settle temporary payments imbalances. For example, in 1929, according to the League of Nations, for 41 countries with a total gold reserve of $9,378 million, only $2,178 million were "surplus" reserves, with the rest required as cover (League of Nations 1944, 12). In fact, this overstates the quantity of truly free reserves, because markets and central banks became very worried when reserves fell within 10% of the minimum. The upshot of this is that deficit countries could lose very little gold before being forced to reduce their domestic money supplies; while, as we have noted, the absence of any maximum reserve limit allowed surplus countries to accept gold inflows without inflating.

The second and related effect of the fractional reserve requirement has to do with the relationship between gold outflows and domestic monetary contraction. With fractional reserves, the relationship between gold outflow and the reduction in the money supply was not one for one; with a 40% reserve requirement, for example, the impact on the money supply of a gold outflow was 2.5 times the external loss. So again, loss of gold could lead to an immediate and sharp deflationary impact, not balanced by inflation elsewhere.

2. *The pyramiding of reserves.* As we have noted, under the interwar gold-exchange standard, countries other than those with reserve currencies were encouraged to hold convertible foreign exchange reserves as a partial (or in some cases, as a nearly complete) substitute for gold. But these convertible reserves were in turn usually only fractionally backed by gold. Thus, just as a shift by the public from fractionally backed deposits to currency would lower the total domestic money supply, the gold-exchange system opened up the

possibility that a shift of central banks from foreign exchange reserves to gold might lower the world money supply, adding another deflationary bias to the system. Central banks did abandon foreign exchange reserves en masse in the early 1930s, when the threat of devaluation made foreign exchange assets quite risky. According to Eichengreen (1987), however, the statistical evidence is not very clear on whether central banks after selling their foreign exchange simply lowered their cover ratios, which would have had no direct effect on money supplies, or shifted into gold, which would have been contractionary. Even if the central banks responded only by lowering cover ratios, however, this would have increased the sensitivity of their money supplies to any subsequent outflow of reserves.

3. *Insufficient powers of central banks.* An important institutional feature of the interwar gold standard is that, for a majority of the important continental European central banks, open market operations were not permitted or were severely restricted. This limitation on central bank powers was usually the result of the stabilization programs of the early and mid 1920s. By prohibiting central banks from holding or dealing in significant quantities of government securities, and thus making monetization of deficits more difficult, the architects of the stabilizations hoped to prevent future inflation. This forced the central banks to rely on discount policy (the terms at which they would make loans to commercial banks) as the principal means of affecting the domestic money supply. However, in a number of countries the major commercial banks borrowed very infrequently from the central banks, implying that except in crisis periods the central bank's control over the money supply might be quite weak.

The loosening of the link between the domestic money supply and central bank reserves may have been beneficial in some cases during the 1930s, if it moderated the monetary effect of reserve outflows. However, in at least one very important case the inability of a central bank to conduct open market operations may have been quite destabilizing. As discussed by Eichengreen (1986), the Bank of France, which was the recipient of massive gold inflows until 1932, was one of the banks that was prohibited from conducting open market operations. This severely limited the ability of the Bank to translate its gold inflows into monetary expansion, as should have been done in obedience to the rules of the game. The failure of France to inflate meant that it continued to attract reserves, thus imposing deflation on the rest of the world.[3]

Given both the fundamental economic problems of the international economy and the structural flaws of the gold standard system, even a relatively minor deflationary impulse might have had significant repercussions. As it happened, both of the two major gold surplus countries—France and the United States, who at the time together held close to 60% of the world's monetary gold—took deflationary paths in 1928–29 (Hamilton 1987).

In the French case, as we have already noted, the deflationary shock took the form of a largely sterilized gold inflow. For several reasons—including a successful stabilization with attendant high real interest rates, a possibly undervalued franc, the lifting of exchange controls, and the perception that France was a "safe haven" for capital—beginning in early 1928 gold flooded into that country, an inflow that was to last until 1932. In 1928, France controlled about 15% of the total monetary gold held by the twenty-four countries in our data set (Board of Governors 1943); this share, already disproportionate to France's economic importance, increased to 18% in 1929, 22% in 1930, 28% in 1931, and 32% in 1932. Since the U.S. share of monetary gold remained stable at something greater than 40% of the total, the inflow to France implied significant losses of gold by countries such as Germany, Japan, and the United Kingdom.

With its accumulation of gold. France should have been expected to inflate; but in part because of the restrictions on open market operations discussed above and in part because of deliberate policy choices, the impact of the gold inflow on French prices was minimal. The French monetary base did increase with the inflow of reserves, but because economic growth led the demand for francs to expand even more quickly, the country actually experienced a wholesale price *deflation* of almost 11% between January 1929 and January 1930.

Hamilton (1987) also documents the monetary tightening in the United States in 1928, a contraction motivated in part by the desire to avoid losing gold to the French but perhaps even more by the Federal Reserve's determination to slow down stock market speculation. The U.S. price level fell about 4% over the course of 1929. A business cycle peak was reached in the United States in August 1929, and the stock market crashed in October.

The initial contractions in the United States and France were largely self-inflicted wounds; no binding external constraint forced the United States to deflate in 1929, and it would certainly have been possible for the French government to grant the Bank of France the power to conduct expansionary open market operations. However, Temin (1989) argues that, once these destabilizing policy measures had been taken, little could be done to avert deflation and depression, given the commitment of central banks to maintenance of the gold standard. Once the deflationary process had begun, central banks engaged in competitive deflation and a scramble for gold, hoping by raising cover ratios to protect their currencies against speculative attack. Attempts by any individual central bank to reflate were met by immediate gold outflows, which forced the central bank to raise its discount rate and deflate once again. According to Temin, even the United States, with its large gold reserves, faced this constraint. Thus Temin disagrees with the suggestion of Friedman and Schwartz (1963) that the Federal Reserve's failure to protect the U.S. money supply was due to misunderstanding of the problem or a lack of leadership; instead, he claims, given the commitment to the gold standard (and, presumably, the absence of effective central bank cooperation), the Fed had little choice but to let the banks fail and the money supply fall.

For our purposes here it does not matter much to what extent central bank choices could have been other than what they were. For the positive question of what caused the Depression, we need only note that a monetary contraction began in the United States and France, and was propagated throughout the world by the international monetary standard.[4]

If monetary contraction propagated by the gold standard was the source of the worldwide deflation and depression, then countries abandoning the gold standard (or never adopting it) should have avoided much of the deflationary pressure. This seems to have been the case. In an important paper, Choudhri and Kochin (1980) documented that Spain, which never restored the gold standard and allowed its exchange rate to float, avoided the declines in prices and output that affected other European countries. Choudhri and Kochin also showed that the Scandinavian countries, which left gold along with the United Kingdom in 1931, recovered from the Depression much more quickly than other small European countries that remained longer on the gold standard. Much of this had been anticipated in an insightful essay by Haberler (1976).

Eichengreen and Sachs (1985) similarly focused on the beneficial effects of currency depreciation (i.e., abandonment of the gold standard or devaluation). For a sample of ten European countries, they showed that depreciating countries enjoyed faster growth of exports and industrial production than countries which did not depreciate. Depreciating countries also experienced lower real wages and greater profitability, which presumably helped to increase production. Eichengreen and Sachs argued that depreciation, in this context, should not necessarily be thought of as a "beggar thy neighbor" policy; because depreciations reduced constraints on the growth of world money supplies, they may have conferred benefits abroad as well as at home (although a coordinated depreciation presumably would have been better than the uncoordinated sequence of depreciations that in fact took place).[5]

Some additional evidence of the effects of maintaining or leaving the gold standard, much in the spirit of Eichengreen and Sachs but using data from a larger set of countries, is given in our tables 2.2 through 2.4. These tables summarize the relationships between the decision to adhere to the gold standard and some key macroeconomic variables, including wholesale price inflation (table 2.2), some indicators of national monetary policies (table 2.3), and industrial production growth (table 2.4). To construct these tables, we divided our sample of twenty-four countries into four categories:[6] 1) countries not on the gold standard at all (Spain) or leaving prior to 1931 (Australia and New Zealand); 2) countries abandoning the full gold standard in 1931 (14 countries); 3) countries abandoning the gold standard between 1932 and 1935 (Rumania in 1932, the United States in 1933, Italy in 1934, and Belgium in 1935); and 4) countries still on the full gold standard as of 1936 (France, Netherlands, Poland).[7] Tables 2.2 and 2.4 give the data for each country, as well as averages for the large cohort of countries abandoning gold in 1931, for the remnant of the gold bloc still on gold in 1936, and (for 1932–35, when there were a significant number of countries in each category) for all gold standard and non–gold standard countries. Since table 2.3 reports data on four different variables, in order to save space only the averages are shown.[8]

The link between deflation and adherence to the gold standard, shown in table 2.2, seems quite clear. As noted by Choudhri and Kochin (1980), Spain's abstention from the gold standard insulated that country from the general deflation; New Zealand and Australia, presumably because they retained links to sterling despite early abandonment of the strict gold standard, did however experience some deflation. Among countries on the gold standard as of 1931, there is a rather uniform experience of about a 13% deflation in both 1930 and 1931. But after 1931 there is a sharp divergence between those countries on and those off the gold standard. Price levels in countries off the gold standard have stabilized by 1933 (with one or two exceptions), and these countries experience mild inflations in 1934–36. In contrast, the gold standard countries continue to deflate, although at a slower rate, until the gold standard's dissolution in 1936.

With such clearly divergent price behavior between countries on and off gold, one would expect to see similarly divergent behavior in monetary policy. Table 2.3 compares the average behavior of the growth rates of three monetary aggregates, called for short M0, M1, and M2, and of changes in the central bank discount rate. M0 corresponds to money and notes in circulation, M1 is the sum of M0 and commercial bank deposits, and M2 is the sum of M1 and savings bank deposits.[9] The expected differences in the monetary polices of the gold and non-gold countries seem to be in the data, although somewhat less clearly than we had anticipated. In particular, despite the twelve percentage point difference in rates of deflation between gold and non-gold countries in 1932, the differences in average money growth in that year between the two classes of countries are minor; possibly, higher inflation expectations in the countries abandoning gold reduced money demand and thus became self-confirming. From 1933 through 1935, however, the various monetary indicators are more consistent with the conclusion stressed by Eichengreen and Sachs (1985), that leaving the gold standard afforded countries more latitude to expand their money supplies and thus to escape deflation.

The basic proposition of the gold standard–based explanation of the Depression is that, because of its deflationary impact, adherence to the gold standard had very adverse consequences for real activity. The validity of this proposition is shown rather clearly by table 2.4, which gives growth rates of industrial production for the countries in our sample. While the countries which were to abandon the gold standard in 1931 did slightly worse in 1930 and 1931 than the nations of the Gold Bloc, subsequent to leaving gold these countries performed much better. Between 1932 and 1935, growth of industrial production in countries not on gold averaged about seven percentage points a year better than countries remaining on gold, a very substantial effect.

In summary, data from our sample of twenty-four countries support the

Table 2.2 Log-differences of the Wholesale Price Index

	1930	1931	1932	1933	1934	1935	1936
1. Countries not on gold standard or leaving prior to 1931							
Spain	−.00	.01	−.01	−.05	.03	.01	.02
Australia (1929)	−.12	−.11	−.01	−.00	.04	−.00	.05
New Zealand (1930)	−.03	−.07	−.03	.03	.01	.03	.01
2. Countries abandoning full gold standard in 1931							
Austria	−.11	−.07	.03	−.04	.02	−.00	−.01
Canada	−.10	−.18	−.08	.01	.06	.01	.03
Czechoslovakia	−.12	−.10	−.08	−.03	.02	.04	.00
Denmark	−.15	−.13	.02	.07	.09	.02	.05
Estonia	−.14	−.11	−.09	.02	.00	−.01	.08
Finland	−.09	−.07	.07	−.01	.01	.00	.02
Germany	−.10	−.12	−.14	−.03	.05	.03	.02
Greece	−.10	−.11	.18	.12	−.01	.02	.02
Hungary	−.14	−.05	−.01	−.14	.00	.08	.03
Japan	−.19	−.17	.05	.11	−.01	.04	.06
Latvia	−.16	−.18	.00	−.02	−.01	.05	.04
Norway	−.08	−.12	.00	−.00	.02	.03	.05
Sweden	−.14	−.09	−.02	−.02	.06	.02	.03
United Kingdom	−.17	−.18	−.04	.01	.04	.04	.06
Average	−.13	−.12	−.01	.00	.02	.03	.04
3. Countries abandoning gold standard between 1932 and 1935							
Rumania (1932)	−.24	−.26	−.11	−.03	.00	.14	.13
United States (1933)	−.10	−.17	−.12	.02	.13	.07	.01
Italy (1934)	−.11	−.14	−.07	−.09	−.02	.10	.11
Belgium (1935)	−.13	−.17	−.16	−.06	−.06	.13	.09
4. Countries still on full gold standard as of 1936							
France	−.12	−.10	−.16	−.07	−.06	−.11	.19
Netherlands	−.11	−.16	−.17	−.03	.00	−.02	.04
Poland	−.12	−.14	−.13	−.10	−.06	−.05	.02
Average	−.12	−.13	−.15	−.07	−.04	−.06	.08
5. Grand averages							
Gold standard countries			−.13	−.07	−.04	−.05	
Non-gold countries			−.01	.00	.03	.04	

Note: Data on wholesale prices are from League of Nations, *Monthly Bulletin of Statistics* and *Yearbook*, various issues. Dates in parentheses are years in which countries abandoned gold, with "abandonment" defined to include the imposition of foreign exchange controls or devaluation as well as suspension; see table 2.1.

Table 2.3 **Monetary Indicators**

	1930	1931	1932	1933	1934	1935	1936
			1. Countries abandoning full gold standard in 1931				
M0 growth	−.04	−.02	−.07	.06	.05	.05	.08
M1 growth	.01	−.11	−.07	.02	.05	.04	.08
M2 growth	.03	−.08	−.04	.03	.05	.05	.06
Discount rate change	−0.8	0.4	−0.2	−1.2	−0.4	−0.1	−0.1
			2. Countries still on full gold standard as of 1936				
M0 growth	.03	.07	−.06	−.02	.01	−.03	.03
M1 growth	.05	−.06	−.07	−.05	.01	−.06	.08
M2 growth	.08	−.00	−.02	−.02	.02	−.03	.05
Discount rate change	−1.4	−0.4	0.1	−0.4	−0.4	0.8	−0.3
			3. Grand averages: Countries on gold				
M0 growth			−.04	−.03	.01	−.02	
M1 growth			−.09	−.04	−.01	−.06	
M2 growth			−.05	−.01	.01	−.02	
Discount rate change			0.2	−0.5	−0.4	0.7	
			4. Grand averages: Countries off gold				
M0 growth			−.07	.05	.03	.06	
M1 growth			−.06	.01	.04	.05	
M2 growth			−.03	.02	.04	.05	
Discount rate change			−0.3	−1.0	−0.4	−0.2	

Note: M0 is money and notes in cirulation. M1 is base money plus commercial bank deposits. M2 is M1 plus savings deposits. Growth rates of monetary aggregates are calculated as log-differences. The discount rate change is in percentage points. The data are from League of Nations, *Monthly Bulletin of Statistics* and *Yearbook,* various issues.

view that there was a strong link between adherence to the gold standard and the severity of both deflation and depression. The data are also consistent with the hypothesis that increased freedom to engage in monetary expansion was a reason for the better performance of countries leaving the gold standard early in the 1930s, although the evidence in this case is a bit less clear-cut.

2.3 The Link Between Deflation and Depression

Given the above discussion and evidence, it seems reasonable to accept the idea that the worldwide deflation of the early 1930s was the result of a monetary contraction transmitted through the international gold standard. But this

Table 2.4 Log-differences of the Industrial Production Index

	1930	1931	1932	1933	1934	1935	1936
1. Countries not on gold standard or leaving prior to 1931							
Spain	−.01	−.06	−.05	−.05	.01	.02	NA
Australia (1929)	−.11	−.07	.07	.10	.09	.09	.07
New Zealand (1930)	−.25	−.14	.05	.02	.13	.09	.14
2. Countries abandoning full gold standard in 1931							
Austria	−.16	−.19	−.14	.03	.11	.13	.07
Canada	−.16	−.18	−.20	.04	.20	.10	.10
Czechoslovakia	−.11	−.10	−.24	−.05	.10	.05	.14
Denmark	.08	−.08	−.09	.14	.11	.07	.04
Estonia	−.02	−.09	−.17	.05	.17	.10	.10
Finland	−.10	−.13	.19	.02	.03	.10	.09
Germany	−.15	−.24	−.24	.13	.27	.16	.12
Greece	.01	.02	−.08	.10	.12	.12	−.03
Hungary	−.06	−.08	−.06	.07	.12	.07	.10
Japan	−.05	−.03	.07	.15	.13	.10	.06
Latvia	.08	−.20	−.08	.31	.15	.05	.04
Norway	.01	−.25	.17	.01	.04	.10	.09
Sweden	.03	−.07	−.08	.02	.19	.11	.09
United Kingdom	−.08	−.10	−.00	.05	.11	.07	.09
Average	−.05	−.12	−.07	.08	.13	.10	.08
3. Countries abandoning gold standard between 1932 and 1935							
Rumania (1932)	−.03	.05	−.14	.15	.19	−.01	.06
United States (1933)	−.21	−.17	−.24	.17	.04	.13	.15
Italy (1934)	−.08	−.17	−.15	.10	.08	.16	−.07
Belgium (1935)	−.12	−.09	−.16	.04	.01	.12	.05
4. Countries still on full gold standard as of 1936							
France	−.01	−.14	−.19	.12	−.07	−.04	.07
Netherlands	.02	−.06	−.13	.07	.02	−.03	.01
Poland	−.13	−.14	−.20	.09	.12	.07	.10
Average	−.04	−.11	−.17	.10	.02	.00	.06
5. Grand averages							
Gold standard countries			−.18	.09	.03	.01	
Non-gold countries			−.06	.08	.12	.09	

Note: Data on industrial production are from League of Nations, *Monthly Bulletin of Statistics* and *Yearbook,* various issues, supplemented by League of Nations, *Industrialization and Foreign Trade,* 1945.

raises the more difficult question of what precisely were the channels linking deflation (falling prices) and depression (falling output). This section takes a preliminary look at some suggested mechanisms. We first introduce here two principal channels emphasized in recent research, then discuss the alternative of induced financial crisis.

1. *Real wages.* If wages possess some degree of nominal rigidity, then falling output prices will raise real wages and lower labor demand. Downward stickiness of wages (or of other input costs) will also lower profitability, potentially reducing investment. This channel is stressed by Eichengreen and Sachs (see in particular their 1986 paper) and has also been emphasized by Newell and Symons (1988).

Some evidence on the behavior of real wages during the Depression is presented in table 2.5, which is similar in format to tables 2.2–2.4. Note that table 2.5 uses the wholesale price index (the most widely available price index) as the wage deflator. According to this table, there were indeed large real wage increases in most countries in 1930 and 1931. After 1931, countries leaving the gold standard experienced a mild decline in real wages, while real wages in gold standard countries exhibited a mild increase. These findings are similar to those of Eichengreen and Sachs (1985).

The reliance on nominal wage stickiness to explain the real effects of the deflation is consistent with the Keynesian tradition, but is nevertheless somewhat troubling in this context. Given (i) the severity of the unemployment that was experienced during that time; (ii) the relative absence of long-term contracts and the weakness of unions; and (iii) the presumption that the general public was aware that prices, and hence the cost of living, were falling, it is hard to understand how nominal wages could have been so unresponsive. Wages had fallen quickly in many countries in the contraction of 1921–22. In the United States, nominal wages were maintained until the fall of 1931 (possibly by an agreement among large corporations; see O'Brien 1989), but fell sharply after that; in Germany, the government actually tried to depress wages early in the Depression. Why then do we see these large real wage increases in the data?

One possibility is measurement problems. There are a number of issues, such as changes in skill and industrial composition, that make measuring the cyclical movement in real wages difficult even today. Bernanke (1986) has argued, in the U.S. context, that because of sharp reductions in workweeks and the presence of hoarded labor, the measure real wage may have been a poor measure of the marginal cost of labor.

Also in the category of measurement issues, Eichengreen and Hatton (1987) correctly point out that nominal wages should be deflated by the relevant product prices, not a general price index. Their table of product wage indices (nominal wages relative to manufacturing prices) is reproduced for 1929–38 and for the five countries for which data are available as our table 2.6. Like table 2.5, this table also shows real wages increasing in the early

Table 2.5 **Log-differences of the Real Wage**

	1930	1931	1932	1933	1934	1935	1936
1. Countries not on gold standard or leaving prior to 1931							
Spain				not available			
Australia (1929)	.10	.01	−.05	−.04	−.03	.01	−.03
New Zealand (1930)	.03	.00	−.00	−.05	−.01	−.01	.10
2. Countries abandoning full gold standard in 1931							
Austria	.14	.05	−.04	−.00	−.05	−.03	.06
Canada	.11	.15	.00	−.06	−.05	.02	−.01
Czechoslovakia	.14	.11	.08	.02	−.04	−.05	−.00
Denmark	.17	.11	−.03	−.07	−.09	−.01	−.04
Estonia	.16	.07	.02	−.06	−.01	.06	−.03
Finland				not available			
Germany	.12	.06	−.03	−.00	−.07	−.03	−.02
Greece				not available			
Hungary	.14	−.00	−.07	.09	−.06	−.11	−.00
Japan	.05	.21	−.04	−.12	.02	−.05	−.05
Latvia	.20	.18	−.15	−.05	.01	−.05	−.02
Norway	.08	.08	.02	−.02	−.01	−.03	−.02
Sweden	.17	.09	.01	−.02	−.06	−.01	−.02
United Kingdom	.17	.16	.02	−.02	−.03	−.03	−.03
Average	.14	.11	−.02	−.03	−.04	−.03	−.02
3. Countries abandoning gold standard between 1932 and 1935							
Rumania (1932)	.20	.14	−.10	−.05	−.02	−.15	−.12
United States (1933)	.10	.13	−.01	−.03	.04	−.03	.02
Italy (1934)	.10	.07	.05	.07	−.01	−.11	−.06
Belgium (1935)	.19	.10	.07	.04	.01	−.16	−.02
4. Countries still on full gold standard as of 1936							
France	.21	.09	.12	.07	.06	.09	−.06
Netherlands	.12	.14	.09	−.02	−.04	−.01	−.06
Poland	.11	.06	.05	.00	.01	.02	−.03
Average	.15	.10	.09	.02	.01	.03	−.05
5. Grand averages							
Gold standard countries			.05	.03	.01	.02	
Non-gold countries			−.02	−.03	−.03	−.04	

Note: The real wage is the nominal hourly wage for males (skilled, if available) divided by the wholesale price index. Wage data are from the International Labour Office, *Year Book of Labor Statistics,* various issues.

Table 2.6 **Indices of Product Wages**

Year	United Kingdom	United States	Germany	Japan	Sweden
1929	100.0	100.0	100.0	100.0	100.0
1930	103.0	106.1	100.4	115.6	116.6
1931	106.4	113.0	102.2	121.6	129.1
1932	108.3	109.6	96.8	102.9	130.0
1933	109.3	107.9	99.3	101.8	127.9
1934	111.4	115.8	103.0	102.3	119.6
1935	111.3	114.3	105.3	101.6	119.2
1936	110.4	115.9	107.7	99.2	116.0
1937	107.8	121.9	106.5	87.1	101.9
1938	108.6	130.0	107.7	86.3	115.1

Source: Eichengreen and Hatton (1987, 15).

1930s, but overall the correlation of real wage increases and depression does not appear particularly good. Note that Germany, which had probably the worst unemployment problem of any major country, has almost no increase in real wages;[10] the United Kingdom, which began to recover in 1932, has real wages increasing on a fairly steady trend during its recovery period; and the United States has only a small dip in real wages at the beginning of its recovery, followed by more real wage growth. The case for nominal wage stickiness as a transmission mechanism thus seems, at this point, somewhat mixed.

2. *Real interest rates.* In a standard IS-LM macro model, a monetary contraction depresses output by shifting the LM curve leftwards, raising real interest rates, and thus reducing spending. However, as Temin (1976) pointed out in his original critique of Friedman and Schwartz, it is real rather than nominal money balances that affect the LM curve; and since prices were falling sharply, real money balances fell little or even rose during the contraction.

Even if real money balances are essentially unchanged, however, there is another means by which deflation can raise ex ante real interest rates: Since cash pays zero nominal interest, in equilibrium no asset can bear a nominal interest rate that is lower than its liquidity and risk premia relative to cash. Thus an expected deflation of 10% will impose a real rate of at least 10% on the economy, even with perfectly flexible prices and wages. In an IS-LM diagram drawn with the nominal interest rate on the vertical axis, an increase in expected deflation amounts to a leftward shift of the IS curve.

Whether the deflation of the early 1930s was anticipated has been extensively debated (although almost entirely in the United States context). We will add here two points in favor of the view that the extent of the worldwide deflation was less than fully anticipated.

First, there is the question of whether the nominal interest rate floor was in fact binding in the deflating countries (as it should have been if this mechanism was to operate). Although interest rates on government debt in the United States often approximated zero in the 1930s, it is less clear that this was true for other countries. The yield on French treasury bills, for example, rose from a low of 0.75% in 1932 to 2.06% in 1933, 2.25% in 1934, and 3.38% in 1935; during 1933–35 the nominal yield on French treasury bills exceeded that of British treasury bills by several hundred basis points on average.[11]

Second, the view that deflation was largely anticipated must contend with the fact that nominal returns on safe assets were very similar whether countries abandoned or stayed on gold. If continuing deflation was anticipated in the gold standard countries, while inflation was expected in countries leaving gold, the similarity of nominal returns would have implied large expected differences in real returns. Such differences are possible in equilibrium, if they are counterbalanced by expected real exchange rate changes; nevertheless, differences in expected real returns between countries on and off gold on the order of 11–12% (the realized difference in returns between the two blocs in 1932) seem unlikely.[12]

3. *Financial crisis*. A third mechanism by which deflation can induce depression, not considered in the recent literature, works through deflation's effect on the operation of the financial system. The source of the non-neutrality is simply that debt instruments (including deposits) are typically set in money terms. Deflation thus weakens the financial positions of borrowers, both nonfinancial firms and financial intermediaries.

Consider first the case of intermediaries (banks).[13] Bank liabilities (primarily deposits) are fixed almost entirely in nominal terms. On the asset side, depending on the type of banking system (see below), banks hold either primarily debt instruments or combinations of debt and equity. Ownership of debt and equity is essentially equivalent to direct ownership of capital; in this case, therefore, the bank's liabilities are nominal and its assets are real, so that an unanticipated deflation begins to squeeze the bank's capital position immediately. When only debt is held as an asset, the effect of deflation is for a while neutral or mildly beneficial to the bank. However, when borrowers' equity cushions are exhausted, the bank becomes the owner of its borrowers' real assets, so eventually this type of bank will also be squeezed by deflation.

As pressure on the bank's capital grows, according to this argument, its normal functioning will be impeded; for example, it may have to call in loans or refuse new ones. Eventually, impending exhaustion of bank capital leads to a depositors' run, which eliminates the bank or drastically curtails its operation. The final result is usually a government takeover of the intermediation process. For example, a common scenario during the Depression was for the government to finance an acquisition of a failing bank by issuing its own debt; this debt was held (directly or indirectly) by consumers, in lieu of (vanishing) commercial bank deposits. Thus, effectively, government agencies became part of the intermediation chain.[14]

Although the problems of the banks were perhaps the more dramatic in the Depression, the same type of non-neutrality potentially affects nonfinancial firms and other borrowers. The process of "debt deflation", that is, the increase in the real value of nominal debt obligations brought about by falling prices, erodes the net worth position of borrowers. A weakening financial position affects the borrower's actions (e.g., the firm may try to conserve financial capital by laying off workers or cutting back on investment) and also, by worsening the agency problems in the borrower-lender relationship, impairs access to new credit. Thus, as discussed in detail in Bernanke and Gertler (1990), "financial distress" (such as that induced by debt deflation) can in principle impose deadweight losses on an economy, even if firms do not undergo liquidation.

Before trying to assess the quantitative impact of these and other channels on output, we briefly discuss the international incidence of financial crisis during the Depression.

2.4 Interwar Banking and Financial Crises

Financial crises were of course a prominent feature of the interwar period. We focus in this section on the problems of the banking sector and, to a lesser extent, on the problems of domestic debtors in general, as suggested by the discussion above. Stock market crashes and defaults on external debt were also important, of course, but for the sake of space will take a subsidiary role here.

Table 2.7 gives a chronology of some important interwar banking crises. The episodes listed actually cover a considerable range in terms of severity, as the capsule descriptions should make clear. However the chronology should also show that (i) quite a few different countries experienced significant banking problems during the interwar period; and (ii) these problems reached a very sharp peak between the spring and fall of 1931, following the Creditanstalt crisis in May 1931 as well as the intensification of banking problems in Germany.

A statistical indicator of banking problems, emphasized by Friedman and Schwartz (1963), is the deposit-currency ratio. Data on the changes in the commercial bank deposit-currency ratio for our panel of countries are presented in table 2.8. It is interesting to compare this table with the chronology in table 2.7. Most but not all of the major banking crises were associated with sharp drops in the deposit-currency ratio; the most important exception is in 1931 in Italy, where the government was able to keep secret much of the banking system's problems until a government takeover was affected. On the other hand, there were also significant drops in the deposit-currency ratio that were not associated with panics; restructurings of the banking system and exchange rate difficulties account for some of these episodes.

What caused the banking panics? At one level, the panics were an endogenous response to deflation and the operation of the gold standard regime.

Table 2.7 A Chronology of Interwar Banking Crises, 1921–36

Date	Country	Crises
June 1921	SWEDEN	Beginning of deposit contraction of 1921–22, leading to bank restructurings. Government assistance administered through Credit Bank of 1922.
1921–22	NETHERLANDS	Bank failures (notably Marx & Co.) and amalgamations.
1922	DENMARK	Heavy losses of one of the largest banks, Danske Landmandsbank, and liquidation of smaller banks. Landmandsbank continues to operate until a restructing in April 1928 under a government guarantee.
April 1923	NORWAY	Failure of Centralbanken for Norge.
May 1923	AUSTRIA	Difficulties of a major bank, Allgemeine Depositenbank; liquidation in July.
September 1923	JAPAN	In wake of the Tokyo earthquake, bad debts threaten Bank of Taiwan and Bank of Chosen, which are restructured with government help.
September 1925	SPAIN	Failure of Banco de la Union Mineira and Banco Vasca.
July–September 1926	POLAND	Bank runs cause three large banks to stop payments. The shakeout of banks continues through 1927.
1927	NORWAY, ITALY	Numerous smaller banks in difficulties, but no major failures.
April 1927	JAPAN	Thirty-two banks unable to make payments. Restructuring of 15th Bank and Bank of Taiwan.
August 1929	GERMANY	Collapse of Frankfurter Allgemeine Versicherungs AG, followed by failures of smaller banks, and runs on Berlin and Frankfurt savings banks.
November 1929	AUSTRIA	Bodencreditanstalt, second largest bank, fails and is merged with Creditanstalt.
November 1930	FRANCE	Failure of Banque Adam, Boulogne-sur-Mer, and Oustric Group. Runs on provincial banks.
	ESTONIA	Failure of two medium-sized banks, Estonia Government Bank Tallin and Reval Credit Bank; crisis lasts until January.
December 1930	U.S.	Failure of Bank of the United States.
	ITALY	Withdrawals from three largest banks begin. A panic ensues in April 1931, followed by a government reorganization and takeover of frozen industrial assets.
April 1931	ARGENTINA	Government deals with banking panic by allowing Banco de Nacion to rediscount commercial paper from other banks at government-owned Caja de Conversión.

(continued)

Table 2.7 (continued)

Date	Country	Crises
May 1931	Austria	Failure of Creditanstalt and run of foreign depositors.
	Belgium	Rumors about imminent failure of Banque de Bruxelles, the country's second largest bank, induce withdrawals from all banks. Later in the year, expectations of devaluation lead to withdrawals of foreign deposits.
June 1931	Poland	Run on banks, especially on Warsaw Discount Bank, associated with Creditanstalt; a spread of the Austrian crisis.
April–July 1931	Germany	Bank runs, extending difficulties plaguing the banking system since the summer of 1930. After large loss of deposits in June and increasing strain on foreign exchanges, many banks are unable to make payments and Darmstädter Bank closes. Bank holiday.
July 1931	Hungary	Run on Budapest banks (especially General Credit Bank). Foreign withdrawals followed by a foreign creditors' standstill agreement. Bank holiday.
	Latvia	Run on banks with German connections. Bank of Libau and International Bank of Riga particularly hard hit.
	Austria	Failure of Vienna Mercur-Bank.
	Czechoslovakia	Withdrawal of foreign deposits sparks domestic withdrawals but no general banking panic.
	Turkey	Run on branches of Deutsche Bank and collapse of Banque Turque pour le Commerce et l'Industrie, in wake of German crisis.
	Egypt	Run on Cairo and Alexandria branches of Deutsche Orientbank.
	Switzerland	Union Financière de Genève rescued by takeover by Comptoir d'Escompte de Geneve.
	Rumania	Collapse of German-controlled Banca Generala a Tarii Românesti. Run on Banca de Credit Roman and Banca Romaneasca.
	Mexico	Suspension of payments after run on Credito Espanol de Mexico. Run on Banco Nacional de Mexico.
August 1931	U.S.	Series of banking panics, with October 1931 the worst month. Between August 1931 and January 1932, 1,860 banks fail.
September 1931	U.K.	External drain, combined with rumors of threat to London merchant banks with heavy European (particularly Hungarian and German) involvements.
	Estonia	General bank run following sterling crisis; second wave of runs in November.

Table 2.7 (continued)

Date	Country	Crises
October 1931	RUMANIA	Failure of Banca Marmerosch, Blank & Co. Heavy bank runs.
	FRANCE	Collapse of major deposit bank Banque Nationale de Crédit (restructured as Banque Nationale pour le Commerce et l'Industrie). Other bank failures and bank runs.
March 1932	SWEDEN	Weakness of one large bank (Skandinaviska Kreditaktiebolaget) as result of collapse of Kreuger industrial and financial empire, but no general panic.
May 1932	FRANCE	Losses of large investment bank Banque de l'Union Parisienne forces merger with Crédit Mobilier Français.
June 1932	U.S.	Series of bank failures in Chicago.
October 1932	U.S.	New wave of bank failures, especially in the Midwest and Far West.
February 1933	U.S.	General banking panic, leading to state holidays and a nationwide bank holiday in March.
November 1933	SWITZERLAND	Restructuring of large bank (Banque Populaire Suisse) after heavy losses.
March 1934	BELGIUM	Failure of Banque Belge de Travail develops into general banking and exchange crisis.
September 1934	ARGENTINA	Bank problems throughout the fall induce government-sponsored merger of four weak banks (Banco Espanol del Rio de la Plata, Banco el Hogar Argentina, Banco Argentina-Uruguayo, Ernesto Tornquist & Co.).
October 1935	ITALY	Deposits fall after Italian invasion of Abyssinia.
January 1936	NORWAY	After years of deposit stability, legislation introducing a tax on bank deposits leads to withdrawals (until fall).
October 1936	CZECHOSLOVAKIA	Anticipation of second devaluation of the crown leads to deposit withdrawals.

When the peak of the world banking crisis came in 1931, there had already been almost two years of deflation and accompanying depression. Consistent with the analysis at the end of the last section, falling prices lowered the nominal value of bank assets but not the nominal value of bank liabilities. In addition, the rules of the gold standard severely limited the ability of central banks to ameliorate panics by acting as a lender of last resort; indeed, since banking panics often coincided with exchange crises (as we discuss further below), in order to maintain convertibility central banks typically *tightened* monetary policy in the face of panics. Supporting the connection of banking problems with deflation and "rules of the game" constraints is the observation that there were virtually no serious banking panics in any country after aban-

Table 2.8 Log-differences of Commercial Bank Deposit-Currency Ratio

Country	1930	1931	1932	1933	1934	1935	1936
Australia	−.05	−.12*	.05	.01	.05	−.03	−.01
Austria	.17	−.40*	−.06	−.20*	−.07	−.01	−.02
Belgium	−.13*	−.22*	−.10*	.07	−.13*	−.27*	−.02
Canada	.07	−.01	.03	−.05	.00	.01	−.06
Czechoslovakia	−.11	−.08	.07	.02	.07	−.03	−.11*
Denmark	.08	−.03	.00	−.07	.02	.02	−.00
Estonia	.16	−.29*	−.02	−.05	.10	.05	.13
Finland	.09	−.05	.14	−.04	−.06	−.04	−.09
France	−.07	−.12*	−.01	−.10*	−.07	−.10	−.03
Germany	−.11*	−.40*	.05	−.09	−.01	−.08	−.02
Greece	.17	.07	−.27*	−.03	.06	−.04	.02
Hungary	.07	−.07	.10	−.03	−.08	−.05	−.03
Italy	.04	−.01	.05	.06	.01	−.20*	.08
Japan	.09	.03	−.12*	−.04	.03	−.00	.09
Latvia	.03	−.57*	.11	−.06	.12	.10	.45
Netherlands	.10	−.36*	−.05	−.06	−.05	−.08	.24
Norway	.04	−.15*	−.06	−.09	−.01	.03	−.23*
New Zealand	.04	−.11*	.03	.07	.15	−.08	−.32*
Poland	.07	−.29*	−.02	−.08	.10	−.06	.10
Rumania	.11	−.76*	−.05	−.11*	−.28*	.10	−.16*
Sweden	−.00	−.00	−.02	−.06	−.11*	−.08	−.07
Spain	.00	−.24*	.08	.03	.01	.06	N.A.
United Kingdom	.03	−.07	.10	−.07	−.02	.01	−.03
United States	.00	−.15*	−.26*	−.15*	.14	.05	.02

Note: Entries are the log-differences of the ratio of commercial bank deposits to money and notes in circulation. Data are from League of Nations, *Monthly Bulletin of Statistics* and *Yearbook,* various issues.

*Decline exceeds .10.

donment of the gold standard—although it is also true that by time the gold standard was abandoned, strong financial reform measures had been taken in most countries.

However, while deflation and adherence to the gold standard were necessary conditions for panics, they were not sufficient; a number of countries made it through the interwar period without significant bank runs or failures, despite being subject to deflationary shocks similar to those experienced by the countries with banking problems.[15] Several factors help to explain which countries were the ones to suffer panics.

1. *Banking structure.* The organization of the banking system was an important factor in determining vulnerability to panics. First, countries with "unit banking," that is, with a large number of small and relatively undiversified banks, suffered more severe banking panics. The leading example is of course the United States, where concentration in banking was very low, but a high incidence of failures among small banks was also seen in other countries (e.g., France). Canada, with branch banking, suffered no bank failures during

the Depression (although many branches were closed). Sweden and the United Kingdom also benefited from a greater dispersion of risk through branch systems.[16]

Second, where "universal" or "mixed" banking on the German or Belgian model was the norm, it appears that vulnerability to deflation was greater. In contrast to the Anglo-Saxon model of banking, where at least in theory lending was short term and the relationship between banks and corporations had an arm's length character, universal banks took long-term and sometimes dominant ownership positions in client firms. Universal bank assets included both long-term securities and equity participations; the former tended to become illiquid during a crisis, while the latter exposed universal banks (unlike Anglo-Saxon banks, which held mainly debt instruments) to the effects of stock market crashes. The most extreme case was probably Austria. By 1931, after a series of mergers, the infamous Creditanstalt was better thought of as a vast holding company rather than a bank; at the time of its failure in May 1931, the Creditanstalt owned sixty-four companies, amounting to 65% of Austria's nominal capital (Kindleberger 1984).

2. *Reliance of banks on short-term foreign liabilities.* Some of the most serious banking problems were experienced in countries in which a substantial fraction of deposits were foreign-owned. The so-called hot money was more sensitive to adverse financial developments than were domestic deposits. Runs by foreign depositors represented not only a loss to the banking system but also, typically, a loss of reserves; as we have noted, this additional external threat restricted the ability of the central bank to respond to the banking situation. Thus, banking crises and exchange rate crises became intertwined.[17] The resolution of a number of the central European banking crises required "standstill agreements," under which withdrawals by foreign creditors were blocked pending future negotiation.

International linkages were important on the asset side of bank balance sheets as well. Many continental banks were severely affected by the crises in Austria and Germany, in particular.

3. *Financial and economic experience of the 1920s.* It should not be particularly surprising that countries which emerged from the 1920s in relatively weaker condition were more vulnerable to panics. Austria, Germany, Hungary, and Poland all suffered hyperinflation and economic dislocation in the 1930s, and all suffered severe banking panics in 1931. While space constraints do not permit a full discussion of the point here, it does seem clear that the origins of the European financial crisis were at least partly independent of American developments—which argues against a purely American-centered explanation of the origins of the Depression.

It should also be emphasized, though, that not just the existence of financial difficulties during the 1920s but also the policy response to those difficulties was important. Austria is probably the most extreme case of nagging banking problems being repeatedly "papered over." That country had banking problems throughout the 1920s, which were handled principally by merging failing banks into still-solvent banks. An enforced merger of the Austrian Bodencreditanstalt with two failing banks in 1927 weakened that institution, which was part of the reason that the Bodencreditanstalt in turn had to be forceably merged with the Creditanstalt in 1929. The insolvency of the Creditanstalt, finally revealed when a director refused to sign an "optimistic" financial statement in May 1931, sparked the most intense phase of the European crisis.

In contrast, when banking troubles during the earlier part of the 1920s were met with fundamental reform, performance of the banking sector during the Depression was better. Examples were Sweden, Japan, and the Netherlands, all of which had significant banking problems during the 1920s but responded by fundamental restructurings and assistance to place banks on a sound footing (and to close the weakest banks). Possibly because of these earlier events, these three countries had limited problems in the 1930s. A large Swedish bank (Skandinaviska Kreditaktiebolaget) suffered heavy losses after the collapse of the Kreuger financial empire, and a medium-sized Dutch bank (Amstelbank) failed because of its connection to the Creditanstalt; but there were no widespread panics, only isolated failures.

A particularly interesting comparison in this regard is between the Netherlands and neighboring Belgium, where banking problems persisted from 1931 to 1935 and where the ultimate devaluation of the Belgian franc was the result of an attempt to protect banks from further drains. Both countries were heavily dependent on foreign trade and both remained on gold, yet the Netherlands did much better than Belgium in the early part of the Depression (see table 2.4). This is a bit of evidence for the relevance of banking difficulties to output.

Overall, while banking crises were surely an endogenous response to depression, the incidence of crisis across countries reflected a variety of institutional factors and other preconditions. Thus it will be of interest to compare the real effects of deflation between countries with and without severe banking difficulties.

On "debt deflation," that is, the problems of nonfinancial borrowers, much less has been written than on the banking crises. Only for the United States has the debt problem in the 1930s been fairly well documented (see the summary in Bernanke 1983 and the references therein). In that country, large corporations avoided serious difficulties, but most other sectors—small businesses, farmers, mortgage borrowers, state and local governments—were severely affected, with usually something close to half of outstanding debts being in default. A substantial portion of New Deal reforms consisted of various forms of debt adjustment and relief.

For other countries, there are plenty of anecdotes but not much systematic data. Aggregate data on bankruptcies and defaults are difficult to interpret because increasing financial distress forced changes in bankruptcy practices and procedures; when the League of Nations' *Monthly Bulletin of Statistics* dropped its table on bankruptcies in its December 1932 issue, for example, the reason given therein was that "the numerous forms of agreement by which open bankruptcies are now avoided have seriously diminished the value of the table" (p. 529). Perhaps the most extreme case of a change in rules was Rumania's April 1932 Law on Conversion of Debts, which essentially eliminated the right of creditors to force bankruptcy. Changes in the treatment of bankruptcy no doubt ameliorated the effects of debt default, but the fact that these changes occurred indicates that the perceived problem must have been severe. More detailed country-by-country study of the effects of deflation on firm balance sheets and the relation of financial condition to firm investment, production, and employment decisions—where the data permit—would be extremely valuable. A similar comment applies to external debt problems, although here interesting recent work by Eichengreen and Portes (1986) and others gives us a much better base of knowledge to build on than is available for the case of domestic debts.

2.5 Regression Results

In this section we present empirical results based on our panel data set. The principal question of interest is the relative importance of various transmission mechanisms of deflation to output. We also address the question, so far not discussed, of whether banking crises could have intensified the deflation process itself.

The basic set of results is contained in table 2.9, which relates the log-differences in industrial production for our set of countries to various combinations of explanatory variables. The definitions of the right-hand-side variables are as follows:

$\Delta \ln PW$: log-difference of the wholesale price index;
$\Delta \ln EX$: log-difference of nominal exports;
$\Delta \ln W$: log-difference of nominal wage;
DISC: central bank discount rate, measured relative to its 1929 value (a government bond rate is used for Canada; since no 1929 interest rate could be found for New Zealand, that country is excluded in regressions including DISC);
PANIC: a dummy variable, set equal to the number of months during the year that the country experienced serious banking problems (see below);
$\Delta \ln M0$: log-difference of money and notes in circulation.

Exports are included to control for trade effects on growth, including the benefits of competitive devaluation discussed by Eichengreen and Sachs (1986); and the wage is included to test for the real wage channel of transmission from deflation to depression. Of course, theory says that both of these variables should enter in real rather than in nominal terms; unfortunately, in practice the theoretically suggested deflator is not always available (as we noted in our discussion of the real wage above). We resolve this problem by supposing that the true equation is, for example,

$$(1) \quad \Delta \ln IP = \beta_e (\Delta \ln EX - \Delta \ln P_e) + \beta_w (\Delta \ln W - \Delta \ln P_w) + \text{error}$$

where P_e and P_w, the optimal deflators, are not available. Let the projections of log-changes in the unobserved deflators on the log-change in the wholesale price deflator be given by

$$(2) \quad \Delta \ln P_i = \psi_i \Delta \ln PW + u_i \quad i = e,w$$

where the u_i are uncorrelated with $\Delta \ln PW$ and presumably the ψ_i are positive. Then (1) becomes

$$(3) \quad \Delta \ln IP = -(\beta_e \psi_e + \beta_w \psi_w) \Delta \ln PW + \beta_e \Delta \ln EX + \beta_w \Delta \ln W + \text{new error}$$

This suggests allowing $\Delta \ln PW$ and the nominal growth rates of exports and wages to enter the equation separately, which is how we proceed.[18] Putting $\Delta \ln PW$ in the equation separately has the added advantage of allowing us to account for any additional effect of deflation (such as debt deflation) not explicitly captured by the other independent variables.

The discount rate *DISC* is included to allow for the interest rate channel and as an additional proxy for monetary policy. Since $\Delta \ln PW$ is included in every equation, inclusion of the nominal interest rate *DISC* is equivalent to including the actual ex post real interest rate, that is, we are effectively assuming that deflation was fully anticipated; this should give the real interest rate hypothesis its best chance.

In an attempt to control for fiscal policy, we also included measures of central government expenditure in our first estimated equations. Since the estimated coefficients were always negative (the wrong sign), small, and statistically insignificant, the government expenditure variable is excluded from the results reported here.

Construction of the dummy variable *PANIC* required us to make a judgment about which countries' banking crises were most serious, which we did from our reading of primary and secondary sources. We dated periods of crisis as starting from the first severe banking problems; if there was some clear demarcation point (such as the U.S. bank holiday of 1933), we used that as the ending date of the crisis; otherwise we arbitrarily assumed that the effects of the crisis would last for one year after its most intense point. The banking crises included in the dummy are as follows (see also table 2.7):

1. Austria (May 1931–January 1933): from the Creditanstalt crisis to the date of official settlement of the Creditanstalt's foreign debt.
2. Belgium (May 1931–April 1932; March 1934–February 1935): for one year after the initial Belgian crisis, following Creditanstalt, and for one

year after the failure of the Banque Belge de Travail led to a general crisis.

3. Estonia (September 1931–August 1932): for one year after the general banking crisis.
4. France (November 1930–October 1932): for one year following each of the two peaks of the French banking crises, in November 1930 and October 1931 (see Bouvier 1984).
5. Germany (May 1931–December 1932): from the beginning of the major German banking crisis until the creation of state institutes for the liquidation of bad bank debts.
6. Hungary (July 1931–June 1932): for one year following the runs in Budapest and the bank holiday.
7. Italy (April 1931–December 1932): from the onset of the banking panic until the takeover of bank assets by a massive new state holding company, the Istituto por le Riconstruzione Industriale (IRI).
8. Latvia (July 1931–June 1932): for one year following the onset of the banking crisis.
9. Poland (June 1931–May 1932): for one year following the onset of the banking crisis.
10. Rumania (July 1931–September 1932): from the onset of the crisis until one year after its peak in October 1931.
11. United States (December 1930–March 1933): from the failure of the Bank of the United States until the bank holiday.

The inclusion of Austria, Belgium, Estonia, Germany, Hungary, Latvia, Poland, Rumania, or the United States in the above list cannot be controversial; each of these countries suffered serious panics. (One might quibble on the margin about the exact dating given—for example, Temin [1989] and others have argued that the U.S. banking crisis did not really begin until mid 1931—but we doubt very much that changes of a few months on these dates would affect the results.) The inclusion of France and Italy is more controversial. For example, Bouvier (1984) argues that the French banking crisis was not as serious as some others, since although there were runs and many banks failed, the very biggest banks survived; also, according to Bouvier, French banks were not as closely tied to industry as other banking systems on the Continent. For Italy, as we have noted, early and massive government intervention reduced the incidence of panic (see Ciocca and Toniolo 1984); however, the banks were in very poor condition and (as noted above) eventually signed over most of their industrial assets to the IRI.

To check the sensitivity of our results, we reestimated the key equations omitting first the French crisis from the *PANIC* variable, then the French and Italian crises. Leaving out France had a minor effect (lowering the coefficient on *PANIC* and its *t*-statistic about 5% in a typical equation); the additional exclusion of the Italian crisis has essentially no effect.[19]

As a further check, we also reestimated our key equations omitting, in separate runs, (i) the United States; (ii) Germany and Austria; and (iii) all eastern European countries. In none of these equations were our basic results substantially weakened, which indicates that no single country or small group of countries is driving our findings.

The first seven equations in table 2.9 are not derived from any single model, but instead attempt to nest various suggested explanations of the link between deflation and depression. Estimation was by OLS, which opens up the possibility of simultaneity bias; however, given our maintained view that the deflation was imposed by exogenous monetary forces, a case can be made for treating the right-hand-side variables as exogenous or predetermined.

The principal inferences to be drawn from the first seven rows of table 2.9 are as follows:[20]

1. Export growth consistently enters the equation for output growth strongly, with a plausible coefficient and a high level of statistical significance.

2. When wage growth is included in the output equation along with only wholesale price and export growth (row 5), it enters with the wrong sign.

Table 2.9 Determinants of the Log-difference of Industrial Production (dependent variable: $\Delta \ln IP$)

	Independent Variables					
Equation	$\Delta \ln PW$	$\Delta \ln EX$	$\Delta \ln W$	*DISC*	*PANIC*	$\Delta \ln M0$
(1)	.855 (.098)					
(2)	.531 (.095)				−.0191 (.0026)	
(3)	.406 (.121)	.231 (.043)				
(4)	.300 (.111)	.148 (.041)			−.0157 (.0027)	
(5)	.364 (.141)	.231 (.046)	.272 (.206)			
(6)	.351 (.128)	.150 (.044)	−.072 (.197)		−.0156 (.0029)	
(7)	.296 (.123)	.103 (.044)	−.119 (.189)	−.0358 (.0102)	−.0138 (.0028)	
(8)		.217* (.048)	−.015 (.189)		−.0126 (.0031)	.405 (.098)

Note: For variable definitions, see text. The sample period is 1930–36. The panel consists of twenty-four countries except that, due to missing wage data, Finland, Greece, and Spain are excluded from equations (5)–(8). Estimates of country-specific dummies are not reported. Standard errors are in parentheses.

*Export growth is measured in real terms in equation (8).

Only when the *PANIC* variable is included does nominal wage growth have the correct (negative) sign (rows 6 and 7). In the equation encompassing all the various channels (row 7), the estimated coefficient on wage growth is of the right sign and a reasonable magnitude, but it is not statistically significant.

3. The discount rate enters the encompassing equation (row 7) with the right sign and a high significance level. A 100-basis-point increase in the discount rate is estimated to reduce the growth rate of industrial production by 3.6 percentage points.

4. The effect of banking panics on output is large (a year of panic is estimated in equation (7) to reduce output growth by 12 × .0138, or more than 16 percentage points) and highly statistically significant (*t*-statistics of 4.0 or better). The measured effect of the *PANIC* variable does not seem to depend much on what other variables are included in the equation.

5. There may be some residual effect of deflation on output not accounted for by any of these effects. To see this, note that in principle the coefficient on $\Delta \ln PW$ in equation (7) of table 2.9 should be equal to and opposite the weighted sum of the coefficients on $\Delta \ln EX$, $\Delta \ln W$, and *DISC* (where the weights are the projection coefficients of the respective "true" deflators on $\Delta \ln PW$). Suppose for the sake of illustration that each of the projection coefficients equals one (that is, the wholesale price index is the correct deflator). Then the expected value of the coefficient on $\Delta \ln PW$ should be approximately .052; the actual value is .296, with a standard error of .123. Thus there may be channels relating deflation to depression other than the ones explicitly accounted for here. One possibility is that we are simply picking up the effects of a simultaneity bias (a reverse causation from output to prices). Alternatively, it is possible that an additional factor, such as debt deflation, should be considered.

As an alternative to the procedure of nesting alternative channels in a single equation, in equation (8) of table 2.9 we report the results of estimating the reduced form of a simple aggregate demand–aggregate supply (AD-AS) system. Under conventional assumptions, in an AD-AS model output growth should depend on money growth and autonomous spending growth (represented here by growth in *real* exports[21]), which shift the AD curve; and on nominal wage growth, which shifts the AS curve. In addition, we allow *PANIC* to enter the system, since banking panics could in principle affect both aggregate demand and aggregate supply. The results indicate large and statistically significant effects on output growth for real export growth, money growth, and banking panics. Nominal wage growth enters with the correct sign, but the coefficient is very small and statistically insignificant.

We have so far focused on the effects of banking panics (and other variables) on output. There is an additional issue that warrants some discussion here; namely, the possibility that banking panics might have themselves worsened the deflationary process.

Some care must be taken with this argument. Banking panics undoubtedly had large effects on the composition of national money supplies, money multipliers, and money demand. Nevertheless, as has been stressed by Temin (1989), under a gold standard, small country price levels are determined by international monetary conditions, to which domestic money supplies and demands must ultimately adjust. Thus banking panics cannot intensify deflation in a small country.[22] Indeed, a regression (not reported) of changes in wholesale prices against the *PANIC* variable and time dummies (in order to isolate purely cross-sectional effects) confirms that there is very little relationship between the two variables.

The proposition that bank panics should not affect the price level does not necessarily hold for a large country, however. In econometric language, under a gold standard the price level of a large country must be cointegrated with world prices; but while this means that domestic prices must eventually adjust to shocks emanating from abroad, it also allows for the possibility that domestic shocks will influence the world price level. Notice that if banking panics led to deflationary shocks in a large country and these shocks were transmitted around the world by the gold standard, a cross-sectional comparison would find no link between panics and the price level.

The discussion of the gold standard and deflation in section 2.2 cited Hamilton's (1987) view that the initial deflationary impulses in 1928–29 came from France and the United States—both "big" countries, in terms of economic importance and because of their large gold reserves. This early deflation obviously cannot be blamed on banking panics, since these did not begin until at least the end of 1930. But it would not be in any way inconsistent with the theory of the gold standard to hypothesize that banking panics in France and the United States contributed to world deflation during 1931–32.[23]

Empirical evidence bearing on this question is presented in table 2.10. We estimated equations for wholesale price inflation in the United States and France, using monthly data for the five-year period 1928–32. We included an error-correction term in both equations to allow for cointegration between the U.S. and French price levels, as would be implied by the gold standard. This error-correction term is the difference between the log-*levels* of U.S. and French wholesale prices in period $t - 1$; if U.S. and French prices are in fact cointegrated, then the growth rate of U.S. prices should respond negatively to the difference between the U.S. price and the French price, and the French growth rate of prices should respond positively. Also included in the equations are lagged inflation rates (to capture transitory price dynamics), current and lagged base money growth, and current and lagged values of the deposits of failing banks (for the United States only, due to data availability).

The results are interesting. First, there is evidence for cointegration: The error-correction terms have the right signs and reasonable magnitudes, although only the U.S. term is statistically significant. Thus we may infer that shocks hitting either French or U.S. prices ultimately affected both price levels. Second, both U.S. base money growth and bank failures are important

Table 2.10 Error-correction Equations for U.S. and French Wholesale Prices

	Dependent Variable	
	Δln*USAWPI*	Δln*FRAWPI*
Constant	.044 (t = 3.81)	−.006 (t = 1.57)
Log *USAWPI* − log *FRAWPI* (lagged once)	−.166 (t = 2.77)	.071 (t = 1.10)
Four lags of own WPI growth	−.530 (F = 1.57; p = .202)	.320 (F = 2.48; p = .057)
Current and four lags of base money growth	1.412 (F = 5.62; p = .0005)	.519 (F = 0.78; p = .569)
Current and four lags of deposits of failing U.S. banks, in logs	−.020 (F = 5.61; p = .0005)	
R^2	.531	.307
D-W	1.62	1.87

Note: Deposits of failing banks are from the *Federal Reserve Bulletin*. *USAWPI* and *FRAWPI* are wholesale price indexes for the United States and France, respectively. Monthly data from 1928 to 1932 are used.

determinants of the U.S. (and by extension, the French) deflation rates; these two variables enter the U.S. price equation with the right sign and marginal significance levels of .0005.

With respect to the effect of banking panics on the price level, then, the appropriate conclusion appears to be that countries with banking panics did not suffer worse deflation than those without panics;[24] however, it is possible that U.S. banking panics in particular were an important source of *world* deflation during 1931–32, and thus, by extension, of world depression.

2.6 Conclusion

Monetary and financial arrangements in the interwar period were badly flawed and were a major source of the fall in real output. Banking panics were one mechanism through which deflation had its effects on real output, and panics in the United States may have contributed to the severity of the world deflation.

In this empirical study, we have focused on the effects of severe banking panics. We believe it likely, however, that the effects of deflation on the financial system were not confined to these more extreme episodes. Even in countries without panics, banks were financially weakened and contracted their operations. Domestic debt deflation was probably a factor, to a greater or lesser degree, in every country. And we have not addressed at all the effect of deflation on the burden of external debt, which was important for a number of countries. As we have already suggested, more careful study of these issues is clearly desirable.

Notes

1. The original diagnosis of the Depression as a monetary phenomenon was of course made in Friedman and Schwartz (1963). We find the more recent work, though focusing to a greater degree on international aspects of the problem, to be essentially complementary to the Friedman-Schwartz analysis.

2. Eichengreen and Sachs (1985) discuss several mechanisms and provide some cross-country evidence, but their approach is somewhat informal and they do not consider the relative importance of the different effects.

3. To be clear, gold inflows to France did increase the French monetary base directly, one for one; however, in the absence of supplementary open market purchases, this implied a rising ratio of French gold reserves to monetary base. Together with the very low value of the French money multiplier, this rising cover ratio meant that the monetary expansion induced by gold flowing into France was far less significant than the monetary contractions that this inflow induced elsewhere.

4. Temin (1989) suggests that German monetary policy provided yet another contractionary impetus.

5. There remains the issue of whether the differences in timing of nations' departure from the gold standard can be treated as exogenous. Eichengreen and Sachs (1985) argue that exogeneity is a reasonable assumption, given the importance of individual national experiences, institutions, and fortuitous events in the timing of each country's decision to go off gold. Strong national differences in attitudes toward the gold standard (e.g., between the Gold Bloc and the Sterling Bloc) were remarkably persistent in their influence on policy.

6. The countries in our sample are listed in table 2.1. We included countries for which the League of Nations collected reasonably complete data on industrial production, price levels, and money supplies (League of Nations' *Monthly Bulletin of Statistics and Yearbooks,* various issues; see also League of Nations, *Industrialization and Foreign Trade,* 1945). Latin America, however, was excluded because of concerns about the data and our expectation that factors such as commodity prices would play a more important role for these countries. However, see Campa (forthcoming) for evidence that the gold standard transmitted deflation and depression to Latin America in a manner very similar to that observed elsewhere.

7. We define abandonment of the gold standard broadly as occurring at the first date in which a country imposes exchange controls, devalues, or suspends gold payments; see table 2.1 for a list of dates. An objection to this definition is that some countries continued to try to target their exchange rates at levels prescribed by the gold standard even after "leaving" the gold standard by our criteria; Canada and Germany are two examples. We made no attempt to account for this, on the grounds that defining adherence to the gold standard by looking at variables such as exchange rates, money growth, or prices risks assuming the propositions to be shown.

8. In constructing the grand averages taken over gold and non-gold countries, if a

country abandoned the gold standard in the middle of a year, it is included in both the gold and non-gold categories with weights equal to the fraction of the year spent in each category. We use simple rather than weighted averages in the tables, and similarly give all countries equal weight in regression results presented below. This was done because, for the purpose of testing hypotheses (e.g., about the relationship between deflation and depression) it seems most reasonable to treat each country (with its own currency, legal system, financial system, etc.) as the basic unit of observation and to afford each observation equal weight. If we were instead trying to measure the overall economic significance of, for example, an individual country's policy decisions, weighted averages would be more appropriate.

9. The use of the terms M1 and M2 should not be taken too literally here, as the transactions characteristics of the assets included in each category vary considerably among countries. The key distinction between the two aggregates is that commercial banks, which were heavily involved in commercial lending, were much more vulnerable to banking panics. Savings banks, in contrast, held mostly government securities, and thus often gained deposits during panic periods.

10. However, it must be mentioned that recent exponents of the real wage explanation of German unemployment invoke it to account for high levels of unemployment throughout the mid and late 1920s, and not just for the period after 1929 (Borchardt 1979).

11. In the French case, however, there may have been some fear of government default, given the large deficits that were being run; conceivably, this could explain the higher rate on French bills.

12. A possible response to this point is that fear of devaluation added a risk premium to assets in gold standard countries. This point can be checked by looking at forward rates for foreign exchange, available in Einzig (1937). The forward premia on gold standard currencies are generally small, except immediately before devaluations. In particular, the three-month premium on dollars versus the pound in 1932 had a maximum value of about 4.5% (at an annual rate) during the first week of June, but for most of the year was considerably less than that.

13. The effect of deflation on banks, and the relationship between deflation and bank runs, has been analyzed in a theoretical model by Flood and Garber (1981).

14. An important issue, which we cannot resolve here, is whether government takeovers of banks resulted in some restoration of intermediary services, or if, instead, the government functioned primarily as a liquidation agent.

15. In the next section we divide our sample into two groups: eleven countries with serious banking problems and thirteen countries without these problems. In 1930, the year before the peak of the banking crises, the countries that were to avoid banking problems suffered on average a 12% deflation and a 6% fall in industrial production; the comparable numbers for the group that was to experience panics were 13% and 8%. Thus, there was no large difference between the two groups early in the Depression. In contrast, in 1932 (the year following the most intense banking crises), industrial production growth in countries without banking crises averaged −2%; in the group that experienced crises the comparable number was −16%.

16. Although this correlation seems to hold during the Depression, we do not want to conclude unconditionally that branch banking is more stable; branching facilitates diversification but also increases the risk that problems in a few large banks may bring down the entire network.

17. Causality could run in both directions. For example, Wigmore (1987) argues that the U.S. banking panic in 1933 was in part created by a run on the dollar.

18. It has been pointed out to us that if nominal wages were literally rigid, then this approach would find no effect for wages even though changes in the real wage might

be an important channel for the effects of deflation. The reply to this is that, if nominal wages are completely rigid, the hypothesis that real wages are important can never be distinguished from an alternative which proposes that deflation has its effects in some other way.

19. In another sensitivity check, we also tried multiplying *PANIC* times the change in the deposit-currency ratio, to allow for differential severity of panics. The results exhibited an outlier problem. When Rumania (which had a change in the deposit-currency ratio of −.76 in 1931) was excluded, the results were similar to those obtained using the *PANIC* variable alone. However, inclusion of Rumania weakened both the magnitude and statistical significance of the effect of panics on output. The "reason" for this is that, despite its massive deposit contraction, Rumania experienced a 5% growth of industrial production in 1931. Whether this is a strong contradiction of the view that panics affect real output is not clear, however, since according to the League of Nations the peak of the Rumania crisis did not occur until September or October, and industrial production in the subsequent year fell by 14%. Another reason to downplay these results is that the change in the deposit-currency ratio may not be a good indicator of the severity of the banking crisis, as the Italian case indicates.

20. Results were unchanged when lagged industrial production growth was added to the equations. The coefficient on lagged production was typically small and statistically insignificant.

21. Deflation is by the wholesale price index.

22. A possible exception to this proposition for a small country might be a situation in which there are fears that the country will devalue or abandon gold; in this case the country's price level might drop below the world level without causing inflows of reserves. An example may be Poland in 1932. A member of the Gold Bloc, Poland's wholesale price level closely tracked that of France until mid 1931, when Poland experienced severe banking problems and withdrawals of foreign deposits, which threatened convertibility. From that point on, even though both countries remained on the gold standard, money supplies and prices in Poland and France began to diverge. From the time of the Polish crisis in June 1931 until the end of 1932, money and notes and circulation dropped by 9.1% in Poland (compared to a gain of 10.5% in France); Polish commercial bank deposits fell 24.5% (compared to a 4.1% decline in France); and Polish wholesale prices declined 35.2% (compared to a decline of 18.3% in France). Despite its greater deflation, Poland lost about a sixth of its gold reserves in 1932, while France gained gold.

23. This hypothesis does not bear on Temin's claim that there was little that central banks could do about banking crises under the gold standard; rather, the argument is that if, fortuitously, French and U.S. banking panics had not occurred, world deflation in 1931–32 would have been less severe.

24. Indeed, if banking panics induced countries to abandon gold, they may have indirectly contributed to an eventual rise in price levels.

References

Bernanke, Ben. 1983. Non-monetary effects of the financial crisis in the propagation of the Great Depression. *American Economic Review* 73: 257–76.

———. 1986. Employment, hours, and earnings in the Depression: An analysis of eight manufacturing industries. *American Economic Review* 76: 82–109.

Bernanke, Ben, and Mark Gertler. 1990. Financial fragility and economic performance. *Quarterly Journal of Economics* 105: 87–114.

Board of Governors of the Federal Reserve System. 1943. *Banking and monetary statistics, 1919–41*. Washington, DC: Government Printing Office.

Borchardt, Knut. 1979. Zwangslagen und Handlungsspielraume in der grossen Wirtschaftskrise der fruhen dreissiger Jahren: Zur Revision des uberlieferten Geschichtesbildes. *Jahrbuch der Bayerische Akademie der Wissenschaften*, 87–132. Munich.

Bordo, Michael, and Finn Kydland. 1990. The gold standard as a rule. Typescript, Rutgers University and Carnegie-Mellon University.

Bouvier, Jean. 1984. The French banks, inflation and the economic crisis, 1919–1939. *Journal of European Economic History* 13: 29–80.

Campa, Jose Manuel. Forthcoming. Exchange rates and economic recovery in the 1930s: An extension to Latin America. *Journal of Economic History.*

Choudhri, Ehsan U., and Levis A. Kochin. 1980. The exchange rate and the international transmission of business cycle disturbances: Some evidence from the Great Depression. *Journal of Money, Credit, and Banking* 12: 565–74.

Ciocca, Pierluigi, and Gianni Toniolo. 1984. Industry and finance in Italy, 1918–40. *Journal of European Economic History* 13: 113–36.

Eichengreen, Barry. 1986. The Bank of France and the sterilization of gold, 1926–1932. *Explorations in Economic History* 23: 56–84.

———. 1987. The gold-exchange standard and the Great Depression. Working Paper no. 2198 (March). Cambridge, Mass.: National Bureau of Economic Research.

Eichengreen, Barry, and T. J. Hatton. 1987. Interwar unemployment in international perspective: An overview. In *Interwar unemployment in international perspective*, ed. B. Eichengreen and T. J. Hatton, 1–59. Boston: Kluwer Academic Publishers.

Eichengreen, Barry, and Richard Portes. 1986. Debt and default in the 1930s: Causes and consequences. *European Economic Review* 30: 599–640.

Eichengreen, Barry, and Jeffrey Sachs. 1985. Exchange rates and economic recovery in the 1930s. *Journal of Economic History* 45: 925–46.

———. 1986. Competitive devaluation in the Great Depression: A theoretical reassessment. *Economic Letters* 21: 67–71.

Einzig, Paul. 1937. *The theory of forward exchange*. London: Macmillan.

Fisher, Irving. 1933. The debt-deflation theory of great depressions. *Econometrica* 1: 337–57.

Flood, Robert P., Jr., and Peter M. Garber. 1981. A systematic banking collapse in a perfect foresight world. NBER Working Paper no. 691 (June). Cambridge, Mass.: National Bureau of Economic Research.

Friedman, Milton, and Anna J. Schwartz. 1963. *A monetary history of the United States, 1867–1960*. Princeton: Princeton University Press.

Haberler, Gottfried. 1976. The world economy, money, and the Great Depression. Washington, DC: American Enterprise Institute.

Hamilton, James. 1987. Monetary factors in the Great Depression. *Journal of Monetary Economics* 19: 145–69.

———. 1988. The role of the international gold standard in propagating the Great Depression. *Contemporary Policy Issues* 6: 67–89.

Kindleberger, Charles P. 1984. Banking and industry between the two wars: An international comparison. *Journal of European Economic History* 13: 7–28.

League of Nations. 1926. *Memorandum on Currency and Central Banks*, 1913–1925. Geneva.

———. 1935. *Commercial banks, 1929–1934*. Geneva.

———. 1944. *International currency experience: Lessons of the inter-war period.* Geneva.

Lindert, Peter. 1969. Key currencies and gold, 1900–1913. *Princeton Studies in International Finance*, no. 24.

Newell, Andrew, and J. S. V. Symons. 1988. The macroeconomics of the interwar

years: International comparisons. In *Interwar unemployment in international perspective,* ed. B. Eichengreen and T. J. Hatton, 61–96. Boston: Kluwer Academic Publishers.
O'Brien, Anthony. 1989. A behavioral explanation for nominal wage rigidity during the Great Depression. *Quarterly Journal of Economics* 104: 719–35.
Temin, Peter. 1976. *Did monetary forces cause the Great Depression?* New York: W. W. Norton.
———. 1989. *Lessons from the Great Depression.* Cambridge, Mass.: MIT Press.
Wigmore, Barrie. 1987. Was the Bank Holiday of 1933 a run on the dollar rather than the banks? *Journal of Economic History* 47: 739–56.

3 Asymmetric Information and Financial Crises: A Historical Perspective

Frederic S. Mishkin

In recent years there has been a growing concern with the fragility of the financial system. Increasing defaults on junk bonds and the stock market crash of October 1987 have raised the specter of major financial crises which might inflict severe damage on the economy. Policymakers, particularly those in the central bank, are faced with the questions of what they should do to prevent financial crises and what their response should be when a financial crises appears imminent. In order to start providing intelligent answers to these questions, we must first understand the nature of financial crises and how they might affect the aggregate economy.

This paper seeks to understand the nature of financial crises by examining their history in the United States using the new and burgeoning literature on asymmetric information and financial structure, which has been excellently surveyed recently by Gertler (1988a). After describing how an asymmetric information approach helps to understand the nature of financial crises, the paper focuses on a historical examination of a series of financial crises in the United States, beginning with the panic of 1857 and ending with the stock market crash of 19 October 1987. The asymmetric information approach accounts for patterns in the data and many features of these crises which are

Frederic S. Mishkin is professor of money and financial markets at the Graduate School of Business, Columbia University, and a research associate of the National Bureau of Economic Research.

The author gives special thanks to Mark Gertler, who during many after-lunch strolls educated him about the literature on asymmetric information and financial structure. He also thanks Robert Barro, Glenn Hubbard, Michael Bordo, Ben Friedman, Gary Gorton, Hugh Rockoff, Gene White, and participants in the Conference on Financial Crisis, the NBER Macro History Workshop, and a seminar at Rutgers University for their helpful comments; Jinho Kim for his able research assistance; and Dick Sylla and Bill Schwert for sending him data. The paper is part of the NBER's research programs on Financial Markets and Monetary Economics and on Economic Fluctuations. Any opinions expressed are those of the author, not those of the National Bureau of Economic Research.

otherwise hard to explain. It also suggests why financial crises have had such important consequences for the aggregate economy over the past one hundred and fifty years.

3.1 The Nature of Financial Crises

There are two polar views of the nature of financial crises in the literature. Monetarists beginning with Friedman and Schwartz (1963) have associated financial crises with banking panics. They stress the importance of banking panics because they view them as a major source of contractions in the money supply which, in turn, had led to severe contractions in aggregate economic activity in the United States. Their view of financial crisis leads monetarists to advocate a lender-of-last-resort role for the central bank, so that banking panics and the subsequent monetary instability will be prevented. Events in which there is a sharp drop in wealth but no potential for a banking panic and a resulting sharp decline in the money supply are not seen by monetarists as real financial crises that require any central bank intervention. Indeed, Schwartz (1986) characterizes these situations as "pseudo financial crises." Central bank intervention in a pseudo financial crises is viewed as unnecessary and, indeed, possibly harmful; that is, it may lead to a decrease in economic efficiency because firms that deserve to fail are bailed out or because it results in excessive money growth that stimulates inflation.

An opposite view of financial crises is held by Kindleberger (1978) and Minsky (1972), who have a much broader definition of what constitutes a real financial crisis than monetarists. They argue that financial crises involve either sharp declines in asset prices, failures of large financial and nonfinancial firms, deflations or disinflations, disruptions in foreign exchange markets, or some combination of all of these. Since they perceive any one of these disturbances as having potentially serious consequences for the aggregate economy, they advocate a much-expanded role for government intervention when a financial crisis, broadly defined, occurs.

One problem with the Kindleberger-Minsky view of financial crises is that it does not supply a rigorous theory of what characterizes a financial crisis, and thus lends itself to being used too broadly as a justification for government interventions that might not be beneficial for the economy. Indeed, this is the basis of Schwartz's (1986) attack on the Kindleberger-Minsky view. At the other extreme, the monetarist view of financial crises is overly narrow because it focuses only on bank panics and their effect on the money supply. In contrast to both these views, the recent literature on asymmetric information and financial structure provides a broad definition of the nature of financial crises, while supplying a theory which does not automatically justify government interventions when there is a sharp drop in wealth.

The asymmetric information literature which looks at the impact of financial structure on economic activity focuses on the differences in information available to different parties in a financial contract. Borrowers have an informational advantage over lenders because borrowers know more about the investment projects they want to undertake. This informational advantage results in adverse selection and the classic "lemons" problem first described by Akerlof (1970). A lemons problem occurs in the debt market because lenders have trouble determining whether a borrower is a good risk (he has good investment opportunities with low risk) or, alternatively, is a bad risk (he has poorer investment projects with high risk). If the lender cannot distinguish between the borrowers of good quality and bad quality (the lemons), he will only make the loan at an interest rate that reflects the average quality of the good and bad borrowers. The result is that high-quality borrowers will be paying a higher interest rate than they should because low-quality borrowers pay a lower interest rate than they should. One result of this lemons problem is that some high-quality borrowers may drop out of the market, with what would have been profitable investment projects not being undertaken.[1]

Another result, as demonstrated by Stiglitz and Weiss (1981), is that information asymmetry can result in credit rationing in which some borrowers are arbitrarily denied loans. This occurs because a higher interest rate leads to even greater adverse selection: the borrowers with the riskiest investment projects will now be the likeliest to want to take out loans at the higher interest rate. If the lender cannot identify the borrowers with the riskier investment projects, he may want to cut down the number of loans he makes, which causes the supply of loans to decrease rather than increase with the higher interest rate.[2] Thus, even if there is an excess demand for loans, a higher interest rate will not equilibrate the market because additional increases in the interest rate will only decrease the supply of loans and worsen the excess demand for loans even further. Indeed, as Mankiw (1986) has demonstrated, a small rise in the riskless interest rate can lead to a very large decrease in lending and possibly even a collapse in the market.

The adverse selection–lemons analysis above indicates how a disruption can occur in financial markets that adversely affects aggregate economic activity. If market interest rates are driven up sufficiently because of increased demand for credit or because of a decline in the money supply, the adverse selection problem might dramatically worsen and there will be a significant decline in lending, which, in turn, results in a substantial decrease in investment and aggregate economic activity. In addition, if uncertainty increases in a financial market such that it becomes harder for lenders to screen out good borrowers from bad borrowers, the adverse selection problem would also increase dramatically and, again, could lead to a sharp decline in investment and aggregate activity.

These mechanisms suggest that an important manifestation of a financial crisis would be a large rise in interest rates to borrowers for whom there is substantial difficulty in obtaining reliable information about their characteristics; that is, for whom there is a serious asymmetric information problem. At the same time, there would be a much smaller effect on interest rates to borrowers for whom almost no asymmetric information problem exists because information about their characteristics is easily obtainable. Since low-quality borrowers are more likely to be those firms for which information about their characteristics is difficult to obtain, while high-quality borrowers are more likely to be ones for which the asymmetric information problem is least severe, a rise in the spread between interest rates on low-quality versus high-quality bonds can provide information on when the adverse selection problem becomes more severe in debt markets.

One way that lenders can reduce the adverse selection problem in debt markets is to have the borrower provide collateral for the loan. Thus, if the borrower defaults on the loan, the lender can take title to the collateral and sell it to make up the loss. Note that if the collateral is of good enough quality, then it is no longer as important whether the borrower is of good or bad quality since the loss incurred by the lender if the loan is defaulted on is substantially reduced. With collateral, therefore, the fact that there is asymmetric information between the borrower and lender is no longer as important a factor in the market.

The importance of collateral for reducing the adverse selection problem in debt markets suggests another mechanism whereby financial disruption adversely affects aggregate economic activity. As emphasized by Calomiris and Hubbard (1990) and Greenwald and Stiglitz (1988), a sharp decrease in the valuation of firms' assets in a stock market crash lowers the value of collateral and thereby makes adverse selection a more important problem for lenders since the losses from loan defaults are now higher. Note that this decline in asset values could occur either because of expectations of lower future income streams from these assets or because of a rise in market interest rates which lowers the present discounted value of future income streams. The lemons problem analysis indicates that the increased importance of adverse selection will lead to a decline in lending and, therefore, a decline in investment and aggregate economic activity. Again, we would expect that this increase in the adverse selection problem would affect interest rates for lower-quality firms more than for higher-quality firms, about whose characteristics there is better information. Hence, the problem would be manifested by an increase in the interest-rate spread for high- versus low-quality borrowers.

Asymmetric information between borrowers and lenders also results in a moral hazard problem which affects the efficiency of financial markets. Because leaders have trouble ascertaining the quality of investment projects that borrowers wish to undertake, the borrower has incentives to engage in activities that may be personally beneficial but will increase the probability of default and thus harm the lender. For example, the borrower has incentives to cheat by misallocating funds for his own personal use, either through embezzlement or by spending on perquisites which do not lead to increased profits.[3] Also the borrower has incentives to undertake investment in unprofitable projects that increase his power or stature or to invest in projects with higher risk, in which the borrower does well if the project succeeds but the lender bears most of the loss if the project fails. In addition, the borrower has incentives to shirk and to just not work very hard. The conflict of interest between the borrower and lender (the agency problem) implies that lending and investment will be at suboptimal levels. Indeed, as indicated by Bernanke and Gertler (1989), a lower amount of a borrower's net worth increases the agency problem because the borrower has less to lose by engaging in moral hazard. Hence, a decline in borrowers' net worth leads to a decrease in lending, and thus a decline in investment and aggregate economic activity.

The agency and adverse-selection problems provide additional mechanisms for financial crises to affect the aggregate economy. An unanticipated deflation or a disinflation redistributes wealth from debtors to creditors by increasing the real value of debt, and thereby reducing borrowers' net worth. The resulting increase in adverse selection and agency problems causes a decline in investment and economic activity.[4] The presence of asymmetric information thus provides a rationale for Irving Fisher's (1933) debt-deflation analysis of depressions which points to a decreasing price level and increased real indebtedness as a major source of the economic contraction during the Great Depression. In a multiperiod context, Gertler (1988b) shows that the concept of a borrower's net worth can be broadened to include the discounted value of future profits. Thus a stock market crash which represents a decreased valuation of firms' discounted future profits also increases adverse selection and agency problems and can lead to a decline in investment and a business-cycle contraction.

Firms with high net worth and a high value of discounted future profits—that is, high-quality firms—are much less likely to have greatly increased agency costs (costs due to asymmetric information in the market) when a stock market crash or a deflationary shock occurs, than low-quality firms with low net worth and a low value of discounted future profits. An increase in agency costs stemming from either disinflation or a stock market crash, therefore, should also be reflected in a rise in the interest-rate spread for high- versus low-quality borrowers.

An important feature of the recent literature on asymmetric information and financial structure is that it suggests why banks play a prominent role in financial markets. Banks are eminently well suited to solve many of the adverse selection and moral hazard problems inherent in credit markets. They have expertise in collecting information about firms, and thus are better able to screen good borrowers from bad borrowers at a low cost. This is especially true because they are not as subject to the free-rider problem which exists for individual purchasers of marketable securities who can costlessly take advantage of information that other purchasers of marketable securities produce. The advantages of banks in information-collection activities are also enhanced by their ability to engage in long-term customer relationships and to issue loans using lines-of-credit arrangements. In addition, they can engage in lower-cost monitoring than individuals, as is demonstrated in Diamond (1984), and have advantages in enforcement of restrictive covenants, both of which reduce the potential for moral hazard by borrowers.[5] The existence of asymmetric information in credit markets provides a compelling rationale for the importance of banks in getting funds from savers to borrowers who have the most attractive investment opportunities, thereby enhancing economic efficiency.

The importance of asymmetric information provides another mechanism by which financial crises reduce economic activity. The analysis above indicates that banks perform an important role in generating productive investment for the economy. Thus, as is described in Bernanke (1983), disturbances in financial markets that reduce the amount of financial intermediation that can be undertaken by banks will lead to a reduction in lending to borrowers with profitable investment opportunities, resulting in a contraction of economic activity.

Bank panics are clearly one major way for banks to find themselves unable to fully perform their intermediation role.[6] In a panic, depositors, fearing the safety of their deposits, withdraw them from the banking system, causing a contraction in loans and a multiple contraction in deposits. Here, again, an asymmetric information problem is at the source of the financial crisis because depositors rush to make withdrawals from solvent as well as insolvent banks since they cannot distinguish between them. Furthermore, banks' desire to protect themselves from possible deposit outflows leads them to increase their reserves relative to deposits, which also produces a contraction in loans and deposits. The net result is that a bank panic reduces the funds available to banks to make loans, and thus the cost of financial intermediation rises, causing a reduction in investment and a decline in aggregate economic activity.

A bank panic also has the feature of decreasing liquidity, which will lead to higher interest rates. As we have seen before, the rise in interest rates directly increases adverse selection problems in credit markets and can reduce the value of firms' net worth, which also increases adverse selection as well as agency problems. Thus, since bank panics have the secondary effect of increasing adverse selection and agency problems in financial markets, they lead to economic contraction through these channels as well. We should then expect to see that bank panics are also associated with a larger interest-rate spread between higher- and lower-quality debt instruments.

The monetarist literature on the role of bank panics in economic contractions offers an additional channel by which financial crises affect the aggregate economy. Friedman and Schwartz (1963) document how bank panics in the United States led to sharp contractions in the money supply as a result of depositors' movement out of deposits into currency and banks' movement out of loans into reserves. These contractions in the money supply are then seen as being responsible for substantial declines in economic activity and the price level.

The recent literature on the impact of asymmetric information on aggregate economic activity provides a view complementary to that of the monetarists on the importance of bank panics. Indeed, the asymmetric information approach supplies a transmission mechanism for a decline in the money supply to lead to a decline in aggregate economic activity. The deflation that stems from a decline in the money supply increases adverse selection and agency problems, which then cause a decline in investment and aggregate economic activity. However, the asymmetric information approach suggests that a decline in the money supply as a result of a financial crisis is not the whole story of why financial crises affect the aggregate economy. Instead, it takes a much broader view of what a financial crisis is and puts a very different light on when a financial crisis is real rather than a pseudo crisis.

3.2 A Historical Analysis of Pre–World War II Financial Crises

To obtain evidence on how we should characterize financial crises, I examine a series of episodes in the 1857–1941 period in which it is generally agreed that financial crises occurred. Then in section 3.3, I examine two postwar episodes in which there was Federal Reserve intervention to prevent a financial crisis. The analysis in the previous section suggests that a critical variable for assessing the nature of a particular financial crisis is the spread between interest rates for high- and low-quality borrowers. For the period beginning in 1919, the analysis uses the spread between Moody's Baa corporate bond rate and the long-term Treasury bond rate averaged over the month, the same spread variable used by Bernanke (1983). However, since this series is not available prior to 1919, an alternative measure must be used before that date. Macaulay (1938) provides monthly yield data for high-grade railroad bonds from 1857 to 1935 which are essentially averages over the month—they are calculated from the average of the high and low bond price for that month. The spread measure was constructed from this data by subtracting the average yield on the best one-fourth of the bonds from the average yield on the worst one-fourth of the bonds (i.e., three bonds in the best and worst categories were used for 1857–66, five bonds for 1867–81, eight bonds for 1882–87, and ten bonds for 1888–1935).[7] One-fourth as the fraction of bonds in the best and worst categories were chosen because this fraction led to the highest correlation of the Macaulay spread variable with the Bernanke spread variable in the 1919–35 period, when the two series overlap. However, the choice of the fraction of bonds to include in each category is not crucial. The correlation coefficient between Macaulay spread variables using a different choice for the number of bonds in each category is always above .95 in the 1857–1918 period, and the conclusions for each episode studied are not affected by a different choice for the number of bonds in each category.

The Macaulay spread variable has several problems in comparison with the Bernanke spread variable. First, there is no guarantee using the Macaulay variable that the worst or the best bonds remain in the same rating class throughout the time period studied. This cannot be helped because ratings for these bonds are not available. It should be noted that the Bernanke spread variable is not perfect on these grounds either, because, as Temin (1976) points out, during periods when default risk was changing rapidly, it is not clear that the Moody's ratings continued to have the same meaning. Another potential problem is that the Macaulay bonds are all of fairly high grade: for the 1919–35 period, the worst Macaulay bond still has an interest rate below the Moody's Baa corporate bond rate, while the best bond has a rate below the Aaa corporate bond rate. There is a possibility that the Macaulay bonds might not have a sufficient difference in their grades to pick up the changes in the interest rates for high- and low-quality borrowers.

Despite these limitations, the Macaulay measure seems to perform well. The Macaulay spread variable, denoted as SPREADM, is plotted for 1857–1918 in figure 3.1, panel A. Panel B plots the Bernanke spread variable, SPREADB, over the 1919–88 period along with the Macaulay variable from 1919 to 1935. As is evident in panel B, the Macaulay variable is highly correlated with the Bernanke variable: the correlation coefficient between the two variables during 1919–35 is 0.88. Both variables tell similar stories in that period—they rise during the 1920–21 recession, decline thereafter to a low point in the late twenties, climb dramatically with the onset of the banking panics in late 1930, and then fall to substantially lower levels by the end of 1935. Furthermore, as we will see, the Macaulay spread variable seems to have a consistent relationship with stock market and commercial-paper-rate variables in the pre-1919 episodes studied below, adding further confidence in its validity.

The analysis of the nature of financial crises in the previous section also suggests that we should look at stock prices and interest rates when we analyze individual episodes of financial crisis. The level of stock prices, denoted as STOCK, is constructed as the cumulative geometric sum of the stock-market-return series from Wilson, Sylla, and Jones (1990),[8] and is thus meant to be an end-of-month series. However, the earlier data in the stock market series (up until the 1920s) are monthly averages or the averages of the high and low stock prices for the month. Thus, even though the stock price series used here is meant to be thought of as an end-of-month series, it is actually closer to a monthly average, up until the 1920s. Furthermore, before 1890, the stock price series is primarily from railroad stocks.

The interest rates examined are those on high-grade commercial paper, RCP, and those on call loans to stock and bond brokers in New York, RCALL. For 1857–1918, the commercial-paper-rate series is choice 60- to 90-day, two-name paper from Macaulay (1938), while after this date it is the rate on 4- to 6-month commercial paper obtained from *Banking and Monetary Statistics, 1914–1940* and *1941–1970*, published by the Board of Governors of the Federal Reserve System, and from the *Federal Reserve Bulletin,* various years. The call-loan-rate series is taken from Wilson, Sylla, and Jones (1990), and it, along with the commercial-paper-rate series, are monthly averages of daily

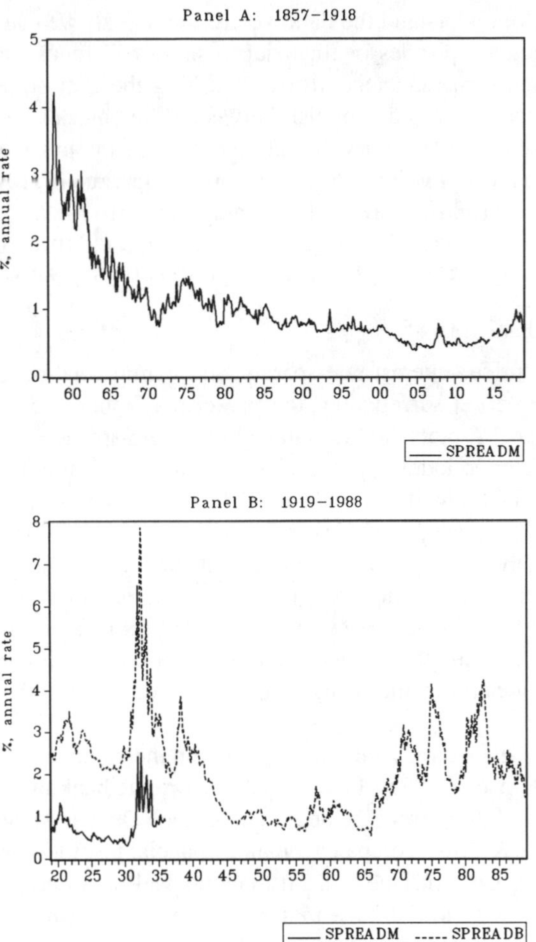

Fig. 3.1 Interest rate spreads

rates. In the following analysis of financial crises, more attention will be focused on the commercial paper rate when discussing interest rate movements. This makes sense because commercial paper rates should be closer to the interest rates that affect business firms' decisions to invest, while call loan rates are influenced by peculiarities of events in the stock market.

There are clearly many other variables that we might want to examine in order to better understand what is going on during financial crises—for example, business failures, the price level, commodity prices, and industrial production. However, in this paper I will be conducting a more preliminary analysis and will only be examining financial market variables. In future work, I hope to be able to use such data to engage in a fuller treatment of the financial crisis phenomenon.

Now that we understand the data we are looking at, we can turn to discussion of particular episodes of financial crisis. I will focus especially on the timing of events and financial variables during these episodes, because the timing will enable us to distinguish between different views of the nature of financial crises. The crises I will examine first are the pre-World War II episodes that are most prominent in discussions by Sprague (1910), Kindleberger (1978), Bordo (1986), Gorton (1988) and Schwert (1989a).[9] Historical descriptions of these episodes are found in Sprague (1910), Collman (1931), Smith and Cole (1935), Friedman and Schwartz (1963), and Sobel (1968).

3.2.1 The Panic of 1857

The stock price, interest-rate-spread, and commercial-paper-rate data for the two-year period surrounding the panic in October 1857 are reported in figure 3.2. Panel A plots the Macaulay interest-rate-spread variable, SPREADM, and the stock price index, STOCK. The left-hand vertical axis corresponds to the spread variable, while the right-hand vertical axis corresponds to the stock price index. The stock price index is normalized to equal 100 at its peak value. Panel B plots the commercial paper rate, RCP, and the call rate, RCALL. In both panels, the date set by the National Bureau of Economic Research for the beginning of the 1857–58 recession, July 1857, is marked on the horizontal axis with an *R*, while the October 1857 date for the banking panic is marked by a *P*. This general format is used in the figures for the other episodes discussed later.

The interest-rate-spread variable, along with the commercial paper rate, begins to climb in July 1857, three months before the banking panic, while the stock market is falling from the beginning of the year. On August 25, the Ohio Life Insurance & Trust Company, a major financial institution with substantial investments in western land and railroads as well as in commodity futures, failed. This was followed by a major stock market crash in September and October. The market returns of −14.46% in September and −15.26% in October were the tenth and eleventh worst monthly returns tabulated by Wilson, Sylla, and Jones (1990) for their entire sample period of January 1834–August 1988. With the failure of the Ohio Life & Trust Co., reserves began to be pulled from New York, and the first bank failures there occurred in September. Interest rates shot through the roof, with the commercial paper rate rising to 18% in September and a peak of 24% in October. Thinly capitalized railroads, such as the Delaware, Lackawanna & Western, the Fond du Lac, and several smaller railroads, went bankrupt in September. Major runs on the New York banks began in October, finally culminating in a suspension of specie payments in mid October, and bank panics spread throughout the country. Failures of major railroads, such as the Erie & Pittsburgh, the Fort Wayne & Chicago, the Reading, and Illinois Central, occurred in October. The outcome was a severe recession which ended in December 1858.

The timing of events in the panic of 1857 seem to fit an asymmetric infor-

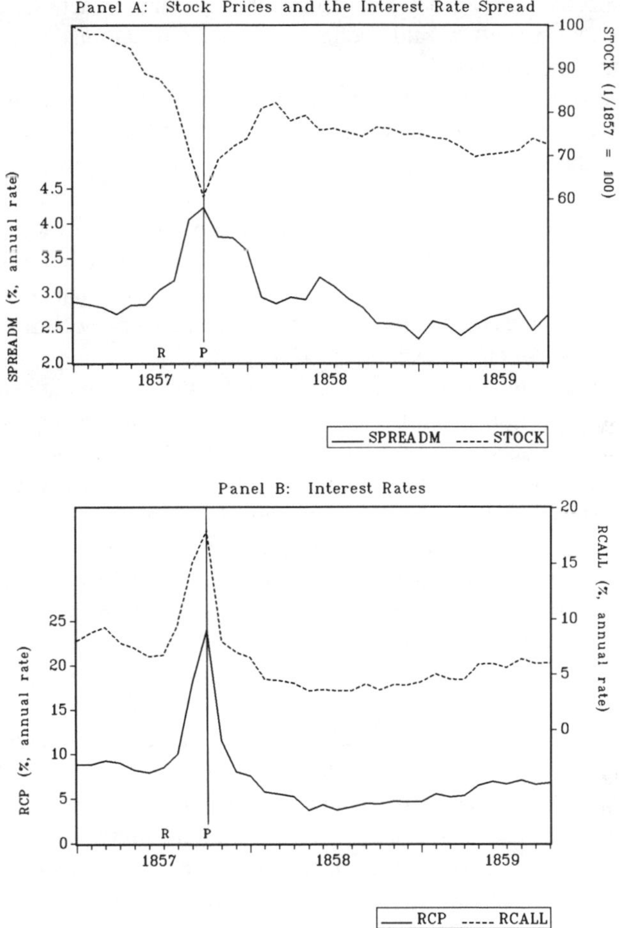

Fig. 3.2 The panic of 1857

mation interpretation of the financial crisis. Rather than starting with the bank panic in October 1857, the disturbance to the financial markets seems to arise several months earlier with the rise in interest rates, the stock market decline, the major failure of a financial firm, and the widening of the interest rate spread. The asymmetric information story provides an explanation of how the financial crisis could have led to a severe economic downturn. The rise in interest rates and the stock market decline, along with the failure of Ohio Life & Trust Co. which increased uncertainty, would magnify the adverse selection and agency problems in the credit markets. Indeed, the stock market crash might be linked to the general rise in interest rates which would have lowered the present discounted value of future income streams. In this case, the panic of 1857 can be viewed as a liquidity crisis. The net result from the increase in adverse selection and agency problems is that investment activity and aggregate economic activity would decline, causing expectations of further economic contraction and business failures.

As pointed out in Gorton (1988), depositors would now want to withdraw their funds from the banking system, because the bleak business conditions would lead them to expect losses on deposits left in the banks and this would be especially undesirable at a time when their consumption might be falling owing to the economic downturn. The outcome of the process would be a run on the banks, and the resulting panic would raise interest rates further, cause the stock market to decline even more, and worsen agency and adverse selection problems in the credit markets. That a severe economic contraction would develop is a logical outcome of this process.

Finally, after suspension of specie payments, the intervention of clearinghouse associations, as noted in Gorton (1985) would help to separate solvent from insolvent banks.[10] The banking panic would then subside and, with the restoration of liquidity in the banking system, interest rates would fall, the stock market might undergo a recovery, and, if economic uncertainty and deflation were not too severe, agency and adverse selection problems would diminish, leading to a decline in the interest-rate-spread variable and setting the stage for an eventual recovery of the economy. This scenario seems to describe the data and the events in 1857–58 quite well.

A monetarist interpretation cannot explain these events as effectively because it does not explain the timing of the events and the financial variables, that is, it does not explain why the banking panic occurred when it did and why the spread between interest rates for high- and low-quality borrowers rises dramatically before the panic and then declines after the panic subsides. The asymmetric information story does not rule out important effects on aggregate economic activity from the decline in the money supply that a banking panic produces, it just suggests that there is more to the story of a financial crisis than its effects on the money supply.

3.2.2 The Panic of 1873

The data for the period surrounding the banking panic of September 1873 is found in panels A and B of figure 3.3. (the format is identical to that in fig. 3.2). Compared to all of the other panics studied in this paper, the panic of 1873 is somewhat unusual. First, it occurs before the business-cycle peak, as can be seen in figure 3.3, and second, it was apparently quite unanticipated since it was not preceded by a rise in the interest rate spread.

The initial disturbance for the panic seems to have originated with the financial difficulties of the railroad sector. On 8 September 1873, the New York Warehouse & Security Company, which had made substantial loans to the Missouri, Kansas & Texas Railroad as well on grain and produce, suspended. This suspension was soon followed by the failure of the banking house of Kenyon, Cox & Co. as a result of endorsements on $1.5 million of paper

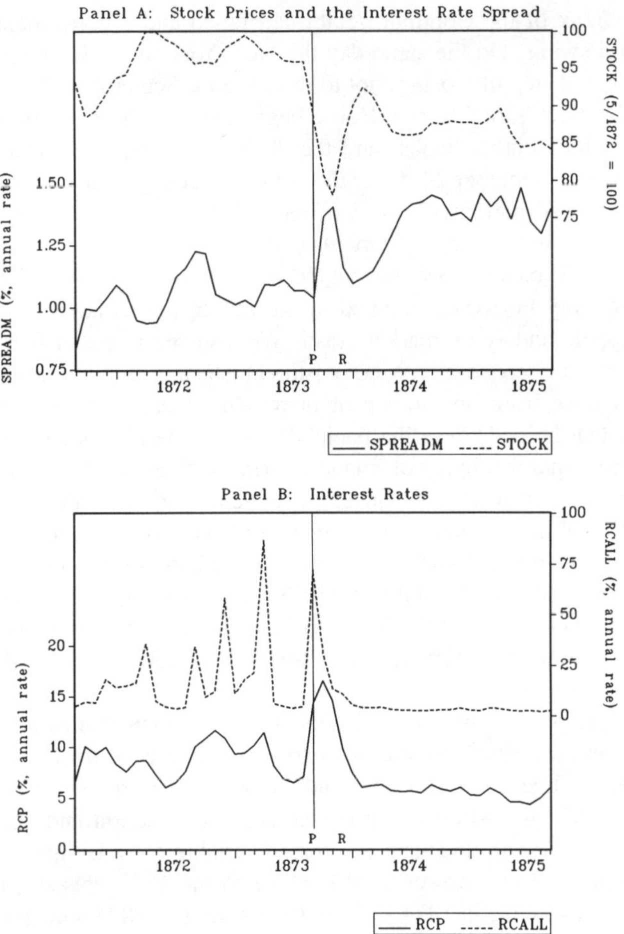

Fig. 3.3 The panic of 1873

issued by the Canada Southern Railroad. At the time, neither of these failures was considered to be of major importance, but they were followed on September 18 by the suspension of Jay Cooke & Co., one of the most respected and important financial institutions in the United States, and by the suspension of Fisk & Hatch the next day. The collapse of Jay Cooke & Co. also stemmed from financial difficulties in the railroad sector, specifically, problems with its loans to Northern Pacific Railroad, which Jay Cooke & Co., controlled. With the announcement of the Jay Cooke & Co. failure, the stock market went into a nose dive, with the result that 18 September 1873 was dubbed "Black Thursday" and the decline in stock prices was over 7% in the month of September. Immediately, runs began on the Fourth National Bank and the Union Trust Company. By Saturday, September 20, both the Union Trust Company and the

National Bank of the Commonwealth had failed and a major banking panic was in full swing. On the same day the New York Stock Exchange took the unprecedented step of closing, not to reopen until September 30. On September 20, the New York Clearing House began to issue clearing-house loan certificates to its member banks, and the decision to suspend specie payments was made on September 24. Over the next several days, suspension of specie payments spread nationwide. It was not until the end of October that banks almost fully resumed specie payments to depositors.

In figure 3.3, panel A, we see that the spread between interest rates on high- and low-quality borrowers jumped in the month immediately following the banking panic and stock market crash. We also see in panel B that interest rates began to rise one month before the crash, and thus the higher interest rates may have been one source of increased adverse selection and agency problems that helped cause the panic. However, the abruptness of the panic suggests that major failures of financial firms such as Jay Cooke & Co. may have increased informational uncertainty, depressed the value of net worth relative to liabilities, and thereby increased adverse selection and agency costs. The runs on banks which occurred immediately after the failure of Jay Cooke & Co. reduced the ability of the banks to perform their intermediation role and are another potential factor in inducing an investment decline and a general economic contraction, which began, according to the NBER dating, in November 1873.

Again, the process of sorting insolvent from solvent banks and insolvent from solvent business firms after the panic would reduce informational uncertainty. The decline in interest rates and the recovery of the stock market after November 1873 would also help reduce adverse selection and agency problems. Consistent with this view, the spread variable does decline immediately after November 1873; however, in contrast to the 1857 episode, the spread variable begins to rise in 1874 and, for the last half of 1874 and all of 1875, is at levels near the peak value reached in October and November of 1873. The high values of the interest-rate spread in 1874 and 1875 are explained by the substantial deflation that sets in after the 1873 panic. As we have seen, a sharp deflation transfers wealth from borrowers to creditors, causing a deterioration in business firms' net worth. The resulting increase in asymmetric information problems, which is reflected in the rise in the interest rate spread, can thus be a major propagation mechanism during the recession.[11] The recession which began in November 1873 was especially long lived and, according to NBER dating, did not end until March 1879. It is often considered to be one of the more severe economic contractions in U.S. history and by some writers is categorized as being the second most severe, only to be outdone by the Great Contraction of 1929–33.

The data in figure 3.3 are quite consistent with an asymmetric information interpretation of the 1873 panic and the severe recession following. However, it gives a prominent role to the banking panic and effects on the economy from declines in the money supply. As Friedman and Schwartz (1963) point out, the period from 1873 to 1879 has an unusual number of years in which declines in the money supply occur. These declines were probably an important factor in the decrease in aggregate demand in this period. The resulting extraordinary and prolonged deflation was then likely to have been an important factor in the rise of asymmetric information problems because of the resulting deterioration in firms' balance sheet positions, which further encouraged a contraction in aggregate economic activity.

3.2.3 The Panic of 1884

We will devote somewhat less discussion to the panic of May 1884 because it was not a particularly severe crisis. However, in figure 3.4 the patterns in the data around the panic date are very similar to the patterns we see in other financial crises. A recession had begun in April 1882, well before the panic, and the interest-rate-spread variable had been declining, with the exception of one large upward blip toward the beginning of 1884. With the decline of stock prices after February 1884, the spread variable again begins to rise. Then, as Sprague (1910, 110) puts it, "within little more than a week an astonishing series of instances of fraud and defalcation, unexplained in our history, were brought to light."[12] On May 8 the firm of Grant & Ward, in which the son of Ulysses S. Grant was a major partner, failed. When audited the firm was found to have assets of only $67,174 and liabilities of $16,792,640. The Marine National Bank, whose president, James D. Fish, was a partner in Grant & Ward, failed immediately when it came to light that the bank had illegally certified one of Grant & Ward's checks for $750,000. On May 13, it became known that John C. Eno, the president of the Second National Bank, has absconded with over $3 million of the bank's securities. The next day, the Metropolitan National Bank closed its doors when it was learned that its president, George Seney, had used bank funds to speculate in railroad stocks which had declined precipitously in value. On the morning of May 16, A. W. Dimock & Co. failed, while in the afternoon, Fisk & Hatch (which had been able to reopen after the panic of 1873) followed suit, taking down with it several banks connected with the firm.

The conditions seemed ripe for a full-scale panic, and we see in panel A of figure 3.4 the typical pattern associated with a panic of a sharp increase in interest rates, especially for call loans, a sharp decline in stock prices (over 8% in May), and a sharp rise in the interest rate spread. However, a panic of the 1873 magnitude was avoided by the timely action of the New York Clearing House Association. On the afternoon of May 14, the New York Clearing House met and approved the issue of clearing-house certificates to the Metropolitan National Bank. The bank was thereby enabled to resume operations the next day and was reorganized with a new president. In addition, the Second National Bank was able to meet all payments because the father of the bank's president repaid the funds stolen by his son. The net result was that the

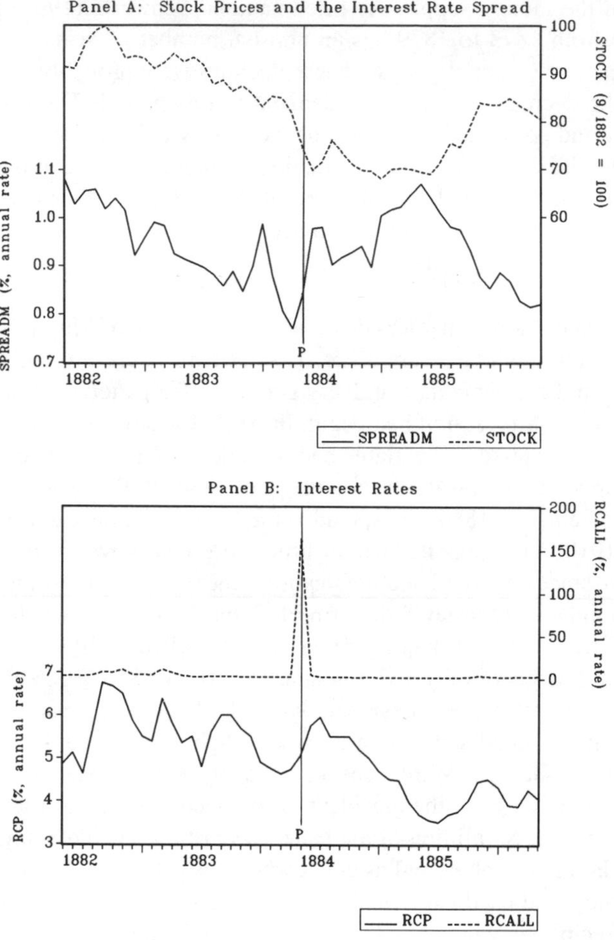

Fig. 3.4 The panic of 1884

bank panic subsided and there was no general suspension of specie payments in the banking system. In the aftermath of the financial crisis, we see the usual pattern that interest rates decline along with the interest rate spread. We also see a pattern that was found after the 1873 panic: the interest rate spread rose again after the decline immediately following the panic. The continuing deflation, which caused a deterioration of firms' balance sheet positions, and continuation of the recession, which increased uncertainty, help explain this rise in the interest rate spread.

3.2.4 The Panic of 1890

The panic of 1890, like that of 1884, was only a minor crisis, in large part because of the swift action by the Clearing House Association. In figure 3.5,

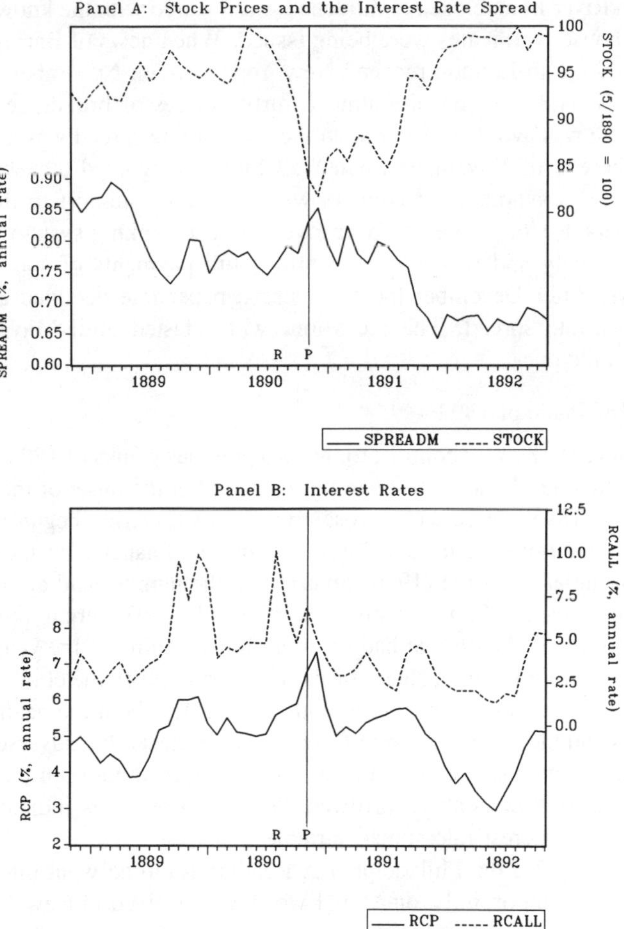

Fig. 3.5 The panic of 1890

we see the usual pattern of stock prices, interest rate spread, and interest rates before the panic in November 1890. Interest rates begin to rise and the stock market begins to fall several months before the panic, and at the same time the interest rate spread begins to widen. On November 7, the Bank of England raised its discount rate from 5% to 6%, which created concern in the New York money market. Heavy selling in the London stock market on November 10 was followed by substantial declines in stock prices in New York, and at 2 P.M. (EST) the failure of Decker, Howell & Co. was announced, which also involved the Bank of North America. The Clearing House Association then immediately decided to issue clearing-house certificates, although this action did not become known until after the close of business on the eleventh. Although the next day the brokerage firm of J. C. Walcott & Co. suspended and the North River Bank closed, confidence was restored with the knowledge that clearing-house certificates were being issued. When news of Baring Brothers & Co.'s failure in London reached New York early on November 15, stocks fell sharply. However, despite almost thirty failures of brokerage houses, a major panic was avoided. The rise in the interest rate spread was quite small, and by the end of November when Wall Street recognized that the Bank of England and a syndicate of bankers were providing support to the London money market, stock prices were recovering. The banking system weathered the panic nicely and was able to continue full payments of specie to their depositors. After December the commercial paper rate declined along with the interest-rate spread. The recession, which lasted until May 1891, remained a mild one.

3.2.5 The Panic of 1893

The panic of 1893, in contrast to the two previous panics of 1884 and 1890, was a severe one. As we can see in figure 3.6, after the onset of the recession in February 1893, interest rates rose and the stock market began to decline. Business conditions were very unsettled, and nonfinancial business failures were substantial. Sprague (1910) reports that the number and amount of liabilities of mercantile failures from January to July 1893 were unprecedented. In addition, the deflation that had set in at the beginning of the year was producing a deterioration in business firms' net worth. Given the climb in interest rates and fall in stock prices, along with uncertainty about the health of business firms and the deterioration in firms' balance sheets, the adverse selection and agency problems began to increase and the spread between interest rates on high- versus low-quality borrowers began to rise, as is indicated by the increase in the interest-rate-spread variable.

On February 26, the Philadelphia & Reading Railroad went into receivership, but more importantly, on May 4 word was received in New York of the failure of the National Cordage Co., a stock market favorite, and a stock market crash ensued. At this stage, the New York banks appeared to be weathering the crisis. However, banks in the West and the South, which were burdened with many problem loans, began to face bank runs, and in June this led to substantial withdrawal of funds by these banks from the banks in New York. Although the wave of bank failures was subsiding by the beginning of July, a second wave of panic hit the western and southern banks in the third week of July. On July 25, the New York, Lake Erie & Western Railroad and the Wisconsin Marine & Fire Insurance Company suspended and there was another sharp drop in the stock market. The bank panics in the South and West, the resulting withdrawals by these banks from the New York banks, and the loss of confidence in the New York banks meant that they too would succumb to the crisis, despite provisions early on by the Clearing House Association to issue loan certificates. Finally, by the beginning of August there was a general suspension of specie payments to bank depositors.

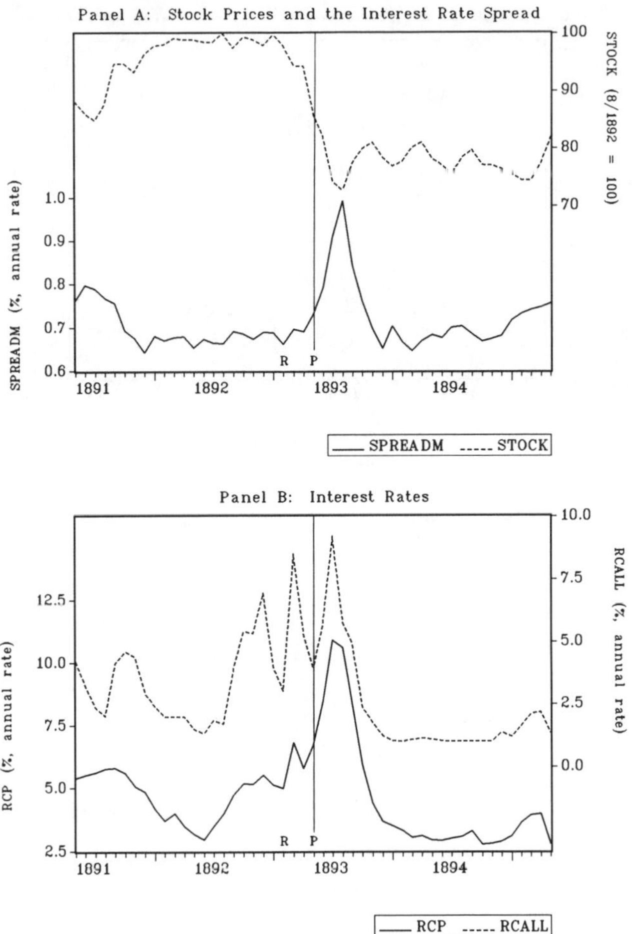

Fig. 3.6 The panic of 1893

The contraction of lending by the banking system as a result of its troubles reduced its role in solving adverse selection and agency problems and clearly made these problems worse in the financial markets. The seriousness of the asymmetric information problems is reflected in the high values of the interest-rate-spread variable in panel A of figure 3.6, which peaked in August 1893. Our asymmetric information analysis indicates that the events of the 1893 panic were then a major factor in the very severe economic contraction that occurred from February 1893 to June 1894. Sobel (1963) reports that besides the more than 600 bank failures as a result of the panic (5% of all American banks), there were over 15,000 commercial bankruptcies, which included such prominent railroads as the Northern Pacific, the Atchison, Topeka & Santa Fe, and the New York & New England.

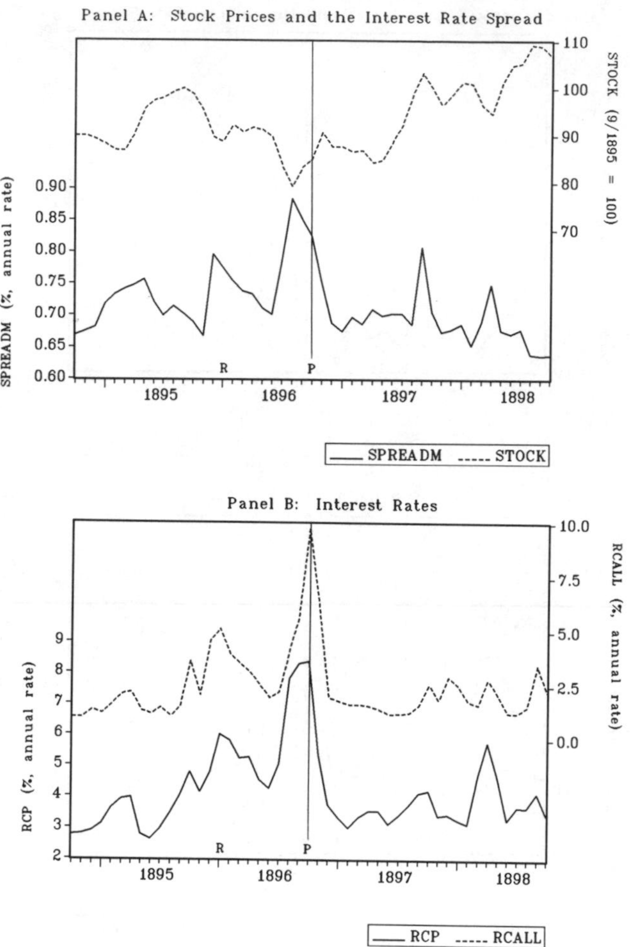

Fig. 3.7 The panic of 1896

3.2.6 The Panic of 1896

Little seems to be written about the panic of 1896, but since Gorton (1988) includes it in his listing of bank panics, the data surrounding his date for the panic in October 1896 is reported in figure 3.7. The data show the typical patterns found in the other panics. Interest rates rise and stock market prices fall several months prior to the panic date and, as our asymmetric information story indicates, there is also a rise in the interest-rate-spread variable. After the panic subsides, interest rates and the interest rate spread fall, while stock prices recover. Another typical pattern is that the panic occurs after the onset of the recession in January 1896, which ends in June 1897. Both the panic and the recession are mild ones, and there is no suspension of specie payments, as in the panic of 1893.

3.2.7 The Panic of 1907

The panic of October 1907 is one of the more severe panics to be discussed in this paper. The traditional story about the beginning of the panic (see, e.g., Sprague 1910, Collman 1931, Friedman and Schwartz 1963, and Sobel 1968) emphasizes the difficulties of a group of banks associated with businessmen F. A. Heinze, C. F. Morse, E. R. Thomas, and O. F. Thomas, who used them to finance their speculative activities. Their grand scheme was to establish a corner in the United Copper Company, which they owned, and to make a killing by squeezing the short sellers. When they suffered large losses with the collapse of the corner on Monday, October 14, the eight banks associated with their activities came under suspicion and were forced to seek assistance from the New York Clearing House Association during that week. By Monday, October 21, the Clearing House Association appeared to have put the affairs of these banks in order, when it was then learned that the president of the Knickerbocker Trust Company, the third largest trust company in New York, was involved with Morse's investment activities. The loss of confidence in Knickerbocker Trust resulted in unfavorable clearing balances, and on the following day, October 22, the National Bank of Commerce announced that it would no longer continue to clear for Knickerbocker Trust. The Clearing House Association did not extend assistance to Knickerbocker Trust, and this is generally viewed as having been a serious mistake. The ensuing run on Knickerbocker Trust forced the bank to close its doors on October 22. The following day, a run began on the second largest trust company, the Trust Company of America, and on October 24, the Lincoln Trust Company was also subjected to a run. Although these trust companies were provided with assistance, the steps taken were too slow and not sufficiently dramatic to restore confidence, as Sprague (1910) and Friedman and Schwartz (1963) have noted. The stock market crashed on October 24, and the monthly return for October 1907 was -10.9%, the thirty-first largest negative return for the 1834–1988 period documented by Wilson, Sylla, and Jones (1990). With the assistance of J. P. Morgan, $35 million was raised by the end of the week to assist the Trust Company of America, and the bank panic in New York seemed to be under control. By then, however, fear had spread throughout the United States, and country banks withdrew large amounts of funds from their New York correspondent banks. Only when the situation was grave for the New York banks did the Clearing House Association finally issue clearing-house loan certificates on October 26. This action was too late because the New York banks still suspended payments of specie to depositors, and the suspension of specie payments then spread nationwide. Payments of specie to depositors was not resumed until the beginning of January 1908.

The traditional story about the 1907 panic places much of the responsibility on securities manipulation and inadequate action by the Clearing House Association to prevent a major disruption of the banking system. Friedman and Schwartz (1963) view the substantial decline in the money supply that fol-

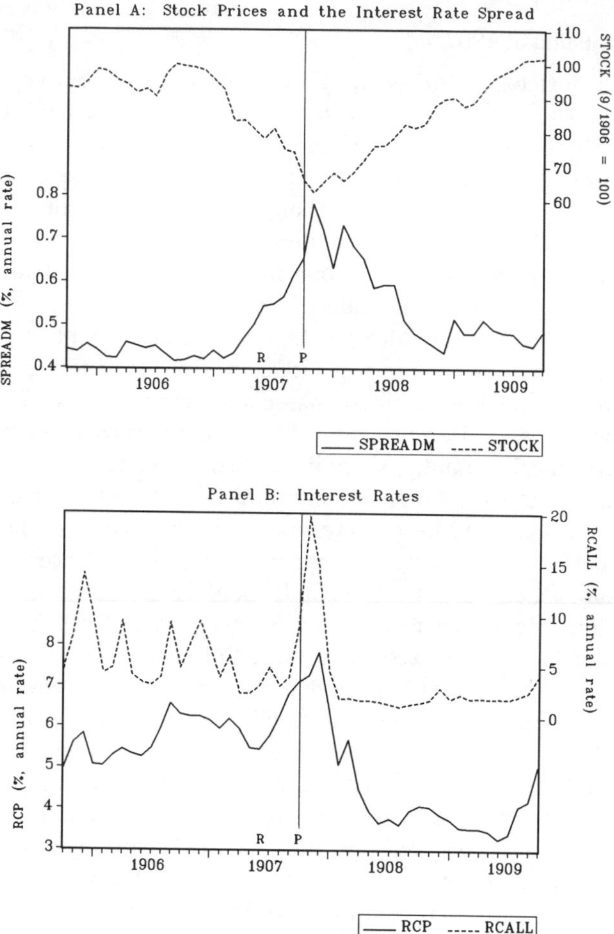

Fig. 3.8 The panic of 1907

lowed the panic to have turned a mild recession into the severe recession that extended from June 1907 to June 1908. The data in figure 3.8 suggest that there may be more to the story. The most striking feature of the data, as can be seen in panel A, is the substantial increase in the interest-rate-spread variable that begins in early 1907, six months before the panic. Indeed, most of the rise in the spread variable has already occurred by the time of the October banking panic. As shown in panel A, the banking panic apparently raised the interest-rate-spread higher and helped prolong its high values in the first half of 1908, but most of the rise cannot be attributed to the bank panic itself.

The rise in the spread variable before the bank panic is easily explained by our asymmetric information story. The stock market begins to decline at the end of 1906, and the negative return in March of −9.8% is the fortieth largest negative return in the 1834–1988 period. Before the panic begins in October, the stock market has declined even further, by 25% from its peak in late 1906. As I have discussed previously, the decline in the valuation of firms by this substantial amount raises adverse selection and agency problems for borrowing firms because it has, in effect, lowered their net worth.

The onset of the recession in June 1907 before the panic, which raised uncertainty about the quality of firms' investment projects, also increased the adverse selection problem. In addition, the rise in the commercial paper rate starting in June 1907, from 5.4% to 6.8% by September, further worsened the potential for adverse selection. The resulting increases in the degree of asymmetric information problems even before the October banking panic, should raise the spread between interest rates for high- and low-quality borrowers, and hence the SPREADM variable. Indeed, since most of the rise in the commercial paper rate and decline in the stock market has already occurred before the onset of the panic, not surprisingly most of the rise in the SPREADM variable has already occurred. The presence of severe asymmetric information problems, even before the banking panic, suggests that they were potentially important factors in creating a severe business-cycle contraction. The decline in the money supply resulting from the bank panics is almost surely another important factor in the severity of the contraction, but the evidence here suggests that it is far from being the whole story.

3.2.8 The Great Depression

The Great Depression differs significantly from other periods of financial panic analyzed above owing to the presence of the Federal Reserve System, which began its operations in 1914. Although the Great Depression is dated by the NBER as beginning in September 1929, the public always associates the onset of the Depression with the stock market crash of October 1929. The outcome of the panic period starting October 23 and culminating in the crash on October 29 was a negative return for the month of October of close to 20%. This was the largest monthly negative return in the stock market up to that time. The data in figure 3.9, however, indicate that this financial panic differed substantially from those in previous periods.

Because of the large swing in the interest-rate-spread variable in 1929–35, it is hard to discern its movements in the early phase of the Great Depression shown in panel A of figure 3.9. Thus, an extra panel, panel C, has been added to the figure to show the stock price and interest-rate-spread data for 1929–31. In figure 3.9, *C* marks the October 1929 stock market crash, *P1* the first banking panic of November 1930, *P2* the second banking panic of March 1931, *P3* Britain's departure from gold in September 1931, and *PH* the bank holiday of March 1933.

As we have seen in the analysis of previous panics, the usual pattern is for a stock market crash to be accompanied by a sharp rise in both the level of interest rates and the interest rate spread. Although in panel C of figure 3.9

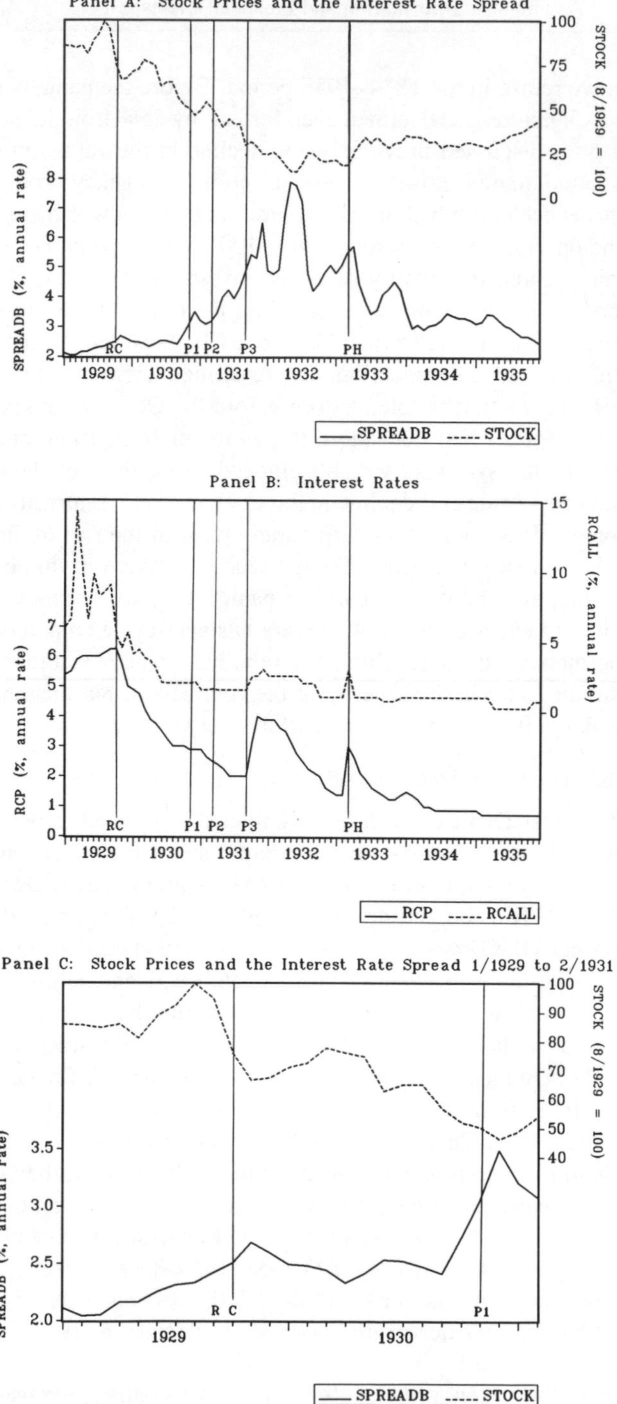

Fig. 3.9 The Great Depression

there is some rise in the interest rate spread when the crash occurs, the increase is fairly small. In addition, panel B indicates that interest rates did not rise, the commercial paper rate held steady, while call loan rates actually fell. Although the stock market crash had such a great impact on a whole generation, it does not appear to have developed into a full-fledged financial crisis, as in the other episodes I have examined. The credit for this goes to the prompt action by the Federal Reserve Bank of New York to provide reserves to the New York banks. During the panic period, banks and lenders outside of New York rushed to liquidate their call loans to brokers. In order to keep market conditions from getting more unsettled, the Federal Reserve Bank of New York, as described by its president, George L. Harrison, kept its "discount window wide open and let it be known that member banks might borrow freely to establish the reserve required against the large increase in deposits resulting from the taking over of loans called by others" (Friedman and Schwartz 1963, 339). In addition, the New York Fed made open market purchases of $160 million during this period, even though this amount was far in excess of what was authorized by the Federal Reserve System's Open Market Investment Committee.

The aftermath of the New York Fed's action to provide sufficient liquidity for the economy was a decline of the interest rate spread to levels below those before the stock market crash and a continuing low level up until October 1930. What is quite remarkable about the level of the interest rate spread before October 1930 is that it remained so low despite the sharp economic contraction up to that point and the more than 40% decline in the value of common stocks. Friedman and Schwartz (1963, 306) state that, from the peak in August 1929 through October 1930, industrial production fell 26%, wholesale prices by 14%, and personal income by 16%. The failure of the interest rate spread to rise seems to indicate that asymmetric information problems had not yet become severe in financial markets.[13]

Just prior to the first banking panic in November–December 1930, the interest rate spread began to increase and reached a temporary peak at the height of the bank panic in December 1930. The first banking panic is described by Friedman and Schwartz (1963, 308) as starting in agricultural regions, where a "contagion of fear spread among depositors," leading to the failure of 256 banks with $180 million of deposits in November and the failure of 352 banks with over $372 million of deposits in December, including the failure on December 11 of the Bank of United States with over $200 million in deposits. Friedman and Schwartz viewed the nature of the economic contraction as changing at this stage. The continuing bank panics, which by the time of the Banking Holiday in March 1933 had reduced the number of banks by over a third, was the unique feature of the Great Depression that Friedman and Schwartz saw as the force behind a steep but normal recession turning into the largest economic contraction ever experienced in U.S. history.

An asymmetric information analysis of the Great Depression, first outlined in Bernanke (1983), agrees with this view, but it does not see the decline in the money supply resulting from the banking panics as being the sole cause of the prolonged depression.[14] Instead the collapse of the banking system is seen as preventing banks from engaging in financial intermediation activities that would reduce asymmetric information problems. The resulting increase in asymmetric information problems in credit markets led to a decline in investment by those with otherwise profitable investment opportunities. Further, the debt deflation, in which the decline in prices transfers resources from debtors to creditors, and the continuing decline in the stock market until the middle of 1932 led to a deterioration in firms' balance sheets. This increased adverse selection and agency problems, so that lending decreased and investment then fell. In addition, as pointed out by Mishkin (1978), a similar deterioration in the balance sheets of consumers led them to reduce their spending. A further effect could have come from the behavior of real interest rates in this period. As shown in Mishkin (1981), although nominal interest rates on high-quality bonds fell during this period, real interest rates climbed to exceedingly high levels during 1931–33.[15] The high level of real interest rates increased the adverse selection problem in credit markets and is one more reason for a decline in investment spending.

All of these effects helped make the Great Depression the most severe in U.S. history. Consistent with this story is the increase in the spread variable to unprecedented levels. By the middle of 1932, the spread between interest rates on corporate Baa and Treasury bonds had risen to above 7.5%, over 5 percentage points higher than the level before October 1930. Indeed, it was not until the end of 1936 that the spread variable fell to levels below those found before October 1930. The fact that the spread between interest rates for low- versus high-quality borrowers remained so high for so long indicates that asymmetric information problems were severe in this period. The continuing severity of asymmetric information problems provides an explanation for why the Great Depression was so prolonged.

The fact that aggregate output remained so far below its potential for such a long period of time has always been a puzzle for neoclassical analysis. Bernanke's (1983) documentation of the disruption of the credit markets during 1931–35 and the attendant asymmetric information problems provides one explanation. An overlooked fact, however, is that another financial crisis appears to have occurred in 1937–38. From its peak in February 1937 until its trough in March 1938, the stock market declined by over 50%. Indeed, four of the fifty largest negative monthly returns from 1834 to 1988, as tabulated by Wilson, Sylla, and Jones (1990), are found in this one-year period. And the stock market return of −23.9% in March 1938 is the second largest negative return (September 1931 is the largest, with a return of −29.3%). As we can see in figure 3.10, which plots the data for 1936–41, there is another rapid run up of the interest rate spread, which peaks in April 1938, one month after the stock market trough. Indeed, in the first half of 1938 the interest rate spread is back at the levels found in 1934. The large spread between interest

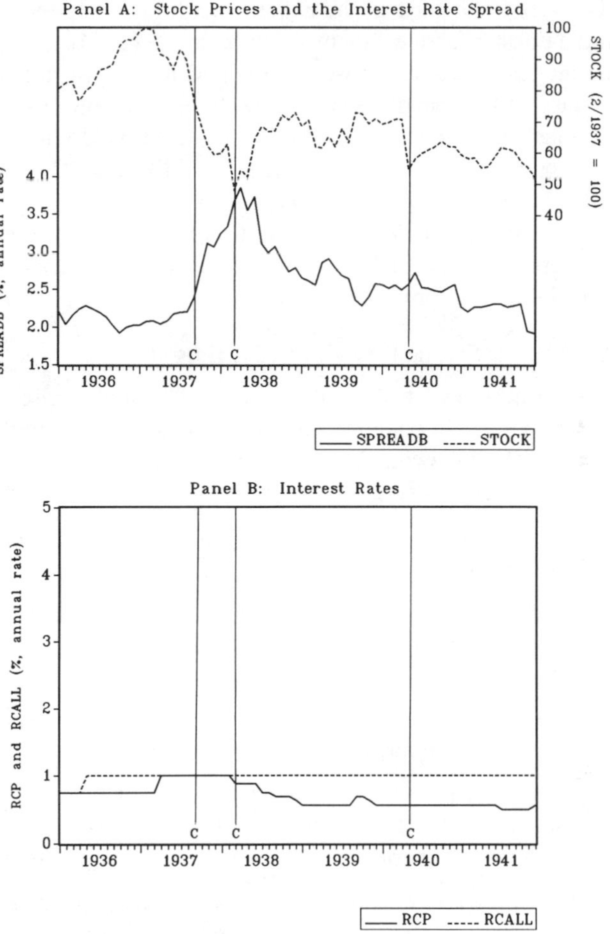

Fig. 3.10 The 1936–41 period

rates on low- and high-quality borrowers suggests that asymmetric information problems were again becoming serious in 1937–38, and this helps explain why the economic contraction during this recession was so severe.

The source of the difficulties in financial markets at this time is not absolutely clear. The increase in reserve requirements in August 1936, March 1937, and May 1937 is one possibility, either through its effects on the money supply, which declined from March 1937 until May 1938, or by decreasing the ability of banks to extend loans because of their need to increase the ratio of their reserves to deposits. Regardless of the cause, the financial disruption in 1937–38 may help to explain why the U.S. economy did not really come out of the shadow of the Depression until World War II.

There is one last episode in the 1936–41 period depicted in figure 3.10 that deserves some comment. May 1940 had a larger decline in stock market prices than did October 1929. Indeed, the negative return of −22.6% in May 1940 is the third largest negative monthly return in the 1834–1988 period. Although the interest rate spread rose in May and June 1940, the increase was very temporary and its magnitude was very slight. The downward trend in the spread variable which started after April 1938 continued after this episode, leading to a spread below 1% by the end of World War II. This illustrates the following important point: *a stock market crash by itself does not necessarily imply that a financial crisis has occurred.* There is no evidence that there was a serious disruption in financial markets after the May 1940 crash which could have created difficulties for the economy.

3.2.9 An Overview of the Financial Crisis Episodes

Now that we have analyzed a whole series of financial crises, it is worth asking what they have in common and what this tells us about the nature of financial crises. The following facts emerge from the study of episodes in the last half of the nineteenth century and the first half of the twentieth:

1. with one exception in 1873, financial panics always occurred after the onset of a recession;
2. with the same exception in 1873, stock prices declined and the spread between interest rates on low- and high-quality bonds rose before the onset of the panic;
3. many panics seem to have features of a liquidity crisis in which there are substantial increases in interest rates before the panic;
4. the onset of many panics followed a major failure of a financial institution, not necessarily a bank. Furthermore, this failure was often the result of financial difficulties experienced by a nonfinancial corporation;
5. the rise in the interest rate spread associated with a panic was typically soon followed by a decline. However, in several cases, most notably after the 1873 panic, the 1907 panic, and the Great Depression, the interest rate spread increased again when there was deflation and a severe recession;
6. the most severe financial crises were associated with severe economic contractions. The most severe panic episodes were in 1857, 1873, 1893, 1907, and 1930–33, while 1857–58, 1873–79, 1893–94, 1907–8, and 1929–33 are all considered to be among the most severe economic contractions;
7. although stock market crashes often appear to be a major factor in creating a financial crisis, this was not always the case. The crash of the stock market in October 1929 and in May 1940 did not have appreciable effects on the interest-rate spread. Therefore, the evidence that there was a serious disruption in financial markets after these crashes is weak.

There are several conclusions that can be drawn from the facts listed above. The timing and the pattern of the data in the episodes studied here seem to fit an asymmetric information interpretation of financial crises. Rather than starting with bank panics, most of the financial crises began with a rise in interest rates, a stock market decline, and the widening of the interest rate spread. Furthermore, a financial panic was frequently immediately preceded by a major failure of a financial firm, which increased uncertainty in the marketplace. The increase in uncertainty and the rise in interest rates would magnify the adverse selection–lemons problem in the credit markets, while the decline in the stock market increased agency and adverse selection problems, both of which are reflected in the rise in the spread between interest rates for low- and high-quality borrowers. The increase in adverse selection and agency problems would lead to a decline in investment activity and aggregate economic activity.

Depositors would then want to withdraw their funds from the banking system because the poor business conditions would lead them to expect losses on deposits left in the banks. The resulting bank panic would raise interest rates further, cause the stock market to decline even more, and worsen agency and adverse selection problems in the credit markets. This would further encourage a severe economic contraction.

Finally, there would be a sorting of solvent from insolvent firms by bankruptcy proceedings and a sorting of solvent from insolvent banks, often with the help of public authorities and clearing-house associations. The panic would then subside, the stock market might undergo a recovery, interest rates would fall, and if economic uncertainty and deflation were not too severe, adverse selection and agency problems would diminish, leading to a decline in the interest-rate-spread variable and setting the stage for an eventual recovery of the economy. This process might get short circuited if a substantial deflation sets in, leading to a debt-deflation process which transfers resources from debtors to creditors, thereby leading to a deterioration in business firms' net worth. The deterioration of firms' balance sheet positions would lead to increased asymmetric information problems, reflected by a continuation of a large spread between interest rates for low- and high-quality borrowers. Investment spending and aggregate economic activity would then remain depressed for a prolonged period of time.

A monetarist interpretation of financial panics cannot explain the events and their timing as effectively as the asymmetric information approach because the monetarist view does not explain why the spread between interest rates for high- and low-quality borrowers rises dramatically before the panic and then declines after the panic subsides. However, the asymmetric information story does not rule out important effects on aggregate economic activity from the decline in the money supply that a banking panic produces. It just suggests that there is more to the story of a financial crisis than its effects on the money supply.

A monetarist explanation of financial panics is also not able to explain why the banking panics occurred when they did. The facts about the panic episodes discussed in this paper are entirely consistent with Gorton's (1988) view that bank panics are predictable. His analysis depends on asymmetric information because he sees a bank panic as occurring as a result of the inability of depositors to evaluate the risk in individual bank liabilities, so they cannot easily screen out good from bad banks. Hence, when information such as high interest rates, a major failure of a corporation, or weak business conditions stemming from a recession occurs, depositors worry about potential losses on their deposits and withdraw funds from the banking system, precipitating a panic. Gorton finds that unanticipated changes in the liabilities of failed businesses in the best predictive variable for the occurrence of a bank panic. The analysis in this paper suggests that since stock market declines and widening of the interest rate spread often precede bank panics, stock price and interest-rate-spread variables, which were not used in Gorton's analysis, might also appreciably help in the prediction of bank panics.

The successful intervention of the New York Clearing House Association in the 1884 and 1890 episodes and of the New York Federal Reserve Bank during the October 1929 stock market crash illustrates how an effective lender-of-last-resort role can minimize the impact of a financial crisis on the economy. We now turn to two postwar episodes of financial disturbances in which the Federal Reserve actively performed this role, even though the banking system was not directly threatened.

3.3 Two Postwar Episodes of Financial Disturbances

The postwar period differs from the pre–World War II period in one important respect. Since 1945, the banking system has not been subjected to a banking panic and in no instance has there been a financial crisis that has had serious adverse consequences for the aggregate economy. Examining episodes of financial disturbances in the postwar period in which banking panics were not an issue should be particularly instructive because the monetarist interpretation does not view them as real financial crises. However, if we do find that these financial disturbances have many of the same patterns in the data as prewar financial crises, and thus appear to exhibit the potential for serious asymmetric information problems in credit markets, this would lend additional support to the asymmetric information approach to financial crises. Two episodes, the Penn Central bankruptcy of June 1970 and the stock market crash of 19 October 1987, are postwar examples of financial disturbances in which banking panics were not an issue. In both episodes the Federal Reserve actively provided liquidity to a specific financial sector outside of the banking system and thus engaged in a broader lender-of-last-resort role.

3.3.1 The Penn Central Bankruptcy

Prior to 1970, commercial paper was considered one of the safest money market instruments because only corporations with very high credit ratings issued it. It was common practice for corporations to continually roll over their commercial paper, that is, issue new commercial paper to pay off the old. Penn Central Railroad was a major issuer of commercial paper, with more than $200 million outstanding, but by May 1970 it was on the verge of bankruptcy and it requested federal government assistance from the Nixon administration.[16] Despite administration support for a bailout of Penn Central, after six weeks of debate Congress decided not to pass bailout legislation. Meanwhile, the Nixon administration asked the Board of Governors of the Federal Reserve System to authorize a direct loan from the Federal Reserve Bank of New York to Penn Central. On Thursday, June 18, the New York Fed informed the Board of Governors that its staff studies indicated that Penn Central would not be able to repay the loan and, as a result, the Board decided not to authorize the loan. Without this loan, Penn Central was forced to declare bankruptcy on Sunday, 21 June 1970.

Once the Federal Reserve made the decision to let Penn Central go into bankruptcy, it was concerned that Penn Central's default on its commercial paper would, as Brimmer (1989, 6) puts it, have a "chilling effect on the commercial paper market", making it impossible for other corporations to roll over their commercial paper. The Penn Central bankruptcy, then, had the potential for sending other companies into bankruptcy which, in turn, might have triggered further bankruptcies, leading to a full-scale financial panic. To avoid this scenario, the New York Fed got in touch with a number of large money-center banks on Saturday and Sunday, June 20 and 21, alerted them to the impending Penn Central bankruptcy, encouraged them to lend to their customers who were unable to roll over their commercial paper, and indicated that the discount window would be made available to the banks so that they could make these loans.[17] Indeed, the banks did as they were told and made these loans, receiving as much as $575 million through the discount window for this purpose. In addition, on June 22 the Fed decided to suspend Regulation Q ceilings on deposits of $100,000 and over, in order to keep short-term interest rates from rising, and the formal vote was taken the next day to allow the Federal Deposit Insurance Corporation and the Federal Home Loan Bank Board to take parallel action. The net result was that the Federal Reserve provided liquidity so that the commercial paper market would keep functioning.

The rationale for the Fed's action was that lenders would not be able to screen out good borrowers in this market from bad borrowers. Was this rationale plausible? The data in figure 3.11 are suggestive that it was. Panel A has the same format as previous figures, with the onset of the recession in January 1970 marked with an *R*, the Penn Central bankruptcy date marked by a *P*, and data on the stock market and the SPREADB interest-rate-spread variable. Panel B contains data on the commercial paper rate and on the interest rate spread between commercial paper (4–6 month) and the 6-month Treasury bill, denoted by SPREADC (replacing the rate on call loans, which were no longer a major element in money markets).

The data in panel A display the typical pattern that we saw for prewar finan-

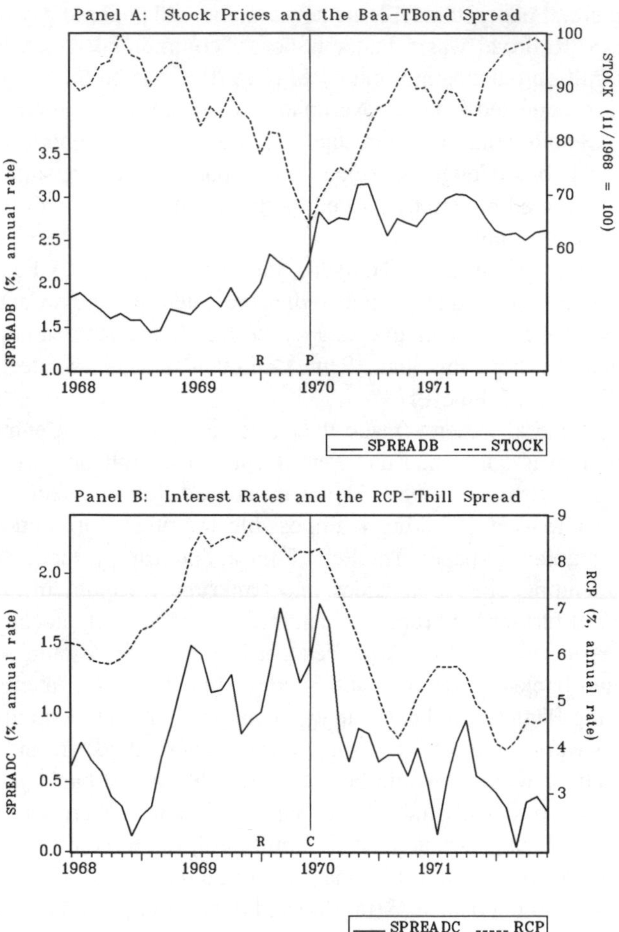

Fig. 3.11 The Penn Central bankruptcy

cial crises. The high level of interest rates reached in late 1969–early 1970, and the increase in uncertainty with the onset of the recession in January 1970 are likely to have increased the adverse selection problem in the credit markets. Furthermore, by May 1970 the stock market had declined over 35% from its peak value in November 1969. This decline in the valuation of firms resulted in a decrease in net worth and increased agency and adverse selection problems in the credit markets. Consistent with the rise in asymmetric information difficulties for the credit markets, there is a rise in both of the interest-rate-spread variables, SPREADB (for long-term bonds) and SPREADC (for commercial paper). Furthermore, despite the Fed's actions, there is also a jump in the interest-rate-spread variables at the time of the Penn Central bankruptcy in

June 1970. The fact that the spread between interest rates on corporate Baa and Treasury bonds rises along with the commercial paper–Treasury spread variable indicates that the problems in the commercial paper market had a potential for spreading to other sectors of the capital market. As we saw after other financial disturbances, the interest-rate spread declines after the crisis, and this pattern is especially pronounced for the commercial paper–Treasury spread variable in panel B, which returns to 1968 levels by the end of 1970. The SPREADB variable, on the other hand, continues to remain high for over two years after the Penn Central bankruptcy. However, the increase in the SPREADB variable resulting from the Penn Central bankruptcy was not large by the standards of earlier financial crises. A major disturbance to the credit markets as a result of increased asymmetric information problems seems to have been avoided by the Fed's willingness to perform its lender-of-last-resort function.

3.3.2 The Stock Market Crash of 19 October 1987

The causes of the stock market crash are still being hotly debated, but the biggest danger to the economy appears not to have come from the decline in wealth resulting from the crash itself, but rather from the threat to the clearing and settlement system in the stock and futures markets.[18] From the peak on 25 August 1987 until October 16, just prior to the crash, the Dow Jones Industrial Average (DJIA) had declined 17.5%. On Monday, October 19, the market fell by 22.6% (as measured by the DJIA) on record volume of 604 million shares. Although 19 October 1987, dubbed "Black Monday," will go down in history as the largest one-day decline in stock prices to date, it was on Tuesday, October 20, that financial markets received their worst threat. In order to keep the stock market and the related index futures market functioning in an orderly fashion, brokers needed to extend massive amounts of credit on behalf of their customers for their margin calls. The magnitude of the problem is illustrated by the fact that two brokerage firms, Kidder, Peabody and Goldman, Sachs, alone had advanced $1.5 billion in response to margin calls on their customers by noon of October 20. Clearly, brokerage firms as well as specialists were severely in need of additional funds to finance their activities. However, understandably enough, banks were growing very nervous about the financial health of securities firms and so were reluctant to lend to the securities industry at a time when it was most needed.

Upon learning of the plight of the securities industry, Alan Greenspan, chairman of the Board of Governors, and E. Gerald Corrigan, president of the New York Federal Reserve Bank and the Fed official most closely in touch with Wall Street, began to fear a breakdown in the clearing and settlement systems and the collapse of securities firms. To prevent this from occurring, Alan Greenspan announced before the market opened on Tuesday, October 20, the Federal Reserve System's "readiness to serve as a source of liquidity to support the economic and financial system." In addition to this extraordinary announcement, the Fed encouraged key money-center banks to lend freely to their brokerage firm customers and, as in the Penn Central bankruptcy episode, made it clear that it would provide discount loans to banks so that they could make these loans. Again, the banks did as they were told, and by October 21 had increased by $7.7 billion their loans to brokers and to individuals to purchase or hold securities. As a result, the markets kept functioning on Tuesday, October 20, and a market rally ensued that day, raising the DJIA by over 100 points (over 5%). This action by the Fed is reminiscent of the actions it took in the October 1929 panic period, during which it provided liquidity to enable money-center banks to take over call loans which had been called by others.

The data for the period surrounding the October stock market crash are found in figure 3.12. Panels A and B have the same format as those in figure 3.11, while an additional panel, panel C, is shown which contains weekly data on interest spread variables for the six months surrounding the crash. Panel C also plots a series obtained from weekly issues of *Barrons,* the spread between interest rates on junk bonds (those with ratings below Baa) and Treasury bonds, denoted by SPREADJ.

The data in figure 3.12 again display patterns seen in other financial crises. The commercial paper rate had been rising for a year before the stock market crash because of the tight money policy followed by the Fed, while stock prices began a decline over a month earlier. The evidence for increased asymmetric information problems in credit markets before the crash, however, is not particularly strong. The commercial paper–Treasury bill interest-rate-spread variable, SPREADC, also had been rising for a year before the crash, and yet the junk bond–Treasury and Baa-Treasury spread variables, SPREADJ and SPREADB, did not rise until the stock market crash, when they immediately jumped. Not surprisingly, given that asymmetric information effects should have more effect on low-quality borrowers than on high-quality borrowers, the junk bond–Treasury spread shows the largest jump. In the week of the stock market crash, it jumped by 130 basis points (1.3 percentage points) and rose another 60 basis points over the next two weeks. However, as usually occurs after a panic, the junk bond–Treasury spread fell quickly thereafter, and within two months of the crash was back to pre-crash levels. The commercial paper–Treasury spread, SPREADC, followed a similar pattern by returning quickly to its pre-cash levels, but the Baa–Treasury spread, SPREADB, declined more slowly and only reached its pre-crash level six months after the crash.

The fact that the spread variables seem to fit a classic pattern for financial crises suggests that the October 1987 stock market crash had the potential to create major asymmetric information problems in the credit markets. However, the prompt action by the Fed to perform its lender-of-last-resort role kept the asymmetric information problem from getting out of hand, as is indicated

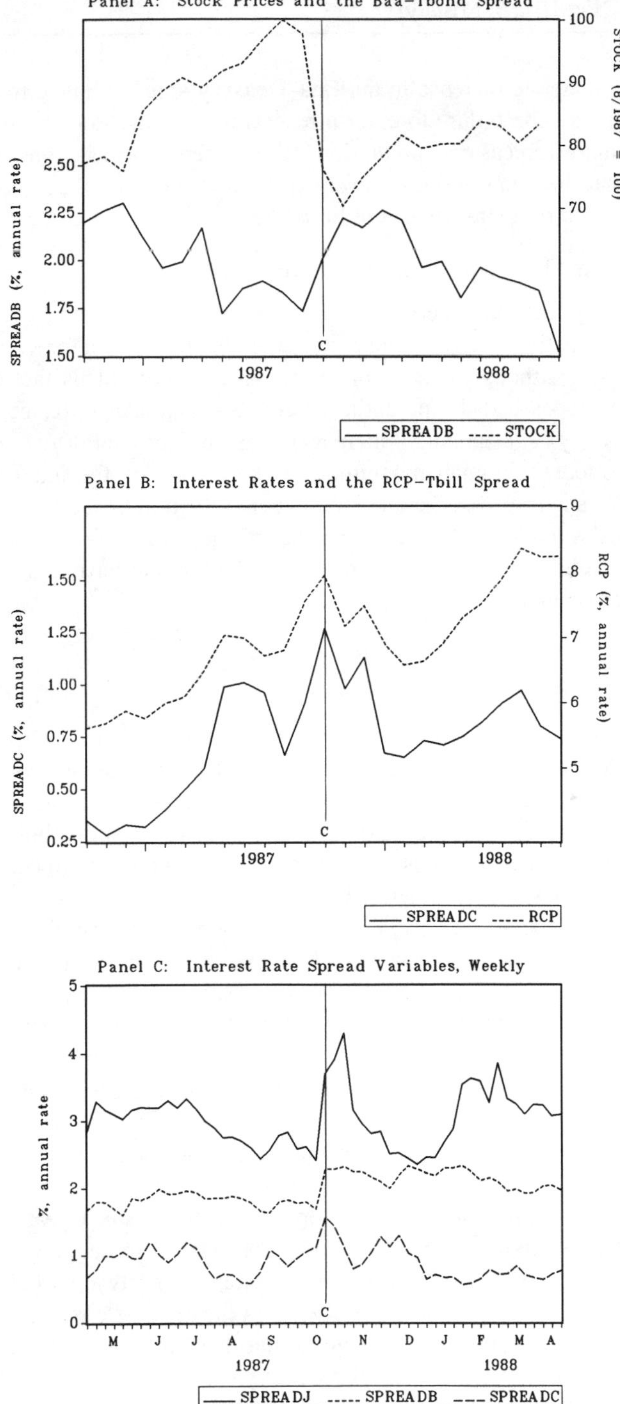

Fig. 3.12 The stock market crash of October 1987

by the moderate increase in the Baa-Treasury spread relative to earlier financial panics. The failure to enter a recession after the stock market crash, despite many forecasters' predictions along these lines, is consistent with the view that the Fed's actions prevented the development of serious asymmetric information problems in the credit markets.

3.3.3 An Overview of the Postwar Episodes

The key fact that emerges from the postwar episodes analyzed here is that they display the typical timing patterns visible in the data for the prewar financial crises, although with a much-muted amplitude. This fact suggests that these episodes had the potential to create a major disturbance to the credit markets by substantially increasing asymmetric information problems. Furthermore, the small magnitude of the effects on the interest-rate-spread variables suggests that the quick and decisive action by the Federal Reserve to perform as lender-of-last resort prevented more serious asymmetric information disturbances to the credit markets which could have had significant adverse consequences for the aggregate economy.

3.4 Conclusions

The asymmetric information approach to financial crises explains the timing patterns in the data and many features of these crises which are otherwise hard to explain. It also suggests why financial crises have had such important consequences for the aggregate economy over the past one hundred and fifty years. The evidence thus seems to favor as asymmetric information view of financial crises over a monetarist view.

However, the asymmetric information approach can be viewed as complementary to the monetarist view of financial crises since it provides an important transmission mechanism for how banking panics and monetary disturbances affect aggregate economic activity. Yet, the asymmetric information approach does not view banking panics and money supply declines as the only financial disturbances that can have serious adverse effects on the aggregate economy. Financial crises have effects over and above those resulting from banking panics, and analysis of such episodes as the stock market collapse in 1937–38 suggests that a financial crisis which has serious adverse consequences for the economy can develop, even if there is no threat to the banking system. The asymmetric information approach also suggests that financial disturbances outside of the banking system in the postwar period have had the potential to have serious adverse effects on the aggregate economy.

The analysis in this paper suggests that there could be benefits to a lender-of-last-resort role for the central bank to provide liquidity to nonbanking sectors of the financial system in which asymmetric information problems have developed. However, there are also potential costs to such an expanded lender-of-last-resort role since it might encourage too much risk-taking on the part of nonfinancial corporations. There are thus complex issues involved in deciding whether an expanded lender-of-last-resort role will, on the whole, be beneficial and how it should be executed. This is a topic that I plan to pursue in further research.

Notes

1. The lemons problem also can be important in equity markets. Myers and Majluf (1984) and Greenwald, Stiglitz, and Weiss (1984) describe how the inability of investors to distinguish between good and bad issuers of equity means that the price they will pay for shares will reflect the average quality of the issuers. The result is that high-quality firms receive a lower price for their shares than the fair market value, while low-quality firms receive a price above the fair market value. As a result, some high-quality firms will not issue shares, and thus investment projects with a positive net present value will not be undertaken.

2. Asymmetric information can also explain credit rationing in which there are restrictions on the size of loans, as in Jaffee and Russell (1976).

3. F. Ross Johnson, the former CEO of RJR-Nabisco, is reputed to have had RJR-Nabisco pay for two personal maids, two dozen country club memberships, and a fleet of ten corporate planes nicknamed the "RJR Airforce."

4. Calomiris and Hubbard (1989) emphasize this mechanism in their econometric analysis of the 1894–1909 period.

5. In addition, as pointed out by Stiglitz and Weiss (1983), banks have an advantage in minimizing moral hazard on the part of borrowers because banks can use the threat of cutting off lending in the future to improve borrowers' behavior.

6. Credit controls, such as those imposed in 1980, or disintermediation arising out of deposit rate ceilings are another possible way in which banks may find themselves unable to fully perform their intermediation role.

7. Note that the dates at which the number of bonds in each category changes do not fall within any of the subsamples analyzed in the paper. This avoids the potential for discontinuities in the interest-rate-spread series during the episodes studied.

8. The stock price series developed by Schwert (1989b) is very close to that of Wilson, Sylla, and Jones (1990), and its use would not change any conclusions in the analysis here.

9. The financial crisis associated with the beginning of World War I in August 1914 is not examined in this paper because data are not available from August to November 1914, when the New York Stock Exchange was closed.

10. Another important role of the clearing-house associations mentioned by Gorton (1985) is that they would provide liquidity to the banking system by issuing clearing-house certificates during a panic. The clearing-house associations had not yet taken on this role in 1857, but did so in later banking panics.

11. A similar phenomenon can also affect consumer spending, as discussed in Mishkin (1978).

12. For those who, like myself, do not know the meaning of the word "defalcation," it is a misappropriation of funds held by a trustee or other fiduciary.

13. The failure of the interest rate spread to rise also casts some doubt on the story put forward by Romer (1988) that the initial severity of the Great Depression may have resulted from increased uncertainty. Since such uncertainty should increase adverse selection and thereby increase the interest rate spread, and yet this does not seem to

happen before October 1930, it is not at all clear that uncertainty rose appreciably in this period.

14. See also Hamilton (1987).

15. Hamilton (1987) disputes the view that real interest rates were high during this period because he finds that futures prices in commodity markets were not indicating an expected deflation in this period. Mishkin (1990), however, demonstrates that futures prices in commodity markets are not capable of informing us about expected inflation for aggregate price indices. Cecchetti (1989), using additional evidence, also criticizes Hamilton's position that the deflation in this period was not anticipated. More recent work by Hamilton (1990) is more favorable to the view that real interest rates rose during the 1931–33 period. Indeed, an interesting finding in the Hamilton paper is that substantial anticipated deflation, and hence high real rates, did not occur until late 1930, and this is exactly when we start to see evidence that serious asymmetric information problems are beginning to appear in the U.S. economy.

16. See Maisel (1973) and Brimmer (1989) for further discussion of the Penn Central bankruptcy episode.

17. It is noteworthy that when the Fed advanced discount loans to banks lending to customers who needed to roll over their commercial paper, the banks were told that they would be responsible for the credit risk involved in this lending; see Brimmer (1989, 6).

18. See the *Wall Street Journal* (1987) and Brimmer (1989) for a description of the events surrounding the stock market crash.

References

Akerlof, George. 1970. The Market for Lemons: Quality Uncertainty and the Market Mechanism. *Quarterly Journal of Economics* 84 (August): 488–500.

Bernanke, Ben S. 1983. Non-Monetary Effects of the Financial Crisis in the Propagation of the Great Depression. *American Economic Review* 73 (June): 257–76.

Bernanke, Ben S., and Mark Gertler. 1989. Agency Costs, Collateral, and Business Fluctuations. *American Economic Review* 79 (March): 14–31.

———. 1990. Financial Fragility and Economic Performance. *Quarterly Journal of Economics* 55 (February): 87–114.

Bordo, Michael D. 1986. Financial Crises, Banking Crises, Stock Market Crashes and the Money Supply: Some International Evidence, 1870–1933. In *Financial Crises and the World Banking System,* ed. F. Capie and G. E. Wood, 190–248. London: Macmillan.

Brimmer, Andrew F. 1989. Distinguished Lecture on Economics in Government: Central Banking and Systemic Risks in Capital Markets. *Journal of Economic Perspectives* 3 (Spring): 3–16.

Calomiris, Charles W., and R. Glenn Hubbard. 1989. Price Flexibility, Credit Availability, and Economic Fluctuations: Evidence from the United States, 1894–1909. *Quarterly Journal of Economics* 54 (August): 429–52.

———. 1990. Firm Heterogeneity, Internal Finance, and "Credit Rationing." *Economic Journal* 100 (March): 90–104.

Cecchetti, Steven. 1989. Prices During the Great Depression: Was the Deflation of 1930–32 Really Unanticipated? National Bureau of Economic Research Working Paper no. 3174 (November).

Collman, Charles Albert. 1931. *Our Mysterious Panics.* New York: William Morrow & Co.
Diamond, Douglas. 1984. Financial Intermediation and Delegated Monitoring. *Review of Economic Studies* 51 (July): 393–414.
Fisher, Irving. 1933. The Debt-Deflation Theory of Great Depressions. *Econometrica* 1 (October): 337–57.
Friedman, Milton, and Anna J. Schwartz. 1963. *A Monetary History of the United States, 1867–1960.* Princeton: Princeton University Press.
Gertler, Mark. 1988a. Financial Structure and Aggregate Economic Activity: An Overview. *Journal of Money, Credit and Banking* 20 (August, 2): 559–88.
———. 1988b. Financial Capacity, Reliquification, and Production in an Economy with Long-Term Financial Arrangements. University of Wisconsin, mimeo (October).
Gorton, Gary. 1985. Clearing Houses and the Origins of Central Banking in the U.S. *Journal of Economic History* 45: 277–84.
———. 1988. Banking Panics and Business Cycles. *Oxford Economic Papers* 40: 751–81.
Greenwald, Bruce, and Joseph E. Stiglitz. 1988. Information, Finance Constraints, and Business Fluctuations. In *Expectations and Macroeconomics,* ed. Meir Kahn and S. C. Tsiang. Oxford: Oxford University Press.
Greenwald, Bruce, Joseph E. Stiglitz, and Andrew Weiss. 1984. Information Imperfections in the Capital Market and Macroeconomic Fluctuations. *American Economic Review* 74 (May): 194–99.
Hamilton, James. 1987. Monetary Factors in the Great Depression. *Journal of Monetary Economics* 19 (March): 145–70.
———. 1990. Was the Deflation During the Great Depression Anticipated? Evidence from the Commodity Futures Market. University of Virginia, mimeo (March 23).
Jaffee, Dwight, and Thomas Russell. 1976. Imperfect Information, Uncertainty, and Credit Rationing. *Quarterly Journal of Economics* 90 (November):651–66.
Kindleberger, Charles P. 1978. *Manias, Panics and Crashes.* London: Macmillan.
Macaulay, Frederick R. 1938. *The Movements of Interest Rates, Bond Yields and Stock Prices in the United States Since 1856.* New York: National Bureau of Economic Research.
Maisel, Sherman J. 1973. *Managing the Dollar.* New York: Norton.
Mankiw, N. Gregory. 1986. The Allocation of Credit and Financial Collapse. *Quarterly Journal of Economics* 101 (August): 455–70.
Minsky, Hyman P. 1972. Financial Stability Revisited: The Economics of Disaster. In *Reappraisal of the Federal Reserve Discount Mechanism,* vol. 3: 95–136. Washington, DC: Board of Governors of the Federal Reserve System.
Mishkin, Frederic S. 1978. The Household Balance Sheet and the Great Depression. *Journal of Economic History* 38 (December): 918–37.
———. 1981. The Real Rate of Interest: An Empirical Investigation. In *The Cost and Consequences of Inflation.* Carnegie-Rochester Conference Series on Public Policy, no. 15: 151–200.
———. 1990. Can Futures Market Data Be Used to Understand the Behavior of Real Interest Rates. *Journal of Finance* 45 (March): 245–57.
Myers, Stewart C., and N. S. Majluf. 1984. Corporate Financing and Investment Decisions When Firms Have Information that Investors Do Not Have. *Journal of Financial Economics* 13 (June): 187–221.
Romer, Christina. 1988. The Great Crash and the Onset of the Great Depression. National Bureau of Economic Research Working Paper no. 2639 (June).
Schwartz, Anna J. 1986. Real and Pseudo-Financial Crises. In *Financial Crises and*

the World Banking System, ed. F. Capie and G. E. Wood, 11–31. London: Macmillan.

Schwert, G. William. 1989a. Business Cycles, Financial Crises and Stock Volatility. National Bureau of Economic Research Working Paper no. 2957 (May).

———. 1989b. Indexes of United States Stock Prices From 1802 to 1987. National Bureau of Economic Research Working Paper no. 2985 (May).

Smith, Walter B., and Arthur H. Cole. 1935. *Fluctuations in American Business 1790–1860.* Cambridge, Mass.: Harvard University Press.

Sobel, Robert. 1968. *Panic on Wall Street: A History of America's Financial Disasters.* London: Macmillan.

Sprague, O. M. W. 1910. *History of Crises under the National Banking System.* Washington, DC: National Monetary Commission, U.S. Government Printing Office.

Stiglitz, Joseph, and Andrew Weiss. 1981. Credit Rationing in Markets with Imperfect Information. *American Economic Review* 71 (June): 393–410.

———. 1983. Incentive Effects of Terminations: Applications to Credit and Labor Markets. *American Economic Review* 73 (December): 912–27.

Temin, Peter. 1976. *Did Monetary Forces Cause the Great Depression?* New York: W. W. Norton.

Wall Street Journal. 1987. Terrible Tuesday: How the Stock Market Almost Disintegrated a Day After the Crash. November 20.

Wilson, Jack, Richard Sylla, and Charles P. Jones. 1990. Financial Market Volatility, Panics Under the National Banking System Before 1914, and Volatility in the Long Run, 1830–1988. In *Crashes and Panics: A Historical Perspective,* ed. Eugene N. White. Dow Jones/Irwin: Homewood.

4 The Origins of Banking Panics: Models, Facts, and Bank Regulation

Charles W. Calomiris and Gary Gorton

4.1 Introduction

The history of U.S. banking regulation can be written largely as a history of government and private responses to banking panics. Implicitly or explicitly, each regulatory response to a crisis presumed a "model" of the origins of banking panics. The development of private bank clearing houses, the founding of the Federal Reserve System, the creation of the Federal Deposit Insurance Corporation, the separation of commercial and investment banking by the Glass-Steagall Act, and laws governing branch banking all reflect beliefs about the factors that contribute to the instability of the banking system.

Deposit insurance and bank regulation were ultimately successful in preventing banking panics, but it has recently become apparent that this success was not without costs. The demise of the Federal Savings and Loan Insurance Corporation and state-sponsored thrift insurance funds and the declining competitiveness of U.S. commercial banks have had a profound effect on the debate over proper bank regulatory policy. Increasingly, regulators appear to be seeking to balance the benefits of banking stability against the apparent costs of bank regulation.

This changing focus has provided some of the impetus for the reevaluation

Charles W. Calomiris is an assistant professor of economics at Northwestern University and a research associate of the Federal Reserve Bank of Chicago. Gary Gorton is an associate professor of finance at the Wharton School, University of Pennsylvania.

The authors would like to thank George Benston, Ben Bernanke, John Bohannon, Michael Bordo, Barry Eichengreen, Joe Haubrich, Glenn Hubbard, and Joel Mokyr for their comments and suggestions.

of the history of banking crises to determine how banking stability can be achieved at a minimum cost. The important question is: What is the cause of banking panics? This question has been difficult to answer. Theoretical models of banking panics are intertwined with explanations for the existence of banks and, particularly, of bank debt contracts which finance "illiquid" assets while containing American put options giving debt holders the right to redeem debt on demand at par. Explaining the optimality of this debt contract, and of the put option, while simultaneously explaining the possibility of the apparently suboptimal event of a banking panic has been very hard.

In part, the reason it is difficult is that posing the problem this way identifies banks and banking panics too closely. In the last decade attempts to provide general simultaneous explanations of the existence of banks and banking panics have foundered on the historical fact that not all countries have experienced banking panics, even though their banking systems offered the same debt contract. Empirical research during this time has made this insight more precise by focusing on how the banking market structure and institutional differences affect the likelihood of panic. Observed variation in historical experience which can be attributed to differences in the structure of banking systems provides convincing evidence that neither the nature of debt contracts nor the presence of exogenous shocks which reduce the value of bank asset portfolios provide "sufficient conditions" for banking panics.

Empirical research has demonstrated the importance of such institutional structures as branch bank laws, bank cooperation arrangements, and formal clearing houses, for the probability of panic and for the resolution of crisis. The conclusion of this work and cross-country comparisons is that banking panics are not inherent in banking contracts—institutional structure matters. This observation has now been incorporated into new generations of theoretical models. But, while theoretical models sharpen our understanding of how banking panics might have occurred, few of these models have stressed testable implications. In addition, empirical work seeking to isolate precisely which factors caused panics historically has been hampered by the lack of historical data and the fact that there were only a relatively small number of panics. Thus, it is not surprising that research on the origins of banking panics and the appropriate regulatory response to their threat has yet to produce a consensus view.

While the original question of the cause of banking panics has not been answered, at least researchers appear to be looking for the answer in a different place. Our goal in this essay is to evaluate the persuasiveness of recent models of the origins of banking panics in light of available evidence. We begin, in section 4.2, with a definition of a banking panic, followed by a discussion of panics in U.S. history. A brief set of stylized facts which a theory must confront is developed. In section 4.3, recent empirical evidence on panics which strongly suggests the importance of the institutional structure is reviewed. Theories of panics must be consistent with this evidence.

Theoretical models of panics are discussed in section 4.4, where we trace the evolution of two competing views about the origins of banking panics. In the first view, which we label the "random withdrawal" theory, panics were caused historically by unexpected withdrawals by bank depositors associated primarily with real location-specific economic shocks, such as seasonal demands for currency due to agricultural payment procedures favoring cash. The mechanism which causes the panic in this theory suggests that the availability of reserves, say through central bank open market operations, would eliminate panics.

The second view, which we label the "asymmetric information" theory, sees panics as being caused by depositor revisions in the perceived risk of bank debt when they are uninformed about bank asset portfolio values and receive adverse news about the macro economy. In this view, depositors seek to withdraw large amounts from banks when they have reason to believe that banks are more likely to fail. Because the actual incidence of failure is unknown, they withdraw from all banks. The availability of reserves through central bank action would not, in this view, prevent panics.

The two competing theories offer different explanations about the origins and solutions to panics. A main goal of this essay is to discriminate between these two views, so we focus on testing the restrictions that each view implies. Section 4.5 describes the empirically testable differences between the competing hypotheses and provides a variety of new evidence to differentiate the two views. We employ data from the National Banking period (1863–1913), a single regulatory regime for which data are easily available for a variety of variables of interest. The two hypotheses have three testable implications that are explored in this paper. First, with respect to the shock initiating the panic, each theory suggests what is special about the periods immediately preceding panics. Second, the incidence of bank failures and losses is examined. Finally, we look at how crises were resolved.

Isolating the historical origins of banking panics is an important first step toward developing appropriate policy reforms for regulating and insuring financial intermediaries. In this regard, it is important to differentiate between the two views of the causes of panics because each has different policy implications. While we do not make any policy recommendations, in the final section, section 4.6, we discuss policy implications.

4.2 Definitions and Preliminaries

Essential to any study of panics is a definition of a banking panic. Perhaps surprisingly, a definition is not immediately obvious. Much of the empirical debate turns on which events are selected for the sample of panics. This section begins with a definition, which is then applied to select events from U.S. history which appear to fit the definition. In doing this we suggest a set of facts which theories of panics must address.

4.2.1 What Is A "Banking Panic"?

The term banking panic is often used somewhat ambiguously and, in many cases, synonymously with events in which banks fail, such as a recession, or in which there is financial market turmoil, such as stock market crashes. Many researchers provide no definition of a panic, relying instead on the same one or two secondary sources for an identification of panics.[1] But it is not clear whether these sources are correct nor whether the definitions implicit in these sources apply to other countries and periods of history.

One result of the reliance on secondary sources is that most empirical research has restricted attention to the U.S. experience, mostly the post–Civil War period, and usually with more weight placed on the events of the Great Depression. Moreover, even when using the same secondary sources, different researchers consider different sets of events to be panics. Miron (1986), for example, includes fifteen "minor" panics in his study. Sobel (1968) discusses twelve episodes, but mentions eleven others which were not covered. Donaldson (1989a) equates panics with unusual movements in interest rates.

Historically, bank debt has consisted largely of liabilities which circulate as a medium of exchange—bank notes and demand deposits. The contract defining this debt allowed the debt holder the right to redeem the debt (into hard currency) on demand at par. We define a banking panic as follows: A *banking panic* occurs when bank debt holders at all or many banks in the banking system suddenly demand that banks convert their debt claims into cash (at par) to such an extent that the banks suspend convertibility of their debt into cash or, in the case of the United States, act collectively to avoid suspension of convertibility by issuing clearing-house loan certificates.[2]

Several elements of this definition are worth discussing.[3] First, the definition requires that a significant number of banks be involved. If bank debt holders of a single bank demand redemption, this is not a banking panic, though such events are often called "bank runs." The term banking panic is so often used synonymously with "bank run" that there is no point attempting to distinguish between the two terms. Whether called a "bank run" or a "bank panic," the event of interest involves a large number of banks and is, therefore, to be distinguished from a "run" involving only a single bank. Thus, the events surrounding Continental of Illinois do not constitute a panic. On the other hand, a panic need not involve all the banks in the banking system. Rarely, if ever, have all banks in an economy simultaneously been faced with large demands for redemption of debt. Typically, all banks in a single geographical location are "run" at the same time, and "runs" subsequently occur in other locations.

The definition requires that depositors *suddenly* demand to redeem bank debt for cash. Thus, protracted withdrawals are ruled out, though sometimes the measured currency-deposit ratio rises for some period before the date taken to be the panic date. In the United States, panics diffused across the country in interesting ways. Panics did not occur at different locations simultaneously; nevertheless, at each location the panic occurred suddenly.

A panic requires that the volume of desired redemptions of debt into cash be large enough that the banks suspend convertibility or act collectively to avoid suspension. There are, presumably, various events in which depositors might wish to make large withdrawals. Perhaps a single bank, or group of banks at a single location, could honor large withdrawals, even larger than those demanded during a panic, if at the same time other banks were not faced with such demands.[4] But, if the banking system cannot honor demands for redemption at the agreed-upon exchange rate of one dollar of debt for one dollar of cash, then suspension occurs. Suspension signals that the banking system cannot honor the redemption option.

It is important to note that a banking panic cannot be defined in terms of the currency-deposit ratio. Since banks suspend convertibility of deposits into currency, the measured currency-deposit ratio will not necessarily show a sharp increase at, or subsequent to, the panic date. The desired currency-deposit ratio may be higher than the measured number, but that is not observable. Also, clearing-house arrangements (discussed below) and suspension allowed banks to continue loans that might otherwise have been called.[5] In fact, in some episodes lending increased. Thus, there is no immediate or obvious way to identify a banking panic using interest rate movements related to credit reductions. Moreover, since panics in the United States have tended to be associated with business cycle downturns, and also with fall and spring, interest rate movements around panics may be quite complicated. Associations between interest rate movements and panics as part of a definition seem inadvisable.

4.2.2 Panics in the United States

Even if there was agreement on a definition of a banking panic, it is still difficult to determine practically which historical events constitute panics. Many historical events do not completely fit the definition. Thus, there is some delicacy in determining which historical events in American history should be labelled panics. Table 4.1 lists the U.S. events which arguably correspond to the definition of panics provided above.

Consider, first, the pre–Civil War period of American history. During this period, bank debt liabilities mostly consisted of circulating bank notes. We classify six events as panics during this period: the suspensions of 1814, 1819, 1837, 1839, 1857, and 1861. Data limitations prevent a detailed empirical analysis of the earliest panics. Moreover, some of these are associated with "special" historical circumstances, and this argues against their relevance to the general question of the sources of banking instability. The Panics of 1814 and 1861 both followed precipitous exogenous declines in the value of government securities during wartime (related to adverse news regarding the probability of government repayment). Mitchell (1903) shows that bad finan-

Table 4.1 Banking Panics and Business Cycles

Height of Panic	Nearest Previous Peak	Notation
August 1814–January 1817[a]	January 1812	War-related
April–May 1819	November 1818	
May 1837	April 1837	
October 1839–March 1842[b]	March 1839	
October 1857	May 1857	
December 1861	September 1860	War-related
September 1873	September 1873	
May 1884	May 1884	
November 1890	November 1890	
June–August 1893	April 1893	
October 1896	March 1896	
October 1907	September 1907	
August–October 1914	May 1914	War-related

Sources: Peaks are defined using Burns and Mitchell (1946, 510), and Frickey (1942, 1947), as amended by Miron and Romer (1989). For pre-1854 data we rely on the Cleveland Trust Company Index of Productive Activity, as reported in Standard Trade and Securities (1932, 166).

[a]Suspension of convertibility lasted through February 1817. Discount rates of Baltimore, Philadelphia, and New York banks in Philadelphia roughly averaged 18, 12, and 9 percent, respectively, for the period of suspension prior to 1817. See Gallatin (1831, 106).

[b]Bond defaults by states in 1840 and 1841 transformed a banking suspension into a banking collapse.

cial news in December 1861 came at a time when banks in the principal financial centers were holding large quantities of government bonds (also see Dewey 1903, 278–82).

During the National Banking Era, there were four widespread suspensions of convertibility (1873, 1893, 1907, 1914) and six episodes where clearinghouse loan certificates were issued (1873, 1884, 1890, 1893, 1907, 1914). In October 1896 the New York Clearing House Association authorized the issuance of loan certificates, but none were actually issued. Thus, one could rank panics in order of the severity of the coordination problem faced by banks into three sets: suspensions (1873, 1893, 1907, 1914); coordination to forestall suspensions (1884, 1890); and a perceived need for coordination (1896). We leave it as an open question whether to view 1896 as a panic, as our results do not depend on its inclusion or exclusion.

The panics during the Great Depression appear to be of a different character than earlier panics. Unlike the panics of the National Banking Era, these events did not occur near the peak of the business cycle and did result in widespread failures and large losses to depositors. The *worst* loss per deposit dollar during a panic (from the onset of the panic to the business cycle trough) in the National Banking Era was 2.1 cents per dollar of deposits. And the *worst* case in terms of numbers of banks failing during a panic was 1.28 percent, during the Panic of 1893. The panics during the Great Depression resulted in significantly high loss and failure rates. During the Great Depression the percentage of national banks which failed was somewhere between 26 and 16 percent, depending on how it is measured. The losses on deposits were almost 5 percent (see Gorton 1988).

Many authors have argued that the panics during the 1930s were special events explicable mainly by the pernicious role of the Federal Reserve (Friedman and Schwartz 1963) or, at least, by the absence of superior preexisting institutional arrangements or standard policy responses which would have limited the persistence or severity of the banking collapse (Gorton 1988; Wheelock 1988). From the standpoint of this literature, the Great Depression tells one less about the inherent instability of the banking system than about the extent to which unwise government policies can destroy banks. For this reason we restrict attention to pre–Federal Reserve episodes.

As can be seen in table 4.1, the National Banking Era panics, together with the Panic of 1857, all happened near business cycle peaks. Panics tended to occur in the spring and fall. Finally, panics and their aftermaths did not result in enormously large numbers of bank failures or losses on deposits. These observations must be addressed by proposed explanations of panics.

A final interesting fact about panics in the United States during the National Banking Era is their peculiarity from an international perspective. Bordo (1985) concludes, in his study of financial and banking crises in six countries from 1870 to 1933, that "the United States experienced banking panics in a period when they were a historical curiosity in other countries" (73). Explanations of the origins of panics must explain why the U.S. experience was so different from that of other countries.

4.3 Market Structure and Bank Coalitions

Proposed explanations of panics must also be consistent with, if not encompass the abundant evidence suggesting that differences in branch-banking laws and interbank arrangements were important determinants of the likelihood and severity of panics. International comparisons frequently emphasize this point. Also, within the United States the key observation is that banking systems in which branch banking was allowed or in which private or state-sponsored cooperative arrangements were present, such as clearing houses or state insurance funds, displayed lower failure rates and losses. Since there now seems to be widespread agreement on the validity of these conclusions, theories of banking panics must be consistent with this evidence.

The institutional arrangements which mattered were of three types. First, there were more or less informal cooperative, sometimes spontaneous, arrangements among banks for dealing with panics. These were particularly prevalent in states that allowed branch banking. Secondly, some states sponsored formal insurance arrangements among banks. And finally, starting in the 1850s in New York City there were formal agreements originated privately by clearing houses. We briefly review the evidence concerning the importance of these institutional arrangements in explaining cross-country and intra-U.S. differences in the propensity of panics and their severity.

4.3.1 International Comparisons

Economies in which banks issue circulating debt with an option to redeem in cash on demand (demandable debt) have historically had a wide range of experiences with respect to banking panics. While some of these countries did not experience panics at all, other countries experienced panics in the seventeenth and early eighteenth centuries but not thereafter. In the United States and England, panics were persistent problems. This heterogeneous experience is a challenge to explanations of panics.

In England, panics recurred fairly frequently from the seventeenth century until the mid nineteenth century. The most famous English panics in the nineteenth century are those associated with Overend, Gurney & Co. Ltd. in 1866, and those of 1825, 1847, and 1857. Canada experienced no panics after the 1830s. Bordo (1985) provides a useful survey of banking and securities-market "panics" in six countries from 1870 to 1933. Summarizing the literature, Bordo attributes the U.S. peculiarity in large part to the absence of branch banking.

Recent work has stressed, in particular, the comparison between the U.S. and Canadian performance during the National Banking Era and the Great Depression. Unlike the United States, Canada's banking system allowed nationwide branching from an early date and relied on coordination among a small number (roughly forty in the nineteenth century, falling to ten by 1929) of large branch banks to resolve threats to the system as a whole. Haubrich (1990) and Williamson (1989) echo Bordo's emphasis on the advantages of branch banking in their studies of the comparative performance of U.S. and Canadian banks. Notably, suspensions of convertibility did not occur in Canada. The Canadian Bankers' Association, formed in 1891, was the formalization of cooperative arrangements among Canadian banks which served to regulate banks and mitigate the effects of failures. As in Scotland and other countries, the largest banks acted as leaders during times of crisis. In Canada the Bank of Montreal acted as a lender of last resort, stepping in to assist troubled banks (see Breckenridge 1910 and Williamson 1989).

The incidence of bank failures and their costs were much lower in Canada. Failure rates in Canada were much lower, but they do not accurately portray the situation since the number of banks in Canada was so small. However, calculation of failure rates based on the number of branches yields an even smaller failure rate for Canada. The failure rate in the United States for national banks during the period 1870–1909 was 0.36, compared to a failure rate in Canada, based on branches, of less than 0.1 (see Schembri and Hawkins 1988). Comparing average losses to depositors over many years produces a similar picture. Williamson (1989) compares the average losses to depositors in the United States and Canada and finds that the annual average loss rate was 0.11 percent and 0.07 percent, respectively.

Haubrich (1990) analyzes the broader economic costs of bank failures and of a less-stable banking system more generally. He investigates the contribution of credit market disruption to the severity of Canada's Great Depression. In sharp contrast with Bernanke's (1983) and Hamilton's (1987) findings for the United States, international factors rather than indicators of financial stress in Canada (commercial failures, deflation, money supply) were important during Canada's Great Depression. One way to interpret these findings is that, in the presence of a stable branch-banking system, financial shocks were not magnified by their effects on bank risk and, therefore, had more limited effects on economic activity.

4.3.2 Bank Cooperation and Institutional Arrangements in the United States

Redlich (1947) reviews the history of early interbank cooperation in the northern United States, arguing that this cooperation was at a nadir in the 1830s. Govan (1936) studies the ante-bellum southern U.S. branch-banking systems, describing cooperative state- and regional-level responses to banking panics as early as the 1830s. The smaller number of banks, the geographical coincidence of different banks' branches, and the clear leadership role of the larger branching banks in some of the states allowed bankers to coordinate suspension and resumption decisions, and to establish rules (including limits on balance sheet expansion) for interbank clearings of transactions during suspension of convertibility. The most extreme example of bank cooperation during the ante-bellum period was in Indiana, from 1834 to 1851.[6] Golembe and Warburton (1958) describe the innovative "mutual-guarantee" system in that state, which was later copied by Ohio (1845) and Iowa (1858). In this system, banks made markets in each other's liabilities, had full regulatory powers over one another through the actions of the Board of Control, and were liable for the losses of any failed member banks.

As early as the Panic of 1839, these differences in banking structure and potential for coordination seem to have been an important determinant of the probability of failure during a banking panic. *Hunt's Merchants' Magazine* reports the suspension and failure propensities of various states from the origin of the panic on 9 October 1839 until 8 January 1840. Banks in the centralized, urban banking systems of Louisiana, Delaware, Rhode Island, and the District of Columbia all suspended convertibility during the panic, and none failed in 1839. Similarly, the laissez-faire, branch-banking states of the South (Virginia, North Carolina, South Carolina, Georgia, and Tennessee) saw nearly universal suspension of convertibility (with 92 out of 100 banking facilities suspending) and suffered only four bank failures in 1839, all small newly organized unit banks in western Georgia.[7] Indiana's mutual-guarantee banks all suspended, but would never suffer a single failure from their origin in 1834 to their dissolution in 1865, and after suspending in 1839 would never again find it necessary to suspend convertibility (see Golembe and Warburton 1958, and Calomiris 1989a).

Other states typically had fewer suspensions, less uniformity among banks in the decision to suspend, and a higher incidence of bank failure. In New England, outside of Rhode Island, only four out of 277 banks suspended and remained solvent, while eighteen (6.5 percent) failed by the end of 1839. In the mid-Atlantic states, outside of Delaware and the District of Columbia, 112 out of 334 banks suspended and remained solvent, while 22 (6.6 percent) failed. In the southeastern states of Mississippi and Alabama, 23 of 37 banks suspended and two (5.4 percent) failed. In the northwestern states of Ohio, Illinois, and Michigan, 46 out of 67 banks suspended, while nine (13.4 percent) failed.

Calomiris and Schweikart (1991) and Calomiris (1989a) demonstrate that the importance of branch-banking laws and banking cooperation is just as apparent in the experiences of banks during the crisis of 1857. They document that the branch-banking South and the mutual-guarantee coinsurance systems of Indiana and Ohio enjoyed a lower ex ante risk evaluation on their bank notes and suffered far lower bank failure rates than the rest of the country during the Panic of 1857.[8]

None of Indiana's or Ohio's mutual-guarantee banks failed or suspended convertibility during the Panic of 1857. Both Ohio and Indiana chartered free banks, in addition to the coinsuring systems of banks. During the regional crisis of 1854–55, 55 of Indiana's 94 free banks failed, and during the Panic of 1857, 14 out of Indiana's 32 free banks failed. In Ohio, failure rates were lower, with only one bank failing in the Panic of 1857. The difference between Ohio's and Indiana's free banks cannot be attributed to observed differences in the size of the shocks affecting the two locations. For example, the magnitudes of the declines in bond prices were roughly comparable.[9] What set Indiana's newer free banks apart from those of Ohio was their failure to coordinate suspension or to obtain aid from the coinsuring banks.

Ohio banks received assistance from the coinsuring banks during the panic. In Indiana, the free banks and the coinsuring banks did not cooperate. Moreover, the free banks had not had the time to establish an independent coordination mechanism. Ironically, just prior to the Panic of 1857, Indiana free banks began to discuss forming a clearing association for their mutual benefit.[10]

Branch-banking systems tended to be less prone to the effects of panics. Evidence on the importance of branch banking in the United States is provided by Calomiris (1989b, 1990) in a detailed, state-by-state examination of the response of banks in agricultural states to the large adverse asset shocks of the 1920s. Controlling for differences in the severity of shocks, states that allowed branch banking weathered the crisis much better than unit-banking states. Bank failure rates for (grandfathered) branching banks in unit-banking states, and for branching banks in free-entry branching states, were a fraction of those of unit banks. Furthermore, in states that allowed branching it was much easier for weak banks to be acquired or replaced by new entrants.

Private banking associations in the form of clearing houses provided mechanisms for coordinating bank responses to banking panics. During the nineteenth century, starting in New York City in 1853, clearing houses evolved into highly formal institutions. These institutions not only cleared interbank liabilities but, in response to banking panics, they acted as lenders of last resort, issuing private money and providing deposit insurance. As part of the process of performing these functions, clearing houses regulated member banks by auditing member risk-taking activities, setting capital requirements, and penalizing members for violating clearing-house rules.

During banking panics, clearing houses created a market for the illiquid assets of member banks by accepting such assets as collateral in exchange for clearing-house loan certificates which were liabilities of the association of banks. Member banks then exchanged the loan certificates for depositors' demand deposits. Clearing-house loan certificates were printed in small denominations and functioned as a hand-to-hand currency. Moreover, since these securities were the liability of the association of banks rather than of any individual bank, depositors were insured against the failure of their individual bank.[11] Initially, clearing-house loan certificates traded at a discount against gold. This discount presumably reflected the chance that the clearing house would not be able to honor the certificates at par. When this discount went to zero, suspension of convertibility was lifted. Cannon (1910) and Sprague (1910) trace these increasingly cooperative reactions of city bank clearing houses to panics during 1857–1907. Gorton (1985, 1989b) and Gorton and Mullineaux (1987) also analyze these clearing arrangements.

Bank clearing houses, and their cooperative benefits, were limited to citywide coalitions in the United States because of branching restrictions. The sharing of risk inherent in these cooperative arrangements required effective monitoring and enforcement of self-imposed regulations. Banks could only monitor and enforce effectively if they were geographically coincident. Moreover, as the number of banks in a self-regulating coalition increases, the incentives for effective supervision decline because the cost of monitoring is borne individually, while the benefits are shared among all members of the group.

4.3.3 Summary

The variety of institutional arrangements discussed above resulted in different propensities for panics and different abilities to respond to panics when they occurred. Internationally, not all countries experienced panics, even when the banking contracts appeared similar to those present in the United States. In the case of the United States, as reviewed above, there is direct evidence that these institutional arrangements resulted in different loss and failure experiences. Also, there is evidence from the Free Banking Era (1838–63), during which bank notes traded in markets, that these differences were priced by markets. As shown by Gorton (1989a, 1990), the note prices varied depending on the presence or absence of arrangements such as insurance, clearing house, and so on.

The evidence on the importance of market and institutional structure strongly suggests the importance of asymmetric information in banking. If full information for all agents characterized these markets, then institutional differences would not matter. We interpret this evidence as implying a set of stylized facts with which a theory of banking panics must be consistent. A theory must not only explain why such institutional structure matters, but also the origins of such structures as responses to panics.

4.4 Models of Banking Panics

A decade ago, theoretical work on banks and banking panics was aimed at addressing the following questions: How can bank debt contracts be optimal if such contracts lead to banking panics? Why would privately issued circulating bank debt be used to finance nonmarketable assets if this combination leads to socially costly panics? Posed in this way, explaining panics was extremely difficult. In the last decade, two distinct theories have developed to explain the origins of banking panics. While these two lines of argument do not exhaust the explanations of panics, they seem to be the explanations around which research has coalesced.[12] In this section we briefly review the evolution of this research, stressing the testable implications of each.

One line of argument, initiated by the influential work of Diamond and Dybvig (1983), began by arguing that bank contracts, while optimal, necessarily lead to costly panics. Banks and banking panics were seen as inherently intertwined. Over the last decade, confronted with the historical evidence that panics did not accompany demandable-debt contracts in all cases, this view has evolved to include institutional structure as a central part of the argument. Nevertheless, as we trace below, the essential core of the theory remains unchanged, namely, that panics are undesirable events caused by random deposit withdrawals. We, therefore, label this view the "random withdrawal" theory of panics.

The second line of argument on the origins of panics emphasizes the importance of market structure in banking when depositors lack information about bank-specific loan risk. While it is important to explain the existence of banks as institutions, the second view essentially starts with the unit-banking system as given. In this view, runs on banks may be an optimal response of depositors. A key to this argument is the hypothesis that bank depositors cannot costlessly value individual banks' assets. In other words, there is asymmetric information. In such a world, depositors may have a difficult time monitoring the performance of banks. A panic can be viewed as a form of monitoring. If depositors believe that there are some under-performing banks but cannot detect which ones may become insolvent, they may force out the undesirable banks by a systemwide panic. This line of argument, then, emphasizes sudden, but rational, revisions in the perceived riskiness of bank deposits when nonbank-specific, aggregate information arrives. We label this view the "asymmetric information" theory of panics.

These two lines of thought have different visions of why banks exist, though there are also important overlaps in the arguments. These theoretical considerations are discussed in the final subsection.

4.4.1 Random Withdrawal Risk

The model of Diamond and Dybvig (1983) was the first coherent explanation of how bank debt contracts could be optimal and yet lead to banking panics. An essential feature of the Diamond and Dybvig model is the view of banks as mechanisms for insuring against risk. In their model, agents have uncertain needs for consumption and face an environment in which long-term investments are costly to liquidate. Agents would prefer the higher returns associated with long-term investments, but their realized preferences may turn out to be for consumption at an earlier date. Banks exist to insure that consumption occurs in concert with the realization of agents' consumption preferences. The bank contract, offering early redemption at a fixed rate, is interpreted as the provision of "liquidity." This idea, further developed by Haubrich and King (1984), will not suffice, by itself, to explain panics.

In order for panics to occur, two further, related ingredients were needed. First, as Cone (1983) and Jacklin (1987) made clear, markets had to be incomplete in an important way, namely, agents were not allowed to trade claims on physical assets after their preferences for consumption had been realized.[13] Thus, stock markets or markets in bank liabilities were assumed to be closed. Second, deposit withdrawals were assumed to be made according to a first-come-first-served rule, or sequential-service constraint. These two assumptions, particularly the latter, were able to account for panics which were caused by random withdrawal risk.

A panic could occur as follows. In the Diamond and Dybvig model, a bank cannot honor all its liabilities at par if all agents present them for redemption. The problem is that liquidation of the bank's long-term assets is assumed to be costly. But, the essential mechanism causing the possibility of panic is the sequential-service constraint. With this rule, a panic can occur as a self-fulfilling set of beliefs. If agents think that other agents think there will be many withdrawals, then agents at the end of the sequential-service line will suffer losses. Thus, all agents, seeking to avoid losses associated with being at the end of the line, may suddenly decide to redeem their claims, causing the very event they imagined. The first-come-first-served rule prevents allocation of the bank's resources on a pro rata basis, which would have prevented the panic.

A key question for the original Diamond and Dybvig model concerned the causes of panics. Why would agents sometimes develop beliefs leading to a panic, while at other times believe that there would be no panic? This question, the answer to which was essential for any empirical test of the theory, was not really addressed. Diamond and Dybvig suggested that such beliefs may develop because of "a random earnings report, a commonly observed run at some other bank, a negative government forecast, or even sunspots" (1983, 410).

In the Diamond and Dybvig model, panics are due to random withdrawals caused by self-fulfilling beliefs. The difficulties with this hypothesis were quickly recognized. As mentioned above, Cone (1983) argued that panics would be eliminated if banking was conducted without the sequential-service constraint. Wallace (1988) observed that the explanation for the existence of the crucial sequential-service constraint was "vague." Jacklin (1987) made the observation about the required market incompleteness. Postlewaite and Vives (1987) observed that the optimality of the Diamond and Dybvig bank could not be demonstrated if probabilities could not be attached to the possibilities of self-fulfilling beliefs occurring. Gorton (1988) pointed out that the model was untestable because it did not specify how beliefs were formed or changed as a function of observables.

These difficulties with the Diamond and Dybvig model motivated further research along two lines. First, some justification for the sequential-service constraint had to be found. In Diamond and Dybvig this constraint, clearly not optimal from the point of view of the agents in the model, was assumed to be part of the physical environment. Without the constraint, panics would not arise. Second, the model had to be refined to make clear what types of events would cause beliefs to change such that a panic would occur. The Diamond and Dybvig model theoretically equated the existence of banks as providers of liquidity with the possibility of banking panics. But, in reality, not all banking systems experienced panics. Consequently, as argued by Smith (1987), explaining what shocks would cause agents to withdraw would require more attention to market structure in banking.

Wallace (1988) addressed the issue of the existence of the sequential-service constraint by introducing spatial separation of agents. The assumed isolation of agents prevents them from coordinating their withdrawals. In particular, they cannot organize a credit market at the time when withdrawal choices must be made.[14] This interpretation formally rationalized the existence of the constraint, but it was difficult to recognize as an historical phenomenon. Bhattacharya and Gale (1987), Smith (1987), and Chari (1989) interpreted the spatial separation of agents as corresponding to the institutional features of the U.S. banking system during the nineteenth century. While differing in some important respects, the common thread among these papers is the recognition that the United States had a large number of geographically separated banks due to prohibitions on interstate banking. Banks were linked by the regulatory structure of the National Banking System which required small country banks to hold reserves in specified reserve-city banks. New York City, deemed the central reserve city, was at the top of the reserve pyramid.

This reinterpretation remedied the two defects of the Diamond and Dybvig model in one stroke. The sequential-service constraint appeared to be imposed on the system by the three-tiered reserve system.[15] Isolation corresponded to the spatial separation of the country banks. Reinterpreting the Diamond and Dybvig model in this historical context meant locating a causal panic shock in the countryside. The gist of the causal mechanism now was that country banks, facing a withdrawal shock, would demand that their reserves from city banks be shipped to the interior. If enough country banks in various locations faced problems at the same time, then they would demand their reserves from their reserve-city banks. The reserve-city banks, in turn, would demand their reserves from their central reserve-city banks in New York City. Thus, panics were not inherent to banking, but were linked to a particular institutional structure, namely, unit banking and reserve pyramiding.

Vulnerability to panics was identified with the spatial separation of banks. But, in order for a panic to occur, the spatially separated banks must be unable to form an effective interbank insurance arrangement. If a coalition of banks could form, then banks could self-insure, moving reserves about through interbank loan markets. Chari (1989) argues that difficulties in unit banks monitoring each other's holdings of reserves vitiated credible interbank arrangements. In the absence of effective monitoring, banks will have an incentive to hold too little in reserves (and place reserves in interest-bearing loans), thus making coinsurance of withdrawal risk infeasible. According to Chari (1989), geographically separate unit banks should be forced to hold reserves by government regulation. The government would then enforce this regulation, and thereby make interbank lending feasible.

In the refined version of Diamond and Dybvig an important question still remained: what was the shock which caused the panic? In order to confront the data, this question must be answered. Unfortunately, not much of an answer has been provided. Bhattacharya and Gale (1987) refer only to "local" shocks in a model of spatially separated banks. Smith (1987) is also vague. Only Chari (1989) explicitly provides an explanation:

> The idea that the demand for currency can vary within communities is not implausible. In the second half of the 19th century an important source of these variations was agriculture. The demand for farm loans rose during the planting season and fell in the harvest. Since cash was required for many farm transactions, the demand for currency in agricultural communities was high at both planting and harvesting times and low at other times of the year. (11)

Indeed, there is a long literature on the seasonality of the demand for currency in the United States.[16] And, the identification of unexpectedly large demands for currency in the countryside as the cause of panics also has a long history.[17] Thus, the modern theory of panics which associates panics with random withdrawal risk due to seasonal fluctuations theoretically rationalizes a traditional view of panics.

To summarize, the theoretical development of the random-withdrawal risk theory of panics has resulted in a view which assigns the origin of the panic-causing shock to the countryside. Only one kind of shock has been proposed, namely, seasonally related demand for money shocks. This has testable implications for the random withdrawal theory, which are developed below.

4.4.2 Asymmetric Information

The alternative theory of banking panics is based on identifying the conditions under which bank depositors would rationally change their beliefs about the riskiness of banks. Then the theoretical task is to identify banking system features under which such changes in beliefs are manifested in panics. The core of the theory is that banking panics serve a positive function in monitoring bank performance in an environment where there is asymmetric information about bank performance. Panics are triggered by rational revisions in beliefs about bank performance.

Banks are not viewed as providing insurance in the asymmetric information theory. Rather, banks are seen as providing valuable services through the creation of nonmarketable bank loans together with the provision of a circulating medium.[18] Since banks are involved in the creation of nonmarketable assets, they may be difficult to value, and bank managements difficult to monitor. There is, thus, asymmetric information between banks and depositors concerning the performance of bank managements and portfolios. In an environment where there are many small, undiversified banks, these problems may be particularly severe.[19] Arguments for the existence of banks' value-creating activities in making loans depend on depositors' abilities to monitor the unobservable performance of bank managements.[20] The view of the asymmetric information theory of panics is that the sequential-service constraint and, indeed, panics themselves, are mechanisms for depositors to monitor the performance of banks.

In an environment with asymmetric information, a panic can occur as follows. Bank depositors may receive information leading them to revise their assessment of the risk of banks, but they do not know which individual banks are most likely to be affected. Since depositors are unable to distinguish individual bank risks, they may withdraw a large volume of deposits from all banks in response to a signal. Banks then suspend convertibility, and a period of time follows during which the banks themselves sort out which banks among them are insolvent. Indeed, it is possible to view panics as a means for depositors to force banks to resolve asymmetries of information through collective action (i.e., monitoring and closure). The efficiency of this mechanism derives from a supposed comparative advantage (low costs) that banks possess.

No single model has given rise to the view that banking panics are essentially due to revisions of the perceived risk of bank debt in an environment where there is asymmetric information about bank asset portfolios. A number of researchers, including Calomiris (1989a), Calomiris and Schweikart (1991), Chari and Jagannathan (1988), Gorton (1987, 1989b), Gorton and Mullineaux (1987), Jacklin and Bhattacharya (1988), Williamson (1989), and others, have argued for this asymmetric information–based view of banking panics. These models are broadly consistent with the arguments of Sprague (1910) and Friedman and Schwartz (1963) which stress real disturbances, causing erosion of trust in the banking system, as precursors to panics. Although these viewpoints differ in important respects, they seem to have a similar idea at core.

The evolution of the asymmetric information view is not as straightforward as the random withdrawal theory, but there is some logic to its development. To see how the asymmetric information view differs from the random withdrawal theory and to trace some of its development, we will focus on the sequential-service constraint. The asymmetric information theory of banking panics views the sequential-service constraint in a fundamentally different way than the random withdrawal theory.

A convenient beginning point is Chari and Jagannathan (1988). They assumed a setting in which depositors are uninformed about the true values of banks. In their model, depositors randomly fall into one of three groups: those who become informed about the state of bank portfolios; those who withdraw because they wish to consume, independently of the state of banks; and those who are uninformed and do not wish to consume. Their basic idea was that some bank depositors might withdraw money for consumption purposes while other depositors might withdraw money because they knew that the bank was about to fail.[21] In this environment, the group of depositors which cannot distinguish whether there are long lines to withdraw at banks because of consumption needs or because informed depositors are getting out early may also withdraw. The uninformed group learns about the state of the bank only by observing the line at the bank. If there happens to be a long line at the bank, they infer (rightly or wrongly) that the bank is about to fail and seek to withdraw also.[22]

This view of panics assumes the sequential-service constraint and asymmetric information, but introduces the idea of heterogeneously informed depositors (also see Jacklin and Bhattacharya 1988). Heterogeneously informed depositors became the basis for Calomiris and Kahn's (1991) and Calomiris, Kahn, and Krasa's (1990) argument that a debt contract, together with the sequential-service constraint, is an optimal arrangement in banking when depositors are uninformed about the bank's assets and managers' actions. To see the basic idea, suppose that information about the bank is costly to obtain. In order to monitor bank performance, some depositors must be induced to undertake costly information production. A sequential-service constraint rewards those who arrive first to withdraw their money because their deposit contracts are honored in full. Since informed agents would know when to withdraw, they would arrive first, receiving a larger return; those at the end of the line, the uninformed, would get less since the bank would have run out of cash. Thus, the sequential-service constraint induces efficient monitoring of banks by depositors.

In this context, however, the sequential-service constraint does not inevitably lead to banking panics. Instead, the above scenario would occur at specific banks which faced problems, but would not necessarily occur at many banks simultaneously. Banking panics do not occur unless there are a large number of undiversified banks. Some details about the reasons for this were provided by Gorton (1989b). He argued that a bank debt contract and sequential-service constraint, as implied by Calomiris and Kahn (1989), can be a costly way to monitor banks if it requires a large equity-to-debt ratio. (Equity is owned by the managers, so the managers' stake in the bank can be threatened by withdrawal.) For Gorton, bank debt has a role independent of the banks' value-adding activities in creating loans. Bank debt circulates as a medium of exchange. In that setting there must be some mechanism to clear bank liabilities. Gorton compares two institutional arrangements for clearing in the banking industry. The first was similar to American free banking in that bank debt liabilities were like bank notes. That is, bank debt traded in secondary markets. The market prices of these notes revealed information about bank-specific risks. Hence, there is no asymmetric information in this setting. As a result, bank managers are induced to perform their tasks of monitoring or information production because of the threat of redemption. But, optimal performance is only achieved if enough equity is at stake.

Now consider a second way of organizing the banking industry in which there is no market in which bank debt is traded. Instead of clearing bank debt through trade in a market, suppose that bank liabilities clear through a clearing house. This arrangement would create an information asymmetry since there are no publicly observed market prices of different banks' debts. The market incompleteness, assumed in some other models, arises endogenously if this clearing arrangement is chosen. Gorton shows that panics can occur under this second system, but that the costs of monitoring banks can be reduced. The reason is that, with the information asymmetry, banks are forced to internalize the monitoring. The threat of a panic induces banks to form clearing houses which monitor member banks and act as the lender of last resort. The equity-debt ratio can be reduced, economizing on resources. In this view, panics are part of an optimal arrangement for monitoring banks.

While the assumption of information-revealing note prices, revealing bank-specific risk, may be a bit extreme, the essential point is that the need for bank debt holders to place a collective burden on banks to resolve information asymmetries is much greater under deposit banking than under note banking.[23] The clearing-house coalition is the natural group to resolve asymmetric information problems. Banks as a group have a collective interest in the smooth functioning of the payments system and comparative advantage in monitoring and enforcement.

Notice that there is a subtle difference between the arguments of Calomiris and Kahn (1991) and Gorton (1989b). Calomiris and Kahn argue that the sequential-service constraint provides an efficient way for depositors to monitor individual banks, though it may have the disadvantage of allowing systemic panics to occur. Gorton, however, sees the operation of the sequential-service constraint during panics as adding to the advantages of demandable debt.

The asymmetric information theory argues that insufficient diversification of asset risk among banks occurs under unit banking. Bank depositors do not know the value of bank asset portfolios. A panic may occur when depositors observe a public signal correlated with the value of banking-system assets. In Gorton (1988) the signal is an increase in a leading indicator of recession. In Calomiris and Schweikart (1991) the signal is a decline in the net worth of a particular class of bank borrowers. The signal may imply very slight aggregate losses to banks as a whole, but depositors are unable to observe the incidence of the shock across the many banks in the banking system. Conditional on the signal, deposits are riskier.[24] At some point, as the risk associated with asymmetric information rises, depositors prefer to withdraw their funds or force a suspension of convertibility which will resolve the information asymmetry.

4.4.3 Theoretical Considerations

The competing theoretical constructs discussed above propose different visions of the nature of banks and banking, though there is some common ground. The varying perspectives on the nature of banking are not unrelated to the resulting different theories of panics. From a purely theoretical point of view, there are desirable and undesirable features of the two theories. In this section we indicate these differences and commonalities.

Banks are unique institutions because of services that are provided on each side of the balance sheet. Examining the asset side of the balance sheet first, the two theories appear to agree on the nature of banks' value-adding activities with respect to the creation of bank loans. Monitoring borrowers and information production about credit risks are activities that banks undertake which cannot be replicated by capital markets. The arguments for this are articulated by Diamond (1984) and Boyd and Prescott (1986), among others. The essential idea is that bank production of these activities requires that the bank loan which is created be nonmarketable or, synonymously, illiquid, that is, that it not be traded once created. If the loan could subsequently be sold, then the originating bank would not face an incentive to monitor or produce information. This argument depends on the banks' activities being unobservable, so that the only way of insuring that banks undertake the activities they promise is by forcing them to maintain ownership of the loans they create. This need for incentive compatibility makes bank loans nonmarketable.

The nonmarketability or illiquidity of bank loans plays an essential role in each theory of banking panics. The random-withdrawal risk theory requires that the liquidation of long-term bank assets be costly. Though never clearly stated, presumably the reason for this cost assumption is that bank loans are not marketable. The asymmetric information theory also assumes that bank loans are nonmarketable. If banks' monitoring and information production activities were observable, then there would be no information asymmetry. Bank loans are not traded because bank activity is hard to observe and monitor.

The two theories significantly differ concerning the nature of bank liabilities. The key question concerns the meaning of "liquidity." The random withdrawal theory sees banks as institutions for providing insurance against random consumption needs. The high-return, long-term investment can only be ended, and transformed into cash or consumption goods, at a cost (for the reasons discussed above). While agents prefer the high-return, long-term investment project, they may want to consume at an earlier date. The bank, by pooling the long- and short-term investments in the right proportions, can issue a security which insures against the risk of early consumption. The idea, articulated by Diamond and Dybvig (1983, 403), is that "banks are able to transform illiquid assets by offering liabilities with a different, smoother pattern of returns over time than the illiquid assets offer." Thus, the insurance feature of the bank contract is interpreted as the provision of "liquidity."

In the random withdrawal theory the illiquidity or nonmarketability of bank assets provides the rationale for the special feature of bank liabilities. In fact, precisely *because* the long-term investments are illiquid, the bank is needed. The banks' liabilities do not circulate as a medium of exchange in this model, so there is no sense in which demand deposits function like money. This appears to be a weakness of the model. But, the model provides a rationale for banks appearing to be financing illiquid assets with liabilities which have a redemption option. In the random withdrawal theory, liquidity means intertemporal consumption flexibility.

The asymmetric information theory also offers a definition of the "liquidity" of bank liabilities. This notion of liquidity refers to the ease with which a security can be valued and, hence, traded. (This definition of liquidity is based on Akerlof 1970.) Importantly, this notion of liquidity is related to explaining the combination of nonmarketable or illiquid bank loans with liabilities offering the redemption option. As mentioned above, Calomiris and Kahn (1991) argue that the illiquidity of bank loans makes bank debt, together with the sequential-service constraint, optimal. Here, uninformed depositors learn about the state of the bank by observing whether informed depositors have run the bank. Thus, information about the value of bank debt is created. An implication would be that bank debt can be used as a medium of exchange. Gorton (1989b) and Gorton and Pennacchi (1990) also argue that bank liabilities are special because they circulate as a medium of exchange. In Gorton and Pennacchi (1990) the same notion of liquidity is articulated. The basic point is that bank debt is designed to be valued very easily because it is essentially riskless. This makes it ideal as a medium of exchange.

Gorton and Pennacchi consider a set-up similar to Diamond and Dybvig (1983) in that consumption needs are stochastic for some agents. But, other agents do not have random consumption and are informed about the state of the world. The informed agents can take advantage of the uninformed agents who have urgent needs to consume. This is accomplished by successful insider trading. Insiders can profit at the expense of the uninformed agents because these agents need to trade to finance consumption and do not know the true value of the securities they are exchanging for consumption goods. Gorton and Pennacchi show that market prices do not reveal this information. This problem creates the need for a privately produced trading security with the feature that its value is always known by the uninformed. A bank can prevent such trading losses by issuing a security which is riskless.

Banks can design a riskless security by creating liabilities which are, first of all, debt, and secondly, backed by a diversified portfolio. Debt contracts reduce the variance of the security's price. In addition, banks are in a relatively unusual position to back these liabilities with diversified portfolios, because banks make loans to many firms and, thus, hold large portfolios against which debt claims can be issued. For this reason, it is banks which issue trading securities, such as demand deposits.

The asymmetric information theory articulates a notion of liquidity that corresponds closely to the idea that bank liabilities have unique properties making them suitable as a circulating medium. Banks create securities with the property that they can be easily valued because they are riskless. The property of risklessness makes these securities desirable as a medium of exchange. The random withdrawal theory has a notion of liquidity corresponding to a type of insurance which banks are viewed as being in a unique position to offer. Bank debt does not circulate, but functions to insure against the liquidation of bank assets which would be costly. We leave it to the reader to judge whether any weight should be attached to these theoretical distinctions.

4.5 Confronting the Data: The United States During the National Banking Era

Having established the importance of banking institutions and market structure in generating banking panics, we proceed, in this section, to an examination of the comparative empirical performance of the two competing theories of the origins of banking panics. At the outset it is worth noting the substantial overlap in the predictions of the two views.

First, both views predict widespread banking contraction coinciding with suspension of convertibility. Second, the order in which suspension occurs in different regions (that is, typically moving from East to West) is consistent with either view, as well. According to both views, because of interbank reserve pyramiding, a nationwide move to withdraw funds for whatever reasons will concentrate pressure on eastern financial centers first. Because peripheral banks had substantial deposits in New York, and because depositors often moved to withdraw funds from banks in one location to compensate for suspension elsewhere, suspension in New York City or Philadelphia would precipitate widespread suspension by banks elsewhere. Suspension of convertibility typically spread from eastern cities to other locations within a day or two of suspension in the financial centers (see Calomiris and Schweikart 1991, and Sprague 1910).

Third, as noted above, both views predict that branch banking or deposit insurance would be associated with an increase in banking stability, that is, a reduction in the incidence and severity of banking panics. Branch banking diversifies, and deposit insurance protects against, both asset and withdrawal risks, and either removes the incentive for preemptory runs by depositors which both the withdrawal risk and asymmetric information views predict.[25]

Fourth, the two approaches are consistent with the fact that bank panics occurred in certain months of the year. The withdrawal risk approach views the seasonality of banking panics as evidence of the role of seasonal money-demand shocks in precipitating panics. According to the asymmetric information view, seasonal patterns in the incidence of banking panics, noted by Andrew (1907), Kemmerer (1910), and Miron (1986), indicate that the banking system was more *vulnerable* to asset-side shocks during periods of low reserve-to-deposit and capital-to-deposit ratios, but exogenous withdrawals by themselves were not the cause of panics. This is the argument for the seasonality of panics found in Sprague (1910) and Miron (1986). We provide further evidence for this argument below.

Despite the substantial agreement in the predictions of the two views, there are some important differences in their empirical implications. We have identified three verifiable areas of disagreement. First, because the two views differ over the sources of shocks, they differ in their predictions about what aspects of panic years were unusual, particularly the weeks or months immediately preceding the panic. The withdrawal risk approach implies an unusual increase in withdrawals from banks typically combined with an unusually large interregional flow of funds at the onset of a panic. In particular, Chari (1989) argues that unusually large demands for money in the periphery for planting and harvesting crops were an important source of disturbance. Eichengreen (1984) provides some supporting evidence for this point by showing that the propensity to hold currency relative to deposits was higher in agricultural areas. During the planting and harvesting seasons, when the composition of money holdings shifted to the West, the money multiplier fell.

In contrast, the asymmetric information approach predicts unusually adverse economic news prior to panics, including increases in asset risk, declines in the relative prices of risky assets, increases in commercial failures, and the demise of investment banking houses. The importance of this news for banking panics depends on the links between the news and the value of bank assets.

A second difference between the two approaches concerns predictions about the incidence of bank liquidations during panics. According to the asymmetric information view of panics, the incidence of bank failures will reflect, in large part, the interaction between different bank loan portfolios and a systemic disturbance. Bank-failure propensities should vary according to the links between bank assets and the shock. For example, a shock which affects western land values or railroads' values clearly should tend to bankrupt banks holding western mortgages or railroad bonds more than other banks. According to models of random withdrawal risk, banks should fail disproportionately in locations with pronounced idiosyncratic money-demand shocks. Or banks fail because they have connections to those regions through correspondent relationships (which transmit the money-demand shocks).[26] Furthermore, the asymmetric information view predicts that the aggregate ratio of bank failures to suspensions should depend on the severity of the shock that initiates suspension, while the withdrawal risk approach would link the severity and suddenness of the withdrawal from banks to the ratio of suspensions to subsequent bank liquidations over different panics.

The third area of disagreement refers to sufficient conditions to resolve a panic. That is, the causes of banking panics can be inferred by the types of measures that are capable of resolving crises. (This has regulatory implications, discussed in the final section.) While both views of panics agree that bank coordination ex ante will probably mitigate the likelihood of panics and the effects of panics when they do occur, the two views have different implications for what efforts are sufficient to resolve panics. The withdrawal risk model predicts that panics take time to resolve because of the difficulty banks face in transforming assets into cash quickly. Historically, however, a large proportion of bank assets took the form of internationally marketable securities, including bills of exchange and high-grade commercial paper which were convertible into gold in international markets (see Myers 1931). In some instances there were more immediate sources of funds available. We investigate whether the time it would have taken to perform this conversion corresponds to the duration of suspension.

Alternatively, the asymmetric information view sees the duration of suspension as an indicator of how long it takes to resolve confusion about the incidence of asset shocks. The availability of specie per se may be insufficient to resolve panics, especially if many banks' assets are not "marked to market" and are viewed as suspect. Furthermore, the asymmetric information view predicts that interbank transfers of wealth can resolve asset-risk concerns without necessarily taking the form of specie movements and, thus, can put an end to crises. We consider examples of private and public bailouts that took this form.

4.5.1 How Were Pre-Panic Periods Unusual?

We begin by examining whether pre-panic periods were characterized by unusually large withdrawals and interregional flows of funds. Consistent with our definition of panics, we date the beginning of trouble by reference to the timing of a cooperative emergency response by banks, such as providing for the issue of clearing-house loan certificates. This will produce an upwardly biased measure of the withdrawals during panic years, since by the time banks had recognized and acted upon a problem, some endogenous preemptive withdrawals may already have occurred. Thus, our inter-year comparisons of shocks are biased in favor of finding large withdrawals in advance of panics. In other words, a negative finding would provide an a fortiori argument against the importance of random withdrawals.

All comparisons are made across years for the same week of the year. This allows one to abstract from predictable seasonal components of withdrawals.

Our first measures refer to the condition of New York City banks at the beginnings of panics so defined, using data compiled up to 1909 by the National Monetary Commission (see Andrew 1910). We focus on the percentage of deposits withdrawn and the ratio of reserves to deposits as indicators of the New York banks' vulnerability or illiquidity. The two measures are complementary. Because weekly disturbances in money demand are likely to be serially correlated within the year (the sine qua non of the seasonal withdrawal-risk approach), it is useful to focus not only on the reserve ratio but also on the amount actually withdrawn from banks, as an indication of how much is likely to be withdrawn for similar purposes in the following weeks. At the same time, a large withdrawal during times when banks are holding large reserves will be of little consequence, so one must also pay attention to the reserve ratio when comparing years of similar seasonal withdrawal shocks.

Introducing two complementary measures of seasonal "illiquidity risk" complicates matters slightly for determining the extent to which pre-panic episodes were unusual. How does one compare years where the two measures provide opposite results for the degree of "tightness"? We adopt the following conventions: A year is said to be *unambiguously tighter* than another year (during a particular week) if its reserve ratio is lower and the percentage of deposits withdrawn in the immediate past is higher during a given week. A year is defined as *possibly tighter* if the percentage of withdrawals is higher and the reserve ratio differs by less than 1 percent.

We also had to choose a definition of the *immediate past.* Seasonal withdrawals associated with planting and harvesting tend to be spread over periods of one to two months (more on this below). Clearly, protracted steady withdrawals of funds over a two-month period would not have posed nearly the threat to banks that a sudden withdrawal of the same amount would have posed. The transatlantic cable was in operation beginning in 1866, and it took roughly ten days for a steamship to cross the Atlantic to exchange European specie for marketable bills of exchange and commercial paper. Calomiris and Hubbard (1989b) show that specie flows across the Atlantic and within the country responded extremely rapidly to specie demands, with most long-run adjustments to a shock occurring in the first month. We decided on four weeks as a reasonable time horizon for withdrawal risk since it would take at least two weeks after recognizing a threat to liquidity to retrieve the gold from abroad and distribute it.[27]

Table 4.2 is divided into five pairs of columns, which provide data from 1871 to 1909 on reserve ratios and the percentage change in deposits immediately prior to benchmark weeks that witnessed the onset of banking panics. Panics originated in week 19 (mid May 1884), week 22 (early June 1893), week 37 (late September 1873), week 42 (late October 1907), and week 45 (mid November 1890).

The "quasi panic" of 1896 is excluded from our list. Its inclusion would strengthen the conclusions reported below, since its onset did not correspond to unusually large seasonal withdrawals. Our conclusions would also be strengthened by extending comparisons to include weeks other than 19, 22, 37, 42, and 45. That is, one could seasonally adjust the complete data set on withdrawals and reserve ratios and perform comparisons across weeks, as well.[28] By restricting our attention to the five clear panic cases and to inter-year comparisons for panic weeks, we biased our results in favor of concluding that panic episodes were times of unusually large withdrawals. This will strengthen the interpretation of our findings below. We also chose not to detrend the reserve ratios in table 4.2 for the same reason. Detrending the reserve ratio increases the number of episodes in which we find "unambiguously tighter" conditions than those preceding panics.

The measures reported in table 4.3 do not support the notion that panics were preceded by unusually large seasonal shocks or that panics resulted from tripping a threshold of bank liquidity, as measured either by reserve ratios or rates of deposit withdrawal. As shown in table 4.3, even using our extremely conservative methods, we find eighteen episodes in which panics did *not* occur, even though seasonal "liquidity risk" at New York City banks was unambiguously more acute than in periods preceding panics. Three additional episodes involved comparable or larger withdrawals than panic years, with only slightly higher reserve ratios (1900, 45; 1905, 42; 1909, 42). Measures of stringency just prior to the Panics of 1907 and 1893 were roughly at their median levels for the same weeks in other years.

Table 4.2 **Four-Week Percentage Change in Deposits and Reseve Ratios of New York City Banks Prior to Weeks when Panics Occurred**

	Panic of 1884, Week 19		Panic of 1893, Week 22		Panic of 1873, Week 37		Panic of 1907, Week 42		Panic of 1890, Week 45	
	%Δ	Reserve Ratio	%Δ	Reserve Ratio	%Δ	Reserve Ratio	%Δ	Reserve Ratio	%Δ	Reserve Ratio
1871	7.4	34.67	5.7	35.06	−0.2	29.98	−16.4	29.50	−0.4	32.39
1872	11.0	30.98	6.4	33.14	−12.5	29.01	−0.0	32.38	6.7	30.28
1873	7.9	30.67	5.6	30.65	**−13.3**	**27.54**	—	—	—	—
1874	−1.0	35.56	−0.9	37.39	−0.0	35.78	−2.9	32.84	−3.0	31.71
1875	4.1	29.89	5.1	32.13	−2.2	32.38	−4.9	27.49	−3.7	29.09
1876	1.2	29.60	2.6	32.79	3.5	34.85	−4.7	29.99	−4.3	29.09
1877	3.2	32.70	−1.6	33.88	−2.4	30.64	−5.7	28.84	−1.9	29.56
1878	−0.4	32.86	0.4	32.14	0.2	30.90	−4.4	27.30	−0.3	31.09
1879	13.2	32.14	5.1	26.83	−10.2	26.31	2.0	25.54	−0.3	24.71
1880	0.8	27.35	3.9	31.13	−0.1	26.91	1.2	26.57	2.2	25.56
1881	3.6	29.67	10.2	27.79	−5.7	25.14	−9.7	25.66	0.2	26.02
1882	3.0	27.72	−1.3	26.32	−6.6	24.66	−4.3	25.97	−1.2	23.98
1883	6.4	26.64	1.3	27.91	−1.8	26.17	−1.7	24.99	−2.2	26.56
1884	**−4.4**	**26.35**	—	—	—	—	—	—	—	—
1885	2.1	40.28	0.9	41.81	1.0	38.28	−0.6	35.36	−0.2	32.39
1886	−0.2	27.37	−2.1	28.77	−6.8	27.20	−1.5	26.31	0.2	26.60
1887	−0.2	26.10	−1.4	26.16	−1.3	26.11	4.2	27.62	0.3	27.69
1888	NA	NA	NA	NA	NA	NA	NA	NA	NA	NA
1889	1.6	27.10	0.5	28.29	−1.4	26.21	−3.8	25.22	−1.4	24.56
1890	−0.9	25.36	−0.2	26.21	−4.3	24.13	−3.4	24.91	−3.7	25.35
1891	−3.1	26.18	−5.2	26.94	−0.7	27.15	1.6	27.19	2.9	26.19
1892	0.7	27.78	0.1	29.59	−5.0	25.95	−5.1	25.11	−3.6	25.57
1893	−1.1	29.09	**−0.3**	**29.84**	—	—	—	—	—	—
1894	2.7	38.92	−1.1	38.62	0.3	35.21	1.1	35.51	0.2	35.41
1895	6.3	30.77	6.9	32.28	−1.0	29.66	−5.0	27.88	−1.0	28.64
1896	2.4	29.08	0.8	29.45	−4.9	26.96	1.7	27.62	−4.6	27.10
1897	0.8	32.73	−0.2	33.09	1.8	29.15	−3.2	27.37	2.5	28.34
1898	0.5	32.04	7.0	32.35	−7.4	25.61	6.0	28.13	6.4	26.92
1899	1.4	28.00	−1.1	29.78	−3.9	25.03	−3.9	25.17	−4.0	24.62
1900	3.8	26.76	2.1	27.26	1.4	27.29	−6.0	25.34	−3.7	25.55
1901	0.8	25.83	−2.2	27.22	−3.6	25.76	1.6	26.63	0.8	25.89
1902	0.3	25.35	−2.1	26.25	−5.7	25.07	−2.1	25.64	1.5	27.00
1903	3.5	26.08	0.8	26.06	1.6	26.66	−2.0	26.95	−3.4	25.61
1904	4.1	27.00	−1.4	27.69	1.2	28.14	−2.6	26.33	−0.8	25.84
1905	0.9	26.44	−0.7	25.53	−8.4	25.42	−5.8	26.22	0.2	24.75
1906	3.2	26.26	0.9	25.65	−4.8	25.34	3.7	25.57	−5.2	24.84
1907	2.1	25.75	0.7	26.13	−1.4	25.65	**−2.1**	**26.08**	—	—
1908	3.6	30.03	2.2	28.72	2.4	28.84	0.3	27.39	−0.4	27.33
1909	1.6	26.08	0.8	26.37	−3.8	25.58	−8.3	26.37	−2.6	25.59
Median	1.6	27.78	0.7	29.45	−1.8	26.96	−2.6	26.95	−0.8	26.92

Source: Andrew (1910, 79–117).

Table 4.3 **Times of Greater "Seasonal Withdrawal Stress" than During Panic Years (within-week comparison)**

Unambiguously Greater		Possibly Greater	
Year	Week	Year	Week
1881	42		
1882	22		
1882	42		
1886	22		
1887	22		
1889	42		
1891	22		
1892	42		
1899	22		
1899	42		
1899	45		
1900	42		
		1900	45
1901	22		
1902	22		
1902	42		
1904	22		
1905	22		
		1905	42
1906	45		
		1909	42

Source: Table 4.2

Clearly, seasonal withdrawals from, and reserve ratios of, New York City banks were not "sufficient statistics" for predicting panics. Tables 4.4 and 4.5 provide additional evidence that pre-panic periods were not episodes of unusually large seasonal flows of funds to the interior. Andrew (1910) reports weekly data on shipments of gold between New York City banks and the interior beginning in 1899. These data were used to construct measures of net cash flows from New York to the interior for the four- and eight-week periods prior to the Panic of 1907, and prior to comparable weeks in earlier years. According to these measures, 1900, 1901, and 1906 witnessed greater or comparable withdrawals for *both* time horizons relative to 1907. For the eight-week period, six out of eight years witnessed larger seasonal net outflows.

Andrew (1910) compiled monthly data on cash shipments to and from New York City by region of origin and destination beginning in 1905. Data for September (the month in which harvesting payments are most concentrated, as discussed below) are used to construct table 4.5. Again, 1906 shows a much larger outflow in September. Furthermore, since the Chari (1989) model emphasizes regional variation, it is interesting to note that both 1905 and 1906 show larger region-specific outflows than any in 1907. In September 1906,

Table 4.4 **Net Flows of Cash from New York City Banks to Interior, 1899–1907**

	For 4 Weeks Prior to October 21, or Comparable Dates[a]	For 8 Weeks Prior to October 21, or Comparable Dates[a]
1899	9,682	26,273
1900	25,190	34,836
1901	15,585	27,266
1902	6,973	16,050
1903	10,636	16,127
1904	9,968	22,962
1905	6,764	23,832
1906	21,649	37,076
1907	17,700	18,248

[a]Comparable dates are as follows: 20 October 1899; 19 October 1900; 18 October 1901; 24 October 1902; 23 October 1903; 21 October 1904; 20 October 1905; 19 October 1906; 18 October 1907.
Source: Andrew (1910, 172–77).

Table 4.5 **Net Shipments of Cash for Month of September 1905–1907, from New York City Clearing House Banks to Interior**

Region	1905	1906	1907
New England	2,640	3,453	3,846
Eastern states	3,130	6,616	809
Southern states	8,035	3,921	4,834
Middle West	1,965	7,886	6,611
Western states	−5	−2	89
Pacific states	−496	−107	−95
Aggregate			
Sum of balances	15,269	21,767	16,094
Mean of balances	2,545	3,628	2,682

Source: Andrew (1910, 232–39).

two regions received net transfers of cash in excess of the largest amount received by any region in September 1907, while in September 1905 one region did.

Advocates of random withdrawal risk might object to these findings on the grounds that it was *anticipated* future seasonal withdrawals, not past withdrawals, that caused banking panics. To this objection we have four responses. First, anticipations of cash needs in the West and South for planting and harvesting should be closely related to previous weeks' withdrawals, since not all farmers plant or harvest crops in the same week. Thus, years of unusual expected withdrawals (e.g., large harvest years) typically will be years of unusual withdrawals in the immediate past.

Second, information on the volume of crops harvested, which provides independent information on the expected payments required for harvesting, indicates that years in which panics occurred in the fall (1873, 1890, 1907) were not years of unusually large harvests for corn, wheat, and cotton. Table 4.6 reports data on the percentage differences between the annual volume of these three crops compared to five-year moving averages centered in that year, from 1871 to 1907. As can be seen, in 1873, 1890, and 1907, the harvests were not unusually large. In fact, in many cases they were unusually small.

Table 4.6 **Percentage Difference Between Annual Harvest of Corn, Wheat, and Cotton and Respective Five-Year Moving Averages Centered in that Year[a]**

	Corn (thousand bushels)	Wheat (thousand bushels)	Cotton (thousand bales)
1871	−0.5	−8.0	−19.3
1872	10.1	−4.2	2.0
1873	−9.7	3.3	6.7
1874	−22.4	8.5	−9.8
1875	15.3	−4.9	5.9
1876	3.7	−13.6	−1.8
1877	−2.5	0.3	−3.4
1878	−4.7	4.0	−4.9
1879	7.6	6.1	4.0
1880	15.0	−9.6	10.7
1881	−1.8	−15.1	−10.5
1882	2.7	8.6	14.2
1883	−4.2	−3.4	−6.0
1884	4.8	14.0	−7.7
1885	15.2	−19.0	4.2
1886	−5.8	3.9	−0.7
1887	−20.3	4.8	2.0
1888	14.1	−6.3	−5.3
1889	16.0	3.4	10.5
1890	−19.7	−18.1	11.5
1891	15.6	26.7	14.6
1892	1.6	8.2	−19.9
1893	−6.6	−19.2	−6.4
1894	−31.8	1.5	1.1
1895	17.3	2.4	−19.7
1896	17.0	−16.4	−9.3
1897	−8.0	0.0	16.9
1898	−6.6	25.0	10.6
1899	9.0	−9.4	−8.1
1900	3.6	−17.4	−0.1
1901	−27.3	19.7	−5.3
1902	16.2	7.0	0.6
1903	1.3	−3.2	−8.4
1904	−4.2	−16.1	1.6
1905	4.7	6.6	−0.8
1906	9.5	12.0	6.5
1907	−5.2	−8.5	−4.3

Source: Andrew (1910, 14).
[a]Calculated as a percentage of the value of the moving average.

Third, the timing of panics (with the possible exception of the Panic of 1873) places them *after* weeks of seasonal shocks associated with planting and harvesting, so that any money flows for these purposes would have occurred prior to the dates when panics began. Kemmerer's (1910) and Swift's (1911) analyses of seasonal patterns for interregional currency transfers and agricultural trade make clear that planting was associated with large retentions of funds in the interior in February through April, with large seasonal flows to New York beginning in May. Similarly, late August through early October marked the height of the fall currency transfer. Average seasonal deviations reported by Swift and Kemmerer are given in table 4.7. Data on seasonal variation in currency premia across cities within the United States point to the same seasonal pattern of currency scarcity as in New York, as shown in table 4.8.

Swift (1911) and Allen (1913a) emphasize the difference between the early autumn movement of currency to finance harvesting and the late autumn increase in loans (associated with *increased* deposits in the banking system) to finance the movement of the crops. Allen cites the description of this difference given by the New York Chamber of Commerce Currency Committee:

> These harvests and the marketing of the crops bring to bear upon the banks a two-fold strain, one for capital, the other for currency. The demand for

Table 4.7 Average Seasonal Currency Flows, 1899–1906[a]

	Average Net Inflow of Funds from Interior to New York City Banks (million $)	Deviation from Average Monthly Flow Over the Year (million $)
January	23.8	18.8
February	10.0	5.0
March	4.1	−0.9
April	7.7	2.7
May	9.5	4.5
June	12.3	7.3
July	13.4	8.4
August	3.8	−1.2
September	−15.6	−20.6
October	−13.1	−18.1
November	−0.3	−5.3
December	3.9	−1.1
Average over the year	5.0	0.0

Source: Kemmerer (1910, 358–59).

[a]Figures for weekly flows were compiled by the *Commercial and Financial Chronicle* and reported in Kemmerer (1910). Goodhart (1969) argues that these are the most reliable of available data. The data reported here do not include 1907 and 1908 (because of the panic, the last three months of 1907 witnessed unusual interbank outflows from New York, with correspondingly unusual inflows in early 1908). According to Kemmerer's (1910) definition of "months," some months contain five weeks, while others contain four. April, July, September, and December each contain five weeks.

Table 4.8 **Seasonal Variations in the Relative Demand for Money in Chicago, St. Louis, and New Orleans, as Evidenced by Exchange Rates in New York City (average figures, 1899–1908, per $100)**

Month and Week	Chicago Average Rate	St. Louis Average Rate	New Orleans Average Rate
January			
1	2.5¢p	7¢p	35.5¢d
2	5¢p	3¢d	15.5¢d
3	5¢p	7.8¢p	0.5¢d
4	10¢p	1.5¢p	8¢d
February			
5	2¢p	8¢d	19¢d
6	6¢d	13¢d	26.5¢d
7	9¢d	7¢d	24¢d
8	20¢d	4.5¢p	26¢d
March			
9	29.5¢d	5.5¢d	13¢d
10	23¢d	.05¢d	18.5¢d
11	13¢d	2¢p	15.5¢d
12	14.5¢d	3.5¢p	17¢d
April			
13	5¢d	2¢p	22.5¢d
14	14¢d	5¢d	18.5¢d
15	7.5¢d	8¢d	18¢d
16	4¢p	4¢p	20¢d
17	9¢d	1.5¢d	21.5¢d
May			
18	3.5¢d	4.5¢d	45¢d
19	2.5¢p	7.5¢p	46¢d
20	16¢p	20.5¢p	45¢d
21	16¢p	35¢p	37.5¢d
June			
22	10¢p	24¢p	20¢d
23	5¢p	7¢p	8.5¢d
24	4¢p	8¢p	12.5¢d
25	10.5¢p	12¢p	33¢d
July			
26	11.5¢p	2.5¢d	33¢d
27	16.5¢p	18¢d	56.5¢d
28	7.5¢d	21.5¢d	50.5¢d
29	8¢d	11¢d	42¢d
30	10.5¢d	9.8¢d	26¢d
August			
31	11¢d	24.5¢d	35¢d
32	17.5¢d	23.5¢d	28.5¢d
33	19¢d	31.5¢d	42¢d
34	34.5¢d	27¢d	42¢d

(continued)

Table 4.8 (continued)

Month and Week	Chicago Average Rate	St. Louis Average Rate	New Orleans Average Rate
September			
35	37.5¢d	32¢d	59.5¢d
36	36.5¢d	48¢d	65.5¢d
37	25¢d	40.5¢d	79.5¢d
38	26¢d	39¢d	82¢d
39	33¢d	55.5¢d	81¢d
October			
40	32¢d	54¢d	95.5¢d
41	29.5¢d	46.5¢d	85.5¢d
42	27.5¢d	45¢d	85.5¢d
43	31¢d	72.5¢d	82¢d
November			
44	29¢d	60.5¢d	$1.005d
45	20¢d	26.5¢d	$1.09d
46	4.5¢d	11.3¢p	$1.03d
47	13¢p	53.3¢p	91.5¢d
December			
48	2.5¢d	7.3¢p	81.5¢d
49	11.5¢d	2¢d	82.5¢d
50	5¢p	32¢p	74¢d
51	3.5¢p	11.8¢p	86.5¢d
52	3.5¢p	2¢d	66¢d

Source: Kemmerer (1910, 94–95).
Note: "p" = premium; "d" = discount.

> capital comes from the buyers and shippers of agricultural products and is in the main satisfied by an expansion of bank loans and deposits, most of the payments being made by checks and drafts. The demand for currency comes principally from the farmers and planters who must pay their help in cash. In the satisfaction of this demand the banks are unable to make use of their credit, but are obliged to take lawful money from their reserves and send it into the harvest fields. (Quoted in Allen 1913a, 128.)

The upshot of this analysis is that, whatever seasonal currency outflows were associated with planting and harvesting, these flows *preceded* the Panics of May 1884, June 1893, (late) October 1907, and November 1890. Thus, it would be difficult to argue that at these dates people were expecting large seasonal withdrawals of cash to agricultural areas.

Fourth, the observation that a reversal of seasonal flows of cash from New York typically would have been expected beginning in May and late October implies that "illiquidity risk" thresholds consistent with the withdrawal risk approach should have been lower in early spring and autumn. That is, given the expected reversal of fund flows in the summer and winter, a liquidity shock in late spring or fall should have prompted less of a concern than in early spring or fall. Table 4.2 provided evidence that contradicts that implication. The withdrawal shock associated with the onset of the Panic of 1893 (week 22) indicates a *lower* threshold to initiate a panic than for the shock associated with the Panic of 1884 (week 19). Similarly, the panics in 1907 (week 42) and 1890 (week 45) were associated with lower previous percentage withdrawals than the Panic of 1873 (week 37). This evidence leads one to wonder why there were not many more panics in weeks 19 and 37. That is, using a cross-week comparison criterion to predict panics, we predict fifteen additional panics that never occurred, which are listed in table 4.9. Thus, under the assumption that seasonal liquidity-shock thresholds should be smaller during weeks of higher risk of seasonal withdrawals from New York, the number of unrealized, predicted panics rises from 18 (or 21) to 33 (or 36). Furthermore, one could add to this list by considering unusual seasonal withdrawals prior to weeks other than (and before) weeks 19 and 37. One such case would be March 1881 (week 10), with withdrawals equal to 13.4 percent of deposits over the previous four weeks and a reserve ratio of 25.15. In summary, an emphasis on expected future withdrawal risk, rather than actual past withdrawals, strengthens the case against the random-withdrawal risk approach.

We turn now to investigate whether pre-panic periods were unusual in a manner consistent with the predictions of the asymmetric information theory of panics. The accounts of Sprague (1910), Calomiris and Schweikart (1991), and Gorton (1988) emphasize various specific real disturbances prior to panics, some originating in particular markets (e.g., the western land market in 1893), or high-risk railroad securities in several cases, as well as general business contractions. The single time-series most likely to be systematically associated with all of these shocks is the stock price index. Thus, it seems reasonable to require that pre-panic periods be characterized by unusually adverse movements in stock prices. The extent to which such disturbances threaten the banking system, however, will depend on (1) their severity; (2) the extent to which they signal adverse circumstances in other markets; and (3) the extent to which banks are exposed to risk.

As a starting point it is interesting to compare real economic news prior to the 18 (21) "unrealized panics" (using the within-week criterion) to news pre-

Table 4.9 **Times of Greater "Seasonal Withdrawal Stress" than During Panic Years (cross-week comparison)**

Year	Week	Year	Week	Year	Week
1881	37	1892	37	1901	37
1882	37	1893	19	1902	37
1890	19	1896	37	1905	37
1890	37	1898	37	1906	37
1891	19	1899	37	1909	37

Source: Table 4.2.

ceding the five actual panics. Table 4.10 reports the three-month percentage change in nominal and real (WPI-deflated) stock prices prior to all 26 episodes. This time horizon is long enough to allow continuing bad news to become fully reflected in stock prices, but not too long as to include gradual price declines. Whether one focuses on real or nominal stock price changes depends on the extent to which the wholesale price index follows a random walk (i.e., whether short-run changes in commodity prices are a good indicator of long-run expectations). Barsky (1987) shows that, roughly speaking,

Table 4.10 **Stock Price Declines Over Three Months Prior to Periods of "Seasonal Withdrawl Stress" (within-week criterion)**

Actual Panics	Predicted Unrealized Panics[a]	Nominal %Δ[b]	Real %Δ (WPI deflated)[c]
1873 (37)		**−7.9**	**−7.9**
	1881 (42)	−3.2	−10.1
	1882 (22)	−1.6	−3.5
	1882 (42)	0.8	−1.1
1884 (19)		**−12.6**	**−8.5**
	1886 (22)	−5.0	−0.2
	1887 (22)	6.3	6.3
	1889 (42)	2.3	1.0
1890 (45)		**−8.4**	**−13.3**
	1891 (22)	1.2	−0.4
	1892 (42)	0.6	−0.7
1893 (22)		**−12.2**	**−7.4**
	1899 (22)	−1.9	−3.9
	1899 (42 and 45)	0.8	−5.9
	1900 (42 and [45])	2.7	3.6
	1901 (22)	6.6	7.7
	1902 (22)	3.2	0.4
	1902 (42)	−1.0	−7.9 (−3.7)[c]
	1904 (22)	0.0	3.6
	1905 (22)	−3.3	−0.5
	[1905 (42)]	5.4	4.6
	1906 (45)	10.0	4.8
1907 (42)		**−18.6**	**−19.8**
	[1909 (42)]	2.8	−0.6

Source: U.S. Department of Commerce (1949), 344–45), and table 4.2.

[a]Episodes of "possibly greater" seasonal stress than preceding panics appear in brackets.

[b]Stock price changes are measured using monthly data as follows: for week 19 and week 22 we use February and May prices to calculate the percentage change; for week 37 we use June and September prices; and for week 42 and week 45 we use July and October prices. Evidence on daily stock price changes from the *Commercial and Financial Chronicle* indicates that most of the stock price declines measured in May 1884, September 1873, and October 1907 preceded the onset of panic. In the two remaining panics the monthly stock price changes reported here entirely predate the panics.

[c]The wholesale price index shows an unusually large upward movement in October 1902, which is reversed immediately thereafter. Real percentage change computed using November's price level is given in parentheses.

price movements can be characterized this way, although Calomiris (1988) shows that 1869–79 (and especially 1876–79) was an exceptional period of deflationary expectations in anticipation of the resumption of greenback convertibility. Thus, with the exception of the 1870s, deflated stock price movements are probably the best indicator of real change. At the same time, the existence of measurement error in the wholesale price index argues against identifying a large real stock price movement that does not coincide with nominal movements in stock prices.

The evidence presented in table 4.10 supports the view that large withdrawals only threatened the banking system when they were accompanied by (perhaps precipitated by) real disturbances. The five pre-panic episodes experienced the largest nominal declines in stock prices by far and were all associated with similarly large real declines in stock prices.

Thus far we have shown that adverse stock price movements preceded panics and that unusually large seasonal movements of cash or withdrawals from New York banks were neither necessary nor sufficient conditions for panics. We now ask whether adverse stock price movements by themselves provide sufficient conditions for predicting panics. Specifically, did all sufficiently large percentage declines in stock prices predict panics? Table 4.11 describes all periods of unusual three-month downturns in stock prices, that is, all nonoverlapping three-month intervals in which stock prices fell by more than 5 percent.[29]

Of the 23 intervals of greater than 5 percent nominal decline in stock prices, nine preceded or coincided with panics. Another of these intervals preceded the "quasi panic" of 1896. As table 4.11 shows, these ten pre- and post-panic intervals showed much larger nominal and real declines in stock prices than the remaining thirteen non-panic intervals. The average nominal and real percentage declines for the five pre-panic intervals were −11.9 and −11.4, respectively, while the averages for the thirteen non-panic intervals were 1.7 and 0.07 percent. There were only five non-panic intervals that showed real stock price declines as large as the *minimum* of ten pre- and post-panic intervals. In other words, assuming a threshold of 7.9 percent real decline in stock prices is sufficient to produce a banking panic, one can predict all actual panics (including 1896) and falsely identify only five non-panics as panics.

Of course, the asymmetric information view need not see stock price declines as a sufficient condition for producing panics. As already noted, it is the threat to banks that matters. Stock price declines will have more severe consequences for banks the more they are associated with widespread commercial defaults, and the more banks' portfolio positions expose themselves to loan-default risk.

In table 4.11, we also present data on seasonal differences in the liabilities of business failures for the periods of stock market price declines beginning in 1875. These are the percentage change in the liabilities of business failures for the given interval relative to the previous year's interval. This allows us to

Table 4.11 Three-Month Periods of Unusual Stock Price Decline, 1871–1909

	Nominal %Δ	Real %Δ	Seasonal Difference (%Δ) in Liabilities of Commercial Failures[a]
1873 (June–September)	−7.9	−7.9	NA
1874 (February–May)	−6.3	−4.0	NA
1876 (February–May)	−7.9	−3.3	30.0
1877 (January–April)	−17.2	−12.9	−8.1[b]
1880 (February–May)	−8.3	−2.6	−11.5
1882 (August–November)	−5.6	−1.1	26.6[c]
1883 (May–August)	−5.4	−0.5	115.8[d]
1884 (February–May)	−12.6	−8.5	202.9
1884 (August–November)	−8.8	−4.5	−6.3[c]
1886 (February–May)	−5.0	−0.2	−27.3
1887 (May–August)	−7.7	−6.5	168.4[d]
1890 (July–October)	−8.4	−13.3	50.3[c]
1893 (February–May)	−12.2	−7.4	428.3
1893 (May–August)	−15.4	−6.6	389.2[d]
1895 (September–December)	−10.2	−8.8	25.2
1896 (May–August)	−13.1	−11.1	71.2
1900 (April–July)	−7.4	−5.0	148.0
1902 (September–December)	−8.8	−13.6	−3.8
1903 (February–May)	−9.5	−4.7	23.3
1903 (May–August)	−12.9	−12.6	22.7
1907 (January–April)	−12.3	−13.1	−7.7
1907 (May–August)	−7.1	−7.9	110.0
1907 (August–November)	−17.0	−14.7	143.5

Source: U.S. Department of Commerce (1949, 344–45, 349).
[a]Data on seasonal differences in liabilities of business failures are for four-month period ending the month after the corresponding stock decline, unless otherwise noted.Quarterly data exist for 1875–94; monthly data exist after 1894.
[b]Uses average of first- and second-quarter data.
[c]Uses average of third- and fourth-quarter data.
[d]Uses average of second- and third-quarter data.

abstract from the pronounced seasonality in the series owing to the seasonality in the settlement of debts (see Kemmerer 1910, 219; and Swift 1911).[30] Not surprisingly, the intervals of the sharpest stock price declines also tend to be the intervals of greatest increase in the seasonal difference of the liabilities of commercial failures.

If one asks which periods (for which data are available, i.e., 1875 and after) of the most extreme adverse economic news (real stock price declines in excess of 7.4 percent) are also periods of unusually large business failure (seasonal differences of greater than 50 percent), one is left with only the actual panic episodes and the quasi panic of 1896. In other words, if one posits that the simultaneous violations of thresholds for percentages of real stock price decline and commercial failure increase are sufficient conditions for panic, one can predict panics perfectly. Indeed, one would even be able to predict that the stock price decline of 1896 would not be as severe a threat to banks as the other episodes, since business failures increased by a somewhat smaller percentage.

An analysis of national bank portfolio risk exposure is also consistent with the predictions of the asymmetric information approach and helps explain why panics tended to occur when they did (near business-cycle peaks, in the fall and spring). According to the asymmetric information view, panics are most likely when bad news immediately follows a period of high loan demand and sanguine expectations. These will be periods when the leverage of banks and their borrowers is highest. This explains why in panic periods, adverse news was translated into unusually large declines in securities' prices and high borrower-default rates.

Because the dates of call reports for national banks vary greatly across years, the potential for meaningful specific inter-year comparisons of bank balance sheet positions is limited. Nevertheless, two broad patterns are unmistakable. First, the risk exposure of banks is highest in spring and fall, and lowest in winter and summer. Second, years of cyclical peaks are associated with unusually high risk exposure. These patterns are demonstrated in table 4.12.

Bank leverage was highest at cyclical peaks (including panic years). Reading down any column in panel A of table 4.12, one compares average loan-to-reserve ratios at different cyclical points, holding the time of year constant. In every case, the ratio is higher at peaks than at troughs and, in most cases, peaks show the highest loan-to-reserve ratios. Clearly, the longer an economic downturn is maintained (as one approaches troughs), the lower is the ratio of loans to reserves. Table 4.12 also provides data on loan-to-reserve ratios at different times of the year and at different points in the business cycle.

Reading across panel A, one can see how seasonality influenced bank loan risk exposure. Typically, March, October, and November calls saw seasonal peaks in the ratio, with declines from March to June, and from November to December. Panics occurred at times of the year when banks were unusually vulnerable to loan-default risk.[31] While *withdrawal* risk was low during pre-panic periods, loans (and hence, loan-default risk) were high in late autumn, when most panics occurred (see Allen 1913a; Swift 1911; and Kemmerer 1910). It is interesting to note in table 4.11, however, that periods of severe bad news in risky-asset pricing are typically confined to these same seasons. Notice how few of the precipitous declines in stock prices occur from November to February, or from April to July. Intervals ending in April or May account for nine incidents of severe decline, and declines for intervals ending in August through November account for eleven more. This leaves three episodes which occurred in other times of the year, namely, two intervals ending in December (1895 and 1902), and one in July (1900). No intervals of decline ended in January, February, March, and June. More formally, using a chi-squared test we were able to reject the null hypothesis that the probability of a

Table 4.12 **Cyclical and Seasonal Influences on the Ratio of National Bank Loans to Reserves, 1870–1909**

A. Mean Loan-to-Reserve Ratios

	March 10[c]	May 17[d]	June 11[e]	October 3[f]	November 12[g]	December 13[h]
Trough and early recovery[a]	4.62	5.19	4.77	5.74	5.96	5.30
Recovery and expansion	NA	5.87	5.93	6.40	6.65	6.24
Peaks and early decline[b]	6.72	6.45	6.06	6.84	6.68	6.05
Decline	6.89	NA	NA	6.64	NA	6.54

B. Data for Specific Calls

Date	Business-Cycle Reference	Loan-to-Reserve Ratios
March 10 Calls[c]		
Comparable March calls		
10 March 1876	Decline	6.96
11 March 1881	Peak	6.57
11 March 1882	Early decline	6.72
13 March 1883	Decline	7.47
7 March 1884	Decline	6.23
10 March 1885	Trough	4.72
6 March 1893	Peak	6.88
9 March 1897	Trough	4.52
May 17 Calls[d]		
Comparable May calls		
19 May 1882	Early decline	6.30
13 May 1887	Peak	6.12
13 May 1889	Recovery	5.87
17 May 1890	Peak	6.94
17 May 1892	Early recovery	5.65
14 May 1897	Trough	4.72
June 11 Calls[e]		
Comparable June calls		
9 June 1870	Trough	4.25
10 June 1871	Early recovery	4.57
10 June 1872	Expansion	5.47
13 June 1873	Peak	5.89
14 June 1879	Recovery	6.21
11 June 1880	Expansion	5.64
9 June 1903	Peak	6.23
9 June 1904	Trough	5.50
October 3 Calls[f]		
Comparable October calls		
2 October 1871	Recovery	5.63
3 October 1872	Expansion	6.79
2 October 1874	Decline	5.81
1 October 1875	Decline	7.39
2 October 1876	Decline	6.91
1 October 1877	Decline	7.25
1 October 1878	Trough	6.53

Table 4.12 (continued)

Date	B. Data for Specific Calls	
	Business-Cycle Reference	Loan-to-Reserve Ratios
2 October 1879	Early recovery	6.36
1 October 1880	Recovery	6.00
1 October 1881	Peak	6.74
3 October 1882	Early decline	7.11
2 October 1883	Decline	6.95
1 October 1885	Trough	4.96
5 October 1887	Early decline	6.48
4 October 1888	Early recovery	6.28
30 September 1889	Expansion	6.88
2 October 1890	Early decline	7.03
30 September 1892	Recovery	6.63
2 October 1894	Early recovery	4.98
6 October 1896	Decline	5.52
5 October 1897	Early recovery	5.31
30 September 1901	Recovery	6.49
November 12 Calls[g]		
Comparable November calls		
17 November 1903	Early decline	6.68
10 November 1904	Early recovery	5.96
9 November 1905	Expansion	6.54
12 November 1906	Expansion	6.97
16 November 1909	Expansion	6.45
December 13 Calls[h]		
Comparable December calls		
16 December 1871	Recovery	5.65
17 December 1875	Decline	8.10
12 December 1879	Expansion	6.46
12 December 1888	Recovery	6.34
11 December 1889	Expansion	6.85
13 December 1895	Peak	6.05
17 December 1896	Decline	4.98
15 December 1897	Early recovery	5.12
13 December 1900	Early recovery	5.48
10 December 1901	Recovery	5.92
Other Dates of interest		
12 September 1873	Early decline	5.89
24 April 1884	Peak	6.52
4 May 1893	Peak	6.70
25 November 1902	Expansion	6.28

Sources: Andrew (1910, 63–66); and Burns and Mitchell (1946, 111–12), based on Frickey (1942, 328).

[a]Business cycles are defined relative to the Frickey (1942) index, reported in Burns and Mitchell (1946). "Early" recovery refers to a date no more than six months after the trough.

[b]"Early" decline refers to a date no more than six months after the peak.

[c]"March 10 calls" include all call reports from March 6 to March 13.

[d]"May 17 calls" include all call reports from May 13 to May 19.

[e]"June 11 calls" include all call reports from June 9 to June 14.

[f]"October 3 calls" include all call reports from September 30 to October 6, except for the unusual post-panic year 1893.

[g]"November 12 calls" include all call reports from November 9 to November 17.

[h]"December 13 calls" include all call reports from December 10 to December 17.

severe decline in the stock market was randomly distributed over the year at the 0.004 significance level. More contemporary patterns are also consistent with these findings. The stock market crashes of 1929, 1987, and 1989 all occurred in mid to late October.

Thus, it is not possible to argue that bank or borrower leverage transformed normal disturbances into panics. From a cyclical perspective, bad news and high leverage are both associated with cyclical peaks. Furthermore, fundamental seasonal patterns in the economy seem to concentrate adverse news in the spring and fall, at times when leverage is also high. What can explain these patterns? It is not difficult to explain why cyclical peaks are times of bad news (ex post), otherwise they would not have been cyclical peaks, and the high leverage of banks in these times is explicable by reference to previous rosy circumstances (given the evidence that economic activity during this period was strongly autoregressive; see Calomiris and Hubbard 1989a, 442–43). The simplest explanation for the seasonal pattern is that seasons of greatest economic activity will witness both higher borrowing and more news.[32]

Of course, very bad news and high leverage were not always coincident, and these episodes reinforce the notion that both bad news and risk exposure are necessary to produce a panic. The (nominal and real) stock price declines of December 1895 and December 1902 were larger than the average declines that preceded panics, but these did not produce panics, occurred "off season" at times when bank and borrower leverage was low (see table 4.12), and were associated with less-pronounced business failure increases.

Before moving on to the next section, it may be useful to make a methodological point regarding what we have *not* done in this section. We did not use linear regression analysis, with adjustments for seasonal factors, to test models. Given the oscillation between panic and non-panic episodes, it would be difficult to argue that bank balance sheet variables are a stationary process. Thus, direct comparison across plausibly comparable episodes seemed to us a better way to proceed. Moreover, as we have stressed, the implications of the two approaches are best stated in terms of responses to violations of thresholds and nonlinear combinations of such violations (news and leverage). More formal technical analysis of these nonlinearities would be possible, but given the conclusiveness of the simple approach, we found this was not necessary.

The results of this subsection suggest that seasonal money-demand shocks originating in the countryside cannot possibly be the cause of panics. Rather, the results are consistent with the view that "bad" macroeconomic news combined with the vulnerability of banks to shocks, a vulnerability which is associated with banking activities in a natural way, accounts for panics. These results confirm the time-series econometric work of Gorton (1988) which shows that panics are associated with a threshold level of news receipt concerning the growth in liabilities of failed businesses, which is a leading indicator of recession (see also Calomiris and Hubbard 1989a). Gorton (1988) argued that panics in the United States occurred every time measures of the liabilities of failed businesses reached a critical threshold, and did not occur otherwise.

4.5.2 Bank Liquidations and Deposit Losses During Panics

We now analyze the data on bank failures during panics to compare the predictions of the asymmetric information and random-withdrawal risk views. Both predict that cooperation among banks (branching or coinsurance) reduces the incidence of bank failure during panics. As noted above, there is abundant evidence to support this view. But the two theories differ in many of their implications regarding which banks are mostly likely to fail, as well as the extent and regional distribution of bank failures in different panics.

The withdrawal risk approach sees the greatest threat to banks as coming from regionally concentrated shocks transmitted through the correspondent network. Regionally concentrated shocks should be especially problematic for banks in the region of the shock, especially those in regional reserve centers and their correspondents in other regions. Episodes of greatest money-demand shocks or vulnerability to money-demand shocks should correspond to those with the highest incidence of bank failure. Finally, bank failures during panics are mainly attributable to the exogenous money-demand disturbance, rather than to the investment decisions of bankers.

The asymmetric information approach has strong testable implications for bank failure, since it identifies asset shocks as the source of panics and sees panics as an attempt by the banking system as a whole to resolve asymmetric information by closing insolvent banks, that is, those which have suffered the greatest declines. Thus, there should be a direct link between ultimate bank failures and the asset shock that triggers the panic. Regions with relatively large asset shocks (such as region-specific agricultural commodity and land price declines) should show higher incidences of failure. Also, within regions, banks with the greatest exposure to the asset shocks that induce the panic should be more likely to fail (some shocks are more likely to affect city banks than country banks because of their different loan portfolios). Across panics, the aggregate failure rate should depend on the severity of the disturbance *as well as the concentration* (more regionally concentrated shocks induce higher average failure rates). Finally, individual banker behavior in undertaking risky investments could be an important determinant of within-region variation in failures.

Table 4.13 presents state and regional data on the number of national banks and national bank failures for intervals surrounding panics, including the quasi panic of 1896. Table 4.14 provides data on individual bank failures during panics and their causes, according to the brief summary of each case provided by the Comptroller of the Currency in his *Annual Report* of 1920.

With respect to the stated causes of bank failures, the data in table 4.14 are

Table 4.13 **The Number of National Banks and National Bank Failures During Panics, by State and Region, 1873–1907**[a]

	1873		1884		1890		1893		1896		1907	
Region and State	Banks	Failures	Banks	Failures	Banks	Failures	Banks	Failures	Banks	Failures	Banks	Failures
New England												
ME	63	0	72	0	78	0	83	0	82	0	79	0
NH	42	0	49	0	51	0	53	2	50	0	57	0
VT	42	0	47	1	51	0	48	0	49	0	50	0
RI	62	0	63	0	59	0	59	0	57	0	23	0
MA	217	0	246	0	260	0	268	0	268	0	203	0
CT	80	0	88	0	84	0	84	0	82	0	80	0
	506	0	565	1	583	0	595	2	586	0	482	0
East												
NY	277	1*	314	2*	319	0	336	2*	330	3	401	0
NJ	62	0	69	0	94	0	99	0	102	0	168	0
PA	202	1	270	0	349	0	399	0	419	0	722	1
DE	11	0	15	0	18	0	18	0	18	0	24	0
MD	33	0	41	0	59	0	68	0	68	0	97	0
DC	5	1	6	0	12	0	13	0	14	0	12	0
	590	3	715	2	851	0	933	2	951	3	1,424	1

South												
VA	24	2	23	0	32	0	36	0	37	0	96	0
WV	17	0	19	0	21	0	30	0	33	0	38	0
NC	10	0	15	0	21	1	24	0	28	0	57	0
SC	12	0	13	0	16	0	14	0	15	0	25	0
GA	13	0	13	0	30	0	30	3	30	0	36	0
FL	0	0	2	0	15	0	18	1	17	0	35	0
AL	9	0	9	0	30	0	30	1	27	0	73	0
MS	0	0	3	0	12	0	13	1	10	0	26	0
LA	9	1*	8	0	19	0	20	0	21	1*	36	0
TX	8	0	44	0	189	0	226	4	209	3	510	1
AR	2	0	5	1	9	0	9	0	9	0	35	0
KY	36	0	64	0	76	0	81	1	77	2	139	0
TN	24	0	30	0	51	0	55	4	48	0	77	0
	164	3	248	1	521	1	586	15	561	6	1,233	1
Middle West												
OH	169	1	200	0	233	0	244	1	249	1	358	2
IN	93	1	97	2	100	0	120	2	113	0	219	1
IL	137	0	161	1	192	0	216	3**	220	2*	339	0
MI	77	0	87	0	110	0	102	2	92	4	91	0
WI	45	0	45	0	68	0	82	0	81	0	125	0
MN	32	0	43	0	60	0	77	0	76	2*	245	0
IA	75	0	108	0	139	0	170	1	168	2	301	1
MO	36	0	34	0	79	0	79	0	68	1*	113	0
	664	2	775	3	981	0	1,090	9	1,067	12	1,841	4

(continued)

Table 4.13 (continued)

Region and State	1873 Banks	1873 Failures	1884 Banks	1884 Failures	1890 Banks	1890 Failures	1893 Banks	1893 Failures	1896 Banks	1896 Failures	1907 Banks	1907 Failures
West												
ND	1	0	30	0	29	0	35	3	29	4	121	0
SD		0		0	39	0	39	2	31	1	83	0
NE	10	0	41	0	135	1	137	2	114	1	193	0
KS	26	1	35	0	159	7	138	1	105	2	199	0
MT	5	0	10	1	25	0	28	3	26	1	37	0
WY	2	0	4	0	11	0	13	1	11	0	29	0
CO	7	0	22	0	46	0	53	1	42	0	97	0
NM	0	0	6	0	9	0	11	1	7	1	36	0
OK	0	0	0	0	5	0	6	0	13	0	294	0
	51	1	148	1	458	8	460	14	378	10	1,089	0

Pacific												
WA	0	0	12	0	51	1	66	5	41	2	41	0
OR	1	0	6	0	37	0	40	1	33	0	53	0
CA	5	0	13	0	37	0	37	1	31	1	126	0
ID	1	0	3	0	7	0	13	0	11	0	34	0
UT	3	0	4	0	10	0	14	0	11	0	18	0
NV	0	0	1	0	2	0	2	0	1	0	7	0
AZ	0	0	1	0	2	0	5	0	5	0	14	0
	10	0	40	0	146	1	177	7	133	3	293	0
Total	1,985	9	2,491	8	3,540	10	3,841	49	3,676	34	6,412	6
Reserve center banks		2		1		0		3		4		0

Sources: U.S. Comptroller of the Currency, *Annual Report* (1873, 1884, 1890, 1893, 1920).
Notes: "Banks" means the number of banks in existence prior to panics. "Failures" means bank failures at or near the time of panic (only liquidated banks are included). Specifically, we include bank failures that occurred within the following intervals: June–December 1873; March–August 1884; August 1890–February 1891; April–October 1893; July 1896–January 1897; August 1907–February 1908.
*Denotes a reserve-center bank failure.
**Denotes two reserve-center bank failures.

Table 4.14 The Causes of National Bank Failures During Panics[a]

	1873	1884	1890	1893	1896	1907
Total number of failures	9	6	10	49	34	6
Number attributed to asset depreciation alone	4	2	5	31	26	3
Number attributed to fraud alone	0	2	0	7	3	2
Number attributed to both asset depreciation and fraud	5	4	5	11	5	0
Asset depreciation attributed to monetary stringency	0	0	0	17	8	0
Asset depreciation only; attributed to real estate	0	1	2	0	4	0
Bank failure attributed to real estate depreciation and fraud	0	1	2	0	1	0
Bank failure attributed to run on bank	0	0	0	0	0	1

Source: U.S. Comptroller of the Currency, *Annual Report* (1920, 56–73).
[a]Relevant intervals for bank failures are defined in table 4.13.

strongly supportive of the asymmetric information view and provide virtually no evidence that money-demand shocks provided necessary or sufficient conditions for banks to fail. Of the 116 bank failures that occurred during intervals surrounding panics, 101 were attributed to asset depreciation, with eleven of these cases mainly involving real estate–related investments (all from 1884 to 1896). Thirty of these 101 failures involved fraudulent activities. An additional fourteen failures were attributed solely to fraud. The single remaining failure was attributed to a bank run (in 1907). These data clearly indicate that bank failures during panics often involved shady activities by bankers (44 out of 116 cases), which typically made banks' assets especially vulnerable to bad news (hence the association between asset depreciation and fraud in most of the fraud cases). The fact that bank failure is linked to asset depreciation does not itself contradict the withdrawal risk approach, since advocates of this view argue that panics themselves caused asset depreciation of banks. In 25 cases, asset depreciation was deemed the result of high market interest rates during the panics. Nevertheless, in the overwhelming majority of cases (91 of the 116), failure was not attributed to panic-induced stringency in the money market. Furthermore, the fact that the Comptroller only attributed one failure to a bank run per se shows that the *direct* link between bank runs and bank failures during panics was not important.

The withdrawal risk and asymmetric information views also differ in their implications regarding the relative severity of bank failure rates during the various panics. According to the withdrawal risk approach, inadequacy of reserves to meet withdrawal needs is the key factor in causing suspensions and failures alike. Thus, the degree to which panics were associated with illiquidity in the banking system should be reflected in bank failure rates as well. In other words, the three widespread suspensions of convertibility (1873, 1893, and 1907) should be associated with the largest failure rates, followed by the Panics of 1884 and 1890 in which there was bank coordination without widespread suspension, with the quasi panic of 1896 showing the least-severe failure experience of all. Moreover, within the group of suspensions, 1893 should have been milder than 1873 or 1907, since it followed especially small spring seasonal money flows and occurred in the middle of the year (rather than in the fall), when anticipated interregional flows favored New York City and reserve ratios of the system as a whole rose (as shown in table 4.12). Thus, one should find that the failure rates are ranked in four groups roughly as follows: 1873 and 1907; 1893; 1884 and 1890; and 1896.

The predictions of the asymmetric information approach regarding the relative severity of bank failures during these panics could be quite different. The asymmetric information approach does not equate systemic illiquidity risk of banks with failure risk. It can envision cases in which the aggregate illiquidity of the banking system is severe but the ex post failures are relativity few. It can also envision cases where large *observable* shocks to a subset of banks could cause many failures without leading to a suspension of convertibility for the banking system as a whole. In particular, panics that are associated with large region-specific asset shocks may produce larger failure rates in one region, while posing a relatively small problem for systemic convertibility of deposits on demand. In the asymmetric information approach, nationwide commercial-failure rate and production data, as well as other *region-specific* proxies for real shocks preceding panics, would be useful guides for ranking the likely consequences for bank failures.

For aggregate data we consider the new Miron and Romer (1989) monthly production index (augmented by Frickey [1942, 1947] for the period prior to 1884) and liabilities of commercial failures. A consistent monthly series of commercial failures at the national level is not available for the entire period from 1873 to 1907. Limited comparisons that are possible using quarterly and monthly data for 1875 to 1907, however, provide a rough ranking of commercial failure severity, again using seasonal difference as our measure. Table 4.15 reports data for the liabilities of commercial failures and industrial production growth for the bank failure intervals used to construct table 4.13.

Interestingly, if one confines oneself to these two aggregate measures, the predicted ranking of bank failure severity for panics is very close to that of the withdrawal risk view above. The ranking would be: 1893, 1907, 1873, 1884, 1890, 1896. If the positions of 1893 and 1873 are switched, the ranking becomes the same as that implied by the random withdrawal approach.

The actual ranking of bank failure rate and depositor loss rate severity for national banks as a whole is different from the predicted ranking of the withdrawal risk view and the predicted ranking from economywide measures of real shocks. The ranking, with the percentage of national banks failing given

Table 4.15 Liabilities of Commercial Failures and Industrial Production During Panic Intervals

	Liabilities	Industrial Production (%Δ)
June–December 1873	NA	−6.9 (−12.9)[a]
April–September 1884[b]	140.8	−4.0
April–September 1883	77.9	
seasonal difference	80.7%	
October 1890–March 1891[b]	131.3	−2.9
October 1889–March 1890	80.6	
seasonal difference	62.9%	
April–September 1893[b]	204.0	−26.6
April–September 1892	41.7	
seasonal difference	389.2%	
July 1896–January 1897	146.7	2.0
July 1895–January 1896	106.2	
seasonal difference	38.1%	
August 1907–February 1908	169.6	−28.5
August 1906–February 1907	73.6	
seasonal difference	130.4%	

Sources: U.S. Department of Commerce (1949, 349), Miron and Romer (1989); Frickey (1947, 120; 1942, 328).

[a]Miron and Romer (1989) begin their index in 1884. Frickey's (1947) monthly index of production for transportation and communication is reported instead, as well as Frickey's (1942) quarterly index of economic activity (in parentheses).

[b]Intervals were dictated by the use of quarterly data for commercial failures prior to 1894 and differ slightly from bank-failure intervals reported in table 4.13.

in parentheses, is: 1893 (1.28 percent), 1896 (0.92 percent), 1873 (0.45 percent), 1884 (0.32 percent), 1890 (0.28 percent), and 1907 (0.09 percent). The relative positions of 1893 and 1873 in this ranking correspond to the predictions of the asymmetric information approach, but in other respects this ranking differs drastically from either of the two "predicted" rankings.

First, the Panic of 1907 is practically a non-event from the standpoint of national bank failures. Indeed, it was a time of unusually *low* bank failures during the National Banking Era. For the entire period of 1865 to 1909, there were 0.94 bank failures per month on average. There were only six failures during the seven-month interval we examined for the Panic of 1907, implying a rate of 0.86 failures per month. Considering the more than tripling of the number of banks over this period, this amounts to a substantially lower failure rate (per bank, per month) than the average rate for the entire period.

Second, the quasi panic of 1896 was a time of substantially above-average bank failure, even though it did not result in suspension. According to the asymmetric information approach, this would imply that the shocks of 1896 were not accompanied by a great deal of confusion regarding their incidence.

To summarize, the data on actual bank failures support the asymmetric information approach more than the random withdrawal approach, but they also pose a challenge, namely, to explain the lack of bank failures during the severe contraction of 1907 and the unusually large incidence of failure during the relatively mild business-cycle downswing of 1896.

With respect to the low national bank failure rate during the Panic of 1907, a recent paper on the panic by Moen and Tallman (1990) points out that national banks and state banks fared much better than trusts in New York City during the panic:

> Depositor runs on trust companies in 1907 occurred without similar runs on New York City national banks. . . . The balance sheets of trust companies in New York City suggest that their asset values were subject to greater volatility than the other intermediaries. . . . In addition, it is notable that the initial runs on intermediaries in 1907 occurred at the trust companies, institutions that were not eligible to hold legal reserve funds for interior banks. Thus, the onset of the Panic does not appear to be a result of the institutional structure of reserves held at national banks, often referred to as the "pyramid" of reserves.

Moen and Tallman show that trusts had much greater proportions of investments in securities and in call loans, which were collateralized by securities. This made them more vulnerable to the stock market decline that preceded the panic. They also find that practically all of the contraction in New York City loans during the panic is attributable to the trust companies. On the basis of this evidence, Moen and Tallman argue that the Panic of 1907 is best understood as a consequence of adverse news about the value of a subset of assets in the economy.

One does not need to search too hard to find reasons for the unusually high failure rates during 1896. Table 4.13 shows that failures were concentrated in a few states, while many other states avoided failures altogether during the panic. This was also true in 1890 and 1893. In 1890, eight out of ten failures occurred in Kansas and Nebraska, producing a combined failure rate in these states of 4.1 percent. In 1893 the outliers were the western states, with a 3.0 percent overall failure rate, and a combined failure rate for Montana and the Dakotas of 7.3 percent. Washington had a failure rate of 7.6 percent. The southern states (especially Texas, Tennessee, and Georgia) failed at a rate of 2.6 percent. In the Middle West during the Panic of 1893, the states of Illinois, Indiana, and Michigan experienced a combined failure rate of 1.6 percent.

In 1896 the pattern is quite similar. Western states' national banks failed at the rate of 2.6 percent, with a failure rate in the Dakotas of 13.8 percent. Texas and Kentucky, in the South, suffered a combined failure rate of 1.7 percent, while 4.9 percent of Washington's national banks failed. In Michigan, Iowa, and Illinois the combined failure rate was 1.7 percent. Explaining unusually high failure experiences of national banks during panics, therefore, reduces to explaining why scattered states in the Middle West, West, Pacific, and South regions experienced high failure rates during the 1890s.

The regional pattern of failures seems incompatible with the withdrawal risk view of panics. States with high failure rates in any one panic were often quite distant, differed in planting and harvesting times, and were oriented toward different financial centers. Thus, it would be unlikely for them to experience simultaneous liquidity shocks. For example, Washington, Kentucky, Texas, Michigan, and the Dakotas (in 1896) are unrelated in terms of correspondent relations, harvest and planting timing, and geographical proximity. Georgia, Texas, Tennessee, the Dakotas, and Montana are similarly unrelated (in 1893).

What does explain the regional patterns of bank failure, and why is it that high regional bank failures in 1890 and 1896 were not associated with systemic illiquidity? The answer seems to be that the 1890s were a time of unusually adverse shocks concentrated in agricultural product and land markets. These shocks were known to be isolated to particular markets and had especially adverse consequences for borrowers and bankers whose portfolio values varied with the value of investments in newly cleared land.

Allan Bogue's (1955) classic study of the speculative land boom and bust of 1873–96 documents the changing fortunes of mortgage brokers who acted as intermediaries between western landowners and mortgage investors throughout the country. During the boom of the 1870s and early 1880s, agricultural prices and land prices rose, and many mortgages were bought by banks in other regions. A series of ever-worsening economic news for agriculture created waves of foreclosures, bankruptcy, and bank failure. Bogue writes:

> Between 1888 and 1894 most of the mortgage companies failed. The causes of failure were closely interrelated. The officers of the mortgage agencies had misunderstood the climatic vagaries of the plains country. They had competed vigorously to finance the settlement of areas beyond the ninety-eighth meridian (e.g., western Kansas and Nebraska). Beginning in 1887 the plains country was struck by a series of disastrously dry years. The effects of drought and short crops are sometimes alleviated by high prices, but in these years the prices of agricultural products were depressed. Many of the settlers along the middle border failed to meet their obligations. The real estate holdings of the companies grew to unmanageable size; operating capital was converted into land at a time when the bottom had dropped out of the land market. (267)

Panics in the 1890s were associated with large declines in productivity and the terms of trade for agriculture. In each of the years prior to the panics of 1890 and 1893, the terms of trade in agriculture, as measured by the ratio of the price of wheat to the wholesale price index, declined by approximately 30 percent.

The hypothesis that the unusual failure experience of certain states in the

1890s can be explained by the collapse of the high-risk mortgage market in certain agricultural areas has testable implications. First, the Comptroller of the Currency identifies cases of national bank failure that are primarily attributable to real estate depreciation. As table 4.14 shows, almost all real-estate-related failures of national banks that accompanied panics occurred during the Panics of 1890 and 1896.

Of course, national banks faced restrictions on mortgage lending which limited their direct exposure to land price declines. State banks, however, tended to permit greater involvement in mortgage lending. Hence, another testable implication of the land-value-shock explanation of bank failures during the 1890s is that state banks in Kansas and Nebraska should have had *unusually high* rates of bank failure compared to their counterparts in the national banking system in those same states. In other panics, rates of failure in those states should have been lower and more similar between national and state banks.

As a first step toward testing this proposition, we collected data on state bank failures during panic intervals for the Panics of 1893 and 1907 from state banking reports available at the Library of Congress. These data are provided in table 4.16. We find that state bank failure rates were high relative to national bank failure rates in Kansas and Nebraska in 1893. This same pattern is not visible in other states in 1893. Furthermore, in 1907, Kansas and Nebraska state banks had failure records similar to western national banks.

These data provide some support for the notion that region-specific asset shocks in western lands were important in explaining the peculiar regional patterns of bank failures in the 1890s. They also provide evidence supporting the general importance of asset risk in explaining the incidence of bank fail-

Table 4.16 **State and National Bank Failure Rates from Available States During Panic Intervals in 1893 and 1907[a]**

	State Bank Failure Rate[b] (%)		National Bank Failure Rate (%)	
	1893	1907	1893	1907
Massachusetts	0	0	0	0
New Jersey	0[c]	0	0	0
New York	0.7	0.9	0.6	0
Kansas	8.1	0.1	0.7	0
Nebraska	2.0	0.3	1.5	0
Michigan	0.7	0	2.0	0

Sources: U.S. Comptroller of the Currency, *Annual Report* (1920); the reports of banking authorities of various states; Board of Governors of the Federal Reserve System (1959, passim).

[a]Panic intervals are April–October 1893 and August 1907–February 1908.

[b]For 1893 the number of state banks is assumed to be roughly equal to the number in existence in 1896 for which data are available.

[c]One bank failed, but it was able to pay its depositors in full.

ure, which is essential to the asymmetric information approach. In future research we plan to extend our sample to include other states and episodes.

4.5.3 Sufficient Conditions for Ending Panics

The mechanisms for resolving banking panics, by bringing suspension of convertibility to an end, provide a way of discriminating between the two hypotheses concerning the origins of banking panics. In this section we first ask whether physical inflows of gold or the availability of cash per se were sufficient to bring an end to suspensions of convertibility. Cash availability includes the possibility of borrowing from the discount window during the Great Depression. Then we ask whether coinsurance in the absence of aggregate increases in gold is sufficient to end banking panics. Here we consider some cooperative arrangements of banks to mitigate the effects of panics. We also examine the experiences of branches of Canadian banks in the United States during panics.

If suspension of convertibility is made necessary by a scarcity of cash in the banking system, then shipments of gold should be able to resolve the problem. The asymmetric information view also predicts that shipments of gold will occur during panics, in part as a means for banks to signal their creditworthiness to depositors. But according to the asymmetric information view, gold shipments into the country are neither a necessary nor a sufficient condition for bringing panics to an end. Gold shipments are not a necessary condition for ending panics because a sufficient degree of asset insurance or coinsurance might itself resolve problems of asymmetric information, potentially even in the absence of gold inflows. Gold shipments are not a sufficient condition because it is the transfer of gold to *banks,* rather than the physical fact of gold availability per se, that brings an end to the panic.

As Myers (1931) shows, New York City banks held substantial amounts of internationally traded securities, including bills of exchange and commercial paper, in their portfolios in the nineteenth century. While the proportion of commercial paper to other investments declined over the period, even as late as 1909, banks in New York City held 30–40 percent of their interest-bearing assets in this form (Myers 1931, 336). From 1866 on, the transatlantic cable connected New York to the major financial centers of Europe and allowed financial transactions to take place at a moment's notice. Finally, it took approximately ten days for a steamship to travel from London to New York. Thus, upon suspending convertibility it should have been possible for New York City banks to wire to have a shipment of gold sent to alleviate any money-demand shocks. They could have paid for the gold with their substantial holdings of prime-grade paper. Allowing for railroad delivery lags within the United States, the process of shipping and distributing the currency should have taken no longer than two or three weeks. Calomiris and Hubbard (1989b) show that international gold flows moved rapidly across the Atlantic during the Panic of 1907, and coincided with internal movements of gold flows which indicate extremely rapid adjustment to changes in the demand for gold, most of which was accomplished within a month of the initial shock.

Yet the duration of suspensions of convertibility could be substantially longer than the time horizon for the delivery of gold. The durations of the suspensions of 1873 and 1893 were roughly a month (see Sprague 1910, 53–58, 180–86), but the suspension during the Panic of 1907 lasted from 26 October 1907 until 4 January 1908 (277–82). While Sprague chides the New York banks for not resuming sooner, the currency premium on certified checks was still roughly 1 percent as late as December 20.

Another way to consider whether the availability of cash can end a panic, as suggested by the random withdrawal theory, is to examine the behavior of banks during the Great Depression. A basic purpose of the Federal Reserve Act was to establish a lender of last resort which would provide cash when necessary. The Fed's discount window would appear to provide a mechanism for obtaining ample amounts of cash to banks, even if the Fed did not engage in open market operations. Yet, during the 1930s, banking panics did occur and banks did not avail themselves of the discount window opportunity. This contradicts the random withdrawal theory. Even if the Fed made discount window borrowings relatively expensive, as suggested by Gendreau (1990), banks presumably would have preferred to pay a high price at the discount window rather than become insolvent. And yet, they did not.

The behavior of banks during the Great Depression is consistent with the asymmetric information theory, however. In this view, the basic problem is that depositors do not know which banks are most likely to fail. A bank which went to the discount window would be publicly identifying itself as a weak bank, would immediately face a run, and could go bankrupt. The information asymmetry would be resolved if the weak banks went to the discount window. It was for precisely this reason that, during the panics of the National Banking Era, clearing houses never revealed the identities of banks which had received the largest quantities of loan certificates. The need for secrecy was paramount if the interests of all banks were to be protected (see Gorton 1985, and Gorton and Mullineaux 1987).

In summary, monetary scarcity per se was not a sufficient condition for prolonging or avoiding suspensions of convertibility. On the other hand, the availability of cash, through gold flows or the discount window, was not a sufficient condition for ending a panic either. We now turn to the question of whether crises could be avoided or brought to an end by collective action that did not involve aggregate increases in specie. The clearest and most famous example is the resolution of the Baring crisis, as recounted by Kindleberger (1978).

The possible insolvency of Baring Brothers investment banking house in London in November 1890, to which Sprague (1910) attributed the Panic of

1890 in the United States, threatened a more general financial crisis in Britain, presumably because of asymmetric information about the precise causes and extent of its insolvency, and its possible links to commercial banks or their borrowers. Evidence on the importance of these information externalities comes mainly from the behavior of London bankers themselves. As it became clear that Baring was insolvent, London bankers cooperated to assume full mutual liability through an insurance fund to guarantee against any losses to Baring's creditors.

Three points deserve emphasis here. First, there was no money-demand shock and no bank run on Baring. Baring was not a commercial bank. Thus, there was no question of its failure resulting from money-demand shocks or low reserves. Second, the banks' commitment was sufficient to quell whatever incipient disturbance they had feared. Third, the banks voluntarily assumed liability without compensation for a firm that was clearly insolvent. If there were not substantial externalities associated with asymmetric information and if it did not pay the banks to dispel doubts about the incidence of the disturbance, then why would banks have volunteered to provide a bailout?

A final important experiment which helps to test the withdrawal risk view against the asymmetric information view concerns the role of Canadian banks in the United States during banking panics. Earlier we discussed the fact that Canadian banks were heavily branched and cooperated to regulate themselves through the Canadian Bankers' Association. The result was that Canada did not experience banking panics, and had significantly lower loss and failure rates compared to the U.S. experience. These Canadian banks also had American branches. If the withdrawal risk theory is correct, then during a panic, branches of Canadian banks should have experienced specie withdrawals similar to those of American banks in the same location. However, Schembri and Hawkins (1988) argue that, rather than suffering the same disintermediation as their American counterparts, Canadian branches were viewed as a "safe haven" during the crisis and received net inflows at that time.

4.6 Bank Regulation and Financial History

Banking panics have long been a motivating factor in the development of financial regulation and monetary policy. Ideally, public policy should reflect the "lessons of history," once relevant differences between historical and contemporary environments are considered. Designing public policy is complicated not only because it is difficult to distill the appropriate lessons from history but also because banking and capital markets continue to be transformed by technological change. That is to say, history does not end. Possibly, the lessons of history are not relevant in the new environment. In this section we briefly consider some of these issues in the context of our conclusion that the historical evidence is consistent with the asymmetric information hypothesis. Since this conclusion contradicts a long history of received wisdom, we begin by asking why the alternative view—that seasonal money shocks cause panics—has had such a long history. It may be that the answer to this puzzle is very important for understanding public policy.

4.6.1 The Politics of Panics

Why does the previous literature on the origins of banking panics, including, in particular, some of the studies of the National Monetary Commission, view monetary shocks as a source of banking instability? We think there are two answers. The first reason for the misinterpretation of the importance of money-demand shocks in causing panics is the political usefulness of this distortion of the facts during the debate over the establishment of the Federal Reserve System, which included the possible regulation of commercial bank lending to securities brokers and of securities markets transactions of banks through underwriting and trust affiliates. The "interior money-demand shock" story exonerated New York City banks and Wall Street speculators from any blame for causing stock market collapses and banking panics. Instead, this story identified decentralized disturbances in the periphery as the cause of both (rather than "excessive" bank credit backed by stocks in New York).

In a series of articles criticizing the money-demand view and its proponents, W. H. Allen (1911, 1913a, 1913b) offered contrary evidence and questioned the motives of Aldrich, Andrew, Kemmerer, Vreeland, and the National Monetary Commission as a whole. He argued against Kemmerer's (1910) use of call loan interest rates (the rate charged to stock brokers) as a guide to general conditions in the money market, and pointed out that seasonal money flows were not large in panic years. He emphasized the difference between money movements in the early fall and credit growth in the late fall. Finally, Allen (1913b) accused the Commission of catering to the interests of Wall Street bankers:

> Wall Street bankers originated the idea of making a financial bogie of crop demands; they also originated this theory of the cause and effect of the concentration of money at New York; and Congress, with all of its investigating, has never even tried to learn if there were not other possible causes of this concentration of money [in the stock market] and the resulting financial ills. . . . The currency committees of the present Congress are, it is believed, freer from outside control than any currency committees that we have had in many years. Nevertheless, they have lapsed into the old habit of looking to our big bankers as the sole depositaries of financial facts. (105)

Allen was not alone in this view. In a speech to the Wisconsin State Bankers' Association in 1903, Andrew J. Frame, president of a rural national bank in Wisconsin, disputed the claim that agriculture-related shocks in the periphery were the main cause of banking instability:

> I challenge any man to prove that since 1893 there have been more than two fall seasons when the money market has been above a normal or reasonable level, and then *speculation and not crop movements were the primary causes of trouble* [emphasis added]. (Frame 1903, 12)

Frame goes on to cite several prominent banking sources who agree with his view that the "excessive speculation" of New York City bankers is the greatest threat to banking stability. While the arguments of these various sources fall far short of proving their case, they do offer insight into the conflicting opinions and motivations of bankers, who tried to influence opinion on currency reform. Given the political benefits to New York City bankers of the National Monetary Commission's recommendations, one is led to wonder whether the Commission was "captured" by the most powerful group having a stake in its banking reform proposals.

A second reason for the persistence of the seasonal money-shock view is that authors frequently used the terms "money" and "money market" loosely, sometimes meaning cash, sometimes credit. This has led to confusion regarding the views of earlier scholars. As noted before, Sprague (1910) clearly focused on asset shocks, but saw seasonal money *market* strain as one of many factors influencing bank vulnerability. While Kemmerer (1910) did emphasize money-demand shocks in much of his discussion, he also discussed credit seasonality and was often unclear about whether he viewed seasonality as mainly influencing bank leverage (and hence vulnerability to asset shocks) or withdrawal risk per se. His direct references to panics occupy only three pages of his 500-page statistical tome. Even there, in his reference to Jevons' (1884) discussion of seasonality, Kemmerer seems to emphasize credit risk rather than money demand as the primary determinant of the seasonality of panics.

4.6.2 Bank Regulation and the Historical Record

What conclusions can be drawn from the evidence on the origins of panics for regulation of banks? We divide our discussion of the implications of the asymmetric information view of the causes of historical banking panics into two parts. First, we describe the broad implications of the above analysis. Then we explore the general relevance of the historical record for today's financial system.

As we have noted, both views of banking panics agree that a banking system composed of a small number of nationwide branching banks would have been much more stable. According to Chari (1989), stability would have come from diversification of withdrawal risk. According to the asymmetric information view, diversification ex ante and credible coinsurance ex post would have substantially reduced, if not eliminated entirely, the possibility and costliness of banking panics historically. Therefore, there is a consensus that a smaller number of larger, branched, more diversified banks, approximating the Canadian system, would likely prevent panics. Short of this conclusion, however, there is disagreement between the two views about appropriate public policies towards banks.

According to the random withdrawal risk view, under the historical conditions of the United States, with unit banking and before federal deposit insurance, the basic problem is that there are not enough reserves to go around in time of crisis. When there is a seasonal, unusually high desired currency-deposit ratio, the economy needs cash. Notably, the implication of this view is that an increase in cash through open market operations would be effective in forestalling panics. During the National Banking Era the government was unable to conduct open market operations to inject cash. The U.S. Treasury was unable to purchase securities in sufficient amounts to prevent panics or effectively aid in their resolution.

Moreover, in the random withdrawal risk view, banks themselves were unable to form effective coalitions to mitigate the effects of panics. Banks as a group were unable to diversify withdrawal risk because reserves were unobservable. Taken literally, this view suggests intervention in the form of open market operations or reserve requirements, which may make feasible private bank coalitions for diversifying withdrawal risk.

The asymmetric information view suggests different directions for future research. First, in this view, open market operations by themselves will not be effective in preventing or easing panics. The problem is not that depositors want cash for its own sake, as in the random withdrawal view, but are concerned that their bank will fail. In this case, discount loans can (in the absence of deposit insurance) be an effective way to transform illiquid bank assets into a security that depositors can easily value, namely cash. Private clearing houses historically provided the discount window through the issurance of clearing-house loan certificates. Both government lending to banks and deposit insurance share the same essential feature, namely, the government is willing to bear risks that are peculiar to the banking system, either by making loans to banks or by guaranteeing bank deposits.

It is difficult to determine the potential importance of asymmetric information problems for today's banks. The very fact that banks are regulated prevents a clear determination of how banks would have evolved in the absence of this regulation. To some extent, perhaps to an extreme degree, regulation prevents the evolution of the banking system in ways that may be very desirable. The fact that such evolution is not directly observable prevents us from finding persuasive evidence that it would not occur in a different regulatory environment. There are two final observations we wish to make about the current environment in this regard.

The first observation is that the historical efficacy of bank self-regulation seems (to us) not to have been well understood in the literature. Private bank coalitions were surprisingly effective in monitoring banks and mitigating the effects of panics, even if panics were not eliminated. While in today's thrift debacle we observe the costs of having eliminated panics through government deposit insurance, this does not imply that all insurance is undesirable. Private self-regulation may be quite effective, especially when combined with some government policies. One does find examples in other less-regulated financial markets of coinsurance arrangements and problems of asymmetric information. For example, futures-market clearing house members coinsure against each other's default by standing between all market transactions, as a group.[33]

The second observation is that the business of banking has changed in some important respects over the last decade, partly in response to regulation. The regulatory costs for financial intermediaries of increasing the size of their balance sheets (reserve requirements, insurance premia, etc.), along with the advantages of diversification, have encouraged them to initiate and re-sell loans. While initially this was confined mainly to mortgages, commercial loan sales have become increasingly common in the last decade (see Gorton and Haubrich 1989). There still may be a substantial proportion of small- and medium-sized borrowers whose loans are not saleable. Nonetheless, to the extent that loans can be sold on the open market, asymmetric information is less of a concern. The fact that loans can be sold indicates that information-sharing technology has improved, and hence that asymmetries are likely to be less dramatic. The ability of banks to sell loans, even if only among themselves, provides an important means for asset diversification, as well. Investigating the extent to which loan sales by intermediaries reflect fundamental changes in information sharing and the regulatory implications of these changes is an important area for future research.

Notes

1. The two secondary sources which are widely used are Kemmerer (1910) and Sprague (1910). Neither author provides a definition of a banking panic. Both works are concerned with the U.S. National Banking Era. Sprague details what occurred during the events of 1873, 1884, 1890, 1893, and 1907. Kemmerer arbitrarily identifies panics, finding six major and fifteen minor panics during the period 1890–1908 (see pp. 222–23, 232).

2. Clearing-house loan certificates were the joint liabilities of all members of the clearing house. They were issued during banking panics. See Gorton (1985) and Gorton and Mullineaux (1987) for further discussion.

3. The definition is in terms of bank debt which circulates as a medium of exchange and which contractually allows redemption on demand at par. But, the definition does not otherwise distinguish between different types of bank liabilities. There may have been an important difference, however, between bank notes, which were noninterest-bearing bearer liabilities, and bank deposits, which bore interest and were not bearer liabilities, being checking accounts of the type familiar. Since banks often issued both types of liabilities, especially in the United States, effects of the distinction are difficult to detect empirically. But theoretically, different theories make important distinctions.

The main difference, discussed later, concerns the existence or nonexistence of secondary markets. In the United States, such markets existed for bank notes but not for demand deposits. On this point, however, the definition is left vague.

4. Nicholas (1907) provides evidence that idiosyncratic money-demand shocks to a particular bank were offset by interbank loans.

5. Suspension of convertibility did not mean that banks ceased to clear transactions or make loans. Indeed, suspension was usually the beginning of the end of the contraction, and marked a period of loan and deposit recovery, albeit at slow rates initially as banks strived to accumulate specie reserves to facilitate resumption. Sprague (1910, 56–58, 186–91, 280–82) documents the existence of a secondary market for bank deposits during suspensions under the National Banking System as early as 1873. Certified checks of suspended banks typically traded at slight discounts of no more than 4 percent and usually less than 1 percent. Thus, while suspension placed limits on the movement of specie out of the banking system, it allowed depositors and merchants to exchange one form of bank liability for another, both within a locality and, to a lesser extent, across localities.

6. In 1851 a free-banking statute created a second group of uncoordinated banks in the state.

7. As Schweikart (1987) argues, the performance of Mississippi, Florida, and Alabama banks during this period mainly reflected government use of banks as a fiscal tool. These states are excluded from the comparison.

8. Bank failure rates were low throughout the South and, unlike the North, confined almost entirely to small rural banks. Recovery of bank balance sheets was relatively rapid in the South, and many banks continued operations in an atmosphere of relative normalcy in comparison to the North. These differences can be traced to differences in bank coordination, particularly interbank lending during the crisis, rather than to a different incidence of fundamental shocks in the North and South.

9. Rolnick and Weber (1984) argue that free bank failures were caused by exogenous asset depreciation. During banking panics, however, coordination among banks, or a lack thereof, also seems important.

10. Interestingly, ex ante pricing of bank note risk prior to the Panic of 1857 mirrored these ex post differences in the relative performance of free banks in Indiana and Ohio. Ohio's mutual liability and free banks, and Indiana's mutual liability banks, all enjoyed a common discount rate in New York City of 1 percent, while the Indiana free banks were discounted at 1.5 percent. For data on bank note discount rates in the Philadelphia market and a model of bank note risk pricing, see Gorton (1990, 1989a).

11. Clearing houses created significant amounts of money. During the Panic of 1893, clearing houses issued $100 million of loan certificates, about 2.5 percent of the money stock. During the Panic of 1907, about $500 million was issued, about 4.5 percent of the money stock. This private money circulated as hand-to-hand currency, initially at a slight discount from par. See Gorton (1985) and Gorton and Mullineaux (1987).

12. Other panic theories are provided by Bryant (1980), Donaldson (1989b), and Waldo (1985). Also, see Minsky (1975) and Kindleberger (1978).

13. Jacklin (1987) shows that dividend-paying equity shares dominate demand deposits in the Diamond and Dybvig (1983) model, but that this depends on the specific nature of the preferences assumed by Diamond and Dybvig. It does not hold for fairly general preference structures. Nevertheless, trading restrictions are a necessary ingredient to the Diamond and Dybvig argument, as Jacklin shows.

14. A market would allow for agents' beliefs to be coordinated, eliminating panic-causing conjectures about other agents' beliefs. Pre–Civil War America, with active markets for bank liabilities, appears to contradict this view of spatial separation.

15. Typically, in these models the sequential-service constraint still applies to the depositors of each individual bank. But, while the initiating shock may thus be the same as in the original Diamond and Dybvig model, the main point is the reserve pyramiding which causes country banks to essentially behave as individual depositors with respect to the central-reserve city bank.

16. The importance of seasonality is discussed by Andrew (1907) and Kemmerer (1910). Goodhart (1969, 3) writes: "Financial crises were attributed, with a great deal of truth, not so much to cyclical factors as to the natural results of the recurring autumnal pressures upon the money-market; these seasonal pressures were so extreme that it took only a little extra strain—in the form of overheated boom conditions or the bursting bubbles of Wall Street speculation—to turn tightness into distress."

17. See Eichengreen (1984) for a review. Eichengreen finds substantial interregional variation in the propensity to hold cash relative to demand deposits. Thus, variations across regions in the demand for money would be associated with interregional flows of currency. Furthermore, seasonal demands for money in the West (where cash-to-deposit ratios were high) would cause an aggregate contraction in the money supply (shrinkage in the money multiplier).

18. The appropriate literature discussing bank activities on the asset side of the balance sheet consists of Diamond (1984), Boyd and Prescott (1986), Campbell and Kracaw (1980), among others. On bank liabilities as a circulating medium see Gorton (1989b), Gorton and Pennacchi (1990), and Calomiris and Kahn (1991). These ideas are discussed further in subsection 4.4.3.

19. In the United States, most banks have not had traded equity claims historically because the overwhelming number of banks were small institutions. Thus, there were no markets in any bank assets or liabilities.

20. Diamond's (1984) argument explains how it is possible for depositors to monitor the monitor, that is, how the depositors can rely on the bank to monitor the borrowers.

21. In Chari and Jagannathan (1988), as in Diamond and Dybvig (1983), bank liabilities have no discernible role as a circulating medium of exchange. Thus, in Chari and Jagannathan it is not clear why agents withdraw from the bank if they want to consume. Apparently, bank liabilities do not function to satisfy cash-in-advance constraints.

22. There is no explanation in Chari and Jagannathan (1988) for why this would be a systemic event affecting the entire banking system, rather than an event producing a run on a single bank.

23. The assumption of full revelation of bank-specific risk may be extreme for the following reasons. Note brokers sometimes refused to make markets in individual banks' notes, particularly during panics. Furthermore, earlier banking panics, for example, one in Indiana in 1854, took the form of runs by note holders rather than depositors. Gorton's (1990) evidence on the information content of bank notes pertains to state-specific, not bank-specific, risk. The extent to which bank-specific note risk was information revealed by the note market prices remains an area for future research.

24. Moreover, the expected losses on deposits may be expected to occur when consumption is highly valued, during a recession, for example. As shown in Gorton (1988), losses per se cannot explain panics. But, losses occurring during a recession would receive more weight in utility terms. The combination of these events can cause panics. See Gorton (1988) for a model.

25. Chari (1989) argues that the reduction in the "bank failure" rate in the United States upon introducing deposit insurance supports the withdrawal risk view over the asymmetric information view. We do not agree. In an undiversified system of many

unit banks, confusion over the incidence of an asset shock will lead despositors to withdraw, absent the ex post protection of deposit insurance. This will, in turn, cause suspensions of convertibility, disruptions in commerce, deflations, and increased bank insolvency rates.

26. One could argue, from an asymmetric information perspective, that correspondents' asset risks are related and, therefore, the asymmetric information approach could also explain increases in the probability of failure associated with correspondent relations. However, as demonstrated later in our discussion, the asymmetric information approach does not rely on these linkages to explain variations in failure rates within a given region.

27. It is worth noting that experimentation confirms that our results are robust to variations in the choice of time horizon over the interval from two to five weeks.

28. Three particularly large withdrawals (for their respective weeks) occurred before week 50 in 1880 (-15.5 percent, bringing the reserve ratio to 24.96 percent), week 10 in 1881 (-13.4 percent, bringing the reserve ratio to 25.15 percent), and week 33 in 1896 (-8.3 percent, bringing the reserve ratio to 27.01 percent).

29. Each interval of decline is defined as follows. Moving forward in time we compare the price index of each month in the sample to the index three months before. Intervals are defined not to overlap. For example, if stock prices fell from February to May, then fell again in June and rebounded in July, we would register only the February–May interval (not the March–June interval).

30. Seasonal patterns for 1901–10 show the highest commercial failure rates in the months of October through February (see Swift 1911, 40).

31. Banks, of course, would have understood the seasonal vulnerability induced by changes in leverage. One might expect that banks would have responded by importing and exporting reserves to offset seasonally related loan changes. Presumably, the costs of importing and exporting specie, to maintain constant leverage (i.e., the ratio of risky to riskless assets), were high.

32. There is an alternative explanation for these findings. High leverage during times when adverse news is relatively likely is consistent with the view of Minsky (1975) and Kindleberger (1978) that investors and banks were myopic. According to this view, the reason that large stock price declines, higher leverage, and panic are most likely coincident events is that they are all driven by myopic speculative frenzies. Such frenzies are most likely to occur in the months and cyclical phases of greatest economic activity.

33. Also, Calomiris (1989c) describes cooperative arrangements between commercial paper issuers and banks that insure against similar problems.

References

Akerlof, G. 1970. The Market for Lemons: Qualitative Uncertainty and the Market Mechanism. *Quarterly Journal of Economics* 84:488–500.

Allen, W. H. 1913a. Seasonal Variations in Money Rates: A Reply to Professor Kemmerer. *Moody's Magazine* (February).

———. 1913b. A False Diagnosis of Financial Ills. *Moody's Magazine* (November).

———. 1911. The Lie in the Aldrich Bill. *Moody's Magazine* (April).

Andrew, A. Piatt. 1907. The Influence of Crops Upon Business in America. *Quarterly Journal of Economics* 20:323–53.

———. 1910. *Statistics for the United States, 1867–1909.* National Monetary Commission. 61st Cong. 2d sess. Senate Doc. 570. Washington D.C.: U.S. Government Printing Office.

Barsky, Robert B. 1987. The Fisher Hypothesis and the Forecastability and Persistence of Inflation. *Journal of Monetary Economics* 19(1):3–24.

Bernanke, Ben. 1983. Nonmonetary Effects of the Financial Crisis in the Propagation of the Great Depression. *American Economic Review* 73:257–76.

Bhattacharya, Sudipto, and Douglas Gale. 1987. Preference Shocks, Liquidity, and Central Bank Policy. In *New Approaches in Monetary Economics,* ed. William A. Barnett and Kenneth Singleton. New York: Cambridge University Press.

Board of Governors of the Federal Reserve System. 1959. *All-Bank Statistics, 1896–1955.*

Bogue, Allan G. 1955. *Money at Interest: The Farm Mortgage on the Middle Border.* Lincoln, Neb.: University of Nebraska Press.

Bordo, Michael D. 1985. The Impact and International Transmission of Financial Crises: Some Historical Evidence, 1870–1933. *Revista di storia economica,* 2d ser., vol. 2: 41–78.

Boyd, John, and Edward Prescott. 1986. Financial Intermediary Coalitions. *Journal of Economic Theory* 38:211–32.

Breckenridge, R. M. 1910. *The History of Banking in Canada.* National Monetary Commission. 61st Cong., 2d sess. Senate Doc. 332. Washington D.C.: U.S. Government Printing Office.

Bryant, John. 1980. A Model of Reserves, Bank Runs, and Deposit Insurance. *Journal of Banking and Finance* 4:335–44.

Burns, Arthur, and Wesley C. Mitchell. 1946. *Measuring Business Cycles.* NBER Studies in Business Cycles, no. 2. New York: Columbia University Press.

Calomiris, Charles W. 1990. Is Deposit Insurance Necessary?: A Historical Perspective. *Journal of Economic History* 50, no. 2 (June): 283–95.

———. 1989a. Deposit Insurance: Lessons from the Record? Federal Reserve Bank of Chicago, *Economic Perspectives* (May–June).

———. 1989b. Do "Vulnerable" Economies Need Deposit Insurance?: Lessons from the U.S. Agricultural Boom and Bust of the 1920s. Federal Reserve Bank of Chicago, Working Paper no. 89–18.

———. 1989c. The Motivations for Loan Commitments Backing Commercial Paper. *Journal of Banking and Finance* 13:271–77.

———. 1988. Price and Exchange Rate Determination During the Greenback Suspension. *Oxford Economic Papers* 40:719–50.

Calomiris, Charles W., and R. Glenn Hubbard. 1989a. Price Flexibility, Credit Availability, and Economic Fluctuations: Evidence from the United States, 1894–1909. *Quarterly Journal of Economics* 104(3):429–52.

———. 1989b. International Adjustment Under the Classical Gold Standard: Evidence for the U.S. and Britain, 1879–1914. Northwestern University, typescript.

Calomiris, Charles W., and Charles M. Kahn. 1991. The Role of Demandable Debt in Structuring Optimal Banking Arrangements. *American Economic Review,* June (in press).

Calomiris, Charles W., Charles M. Kahn, and Stefan Krasa. 1990. Optimal Contingent Bank Liquidation Under Moral Hazard. Northwestern University, typescript.

Calomiris, Charles W., and Larry Schweikart. 1991. The Panic of 1857: Origins, Transmission, and Containment. *Journal of Economic History* (in press).

Campbell, Tim, and William Kracaw. 1980. Information Production, Market Signalling and the Theory of Financial Intermediation. *Journal of Finance* 35(4):863–81.

Cannon, J. G. 1910. *Clearing Houses.* National Monetary Commission. 61st Cong., 2d sess. Senate Doc. 491. Washington D.C.: U.S. Government Printing Office.

Chari, V. V. 1989. Banking Without Deposit Insurance or Bank Panics: Lessons from a Model of the U.S. National Banking System. Federal Reserve Bank of Minneapolis, *Quarterly Review* (Summer):3–19.

Chari, V. V., and Ravi Jagannathan. 1988. Banking Panics, Information, and Rational Expectations Equilibrium. *Journal of Finance* 43:749–60.

Cone, Kenneth. 1983. Regulation of Depository Institutions. Ph.D. diss., Stanford University.

Dewey, Davis R. 1903. *Financial History of the United States*. New York: Longman's Green and Company.

Diamond, Douglas. 1984. Financial Intermediation and Delegated Monitoring. *Review of Economic Studies* 51:393–414.

Diamond, Douglas, and Phillip Dybvig. 1983. Bank Runs, Liquidity and Deposit Insurance. *Journal of Political Economy* 91:401–19.

Donaldson, R. Glenn. 1989a. Sources of Panics: Evidence From the Weekly Data. Princeton University, typescript.

———. 1989b. Money Moguls, Market Corners and Cash Collusion During Panics. Princeton University, typescript.

Eichengreen, Barry. 1984. Currency and Credit in the Gilded Age. *Research in Economic History*, supp. 3: 87–114.

Frame, Andrew J. 1903. *Sound vs. Soft Money*. Waukesha, Wis.: Wisconsin State Bankers' Association.

Frickey, Edwin. 1947. *Production in the United States, 1860–1914*. Cambridge, Mass.: Harvard University Press.

———. 1942. *Economic Fluctuations in the United States*. Cambridge, Mass.: Harvard University Press.

Friedman, Milton, and Anna Schwartz. 1963. *A Monetary History of the United States, 1867–1960*. Princeton: Princeton University Press.

Gallatin, Albert. 1831. *Considerations on the Currency and Banking System of the United States*. Philadelphia: Carey and Lea.

Gendreau, B. 1990. Federal Reserve Policy and the Great Depression. University of Pennsylvania, typescript.

Golembe, Carter, and Clark Warburton. 1958. Insurance of Bank Obligations in Six States During the Period 1829–1866. Federal Deposit Insurance Corporation, typescript.

Goodhart, C. A. E. 1969. *The New York Money Market and the Finance of Trade, 1900–1913*. Cambridge, Mass.: Harvard University Press.

Gorton, Gary. 1990. Free Banking, Wildcat Banking, and the Market for Bank Notes. The Wharton School, University of Pennsylvania, typescript.

———. 1989a. An Introduction to Van Court's Bank Note Reporter and Counterfeit Detector. The Wharton School, University of Pennsylvania, typescript.

———. 1989b. Self-Regulating Bank Coalitions. The Wharton School, University of Pennsylvania, typescript.

———. 1988. Banking Panics and Business Cycles. *Oxford Economic Papers* 40: 751–81.

———. 1987. Bank Suspension of Convertibility. *Journal of Monetary Economics* 15(2):177–93.

———. 1985. Clearing Houses and the Origin of Central Banking in the U.S. *Journal of Economic History* 45(2): 277–83.

Gorton, Gary, and Joseph Haubrich. 1989. The Loan Sales Market. In *Research in Financial Services*, ed. George Kaufman. Greenwich, Conn.: Jai Press.

Gorton, Gary, and Donald Mullineaux. 1987. The Joint Production of Confidence: Endogenous Regulation and 19th Century Commercial Bank Clearinghouses. *Journal of Money, Credit and Banking* 19(4):458–68.

Gorton, Gary, and George Pennacchi. 1990. Financial Intermediation and Liquidity Creation. *Journal of Finance* 45(1):49–72.

Govan, Thomas. 1936. The Banking and Credit System in Georgia. Ph.D. diss., Vanderbilt University.

Hamilton, James. 1987. Monetary Factors in the Great Depression. *Journal of Monetary Economics* 19:145–69.

Haubrich, Joseph. 1990. Non-Monetary Effects of Financial Crises: Lessons from the Great Depression in Canada. *Journal of Monetary Economics,* 25, no. 2 (March): 223–52.

Haubrich, Joseph, and Robert King. 1984. Banking and Insurance. National Bureau of Economic Research Working Paper no. 1312.

Jacklin, Charles. 1987. Demand Deposits, Trading Restrictions, and Risk Sharing. In *Contractual Arrangements for Intertemporal Trade,* ed. Edward D. Prescott and Neil Wallace. Minneapolis, Minn.: University of Minnesota Press.

Jacklin, Charles, and Sudipto Bhattacharya. 1988. Distinguishing Panics and Information-Based Bank Runs: Welfare and Policy Implications. *Journal of Political Economy* 96(3):568–92.

Jevons, Stanley. 1884. *Investigations in Currency and Finance*. London: Macmillan.

Kemmerer, E. W. 1910. *Seasonal Variations in the Relative Demand for Money and Capital in the United States.* National Monetary Commission. 61st Cong., 2d sess. Senate Doc. 588. Washington, D.C.: U.S. Government Printing Office.

Kindleberger, Charles. 1978. *Manias, Panics, and Crashes: A History of Financial Crises.* New York: Basic Books.

Minsky, Hyman P. 1975. *John Maynard Keynes.* New York: Columbia University Press.

Miron, Jeffrey A. 1986. Financial Panics, the Seasonality of the Nominal Interest Rate, and the Founding of the Fed. *American Economic Review* 76(1):125–40.

Miron, Jeffrey A., and Christina D. Romer. 1989. A New Monthly Index of Industrial Production, 1884–1940. National Bureau of Economic Research Working Paper no. 3172.

Mitchell, Wesley. 1903. *A History of the Greenbacks*. Chicago: University of Chicago Press.

Moen, Jon, and Ellis W. Tallman. 1990. The Bank Panic of 1907: The Role of Trust Companies. Federal Reserve Bank of Atlanta, typescript.

Myers, Margaret G. 1931. *The New York Money Market.* New York: Columbia University Press.

Nicholas, Henry C. 1907. Runs on Banks. *Moody's Magazine* (December).

Postlewaite, Andrew, and Xavier Vives. 1987. Bank Runs as an Equilibrium Phenomenon. *Journal of Political Economy* 95:485–91.

Redlich, Fritz. 1947. *The Molding of American Banking: Men and Ideas.* Reprint. New York: Augustus Kelley, 1968.

Rolnick, Arthur, and Warren E. Weber. 1984. The Causes of Free Bank Failures: A Detailed Examination. *Journal of Monetary Economics* 14:267–91.

Schembri, Lawrence L., and Jennifer A. Hawkins. 1988. The Role of Canadian Chartered Banks in U.S. Banking Crises: 1870–1914. Carleton University, typescript.

Schweikart, Larry. 1987. *Banking in the American South from the Age of Jackson to Reconstruction.* Baton Rouge: Louisiana State University Press.

Smith, Bruce. 1987. Bank Panics, Suspension, and Geography: Some Notes on the "Contagion of Fear" in Banking. Cornell University, typescript.

Sobel, Robert. 1968. *Panic on Wall Street: A History of America's Financial Disasters.* New York: Macmillan.

Sprague, O. M. W. 1910. *A History of Crises Under the National Banking System.*

National Monetary Commission. Washington, D.C.: U.S. Government Printing Office.

Standard Trade and Securities. 1932. *Base Book of the Standard Statistical Bulletin.*

Swift, W. Martin. 1911. The Seasonal Movements of Trade. *Moody's Magazine* (July).

U.S. Comptroller of the Currency. Various issues. *Annual Report.* Washington, D.C.: U.S. Government Printing Office.

U.S. Department of Commerce. 1949. *Historical Statistics of the United States.* Washington, D.C.: U.S. Government Printing Office.

Waldo, Douglas. 1985. Bank Runs, the Deposit-Currency Ratio and the Interest Rate. *Journal of Monetary Economics* 15(3):269–78.

Wallace, Neil. 1988. Another Attempt to Explain an Illiquid Banking System: The Diamond and Dybvig Model With Sequential Service Taken Seriously. Federal Reserve Bank of Minneapolis, *Quarterly Review* (Fall):3–16.

Wheelock, David C. 1988. The Fed's Failure to Act as Lender of Last Resort During the Great Depression, 1929–1933. University of Texas, typescript.

Williamson, Steven. 1989. Bank Failures, Financial Restrictions, and Aggregate Fluctuations: Canada and the United States, 1870–1913. Federal Reserve Bank of Minneapolis, *Quarterly Review* (Summer): 20–40.

5 Before the Accord: U.S. Monetary-Financial Policy, 1945–51

Barry Eichengreen and Peter M. Garber

5.1 Introduction

The 1951 Treasury–Federal Reserve Accord brought to a close an extraordinary period in the monetary and financial history of the United States. For nearly a decade, U.S. Treasury bond yields never rose above 2½ per cent (see fig. 5.1). Long-term interest rates may have been low, but short-term rates were lower still: those on 12-month certificates of indebtedness were capped at ⅞ of 1 per cent to 1¼ per cent; for the first half of the period, 90-day Treasury bill rates never exceeded ⅜ of 1 per cent. Interest rates were low despite an inflation rate that reached 25 per cent in the year ending July 1947 (see fig. 5.2). They were stable despite swings from 25 per cent inflation in 1946–47 to 3 per cent deflation in the year July 1948–July 1949, to 10 per cent inflation in the year March 1950–March 1951. These pronounced fluctuations in ex post real interest rates did not undermine the stability of financial institutions: there were only five bank suspensions between the end of 1945 and the middle of 1950. The stability of interest rates and the absence of bank failures in the turbulent aftermath of World War II seems all the more remarkable following a decade like the 1980s when the volatility of asset prices was so pronounced and the difficulties of financial institutions were so prevalent.[1]

We analyze in this paper U.S. monetary-financial policy in the period leading up to the March 1951 Treasury-Fed Accord. Our point of departure is Friedman and Schwartz's (1963) notion that policy in this period was formu-

Barry Eichengreen is professor of economics at the University of California, Berkeley, and a research associate of the National Bureau of Economic Research. Peter M. Garber is professor of economics at Brown University and a research associate of the National Bureau of Economic Research.

The authors thank Alex Mackler, Carolyn Werley, and Lauren Auchincloss for research assistance, and Glenn Hubbard and Rick Mishkin for helpful comments.

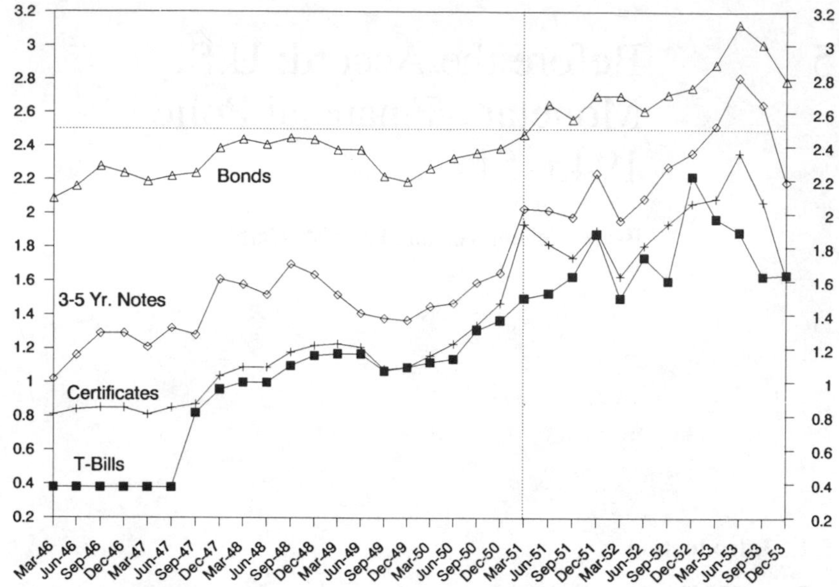

Fig. 5.1 Yields of maturities (%)

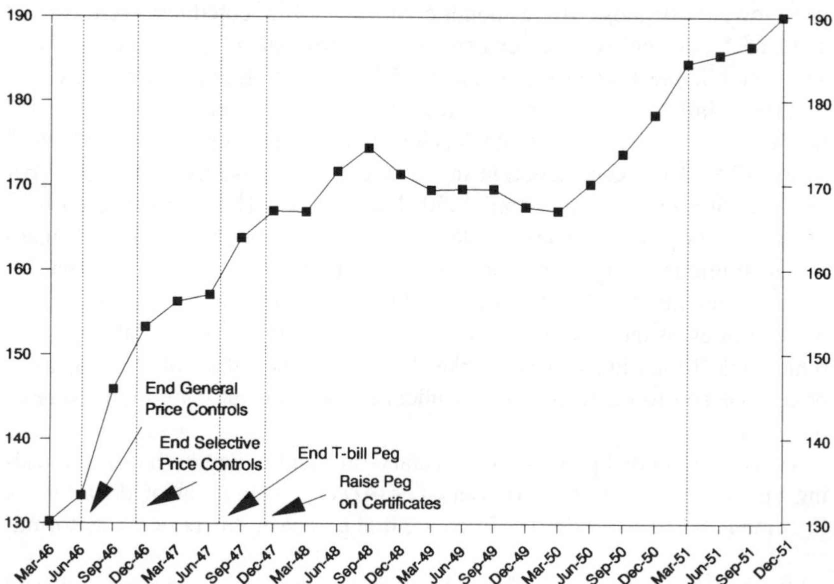

Fig. 5.2 Consumer price index

lated with reference to a price-level target. As soon as the price level deviated sufficiently from its target range, policymakers were expected to intervene to prevent it from straying further. We draw on the recent literature on exchange rate target zones and collapsing exchange rate regimes to formalize this notion and to show how its implications for interest rate behavior can be derived. We model policy in the period as a target zone for the price level, and the mounting difficulties on the eve of the Accord as an incipient run on a collapsing target-zone regime. In the framework we employ, a target zone for the price level plus an intervention rule imply a target zone for the interest rate. Thus, the model provides a framework for analyzing Federal Reserve intervention and an approach to understanding the singular behavior of interest rates.

The model also helps one to understand the economic policies and conditions that rendered the policy of capping interest rates sustainable through 1949 but set the stage for its collapse in 1951. In particular, it directs attention to the financial and monetary objectives of the authorities and the evolution of the real economy. The absence of dramatic real shocks before 1950 minimized the burden on the monetary authorities, while their credible commitment to the price-level target zone enhanced their capacity to absorb those shocks that occurred. Subsequently, real interest rates rose dramatically, intensifying the pressure for monetary policymakers to intervene, while the advent of the Korean War increased the perceived costs of continued adherence to the target-zone regime.

To understand pre-Accord policy—specifically, policymakers' commitment to a regime that entailed an explicit target zone for interest rates and an implicit target zone for prices—and the advent of the Accord in 1951, it is essential to appreciate the threats to financial stability perceived by the authorities and how those perceptions changed over time. Toward the beginning of the period the perceived threat to financial stability lay in the volatility of inflation and interest rates. Hence the authorities' commitment to stabilizing these variables. Toward the end of the period, these fears had receded and policymakers' concern had shifted toward mobilizing the nation's productive capacity for the Korean War. Hence the March 1951 Accord, under which the Fed could turn its attention from stabilizing interest rates to other objectives.

The rest of the paper is organized as follows. Section 5.2 sketches the background to the 1945–51 period and presents a chronology of the principal events. Section 5.3 presents the target-zone model that provides the framework for our subsequent analysis. Section 5.4 shows how the events of the period can be reinterpreted from a target-zone perspective. In section 5.5 we argue that concern for the stability of the U.S. banking system accounts for the Fed's commitment to a target-zone regime designed to stabilize prices and interest rates prior to 1951, and that shifts in the locus of concern associated with changes in commercial bank portfolios and the advent of the Korean War account for the collapse of the target-zone regime and the Accord of 1951. Section 5.6 concludes.

5.2 A Chronology of Events

In this section we sketch the background to postwar monetary policy in the United States and present a chronology of events affecting its formulation. This sketch provides the reader unfamiliar with the episode an overview of events. It also serves to indicate how the events of the period are characterized in the existing literature. In section 5.4 we present a rather different perspective and contrast it with the conventional interpretation given here.

This summary is also intended to bring out a limitation of existing accounts, namely their emphasis on the role of fortuitous events in sustaining the Fed and Treasury's low interest rate policy. The 1948–49 recession, for instance, is portrayed as a fortuitous event relieving inflationary pressure and demolishing inflationary expectations. There is remarkably little discussion of the underlying economic environment or policy regime that rendered the low interest rate policy viable. It is precisely such discussion that, in subsequent sections of the paper, we seek to add to the existing literature.

5.2.1 Precursors of Wartime Policy

The origins of pre-Accord monetary policy in the United States are conventionally traced to World War II. The low interest rate regime is portrayed as a logical extension of wartime debt-management policies. In fact, the origins of U.S. policy in the period 1945–50 go back further, specifically to the monetary policies and problems of the 1930s.

For the Fed to pursue a policy of stabilizing bond prices, it had to have the capacity to intervene in securities markets. That capacity was enhanced by the passage of the Glass-Steagall Act of 1932 (not the 1933 Banking Act of the same name). Glass-Steagall permitted the Federal Reserve System to count government bonds among the eligible securities required as backing for 60 per cent of Federal Reserve notes. This permitted the Federal Reserve to hold directly a much larger quantity of Treasury securities than had been possible before.

Two developments in the 1930s that encouraged the Fed to intervene to stabilize securities prices were rising interest rates and the problem of excess reserves. Both continued to mold the conduct of monetary policy in the 1940s.

Economic recovery after 1933 placed gentle upward pressure on interest rates. Investors began to anticipate inflation. In early 1935, Treasury officials, concerned that rising interest rates might prevent them from attaining their debt-management objectives, inquired whether the Fed might intervene to stabilize bond prices before the Treasury engaged in its March financing operation. System officials resisted pressure to peg government bond prices but acceded to requests that they at least help to dampen fluctuations in the market. In the spring of 1935, to moderate the rise in interest rates, the Fed, for one of the first times in its history, purchased long-term government bonds.

If the Treasury was worried about debt management, the Fed was preoccupied by excess reserves. By late 1933 these had reached $800 million, or more than 40 percent of required reserves. By the end of 1935 they had soared to more than $3 billion, or 115 per cent of required reserves.

The Federal Open Market Committee's (FOMC) concern was that the growth of excess reserves weakened monetary control. Because few member banks had occasion to borrow from the Fed, an increase in reserve bank discount rates would be incapable of reining in inflationary pressure. At the end of 1935, System holdings of securities were only about $2.5 billion. Even if the FOMC sold off the System's entire portfolio, it could not mop up the banks' excess reserves. This concern led ultimately to three controversial increases in reserve requirements in August of 1936, and March and May of 1937.

These increases were not universally supported. Though mopping up excess reserves might enhance monetary control, the higher interest rates it produced might prompt a recession. To acquire reserves, banks would liquidate a portion of their bond portfolios, and the consequent rise in long-term interest rates might abort the recovery. If the fall in bond prices was sufficiently severe, the solvency of banks which had invested heavily in bonds might be threatened.[2]

Hence on 4 April 1937 the FOMC agreed to purchase $25 million of government securities in the coming week as "may be necessary with a view to preserving an orderly market."[3] Interest rates rose, and the Fed continued purchasing long-term government bonds. In pursuit of this "flexible portfolio policy," it acquired $200 million of long-term bonds in exchange for $150 million of short-term bills and notes and $50 million of cash.[4]

To some, such as George Harrison, president of the Federal Reserve Bank of New York, open market purchases were counterproductive. The object of increased reserve requirements was to reduce excess reserves; bond purchases, by replenishing reserves, defeated the purpose. Harrison favored no open market intervention to limit the fall in bond prices. Others, notably Marriner Eccles, chairman of the FOMC, favored large-scale bond purchases to "stabilize the market."[5] The policy adopted was a compromise between the two positions (Friedman and Schwartz 1963, 527). Long-term interest rates were allowed to rise, but only moderately. Excess reserves were allowed to fall, but only moderately.

Long-term rates rose from 2½ to 2¾ per cent before peaking in April 1937. Excess reserves were reduced, temporarily, to less than half of System holdings of government securities. The policy continued into 1939, although it was not necessary for the Fed to conduct purchases on a significant scale.

The importance of the flexible portfolio policy lay in the Fed's acknowledgment of responsibility for what it came to refer to as "orderly conditions in the government securities market." The phrase became commonplace in the resolutions of the FOMC starting in the spring of 1938. In effect, the Fed had assumed responsibility for preventing changes in bond prices that might endanger financial and economic stability. In addition, as a result of this experience, changes in reserve requirements had become one of the leading instruments of monetary control. They would be relied upon heavily in the 1940s.

5.2.2 Wartime Changes

In September 1938 a conference of presidents of Federal Reserve banks met to consider options for wartime policy. By 1939 a consensus had emerged that steps should be taken to stabilize the government securities market. There was a desire to avoid a problem that had plagued European finance during World War I—continually rising rates that induced investors to defer purchases of government securities in anticipation of still higher yields. In April and June the FOMC was authorized to buy government securities to prevent their prices from falling.

Following the outbreak of war in Europe on 1 September 1939, the System purchased $500 million of bonds in the open market.[6] No additional support by the Federal Reserve System was required, however. The outbreak of hostilities in Europe was not accompanied by a financial crisis comparable to the worldwide collapse of securities markets in 1914. The Munich crisis in 1938 provoked more of a security price decline in New York and London than did the outbreak of fighting in 1939. The advent of war came as no surprise. The autarchical policies of the 1930s were ideal precautions against the financial interconnections among belligerants that would have created a financial crisis.

The gross public debt of the United States increased by 33 per cent between 30 June 1939 and 30 November 1941 (Murphy 1950, 30). But the only instance in this period, other than September 1939, when the Fed was forced to purchase Treasury bonds was the spring of 1940, following the invasion of Norway, Denmark, and the Low Countries. Compared to European securities, U.S. Treasury bonds were regarded as safe and attractive assets. The trade balance moved into strong surplus and gold surged toward the United States, augmenting the liquidity of the market. Pearl Harbor, which augered budget deficits and inflation, transformed this situation. Securities prices fell, impelling the Fed to purchase $50 million of bonds and $10 million of bills. Within two weeks of the Japanese attack, Treasury and Federal Reserve officials had agreed to stabilize interest rates.

Though the Fed, compared to the Treasury, preferred higher interest rates, neither agency disputed the desirability of stabilization. Following negotiations, the Fed agreed in March 1942 to support Treasury bill prices once short-term rates reached ⅜ per cent. Reserve banks were ordered by the FOMC to purchase all Treasury bills offered them at this price.[7] No such formal instruction was issued regarding Treasury bonds, but it was understood that long rates would not be permitted to rise above 2½ per cent.[8] Wage and price controls were relied on to prevent the ready availability of credit from generating undue inflation.

A 2-percentage-point differential between short and long rates was almost exactly the differential established previously by the market. Treasury officials regarded it as a necessary premium to induce investors to hold long-term bonds. Pegging short rates at less than ½ per cent was essential, in their view, to prevent long rates from rising above 2½ per cent. What they neglected was the effect of intervention on portfolio preferences. As soon as the Fed's policy was regarded as credible and interest-rate risk vanished, investors came to regard Treasury bills and bonds as virtually perfect substitutes. Investors sold bills for higher yielding bonds, forcing the Fed to do the converse (as indicated by figs. 5.3 and 5.4). By the end of the war, the Federal Reserve System held virtually the entire supply of Treasury bills. Prior to the end of 1947, it held negligible amounts of bonds, though bond yields remained at their ceiling from 1942 until the beginning of 1945.

5.2.3 1945–1947: Inflation

The cap on long-term interest rates did not bind immediately after the war. Massive bond issues might have exhausted the Fed's willingness or ability to peg long-term rates. But with the end of fighting, fresh sales of government securities were almost immediately limited to funding operations. The Victory Loan issued in December 1945 virtually ended Treasury borrowing. The federal budget was balanced in 1946 and in strong surplus in 1947–48. With

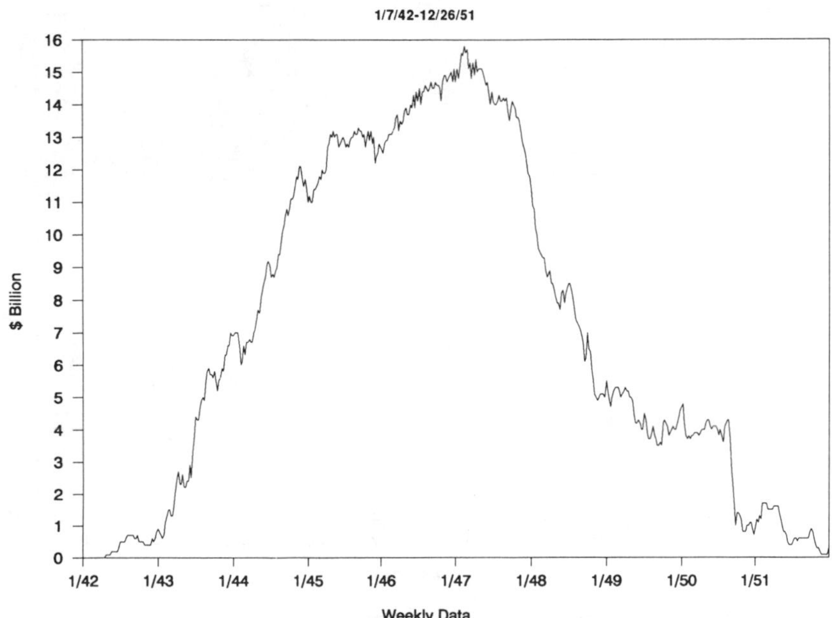

Fig. 5.3 Federal Reserve T-bill holdings

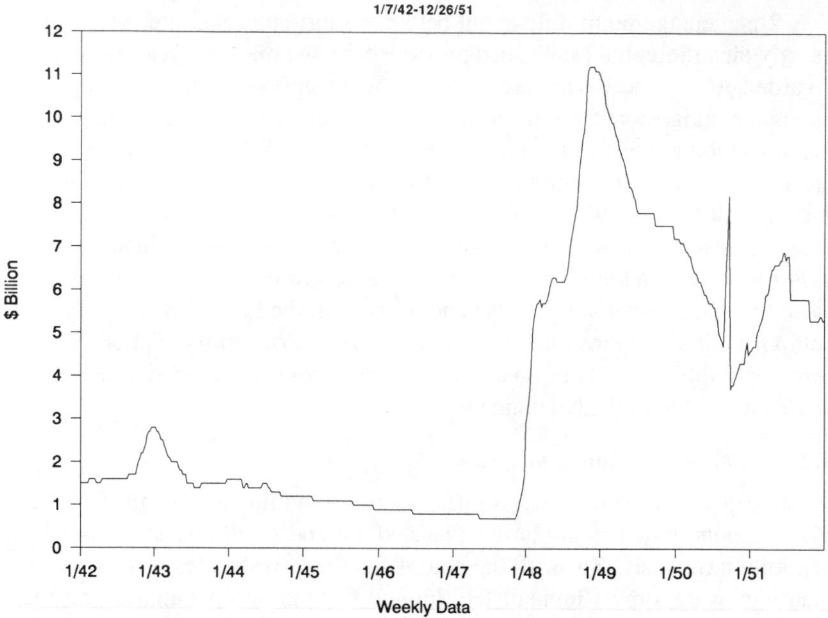

Fig. 5.4 Federal Reserve bond holdings

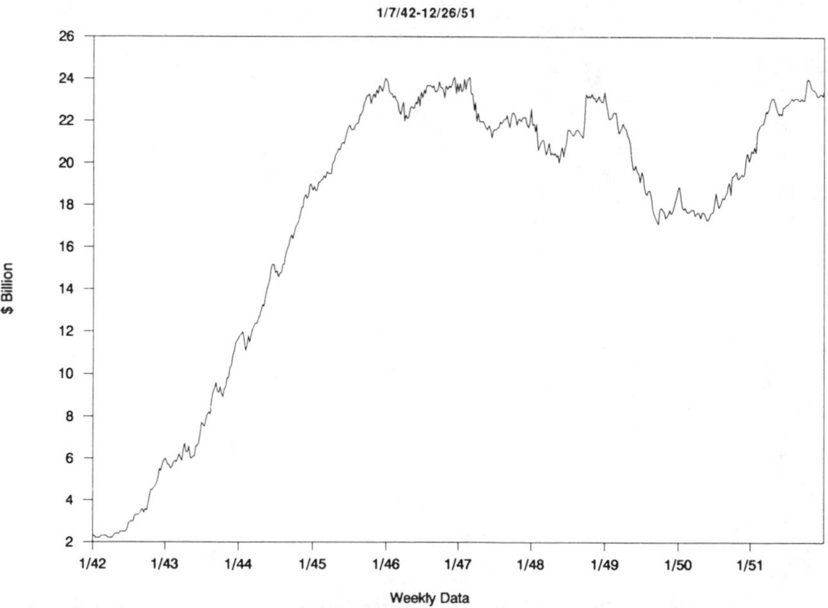

Fig. 5.5 Total Federal Reserve security holdings

the danger of capital losses removed, the two-point yield differential between short- and long-term bonds rendered the latter increasingly attractive. At the end of 1945 the yield on long-term government bonds was slightly more than 2.3 per cent. By the following April it had fallen to less than 2.1 per cent.

Starting in July 1946, the price level began to rise. The end of price control, in conjunction with European demands for American exports, pushed up U.S. wholesale prices by 25 per cent over the succeeding twelve months. In July of 1947, concern over inflation led the Fed, with the concurrence of the Treasury, to abolish the buying rate for Treasury bills. Bowing to Treasury pressure, it continued to support the rate on 9- to 12-month certificates at slightly more than ¾ per cent and bond yields at 2½ per cent. Later in the year, it gradually increased its buying rate for certificates to 1 per cent. Bill rates fluctuated below this level. (Fig. 5.1 plots these rate movements.)

Inflation moderated temporarily, stimulating the demand for government securities. It was mainly the demand for Treasury bills that rose. The gap between bond and bill rates was narrower than two years before, since the Fed no longer supported Treasury bill prices. In addition, since May the Treasury had sold $1.8 billion of bonds from its investment accounts. Treasury bond yields rose from 2.24 per cent in September to 2.39 per cent in December. The Fed was forced to intervene with $2 billion of bond purchases in November and December to limit the rise in yields (Chandler 1949, 12). It purchased an additional $3 billion of bonds in the first quarter of 1948. But the demand for Treasury bills was sufficiently strong that the Fed was able to reduce its overall portfolio of Treasury securities by $1 billion over the period (see figs. 5.3–5.5) (Friedman and Schwartz 1963, 580).

By the second quarter of 1948, inflation had again become the dominant fear. The Fed was forced to purchase bonds with cash. System holdings of Treasury securities (the sum of bonds, bills, and certificates) began to rise. The Treasury resisted any measure to increase short-term rates. Only in August 1948 did it finally accede to an increase in the 12-month rate to 1¼ per cent.

5.2.4 1948–1949: Deflation

Increasingly, price stability and the prevailing level of interest rates seemed at odds. Reserve requirements were raised in February and June to the legal maximum of 24 per cent. In August a special session of Congress called by President Truman to consider anti-inflation legislation passed a bill authorizing further increases in reserve requirements. The September increase in reserve requirements to 26 per cent led the banks to sell $2 billion of government bonds, which the Fed purchased, increasing the supply of high-powered money commensurately (Friedman and Schwartz 1963, 604–5).

The 1948–49 recession brought a fortuitous respite. Wholesale prices stopped rising in August 1948. Industrial production stopped rising in November. As the demand for commercial and mortgage loans softened, banks and insurance companies once again began to purchase Treasury bonds.

Monetary policymakers' dissatisfaction with interest-rate pegging was compounded by the perceived need to sell government bonds during the recession. The Fed had never formally committed itself to prevent interest rates from falling. Nonetheless, the System sold $3 billion of bonds in the first half of 1949, the majority in exchange for cash. The action was widely criticized for aggravating the recession.

This unsatisfactory experience led the Fed to affirm that its primary commitment was to price and income stability, not to the stability of interest rates. Thus, in the *Federal Reserve Bulletin* for July 1949, the FOMC announced its intention "to direct purchases, sales and exchange of Government securities by the Federal Reserve Banks with primary regard to the general business and credit situation" (776). The question was whether the Treasury would go along. This question acquired new urgency once industrial production began to recover in July 1949.

5.2.5 1950–1951: Inflation

Consumer prices resumed their rise in the second quarter of 1950. Long-term bond yields anticipated the trend, bottoming out at the end of 1949. The resurgence of inflationary pressure had an immediate impact on Federal Reserve operations. In the second quarter of 1950, Federal Reserve holdings of U.S. Treasury securities began to rise steadily. By June, fighting in Korea was underway. With market interest rates rising, System purchases of Treasury securities continued at an accelerating pace. The Federal Reserve Board and the FOMC continued to mouth their commitment to the maintenance of orderly conditions in the government securities market but also reaffirmed the priority attached to curbing inflation.[9] In private they pressed the Treasury for higher interest rates. Treasury Secretary John W. Snyder resisted; the Treasury's autumn refunding loan was issued at 1¼ per cent. The Federal Reserve System was forced to purchase the majority of it.

By this time the public had grown concerned over inflation. Congressional criticism of Treasury policy had become increasingly common. The Douglas Committee, which reported in January 1950, criticized the Treasury's insistence on pegging interest rates.[10] In February, Senator Paul H. Douglas made a famous speech critical of the Treasury. The specter of an inflationary crisis prompted a series of staff-level conferences between the Treasury and the Fed. On the last day of February, Secretary Snyder gave in. The Accord between the two organizations was couched in general terms: "The Treasury and the Federal Reserve system have reached full accord with respect to debt-management and monetary policies to be pursued in furthering their common purpose to assure the successful financing of the Government's requirements and, at the same time, to minimize monetization of the public debt."[11]

The exact provisions of the agreement between the Federal Reserve Board and the Treasury were never published. Its essence limited the Fed's commitment to support the 2½ per cent Treasury bonds to $400 million. Other government bond prices fell immediately. By March 13 the funds to support the 2½'s were exhausted, and for the first time their prices were permitted to fall below par. By the end of the year their yield had risen to 2¾ per cent.

5.2.6 Recapitulation

This review of events as they are portrayed in the literature brings out several important points. First, concern over the stability of the banking system figured in the Federal Reserve System's decision to intervene in the bond market at various junctures in the 1930s; this experience laid the groundwork for similar intervention in the 1940s. Second, changes in reserve requirements emerged as one of the principal instruments of monetary control in the 1930s; once again, as a result of this experience the instrument was relied upon heavily in the 1940s. Third, and most importantly from our perspective, the existing literature does not provide a systematic analysis of the policy regime that rendered the Fed's program of bond-market intervention sustainable; it is unclear why investors willingly held Treasury securities at such low interest rates in the 1940s or why this willingness apparently evaporated at the decade's end.

5.3 The Analytical Framework

One way to appreciate the problem this poses for analysis is in terms of the implications of conventional models of interest-rate pegging. Assume that the Fed simply commits to pegging nominal rates at a certain level. Assume next that the rate demanded by investors rises relative to the rate maintained by the Fed. Since bonds are yielding less than the required rate, investors begin to sell them off. The Fed is forced to purchase them for cash. The increase in money supply fuels inflation which places additional upward pressure on nominal interest rates, leading to more bond sales, more monetary expansion, and an explosive inflationary spiral. Analogously, if market rates fall relative to the interest-rate peg, investors purchase bonds from the Fed. This reduces the money supply, creates expectations of deflation, lowers nominal rates, and provokes additional bond purchases, in an implosive spiral. Again, there is nothing to stabilize the financial system until the authorities have sold off their entire bond portfolio and abandoned their interest-rate pegging policy.

The conventional framework suggests that an interest-rate pegging policy will be highly unstable, not remarkably stable, as was the case from 1946 to 1950. Clearly, an alternative framework is required. The framework we propose builds on a previous analysis of the period by Friedman and Schwartz (1963). When describing the Treasury-Fed bond-price support program of 1945–51, Friedman and Schwartz asked why the public did not attack the scheme in 1947–48, when inflation was relatively high, by reducing its holdings of liquid balances, but did attack in similar circumstances in 1951. They emphasized price expectations as the crucial factor supporting the Fed's ability to maintain the program.

> That factor was a continued fear of a major contraction and a continued belief that prices were destined to fall. A rise in prices can have diametrically opposite effects on desired money balances depending on its effect on expectations. If it is interpreted as a harbinger of further rises, it raises the anticipated cost of holding money and leads people to desire lower balances relative to income than they otherwise would. In our view, that was the effect of price rises in 1950. . . . On the other hand, if a rise in prices is interpreted as a temporary rise due to be reversed, as a harbinger of a likely subsequent decline, it lowers the anticipated cost of holding money and leads people to desire higher balances relative to income than they otherwise would. In our view, that was the effect of price rises in 1946 to 1948. . . .
>
> Despite the extent to which the public and government were exercised about inflation, the public acted from 1946 to 1948 as if it expected deflation. There is no real conflict. The major source of concern about inflation at that time was not the evils of inflation per se . . . but the widespread belief that what goes up must come down and that the higher the price rise now the larger the subsequent price fall. In our view, this fear or expectation of subsequent contraction and price decline reconciled the public to only a mild reduction in its liquid asset holdings relative to its income and induced it to hold larger real money balances than it otherwise would have been willing to. In this way, it made the postwar rise more moderate. (1963, 583–84)

We can formalize Friedman and Schwartz's account by applying recent research from the exchange rate target-zone literature.[12] A simple amendment to these models converts them into a model of a price-level target zone. Thus, we interpret Friedman and Schwartz's description of the situation in 1948 in terms of an implicit target-zone model.

Imagine that forces in the economy placed upward pressure on the price level. Below the upper bound of the target zone, prices would be allowed to rise. But once the upper bound of the zone was reached, a change in either underlying real variables or policy would reverse the movement in prices. We focus on the case in which reaching the upper bound triggers intervention by the Fed. Given this policy regime, it was rational to anticipate deflation in the midst of rapid inflation. Similarly, there might be a lower bound on the price level which would prompt intervention as it was approached. This regime decouples inflation from inflationary expectations and nominal interest rates, reconciling a volatile inflation rate with stable bond yields.

5.3.1 The Basic Framework

This target-zone interpretation can be formalized using a straightforward monetary model of the price level. We take real variables as exogenous and concentrate on the relation between money and prices.[13] The central relationship is the standard money equilibrium equation:

$$m - p = ay - b(r + Edp/dt)$$

or

$$p = k + bEdp/dt$$

where $k = m - ay + br$.

The variables m, p, and y represent the logarithms of the money stock, the price level, and real income, respectively; r is the real interest rate; Edp/dt is the expected *change* in p; a and b are parameters.

The problem is to determine the price level. Since real income and the real interest rate are determined in the real economy alone and the money supply is determined by policy, k is a forcing variable. The variable k may be controlled by intervention either at the boundaries or, more generally, inside the boundaries of the target zone whose upper bound is p^u and whose lower bound is p^l. In general, while the price level remains inside the target zone, the variables m, y, and r can evolve randomly with no control exerted over the price level. Once k reaches some critical value, however, it is controlled through monetary intervention. At this moment, changes in the money supply are directed at maintaining the price-level zone.

We assume for simplicity that only the real interest rate r drives k inside the boundary, and that r is a Brownian motion process with no drift.[14] Formally,

$$dr = sdz$$

where z is a Brownian motion process and s is the standard deviation of dr.

This scenario is exactly that developed in Krugman's (1989) study of the collapse of an exchange-rate target zone defended with a limited amount of reserves. The process of collapse, which we study below, is also the same as in Krugman.

If p rises toward its maximum p^u because the real interest rate rises, an intervention involving a decline in the money supply will occur. The decline might be infinitesimal, aimed at offsetting infinitesimal increases in r. Alternatively, the decline in money supply may be discrete and large. If the price level tends to its minimum value p^l because the real interest rate is falling, the intervention would entail an increase in money supply.

Given these assumptions, it is standard to write the solution for the price level as a nonlinear function of the forcing variable r. Since a large literature now exists which presents this solution, we do not develop it here. We simply depict it in figure 5.6. The figure applies to a broad range of intervention policies. For a given money supply, curve 1 represents the price level as a function of r, and r is permitted to reach an upper bound r^u before intervention

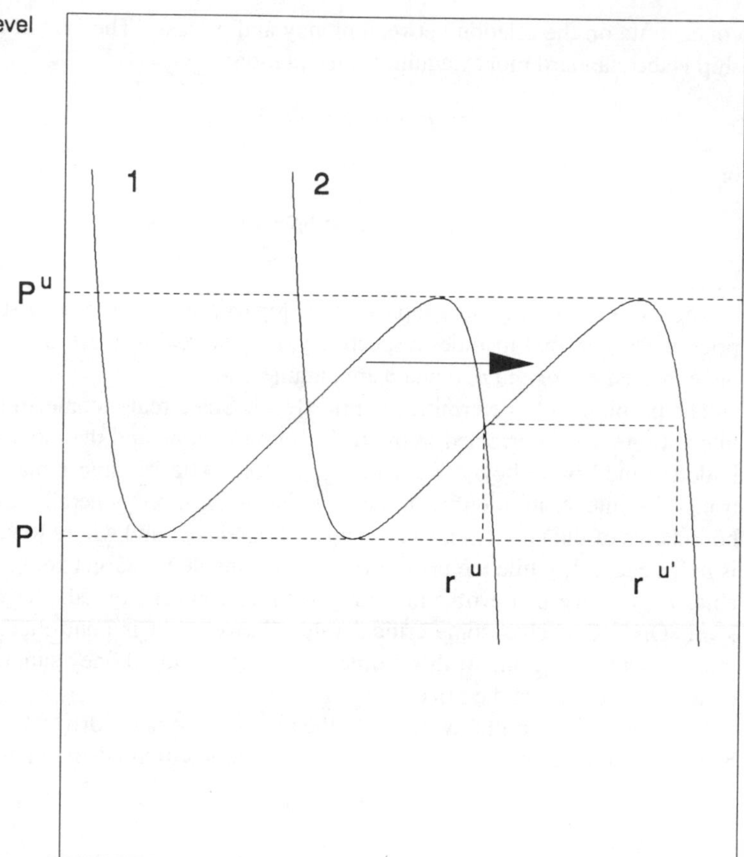

Fig. 5.6 Price-level zone

aimed at maintaining the zone occurs. Thus, as r rises, the price level rises and then falls before intervention occurs. Intervention in this case involves reducing the money supply discretely. Since this is a credible policy, intervention comes as no surprise; there is no jump in the price level at the moment it occurs. Since r is exogenous, it does not change from r^u as a result of the intervention. The monetary contraction has the effect of shifting the price-level function rightward from the curve labelled 1 to the curve labelled 2. The shift occurs by an amount which maintains price-level continuity when the new solution is evaluated at r^u. If r again moves up to $r^{u\prime}$, then another contractionary intervention occurs and the process repeats.

Alternatively, the intervention may be infinitesimal. Such an intervention can be depicted in figure 5.6 by setting r^u equal to r^{max}, the argument at which the price-level function represented by curve 1 is flat. Repeated infinitesimal interventions then slide the solution curve continuously rightward in the zone.

5.3.2 A Range on Nominal Interest Rates

As developed so far, the size of the intervention is arbitrary. Associated with any specified zone on the price level, however, is a range of nominal interest rates that depends on the size of interventions. If an additional limit is placed on the range of the instantaneous interest rate, the intervention rule becomes uniquc.

The expected inflation rate can be depicted in figure 5.7 as a function of *r*. The expected inflation rate associated with the price-level zone is a monoton-

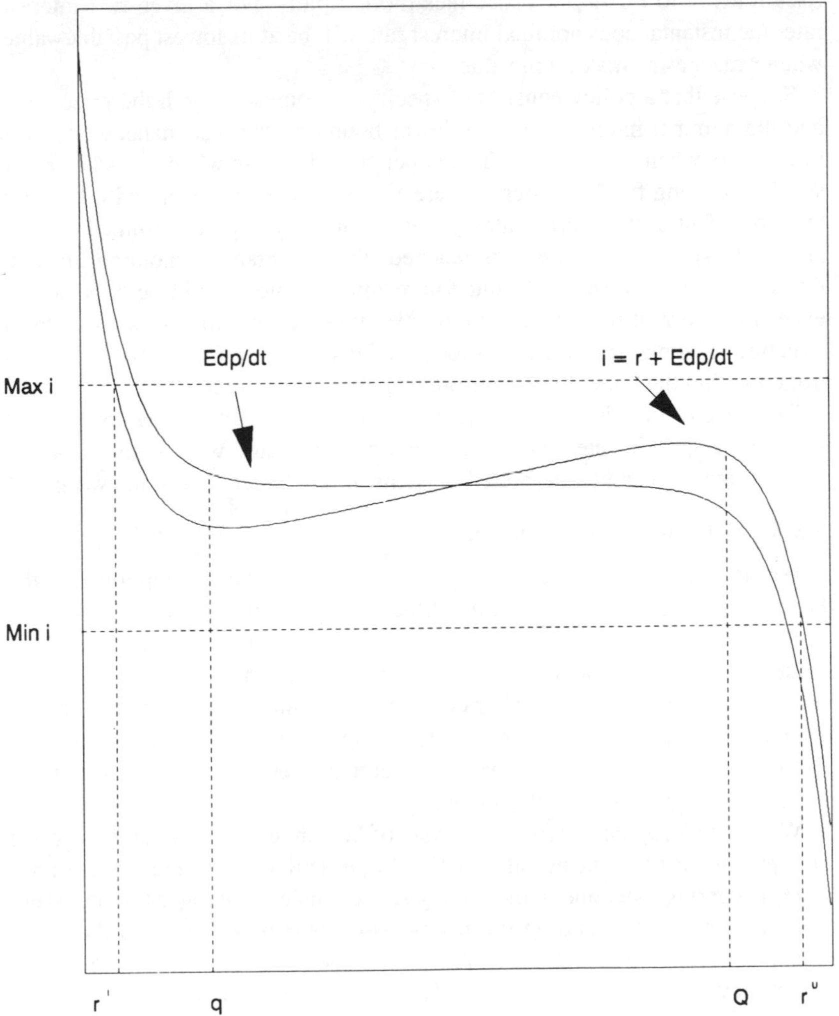

Fig. 5.7 Nominal interest rates and expected inflation rates

ically decreasing function of r, flat in the middle range of r but highly nonlinear near the intervention trigger points. When r approaches its maximum level, a situation which would normally be associated with rising price levels, expected inflation is in fact at its lowest negative value. This is because, as r rises, intervention to reverse the movement of the price level becomes increasingly likely.

From the Fisher equation, the instantaneous nominal interest rate is:

$$i = r + Edp \,/\, dt$$

The nominal interest rate as a function of r also appears in figure 5.7. As r rises linearly to r^u, $Edp \,/\, dt$ declines more rapidly. For a given real interest rate, the instantaneous nominal interest rate will be at its lowest possible value when r reaches its maximum value.

Suppose that a policy consists of specifying bounds on both the price level and the nominal interest rate. The lower bound on the instantaneous interest rate occurs when r reaches r^u. The upper bound occurs when r reaches r^l. A specified ceiling for longer-term interest rates can be consistent with limiting the movement of the shorter rates. Again, that range is predetermined once r^u and r^l are specified. When r^u is reached, the instantaneous nominal interest rate reaches its lowest level, and future interest rates would be expected to exceed the current instantaneous rate. We would expect to have a rising term structure. If longer rates are an average of instantaneous rates, they are controlled within the upper and lower bounds given in figure 5.7.

Thus, we can model interest rate policy prior to 1951 as a price-level target zone and a specific intervention rule. Events associated with maintaining the interest rate cap can be interpreted in terms of this target-zone framework.[15]

5.3.3 Collapse of the Target Zone

We have based our discussion of this regime on the assumption that the Federal Reserve is willing to contract the money supply to whatever extent is necessary to maintain the zone. We now presume that there is some minimum value of the nominal money stock below which the Fed is unwilling to go. As the real interest rate rises, further contractionary interventions are required to maintain the target zone. As these interventions cumulate, the money supply declines toward its minimum value. Eventually, everyone realizes that the target-zone regime will be abandoned.

We utilize Krugman's (1989) analysis of how an exchange-rate target zone collapses to describe the events of 1951. Suppose that, as in figure 5.8, r rises to r^u, triggering a decline in the money stock. Since r is exogenous, intervention has the effect of sliding the price-level function rightward in the zone. This is depicted in figure 5.8 as a shift from curve 1 to curve 2. If the intervention policy is maintained, there is a shift in the upper bound on r at which the intervention is triggered, from r^u to $r^{u\prime}$. Without a lower bound on the money stock, this process can continue indefinitely.

Imagine, however, that there exists such a lower bound. Suppose that when

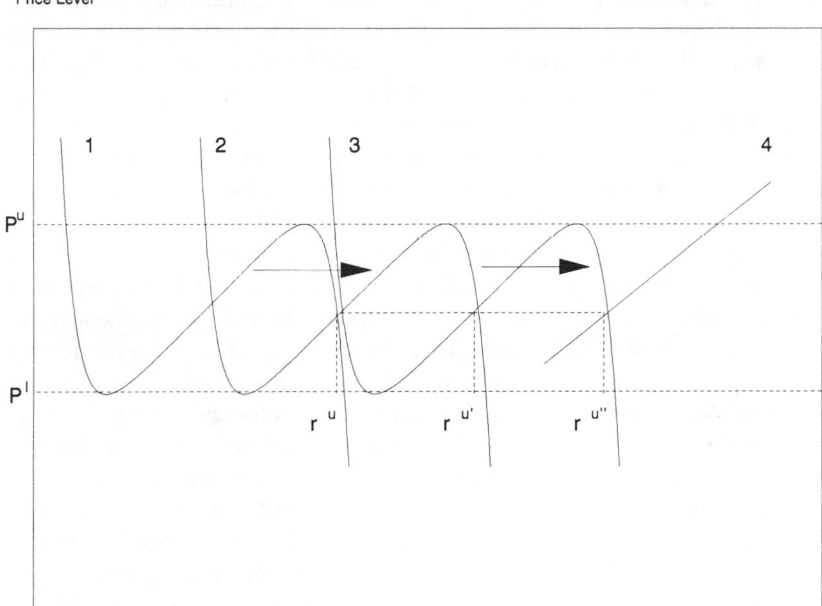

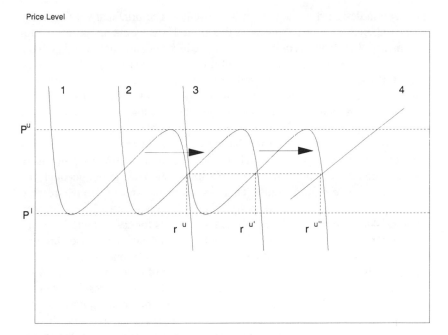

Fig. 5.8 Collapsing price-level zone

r reaches $r^{u'}$, the money stock has declined to such a level that one more intervention will push it exactly to its lower bound. The intervention policy is still credible for one last time, so the price level will move along the new target-zone solution path indicated by curve 3. If r continues to rise to $r^{u''}$, intervention will occur as promised but thereafter further intervention is no longer credible. The price-level solution will follow curve 4, the usual linear function of fundamentals. Note that price-level continuity will be maintained at $r^{u''}$, the real interest rate associated with the regime shift.

We can use this framework to explain the termination of interest rate pegging in 1951. The outbreak of the Korean War drove real interest rates upward, requiring monetary contraction to maintain the price-level zone. The 1949 contraction had already pushed the system toward its limit. Moreover, the perceived costs of further monetary contraction had risen in 1951, given the need to mobilize resources for the Korean War. Thus, the target-zone regime was abandoned, leading to negotiation of the Accord.

5.4 Applying the Target-Zone Framework

Our target-zone framework can be used to analyze the evolution of U.S. monetary-financial policy between 1946 and 1950 and to understand the coming of the Accord in 1951.

Given the focus of the theoretical model, we emphasize Federal Reserve intervention designed to alter the money supply. The principal way in which the Fed altered the money supply in this period was by changing reserve requirements. Increasing required reserves reduced loans, among other bank investments, lowering the money multiplier. From February 1948 through August 1949, however, the required reserve ratio was changed five times. It was altered again at the end of 1950 and the beginning of 1951. This reliance on changes in reserve requirements can be seen as a logical outgrowth of the policy developed in the 1930s in response to the problem of excess reserves.[16]

This is a change in focus from the conventional literature, which emphasizes bond-market intervention. There the Fed is described as purchasing bonds to limit the rise in yields when inflation accelerates. In our account, the Fed raises reserve requirements. There is no inconsistency. Higher reserve requirements induced the banks to sell bonds along with other investments in order to acquire reserves. The Fed purchased bonds for cash which the banks used as the basis for reserves.[17] Although the monetary base rose, broader measures, such as M1, declined owing to the fall in the money multiplier.

We can use this approach to describe the course of events starting in 1946, when serious inflation pressures first surfaced.[18] These pressures reflected the interplay of several factors. First, the failure of the anticipated postwar recession to materialize can be interpreted as a rise in the real interest rate. Investment demand remained strong throughout 1946. Managers attempted to add to capacity, given the exceptional buoyancy of sales. Automobiles, meat, and other consumer goods in short supply were rationed by higher real interest rates which encouraged consumers to defer expenditure (Fforde 1954, 150). Higher real interest rates reduced the demand for money and placed upward pressure on prices. Second, the supply of money expanded steadily during 1946. This reflected gold inflows and the rapid growth of virtually all categories of bank loans. (Both gold inflows and changes in the lending behavior of the banks are exogenous to our model.) Third, the Treasury retired a considerable quantity of debt over the course of the year (see fig. 5.9). This decline in private financial wealth can be thought of as reducing the demand for money, with further inflationary effects.[19]

Though concern over inflation mounted over the course of the year, it never reached the point where the Fed felt compelled to intervene. Investors apparently anticipated a deflation like that which had followed World War I; they did not question the Fed's ability to maintain the current low level of nominal short-term rates. As Goldenweiser characterizes the year, "Federal Reserve policy was essentially static with little done to counteract inflationary forces and little occasion to support the government security market" (1951, 199). In other words, prices had not yet risen to the point where they threatened to violate the upper bound of the implicit price-level target zone.

Worries mounted in 1947, however, as prices continued to rise. Various measures were proposed to restrain inflation. In the autumn, President Truman sent Congress a special message requesting the reimposition of price and wage

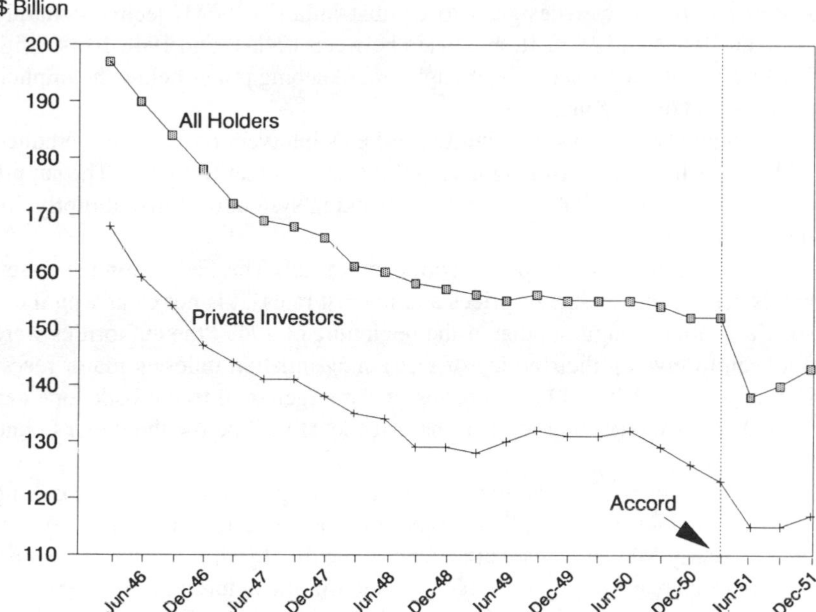

Fig. 5.9 Ownership of U.S. Government marketable securities, 1946–51
Source: Banking and Monetary Statistics (1971, 884, 887)

controls. Marriner Eccles, now chairman of the Federal Reserve Board, proposed a Special Reserves Plan that would have required commercial banks, members and nonmembers alike, to hold large new secondary reserves of Treasury bills.[20] Neither program was adopted. Congress found Truman's controls unpalatable. Others within the Fed, such as Allan Sproul, president of the Federal Reserve Bank of New York, thought that Eccles's plan to discourage bank lending risked initiating a recession.[21] As in the previous year, there was little Fed intervention. According to Goldenweiser, "the Federal Reserve was still acting with great moderation" (1951, 199). Again, the implication was that the price level did not yet threaten to breach the upper bound of the zone.

Nineteen hundred forty-eight provided the first test of the Fed's commitment to limiting the level of prices (Karunatilake 1963, 108). Continued inflation provoked criticism of policy both within and outside the Federal Reserve System.[22] The Fed then reduced the money supply by raising reserve requirements. In January, reserve requirements for banks in central-reserve cities were raised from 20 to 22 per cent of net demand deposits. Toward the middle of the year they were raised to 24 per cent. In August the Board was given permission by Congress to raise reserve requirements still further, which it did in September. Its press releases declared that, as on the previous two occasions, the change was designed to combat inflation.[23] M1 declined sharply between 1948-I and 1948-II, and again between 1948-II and 1948-III (see fig. 5.10). This intervention can be thought of as keeping prices below the implicit upper bound of the zone.

The tightness of money owing to the Fed's intervention is widely credited with provoking or at least magnifying the recession that followed. The supply of liquidity made available through the banking system declined abruptly. Inflationary pressure subsided.

Through most of 1949, prices continued to fall. The Fed continued to sell bonds despite the decline of prices and interest rates. It is not clear why it did so. Karunatilake suggests that at the beginning of 1949 "the authorities were not keen to give up their policy of restraining inflation unless a major recession occurred" (1963, 111). In terms of the target-zone framework, one can view them as intervening to push the price level well below the upper bound of the zone.

Eventually the Fed began to intervene as if the price level was approaching the lower bound of its implicit target zone. Reserve requirements were reduced in early May and again at the end of the fiscal year when the temporary powers to increase required reserves granted in the autumn of 1948 expired. Margin requirements on security loans were reduced to 50 per cent and consumer credit regulation was relaxed. These initiatives stabilized M1 despite

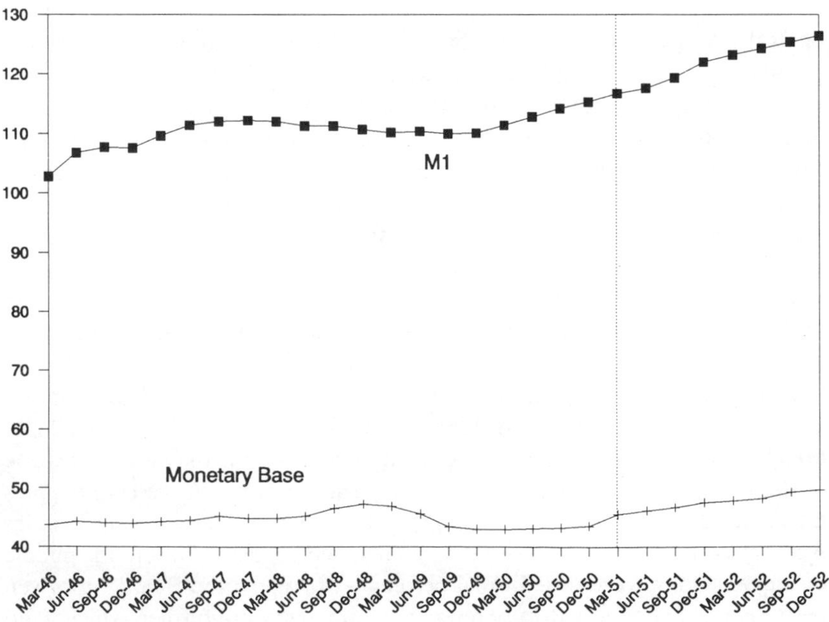

Fig. 5.10 M1 and monetary base

the continued decline of the monetary base. By the final quarter of 1949, M1 had once again begun to rise. (Again, see fig. 5.10.)

M1 rose steadily through 1950 and into early 1951 as commercial banks expanded their loan portfolios. Growing government budget deficits associated with the approach of the Korean War then began putting upward pressure on real interest rates. Markets were characterized by "a boom psychology which was unsurpassed since the end of the war in 1945" (Karunatilake 1963, 117). It became obvious that military expenditures would increase, and a wave of precautionary buying ensued in anticipation of shortages of consumer goods. As James Tobin remarked, "To a nation so recently schooled in the economics of war, Korea foretold both inflation and the eventual rationing, official or unofficial, of civilian goods" (1951, 197). All this implies rising real interest rates. As the demand for money fell, the consumer price index began to rise more rapidly than it had at any time since the end of 1947.

The Fed affirmed its support for "the Government decision to rely in major degree for the immediate future upon fiscal and credit measures to curb inflation."[24] It took steps to limit the rise in prices. It joined with other federal and state supervisory agencies, such as the Home Loan Bank Board, issuing a statement requesting banks to restrict their lending activities. In September it again placed restrictions on consumer installment credit. Finally, after some hesitation, it raised reserve requirements to 24 per cent. Once again the banks obtained the additional reserves by selling $2 billion of government securities, most of which the System purchased.

Owing in part to this hesitancy, doubts arose about the Fed's commitment to maintain the price level within an implicit zone. Previously, when prices had risen, the market was dominated by expectations that the Fed would adopt measures to reduce them. These expectations of deflation, or at least of price stability, stabilized nominal interest rates. Now there was the fear that the imperative of mobilizing resources for the Korean War would preclude deflationary initiatives. "On balance, the scale is tipped heavily toward continued rapid inflation," commented *Business Week* in the first week of 1951 (6 January 1951, 28). Interest rates rose with inflationary expectations. The cap on interest rates was rendered inconsistent with foreign policy imperatives and their fiscal implications. Hence the negotiation of the Accord in 1951, which allowed the Fed to drop its interest-rate target.

5.5 Why Was the Fed Committed to a Price-Level Target Zone?

At the core of our analysis is the notion that the Fed was committed to limiting variations in the price level and, by preventing the emergence of persistent inflation, to stabilizing interest rates. But why should the Fed have been more concerned about price and interest-rate stability in the aftermath of World War II than in other periods?

A common answer, advanced at the time, was that the Federal Reserve System was forced by the Treasury to pursue policies consistent with low interest rates to minimize debt-service costs. This accusation was vehemently denied by System officials. They repeatedly asserted that they themselves were strong supporters of the policy of stabilizing prices and interest rates.[25]

An alternative explanation is that the monetary authorities feared that a rise in interest rates would cause capital losses on commercial bank bond portfolios, undermining the stability of the banking system. System officials recalled the drastic decline of bond prices in 1920 and the difficulties this had created for the banks. They recalled also the deterioration of bond portfolios, especially those heavily weighted toward low-grade issues, in the 1930s, and their contribution to the 1930, 1931, and 1933 banking crises. They envisaged a crisis scenario in which a sudden rise in rates and decline in bond prices would lead panicky investors to throw their holdings on the market.[26] As the point was put in the Board of Governors' *Annual Report* for 1945:

> A major consequence [of] increasing the general level of interest rates would be a fall in the market values of outstanding Government securities. These price declines would create difficult market problems for the Treasury in refunding its maturing and called securities. If the price declines were sharp they could have highly unfavorable repercussions on the functioning of financial institutions and if carried far enough might even weaken public confidence in such institutions.[27]

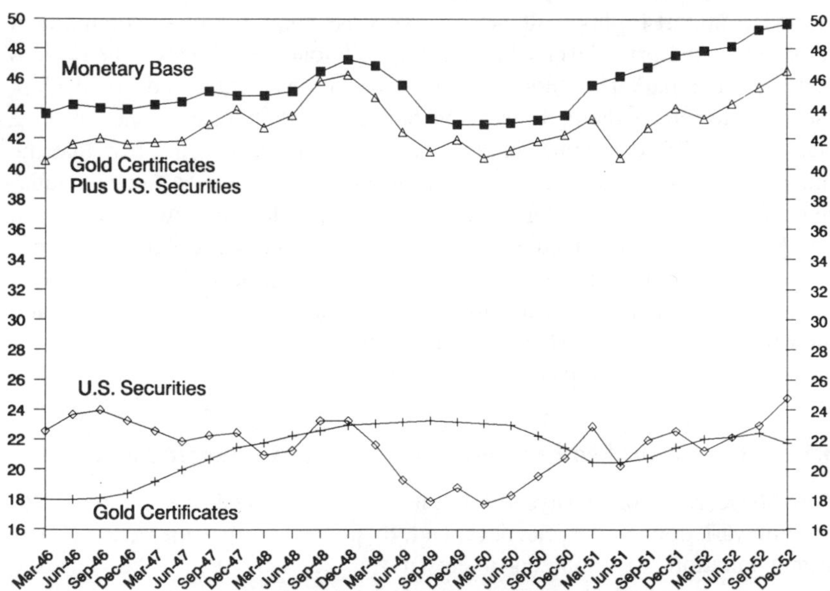

Fig. 5.11 Monetary base and Federal Reserve assets (in $billion)

Or, as Whittlesey put the point, "The Reserve authorities would hardly dare to sell heavily in the open market or force up interest rates, for fear of depressing securities of the types held by member banks to such an extent as either to weaken the banks or to create undue alarm" (1946, 343–44).[28] Others warned against even moderate sales: "The impact effects of a falling bond market . . . could well be dangerous. Even a moderate fall would be unsettling to banks and might set off disorderly selling" (Seltzer 1945, 73).

Concern over capital losses on bond portfolios was no new phenomenon. The Fed had invoked this concern to help justify its bond-market intervention in the 1930s. But the banking system had grown increasingly vulnerable to declining bond prices as a result of its massive investments in government securities over the course of World War II. Moral suasion had been used to induce the banks to absorb debt issued during the war, while wartime disruptions had limited the scope for alternative investments. On 30 June 1945, the banks' government securities holdings came to $82 billion, of which $27.7 billion consisted of maturities of over five years (see table 5.1 for end-year figures). Bank capital was only $8.6 billion. Thus, even a relatively small rise in interest rates could wipe out the banks' capital funds.

Table 5.1 shows bank holdings of government securities at the end of each year between 1945 and 1950. It is evident that the banks reduced their vulnerability to this source of interest-rate risk as the period progressed. The value of insured commercial bank holdings of Treasury securities fell absolutely, from nearly $90 billion at the end of 1945 to little more than $60 billion at the end of 1950, and even more dramatically as a share of bank capital, which had risen to $11.4 billion by the middle of the latter year.[29] This is likely to have reduced the weight the Fed and other bank regulators attached to stable long-term rates.

The question is by how much this risk had been reduced. Table 5.2 reports the market value of bank Treasury security portfolios (net of bills maturing in fewer than twelve months) as a share of two measures of bank capital, both their actual value and under the counterfactual that Treasury security yields at each date doubled relative to their historical values.[30] The comparison over time confirms that the impact of higher interest rates on the value of bond portfolios declined quite significantly. At the end of 1945 a doubling of yields would have led to the loss of nearly 60 per cent of total capital; by the end of 1951 the comparable figure had declined to 30 per cent. (When a narrower measure of bank capital, total stocks, is considered, the comparable figures are 172 and 98 per cent, respectively.) Thus, it was logical that with the passage of time the Fed should have attached less weight to this concern. The calculations also suggest that fears that higher interest rates would leave the banks insolvent were somewhat exaggerated. Many of the long-term bonds held by the banks had been acquired in the 1930s or at the beginning of the 1940s and were approaching maturity. A doubling of yields would nearly

Table 5.1 **Maturities of U.S. Government Obligations Held by Insured Commercial Banks, 1945–1951**

		Direct Marketable Issues								
					Bonds Maturing in:[b]					
December 31	Total	Bills[a]	Certificates[a]	Notes[a]	5 years or less	5–10 years	10–20 years	Over 20 years	Guaranteed Marketable Issues	Nonmarketable Issues[c]
Panel A: Amount (in millions)										
1951	$60,599	$7,223	$ 7,536	$11,274	$19,645	$ 7,024	$3,055	$2,335	$21	$2,486
1950	61,047	4,122	1,937	16,774	22,594	7,737	2,987	2,554	11	2,331
1949	65,847	3,692	12,488	5,812	27,278	7,692	4,461	2,409	6	2,009
1948	61,407	2,822	10,068	3,395	19,374	15,114	6,581	2,059	8	1,986
1947	67,960	2,124	7,555	5,920	18,341	22,202	7,534	2,654	14	1,616
1946	78,575	1,272	12,293	6,781	12,728	29,700	6,597	3,008	15	1,181
1945	88,933	2,456	19,075	16,047	9,030	32,230	6,092	2,787	22	1,194
Panel B: Percentage Distribution										
1951	100.0%	11.9%	12.4%	18.6%	32.4%	11.6%	5.1%	3.9%	<.05%	4.1%
1950	100.0	6.7	3.2	27.5	37.0	12.7	4.9	4.2	<.05	3.8
1949	100.0	5.6	19.0	8.8	41.4	11.7	6.8	3.6	<.05	3.1
1948	100.0	4.6	16.4	5.5	31.6	24.6	10.7	3.4	<.05	3.2
1947	100.0	3.1	11.1	8.7	27.0	32.7	11.1	3.9	<.05	2.4
1946	100.0	1.7	16.7	9.2	17.8	40.4	9.0	4.1	<.05	1.6
1945	100.0	2.8	21.5	18.0	10.2	36.2	6.9	3.1	<.05	1.3

Source: Annual Report of the FDIC (1951, 6).

[a]Treasury bills are generally issued with maturities of 91 days; certificates of indebtedness have maturities of approximately 1 year; and Treasury notes are issued with maturities of from 1 to 5 years.

[b]Based upon number of years to final maturity.

[c]U.S. savings bonds, Treasury bonds (investment series A-1965), and depositary bonds. Prior to 31 December 1947, this item included U.S. savings bonds only. Depositary bonds were included with other U.S. bonds according to maturity.

Table 5.2 **Value of Public Marketable Securities of at Least One Year to Maturity as a Ratio of Bank Capital, 1945–1951: Actual and Counterfactual Values**

	Actual Market Value		Counterfactual Market Value	
End of:	Share of Total Capital	Share of Total Stocks	Share of Total Capital	Share of Total Stocks
1945	10.71	31.34	10.12	29.61
1946	8.47	24.46	7.83	23.53
1947	6.99	21.66	6.46	20.04
1948	5.84	18.48	5.46	17.28
1949	6.15	19.55	5.84	18.56
1950	5.25	17.00	4.91	15.91
1951	4.53	14.74	4.22	13.73

Source: Authors' calculations based on data drawn from *Treasury Bulletin* (various issues) and *Annual Reports* of the Federal Deposit Insurance Corporation (various issues).
Notes: Not including Canal bonds and other issues for which no maturity/coupon information was available. Valuations are based on the assumption that calls are exercised on the first eligible date. Total stocks are the sum of common and preferred issues. Total capital is the sum of total stocks, surplus, reserves for contingencies, and undistributed profits. A figure of 10.71, for example, means that the market value of bonds was slightly more than ten times the value of capital.

halve the value of a portfolio of bonds running many years to maturity; compared to this, the effects shown in table 5.2 are relatively modest.

Though by 1951 the banking system's vulnerability to capital losses had been considerably attenuated, it is an indication of the depth of the authorities' concern that, at the time of the Accord, steps were taken to minimize the extent of such losses. Following the Accord, bond yields immediately rose above 2.5 per cent. The Treasury stepped into the breach; through a bond conversion, it absorbed part of the losses that would have accrued to bondholders.

The Treasury offered the conversion to holders of the various issues of long-term bonds marketed in 1945. The conversion offer did not apply to all long-term bonds, though $19 billion in such bonds were eligible. Marketable long-term bonds could be exchanged at par for nonmarketable Treasury bonds with 2.75 per cent yields. This was a 29-year bond callable in 24 years, so its maturity approximately matched those of the bonds to be converted. Since the bond was nonmarketable, some loss in liquidity offset the capital gain associated with the higher yield. Since the new bonds would be removed from the markets, the maximum potential magnitude of any future intervention by the Fed aimed at stabilizing long-term yields was therefore reduced. The new bond, however, was convertible on demand of the holder into a marketable five-year note paying a yield of 1.5 per cent. This would tend to protect the holder against large rises in bond yields during the life of the bond and minimize the value loss arising from its lack of liquidity.

The bond conversion proceeded as of 1 April 1951, as announced in prior Treasury circulars. Since bond yields rose to the range of 2.75 per cent, bondholders did manage to avoid capital losses. The Treasury absorbed the loss rather than the Fed. Supposing that the holders avoided the entire capital loss of 9 per cent, the Treasury must have absorbed a $1.2 billion loss to keep its creditors whole.[31]

Commercial banks were permitted to convert only one of the bond issues covered by the conversion and only if they had acquired these bonds on original issue or held them in trading accounts.[32] Otherwise, banks could not engage in this transaction. Of course, since they could market their bonds to insurance companies, banks could capture any positive value of the conversion offer.

The transaction was also aimed at insurance companies. Its magnitude is indicated in figure 5.12, which shows a fall in the amount of marketable Treasury bonds, from March to April 1951, of $13.6 billion (from $43.6 billion to $30 billion). Of course, this decline was offset by an increase in nonmarketable debt in that same period, of $13.5 billion of new convertible bonds.[33]

Insurance company holdings of long bonds dropped from March to June 1951, from $11.2 billion to $7.3 billion. Unspecified other private investors reduced their holdings from $13.8 billion to $10.5 billion. U.S. government agencies and trust funds reduced their holdings from $5.5 billion to $2.6 billion. Federal Reserve banks, which had been cumulating these long-term bonds, reduced their holdings from $3.5 billion to $1.4 billion.

5.6 Conclusions

In this paper we have analyzed U.S. monetary-financial policy in the turbulent aftermath of World War II. We have shown that the juxtaposition of periods of rapid inflation and deflation with stable nominal interest rates can be understood as a corollary of the Fed's implicit policy of maintaining a price-level target zone. Because the credible price-level target-zone regime decoupled inflation from inflationary expectations, interest rates were stabilized.

A deeper question is why the Fed adhered to this target-zone regime for prices and interest rates immediately after World War II but not in other periods. The explanation, we argue, lies in policymakers' perceptions of the threats to financial stability. In the aftermath of World War II, higher interest rates were perceived to pose a threat to the stability of the banking system. Only when the banks' exposure to bond-market risk had been reduced in the 1950s was policy reoriented to other targets. Our analysis of bank portfolios suggests that fears for the stability of the banking system may have been overdrawn. But it remains true that concern over financial stability, which originated in memories of widespread bank failures in the 1930s, provides the explanation for the singular policies pursued in the aftermath of World War II.

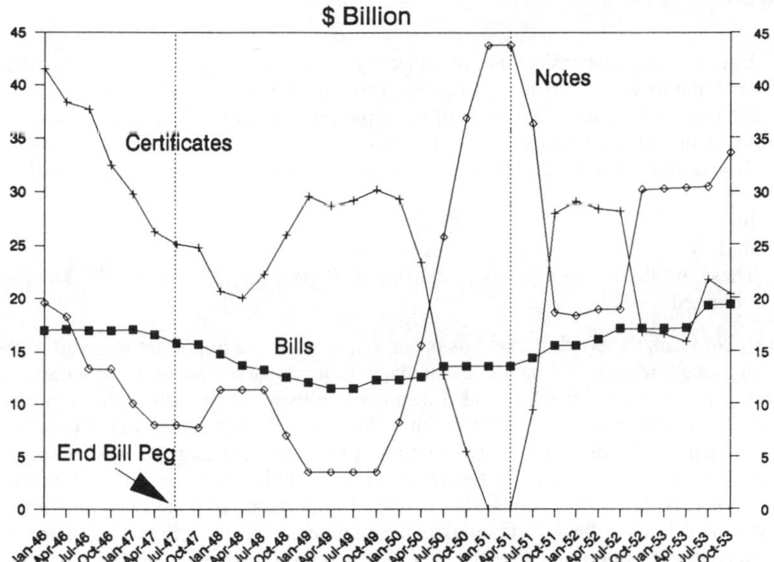
Treasury Bills, Certificates and Notes Outstanding
$ Billion
Notes
Certificates
Bills
End Bill Peg
0
5
10
15
20
25
30
35
40
45
Jan-46
Apr-46
Jul-46
Oct-46
Jan-47
Apr-47
Jul-47
Oct-47
Jan-48
Apr-48
Jul-48
Oct-48
Jan-49
Apr-49
Jul-49
Oct-49
Jan-50
Apr-50
Jul-50
Oct-50
Jan-51
Apr-51
Jul-51
Oct-51
Jan-52
Apr-52
Jul-52
Oct-52
Jan-53
Apr-53
Jul-53
Oct-53

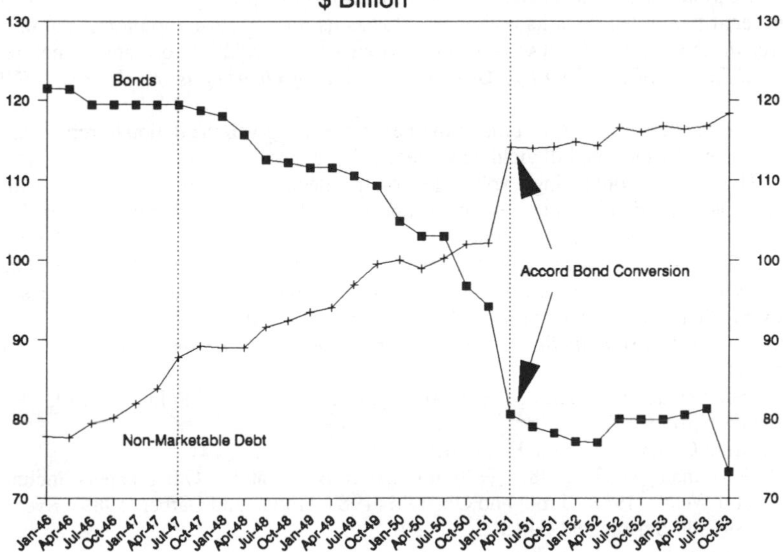
Treasury Bonds and Non-Marketable Debt Outstanding
$ Billion
Bonds
Non-Marketable Debt
Accord Bond Conversion
70
80
90
100
110
120
130
Jan-46
Apr-46
Jul-46
Oct-46
Jan-47
Apr-47
Jul-47
Oct-47
Jan-48
Apr-48
Jul-48
Oct-48
Jan-49
Apr-49
Jul-49
Oct-49
Jan-50
Apr-50
Jul-50
Oct-50
Jan-51
Apr-51
Jul-51
Oct-51
Jan-52
Apr-52
Jul-52
Oct-52
Jan-53
Apr-53
Jul-53
Oct-53

Fig. 5.12

Notes

1. Data on bank suspensions are provided by Simmons (1950, 12). Given the focus of the volume in which our paper appears, this may be thought of as an example of "the dog that didn't bark." But as shall be apparent momentarily, financial instability figures prominently in the analysis that follows.

2. *Annual Report of the Board of Governors Covering Operations for the Year 1937* (1938, 6).

3. Ibid., 214.

4. Ibid., 6–7.

5. These are the Board's words in its *Annual Report* for 1937 (1938, 7). The passage continued,

> In recent years the bond market has become a much more important segment of the open money market, and banks, particularly money-market banks, to an increasing extent use their bond portfolios as a means of adjusting their cash position to meet demands made upon them. At times when the demands increase they tend to reduce their bond portfolios and at times when surplus funds are large they are likely to expand them. Since prices of long-term bonds are subject to wider fluctuations than those of short-term obligations, the increased importance of bonds as a medium of investment for idle bank funds makes the maintenance of stable conditions in the bond market an important concern of banking administration.

6. The Fed invoked both the need to exert a steadying influence on the capital market, which was necessary for economic recovery, and the need to safeguard the stability of the banking system. As the Board described its policy, "While the system has neither the obligation nor the power to assure any given level of prices or yields for Government securities, it has been its policy in so far as its powers permit to protect the market for these securities from violent fluctuations of a speculative, or panicky nature" (*Annual Report of the Board of Governors Covering Operations for the Year 1939* [1940, 5]).

7. Since sellers of Treasury bills to the Fed were also given the option to repurchase at a 3/8 per cent yield, the bill yield was effectively pegged.

8. There is no convincing explanation of the decision to settle on 2½ per cent. Britain had pegged consols at 3 per cent, and U.S. officials argued that superior U.S. credit justified somewhat lower rates. Two and a half per cent was close to the rate previously set by the market. It was an even rate, not a "hat size" like 2⅜ or 2⅝. One Treasury official later justified the rate as consistent with the yields required for solvency by life insurance companies. (Murphy 1950, chap. 8).

9. *Annual Report of the Board of Governors Covering Operations for the Year 1950* (1951, 2).

10. See Senate Subcommittee on Monetary, Credit, and Fiscal Policies (1950, 213–47 and passim).

11. Joint Committee on the Economic Report (1952, pt. 1, 74).

12. Krugman (1987, 1988, 1989) initiated this literature. Other papers include Miller and Weller (1988), Froot and Obstfeld (1989), Flood and Garber (1989), Svensson (1989) and Bertola and Caballero (1989).

13. This is the usual simplifying assumption in the target-zone literature. Feedback from nominal to real variables would greatly complicate the analysis of dynamics. Such a model would typically assume a relation between real variables and a sluggishly moving price level. In such a case, the price level becomes dependent on the path of the exogenous variable. Miller and Weller (1988) explore several such models but find

that closed-form solutions are not generally available. We do, however, allude to such feedback informally in section 5.4 below.

14. The change in r should be thought of as representing the evolution of not only real interest rates but also other variables, such as y, that affect the demand for money, and hence the price level.

15. An alternative hypothesis, which we do not explore here, is that the U.S. commitment to peg the price of gold at $35 an ounce under the Bretton Woods System stabilized price expectations by placing implicit limits on the price level. While this hypothesis is readily incorporated into our target-zone framework, we do not believe that it is the essence of the matter. Given the ample gold reserves the United States possessed after World War II, a very wide range of price levels (and hence persistent expected inflation and highly variable interest rates) were consistent with the $35 peg. This was less the case in the 1960s, when U.S. gold reserves had declined relative to foreign dollar liabilities. Evidence supporting our view may be found in the fact that interest rates became much more variable after February 1951, even though the same Bretton Woods System and $35 gold price prevailed.

16. There were also other forms of intervention, as is clear from figure 5.9. We focus on changes in reserve requirements as the single most important form of intervention, an interpretation we hope to justify in the remainder of this section.

17. This combination of raising reserve requirements and buying bonds had the effect of swapping interest-yielding bank assets for reserves, thereby directly reducing bank income and raising the cost of liquidity across financial markets. Simultaneously, it benefited the Treasury; the Fed acquired relatively high yielding bonds either by expansion of its balance sheet or by partly sterilizing with sales of low-yielding bills and certificates.

18. Obviously, our analytical framework only applies to the period following the removal of general price controls in June 1946.

19. There is no contradiction with the standard logic that a reduction in the supply of debt places downward pressure on interest rates, since, as indicated in figure 5.7, as k rises and the price level increases, expected inflation and therefore nominal interest rates decline.

20. The amounts would have been 25 per cent against demand and 10 per cent against time deposits. See Joint Committee on the Economic Report (1948b, 139–44).

21. Treasury Secretary Snyder also opposed Eccles's plan. For Sproul's views, see Senate Committee on Banking and Currency (1947, 228–30).

22. See Senate Subcommittee on Monetary, Credit, and Fiscal Policies (1950, 40–108) for views on the question. Another source of concern was that nominal interest rates on long-term bonds rose to the cap established by the Fed and the Treasury. This is not a problem for our model, since immediately prior to an intervention to reduce the money supply, short-term rates should be low but long-term rates can be relatively high.

23. *Annual Report of the Board of Governors of the Federal Reserve System Covering Operations for the Year 1948* (1949, 85–86).

24. *Annual Report of the Board of Governors Covering Operations for the Year 1950* (1951, 2).

25. See, for example, the testimony of Thomas B. McCabe, chairman of the Board of Governors of the Federal Reserve System, in Senate Subcommittee on Monetary, Credit, and Fiscal Policies (1950, 21–90). Implicit in the bureaucratic model of the Fed developed by Toma (1982) is the view that the Fed was under pressure to compensate the Treasury for any increase in debt-service costs due to increases in interest rates. While this consideration may have figured in the particular 1947 episode with which Toma is concerned, we question whether it provided the Fed's dominant motivation over the entire period.

26. See, for example, Board of Governors, *Annual Report* for 1945 (1946, 7); *Federal Reserve Bulletin* (January 1948, 11); Joint Committee on the Economic Report (1948b, 140, 620); Joint Committee on the Economic Report (1948a, 101–2).

27. *Annual Report of the Board of Governors Covering Operations for the Year 1945* (1946, 7).

28. Sproul emphasized potential implications for credit supplies and economic activity: "A decline in prices of long-term Treasury bonds more than fractionally below par, under existing conditions, would throw the whole market for long-term securities—corporate and municipal, as well as federal—into confusion. . . . Flotations of long-term securities would be made very difficult if not impossible, until the market became stabilized at a new level" (Joint Committee on the Economic Report 1948a, 101).

29. Data are from *Banking and Monetary Statistics*, table 13.5 (Board of Governors 1971).

30. For example, if certificates were yielding 1.25 per cent while 20-year bonds were yielding 2.42 per cent, we assume that their yields rose to 2.50 and 4.84 per cent, respectively. Bills are omitted for lack of comparable information on coupons and yields. Given their short maturity, capital losses on bills should be of little consequence.

31. For a detailed description of these bonds, see Treasury Department Circular no. 883 (26 March 1951). If the conversion involved a transfer of this magnitude, it is unclear why the entire eligible issue was not converted. About $5 billion of eligible long bonds remained outstanding after the conversion offer, but it is not clear from the evidence who held them.

32. These were bonds which matured on 15 December 1972, issued in November 1945.

33. See *Banking and Monetary Statistics*, vol. 3, table 13.3 (Board of Governors 1971).

References

Bertola, Giuseppe, and Ricardo J. Caballero. 1989. Target Zones and Realignments. Department of Economics, Princeton University, December. Typescript.

Board of Governors of the Federal Reserve System. Various years. *Annual Report*. Washington, DC: GPO.

———. 1971. *Banking and Monetary Statistics*. Washington, DC: GPO.

Chandler, Lester V. 1949. Federal Reserve Policy and the Federal Debt. *American Economic Review* 39: 405–29.

Fforde, J. S. 1954. *The Federal Reserve System, 1945–1949*. Oxford: Clarendon Press.

Flood, Robert, and Peter Garber. 1989. The Linkage Between Speculative Attack and Target Zone Models of Exchange Rates. National Bureau of Economic Research Working Paper no. 2918, April.

Friedman, Milton, and Anna J. Schwartz. 1963. *A Monetary History of the United States, 1867–1960*. Princeton, NJ: Princeton University Press.

Froot, Kenneth, and Maurice Obstfeld. 1989. Exchange Rate Dynamics Under Stochastic Regime Shifts: A Unified Approach. Massachusetts Institute of Technology. Typescript.

Goldenweiser, E. A. 1951. *American Monetary Policy*. New York: McGraw-Hill.

Joint Committee on the Economic Report. 1948a. *Credit Policies: Hearings.* 80th Cong., 2d sess. Washington, DC: GPO.

———. 1948b. *Anti-Inflation Program: Hearings.* 80th Cong., 1st sess. Washington, DC: GPO.

———. Subcommittee on General Credit Control and Debt Management. 1952. *Monetary Policy and the Management of the Public Debt.* 82nd Cong., 2d sess., pt. 1. Washington, DC: GPO.

Karunatilake, H. N. S. 1963. *The Variable Reserve Ratio as an Instrument of Central Bank Policy.* Ceylon: Central Bank of Ceylon.

Krugman, Paul. 1987. Trigger Strategies and Price Dynamics in Equity and Foreign Exchange Markets. National Bureau of Economic Research Working Paper no. 2459, December.

———. 1988. Target Zones and Exchange Rate Dynamics. National Bureau of Economic Research Working Paper no. 2841, January. (Forthcoming, *Quarterly Journal of Economics*).

Krugman, Paul, and J. Rotemberg. 1990. Target Zones with Limited Reserves. Massachusetts Institute of Technology, August. Typescript.

Miller, Marcus, and Paul Weller. 1988. Solving Stochastic Saddlepoint Systems: A Qualitative Treatment with Economic Application. University of Warwick, October. Typescript.

Murphy, Henry C. 1950. *National Debt in War and Transition.* New York: McGraw-Hill.

Seltzer, Lawrence H. 1946. The Changed Environment of Monetary-Banking Policy. *American Economic Review* 36: 65–79.

Senate Committee on Banking and Currency. 1947. *To Provide for the Regulation of Consumer Credit for a Temporary Period: Hearings on S.J.R. 157.* 80th Cong., 1st sess. Washington, DC: GPO.

Senate Subcommittee on Monetary, Credit and Fiscal Policies (Douglas Committee). 1950. *Report.* S. Con. Res. 26, January 4. Washington, DC: GPO.

Simmons, Edward C. 1950. The Monetary Mechanism Since the War. *Journal of Political Economy* 58: 124–41.

Svensson, Lars. 1989. Target Zones and Interest Rate Variability: Where Does the Variability Go, and Is a Fixed Exchange Rate Regime the Limit of a Narrow Zone? Seminar Paper no. 457. Institute for International Economic Studies, Stockholm University.

Tobin, James. 1951. Monetary Restriction and Direct Controls. *Review of Economics and Statistics* 33: 196–98.

Toma, Mark. 1982. Inflationary Bias of the Federal Reserve System: A Bureaucratic Perspective. *Journal of Monetary Economics* 10: 163–90.

Whittlesey, Charles. 1946. Federal Reserve Policy in Transition. *Quarterly Journal of Economics* 60: 340–50.

6 Is There a Corporate Debt Crisis? Another Look

Mark J. Warshawsky

Many have expressed concern about the financial stability of the U.S. corporate sector. This concern stems, in part, from the increased leverage involved in a steady stream of well-publicized mergers, leveraged buyouts, and other corporate restructurings and, in part, from recent defaults. Indeed, aggregate statistics indicate significant increases over the 1980s in net equity retirements and issuance of debt securities. Aggregate ratios of debt outstanding to assets and of interest expense to operating cash flow, computed on the basis of book-value statistics, also have risen steadily for the nonfinancial corporate sector. In a paper published in 1988, "Is There a Corporate Debt Crisis?," Ben S. Bernanke and John Y. Campbell examine these and several other indicators of the financial stability of U.S. nonfinancial corporations in great detail. Bernanke and Campbell rely on samples culled from the COMPUSTAT files, which contain historical data on the balance sheets and income statements of individual large nonfinancial corporations. They also adjust book values to market values, whenever appropriate and possible. Their sample period extends from 1969 through 1986.

This paper expands on the work by Bernanke and Campbell in several ways. First, the sample period is extended through 1988, and thus incorporates the massive restructuring of balance sheets done in 1987 and 1988. Second, the sample is enlarged to include small corporations and corporations that have disappeared over the years owing to mergers, private buyouts, and

The analysis and conclusions of this paper are those of the author and do not indicate concurrence by other members of the research staff, by the Board of Governors, or by the Federal Reserve Banks. Able research assistance was provided by Peter Oberkircher. Helpful insights into the techniques used by Ben Bernanke and John Campbell in their paper were provided by Toni Whited. Helpful comments and suggestions were made by Tom Simpson, Pat Parkinson, John Rea, and Anil Kashyap.

Mark J. Warshawsky is a Senior Economist in the Division of Research and Statistics at the Board of Governors of the Federal Reserve System.

bankruptcy. Third, a measure of financial stability not reported by Bernanke and Campbell, the median bond rating, is examined here. Finally, a simpler and more accurate method of converting the book value into the market value of debt than employed by Bernanke and Campbell is used in this paper. In other respects, including the primary measures examined and the primary methodologies used, however, this paper follows the work by Bernanke and Campbell rather closely.[1]

6.1 Summary of Paper by Bernanke and Campbell

Instead of relying on aggregate statistics based on book values, Bernanke and Campbell compute indicators, based on market values, for samples of large nonfinancial corporations culled from the COMPUSTAT files. They address, in particular, the question of how the mean and the upper tail of the distribution of the debt-asset ratio, at market value, has evolved over the period 1969–86. The upper tail of this distribution is thought to be more relevant to concerns about bankruptcy risk than average measures based on broad book-value aggregates.

Bernanke and Campbell also examine other measures of the financial health of the corporate sector. The distributions of indicators of liquidity, such as the ratios of interest expense to operating cash flow and of interest expense to current assets, are computed for the samples. The authors investigate the degree to which changes in aggregate debt are related to changes in industry composition to ascertain whether industry effects have been an important part of recent aggregate financial behavior. They also estimate a formal model of the determinants of debt-asset ratios to determine whether recent patterns of debt issuance fit the estimated relationship or whether debt issuance has been unusual relative to model expectations. Finally, the authors study how recessions such as those of 1973–74 and 1981–82 would affect the financial structures of the sample of firms if such recessions took place after 1986.

Although the evidence is decidedly mixed, Bernanke and Campbell choose to emphasize two pieces of evidence suggesting that it is appropriate to be concerned about trends in corporate finance during the 1980s. Measures of corporate liquidity, in particular, the ratio of interest expense to operating cash flow, have deteriorated. And, more significantly, a simulation shows that a recession like that of 1973–74 would lead to debt-asset ratios of unprecedented levels, implying bankruptcy for more than 10 percent of the sample of firms. In contrast, however, other evidence suggests a less negative view of recent corporate financial behavior. In the sample of firms examined for 1969–86, there is little upward trend in the mean ratio of debt to assets, whether measured at book or market values. The upper percentiles of distribution of this ratio also do not seem to indicate any significant deterioration in financial structure. In particular, the large increases in equity values during the 1980s led to increases in the denominator of the debt-asset ratio; increases in debt outstanding were therefore supported fully by increased asset values. The stability in debt-asset ratios holds true, whether the industrial composition of the sample is allowed to change or is fixed at 1969–74 or 1986 values, or whether oil-related industries are included or excluded. Furthermore, the model of the determinants of debt indicates that the growth in debt over the 1980s is well explained by the economic variables in the model and has not been unusual in that sense.

6.2 Methodological Contributions of the Bernanke-Campbell Paper

The main contributions of the paper by Bernanke and Campbell are the extensive use of a segment of the COMPUSTAT data base, the calculation of market values of debt, and simulations of the impact of recession on corporate financial structure. Using the "Industrial" COMPUSTAT file, and after eliminating financial corporations and firms with missing essential data, Bernanke and Campbell produce a sample that starts with about 650 firms in 1969 and grows to some 1,400 firms by 1986. They call this sample, which excludes firms that were later acquired or went bankrupt or private, the "growing sample." Data for the initial 650 firms were available consistently throughout the sample period; this "fixed sample" thus excludes firms that came into existence over the period as well as those that were acquired or went bankrupt or private. In general, Bernanke and Campbell report results based on the growing sample, although they indicate that there is little difference if the results are based on the fixed sample. There is some question about how representative are the corporations in either the fixed or growing samples. The Industrial file includes only large well-capitalized corporations whose stock is traded on the NYSE or AMEX and, hence, excludes smaller firms. Furthermore, owing to the exclusion of firms that were acquired or went bankrupt or private, the samples might exhibit a survivorship bias that could lead to an understatement of debt-asset ratios.

The second contribution of the paper is the computation of the market value of debt for a large sample of firms over a substantial period of time. Bernanke and Campbell claim that it is the market value of debt that is significant to evaluating the riskiness of financial structure, because "firms can always refinance existing debt at current interest rates, thereby effectively redeeming their outstanding debt at the market value" (p. 97).

Bernanke and Campbell employ an algorithm first created by William Brainard, John Shoven, and Lawrence Weiss (1980) to calculate the market value of debt. It is assumed that the market value of short-term debt and other current liabilities equals the book value. The algorithm also assumes that, at the starting date of the analysis, the maturity distribution of each firm's long-term debt equals the aggregate average distribution of long-term debt in the corporate sector for that date. The aggregate average distribution is computed from historical statistics on past debt issuance in the corporate sector, using the assumption that bonds with 20-year maturities were issued exclusively. After the starting year, the maturity distribution for each firm is updated under the assumption that, if net issuance for the firm is positive, new issues have a 20-year maturity and that, if net issuance is negative, net retirements apply to all outstanding issues proportionately. Net issuance for each firm is obtained as the change in the total book value of long-term debt, adjusted for maturing issues. The impact of calls, conversions, and other early retirements on the maturity distribution is ignored.

The authors modify the basic algorithm to use information available after 1974 for some firms on the COMPUSTAT files concerning the maturity distribution of long-term debt out to five years' maturity. They replace the first five years of the maturity distribution produced by the basic algorithm with the COMPUSTAT numbers, scaling the remainder of the distribution produced by the basic algorithm up or down in proportion to remain consistent with the COMPUSTAT number on total long-term debt. The modified distribution is then carried forward to the next year and updated by the modified algorithm.

Once the maturity distribution of long-term debt for each firm is obtained, the algorithm assumes that each issue has a coupon rate equal to the Baa rate at the time of issue and a yield to maturity equal to the current Baa rate. The last assumption is equivalent to a market value given by a simple present-value calculation and to assuming that the yield curve is flat. The effects of upgrading or downgrading of bond ratings over time, the actual debt rating when bonds were issued, and of convertibility into stock are ignored.

The impact of call provisions on market prices of bonds also are ignored by Bernanke and Campbell. Utilities are generally constrained by covenants from calling bonds prior to the fifth year after issuance. Industrial firms typically are constrained for ten years. In the sixth (or eleventh) year, however, firms can call bonds at or slightly above par value. Hence, when current interest rates are lower than coupon rates, the issuer is likely to call older bonds, thereby limiting prices of these bonds to the call price. Therefore, the "market" value of debt produced by Bernanke and Campbell using a simple present-value computation likely exaggerates the "up-side" changes in the true market value of newly issued and, certainly, of older bonds when interest rates decline.

The third main contribution of the Bernanke and Campbell paper is to calculate the effect of simulated recessions on current debt-asset ratios, valued at market. For each firm that existed in the base years, 1972 or 1980, Bernanke and Campbell computed the percentage changes in the total market value of the firm (debt and equity) that were observed (in the market or by algorithm) over the two succeeding years. They applied these changes to the denominator of the debt-asset ratio extant in 1986. Instead of applying percentage changes to the numerator, however, Bernanke and Campbell employed a more elaborate technique to simulate the market value of debt in hypothetical recession years following 1986. They assumed that the book value of debt will change by the amount it changed in 1973–74 or 1981–82, and then adjusted the change for growth in corporate assets through 1986. They also simulated the maturity structure of the firm's debt over the hypothetical recession years, using the Bernanke-Campbell algorithm discussed above. Employing the historical percentage changes in interest rates from the appropriate recession, the market value of debt was calculated for each firm in two hypothetical years following 1986. Combining these simulations of market values of debt and of assets, debt-asset ratios were created.

A very dramatic deterioration in debt-asset ratios occurs in the simulation of the 1973–74 recession. During 1973–74, the total market value of COMPUSTAT firms dropped sharply. For the simulation, 10 percent of the firms in the sample have debt-asset ratios exceeding unity, indicating financial trouble. In 1986, firms have higher debt-asset ratios than they had in 1972, and hence are more severely affected by a given drop in total market value than they were in 1973–74. In the 1981–82 recession, by contrast, the stock market was relatively stable and interest rates were high, leading to little deterioration in simulated debt-asset ratios. The very severe results of the 1973–74 simulation, to some extent, come directly from the methodology employed; the denominator of the ratio is changed in simple percentage terms, while the numerator is altered by an elaborately computed change.

Simulations of the ratios of interest expense to operating cash flow and of interest expense to current assets also were done for the two recession scenarios. Bernanke and Campbell took observed changes in earnings and current assets from the historical recessions and scaled them up by the book value of the firm's assets. They used the book-into-market algorithm to estimate interest expenses. In both simulated recessions, the liquidity measures deteriorate; in some instances, the measures deteriorate sharply.

6.3 Improvements Presented in This Paper

Although the paper by Bernanke and Campbell represents a significant advance over other empirical papers in the corporate finance literature, I believe that improvements can be made in the sample and the algorithm used for computing market values of debt. Furthermore, information about average Standard and Poor's (S&P) bond ratings is available and can be used and shown. These improvements might lead to broader applicability and greater realism in the results, although it is difficult to know a priori whether they would tend to buttress or weaken the conclusions drawn by Bernanke and Campbell.

Regarding the sample, COMPUSTAT files for 1987 and 1988 are now available, enabling analysis on the impact of additional restructuring activity. In addition, the "Full Coverage" and "Research" COMPUSTAT files are available, enabling the analysis to include, respectively, smaller corporations whose stocks are traded on the NASDAQ and regional exchanges, and corporations which disappeared by being acquired or by going bankrupt or private. In particular, the issue of survivorship bias can be studied.

Initially I also thought that significant improvements could be made to the market-value-of-debt algorithm used by Bernanke and Campbell by making several adjustments. Foremost among the adjustments was the utilization of information available on COMPUSTAT for years after 1978 on representative S&P bond ratings. For the years prior to 1978 it was assumed that each new bond issue has a coupon rate equal to the rate prevailing at the time of issue on a bond with the corporation's 1978 bond rating. After 1978 the rate at the time of issue on a bond with the corporation's then-current bond rating was used. Also, a rough modification of the simple present-value calculation of market value was made to account for the existence of call provisions in bond covenants. The pricing effect of call provisions was proxied by placing an upper limit of $115 on bond prices produced by the algorithm. Another improvement attempted was the use of firm-specific information in 1988 on the actual maturity distribution of long-term debt; preliminary experimentation with this information, however, did not show significant differences from the results of Bernanke and Campbell, who used the average aggregate maturity distribution in 1969 as initial values in their algorithm.

The extent of the improvement that can be made by these adjustments in the Bernanke-Campbell book-into-market algorithm is shown in table 6.1. For the period 1979–87, the book values of long-term debt of Woolworth and Alcoa reported in Standard and Poor's *Bond Guide* are shown. Also given are the actual market values of the long-term debt for these companies reported in the *Bond Guide*, and estimated market values computed under (a) the adjusted algorithm and (b) the original algorithm used by Bernanke and Campbell.[2] The estimates using the adjusted algorithm of the market values of bonds for these companies are closer to the actual market values than Bernanke and Campbell's estimates. This improvement primarily owes, at least in the cases of Woolworth and Alcoa, to the placement of an upper limit on bond prices. Nevertheless, neither set of estimates captures fully the steep decline in bond prices in 1981; moreover, neither algorithm can capture the depressed market value of Alcoa's convertible bonds over the 1979–87 period resulting from a depressed price for Alcoa's shares. More generally, no simple book-into-market algorithm can replicate changing maturity distributions or value effectively convertible debt or other debt contracts with equity features; at some point, a more accurate research approach may be to simply obtain information on the actual market value of individual bonds.

In the absence of complete historical data on the market value of individual bonds (which, in any case, would not be available for privately placed bonds), however, another simple approach can be employed and compared to the adjusted algorithm. This simple approach entails the application to each company's long-term debt of the ratio of market to par value of all corporate bonds

Table 6.1 Comparison of Calculations of Market Value of Debt (in millions of dollars)

	Standard and Poor's *Bond Guide*		Estimated Market Value	
Year	Book Value	Market Value	Adjusted Algorithm	Bernanke-Campbell Algorithm
F. W. Woolworth Co.				
1979	231	176	191	192
1980	219	144	163	160
1981	217	115	139	145
1982	206	143	159	164
1983	182	126	141	146
1984	182	134	147	152
1985	182	163	166	171
1986	179	177	179	181
1987	169	159	161	162
Alcoa				
1979	574	458	476	476
1980	483	338	370	352
1981	1,161	702	920	1,001
1982	1,389	1,108	1,320	1,434
1983	1,381	1,076	1,287	1,415
1984	1,322	1,070	1,264	1,392
1985	1,322	1,204	1,323	1,578
1986	1,172	1,115	1,232	1,524
1987	855	714	835	1,029

Source: Standard and Poor's *Bond Guide* and author's calculations.

traded on the NYSE.[3] At year-end 1988, a total of 2,259 U.S. corporate debt issues were listed on the NYSE by 793 issuers. The par value of these domestic corporate bonds totaled $294.5 billion and the market value was $243.6 billion. The advantages of this simple aggregate approach are the utilization of actual, not simulated, market values, and the ability to track exactly broad macroeconomic trends. The main drawback, of course, is the discarding of information specific to each individual company's debt structure and bond rating.

The accuracy of the adjusted algorithm and the simple aggregate approach are compared in table 6.2. (A fortiori, the accuracy of the original Bernanke-Campbell algorithm is also being compared.) The mean squared error of estimates of market values of bonds calculated under the adjusted algorithm and the aggregate approach are shown for twelve companies for the years 1979 through 1988. The mean squared error was smaller for the adjusted algorithm

Table 6.2 **Comparison of Adjusted Algorithm and Aggregate Approach to Calculating the Market Value of Debt, 1979–1988**

	Mean Squared Error	
Company	Adjusted Algorithm	Aggregate Approach
Abbott	.04233	.13031
Alcoa	.17520	.01814
AT&T	.19984	.04808
Atlantic Richfield	.01806	.07850
Bethlehem Steel	.51670	.43861
Caterpillar	.09010	.00984
Chrysler	.30205	.28967
Du Pont	.42377	.01402
General Electric	.13434	.06549
Owens-Corning	.10119	.07014
Procter & Gamble	.19326	.07584
TRW	.03154	.06051
Mean for 12 companies	.01860	.01080

Source: Author's calculations.

in only three of the twelve cases; over all companies, the mean squared error is smaller for the aggregate approach than for the adjusted algorithm. Hence, the aggregate approach will be used exclusively in the calculations of the ratio of debt to assets, at market value, reported below.[4] The historical ratio of market to par value of NYSE-listed bonds is shown in figure 6.1.

6.4 Construction of the Samples

As Bernanke and Campbell did, I created two samples of corporations listed on the COMPUSTAT files. The first *fixed* sample consists of 828 domestic nonfinancial corporations for which data are available for *each* year from 1969 through 1988. Of the 828 corporations, 701 come from the Industrial COMPUSTAT file and 127 from the Full Coverage file. The second *fluctuating* sample consists of all corporations for which data on key variables were available for *any* year from 1969 through 1988. The total number of corporations grew from 2,468 in 1969 to 5,120 in 1987. Of the 5,120 corporations in 1987, 1,676 appeared on the Industrial file, 2,908 on the Full Coverage file, and 536 on the Research file. The number of companies dropped to 4,523 in 1988, owing mainly to fewer companies listed on the Research file. Also, I used the September 1989 COMPUSTAT tapes; because some corporations' fiscal years end later than December 31 and because from the end of the fiscal year to the time COMPUSTAT enters annual statement variables as much as eight months can elapse, fewer companies are listed on the Industrial and Full Coverage files in 1988 than in 1987.[5] The number of corporations listed in the Full

Coverage files grew particularly quickly over the 1969 through 1988 period, consistent with the growth in listings on the NASDAQ over the period. The number of corporations listed on the Research file grew slowly through 1976 and then declined through 1988. Because historical data on a disappeared company can be included on the Research file only up to the year of the company's disappearance, it is sensible that the number of companies for which data appear on the Research file declines rapidly in recent years as the active history of the companies disappearing since 1969 recedes in time.

6.5 Distribution of Debt-Asset Ratios

Various perspectives on the debt-asset ratios for 1969–88 in various samples are shown in the next three tables. The ratios are calculated using the aggregate approach to calculating the market value of debt as described above, actual market values of common equity, and the approach used by Bernanke and Campbell to evaluate preferred equity. Assets equal the sum of debt and equity.

Debt-asset ratios for the fixed sample, shown in table 6.3, are calculated, as well, for the Industrial and Full Coverage subsamples. Three different statistics of the distribution for each year are shown: the weighted average, the

Fig. 6.1. The ratio of market to par value of NYSE-listed corporate bonds
Source: NYSE *Fact Book.*

Table 6.3 Debt-Asset Ratio[a], Fixed Sample

	Industrial (701 companies)			Full Coverage (127 companies)			Combined (828 companies)		
Year	Weighted Average	Median	90th Percentile	Weighted Average	Median	90th Percentile	Weighted Average	Median	90th Percentile
1969	.2622	.2967	.5560	.3148	.3297	.5624	.2637	.3006	.5564
1970	.3023	.3542	.6451	.3581	.3662	.6858	.3038	.3562	.6494
1971	.2947	.3401	.6332	.3187	.3315	.6552	.2954	.3373	.6340
1972	.2735	.3590	.6485	.3143	.3475	.6844	.2746	.3587	.6504
1973	.3285	.5096	.7818	.4456	.5424	.7863	.3314	.5162	.7820
1974	.4361	.6085	.8495	.5623	.6437	.8677	.4392	.6157	.8505
1975	.3886	.5193	.7832	.4762	.5880	.8030	.3908	.5313	.7878
1976	.3797	.4652	.7406	.4533	.5200	.7682	.3815	.4743	.7433
1977	.4201	.4758	.7343	.4785	.5150	.7599	.4216	.4833	.7376
1978	.4343	.4911	.7346	.5058	.5154	.7618	.4362	.4939	.7386
1979	.4299	.4577	.7120	.5021	.5054	.7589	.4318	.4636	.7239
1980	.3860	.4211	.6989	.4769	.4509	.7657	.3884	.4309	.7163
1981	.4205	.4412	.7151	.4949	.4572	.7597	.4227	.4434	.7239
1982	.4085	.4188	.7089	.4339	.4489	.7439	.4093	.4202	.7145
1983	.3692	.3677	.6093	.4070	.3742	.6984	.3703	.3687	.6205
1984	.3954	.4019	.6683	.4297	.4326	.7604	.3966	.4049	.6769
1985	.3810	.3934	.6652	.4047	.4035	.7272	.3815	.3959	.6767
1986	.3701	.4041	.6650	.4270	.4065	.7478	.3721	.4044	.6787
1987	.3667	.4247	.7170	.4467	.4570	.7928	.3694	.4279	.7299
1988	.4005	.4083	.7030	.6107	.4741	.9076	.4071	.4158	.7212

Source: COMPUSTAT and author's calculations.
[a]At market values.

median, and the ninetieth percentile. Over the entire period, for all statistics and all subsamples, the debt-asset ratio rose. Companies on the Full Coverage file exhibit consistently higher debt-asset ratios than companies on the Industrial file. The former companies experienced a particularly notable increase in the ratio in 1988, owing largely to the restructuring of a few companies in the subsample. While the significant increases in debt-asset ratios in 1973 and 1974 are due primarily to the large drop in equity prices that occurred over that period, and the steady decline in the ratios through 1983 results from increases in equity prices, the small climb in the ratios since 1983 occurred despite further significant increases in equity prices. Because the ratio of market to par value for bonds in 1988 was nearly identical to the market-par ratio in 1983, the overall rise in the debt-asset ratio since 1983 must have been caused by the considerable issuance of debt and retirement of equity securities through 1988. The statistic on ninetieth percentile indicates that some companies, particularly those in the 1988 Full Coverage subsample, are operating very close to "market value insolvency," which would occur when the ratio equals one.

The same perspectives on debt-asset ratios are offered in table 6.4 for the

Table 6.4 **Debt-Asset Ratio[a], Fluctuating Sample**

	Industrial				Full Coverage				Research				Combined			
Year	No. of Companies	Weighted Average	Median	90th Percentile	No. of Companies	Weighted Average	Median	90th Percentile	No. of Companies	Weighted Average	Median	90th Percentile	No. of Companies	Weighted Average	Median	90th Percentile
1969	837	.2584	.2874	.5510	259	.3729	.3333	.5928	1,372	.3203	.3177	.6075	2,468	.2810	.3098	.5884
1970	869	.2873	.3318	.6456	307	.4151	.3791	.6784	1,376	.3311	.3283	.6174	2,552	.3070	.3342	.6344
1971	917	.2803	.3199	.6216	357	.3985	.3493	.6623	1,545	.3862	.4154	.7120	2,819	.3111	.3704	.6865
1972	953	.2620	.3322	.6411	422	.3900	.3340	.6803	1,611	.3586	.3672	.6737	2,986	.2911	.3533	.6647
1973	1,133	.3572	.5269	.7744	460	.4826	.4932	.7965	1,720	.3488	.3663	.6908	3,313	.3647	.4344	.7395
1974	1,154	.4687	.6244	.8482	507	.5784	.6229	.8831	1,739	.4479	.5439	.8216	3,400	.4730	.5882	.8417
1975	1,170	.4202	.5453	.7799	535	.5059	.5450	.8245	1,745	.5853	.6642	.8899	3,450	.4539	.5995	.8592
1976	1,184	.4101	.4955	.7397	574	.4792	.4972	.7917	1,686	.5167	.5668	.8414	3,444	.4330	.5251	.8072
1977	1,198	.4458	.4962	.7288	610	.4990	.5046	.8032	1,649	.4796	.5224	.8071	3,457	.4563	.5099	.7813
1978	1,216	.4588	.5066	.7272	703	.5258	.4971	.7851	1,545	.4964	.5186	.8042	3,464	.4708	.5104	.7765
1979	1,243	.4538	.4720	.7152	880	.5019	.4406	.7819	1,490	.5110	.5287	.8085	3,613	.4669	.4915	.7720
1980	1,282	.4119	.4329	.7003	1,012	.4355	.3311	.7504	1,495	.4581	.4963	.7989	3,789	.4212	.4371	.7576
1981	1,317	.4446	.4498	.7149	1,364	.4499	.3539	.7675	1,458	.3941	.4247	.7745	4,139	.4364	.4134	.7511
1982	1,339	.4299	.4313	.7089	1,486	.4270	.3150	.7629	1,663	.4740	.4536	.8140	4,488	.4358	.4079	.7616
1983	1,409	.3912	.3709	.6241	1,805	.3563	.2457	.6641	1,492	.4721	.4419	.7984	4,706	.3968	.3471	.7097
1984	1,463	.4181	.4136	.6684	2,019	.4057	.3128	.7121	1,402	.4003	.3586	.7427	4,884	.4146	.3623	.7037
1985	1,512	.4014	.3981	.6652	2,238	.3945	.2867	.6996	1,168	.4520	.4337	.7676	4,918	.4045	.3613	.7068
1986	1,600	.3848	.3966	.6508	2,626	.4167	.2922	.7108	837	.4439	.4222	.7530	5,063	.3917	.3569	.7006
1987	1,676	.3875	.4318	.7097	2,908	.4327	.3494	.7422	536	.4163	.4032	.7634	5,120	.3935	.3873	.7319
1988	1,658	.3990	.4169	.6935	2,622	.4204	.3253	.7227	243	.5316	.4291	.7536	4,523	.4037	.3695	.7155

Source: COMPUSTAT and author's calculations.
[a]At market values.

fluctuating sample. This second sample includes growing subsamples from the Industrial and Full Coverage files and a shrinking subsample from the Research file. The results are similar in a broad way to those in table 6.3. The debt-asset ratio for the fluctuating sample rose during 1969–88, although less significantly than in the fixed sample. The climb in the ratio from 1983 through 1988, in particular, is less noticeable than in the fixed sample. The Full Coverage growing subsample has a lower debt-asset ratio than its fixed subsample counterpart. Apparently, newly listed small companies have lower debt-asset ratios than well-established small companies. By contrast, disappeared companies tend to have slightly higher debt-asset ratios than existing companies, perhaps owing to bankruptcy as one of the causes of disappearance. The survivorship bias, however, does not seem particularly significant.

Debt-asset ratios by industry for selected years are shown in table 6.5. The ratios vary widely by industry, with chemicals, mining, and printing and publishing showing consistently low debt-asset ratios, and petroleum and natural

Table 6.5 **Debt-Asset Ratio: Fluctuating Sample by Industry, Selected Years**[a]

Industry	1969	1974	1979	1984	1985	1986	1987	1988
Laboratory equipment	.251	.611	.399	.233	.238	.227	.281	.283
Printing and publishing	.212	.526	.420	.258	.250	.266	.294	.273
Electronics	.275	.546	.356	.264	.280	.287	.358	.338
Paper	.288	.499	.445	.363	.377	.331	.340	.336
Chemicals	.177	.392	.343	.246	.231	.196	.240	.210
Petroleum and natural gas	.512	.646	.581	.532	.505	.451	.481	.484
Petroleum refining	.287	.499	.466	.523	.587	.484	.467	.432
Mining	.161	.218	.256	.222	.189	.142	.162	.156
Food and tobacco	.314	.546	.496	.403	.359	.321	.341	.306
Retail	.376	.673	.640	.451	.430	.427	.496	.461
Lumber and furniture	.234	.600	.489	.351	.398	.392	.431	.508
Machinery	.291	.566	.398	.274	.281	.292	.349	.339
Glass and concrete	.315	.553	.503	.462	.482	.483	.476	.447
Vehicles	.391	.626	.511	.398	.385	.427	.489	.473
Apparel	.327	.671	.593	.452	.379	.362	.411	.418
Metal products	.318	.577	.470	.398	.412	.422	.487	.443
Rubber and plastics	.342	.578	.540	.374	.364	.315	.346	.335
Construction	.489	.758	.658	.546	.523	.489	.495	.492
Wholesale	.382	.692	.618	.474	.456	.477	.511	.489
Textiles	.365	.694	.562	.488	.486	.446	.487	.438
Steel refining	.418	.574	.527	.546	.504	.518	.496	.427
Transportation	.522	.647	.654	.516	.552	.476	.533	.544
Utilities	.512	.646	.581	.532	.505	.451	.481	.484
Communication	.383	.626	.424	.440	.399	.396	.425	.398

Source: COMPUSTAT and author's calculations.

[a]Debt-asset ratio shown is the median of the distribution, calculated at market values. The sample does not match that in table 6.4 exactly, owing to the omission of a few small industries.

gas, construction, transportation, and utilities showing consistently high ratios. The industries exhibiting the largest increase in debt-asset ratios over the period include petroleum refining, retail, lumber and furniture, glass and concrete, apparel, and metal products. Petroleum refining and retail industries have been prominently involved in merger, restructuring, and buyout activity.

The widely asked question about the relationship between the cyclical risk and the leverage of an industry can be answered by regressing the debt-asset ratio on the variability of detrended industry profits. If the coefficient on the variability factor in such an equation is negative, the intuitive result is implied: lower cyclical risk allows higher leverage. If, however, a counterintuitive zero or positive coefficient is discovered, it would seem that leverage is influenced by other factors more significant than cyclical risk, including, perhaps, tax and regulatory structures, typical company size in the industry, and agency considerations. The dependent variable for a simple cross-section equation which I estimated is the debt-asset ratio, averaged over the three-year period, 1984–86, for each of the twenty-four industries shown in table 6.5. The independent variables are a constant and 1 less than the R^2 computed for profit equations estimated separately for the twenty-four industries over the years 1969–86. The only variable included in these industry profit equations is a simple time trend. The equation estimated over the cross section of the industries, where the t-statistics are in parentheses, follows:

$$X = \underset{(12.789)}{.388} + \underset{(.296)}{.0237}\ Y \qquad R^2 = .0040$$

As is evident, the coefficient on the Y variable measuring the unexplained variability of detrended industry profits is not significantly different from zero. The debt-asset ratio in various industries, the X variable, is apparently not influenced, in any significant way, by cyclical risk.[6]

It is worthwhile to compare table 6.4 with tables 4 and 5 presented in Bernanke and Campbell. In general, the statistics shown in table 6.4, whether weighted average, median, or ninetieth percentile, are higher, particularly toward the end of the period, than the ratios exhibited in Bernanke and Campbell. Furthermore, the positive difference cannot be ascribed to the addition of companies from the Full Coverage and Research files; comparing the Industrial subsample in table 6.4 to the tables in Bernanke and Campbell reveals the same positive differences. Hence, it must be concluded that the reason for differences is the use of the aggregate approach, as opposed to an algorithm, for computing the market value of debt.

6.6 Distributions of the Ratio of Interest Expense to Cash Flow

The next three tables exhibit information about the distribution of the ratio of interest expense to operating cash flow for the various samples and subsamples.[7] As shown in table 6.6, the interest expense–cash flow ratio for the fixed

Table 6.6 Ratio of Interest Expense to Cash Flow, Fixed Sample[a]

Year	Industrial			Full Coverage			Combined		
	Weighted Average	Median	90th Percentile	Weighted Average	Median	90th Percentile	Weighted Average	Median	90th Percentile
1969	.0925	.0927	.2895	.1241	.0882	.3254	.0933	.0924	.2897
1970	.1161	.1302	.4381	.1601	.1161	.8598	.1173	.1281	.4598
1971	.1165	.1256	.4001	.1355	.1166	.4032	.1170	.1247	.3954
1972	.1081	.1095	.3297	.1130	.0883	.3242	.1082	.1070	.3285
1973	.1039	.1179	.3257	.1260	.0961	.2831	.1045	.1147	.3220
1974	.1067	.1400	.4686	.1567	.1435	.5531	.1079	.1405	.4704
1975	.1173	.1410	.4410	.1396	.1319	.5428	.1178	.1389	.4422
1976	.1077	.1108	.3276	.1188	.0997	.3188	.1079	.1096	.3257
1977	.1066	.1088	.3566	.1185	.1123	.3404	.1069	.1106	.3541
1978	.1083	.1141	.3411	.1296	.1359	.4071	.1088	.1164	.3513
1979	.1088	.1248	.3586	.1529	.1424	.4487	.1098	.1280	.3678
1980	.1250	.1462	.4418	.1838	.1762	.6076	.1265	.1491	.4591
1981	.1438	.1537	.4983	.2444	.1666	1.1413	.1461	.1538	.5350
1982	.1669	.1684	1.0214	.2439	.1819	2.4044	.1689	.1708	1.0696
1983	.1513	.1419	.8152	.1855	.1654	.9024	.1522	.1442	.8297
1984	.1446	.1379	.6338	.1782	.1560	9.3768	.1456	.1404	.7027
1985	.1614	.1648	1.4149	.1924	.1714	1.9100	.1623	.1665	1.4364
1986	.1812	.1760	2.3426	.1999	.1562	4.7486	.1819	.1753	2.3869
1987	.1579	.1672	1.2041	.2171	.1861	1.9904	.1598	.1686	1.2082
1988	.1725	.1688	0.9035	.3804	.1999	1.4014	.1781	.1720	.9804

Source: COMPUSTAT and author's calculations.
[a]Cash flow is defined as the sum of before-tax eranings, depreciation, and interest expense. Negative values of the ratio are considered as $+\infty$.

sample nearly doubled, whether calculated as a weighted average or a median, over the years 1969–88. The ratio rose, in particular, since 1979. The ninetieth percentile of the distribution more than tripled over the entire period. According to table 6.6, corporate financial conditions worsened noticeably in the 1981–82, not the 1973–74, recession, and worsened again in 1985 and 1986, when many oil-drilling-equipment and steel companies were experiencing severe difficulties.

A still more somber picture of worsening financial conditions is evident for the larger fluctuating sample shown in table 6.7. In particular, since 1981, for more than 10 percent of the companies on the Full Coverage and Research files, cash flow was negative. For nearly all years, interest expense–cash flow ratios for companies on the Full Coverage and Research files exceed ratios for the larger established companies on the Industrial file. The general trend toward higher interest expense–cash flow ratios also is evident in the industry breakdown shown in table 6.8. Only two industries, laboratory equipment and apparel, exhibited declining ratios, while the ratios for the electronics, glass and concrete, and construction industries tripled over the period of study.

Table 6.7 **Ratio of Interest Expense to Cash Flow, Fluctuating Sample**[a]

	Industrial				Full Coverage				Research				Combined			
Year	No. of Companies	Weighted Average	Median	90th Percentile	No. of Companies	Weighted Average	Median	90th Percentile	No. of Companies	Weighted Average	Median	90th Percentile	No. of Companies	Weighted Average	Median	90th Percentile
1969	837	.0908	.0911	.2942	259	.1329	.1060	.3483	1,372	.1151	.1041	.4597	2,468	.1001	.0990	.3840
1970	869	.1102	.1277	.4393	307	.1707	.1265	.5754	1,376	.1146	.1035	.4592	2,552	.1165	.1145	.4606
1971	917	.1057	.1200	.4019	357	.1649	.1393	.5449	1,545	.1491	.1493	1.9987	2,819	.1199	.1348	.8201
1972	953	.0988	.1031	.3282	422	.1564	.1017	.3740	1,612	.1377	.1270	.7816	2,897	.1117	.1151	.4792
1973	1,133	.1197	.1316	.3528	460	.1651	.1086	.3846	1,720	.1216	.1087	.4237	3,313	.1237	.1167	.3771
1974	1,154	.1339	.1681	.4847	507	.1855	.1561	.8602	1,739	.1271	.1188	.4354	3,400	.1368	.1396	.4860
1975	1,170	.1421	.1595	.4421	535	.1744	.1547	.8728	1,745	.1382	.1545	.6990	3,450	.1438	.1571	.6257
1976	1,184	.1269	.1246	.3412	574	.1478	.1233	.5512	1,686	.1456	.1450	.8090	3,444	.1321	.1349	.5564
1977	1,198	.1239	.1265	.3600	610	.1452	.1246	.6021	1,649	.1328	.1256	.5767	3,457	.1273	.1256	.4687
1978	1,216	.1255	.1337	.3632	703	.1564	.1389	.5520	1,545	.1373	.1274	.5513	3,464	.1301	.1318	.4598
1979	1,243	.1300	.1473	.3922	880	.1692	.1664	1.1502	1,490	.1455	.1493	.6732	3,613	.1365	.1518	.5689
1980	1,282	.1515	.1685	.4724	1,012	.1982	.1829	1.5751	1,495	.1448	.1797	2.1825	3,789	.1549	.1762	.9667
1981	1,317	.1708	.1761	.5112	1,364	.2276	.2019	∞	1,456	.1517	.2065	∞	4,137	.1729	.1951	2.6561
1982	1,339	.1931	.1930	.8517	1,486	.2410	.2499	∞	1,663	.1880	.2457	∞	4,488	.1966	.2258	∞
1983	1,409	.1708	.1635	.7743	1,804	.2026	.2015	∞	1,490	.2345	.2990	∞	4,703	.1811	.2099	∞
1984	1,463	.1633	.1593	.6575	2,017	.2046	.2267	∞	1,402	.2055	.2532	∞	4,882	.1713	.2024	∞
1985	1,512	.1748	.1795	1.3265	2,237	.2229	.2721	∞	1,168	.2246	.2684	∞	4,917	.1829	.2283	∞
1986	1,600	.1875	.1875	2.3597	2,625	.2832	.2804	∞	837	.2775	.3074	∞	5,062	.1999	.2390	∞
1987	1,676	.1704	.1822	1.1704	2,906	.2949	.2993	∞	536	.3443	.3067	∞	5,118	.1837	.2329	∞
1988	1,658	.1868	.1960	1.2076	2,620	.2917	.2656	∞	242	.2456	.1913	∞	4,520	.1952	.2198	∞

Source: COMPUSTAT and author's computations.

[a]Cash flow is defined as the sum of before-tax earnings, depreciation, and interest expense. Negative values of the ratio are considered as $+\infty$.

Table 6.8 **Ratio of Interest Expense to Cash Flow: Fluctuating Sample by Industry, Selected Years[a]**

Industry	1969	1974	1979	1984	1985	1986	1987	1988
Laboratory equipment	.166	.184	.135	.123	.127	.110	.121	.106
Printing and publishing	.069	.098	.076	.077	.082	.089	.122	.103
Electronics	.093	.133	.092	.116	.138	.150	.132	.274
Paper	.084	.089	.088	.149	.166	.153	.126	.117
Chemicals	.067	.080	.194	.136	.153	.159	.128	.105
Petroleum and natural gas	.259	.293	.271	.261	.271	.273	.275	.291
Petroleum refining	.071	.044	.064	.127	.142	.186	.181	.146
Mining	.082	.087	.180	.212	.433	.149	.095	.122
Food and tobacco	.089	.129	.125	.145	.145	.166	.148	.151
Retail	.134	.236	.212	.181	.185	.180	.177	.222
Lumber and furniture	.076	.134	.099	.145	.149	.153	.124	.188
Machinery	.088	.128	.102	.124	.129	.147	.136	.204
Glass and concrete	.074	.130	.120	.170	.202	.182	.224	.218
Vehicles	.099	.156	.114	.110	.109	.124	.128	.262
Apparel	.180	.241	.153	.132	.146	.110	.136	.171
Metal products	.086	.116	.126	.176	.193	.210	.187	.161
Rubber and plastics	.124	.157	.235	.210	.194	.199	.170	.178
Construction	.150	.249	.195	.262	.847	.322	.431	.555
Wholesale	.121	.167	.181	.220	.237	.253	.253	.255
Textiles	.123	.175	.152	.239	.259	.225	.295	.271
Steel refining	.129	.124	.143	.529	1.119	1.236	.241	.157
Transportation	.196	.194	.203	.216	.234	.321	.254	.254
Utilities	.259	.293	.271	.261	.271	.273	.275	.291
Communication	.110	.196	.177	.180	.169	.168	.170	.191

Source: COMPUSTAT and author's calculations.
[a]The ratio shown is the median of the distribution. The sample here does not match the sample in table 6.7 exactly, owing to the omission of a few small industries.

The increase in the interest expense–cash flow ratio over the sample period can be caused by higher interest rates, higher debt outstanding, or relatively lower cash flow. As shown in figure 6.2, the median, for the fluctuating sample, of the ratio of interest expense to debt outstanding (book value), that is, the effective interest rate, climbed rapidly through 1981 to nearly 12 percent, reflecting rising market interest rates. After 1982, however, the effective interest rate declined to about 10 percent by 1988. Hence, through 1982, increases in the ratio of interest expense to cash flow can be attributed, in part, to rising interest rates. Since 1982, however, because cash flow grew rapidly in the economic expansion, the sole culprit for the increasing interest expense–cash flow ratio must be the rapid increase in debt outstanding.

Comparing the results for the fluctuating sample in tables 6.4 and 6.7, the question naturally arises why the interest expense–cash flow ratio increased from 1982 to 1988, while the debt-asset ratio remained relatively stable. The simple arithmetic answer is that the ratio of asset prices (primarily through equity prices) to cash flow rose rapidly over the period. This increase perhaps reflects the view of stock market participants that future strong growth in earnings and lower interest rates would justify fully a very rapid increase in equity prices. If the view of the stock market is realized, clearly there need be little concern about current levels of corporate debt outstanding. If, however, earnings growth were to slow significantly or interest rates were to remain stable, concerns about debt levels would be warranted.

6.7 Average Ratings of Corporate Bonds Outstanding

Figures 6.3 and 6.4 show average ratings of corporate bonds outstanding for 1978–88. Four different measures of average bond rating were computed using the COMPUSTAT files. The average rating fell about a grade and a third over the period, regardless of which of the four measures is used for analysis.

The first two measures (fig. 6.3) are the median and weighted average of the representative Standard and Poor's bond rating for each company in the fixed sample of nonfinancial corporations.[8] The median rating in this sample declined from A in 1978 to BBB in 1988. The average rating, weighted by long-term debt outstanding, declined from AA to just slightly better than A−.

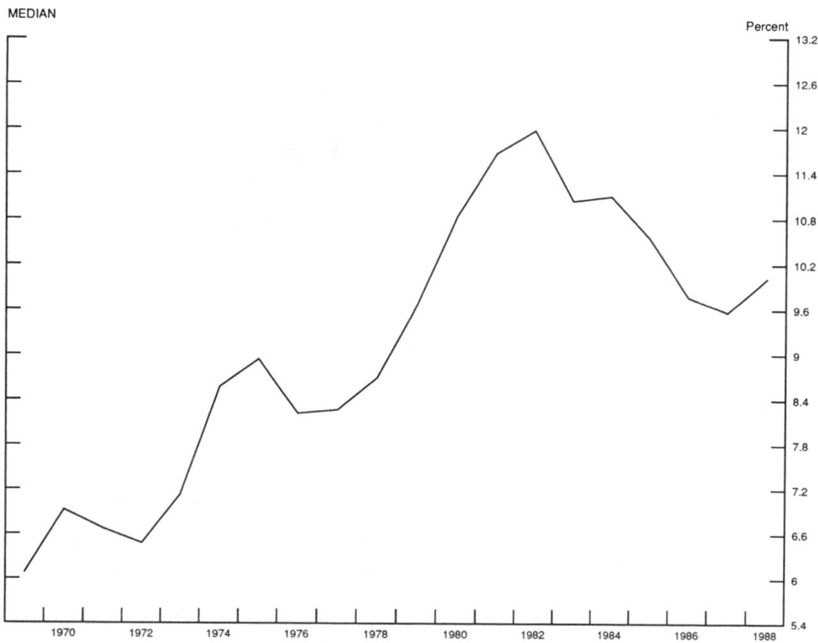

Fig. 6.2 Ratio of interest expense to debt outstanding (book value), fluctuating sample

Source: COMPUSTAT and author's calculations.

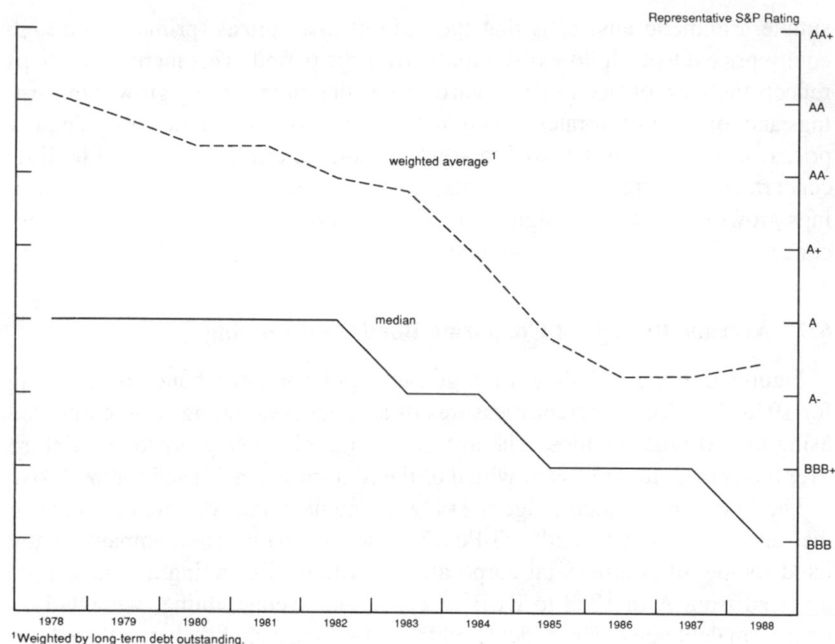

Fig. 6.3 Average rating of corporate bonds outstanding, fixed sample of nonfinancial issuers
Source: COMPUSTAT and author's calculations

Downgradings associated with restructurings and increased access to the junk bond market by many issuers would seem to be the primary explanations for the drop in ratings. The average rating is higher than the median, owing to the existence of a few large issuers with superior bond ratings.

The third and fourth measures (fig. 6.4) are the median and weighted average of the S&P rating for the fluctuating sample. The median rating for this sample declined from A in 1978 to BBB− in 1988. The weighted average rating declined from AA+ to slightly better than A over the period.

6.8 Simulations of Recessions

As did Bernanke and Campbell, to get a sense of the potential effects of a recession on corporate financial structure, I simulated the effects of recessions like those of 1973–74 and 1981–82. For each firm that existed in the base year, 1972 or 1980, and in 1988, I computed the percentage changes in the total market value of the firm (equity and debt) that were observed over the two years succeeding the base year, denoted recession year 1 and recession year 2. I also computed the nominal changes in the book value of the firm's debt and applied these changes, scaled up by the book value of the firm's assets, to the level of debt outstanding in 1988. In addition, I applied the

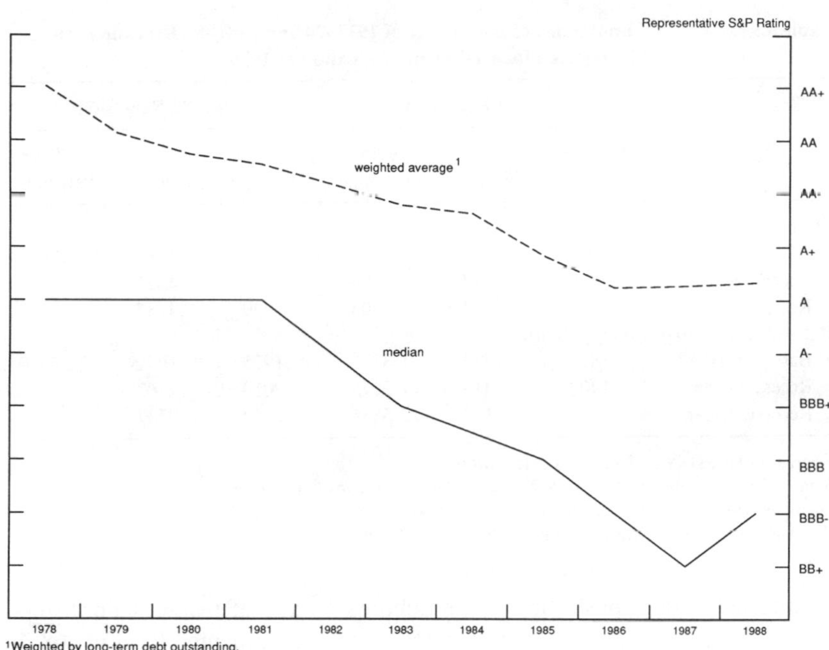

Fig. 6.4 Average rating of corporate bonds outstanding, fluctuating sample of non-financial issuers.
Source: COMPUSTAT and author's calculations

changes in the market-to-par ratios of 1973, 1974, 1981, and 1982 to the market-to-par ratio in 1988. I then used the simulated market-to-par ratio to compute the market value of long-term debt outstanding in the post-1988 recession years. Combining the simulations of market values of debt and assets, it was possible to calculate simulated debt-asset ratios for each firm in two hypothetical recession years after 1988.

In a similar way, I took the observed change in cash flow (excluding interest expense) over the recession years, scaled it up by the book value of the firm's assets, and applied these changes to cash flow (excluding interest expense) in 1988. Simulated interest expense was computed by multiplying the simulated level of debt outstanding (book value) by a simulated effective interest rate for each firm in the recession years.[9] In such a manner, it was possible to construct simulated ratios of interest expense to cash flow. The simulations were done for the fluctuating sample of nonfinancial corporations in the Industrial and Full Coverage files. The results are reported in table 6.9 for the two years of the two simulated recessions.

Even more striking than the results reported by Bernanke and Campbell, the results shown in table 6.9 indicate a significant deterioration in financial conditions if a recession were to hit. More specifically, as shown in the upper panel, a repetition of the 1973–74 recession, when the market values of firms

Table 6.9 **Simulations of the Impact of 1973–74 and 1981–82 Recessions on Corporate Financial Structure Extant in 1988**

	1973–74 Recession[a]			1981–82 Recession[b]		
	Weighted Average	Median	90th Percentile	Weighted Average	Median	90th Percentile
Debt-asset ratio						
Base year (1988)	.3972	.4083	.7315	.4096	.4186	.7230
Recession year 1	.4920	.5587	1.1106	.4328	.4521	.8782
Recession year 2	.6375	.6834	1.4503	.3939	.4185	.9178
Ratio of interest expense to cash flow						
Base year (1988)	.1817	.1722	1.3508	.1975	.1991	22.9530
Recession year 1	.1707	.1818	1.5675	.2010	.2362	∞
Recession year 2	.1767	.2162	72.5834	.2260	.2737	∞

Source: COMPUSTAT and author's calculations.
Note: Also see tables 6.4 and 6.7. Negative values are considered as $+\infty$.
[a]Sample consists of 1,173 corporations that reported data in 1972 and 1988.
[b]Sample consists of 1,925 corporations that reported data in 1980 and 1988.

plummeted, would push the median debt-asset ratio, at market value, from .41 to .56 in the first recession year and to an unprecedented level of .68 in the second recession year. Nearly 25 percent of corporations in the sample would have debt-asset ratios exceeding one by the second recession year, indicating severe financial troubles. About 22 percent of companies in the Industrial subsample would have debt-asset ratios exceeding one, while about 31 percent of companies in the Full Coverage subsample would have debt-asset ratios exceeding one. Around 16 percent of total corporate assets would be in the category of debt-asset ratio exceeding one. A repetition of the 1981–82 recession, when the stock market was fairly robust, would also lead to increases in debt-asset ratios, although the increases would be much less severe than in a 1973–74 recession scenario. Nevertheless, nearly 8 percent of corporations in the sample would have debt-asset ratios exceeding one in the 1981–82 scenario. For the samples used in the simulations, the actual impact of the 1973–74 and 1981–82 recessions on corporate financial structure are shown in table 6.10. Except for the weighted-average ratio for the 1981–82 recession, the simulated debt-asset ratios after 1988 shown in the upper panel of table 6.9 are higher than the actual ratios after 1972 and 1980, shown in the upper panel of table 6.10.

The simulated ratios of interest expense to cash flow are shown in the bottom panel of table 6.9. For the simulation of the 1973–74 recession, the weighted-average ratio actually declines as the effective interest rate declines. The median ratio, however, increases slightly, and the ratio in the ninetieth percentile increases significantly. About 4 percent of the corporations would have negative cash flow *and* a debt-asset ratio exceeding one. For the simulation of the 1981–82 recession, the ratio of interest expense to cash flow, computed either as a weighted average or median, increases noticeably in the recession years. The ratio in the ninetieth percentile is denoted as infinity, as more than 10 percent of the corporations have negative ratios, owing to negative cash flows. Again, comparing with the bottom panel in table 6.10, the simulated interest expense–cash flow ratios after 1988 are uniformly higher than the actual ratios after 1972 and 1980.

Finally, in table 6.11, the prevalence of corporations with interest expense exceeding cash flow is indicated, as a percentage of the number of firms in the sample and as a percentage of total assets. The upper panel shows actual experience, while the lower panel shows simulations of 1973–74 and 1981–82 recessions based on 1988 data and on the samples available for simulation, as indicated in table 6.9. As shown in the upper panel, the prevalence of corporations with interest expense exceeding cash flow has grown significantly, although it is smaller corporations that are predominantly in this category. In the lower panel, simulations show that both 1973–74 and 1981–82 recessions would at least double the percentage of assets represented by corporations with interest expense exceeding cash flow from 1988 levels. By the second year of a 1981–82 recession, almost 27 percent of corporations, with 6 percent of corporate assets, would have interest expense exceeding cash flow.

6.9 Conclusions

The findings here tend to support, and even strengthen, the disturbing conclusions reached by Bernanke and Campbell. The ratios of debt to assets, at market value, increased over the period for most samples, subsamples, industry groupings, and statistical measures, although the highs reached in 1974 remain unsurpassed. The ratio of interest expense to cash flow increased sig-

Table 6.10 **Actual Experience of the Impact of 1973–74 and 1981–82 Recessions on Corporate Financial Structure, Samples Used in Simulations**[a]

	1973–74 Recession			1981–82 Recession		
	Weighted Average	Median	90th Percentile	Weighted Average	Median	90th Percentile
Debt-asset ratio						
Base year (1972 or 1980)	.2695	.3287	.6472	.4044	.3909	.7034
Recession year 1	.3290	.4998	.7837	.4366	.4254	.7220
Recession year 2	.4405	.6106	.8669	.4233	.4027	.7191
Ratio of interest expense to cash flow						
Base year (1972 or 1980)	.1098	.0977	.3334	.1520	.1654	.5705
Recession year 1	.1077	.1081	.3473	.1722	.1751	.6535
Recession year 2	.1127	.1251	.4219	.1938	.1960	1.8180

Source: COMPUSTAT and author's calculations.
[a]See table 6.9.

Table 6.11 Corporations with Interest Expense Exceeding Cash Flow

Year	Percentage of Number in Sample[a]	Percentage of Total Assets
Actual experience		
1972	3.7	0.50
1973	2.6	0.23
1974	7.0	1.21
1980	7.8	2.55
1981	11.2	1.73
1982	17.0	3.56
1988	23.7	3.40
Simulations based on 1988 data[b]		
1973–74 Recession		
Base year (1988)	11.3	2.54
Recession year 1	12.1	2.04
Recession year 2	15.0	6.65
1981–82 Recession		
Base year (1988)	13.9	2.60
Recession year 1	20.8	4.02
Recession year 2	26.7	6.15

Source: COMPUSTAT and author's calculations.
[a]See table 6.7 for sample sizes.
[b]See table 6.9 for description of simulation samples.

nificantly, owing to higher effective interest rates through 1982 and increased levels of debt outstanding through 1988. The current interest expense–cash flow ratio is at or near the highs reached in 1982 and 1986. Small corporations tend to have higher ratios, and hence weaker financial conditions, than large corporations. The median bond rating declined from about A in 1978 to BBB− in 1988. If a severe recession were to hit, as many as 25 percent of corporations, corresponding to as much as 16 percent of total corporate assets, would be placed in severe financial straits, judged by the criterion of simulated debt-asset ratios exceeding one and given the financial structure extant in 1988. Judged by the criterion of simulated interest expense exceeding simulated cash flow, as many as 27 percent of corporations, corresponding to more than 6 percent of corporate assets, would be placed in severe financial straits in a future severe recession.

Bernanke and Campbell examined the possibility that off-balance-sheet considerations give corporations the ability to support higher debt burdens. In particular, they cited arguments advanced by others concerning the emergence of the junk bond market and of corporate pension overfunding. The junk bond argument is that these bonds, owing largely to the dominance of certain underwriters, allow issuers and investors to costlessly renegotiate terms rather than incur the heavy costs of bankruptcy in the event of financial difficulties.

The pension fund argument is that high levels of overfunding may have given corporations the flexibility needed to support heavier debt burdens.

On closer examination, however, these arguments provide little comfort. Recent defaults by large issuers of junk bonds indicate that bankruptcy is still a possibility when financial difficulties are encountered. Furthermore, one of the key arguments used by proponents of corporate restructuring—higher debt levels force corporate managers to focus on improving efficiency—relies on the assumption that default is costly and, hence, to be avoided (Jensen 1988). Yet it is also claimed, with little concern for logical consistency, that insolvency can be handled in a costless manner. And while it is true that the funding of pension liabilities, in the aggregate, has improved considerably, many companies still have underfunded pension liabilities (Warshawsky 1989a). Indeed, the 1980s has witnessed the development of another retiree benefit problem: the rapid rise in unfunded liabilities for retiree health benefits (Warshawsky 1991). Finally, an explanation sometimes given for the increased leverage of U.S. corporations since 1986 is that tax reform provides increased private incentives for higher leverage (Warshawsky 1989b). These private incentives, however, may conflict with the social desire for financial stability. Hence, available evidence and logical considerations indicate that some degree of concern about the financial health of the U.S. nonfinancial corporate sector is appropriate.

Notes

1. Bernanke, Campbell, and Whited (1990) also updated their analysis; they report few changes in results or conclusions from their earlier paper. They, however, did not expand their sample, include any new measures of financial health, or reexamine the book-to-market-value algorithm. In addition, they do not report fully the results of simulations using 1988 data. The samples in their 1988 and 1990 papers do not match exactly, owing to the exclusion of those companies from the later paper's sample which did not restate data to a basis consistent with the new FASB rule requiring consolidation of finance subsidiaries after 1987. In the paper here, I did not use restated data, and hence there may be a slight inconsistency between data reported before 1988 and data reported in 1988. The two large companies most affected by the change in the accounting rule, General Motors and Ford, however, are not included in the fixed sample nor in the flexible sample in 1988 reported in this paper. More generally, only 44 of the 1,931 companies listed on the COMPUSTAT Industrial file in 1987 had a difference greater than 10 percent between historical and restated data for long-term debt.

2. The adjusted algorithm was developed initially by Leland Crabbe; further small revisions were made by Peter Oberkircher.

3. The ratio is calculated based on information reported in successive annual issues of the New York Stock Exchange *Fact Book*.

4. This methodological point also has implications for calculations of q ratios for individual companies.

5. Because observations are entered on a fiscal-year basis and the par-to-market

adjustment using the aggregate approach is done at the end of the calendar year, for those corporations whose fiscal year is not the calendar year, a mismatch occurs.

6. The same exercise was done using R^2's computed from industry profit equations estimated over the period 1977 through 1986; the results did not differ significantly.

7. Operating cash flow is defined as the sum of after-tax earnings, taxes, depreciation, and interest expense.

8. The S&P rating system is an ordinal ranking. For the purpose of computations, the system was enumerated linearly, starting with AAA equal to 2, AA+ equal to 4, AA equal to 5, and so on.

9. The simulated effective interest rates are computed as the effective interest rate extant in 1988, adjusted by the nominal changes in effective interest rates over the recession years.

References

Bernanke, Ben S., and John Y. Campbell. 1988. Is There a Corporate Debt Crisis? *Brookings Papers on Economic Activity* 1: 83–125.

Bernanke, Ben S., John Y. Campbell, and Toni M. Whited. 1990. U.S. Corporate Leverage: Developments in 1987 and 1988. *Brookings Papers on Economic Activity* 1: 255–78.

Brainard, William C., John B. Shoven, and Lawrence Weiss. 1980. The Financial Valuation of the Return to Capital. *Brookings Papers on Economic Activity* 2: 453–502.

Jensen, Michael C. 1988. Takeovers: Their Causes and Consequences. *Journal of Economic Perspectives* (Winter): 21–48.

Warshawsky, Mark. 1991. Postretirement Health Benefit Plans: Costs and Liabilities for Private Employers. In *Corporate Book Reserving for Postretirement Health Care Benefits,* ed. Dwight Bartlett III. Homewood, Ill.: Richard D. Irwin (in press).

———. 1989a. The Adequacy of Funding of Private Defined Benefit Pension Plans. In *Trends in Pensions,* ed. John Turner and Dan Beller. Washington, DC: Department of Labor.

———. 1989b. Tax Reform and Corporate Capital Structure. *Public Finance* 44(2): 295–307.

7 Sustainability, Premia, and the Dollar

Bankim Chadha and Steven Symansky

7.1 Introduction

The 1980s witnessed the emergence of large and persistent current account imbalances among the major industrial countries in the international economic system. The United States is presently running a current account deficit of some 2½ percent of its gross national product (GNP), while Japan and Germany have current surpluses of similar order relative to their output levels. The persistence of these payments imbalances has given rise to unprecedented changes in the stocks of net foreign assets and liabilities of these countries. This process has transformed the United States from the largest net creditor country during most of the postwar period to the world's largest net debtor, with net foreign liabilities estimated officially at $630 billion in 1989.[1] These developments have naturally raised fundamental questions about the magnitude and sustainability of the U.S. external position.

External sustainability of a debtor country is usually defined as a nonexplosive path of net foreign debt relative to some scale variable, that attempts to measure the ability of the country to generate payments to nonresident creditors. In the case of the United States, sustainability could be defined as a stable—or as a path leading to the attainment of a stable—net foreign asset to GNP ratio.[2] Consider now what the path of this ratio may look like with unchanged policies.[3] By the balance of payments identity, the net stock of foreign assets, F_t, can be expressed as

Bankim Chadha is an economist in the External Adjustment Division, Research Department of the International Monetary Fund. Steven Symansky is a senior economist in the External Adjustment Division, Research Department of the International Monetary Fund.

The authors would like to thank Charles Adams, Michael Dooley, Glenn Hubbard, Cara Lown, Paul Masson, and Richard Meese for helpful comments. The views expressed here are those of the authors and should not be interpreted as representing those of the International Monetary Fund.

(1) $$F_t = B_t + (1 + i) \cdot F_{t-1},$$

where B_t represents the trade balance and i the nominal interest rate. Dividing through by nominal GNP, and using lower-case letters to denote ratios to nominal GNP, we have that

(2) $$f_t = b_t + \frac{(1 + r)}{(1 + g)} f_{t-1},$$

or

(3) $$f_t - f_{t-1} = b_t + \frac{(r - g)}{(1 + g)} f_{t-1},$$

where r represents the real interest rate, in terms of domestic goods, and g the growth rate of real GNP. In 1989 the stock of net foreign assets is estimated to have been −12.0 percent of GNP and the trade balance −2.4 percent of GNP. Assuming a constant real interest rate, r, of 3.6 percentage points and a growth rate of real output, g, of 2.8 percent, it follows from (3) that for $r > g$, given that the f-ratio in 1989 was negative, the real interest burden per unit of output is positive. With a positive real interest burden, a necessary condition for the ratio to trough or stabilize over time is that the trade balance fall as a percentage of GNP and eventually go into surplus.

There is a whole set of exchange rate paths, policy changes, and behavioral responses that would lead to a stable f-ratio by pushing the balance of trade sufficiently into surplus to service the debt. One way of tackling the issue is to examine how much exchange rate depreciation is required for the ratio to stabilize. Figure 7.1 presents some illustrative paths for the f-ratio for alternative rates of depreciation of the dollar. The exchange rate paths represent nominal rates of depreciation of the dollar of 1, 2, and 3 percent a year against all currencies. The IMF's MULTIMOD model, which is described in the next section, was used to compute the improvements in the trade balance to GNP ratio, b, in response to an exogenous decline in the exchange rate. Nominal rather than real exchange rate paths were assumed so as to enable the model to endogenously determine the path of the real exchange rate and allow for other feedback effects. It should be noted that in all cases the extent of the real depreciation is substantially smaller, varying from 50 to 70 percent of the nominal depreciation.

Figure 7.1 shows that both the time required for the f-ratio to trough and the level at which it troughs can vary substantially. For a 1 percent rate of nominal depreciation, the ratio troughs at approximately −40 percent, albeit after a substantial period of time, by the year 2017. On the other hand, at a nominal rate of depreciation of 3 percent a year the ratio troughs at −20 percent by 1997. Note that for simplicity and purposes of comparison, the rate of depreciation has been kept constant up to the horizon presented. Therefore, the f-ratio continues to rise once it has troughed. There is of course no reason

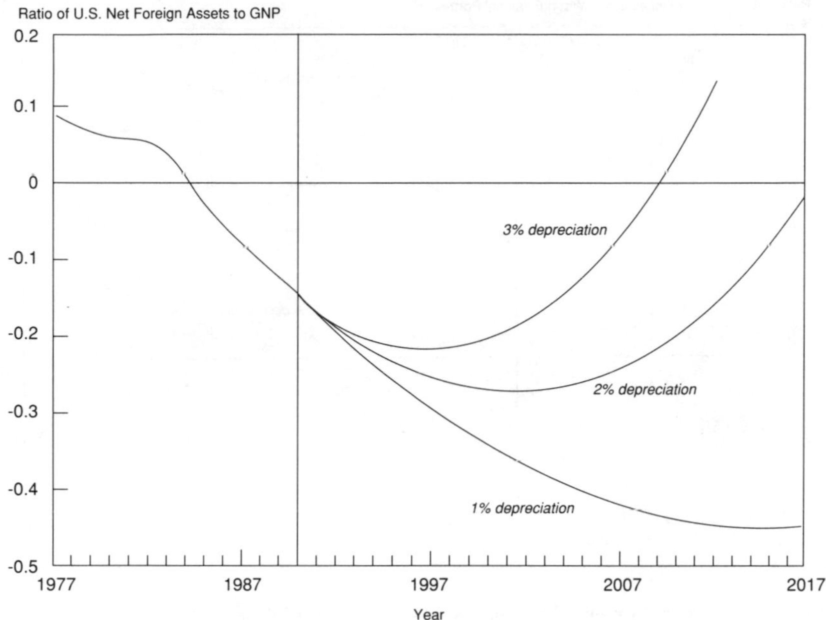

Fig. 7.1 U.S. net foreign assets under alternative exchange rate assumptions

why the exchange rate should continue to depreciate once the balance of trade is sufficiently in surplus to service the debt. If this were the case, the f-ratio would then likely stabilize.

The above discussion of sustainability, while showing that the f-ratio for the United States can easily trough or stabilize for reasonably small rates of depreciation of the dollar, ignores the issue of whether the ratio, even if it were to stabilize, would be consistent with the asset preferences of non-U.S. residents—the ultimate holders of the debt. The counterpart of the current and expected future decline in the U.S. f-ratio has been an increase in the share of holdings of net dollar assets in foreign portfolios. Recently, Dealtry and Van't dack (1989) have examined the impact of changes in the U.S. net external position on foreign portfolios. Their study suggests that the increase in the share of dollar assets in these portfolios has not been substantial. For example, they estimate that gross financial claims on the United States held by private residents of foreign industrial countries increased from 1.8 to 2.8 percent of total business-sector financial assets in these countries from 1981 to 1988, leaving a considerable potential for further increases. Moreover, they project that if the U.S. current account deficit were to persist at its 1988 level of $125 billion, with no change in the pattern of net capital inflows, this share would still be less than 4.5 percent by 1993. Figure 7.2 plots the counterpart of figure 7.1, expressing the ratio of net U.S. foreign assets as a percentage of

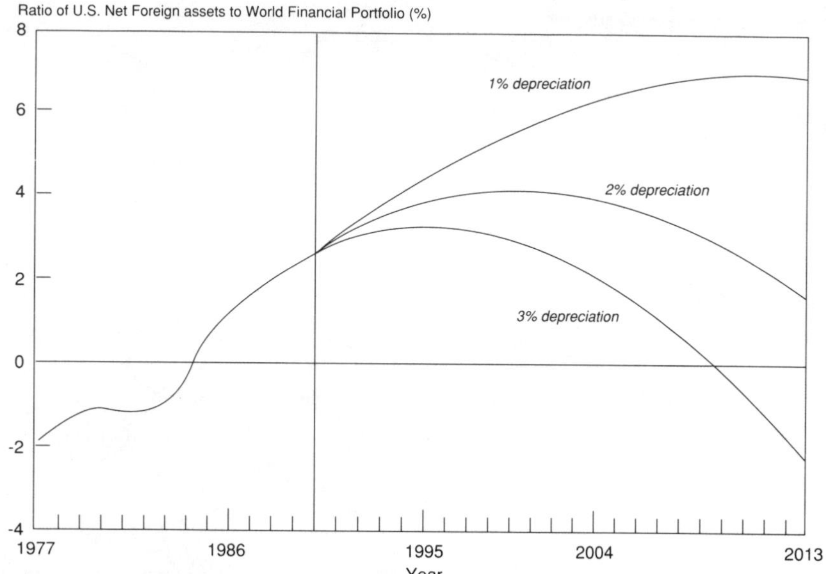

Fig. 7.2 U.S. net external liabilities in world financial portfolio

foreign industrial country financial portfolios, assuming for simplicity a constant financial portfolio to income ratio of three.[4]

The above suggests that (i) the U.S. net foreign asset to GNP ratio can stabilize or trough for reasonably small rates of depreciation of the dollar; and (ii) the associated increase in net U.S. liabilities as a proportion of foreign financial portfolios has been unprecedented but small, and is unlikely to increase substantially as a percentage of these portfolios if the U.S. *f*-ratio troughs or stabilizes. The final verdict on the sustainability of the U.S. external position, however, rests critically on the willingness of foreign investors to allow such an increase, however small, in their portfolios. A primary reason why foreign investors may become increasingly unwilling to hold additional quantities of U.S. debt is, as Dooley and Isard (1986) argue, the possibility of default. Krugman (1988, 1989a) and others have pointed out that for the United States, given its size and relatively limited dependence on foreign trade, the incentives to default may be greater than for other countries. This default does not have to take the form of an explicit refusal to repay. It could take the form of a differential tax levied by residence status, as in Dooley and Isard (1986)—for example, a tax on repatriated interest—or it could take the form of an inflation, or any other measure attempting to reduce the real value of the external debt to domestic residents. Moreover, there exists the possibility that foreign investors may decide to reduce the amount of U.S. debt they are willing to hold. This might happen for reasons that are either exogenous to the United States, for example, an increase in the attractiveness of investing elsewhere; or it could result from a perception that the path of the U.S. f-ratio was either unsustainable or going to become so, for example, because of an expected increase in the fiscal deficit. The situation is not unlike that for the Latin American debtors. Diaz-Alejandro (1984) attributes the build-up of Latin American debt during the 1970s to a one-time stock adjustment in international investors' portfolios, after which net inflows ceased abruptly, precipitating the "debt crisis" and consequent financial squeeze and depression of the 1980s in these economies. Therefore, a primary concern for the United States, resulting from the accumulation of foreign debt, is the exposure and vulnerability of the United States to a portfolio shift.

The purpose of this paper is to examine the effects of a portfolio shift against the dollar in a well-specified macroeconometric model for the industrial countries and the rest of the world. Section 7.2 briefly describes the model used. Section 7.3 then examines the effects of an exogenous shift in portfolio preferences against the dollar. Section 7.4 endogenizes the premium required to hold assets denominated in different currencies in world portfolios by making it a function of expected deviations of countries' f-ratios from arbitrarily specified levels. We examine what the path of the dollar might look like in such a scenario where, for example, there is a "run" on the dollar triggered by expectations that the U.S. external position will deteriorate. A conclusion that emerges from this section is that for reasonable declines in the U.S. f-ratio, such runs on the dollar would be stabilizing in that international investors could successfully impose on the U.S. an arbitrary f-ratio; and if it were to deviate, such a market reaction would bring it back. The economic consequences of such an imposed external adjustment are discussed. It is shown that small premiums can produce substantial movements of exchange rates and, over time, in f-ratios. Section 7.5 concludes the paper.

7.2 Overview of MULTIMOD

The simulations below use MULTIMOD, a multi-region econometric model developed by the IMF staff. While a more complete description of the model is available elsewhere,[5] a brief description is presented here in order to help the reader understand the simulations.

MULTIMOD is a system of linked models designed to analyze the interactions of economic policies and developments among the industrial countries, as well as to examine how changes in economic conditions in the industrial world affect developing countries as a group. It is a dynamic Mundell-Fleming model that incorporates rational expectations in both goods and financial markets. However, policy can be effective in altering output because not all markets clear contemporaneously. In the goods market, for example, it is assumed that there are overlapping contracts and prices are sticky.

The system presently contains econometric models (estimated on the basis of annual data) for each of the G-7 countries (the United States, Canada, Japan, Germany, France, Italy, and the United Kingdom), the smaller industrial countries as a group, high-income (capital-exporting) developing countries as a group, and other (capital-importing) developing countries as a group. Because of the limited degrees of freedom resulting from annual data, most of the equations were estimated using pooled cross-section time-series methods, and coefficients are often the same across countries unless rejected by the data.

The main linkages among the regions are the endogenous determination of prices and volumes of trade in goods and of exchange rates and interest rates. Each of the countries and regions produces manufactured goods which are imperfect substitutes. Imports of manufactured goods by the industrial countries (and capital-exporting developing countries) are functions of relative prices and absorption. Imports by the capital-importing countries depend upon the amount of available foreign exchange (which depends, in turn, on exports and on the region's current and expected ability to service its debt). Each country's (or region's) imports of manufactured goods are allocated as exports across the other countries and regions through a trade matrix, with the initial pattern based on historical trading patterns. Trade shares adjust in response to changes in relative prices. It is assumed that all countries demand oil and that oil is homogeneous, with the developing countries as a group the residual suppliers. Non-oil primary commodities are produced by the developing countries, and the price of this aggregate good adjusts in the short run to clear the market, with production and supply eventually responding to changes in relative prices.

Domestic demand is composed of exogenous government spending on goods and services, as well as behaviorally determined private consumption and investment. Private consumption is derived from intertemporal utility maximization and is determined, in equilibrium, by total wealth (discounted future income plus financial assets); in the short run, it is affected by changes in disposable income. Investment is modeled as a gradual adjustment to an optimal level for the capital stock determined by the production technology. The equation is estimated in error-correction form, with the error-correction term specified as a forward-weighted average of output to capital and a separate term for the user cost of capital

The prices of domestically produced goods are determined in a price-markup Phillips curve relationship that incorporates overlapping wage contracts, so that prices are sticky. Current wage contracts are forward looking, incorporating anticipated future rates of inflation. Export prices are assumed to move with the domestic output price in the long run, but respond in the short run to price movements in export markets. Import prices are a weighted average of the export prices of other countries.

MULTIMOD models the demand for base money, rather than for a broader aggregate. An interest-rate reaction function is used to determine the stance of monetary policy in a country. For example, a fixed exchange rate system is imposed for those countries of the European Monetary System (EMS) who participate in the exchange rate mechanism (ERM). Italy, France, and the smaller industrial countries as a group are assumed to peg their currencies to the German deutsche mark by altering their interest rates in the short run (and, of course, money supplies).[6] This policy regime results in a loss of monetary policy autonomy by all the ERM countries except Germany. In each of the other industrial countries, the monetary authorities set a target path for the monetary base. The actual path of the money supply is determined by the interest-rate reaction function which smoothes interest-rate changes in the short run. The specification of the interest-rate reaction function is used to avoid oscillations and large temporary changes in nominal interest rates (instrument instability), which result if the model is forced to track exactly a target path of the monetary base. In the long run, however, the actual money supply converges to the target path. With respect to monetary shocks, MULTIMOD has the important property that in the long run it is homogeneous of degree one in all nominal variables and degree zero in real variables.

Financial assets of the industrial countries are assumed to be perfect substitutes, and nominal exchange rates are determined by open interest parity. Long-term interest rates are specified as a weighted average of current and expected future short-term rates. An important feature of the model is that expectations about interest rates and exchange rates, as well as prices, are forward looking and consistent with the model's solution in future periods (i.e., expectations are "rational"). Thus current or expected future shocks to the model can result in rather substantial "jumps" in interest rates and exchange rates. These interest rate changes affect investment and consumption demand as well as the return on domestic and international debt stocks. The exchange rate primarily affects exports and imports through a change in relative prices.

A word of caution is necessary regarding the simulations in this paper. All the results are reported as a percentage or level deviation from a baseline value. The baseline for MULTIMOD assumes that over the long run, the noninterest government deficit and the trade balance tend toward balance, real variables grow at the real rate of interest, prices grow at the same rate as money, and thus all stock variables as a ratio to GNP stabilize.[7] These assumptions were made to allow the model to simulate around a reasonable steady state. In general the model is relatively log linear and the choice of a baseline is not crucial. However, for the scenarios discussed in this paper, the baseline does affect the results because of the importance of baseline debt stocks in determining the change in the current account resulting from a change in interest rates. Since the U.S. net foreign asset position in the baseline is negative, the fiscal expansion described in section 7.4 results in a larger deterioration in the U.S. current account balance than if the baseline net foreign asset position were positive. This implies that the exchange rate change necessary to attain any particular improvement in the external position will be larger. While the baseline assumptions affect the magnitude of the results, they do not alter the basic issues described in this paper.

7.3 Exogenous Depreciation of the Dollar

In this section we consider the effects of an exogenous dollar depreciation in order to highlight some of the properties of MULTIMOD.[8] In the IMF's *World Economic Outlook* in October 1988 and the OECD's *Economic Outlook* in June 1988, the effects on the world economy of a dollar depreciation, referred to as the "financial tensions" and "market enforced adjustment" scenarios, respectively, were discussed. In both cases, the analysis was motivated by the belief that the dollar was overvalued at the time, in light of current account imbalances that existed and the expectation that these imbalances would persist over the medium term. In the scenarios referred to above, the exchange rate is the outcome of an increase in the risk premium against dollar assets.[9] In the next section we postulate behavior that can endogenously produce a dollar depreciation, but in the discussion below we restrict the simulation to an exogenous decline in the nominal value of the dollar, with a compensating movement in the risk premium.

In this simulation, we assume that the U.S. dollar depreciates by 10 percent in nominal terms against all the currencies of the industrial countries. Table 7.1 presents the results as deviations from a baseline for the United States, an aggregate of the other industrial countries, and the developing countries.[10] Note that the real exchange rate depreciates by less than 10 percent as domestic prices adjust and offset some of the change in the nominal exchange rate, with the absorption deflator increasing by 3 percent above the baseline for the United States after a few years. On average, the real exchange rate depreciates by 7 percent. The trade balance worsens on impact because of a J-curve effect that lasts one year, but improves in both real and nominal terms over the medium and long run. The trade balance is, on average, about 1 percent of GNP above its baseline value, causing net foreign assets, as a percentage of GNP, to rise continuously over time.

The depreciation of the dollar requires an increase in the spread between U.S. and foreign interest rates. This increase in both real and nominal interest rates causes domestic demand to decline, both in the short run and over the medium term. Private consumption declines as a result of the increase in interest rates which reduces wealth (this decline in wealth more than offsets the increase in wealth arising from the increase in net foreign assets). The rise in the user cost of capital produces a permanent decrease in investment expenditures, and both the capital stock and capacity output decline over the long run. Although U.S. output rises in the short run because of an increase in net exports, it falls below the baseline after three years owing to the sustained

Table 7.1 **10 Percent Nominal Depreciation of the Dollar (deviations from baseline)**

	1990	1991	1992	1993	1994	1995	2000	2010
United States								
National Income								
Real GDP (%)	0.3	0.6	0.2	−0.2	−0.5	−0.7	−0.4	−0.6
Real GDP (growth rate)	0.3	0.2	−0.4	−0.4	−0.3	−0.2	0.1	−0.0
Real GNP (%)	0.4	0.5	0.1	−0.4	−0.7	−0.8	−0.1	0.1
Domestic demand (%)	−0.5	−0.9	−1.5	−2.1	−2.5	−2.7	−2.4	−2.9
Consumption expenditure (%)	−0.6	−1.1	−1.9	−2.7	−3.3	−3.6	−3.4	−3.9
Gross private investment (%)	−0.8	−1.4	−1.9	−2.2	−2.3	−2.1	−1.3	−2.3
Exports of goods and services (%)	2.7	3.7	4.9	5.3	5.3	5.2	5.4	6.6
Imports of goods and services (%)	−4.1	−7.4	−7.8	−7.9	−7.9	−7.9	−8.1	−8.9
Real GNP (1980 $ billion)	13.1	20.2	4.7	−14.3	−28.2	−34.4	−4.1	7.4
Real GDP (1980 $ billion)	13.0	22.7	9.0	−8.6	−22.9	−30.9	−18.2	−39.7
Consumption expenditure (1980 $ billion)	−15.0	−28.2	−49.5	−71.5	−89.8	−102.5	−109.4	−162.3
Gross private investment (1980 $ billion)	−5.4	−10.1	−14.7	−17.8	−19.2	−19.0	−13.3	−30.7
Real net exports (1980 $ billion)	33.4	61.0	73.1	80.7	86.1	90.6	104.4	153.3
Real government expenditure (1980 $ billion)	0.0	0.0	0.0	0.0	0.0	0.0	0.0	0.0
Government								
General government financial balance ($ billion)	−9.2	−17.6	−31.7	−40.5	−39.4	−33.1	10.8	−7.6
General government financial balance/GNP (%)	−0.2	−0.3	−0.5	−0.6	−0.5	−0.4	0.1	−0.0
Government debt ($ billion)	6.2	23.8	56.1	97.7	138.4	172.8	193.0	234.4
Government debt/GNP	−0.1	0.1	0.6	1.2	1.6	2.0	1.5	0.8
Money and interest rates								
Money supply (%)	0.9	0.9	0.7	0.3	−0.0	−0.3	−0.1	−0.0
Money supply (growth rate)	1.0	−0.1	−0.2	−0.3	−0.4	−0.3	0.2	−0.0
Money target (%)	0.0	0.0	0.0	0.0	0.0	0.0	0.0	0.0
Short-term interest rate	0.6	1.1	1.5	1.7	1.7	1.6	0.4	1.0
Long-term interest rate	1.3	1.5	1.6	1.5	1.2	1.0	0.6	0.9

(continued)

Table 7.1 (continued)

	1990	1991	1992	1993	1994	1995	2000	2010
United States								
Prices and supply								
Absorption deflator (%)	1.2	1.6	2.0	2.4	2.7	2.9	2.3	2.3
Absorption deflator (inflation rate)	1.2	0.4	0.4	0.4	0.3	0.2	−0.1	0.0
GNP deflator (%)	0.2	0.5	0.9	1.3	1.6	1.7	1.1	1.1
Export price deflator (%)	1.5	1.7	1.9	2.2	2.3	2.4	1.7	1.4
Import price deflator (%)	8.5	8.0	7.9	7.9	8.0	8.0	8.2	8.5
Capacity utilization rate	0.3	0.6	0.3	−0.1	−0.3	−0.5	0.0	−0.1
Long-term real interest rate	0.9	1.2	1.3	1.3	1.2	1.1	0.6	1.0
Real user cost of capital	0.6	0.8	0.9	1.0	0.9	0.8	0.4	0.8
International accounts								
Trade balance ($ billion)	−5.2	30.7	47.3	59.2	68.2	75.0	102.2	245.7
Current account balance ($ billion)	−5.2	26.2	39.4	47.9	56.8	66.0	133.0	403.2
Net foreign assets ($ billion)	−5.2	21.0	60.4	108.3	165.1	231.1	737.5	3,373.4
As a percent of nominal GNP								
Trade balance	−0.1	0.5	0.8	0.9	0.9	1.0	0.9	1.2
Current account balance	−0.1	0.5	0.6	0.7	0.8	0.9	1.2	1.9
Net foreign assets	−0.0	0.5	1.1	1.7	2.4	3.1	7.0	16.3
Nominal effective exchange rate (%)	−10.0	−10.0	−10.0	−10.0	−10.0	−10.0	−10.0	−10.0
Real effective exchange rate (%)	−7.6	−7.4	−7.0	−6.6	−6.4	−6.3	−7.4	−8.1

Other Industrial Countries								
National income								
Real GDP (%)	−0.2	−0.3	−0.1	0.1	0.3	0.4	0.2	0.3
Real GNP (%)	−0.2	−0.3	−0.1	0.1	0.3	0.3	−0.0	−0.2
Domestic demand (%)	0.3	0.6	1.0	1.3	1.5	1.6	1.4	1.5
Consumption expenditure (%)	0.4	0.7	1.2	1.6	2.0	2.2	2.0	2.1
Gross private investment (%)	0.6	1.1	1.4	1.6	1.6	1.4	1.0	1.4
Exports of goods and services (%)	−0.4	−1.6	−1.4	−1.1	−1.0	−1.1	−1.5	−1.3
Imports of goods and services (%)	1.3	1.4	2.0	2.5	2.6	2.5	2.0	2.3
Government and interest rates								
General government financial balance (local currency)	3.1	7.0	13.0	16.0	14.6	10.9	−3.0	1.6
Short-term interest rate	−0.3	−0.6	−0.9	−1.1	−1.1	−0.9	−0.3	−0.5
Long-term interest rate	−0.8	−0.9	−0.9	−0.9	−0.7	−0.6	−0.4	−0.5
Prices and supply								
Absorption deflator (%)	−0.6	−0.9	−1.2	−1.4	−1.5	−1.5	−1.2	−1.0
GNP deflator (%)	−0.1	−0.4	−0.6	−0.8	−1.0	−1.0	−0.5	−0.3
Export price deflator (%)	−1.1	−1.3	−1.4	−1.5	−1.5	−1.4	−1.0	−0.5
Import price deflator (%)	−2.5	−2.5	−2.6	−2.7	−2.7	−2.7	−2.5	−2.2
Capacity utilization rate	−0.2	−0.3	−0.2	0.0	0.2	0.2	−0.0	−0.0
Long-term real interest rate	−0.6	−0.8	−0.9	−0.8	−0.7	−0.6	−0.4	−0.6
International accounts								
Trade balance (local currency)	−2.6	−18.8	−25.4	−29.4	−31.6	−32.5	−38.1	−71.4
Current account balance (local currency)	−4.9	−19.6	−25.6	−29.6	−32.9	−35.8	−56.6	−151.0
Net foreign assets ($ billion)	10.4	−13.8	−53.4	−103.8	−163.9	−233.0	−732.5	−3,247.5

(continued)

Table 7.1 (continued)

	1990	1991	1992	1993	1994	1995	2000	2010
Other Industrial Countries								
As a percent of nominal GNP								
Trade balance	−0.0	−0.3	−0.3	−0.4	−0.4	−0.4	−0.3	−0.3
Current account balance	−0.1	−0.3	−0.3	−0.4	−0.4	−0.4	−0.5	−0.6
Net foreign assets	−0.4	−0.5	−0.8	−1.0	−1.2	−1.5	−2.8	−5.7
Nominal exchange rate (% in $/local currency)	11.1	11.1	11.1	11.1	11.1	11.1	11.1	11.1
Nominal effective exchange rate (%)	3.9	3.9	3.9	4.0	4.0	4.0	4.0	4.0
Real effective exchange rate (%)	1.5	1.5	1.4	1.4	1.3	1.3	1.6	1.8
Net Debtor Countries								
National income								
Real GDP (%)	−0.0	−0.1	−0.2	−0.2	−0.3	−0.3	−0.2	−0.2
Domestic demand (%)	−0.1	−0.3	−0.3	−0.3	−0.3	−0.3	−0.2	0.1
Consumption expenditure (%)	0.0	−0.0	−0.1	−0.2	−0.2	−0.3	−0.2	0.0
Gross private investment (%)	−0.3	−1.1	−0.9	−0.7	−0.5	−0.4	−0.2	0.3
Exports of goods and services (%)	−0.2	−0.9	−0.8	−0.7	−0.8	−0.8	−0.9	−0.9
Imports of goods and services (%)	−0.4	−1.5	−1.5	−1.4	−1.2	−1.1	−0.7	0.4

Prices and supply								
Absorption deflator (%)	8.3	8.3	8.2	8.1	8.0	8.0	8.3	8.6
GNP deflator (%)	8.2	8.1	8.1	8.0	8.0	8.0	8.3	8.6
Export price deflator (%)	7.8	7.9	7.9	7.9	7.9	7.9	8.1	8.4
Import price deflator (%)	8.6	8.5	8.3	8.2	8.2	8.3	8.3	8.4
International accounts								
Trade balance ($ billion)	−5.5	−0.8	0.3	0.3	−1.2	−3.3	−7.9	−42.4
Current account balance ($ billion)	−5.5	−2.0	−0.9	0.3	1.5	2.5	7.0	24.6
Net debt ($ billion)	4.8	8.3	11.5	14.2	16.5	18.8	33.2	72.5
Interest payments as a % of exports	−1.2	−0.0	0.9	1.7	1.9	1.8	0.2	1.0
As a percent of nominal GDP								
Trade balance	−0.1	0.0	0.1	0.1	0.0	−0.0	−0.0	−0.2
Current account balance	−0.0	0.1	0.1	0.1	0.1	0.1	0.1	0.1
Net debt	−2.2	−2.1	−1.9	−1.8	−1.7	−1.7	−1.6	−1.6
Nominal effective exchange rate (%)	−6.3	−6.3	−6.3	−6.3	−6.3	−6.3	−6.3	−6.3
Real effective exchange rate (%)	−0.0	−0.1	−0.1	−0.2	−0.3	−0.3	−0.2	−0.3
World Prices								
Price of oil	7.0	7.0	6.9	6.9	7.0	7.0	7.0	7.2
Price index of commodities	7.2	8.2	8.6	8.8	8.9	8.8	8.7	8.7

decline in domestic demand. Thus the exogenous nominal depreciation produces a permanent rise in the real interest rate and results in a permanent loss of output. In addition, it is worth noting that the dollar depreciation increases the domestic debt burden of the government. First, the increase in interest rates increases the servicing of the existing stock. Second, real output declines, reducing the tax base. Lastly, nominal government spending and taxes both rise with inflation, but since the government balance is initially in deficit, the rise in domestic prices worsens the deficit.

In general the effect on the aggregate of the other industrial countries is the mirror image of the United States, although the deviations are more modest. The exchange rate change for each of these countries is smaller than for the United States in effective terms, since each country is depreciating against the dollar but remaining unchanged against the other currencies. The developing countries are detrimentally affected by the dollar depreciation as exports from this region decline. Combined with the rise in U.S. interest rates, foreign financing, and therefore imports, decline. Since imports are the primary source of capital formation, output declines over the medium term.

7.4 Endogenous Premia and External Sustainability

In this section we examine, through simulations of MULTIMOD, the possible effects of international investors demanding a premium on holding dollar assets if the U.S. net foreign asset to GNP ratio is expected to deviate from some arbitrarily specified exogenous level, assumed to be perceived by investors to be "sustainable."[11] In the baseline scenario for MULTIMOD, discussed in section 7.2, the ratios of government debt and net foreign assets to GNP stabilize over the long run. These assumptions were made to allow the model to simulate around a reasonable steady state. The first simulation presented below, and shown in table 7.2, assumes that the decline in fiscal expenditures included in the arbitrary baseline does not materialize. Rather, fiscal expenditures are substantially above the baseline values. Since the paths for the fiscal variables in the baseline rest on a policy stance similar to Gramm-Rudmann, it is quite plausible to assume that these goals would not be achieved unless Congress and the White House significantly change their behavior. It appears that the anticipated peace dividends resulting from the easing of tensions in Eastern Europe will likely be spent on increased aid to this region or domestic programs. More precisely, we permanently increase fiscal expenditures by 5 percent of GNP above our baseline, phased in gradually over three years.[12]

The fiscal expansion results in a relatively small and temporary increase in U.S. output, with a substantial increase in the long-term nominal and real interest rates, although short-term rates actually fall on impact.[13] With a prolonged increase in the real interest rate, domestic investment is persistently crowded out and the stock of capital falls over the long run, resulting in a permanent decline in capacity and hence output. The increase in domestic absorption and the appreciation of the real exchange rate produce a substantial increase in the trade deficit. The increase in U.S. nominal interest rates amplifies the deficit on the current account, and the net foreign asset position continues to deteriorate.[14] In fact, it appears that it is on an unstable path. The increase in government spending substantially raises the ratio of domestic government debt to GNP, results in a permanent increase in interest rates and a permanent appreciation of the nominal and the real exchange rate.

The U.S. fiscal expansion increases the output of foreign industrial countries, at least in the short run, primarily through the increase in foreign net exports. However, the appreciation of the dollar puts upward pressure on foreign domestic prices, creating a decline in the real money supply and an increase in interest rates. Therefore, output declines over the medium term because of a fall in both domestic consumption and real investment. The counterpart to the decline in the U.S. net foreign asset position is of course a rise in the net foreign asset position of the other industrial countries. The developing countries are not adversely affected by the U.S. fiscal expansion. Although net lending to the debtor countries falls as the increase in U.S. interest rates reduces the ability of these countries to service the debt, the U.S.-induced increase in export revenues more than compensates and the developing countries are able to increase their imports.

As argued earlier, it seems unreasonable to believe that the industrial countries will continue to build up claims on the United States without some compensating increase in the rate of return on U.S. assets. MULTIMOD assumes that assets denominated in different currencies are perfect substitutes. Therefore, the primary channel remaining to return net asset stocks to their steady-state values is changes in consumption due to wealth transfers. Although these net foreign assets are part of total wealth and their change is rather substantial in the U.S. fiscal expansion, this component of financial wealth represents a relatively small fraction of total wealth. If the model were run for more than fifty years, eventually the change in the net foreign asset positions would dominate total wealth and domestic consumption would respond.[15] But the assumption of perfect asset substitutability becomes less tenable as the size of interest payments made to foreign residents grows substantially, increasing the incentive for either an explicit or implicit default. This could take the form of new tax laws on income to foreigners or possibly some form of capital controls.[16] Krugman (1988), for example, suggests that the United States, probably more than any other country, has the least incentive to abide by the rules of the game. Thus, it is likely that a premium of some form will become necessary for foreign investors to hold U.S. assets if the foreign asset to GNP ratio is expected to continuously worsen, as in this fiscal scenario. Branson and Marchese (1988) posit the existence of such a premium on portfolio-balance grounds.

The approach used here is to assume that there is an arbitrary long-run level of the net foreign assets to GNP ratio, $\bar{f}$, that foreign investors perceive as

Table 7.2 **Rise in U.S. Government Expenditure (deviations from baseline)**

	1990	1991	1992	1993	1994	1995	2000	2010
United States								
National income								
Real GDP (%)	1.3	1.8	2.8	1.5	0.1	−0.9	−1.0	−0.7
Real GDP (growth rate)	1.3	0.5	1.0	−1.3	−1.4	−1.1	0.3	−0.2
Real GNP (%)	1.4	1.9	2.9	1.2	−0.5	−1.8	−2.5	−3.8
Domestic demand (%)	2.3	3.7	5.4	4.3	3.3	2.6	2.4	2.0
Consumption expenditure (%)	0.9	1.0	1.0	−0.3	−1.5	−2.6	−3.2	−3.3
Gross private investment (%)	2.0	1.2	−0.1	−1.6	−2.7	−3.2	−2.0	−3.5
Exports of goods and services (%)	−2.1	−3.6	−5.2	−7.0	−7.8	−8.1	−7.6	−6.6
Imports of goods and services (%)	6.4	10.9	14.0	13.1	13.7	14.3	14.5	11.7
Real GNP (1980 $ billion)	49.2	69.6	108.5	48.5	−18.1	−76.0	−118.6	−232.3
Real GDP (1980 $ billion)	49.2	70.1	113.0	61.5	5.7	−39.8	−48.0	−43.3
Consumption expenditure (1980 $ billion)	22.5	25.7	27.1	−6.9	−42.4	−72.4	−104.4	−139.9
Gross private investment (1980 $ billion)	13.4	8.7	−0.6	−12.9	−22.7	−28.4	−20.1	−46.9
Real net exports (1980 $ billion)	−44.0	−81.8	−114.6	−125.2	−141.1	−156.8	−172.3	−181.3
Real government expenditure (1980 $ billion)	57.2	117.5	201.1	206.5	212.1	217.8	248.8	324.8
Government								
General government financial balance ($ billion)	−57.8	−150.8	−297.3	−377.8	−473.9	−578.7	−1,000.8	−2,742.8
General government financial balance/GNP (%)	−1.0	−2.4	−4.4	−5.2	−6.2	−7.1	−8.7	−12.4
Government debt ($ billion)	58.9	207.6	501.6	877.6	1,352.2	1,933.5	6,182.5	23,871.4
Government debt/GNP	0.5	2.6	6.1	10.9	16.5	22.7	52.9	107.4
Money and interest rates								
Money supply (%)	−0.3	0.3	1.2	1.5	1.3	0.6	−0.6	0.1
Money supply (growth rate)	−0.4	0.7	0.9	0.4	−0.3	−0.7	0.2	−0.1
Money target (%)	0.0	0.0	0.0	0.0	0.0	0.0	0.0	0.0
Short-term interest rate	−0.2	−0.0	0.7	1.6	2.4	2.8	1.1	1.7
Long-term interest rate	0.9	1.5	2.1	2.5	2.5	2.4	1.0	1.4

Prices and supply								
Absorption deflator (%)	−0.7	−0.4	0.4	1.6	2.7	3.7	5.4	6.8
Absorption deflator (inflation rate)	−0.8	0.3	0.9	1.2	1.2	1.0	−0.0	0.3
GNP deflator (%)	0.2	0.8	2.0	3.4	4.9	6.2	7.7	8.7
Export price deflator (%)	−1.1	−0.5	0.5	1.8	3.2	4.5	6.8	8.6
Import price deflator (%)	−6.5	−6.5	−6.7	−7.0	−6.8	−6.5	−4.0	−1.1
Capacity utilization rate	1.3	1.7	2.7	1.4	0.1	−0.8	−0.5	−0.0
Long-term real interest rate	−0.0	0.4	1.0	1.6	1.9	1.9	0.9	1.7
Real user cost of capital	−0.4	−0.1	0.4	0.9	1.2	1.3	0.7	1.4
International accounts								
Trade balance ($ billion)	−11.7	−49.6	−80.4	−84.6	−97.1	−112.0	−160.8	−240.7
Current account balance ($ billion)	−11.7	−51.0	−89.7	−111.4	−148.1	−192.8	−352.8	−988.2
Net foreign assets ($ billion)	−11.7	−62.7	−152.4	−263.9	−412.0	−604.8	−2,104.1	−8,413.3
As a percent of nominal GNP								
Trade balance	−0.2	−0.7	−1.1	−1.1	−1.2	−1.3	−1.3	−1.1
Current account balance	−0.2	−0.8	−1.2	−1.4	−1.8	−2.2	−2.9	−4.4
Net foreign assets	0.0	−0.6	−1.4	−2.8	−4.5	−6.5	−17.0	−36.6
Nominal effective exchange rate (%)	9.6	10.3	11.3	12.1	12.2	11.7	6.9	2.2
Real effective exchange rate (%)	7.5	8.3	9.9	11.7	13.2	14.2	13.5	11.0
Other Industrial Countries								
National income								
Real GDP (%)	0.2	0.2	−0.0	−0.5	−0.7	−0.8	−0.2	−0.5
Real GNP (%)	0.3	0.3	0.1	−0.3	−0.3	−0.2	0.7	1.2
Domestic demand (%)	−0.5	−1.0	−1.7	−2.3	−2.7	−2.8	−2.2	−2.2
Consumption expenditure (%)	−0.5	−1.1	−2.0	−2.9	−3.5	−3.9	−3.3	−3.0
Gross private investment (%)	−1.0	−1.8	−2.5	−2.9	−2.9	−2.7	−1.3	−2.0
Exports of goods and services (%)	1.3	2.3	2.6	1.5	1.5	2.0	3.3	2.5
Imports of goods and services (%)	−1.0	−1.7	−2.7	−4.0	−4.3	−4.3	−2.7	−2.6

(continued)

Table 7.2 (continued)

	1990	1991	1992	1993	1994	1995	2000	2010
Other Industrial Countries								
Government and interest rates								
General government financial balance (local currency)	−2.5	−9.2	−16.0	−22.3	−18.1	−10.7	14.9	10.7
Short-term interest rate	0.4	0.9	1.3	1.5	1.6	1.5	0.5	0.7
Long-term interest rate	1.1	1.4	1.4	1.4	1.2	1.0	0.6	0.7
Prices and supply								
Absorption deflator (%)	0.7	1.1	1.6	1.8	1.9	1.8	0.4	0.4
GNP deflator (%)	0.2	0.5	0.8	1.0	1.0	0.8	−0.6	−0.4
Export price deflator (%)	1.4	1.7	2.2	2.4	2.4	2.1	0.1	−0.4
Import price deflator (%)	2.8	3.3	4.0	4.4	4.6	4.5	2.5	1.5
Capacity utilization rate	0.2	0.2	0.1	−0.3	−0.5	−0.4	0.2	0.0
Long-term real interest rate	0.9	1.2	1.5	1.5	1.4	1.2	0.5	0.8
International accounts								
Trade balance (local currency)	11.2	31.5	46.8	49.0	55.0	61.1	75.7	115.3
Current account balance (local currency)	13.7	34.9	54.0	63.7	78.8	95.0	149.1	382.0
Net foreign assets ($ billion)	7.0	53.5	136.5	238.6	373.4	547.5	1,899.2	7,645.8
As a percent of nominal GNP								
Trade balance	0.2	0.4	0.6	0.6	0.7	0.7	0.6	0.5
Current account balance	0.2	0.5	0.7	0.8	0.9	1.1	1.2	1.6
Net foreign assets	0.5	0.9	1.5	2.1	2.8	3.6	7.4	13.8
Nominal exchange rate (% in $/local currency)	−9.8	−10.4	−11.3	−12.0	−12.2	−11.9	−7.3	−2.8
Nominal effective exchange rate (%)	−3.6	−3.8	−4.2	−4.5	−4.6	−4.5	−2.8	−1.1
Real effective exchange rate (%)	−1.5	−1.7	−2.1	−2.4	−2.6	−2.8	−2.7	−2.3

Net Debtor Countries								
National income								
Real GDP (%)	0.3	0.5	0.7	0.5	0.2	0.1	0.2	0.2
Domestic demand (%)	0.4	0.7	0.9	0.6	0.4	0.3	0.5	0.6
Consumption expenditure (%)	0.1	0.3	0.5	0.5	0.4	0.3	0.3	0.5
Gross private investment (%)	1.5	2.1	2.3	0.7	0.2	0.1	1.3	1.0
Exports of goods and services (%)	1.4	2.2	2.8	1.4	0.8	0.6	1.7	1.1
Imports of goods and services (%)	2.2	3.5	4.1	2.0	1.1	0.8	2.2	2.4
Prices and supply								
Absorption deflator (%)	−6.9	−6.9	−6.9	−7.0	−6.8	−6.4	−3.7	−0.2
GNP deflator (%)	−6.7	−6.7	−6.7	−6.9	−6.7	−6.3	−3.5	−0.1
Export price deflator (%)	−6.1	−6.3	−6.3	−6.9	−7.0	−6.7	−3.5	−0.2
Import price deflator (%)	−7.5	−7.6	−7.7	−7.6	−7.2	−6.6	−3.5	0.0
International accounts								
Trade balance ($ billion)	5.0	2.3	2.5	2.8	1.7	−0.1	−5.3	−39.2
Current account balance ($ billion)	5.0	1.8	0.4	−1.1	−2.9	−4.0	−3.8	−5.0
Net debt ($ billion)	−4.4	−7.6	−10.1	−11.7	−12.2	−12.1	−12.5	6.0
Interest payments as a % of exports	0.8	0.7	1.2	2.9	4.3	5.2	2.7	2.6
As a percent of nominal GDP								
Trade balance	0.1	0.0	0.0	0.0	−0.0	−0.0	−0.1	−0.3
Current account balance	0.0	−0.0	−0.1	−0.1	−0.1	−0.1	−0.1	−0.0
Net debt	2.0	1.8	1.7	1.7	1.7	1.6	0.8	−0.0
Nominal effective exchange rate (%)	5.9	6.3	6.9	7.4	7.5	7.2	4.2	1.4
Real effective exchange rate (%)	0.2	0.4	0.7	0.6	0.4	0.2	0.1	0.1
World Prices								
Price of oil	−6.3	−6.3	−6.3	−6.1	−5.6	−5.0	−2.1	1.2
Price index of commodities	−4.5	−5.6	−5.9	−8.6	−9.8	−9.9	−5.1	−1.9

"sustainable." Investors will demand a premium if it appears that, ex ante, the ratio would deviate from this level because of policy changes or exogenous shocks. We assume that the premium is constant over time and, if the system is stable, the magnitude is enough to force the net foreign asset to GNP ratio back to this prespecified level over a specific time period (twenty years, in this paper). The rule used here is somewhat arbitrary, and it is easy to imagine alternative functional forms. Nevertheless, it provides a useful, model-based way to capture "rational runs" on a currency. Some alternative functional forms are discussed below.

The mechanics of the rule are as follows. We first define a currency premium, η, and a predetermined target value of the foreign asset to GNP ratio, $\bar{f}$. The value of η is determined such that f_T converged to $\bar{f}$ when η is added to the interest-arbitrage condition

(4) $$(1 + i) = (1 + i^*) \cdot (e_{t+1} / e_t) + \eta,$$

where i^* and e are defined, respectively, as multilaterally weighted foreign nominal interest rates and the exchange rate (defined as the number of units of the domestic currency for a unit of the foreign currency).[17] In order to solve for the equilibrium value of η that is consistent with the underlying model and satisfies the above $\bar{f}$ convergence condition, we used the following iterative process. There are eight industrial countries or regions in the model. Therefore we included premia for $N-1$, or 7 countries; the United States was the excluded country. The first step in the procedure is to run a number of simulations on the model. For a specific currency, j, we shock η by adding an arbitrary value to η in equation (4) for the jth currency. We then calculate a vector composed of $\Delta f^i_T / \Delta\eta^j$, for $i = 1$ to 7. We then calculate the other six j vectors by shocking η for the other currencies. We refer to the full 7×7 derivative matrix as Z. The matrix Z is the matrix of (numerical) derivatives of changes in net foreign asset to GNP ratios with respect to changes in the premia.

Taking the first-order Taylor expansion of $f_T(\eta)$, the equation $f_T(\eta) = \bar{f}$ can be written

(5) $$f^k_T = \bar{f} - Z \cdot \Delta\eta,$$

where $f^k{}_T$ is the vector of values of the net foreign asset ratio from any simulation of the model in which η is initially set to zero. Solving (5) for η, we get

(6) $$\eta^{k+1} = \eta^k + Z^{-1} \cdot [\bar{f} - f^k_T].$$

We then add these new values of η to the model, re-solve the model, and recalculate (6) until η converges.

Table 7.3 shows the deviations from the baseline scenario of the combined effects of the premia behavior described above and the fiscal shock. The weighted premium against the dollar turned out to be 1.08 percentage points.

Compared to table 7.2, we find that there has been a substantial reduction in the net foreign asset position of the United States. Although equation (6) implies that there should not be any deviation in the net foreign asset position for any country, the results show modest deviations: for the United States, the deviation is reduced from −36.6 to −4.4 percent by the year 2010; the aggregate of the other industrial countries shows a deviation from the baseline of 1 percent in 2010 compared to 14 percent in the pure fiscal shock. This is because MULTIMOD includes two developing country regions that are not represented in (6), and thus their net foreign asset positions were allowed to deviate from $\bar{f}$. Since world net foreign assets sum to zero in the model and all industrial countries except the United States reduce the deviations of their f-ratios to approximately zero, as implied by equation (6), the negative of the developing country deviation shows up in the U.S. position.

The U.S. dollar, which appreciated in the pure fiscal scenario, now depreciates by 14 percent, although the year-on-year premium is small—little over one percentage point. These results present a "hard landing" for the dollar. While the nominal exchange rate depreciates on impact and hovers permanently in this new range, the real exchange rate depreciates on impact and then appreciates, regaining its baseline level almost exactly by 2010. Short and long, real and nominal interest rates rise by considerably more than in the previous scenario. Moreover, note that the difference in the increase in interest rates between the two scenarios increases over time; that is to say, the effect on interest rates of an increase in the premium against the dollar increases over time. Thus, the financial squeeze resulting from the portfolio shift away from dollar assets increases over time.

This "hard landing" imposes considerable long-run costs on the United States. While output in the United States shows a rather substantial increase on impact, even larger than in the pure fiscal expansion because of an expansion of exports accompanying the exchange rate depreciation, the gain is short lived. After five years, output is below its baseline level and the growth rate is down by two percentage points. Moreover, the long-run decline in capacity, and hence output, is larger. While the dollar depreciation does help the foreign sector, the higher real interest rates seriously discourage domestic consumption and investment. The higher U.S. interest rates also directly increase the domestic and foreign debt-service burdens. There is a worsening of the general government financial balance as a result of increased debt service, an increase in the nominal value of fixed government expenditure in real terms, and a decline in tax revenues as the tax base declines. The brunt of the adjustment required is therefore borne by domestic consumption and investment.

For the other industrial countries, the dollar depreciation causes some short-run costs in the form of a decline in output through net exports, but encourages modest long-term growth through the decline in interest rates. In the pure fiscal scenario, these countries experienced higher interest rates and a long-term loss of output. For the developing countries, this outcome is

Table 7.3 **Rise in U.S. Government Expenditure with Endogenous Risk Premia (deviations from baseline)**

	1990	1991	1992	1993	1994	1995	2000	2010
United States								
National income								
Real GDP (%)	2.1	3.1	3.3	1.1	−0.9	−2.2	−1.8	−1.5
Real GDP (growth rate)	2.2	1.0	0.2	−2.2	−2.0	−1.4	0.6	−0.2
Real GNP (%)	2.2	3.1	3.1	0.4	−1.9	−3.5	−2.8	−2.8
Domestic demand (%)	1.3	1.7	2.1	−0.2	−2.1	−3.4	−3.3	−1.9
Consumption expenditure (%)	−0.3	−1.4	−3.2	−6.1	−8.6	−10.5	−11.3	−8.7
Gross private investment (%)	0.6	−1.4	−3.9	−6.4	−8.0	−8.6	−5.4	−6.8
Exports of goods and services (%)	2.8	3.4	4.4	3.6	3.0	2.7	3.8	1.4
Imports of goods and services (%)	−2.9	−5.9	−3.7	−5.0	−5.4	−5.7	−6.7	−1.8
Real GNP (1980 $ billion)	80.5	114.9	117.4	17.1	−74.7	−143.1	−133.5	−174.3
Real GDP (1980 $ billion)	80.3	121.4	131.9	43.7	−37.7	−96.7	−88.7	−99.5
Consumption expenditure (1980 $ billion)	−8.0	−36.2	−83.4	−163.5	−237.6	−297.3	−364.5	−365.7
Gross private investment (1980 $ billion)	3.9	−10.6	−30.6	−51.8	−67.6	−76.0	−54.5	−90.0
Real net exports (1980 $ billion)	27.2	50.7	44.8	52.5	55.4	58.8	81.5	31.5
Real government expenditure (1980 $ billion)	57.2	117.5	201.1	206.5	212.1	217.8	248.8	324.8
Government								
General government financial balance ($ billion)	−79.4	−192.2	−388.4	−531.5	−688.1	−853.4	−1,398.5	−3,587.4
General government financial balance/GNP (%)	−1.3	−3.0	−5.6	−7.2	−8.8	−10.2	−11.8	−15.9
Government debt ($ billion)	73.9	264.2	650.4	1,182.1	1,873.1	2,731.1	8,878.9	32,240.1
Government debt/GNP	0.4	2.7	7.5	14.3	22.3	31.2	74.1	142.7
Money and interest rates								
Money supply (%)	1.7	2.2	2.6	2.4	1.5	0.4	−1.3	−0.0
Money supply (growth rate)	1.8	0.5	0.4	−0.2	−0.8	−1.2	0.4	−0.1
Money target (%)	0.0	0.0	0.0	0.0	0.0	0.0	0.0	0.0
Short-term interest rate	1.1	2.4	4.0	5.4	6.4	6.7	2.4	2.9
Long-term interest rate	3.8	5.0	5.7	6.0	5.8	5.1	2.0	2.3

Prices and supply								
Absorption deflator (%)	1.8	2.9	4.8	7.1	9.3	11.0	11.6	9.5
Absorption deflator (inflation rate)	1.9	1.1	1.9	2.3	2.2	1.7	−0.6	0.1
GNP deflator (%)	0.6	1.9	3.9	6.4	8.7	10.5	10.7	9.4
Export price deflator (%)	2.4	3.1	4.6	6.7	8.8	10.5	11.3	8.9
Import price deflator (%)	11.8	9.7	9.5	9.9	11.1	12.7	16.1	9.0
Capacity utilization rate	2.1	3.1	3.3	1.2	−0.5	−1.6	−0.4	0.2
Long-term real interest rate	1.8	2.9	3.9	4.7	5.0	4.8	2.3	2.9
Real user cost of capital	0.7	1.5	2.5	3.2	3.7	3.7	1.9	2.4
International accounts								
Trade balance ($ billion)	−29.8	13.5	15.1	35.6	45.7	52.4	82.2	89.2
Current account balance ($ billion)	−29.8	1.5	−13.4	−20.2	−37.2	−58.1	−54.7	−239.1
Net foreign assets ($ billion)	−29.8	−28.3	−41.7	−62.0	−99.2	−157.2	−536.4	−1,500.7
As a percent of nominal GNP								
Trade balance	−0.4	0.3	0.4	0.7	0.7	0.8	0.8	0.4
Current account balance	−0.4	0.2	0.0	−0.1	−0.3	−0.5	−0.3	−0.9
Net foreign assets	−0.1	0.3	0.6	0.4	0.1	−0.4	−2.5	−4.4
Nominal effective exchange rate (%)	−13.9	−12.4	−11.8	−12.1	−13.0	−14.2	−18.0	−10.3
Real effective exchange rate (%)	−10.1	−7.9	−5.7	−3.8	−2.5	−2.0	−5.3	−0.1
Other Industrial Countries								
National income								
Real GDP (%)	−0.8	−1.1	−0.6	−0.3	0.1	0.4	0.4	0.1
Real GNP (%)	−0.9	−1.1	−0.5	−0.1	0.3	0.7	0.5	0.4
Domestic demand (%)	−0.3	−0.2	0.2	0.5	0.9	1.2	1.3	0.1
Consumption expenditure (%)	−0.2	−0.2	0.2	0.7	1.1	1.6	1.9	−0.1
Gross private investment (%)	−1.0	−0.4	0.2	0.8	1.2	1.4	1.[illegible]	0.6
Exports of goods and services (%)	−0.9	−2.3	−1.0	−1.3	−1.0	−0.7	−1.[illegible]	0.1
Imports of goods and services (%)	0.7	0.4	1.2	1.2	1.4	1.6	1.6	0.0

(continued)

Table 7.3 (continued)

	1990	1991	1992	1993	1994	1995	2000	2010
Other Industrial Countries								
Government and interest rates								
General government financial balance (local currency)	0.5	7.7	20.6	28.2	33.2	34.3	16.6	31.1
Short-term interest rate	−0.2	−0.6	−1.0	−1.2	−1.2	−1.1	−0.1	0.4
Long-term interest rate	−0.8	−1.0	−1.1	−1.0	−0.9	−0.7	−0.0	0.7
Prices and supply								
Absorption deflator (%)	−0.8	−1.4	−2.2	−3.1	−3.9	−4.5	−4.4	−3.5
GNP deflator (%)	−0.4	−1.1	−2.0	−3.0	−3.8	−4.4	−4.2	−3.8
Export price deflator (%)	−2.0	−2.2	−2.6	−3.2	−3.8	−4.3	−4.5	−3.2
Import price deflator (%)	−3.7	−3.5	−3.4	−3.7	−4.1	−4.5	−5.2	−2.9
Capacity utilization rate	−0.8	−1.0	−0.5	−0.3	0.1	0.4	0.2	0.0
Long-term real interest rate	−0.0	−0.3	−0.5	−0.6	−0.7	−0.6	−0.2	0.2
International accounts								
Trade balance (local currency)	0.7	−16.8	−17.5	−24.3	−26.2	−26.3	−27.8	15.3
Current account balance (local currency)	−3.5	−16.8	−13.2	−14.2	−12.1	−9.3	−14.9	65.1
Net foreign assets ($ billion)	35.6	33.7	40.3	46.3	63.1	94.8	306.8	1,044.1
As a percent of nominal GNP								
Trade balance	0.0	−0.2	−0.2	−0.3	−0.3	−0.3	−0.2	0.1
Current account balance	−0.0	−0.2	−0.2	−0.1	−0.1	−0.1	−0.1	0.3
Net foreign assets	−0.6	−0.5	−0.5	−0.5	−0.5	−0.5	−0.4	1.0
Nominal exchange rate (% in $/local currency)	22.5	19.8	18.9	19.6	21.5	24.1	31.2	14.9
Nominal effective exchange rate (%)	7.9	7.1	6.8	7.1	7.8	8.8	11.2	5.4
Real effective exchange rate (%)	2.6	2.1	1.6	1.2	1.0	1.0	1.9	0.6

Net Debtor Countries								
National income								
Real GDP (%)	0.2	0.3	0.4	0.0	−0.3	−0.4	−0.2	0.3
Domestic demand (%)	0.1	−0.1	0.2	−0.1	−0.3	−0.3	−0.1	1.0
Consumption expenditure (%)	0.1	0.2	0.2	0.1	0.0	−0.1	−0.0	1.1
Gross private investment (%)	−0.1	−0.9	−0.1	−1.0	−1.2	−1.0	−0.2	0.8
Exports of goods and services (%)	0.5	−0.2	0.7	−0.3	−0.9	−1.2	−0.7	−0.4
Imports of goods and services (%)	0.1	−0.9	0.4	−1.1	−1.6	−1.6	−0.3	3.4
Prices and supply								
Absorption deflator (%)	12.4	11.0	10.5	10.7	11.6	12.8	17.0	9.3
GNP deflator (%)	12.1	10.7	10.4	10.7	11.5	12.7	16.9	9.3
Export price deflator (%)	12.0	11.0	10.9	10.8	11.4	12.6	17.2	9.3
Import price deflator (%)	13.2	11.4	10.7	11.1	12.2	13.8	18.1	9.9
International accounts								
Trade balance ($ billion)	−8.0	−0.7	1.1	0.7	−4.3	−11.4	−26.9	−129.1
Current account balance ($ billion)	−8.0	−3.7	−3.4	−2.4	−1.3	0.9	21.3	36.5
Net debt ($ billion)	7.0	12.7	18.9	25.3	32.4	39.6	60.4	64.3
Interest payments as a % of exports	−1.9	0.6	3.1	6.3	8.1	8.8	3.1	3.5
As a percent of nominal GDP								
Trade balance	−0.1	0.1	0.1	0.1	−0.0	−0.1	−0.2	−0.7
Current account balance	−0.0	0.1	0.0	0.1	0.1	0.1	0.2	0.2
Net debt	−3.3	−2.8	−2.5	−2.3	−2.3	−2.4	−3.3	−1.9
Nominal effective exchange rate (%)	−8.5	−7.6	−7.2	−7.3	−7.9	−8.7	−11.1	−6.2
Real effective exchange rate (%)	0.1	0.2	0.3	0.2	−0.1	−0.3	−0.4	−0.2
World Prices								
Price of oil	11.0	9.7	9.3	9.8	10.9	12.4	16.3	9.0
Price index of commodities	11.8	12.7	13.8	12.4	12.6	13.9	19.4	9.4

worse than the pure fiscal expansion, primarily because of the increased burden of higher U.S. interest rates.

It is interesting to note that a relatively small premium of little over one percentage point a year can bring about sizable movements in exchange rates—a 14 percent nominal and a 10 percent real depreciation on impact—and over time can cause a substantial movement in the f-ratio—more than 32 percentage points in twenty years. This accords well with the observation that though large changes in exchange rates have been observed in the 1980s, observed ex post risk premia have been small.

The functional form employed above describing the dependence of the premium on expected future f positions is, as stated earlier, arbitrary. Branson and Marchese (1988) instead, posit time-varying premia as functions of the contemporaneous level of f. We do not implement such a functional form, primarily because of the potential existence of perverse short-run effects due to the presence of J-curve effects on trade balances, and valuation effects on past holdings of stocks of foreign assets.[18]

7.5 Conclusion

The sustainability of the U.S. external position hinges on the willingness of international investors to add, on net, U.S. liabilities to their portfolios. We have argued that investors are unlikely to allow a "large" build-up of such claims, and an important question is therefore the likely consequences of an unwillingness on their part to add such claims to their portfolios. We have modeled the effects of foreign investors imposing a "sustainable" foreign asset ratio on the United States by positing the existence of a premium on dollar assets when the foreign asset position is expected to deviate from this level. The process presents an example of a self-correcting mechanism for attaining external balance. The results show that the premia required may be modest for "correcting" potentially large movements in net foreign asset positions. However, the costs of such an imposed adjustment can be substantial in terms of lost output. Moreover, the results suggest that in the absence of a fiscal correction, this imposed external adjustment is likely to worsen the fiscal situation, thus increasing the costs of adjustment in terms of private consumption, investment, and hence future output.

Notes

1. Various observers have argued that official U.S. statistics overstate the U.S. net foreign liability position. See Ulan and Dewald (1989) and Danker and Hooper (1990). It seems indisputable, however, that there has been a substantial decline in the position.
2. For a general discussion of movements in such ratios, see Dooley et al. (1986).
3. And what the path of the ratio may look like with unchanged behavioral responses. Krugman (1985, 1988) conducts a similar analysis.

4. The ratio was computed as $f_t^* = -f_t \cdot (\text{GNP}_t / \text{GNP}_t^* \times 3)$, where the asterisk denotes the rest of the industrial countries. For assumptions on the path of foreign variables, see the IMF's *World Economic Outlook* (October 1989).

5. The version of the model we used is based primarily upon Masson, Symansky, and Meredith (1990). However, some of the changes in the model that are described in that paper are very recent and are not incorporated in our version of MULTIMOD. See also Masson et al. (1988) for a description of the first version of MULTIMOD.

6. The form of the interest-rate reaction function does allow for modest deviations of the exchange rate from its target.

7. These are not official IMF assumptions.

8. A simulation is a useful way to understand some of a model's properties. In this section we limit ourselves to an exchange rate scenario. The impact of fiscal and monetary shocks in MULTIMOD are described in detail elsewhere; see Masson et al. (1988) and Masson, Symansky, and Meredith (1990). In addition, a fiscal scenario is discussed in section 7.4.

9. In most models, a constant depreciation of the currency is produced by assuming an exogenous path of the exchange rate and calculating the "add factor" in an exchange rate (or capital account) equation that is consistent with the pre-specified path of the exchange rate. To produce a constant percentage change in the exchange rate in a backward-looking model, the "add factor" risk premium declines over time, while in a forward-looking model, the risk premium increases over time.

A similar analysis was carried out using twelve econometric macro models as part of the Brookings Conference on Empirical Macroeconomics for Interdependent Economies. Detailed tables illustrating the effects of a dollar depreciation for these twelve models can be found in the conference proceedings, collected in a volume edited by Bryant et al. (1988).

10. See Branson and Marchese (1988) for a discussion of the effects of an exogenous change in the exchange rate in both a small theoretical model and in simulations using MULTIMOD and the OECD's INTERLINK model.

11. In a more fully specified model, the determination of such a ratio would, of course, be endogenous. See Dooley and Isard (1987) for discussion of a framework in which such a ratio would be endogenously determined.

12. One change in the structure of MULTIMOD was made for this simulation. MULTIMOD includes a rule that alters taxes to hit a steady-state level of the ratio of government bonds to GNP. This tax reaction function was turned off.

13. If the fiscal expansion was a once and for all change instead of the gradual path used in this simulation, the short-term interest rate would have increased.

14. In the model it is assumed that all external debt is denominated in dollars. The term-structure of debt incurred is assumed to remain constant. In particular, it is assumed that 50 percent is short term, and the other 50 percent long term, which is rolled over every three years.

15. Horne, Kremers, and Masson (1989) attempt to identify empirically relevant channels for external adjustment.

16. The recent change in U.S. tax laws that substantially alters the tax burden on inheritance due non-U.S. residents from assets owned in the United States is an example of a scheme to reduce the return on U.S. assets owned by foreigners.

17. In MULTIMOD, the interest-parity condition is written as a set of bilateral equations with respect to the dollar. Since the model does not account for bilateral foreign asset positions, the arbitrage condition was redefined in multilateral terms in order to use the aggregate foreign asset position in the calculation of η.

18. Branson and Marchese (1988) do not allow for J-curve effects. Krugman (1989b) considers the effects of a once and for all exogenous change in the risk premium against the dollar in a model incorporating J-curve effects on the trade balance.

References

Branson, William. 1985. Causes of appreciation and volatility of the dollar. In *The U.S. Dollar: Prospects and Policy Options*. Federal Reserve Bank of Kansas City.

Branson, William, and Grazia Marchese. 1988. International imbalances in Japan, Germany, and the U.S. Mimeo, October.

Bryant, Ralph C., Dale W. Henderson, Gerald Holtham, Peter Hooper, and Steve Symansky, eds. 1988. *Empirical Macroeconomics for Interdependent Economies*, supplemental vol. Washington, DC: The Brookings Institution.

Danker, Deborah, and Peter Hooper. 1990. International financial markets and U.S. external imbalance. *International Finance Discussion Paper,* no. 372 (January). Washington, DC: Board of Governors of the Federal Reserve System.

Dealtry, Michael, and Josef Van't dack. 1989. The U.S. external deficit and associated shifts in international portfolios. *BIS Economic papers,* no. 25. Basle, Switzerland.

Diaz-Alejandro, Carlos F. 1984. Latin American Debt: I don't think we are in Kansas anymore. *Brookings Papers on Economic Activity* 2:335–89.

Dooley, Michael, William Helkie, Ralph Tryon, and John Underwood. 1986. An analysis of external debt positions of eight developing countries through 1990. *Journal of Development Economics* 21:283–318.

Dooley, Michael, and Peter Isard. 1980. Capital controls, political risk, and deviations from interest rate parity. *Journal of Political Economy* 88(2):370–84.

———. 1981. The portfolio-balance model of exchange rates and some evidence that risk premiums are small. Mimeo, Board of Governors of the Federal Reserve System.

———. 1983. The portfolio-balance model of exchange rates and some structural estimates of the risk premium. *IMF Staff Papers* 30(4):683–702.

———. 1986. Tax avoidance and exchange rate determination. International Monetary Fund, DM/86/1.

———. 1987. Country preferences, currency values and policy issues. *Journal of Policy Modeling* 9(1).

Horne, Jocelyn, Jeroen Kremers, and Paul Masson. 1989. Net foreign assets and international adjustment in the United States, Japan and the Federal Republic of Germany. International Monetary Fund, Working Paper no. 22.

Krugman, Paul. 1985. Is the strong dollar sustainable? In *The U.S. Dollar: Prospects and Policy Options*. Federal Reserve Bank of Kansas City.

———. 1988. Long-run effects of the strong dollar. In *Misalignment of Exchange Rates: Effects on Trade and Industry,* ed. R. Marston, 277–94. Chicago: University of Chicago Press.

———. 1989a. *Exchange Rate Instability.* Cambridge, Mass.: MIT Press.

———. 1989b. The J-curve, the fire sale, and the hard landing. *American Economic Association Papers and Proceedings* 79(2):31–35.

Masson, Paul R., Steven Symansky, Richard Haas, and Mike Dooley. 1988. MULTIMOD: A Multi-Region Econometric Model. *IMF Staff Studies for the World Economic Outlook* (July):50–104.

Masson, Paul R., Steven Symansky, and Guy Meredith. 1990. MULTIMOD: Mark II, The G-7 Version. *IMF Occasional Paper,* no. 71 (July).

Ulan, Michael, and William G. Dewald. 1989. The U.S. net international investment position: The numbers are misstated and misunderstood. U.S. Department of State, Washington, D.C.

8 The Continued Interest-Rate Vulnerability of Thrifts

Patric H. Hendershott and James D. Shilling

U.S. taxpayers are currently making good on a $100 billion or more Federal Savings and Loan Insurance Corporation (FSLIC) loss.[1] At the same time, mounting Federal Deposit Insurance Corporation (FDIC) losses are leading commentators to speculate about the financial condition of that fund. One would hope that the solutions to the depository fund crises would "guarantee" against repetitions of the crises.

The FSLIC debacle is generally viewed as having occurred in two stages.[2] First, sharply rising interest rates easily eliminated the net worth of most thrifts owing to their asset-liability mismatch (borrowing short and lending long). Second, thrifts took substantial risks (doubled their bets) in the 1980s, as one might expect. The latter was made easier by the increase in deposit insurance coverage from $40,000 to $100,000 per account and the enactment of new asset powers (including additional flexibility in writing mortgage contracts). Regulatory forbearance and loose oversight permitted this risk-taking and led, in conjunction with the generous tax provisions of the 1981 Tax Law, to substantial overbuilding in much of the United States and to subsequent real estate depressions in many areas of the country.

Complicating matters has been the erosion in the basic profitability of thrift mortgage portfolio lending. Owing to higher costs of deposit money and increased deposit premiums, thrifts have not been the low-cost supplier of home mortgage credit for some time.[3] With a low basic-profit stream, untoward

Patric H. Hendershott is professor of finance and public policy at Ohio State University and a research associate of the National Bureau of Economic Research. James D. Shilling is associate professor of business at the University of Wisconsin, Madison.

The authors thank James Barth, Edward Kane, and Eduardo Schwartz for their comments on the version of this paper presented at the NBER Conference on Financial Crisis, 24 March 1990.

events (credit problems, rising interest rates) quickly reduce capital, rather than just lowering dividends, and, with little capital, soon increase taxpayer liabilities.

We are now supposedly solving the thrift problem by recapitalizing (forbearance is out), reregulating (new assets powers are out), and reintroducing strict oversight. It is noteworthy, however, that the original source of the problem—the vulnerability of thrifts to periods of sustained increases in interest rates—has not been removed. In fact, lessening this vulnerability has been hampered by the new regulations on trading assets—if thrifts sell any existing fixed-rate mortgages (FRMs), they fear they will have to mark all such investments to market. In early 1989, thrifts were still using roughly 40 percent of their short-term deposits to fund long-term fixed-rate mortgage investments, and many of their adjustable-rate mortgages (ARMs) had rate caps that bind in a period of sustained interest rate increases. Because current thrift regulation concentrates on book, not market, values of assets, thrifts could continue to operate even if their net worth were eliminated by increases in interest rates.

In this paper, we attempt to document just how susceptible the thrift industry continues to be to interest-rate risk. Optimistically assuming a 15 percent pretax return on equity in a recapitalized industry, we find that a repetition of the 1977–86 interest-rate cycle would generate cumulative cash-flow losses of $100 billion to $130 billion within seven years. However, with a profitable, well-capitalized industry, profits and capital could absorb this loss with negligible implications for taxpayers. In contrast, if this cycle should occur today or at any time before significant recapitalization and reprofitization occur, taxpayers would be out another $50 billion to $100 billion.

The first two sections of this paper attempt to establish the appropriate starting point for our analysis of thrift interest-rate sensitivity. Section 8.1 constructs an aggregate thrift balance sheet from individual institution data, where the assets and liabilities are aggregated according to period until they reprice. Nonperforming loans and assets that are now disfavored by regulators are assumed to be sold, and two alternative capital infusions are presumed to be made: $60 billion, to provide all thrifts with capital equal to at least 1.5 percent of tangible assets, or $79 billion, to give all thrifts at least 8 percent of risk-weighted assets. Section 8.2 discusses the structure of thrift mortgage portfolios, indicating the distribution of fixed-rate mortgages by coupon rate and of adjustable-rate mortgages by repricing period, rate caps, and teasers. Section 8.3 describes a method for computing changes in thrift net interest income in response to changes in interest rates and calculates the impact of higher interest rates on thrift net income under a variety of assumptions regarding interest rates, mortgage repayments, and thrift reinvestment. The impact on thrift capital and U.S. taxpayers is discussed. A closing section summarizes our findings, and an appendix describes some of the underlying data.

8.1 Observed and Adjusted Thrift Balance Sheets in Early 1989

Table 8.1 contains the total thrift balance sheet for March 1989, obtained by aggregating across all institutions then insured by FSLIC. The lower-case letters in the table refer to rows in table 8A.1 in the appendix. (The method of computing risk-weighted assets, upon which risk-based capital requirements are calculated, is described in table 8A.1, while the current methods for computing tangible and core capital are reported in table 8A.2.) Balance sheets are also presented separately in table 8.1 for those thrifts with negative and positive generally accepted accounting principles (GAAP) net worth.[4] According to these data, 90 percent of thrift assets are in thrifts with positive GAAP net worth.

Of course, these book net worth numbers have little meaning because many assets have market values far below book. Probably the most egregious example is the $133 billion in other assets. As can be seen in table 8.2, this includes $34 billion in real estate owned (foreclosed on REO) and real estate held for development (REH). Other assets also include $20 billion in goodwill and about $60 billion in other items of dubious value. Based upon data reported in Bovenzi and Murton (1988), we estimate that these assets in the

Table 8.1 Net Balance Sheet, Book Value (billions of $)

	All Thrifts	Thrifts with Negative Net Worth	Thrifts with Positive Net Worth
Net assets:			
Net fixed rate = (a + b + c + d) − (r + s)	403	43	360
Single-family ARMs = e	327	19	308
Adjustable-rate and balloon = f + g	230	23	207
Net intermediate assets = (h + i) − .75q	31	−5	36
Equities except FHLB-FHLMC = m	4	0	4
Other assets = n	129	25	104
Total assets	1,124	105	1,019
Total risk-weighted assets	824	98	726
Net liabilities and net worth:			
Net short-term = (o + p + .25q) − (j + k + l)	1,082	123	959
GAAP net worth = t	42	−18	60
Total liabilities and net worth	1,124	105	1,019
Memo			
RAP capital	36	−20	56
Required risk-based capital (1992)	66	8	58

Source: Appendix table 8A.1.

Table 8.2 **Composition of Other Assets (billions of $)**

	1989 Values	% Markdown[a]	Risk-Weighting
REO and REH, net of valuation allowances (ATREO + AREH − A355)	34	61	200%
Equity in service corporations (A490)	25	20	100[b]
Goodwill (A544)	20	100	100[c]
Purchased servicing (A542)	2	20	100
Other assets, net of val allow (ATOA[d] − A590)	30	20	100
Fixed assets, net of val allow	18	NA	100
Equities except FHLB-FHLMC	4	0	100
Subtotal	133		

Source: Office of Thrift Supervision, quarterly *Thrift Financial Report* (March 1989).
[a]Data on percentage markdowns were obtained from Bovenzi and Murton (1988).
[b]Equity in service corporations that are engaged in impermissible activities is in 100 percent bucket; that in those engaged in permissible activities is in 50 percent bucket (permissible activities have not yet been defined).
[c]Amount counted as assets is the minimum of total goodwill (A544) or 1.5 percent of tangible assets (A800 − A525 − A544 − C992).
[d]ATOA = other assets (A460 through A580 − A490 − A544 − 542) + financing leases (A240 through A260) − deferrals (A525 + C992).

aggregate, excluding fixed assets (branches, etc.), are overstated by $32 billion dollars.[5] In addition, $35 billion of loans are nonperforming (16 percent of loans at thrifts with negative net worth are delinquent). If we value these loans at 80 cents on the dollar, market value is $7 billion below book (we show in section 8.2 that the market value of performing fixed-rate mortgages approximates their book value). Finally, the $15 billion of thrift junk bonds (part of the intermediate assets category in table 8.1) are probably $4 billion below market value. Taking into account all these deviations of market from book values, the market value of net worth for the industry is negative $23 billion, not positive $20 billion. Also, only 50 percent of thrift assets are held by thrifts with positive market-value net worth.

Table 8.3 is an adjusted aggregate balance sheet based on the following assumptions. First, all the other assets in table 8.2, except for fixed assets, are "sold" for $94 billion, and equities (except FHLB-FHLMC stock) are sold for par. Second, $35 billion of loans ($4 billion each of FRMs and ARMs and $27 billion of other adjustable-rate and balloon loans) are sold for $28 billion, and $15 billion in junk bonds are sold for $11 billion. Third, all of the sale proceeds are used to reduce short-term debt. The result is a 15 percent reduction in thrift total assets. Fourth, we infuse the industry with new capital and use this, too, to reduce short-term debt.

We analyze two infusions. In the first, each thrift is given sufficient new capital to raise its capital to 1.5 percent of total assets (the tangible capital requirement). In the second, each thrift is given enough capital to increase its capital to 8 percent of risk-weighted assets, or roughly 5 percent of total assets. The two infusions are $60 billion and $79 billion. With the smaller infusion, short-term deposits are reduced by 14 percent; with the larger infusion, the reduction is 16 percent. We take the resultant balance sheet(s) shown in table 8.3 as the starting point for our analysis (actually, the individual thrift balance sheets that are consistent with this aggregate balance sheet are the starting point).

Table 8.3 indicates that thrifts still have a substantial asset-liability maturity imbalance poblem. A full 40 percent of thrift assets would be long-term fixed-rate loans funded by short-term deposits. (The $399 billion is slightly greater than the dollar value of fixed-rate loans funded by short-term deposits

Table 8.3 **Adjusted Balance Sheet (billions of $)**

	All Thrifts	Thrifts with Negative Net Worth	Thrifts with Positive Net Worth
Net assets:			
Net fixed rate	399[a]	179	220
Single-family ARMs	324[b]	98	226
Adjustable-rate and balloon	202[c]	78	124
Net intermediate assets	16[d]	3	13
Other assets	22[e]	9	13
Total assets	963	367	596
Total risk-weighted assets	635	257	378
Net liabilities and net worth:			
Net short-term	920[f]	358	562
	(901)	(345)	(556)
Market-value net worth	43[g]	9	34
	(62)	(22)	(40)
Total liabilities and net worth	963	367	596
Memo:			
RAP capital before capital infusion	−20	−51	31
Risk-based capital (1992)	51	21	30

[a]Net fixed rate reduced by the $4 billion of fixed-rate mortgage loans assumed to be delinquent.
[b]Single-family ARMs reduced by the $4 billion of adjustable-rate mortgage loans assumed to be delinquent.
[c]Adjustable-rate and balloon reduced by $27 billion estimated to be delinquent.
[d]Net intermediate assets reduced by $15 billion in junk bonds.
[e]Other assets are reduced by $111 billion, as all other assets except fixed assets are assumed to be sold, but increased by $4 billion of appraised equity capital.
[f]Net short-term liabilities are reduced by $102 billion of proceeds from asset sales and $60 billion ($79 billion) infusion of new capital to bring tangible capital (RAP capital) to 1.5 percent of tangible assets (8 percent of risk-weighted assets).
[g]Net worth is reduced by $63 billion loss on asset sales, but increased by an assumed $60 billion ($79 billion) capital infusion. This infusion is the amount of capital needed to bring core capital (RAP capital) to 1.5 percent of tangible assets (8 percent of risk-weighted assets), $58 billion ($71 billion) for thrifts with negative net worth and $2 billion ($8 billion) for other thrifts.

a decade earlier.) In addition, many of the adjustable-rate loans have rate caps that will bind significantly if we experience a period of rates rising as sharply as they did in the late 1970s and early 1980s. While thrifts could be hedging much of this risk through cash markets or with futures, interest-rate swaps, interest-rate caps, and so on, the data indicate little cash-market hedging, and anecdotal evidence suggests little use of other hedging devices.[6]

Table 8.4 shows some detail on how the industry's assets are distributed across thrifts with different percentages of required and actual capital, both before and after our liquidating the below-market thrift assets and injecting new capital into the industry. For the observed balance sheet, we define capital in three ways: 8 percent of risk-weighted assets (the end of 1992 requirement), RAP capital (regulatory accounting capital, see table 8A.2) and actual (our estimate) market-value capital. Note that the end of 1992 regulations require that almost all thrifts have capital greater than 3 percent of total assets. Currently, two-thirds of thrift assets are in thrifts that have 3 percent RAP capital, but only 29 percent of thrift assets are in thrifts with 3 percent market-value capital. Moreover, 44 percent of thrift assets are (as of March 1989) in thrifts with negative market-value capital.

When the balance sheet is adjusted, the required capital-to-total-asset ratio for most thrifts declines because we have liquidated relatively risky assets. Actual capital, of course, rises. With the smaller infusion, all thrifts have

Table 8.4 **Dollars of Assets in Institutions with Different Percentages of Required (Risk-based) and Actual Capital (billions of $)**

	Observed Balance Sheet			Adjusted Balance Sheet		
Capital/ Total Assets	Risk-based	RAP Capital	Market Value[a]	Risk-based	Market Value, $60 billion Infusion[b]	Market Value, $79 billion Infusion[c]
6% +	57	321	129	15	143	200
5–6%	41	176	60	75	59	136
4–5%	255	265	80	706	108	464
3–4%	908	156	133	383	130	339
2–3%	121	100	156	40	160	80
1–2%	6	62	114	4	623	4
0–1%	0	63	112	0	0	0
Negative	0	245	604	0	0	0
Total	1,388	1,388	1,388[d]	1,223	1,223	1,223[e]

[a]Market value capital = GAAP net worth in table 8.1, after assets are marked to market; includes appraised equity capital.
[b]Infusion brings tangible capital up to at least 1.5 percent of tangible assets.
[c]Infusion brings RAP capital up to at least 8 percent of risk-weighted assets.
[d]Book value of total assets from appendix table 8A.1, including loans on deposits and deferred losses.
[e]Adjusted value of total assets = book value of total assets, including loans on deposits − delinquent mortgage loans − junk bonds − equities except FHLB-FHLMC − other assets except fixed + appraised equity capital.

Table 8.5 FRM Balances of Different Maturities Subdivided by Coupon Rate (billions of $)

	Maturity (in years)					
Coupon	5 to 10	10 to 20	Over 20	Total	GNMA Price[a]	Market Value[b]
Less than 8%	5.5	11.2	3.8	20.5	92½	19.0
8–8.99%	5.1	37.4	35.1	77.6	94¾	73.5
9–9.99%	4.4	43.4	60.3	108.1	99½	107.6
10–10.99%	2.6	21.3	39.1	63.0	103½	65.2
11–11.99%	1.1	6.7	8.8	16.6	106¾	17.7
12–13.99%	1.5	3.8	6.3	11.6	110¼	12.8
14% or more	0.3	0.6	0.7	1.6	112	1.8
Total				299.0		297.6

Source: Office of Thrift Supervision, *Thrift Financial Report* (September 1989). We thank Bill McGuire of the Federal Home Loan Bank of Cincinnati for providing us with the FRM balance data.

[a]On 20 February 1990.

[b]Book (total) times GNMA price divided by 100.

capital of at least 1.5 percent of assets, but note that less than half of thrift assets are in thrifts with at least 2 percent market-value capital. With the larger infusion, over 90 percent of thrift assets are in thrifts with over 3 percent market-value capital.

8.2 Thrift Mortgage Portfolios

Both the market values of thrift FRM and ARM portfolios and the sensitivity of these to increases in interest rates depends on the level of the coupons on the mortgages relative to market coupon rates and the tightness of ARM rate caps. This section provides the available data on FRMs and ARMs.

Table 8.5 contains the distribution of FRMs on September 1989 according to coupon and remaining term to maturity. As can be seen, 80 percent had coupons between 8 and 11 percent. The second column from the right gives 20 February 1990 prices on Government National Mortgage Association (GNMA) securities with coupons equal to 8 percent, the midpoint of each of the coupon ranges in column 1 (rows 2–6), and 14.5 percent, respectively. The far right column is an estimate of the market value of the volume in each coupon range. Cumulating over the ranges, one obtains a market-value estimate for the total industry FRM portfolio only $1.3 billion less than book value. That is, in February 1990, below-market FRMs were not an industry problem.

Table 8.6 reports the distribution of ARMs originated at 707 thrifts during May–July of 1986 through 1989, by the years to repricing (≤1 year vs. >1 year), the annual rate cap (1 or 2 percent), and the magnitude of the initial teaser (<0.5 percent up to ≥2.5 percent). The data do not indicate significant

Table 8.6 Distribution of ARMs by Size of Teaser, Years Until Repricing, and Annual Rate Caps

	Years to Reprice		Annual Cap		Teaser			
	≤1	>1	1%	2%	<0.5	0.5–1.5	1.5–2.5	≥2.5
1986	93	7	17	83	42	23	29	6
1987	90	10	19	81	39	13	37	11
1988	93	7	23	77	40	6	36	18
1989	93	7	18	82	38	12	26	24

Source: Appendix table 8A.3.

Table 8.7 Distribution of ARMs by Percentage that Fully Adjusted Rate is Below Maximum Loan Rate (% of ARMs)

Percentage Below Maximum Rate	1-year (and less) Annual Cap		3-year (and more) Annual Cap		
	1%	2%	1%	2%	Total
<1.1%	0.27	0.12	0.00	0.08	0.48
1.1–2.0%	0.48	5.16	0.00	0.16	5.80
2.1–3.0%	2.34	14.29	0.03	0.40	17.06
3.1–4.0%	2.36	12.00	0.02	0.94	15.31
4.1–5.0%	7.38	21.14	0.29	2.53	31.33
5.1–6.0%	2.01	5.95	0.11	1.71	9.77
>6.0%	2.92	14.48	0.29	2.54	20.24
Total	17.75	73.15	0.74	8.36	100.00

Source: Federal Housing Finance Board, Mortgage Interest Rate Survey, May–July of 1986–89.

changes over time in either the years to repricing or the per-period rate cap. Just over 90 percent of ARMs issued in each year reprice within a year, and roughly 80 percent of ARMs have 2 percent annual caps. Virtually all of the ARMs have 5 percent life-of-loan caps.

In contrast, there is a clear trend toward the use of heavily discounted initial interest rates, or teaser rates, after 1986. The percentage of ARMs with a teaser of 2.5 percent or greater rose from only 6 percent in 1986 to 24 percent in 1989. This could be an indication of increased risk-seeking by underwater thrifts. These deep teasers are a potential problem because the effective life-of-loan rate cap on a deep teaser is lower than that on a shallow teaser, that is, rate caps on deep-teaser loans are more likely to bind.

Tables 8.7 and 8.8 illustrate the potential problems with deep-teaser ARMs. In March 1989, 23 percent of ARMs had coupon rates less than 3 percentage points from their maxima, and another 15 percent were within 4 percentage points. As is shown in table 8.8, most (84 percent) of the ARMs within 3 points of their life-of-loan caps were one-year (or less) ARMs with a 2 percent

Table 8.8 **Percentage of ARMs in Institutions Having More Than *X* Percent of ARMs with Fully Adjusted Rate Within 3 Percent of Life-of-Loan Rate Ceiling**

	1-year (and less) Annual Cap		3-year (and more) Annual Cap		
X%	1%	2%	1%	2%	Total
<10%	0.16	0.53	0.03	0.03	0.75
10–19%	0.66	0.84	0.00	0.11	1.61
20–29%	0.89	1.99	0.00	0.18	3.05
30–39%	0.45	5.19	0.00	0.25	5.89
40–49%	0.10	0.84	0.00	0.02	0.96
50–59%	0.00	0.34	0.00	0.00	0.35
>59%	0.86	9.86	0.00	0.06	10.78
Total	3.11	19.59	0.03	0.65	23.38

Source: Federal Housing Finance Board, Mortgage Interest Rate Survey, May–July of 1986–89.

per period cap, and these were concentrated within a few thrifts. More than half of these ARMs were at institutions with over 60 percent of their ARMs within 3 points of the ceiling, and 60 percent were at a single institution.

In the calculations reported in the next section, we assume that ARMs originated by all thrifts throughout 1986–89 were either one- or three-year Treasury ARMs and had terms (teasers, rate caps, and fully adjusted margins) identical to those at the 707 thrifts from which we have data. ARMs originated in 1982–85 are assumed to have been identical to those originated in 1986. We further assume that all originated ARMs have been maintained in the portfolios of the originating institutions. While these assumptions are obviously not fully correct, there is no reason to believe that they bias our loss calculations either up or down.

8.3 The Impact of Increases in Interest Rates

One can compute the impact of changes in interest rates on the thrift industry in two ways. First, one could postulate a one-time change in interest rates and calculate the change in the market values of thrift assets and liabilities, and thus net worth. Second, one could postulate an altered future path of interest rates, calculate the impact on thrift net interest income, and cumulate the net income changes over time. These calculations are related because the market value of an asset is the sum of the asset's expected future cash flows, appropriately discounted. Because computing market values of a wide variety of assets with call options and rate caps is such a formidable task (see, for example, Schwartz and Torous, in this volume), we have chosen the second method. We will, however, analyze a complete cycle—interest rates rising and falling—and we cumulate net income changes for a decade following the completion of the cycle, thereby capturing most of the market-value implications of assets put on the books while interest rates were temporarily high. We begin by describing a method for calculating net interest-income losses and then present the calculations.

8.3.1 Method for Calculating Net Interest Income Losses

When interest rates rise, the net income from FRMs funded with short-term deposits declines and may turn negative. The decline in net income equals the increase in deposit interest paid less any increase in interest income coming from the investment of FRM repayments at higher interest rates. Assume that the initial book value of short-funded FRMs is *FR* and that a constant function, ϕ, of these mortgages repay each year. If deposit rates rise from r_0 to r_1, the interest lost in the next year, assuming 100 percent debt financing, is simply $(r_1 - r_0)(1 - \phi)FR$. This loss is then multiplied by the initial ratio of short-term liabilities to net financial assets, Θ_0, to reflect less than 100 percent debt financing.

The cumulative loss on the initial short-funded FRMs over a twenty-year period, ignoring losses on repayments (or simply assuming they are reinvested at the all-in deposit cost), is

$$FR\sum_{t=1}^{20} (1 - \phi)^t\Theta_0(r_t - r_0).$$

If repayments at the end of year 0, ϕFR, are reinvested in FRMs, they will generate additional future losses if deposit rates continue to rise unexpectedly or will produce future gains if deposit rates return to their initial levels. The cumulative loss over the next twenty years from repayments at the end of year 0 is

$$\phi FR\sum_{t=1}^{20} (1 - \phi)^{t-1}[\Theta_1(r_t - r_0) - (r_1^{FRM} - r_{0A}^{FRM})],$$

where $r_{0A}^{FRM} = \sum_j w_j r_{0-j}^{FRM}$ and w_j is the proportion of the outstanding FRM stock originated *j* periods ago. More generally, the total cumulative loss, assuming that all prepayments are reinvested in FRMs, is

$$\begin{aligned} L_{FRM} = {} & FR\sum_{t=1}^{20}(1 - \phi)^t\Theta_0(r_t - r_0) + \phi FR\sum_{t=1}^{20}(1 - \phi)^{t-1}[\Theta_1(r_t - r_0) \\ (1) \qquad & - (r_1^{FRM} - r_{0A}^{FRM})] + \ldots \\ & + \phi FR\sum_{t=20}^{20}(1 - \phi)^{t-20}[\Theta_{20}(r_t - r_{19}) - (r_{20}^{FRM} - r_{19A}^{FRM})]. \end{aligned}$$

The losses for ARMs are calculated similarly. If the book value of short-funded ARMs is *AR* and deposit rates rise from r_0 to r_1, the interest lost in the next year is $[\Theta_0(r_1 - r_0) - (r_{01}^{ARM} - r_{0A}^{ARM})](1 - \phi)AR$. Of course, if the ARM coupon rises by the increase in deposit costs and 100 percent debt financing is employed ($\Theta = 1$), no interest is lost. The cumulative loss on AR over the twenty-year period, ignoring repayments, is

$$AR\sum_{t=1}^{20}(1 - \phi)^t[\Theta_0(r_t - r_0) - (r_{0t}^{\text{ARM}} - r_{0A}^{\text{ARM}})].$$

If repayments, ϕAR, are reinvested in identical ARMs (except for their higher initial rate), the repayments can also generate losses should rates rise further in the future. This loss over the next twenty years is

$$\phi AR\sum_{t=1}^{20}(1 - \phi)^{t-1}[\Theta_1(r_t - r_1) - (r_{1t}^{\text{ARM}} - r_{1A}^{\text{ARM}})].$$

The total cumulative loss, assuming all prepayments are reinvested in identical ARMs, is

$$\begin{aligned} L_{\text{ARM}} = {} & AR\sum_{t=1}^{20}(1 - \phi)^t[\Theta_0(r_t - r_0) - (r_{0t}^{\text{ARM}} - r_{0A}^{\text{ARM}})] \\ (2) \qquad & + \phi AR\sum_{t=1}^{20}(1 - \phi)^{t-1}[\Theta_1(r_t - r_1) - (r_{1t}^{\text{ARM}} - r_{1A}^{\text{ARM}})] + \dots \\ & + \phi AR \sum_{t=20}^{20}(1 - \phi)^{t-20}[\Theta_{20}(r_t - r_{20}) - (r_{20t}^{\text{ARM}} - r_{20A}^{\text{ARM}})]. \end{aligned}$$

We still need to specify the coupon on existing ARMs. If interest rates have risen since the ARM was originated, the coupon at time t is the minimum of the fully adjusted coupon (r_{jt}^F) and of the coupons resulting from binding annual (c_A) and life-of-loan (c_L) rate caps:[7]

$$(3) \qquad \text{r}_{jt}^{\text{ARM}} = \min(r_{jt}^F, \hat{r}_{jt}^A, \hat{r}^L{}_{jt}),$$

where $\hat{r}_{jt}^A = r_{jt-1}^{\text{ARM}} + c_A$ and $\hat{r}^L{}_{jt} = r_{j0}^{\text{ARM}} + c_L$. If interest rates have fallen, the coupon is the maximum of the fully adjusted coupon and that resulting from a binding annual rate floor (f_A):

$$(4) \qquad r_{jt}^{\text{ARM}} = \max(r_{jt}^F, \hat{\hat{r}}_{jt}),$$

where $\hat{\hat{r}}_{jt} = r_{jt-1}^{\text{ARM}} - f_A$.

The total loss in interest income (for each year from initial year 0), due to a series of upward-interest-rate surprises, is the sum of the losses on FRMs, ARMs, and intermediate assets, minus the gain from less than 100 percent debt financing of fully adjustable rate loans (ADJ). In equation form,

$$(5) \qquad \text{Lost Income} = L_{\text{FRM}} + L_{\text{ARM}} + L_{\text{INT}} - \sum_{t=1}^{N}(1 - \Theta_0)(r_t - r_0)\text{ADJ},$$

where L_{INT} is the negligible loss from short-funding intermediate assets, and the summation measures the gain from fully adjustable rate loans.[8]

The capital loss for a thrift is the difference between lost income and the thrift's earnings in the absence of interest-rate increases. In the absence of rate increases, thrifts would do very well, earning the value of the call options and rate caps on home mortgages they are selling to households plus a normal return on equity. We assume that the value of the call options and rate caps is equivalent to a 0.75 percent annual return on their home mortgage portfolios, or $5 billion a year given an FRM plus ARM base of $732 billion. The value of ARM rate caps obviously varies with the specific terms of the ARM contract—deep teasers and tight caps have greater value to borrowers (see Schwartz and Torous, in this volume)—and with economic conditions—when interest rates are expected to rise and/or rate volatility is high, caps are worth more (Buser, Hendershott, and Sanders 1985). Similarly, the value of the call option is less the lower is the mortgage coupon relative to market coupons and the less likely are interest rates to decline (Buser, Hendershott, and Sanders 1990). We have not attempted to account for these differences; raising or lowering the $5 billion estimate by, say, 25 percent would have little impact on our calculations.

We take the normal pretax return on equity, somewhat optimistically, to be 15 percent. When thrifts have $43 billion in capital (the $60 billion infusion), this implies an average 0.0067 return on total assets (TA) and a $6.5 billion cushion, in the aggregate, against declines in net interest income. We compute the capital loss as [9]

(6) $\text{Capital Loss}_t = \text{Lost Income}_t - 0.0075(\text{FRM}_t + \text{ARM}_t) - 0.0067\text{TA}_0.$

8.3.2 Loss Calculations

Given unchanged asset and liability mixes and no asset sales, net interest income losses depend on three factors: the pattern of future deposit and mortgage interest rates, the rate at which mortgages repay, and the extent to which repayments are reinvested. We do not want to analyze the expected or most likely future path of interest rates because expected future rates likely differ little from current rates. Rather, we want to analyze a "bad case" scenario. We take as our bad scenario—one that might plausibly occur over the next decade or two—that which occurred in the decade 1977–86.

Table 8.9 presents data on interest rates and mortgage repayments during the 1977–86 period. Both one- and three-year Treasury bill rates rose by 8 to 9 percentage points between 1977 and 1981, fell by 4 to 5 points between 1981 and 1983, rose by 1.5 points in 1984, and then fell by over 2 points in 1985 and 1986. The observed ratio of annual aggregate thrift mortgage repayments (amortization plus prepayments) to mortgage loans outstanding was 11 percent in 1977–78, when some of the high-rate mortgages originated in 1973–74 were refinanced, fell to around 7 percent in 1980–82 when mortgage rates peaked, jumped to 15 percent in 1983–85 when many of the 1980–82 mortgages were being refinanced, and increased even further when mortgage

Table 8.9 Interest Rates and Mortgage Repayments

Year	Treasury Yields (%) 1-year	3-year	Mortgage Repayment Rate
1977	6.09	6.69	11.51
1978	8.34	8.29	10.82
1979	10.67	9.71	9.50
1980	12.05	11.55	7.56
1981	14.78	14.44	6.29
1982	12.27	12.92	7.61
1983	9.37	10.45	15.48
1984	10.89	11.89	14.84
1985	8.42	9.64	14.47
1986	6.30	7.06	17.83

Source: Treasury yields are from *Federal Reserve Bulletin,* U.S. Treasury Notes and Bonds Constant Maturities; mortgage repayment rate is from Office of Thrift Supervision, *Savings and Home Financing Source Book.*

rates troughed in 1986. In our bad-case scenario, we let the one- and three-year Treasury rates move exactly as they did in the 1977–86 period and then hold them at their 1977 values for the next decade. Rates on FRMs are assumed to move by 80 percent of the variation in the one-year rate.

A single repayment factor for FRMs is inappropriate given the obvious sensitivity of repayments to interest rates. In the aggregate, FRMs are presumed to repay at the rates observed over the 1977–86 period during the first ten years of our scenario. However, mortgages originated in different years are assumed to repay at different rates. In years 7–9 (1983–85), mortgages originated in years other than 4–6 (1980–82) are presumed to repay at a 9.5 percent rate, and the mortgages for years 4–6 are presumed to repay at a rate sufficient to raise the overall FRM repayment rate to 15 percent. In years 10 and beyond, FRMs originated before year 4 (1980) and after year 9 (1985) are assumed to repay at the 9.5 percent rate; originations in all other years repay at an 18 percent rate.[10] For ARMs, we assume a 10 percent repayment rate.

We also simulate a less-severe interest rate cycle in which interest rates move by half the 1977–86 movement. This is not unlike the movement in interest rates in the 1965–72 period. For FRMs, we keep the basic 9.5 percent repayment rate, varying it in the same years as before but only by half as much. For ARMs, we use the basic 10 percent repayment rate.

The upper panel of table 8.10 contains the scenario where interest rates move as they did in the 1977–86 period (see col. 1 of the table). The tenth year contains the losses for years 10 to 20, present valued to the tenth year using the tenth year one-year Treasury rate, and the far right column gives the totals. The total loss is divided into portions owing to FRMs and ARMs, and the total is reduced by the earnings thrifts would have recorded had interest

Table 8.10 Calculated Value of Cash-Flow Losses on Net Adjusted Assets of Insured S&Ls and Potential Capital Losses (billions of $)

Year	1	2	3	4	5	6	7	8	9	10+	Total
A. Rates Rise as in 1977–86 Period											
Change in 1-year Treasuries	2.25	2.33	1.38	2.73	−2.51	−2.70	1.32	−2.47	−2.12	−0.21	0
Cumulative change in 1-year Treasury	2.25	4.58	5.96	8.69	6.18	3.48	4.80	2.34	0.21	0	0
Loss due to FRMs	8	14	16	21	11	3	5	(1)	(5)	(9)	63
Loss due to ARMs	2	5	7	12	4	(1)	1	(1)	(2)	0	27
Total loss[a]	10	19	22	32	15	2	6	(2)	(7)	(9)	88
Cumulative loss	10	29	51	83	98	100	106	104	97	88	88
Capital loss	1	7	10	21	4	0	0	0	0	0	43
B. Rates Rise Half as Much											
Change in 1-year Treasuries	1.13	1.17	0.69	1.36	−1.25	−1.35	0.66	−1.34	−1.06	−0.11	0
Cumulative change in 1-year Treasury	1.13	2.30	2.99	4.35	3.11	1.76	2.41	1.17	0.11	0	0
Loss due to FRMs	4	7	8	10	6	1	3	(1)	(3)	(4)	31
Loss due to ARMs	1	2	2	3	1	(1)	0	0	0	0	8
Total loss[a]	5	9	10	13	7	0	3	(1)	(3)	(4)	39
Cumulative loss	5	14	24	37	44	44	47	46	43	39	39
Capital loss	0	0	0	2	0	0	0	0	0	0	2

[a]Includes a negligible loss on net intermediate assets and a small gain from less than 100 percent debt financing of fully adjustable rate loans.

rates not risen to give the capital loss. As can be seen in the far right column, the cumulative loss is $88 billion. Moreover, the cumulative losses reach $106 billion in the seventh year. Most of the losses are on FRMs, although ARMs account for $27 billion of the loss. Finally, the cumulative capital loss, that is, the potential cost to the taxpayer is $43 billion.

The lower panel of table 8.10 pertains to a less-severe increase in interest rates; as the first row shows, the rates are up by only half as much as in the top panel. As one would expect, the losses on FRMs are about half as great. For ARMs, though, the losses are only 30 percent as large ($8 billion vs. $27 billion). This is because the 2 percent per annum cap never binds and the life-of-loan cap binds far less than half as much. The cumulative cash-flow loss is still $39 billion, but there is virtually no capital loss.

Table 8.11 gives more detail on the ARM losses and summary statistics for alternative reinvestment scenarios. Looking at column 1 first, we see that most of the ARM losses are due to life-of-loan caps and little result from annual caps. While the annual caps cause some loss in the first two years (after which the life-of-loan cap binds), the annual rate floors save a little interest when interest rates decline. Two reinvestment alternatives are considered. First, we assume that FRM repayments are not reinvested but rather are used to reduce short-term borrowing. Second, we assume that both FRM and ARM repayments are reinvested in ARMs.

In the original calculations, FRM repayments were assumed to be reinvested in FRMs paying the then-higher coupon rate. In the first year or two, when interest rates have not risen sharply, reinvestments increase losses because the higher coupon income over the life of the mortgage will not outweigh the higher deposit costs over the interest rate cycle. However, reinvestments later on, when mortgage rates are near their peak, will generate far more interest income than the temporarily higher deposit costs. On net, rein-

Table 8.11 **Breakdown of Losses Under Alternative Interest Rate Scenarios and Repayment Assumptions (billions of $)**

	Full Rate Rise			Rates Rise Half as Much		
	Base Case	No Reinvestment of FRMs	Reinvestment of FRMs in ARMs	Base Case	No Reinvestment of FRMs	Reinvestment of FRMs in ARMs
Loss due to FRMs	63	111	111	31	53	53
Loss due to ARMs	27	25	32	8	7	13
without annual cap	23	21	27	7	6	11
without life-of-loan cap	11	10	13	6	5	10
Total loss[a]	88	133	141	39	60	65
Capital loss	43	57	66	2	6	9

[a]Includes a negligible loss on net intermediate assets and a small gain from less than 100 percent debt financing of fully adjustable rate loans.

vestment in FRMs reduces losses from the interest rate cycle.[11] Thus, assuming no reinvestment (assuming that the industry is downsized) increases the cumulative losses on FRMs by $48 billion and increases the total loss by $45 billion. However, the aggregate capital loss rises by only $14 billion because most of the additional cash-flow losses come after year 6 and are offset by the basic $11.5 billion cash flow thrifts would earn in the absence of a rise in interest rates.

Given that interest rates eventually decline to their initial values, reinvesting FRM repayments in ARMs makes things even worse because high-coupon ARMs adjust downward when interest rates come back down. Thus the losses from reinvestment of FRMs in ARMs in the early years outweigh the gains from reinvestment in later years (when annual rate floors hold ARM coupons up). This reinvestment increases cumulative ARM losses, the total cumulative loss and the aggregate capital loss by about $8 billion. Overall, these alternative reinvestment scenarios increase the $43 billion aggregate capital loss to $57 billion and $66 billion.

The taxpayers could lose less than the capital losses reported in table 8.11 for two reasons. First, $46 billion to $65 billion of shareholder capital, preferred stock, and subordinated debentures stands between the taxpayer and losses, depending on how well thrifts are recapitalized. Second, regulators could close the thrifts down shortly after interest rates start rising and liquidate their assets before the losses from even higher interest rates cumulate.

To expect such rapid behavior of regulators, especially when over half of thrift assets are in thrifts with capital amounting to less than 2 percent of assets, is unrealistic. Only a year or two of rising interest rates would wipe out that net worth, and by then the market value of existing loans would be far under water (from table 8.5, it would appear that a 2.5 percentage point increase in FRM rates would lower the market value of FRMs by 10 percent, or $40 billion). Moreover, if the thrifts are not closed down, they will be sorely tempted to take greater risks, possibly compounding the losses, as was the case in the 1980s.[12]

8.3.3 Policy Implications

This illustrates the fundamental point of the paper. If thrifts are only weakly recapitalized, taxpayers will continue to be at risk. For example, if the 1977–86 interest rate cycle were to occur today, when thrifts have very little capital or basic cash-flow income to offset reductions in cash flow caused by the increase in interest rates, taxpayers would suffer large losses. Probably 90 percent of the $88 billion to $141 billion total loss would be a capital loss, and with little capital, most of the loss would be passed through to taxpayers. A $50 billion to $100 billion loss would be expected.

In contrast, well-capitalized thrifts have clear incentives not to take significant interest rate risk because their own capital is at risk. Moreover, if they take risks and lose, the taxpayer does not take most of the hit. Finally, the greater capital gives regulators more time to act before net worth goes negative and taxpayers take losses.

Getting an extra $60 billion to $80 billion of capital into the thrift industry is a formidable task. In fact, under current conditions it is impossible. Maybe in a decade, when the industry can again attract funds at reasonable rates owing to reduced deposit insurance premiums and a generally lower cost of funds, equity capital will be attainable. Until then, and possibly even afterward, the interest-rate-risk exposure of thrifts needs to be closely monitored.

A good first start is the new *Thrift Bulletin* (TB13) requirement that thrift boards of directors must consider the sensitivity of thrift market-value net worth to movements in interest rates of 400 basis points (although the wisdom of analyzing a parallel shift in the yield curve when long-term rates are known to move less than short rates is questionable). However, the results of these analyses should be filed quarterly with the supervisory authorities, and specific regulatory actions should be triggered for those thrifts that are increasing interest-rate-risk exposure. In the long run, something like the interest-rate-risk component of the capital requirements contained in the thrift capital requirements developed in response to the recommendations promulgated in 1987 by the Basle Committee on Banking Regulation and Supervisory Practices, may be needed.

8.4 Summary

Our examination of thrift balance sheets in early 1989 suggested an existing capital shortfall in the thrift industry of $60 billion to $79 billion. Unfortunately, the problem does not seem to be being cleaned up in a rapid, efficient manner, so the shortfall is undoubtedly greater now and will be even greater in the future (Kane 1989b). In any event, our analysis begins with assumptions regarding liquidation of nonperforming thrift assets, a 15 percent downsizing of the thrift industry, and either a $60 billion capital infusion to bring market-value capital of each thrift up to at least 1.5 percent of total assets or a $79 billion capital infusion to raise capital to 8 percent of risk-weighted assets. The industry balance sheets, so adjusted, still show the industry short funding $400 billion of long-term fixed-rate loans, a greater absolute maturity mismatch than existed in 1977, and having $325 billion in adjustable-rate loans with interest-rate caps.

A repeat of the 1977–86 interest cycle would be extremely costly to the thrift industry and, unless the industry is adequately recapitalized, ultimately to U.S. taxpayers. Thrifts would suffer cumulative cash-flow losses of $100 billion to $140 billion. About 70 percent of these losses would be due to FRMs; the rest to rate caps on ARMs. If thrifts were both profitable and well capitalized, the basic earnings of thrifts and their capital would be sufficient to cover such losses. However, under current industry conditions, taxpayers would lose $50 billion to $100 billion, and the loss would be magnified if thrifts again took on greater risk. This illustrates a danger in letting the thrift mess drag on. Taxpayers will continue to be at substantial risk until the thrift industry is either recapitalized or liquidated.

Our analysis needs to be qualified because of the many assumptions upon which it is based. For example, we assume that all ARMs originated in the 1980s have been held in portfolio, and this is certainly not correct. For example, half of the ARMs with coupons within 3 percentage points of their life-of-loan rate cap have been originated by a single thrift that is known to sell ARMs. But these ARMs have likely been sold to other thrifts, thrifts with relatively less capital than the originating thrift. That is, the assumption that ARMs are not sold is more likely to understate the vulnerability of the thrift industry to increases in rates than to overstate the vulnerability.

Probably the most controversial assumption is that thrifts are not hedging through interest-rate swaps and caps, and so on. This assumption is obviously incorrect in its extreme form, but again we do not believe that it leads to a serious overstatement of thrift interest-rate sensitivity. Our first defense is that the thrift "experts" we have spoken with do not believe much hedging is going on. A second, and possibly related, defense is that over half of thrift assets are in institutions that have no incentive to hedge: they have few earnings to pay for hedging and little net worth to protect. Locking themselves into a negative, or minimal, net worth position is unlikely to be their preferred strategy.

Appendix

Table 8A.1 Thrift Balance Sheet and Risk Weighting, Book Value (billions of $)

	1989 Values	Risk Weighting	Risk-weighted Assets
Assets:			
Fixed-rate loans			
a. Single-family FRMs (H070 − MBSs)	134[a]	50%[d]	70
b. MBSs:GNMAs	45[b]	0	0
c. MBSs:Other	179[b]	20	36
d. Multifamily and nonresidential (H110)	68	50[e]	36
Adjustable-rate loans and second mortgage			
e. Single-family ARMs (F402)	327[a]	50[d]	169
f. Balloon and adjustable-rate loans, including construction loans, AED loans, etc. (H030 − F402)	214[a]	50[d]	113
g. Second mortgage loans, largely home equity loans (H150)	16	100[f]	17
Intermediate term			
h. Consumer loans, net of loans on deposits (H190 − A170) (plus some seconds)	56[c]	100	56
i. Other investments (including junk bonds, CMOs, and REMICs) (H270 − A370 − A382 − A400)	122[c]	100	122
Short term			
j. Cash and demand deposits (A360)	16	0	0
k. U.S. government and agencies (A370)	37	20	7
l. Commercial loans and accrued interest (H230 + A390)	34[c]	100	34
m. Equities except FHLB-FHLMC (A382)	4	100	4
n. Nonfinancial assets, net of valuation allowances (A800 − H310 − A360 − A390 − A525 − C992)	129	119[i]	153
Total assets, net of deferred losses and loans on deposits	1,381 (1,388)		810 (824)[j]
Liabilities			
o. Deposits (B012 + B014 + B016 + B018)[g]	989		
p. Other short-term borrowing, including commercial bank loans (B030), Reverse repurchase agreements (B040), Consumer retail repurchase agreements (B050), Net demand deposit overdrafts (B060 − A170), Commercial paper (B070), Other liabilities (B110 through B200)	132		

(continued)

Table 8A.1 (continued)

	1989 Values	Risk Weighting	Risk-weighted Assets
Liabilities			
q. Advances plus other borrowing (B020 + B100)[h]	196		
r. Long-term liabilities, other than those listed above (B800 − [deposits + other short-term borrowing + advances + A170])	17		
s. Subordinated debentures (B310 + B312)	5		
t. GAAP net worth[k]	42		
Total liabilities and net worth	1,381		

Source: Office of Thrift Supervision, quarterly *Thrift Financial Report.* In sections A, B, C, F and H of the *Report,* all data are as of March 1989.

Sections A and B provide information on balance sheet items. Section C provides information on modified equity capital items and adjustments to modified equity capital for institutions reporting on a GAAP basis. Section F (supplemental monthly data) reports on activity during the month and balances of loans and commitments outstanding as of the end of the month. Section H (maturity and yield/cost information) provides maturity and yield data on conventional mortgages secured by 1–4 dwelling units with fixed rates, balloon and adjustable-rate mortgage loans, other mortgage loans and contracts, and investment securities.

Note: We thank Carol Wambeke of the Office of Thrift Supervision for providing us with asset risk-weighting.

[a]Net of share of valuation allowances for mortgages (A129 + A131).

[b]MBSs are divided into GNMAs and others based on a survey of commercial banks and savings and loan associations (see Nothaft 1989).

[c]Net of share of valuation allowances for nonmortgages (A270 + A280 + A290).

[d]Delinquent loans are in the 100 percent bucket; in general, delinquent loans equal loans × (delinquent mortgage loans [FDQML]/net mortgage loans & contracts [ATMLCN]).

[e]50 percent weight for properties with under 36 units; 100 percent weight for properties with 36 or more units. We follow the Office of Thrift Supervision in assuming that all properties have under 36 units. Delinquent multifamily and nonresidential loans are in the 100 percent bucket.

[f]Delinquent loans are in the 200 percent bucket.

[g]In 1986, 96 percent of deposits had maturities of 3 years or less; 4 percent had maturities between 5 to 10 years.

[h]In 1986, 70 percent of Federal Home Loan Bank advances had maturities between 2 to 10 years; 76 percent of other borrowings had maturities between 3 to 10 years. Average duration of Federal Home Loan Bank advances is roughly 2 years.

[i]See table 8.2.

[j]Numbers in parentheses represent total assets (risk-based assets), including loans on deposits and deferred losses.

[k]Also includes a minuscule amount of net worth certificates (B320 + B330 + B340 + B350 − B380) and accumulated annual income payments, not due and payable (B360).

Table 8A.2 Measurement of Regulatory Capital (billions of $)

	1989
Core capital (tier 1):	
GAAP net worth	42
− Excluded goodwill (A544 − included goodwill)[a]	11
− Perpetual preferred stock (C012)	2
Total	29
Memo:	
Required core capital[b]	41
Supplementary capital (tier 2):	
Subordinated debentures (B310 + B312)	
+ Perpetual preferred stock (CO12)	
+ Qualifying pledged deposits (C958)	
+ Valuation allowances[c]	
+ Other supplementary capital[d]	
Total, not to exceed core capital	7
RAP capital[e]	36
Memo:	
Tangible capital (core capital − A544)	9
Required tangible capital[f]	20
Required risk-weighted capital at end of 1992[g]	66

Source: Office of Thrift Supervision, *Thrift Financial Report,* March 1989, Section C.
[a]Included goodwill equals min[total goodwill, 0.015*tangible assets].
[b]Required core capital equals 3 percent of tangible assets.
[c]Included valuation allowance equals min[C960, 0.015*risk-weighted assets].
[d]Other supplementary capital includes capital certificates (B320 + B330 + B340 + B350) and accumulated annual income payments, not due and payable (B360).
[e]RAP capital equals core capital plus supplementary capital, where supplementary capital may not exceed core capital.
[f]Required tangible capital equals 1.5 percent of tangible assets.
[g]8 percent of risk-weighted assets.

Table 8A.3 Distribution of ARMs by Size of Teaser, Years Until Repricing, and Annual Rate Caps, 1986–1989 (% of ARMs)

	1-year and less Annual Cap		3-year and more Annual Cap		
Size of Teaser	1%	2%	1%	2%	Total
1986					
<0.5%	8.52	28.01	0.43	4.89	41.85
0.5–1.5%	3.37	18.52	0.32	0.86	23.07
1.6–2.5%	2.83	25.94	0.02	0.47	29.26
>2.5%	1.45	4.27	0.01	0.06	5.79
Total	16.17	76.74	0.78	6.28	100.0
Number of loans	1,095	5,195	54	425	6,769

(continued)

Table 8A.3 (continued)

Size of Teaser	1-year and less Annual Cap 1%	1-year and less Annual Cap 2%	3-year and more Annual Cap 1%	3-year and more Annual Cap 2%	Total
1987					
<0.5%	8.18	24.83	0.39	5.63	39.03
0.5–1.5%	2.22	8.51	0	1.86	12.59
1.6–2.5%	6.96	28.84	0	1.54	37.37
>2.5%	0.79	9.34	0.01	0.91	11.03
Total	18.15	71.50	0.40	9.94	100.0
Number of loans	2,860	11,265	63	1,566	15,754
1988					
<0.5%	8.22	26.74	0.36	4.40	39.72
0.5–1.5%	1.43	3.26	0	1.07	5.76
1.6–2.5%	10.06	24.95	0.01	1.12	36.14
>2.5%	2.47	15.69	0	0.22	18.38
Total	22.18	70.64	0.37	6.81	100.0
Number of loans	4,649	14,814	78	1,428	10,969
1989					
<0.5%	6.69	26.46	0.36	4.13	37.64
0.5–1.5%	2.45	8.43	0.02	0.80	11.79
1.6–2.5%	5.28	19.34	0	1.57	26.19
>2.5%	2.98	21.09	0	0.40	24.47
Total	17.40	75.32	0.38	6.90	100.0
Number of loans	2,350	10,176	52	933	13,511

Source: Federal Housing Finance Board, Mortgage Interest Rate Survey, May–July of 1986–89.

Notes

1. Kane (1989b, table 3–4) estimates a $55 billion loss at thrifts with negative net worth (as measured by generally accepted accounting principles) and tangible-insolvent thrifts as of 30 September 1988, a loss that was increasing by over $1 billion a month.

2. See Kane (1989a, chap. 3) for an enlightening discussion of the development of the debacle.

3. For a discussion of the basic profitability problems of solvent thrifts, see Hendershott (1989).

4. Book net worth exceeds GAAP capital to the extent that the appraised value of fixed assets exceeds their book value.

5. Bovenzi and Murton (1988) break down the total loss on assets at commercial banks into four asset categories: 1) doubtful or loss; 2) substandard; 3) nonclassified risk assets; and 4) income earned but not collected. The estimated losses (per dollar) for each of these four asset categories are $0.92, $0.61, $0.20, and $0.20, respec-

tively. We have assumed that REO and REH are doubtful or loss assets, and equity in service corporations (which is often used to hide underwater assets) and other assets are nonclassified risk assets.

6. Thrifts hold $7 billion in interest-only mortgages, but also $4 billion in principal-only mortgages. In addition, they hold $16 billion in collateralized mortgage obligations (CMOs), but we do not know the maturity of these. We have classified the aggregate of all these assets as intermediate-term loans. See Kaufman (1984) for a primer on hedging the market value of net worth, and Breeden and Giarla (1988) for an advanced treatment.

7. With one exception: the initial coupon on a teaser ARM is set below all of these rates.

8. For net intermediate assets, the increase in interest income per dollar of assets is

$$\Delta r_t^{\mathrm{INT}} = r_t^{\mathrm{INT}} - r_{t-1}^{\mathrm{INT}},$$

where $r_t^{\mathrm{INT}} = \frac{1}{3}(r_t + r_{t-1} + r_{t-2})$. The loss of interest income on intermediate assets, INTER, over the twenty-year period is

$$\mathrm{L}_{\mathrm{INT}} = \sum_{t=1}^{20}(\Theta_t \Delta r_t - \Delta r_t^{\mathrm{INT}})\mathrm{INTER}.$$

This loss is trivial because thrifts have only $12 billion of net intermediate assets.

9. In cases where the capital loss is zero for individual thrifts, e.g., in early periods of the simulation for well-capitalized thrifts, a negative capital loss is set equal to zero, i.e., positive earnings for such thrifts are presumed to be paid out as dividends.

10. In the loss calculations for FRMs, equation (1) was modified to incorporate variable FRM repayment rates.

11. This sounds like a recommendation that thrifts "grow out of the problem," a policy advocated by many in the early 1980s. Such a policy works if (1) the growth is investment in safe long-term assets (long-term Treasuries would be better than FRMs) and (2) interest rates do indeed come back down.

12. For discussion of the perverse incentives facing many thrift managers in the 1980s, see Kane (1989a, chap. 2), Barth, Bartholomew, and Labich (1990), and Benston, Carhill, and Olasov, in this volume.

References

Barth, James R., Phillip F. Bartholomew, and Carol J. Labich. 1990. Moral Hazard and the Thrift Crisis: An Analysis of 1988 Resolutions. *Consumer Finance Law Quarterly Report* 44:344–84.

Bovenzi, J., and A. Murton. 1988. Resolution Cost of Bank Failures. *FDIC Banking Review* (Fall):1–3.

Breeden, Douglas T., and Michael J. Giarla. 1988. Hedging Interest-Rate Risk With Futures, Swaps, and Options. Federal Home Loan Bank Board Research Paper no. 147, June.

Buser, Stephen A., Patric H. Hendershott, and Anthony B. Sanders. 1985. Pricing Life-of-Loan Rate Caps on Default-Free Adjustable-Rate Mortgages. *AREUEA Journal* 13 (Fall):248–60.

———. 1990. Determinants of the Value of Call Options on Default-Free Bonds. *Journal of Business* 63, pt. 2 (January):533–550.

Hendershott, Patric H. 1989. The Future of Thrifts as Mortgage Portfolio Lenders. In *The Future of the Thrift Industry*. Federal Home Loan Bank of San Francisco.

Kane, Edward J. 1989a. *The S&L Insurance Mess: How Did It Happen?* Washington, DC: The Urban Institute Press.

———. 1989b. Principal-Agent Problems in S&L Salvage. Paper presented at the 1989 meetings of the American Finance Association, New York, December.

Kaufman, George G. 1984. Measuring and Managing Interest Rate Risk: A Primer. Federal Reserve Bank of Chicago, *Economic Perspectives* 8 (January–February):16–29.

Nothaft, Frank. 1989. Changes in Housing's Depth Chart. *Secondary Mortgage Markets* 3 (Fall):447–56.

9 Caps on Adjustable Rate Mortgages: Valuation, Insurance, and Hedging

Eduardo S. Schwartz and Walter N. Torous

9.1 Introduction

In April of 1981, federally chartered thrift institutions were permitted to originate adjustable rate mortgages. Prior to this, thrifts primarily originated long-term fixed rate mortgages. As a result, since thrifts are primarily financed with short-term deposits, a gap between their asset and liability maturities arose, thereby exposing thrifts to considerable interest rate risk. Adjustable rate mortgages reduce a thrift's gap, and hence its interest rate risk, since coupon rates vary with the thrift's cost of funds.

As expected, the origination of adjustable rate mortgages became prevalent with thrift institutions. After falling from 75 percent of total thrift originations in August 1984 to 21 percent of originations in June 1986, adjustable rate mortgages rose to an average of 71 percent of originations during 1988. Currently, approximately $300 billion of adjustable rate mortgages are outstanding. However, as the ongoing thrift crisis would indicate, adjustable rate mortgages did not eliminate thrifts' interest rate risk exposure.

Adjustable rate mortgage originators remain exposed to interest rate risk since the many contractual features of a typical adjustable rate mortgage result in an imperfect adjustment of its coupon rate to changes in the thrift's cost of funds. For example, Section 3806 of the Alternative Mortgage Transaction Parity Act of 1982 states that "adjustable rate mortgage loans originated by a

Eduardo S. Schwartz is the California Professor of Real Estate and Professor of Finance at the Anderson Graduate School of Management, University of California at Los Angeles. Walter N. Torous is Associate Professor of Finance at the Anderson Graduate School of Management, University of California at Los Angeles.

The authors would like to thank Patric Hendershott, Glenn Hubbard, James Shilling, and workshop participants at the University of British Columbia for their helpful comments and suggestions.

creditor shall include a limitation on the maximum interest rate that may apply during the term of the mortgage loan" (p. 4361).[1] The presence of a lifetime cap, as well as other contractual features, prevents a timely and full adjustment in the adjustable rate mortgage's coupon rate to changes in a thrift's cost of funds.

The purpose of this paper is to investigate the interest rate risk exposure of thrifts originating adjustable rate mortgages arising from the various contractual features of these mortgage instruments. In particular, we consider how the resultant interest rate risk exposure varies with the adjustable rate mortgage's lifetime cap, periodic cap, adjustment period, teaser rate, and margin. In addition to quantifying this interest rate risk exposure, we also investigate various means of minimizing it. Given the potentially considerable interest rate risk exposure due to the inclusion of lifetime cap provisions, we value lifetime cap insurance which insures against the adjustable rate mortgage's coupon rate exceeding its lifetime cap. We also discuss dynamic hedging strategies which, in lieu of purchasing insurance, can be pursued by thrifts to minimize the interest rate risk associated with the origination of adjustable rate mortgages.

We investigate these various issues within a two-factor adjustable rate mortgage valuation framework which explicitly takes into account the essential contractual features of the adjustable rate mortgage as well as the prepayment behavior of borrowers. Other studies which have investigated the valuation of adjustable rate mortgages include Buser, Hendershott, and Sanders (1985) and Kau et al. (1985). By comparison, both of these studies assume a one-factor framework and ignore the prepayment behavior of borrowers.

In this paper we abstract from the possibility of default by either the borrower or the originating thrift institution. The borrower's default risk can be taken into account by charging an appropriate default insurance premium (see Schwartz and Torous 1990). For our purposes here, this insurance premium can be assumed to be included in the adjustable rate mortgage's servicing fee. By contrast, we do not deal with the potential strategic behavior of an originating thrift institution in financial distress.

The plan of this paper is as follows. In section 9.2 we detail the various contractual features of adjustable rate mortgages. An understanding of these contractual features is necessary to analyze why an adjustable rate mortgage's coupon rate is typically not perfectly indexed to a thrift's cost of funds. Section 9.3 details our two-factor adjustable rate mortgage valuation model. Following Brennan and Schwartz (1982) and Schwartz and Torous (1989), we take the two factors to be the instantaneously riskless rate of interest and the yield on a default-free consol bond. Monte Carlo simulation techniques are used to value adjustable rate mortgages and various cap options embedded in them, as well as to determine the fair fee to charge for lifetime cap insurance. We present these valuation results in section 9.4. In section 9.5 we discuss various techniques to dynamically hedge adjustable rate mortgages' interest rate risk. Section 9.6 provides our conclusions and suggests policy implications arising from this research.

9.2 Contractual Features of Adjustable Rate Mortgages

An ideal adjustable rate mortgage (ARM) would have a coupon rate which adjusts to perfectly reflect changes in the originating thrift's cost of funds. The thrift's assets and liabilities would then be perfectly matched, thereby eliminating interest rate risk. However, in practice the various contractual features of an ARM typically prevent its coupon rate from perfectly responding to changes in a thrift's cost of funds. In this section, we summarize the essential contractual features of ARMs, emphasizing how these features may prevent the ARM coupon rate from being perfectly indexed to the originating thrift's cost of funds and, as such, exposing the thrift to interest rate risk. For further details regarding the various contractual features of ARMs, see Bartholomew, Berk, and Roll (1986).

9.2.1 Index

The ARM's coupon rate varies directly with its contractually specified index. The two most widely used indices are a cost of funds index (COFI) and a constant maturity (1 year or 5 year) Treasury yield index. The former represents a weighted average of the actual book cost of funds of thrifts located in the Federal Home Loan Bank's eleventh district (Arizona, California, and Nevada), while the latter is constructed from the current yields of 1-year or 5-year Treasury securities.

To the extent that a COFI reflects the book rather than market cost of a thrift's funds, changes in this index will not perfectly reflect changes in market interest rate conditions. Similarly, while levels of the Treasury yield indices move extremely closely with levels of corresponding market Treasury rates, the empirical analysis of Roll (1987) concludes that the method of constructing these indices significantly reduces the correlation between changes in these indices and changes in corresponding market rates. As a result, changes in the coupon rate of an ARM based on a Treasury yield index will also not perfectly reflect changes in market interest rate conditions.

9.2.2 Margin

The ARM's coupon rate equals the prevailing level of the index plus the contractually specified margin, subject to initial discounts and restrictions to be discussed shortly. The margin on ARMs have remained relatively level over the recent past. For example, from January 1986 through April 1989, the margin over index for ARMs based on the 1-year Treasury yield index averaged between 200 and 300 basis points (see Gordon, Luytjes, and Feid 1989). The size of the margin reflects the value of the various options embedded in the ARM, including the option to prepay, as well as the costs of servicing the underlying loan.

9.2.3 Adjustment Period

An ARM's coupon rate is not continuously adjusted to changes in the level of the underlying index, but rather is adjusted periodically at a contractually stipulated frequency. An ARM's adjustment period is the minimum period of time over which its coupon rate cannot be changed. Typical adjustment periods are six months or one year. Clearly, the higher an ARM's adjustment frequency, the more responsive its coupon rate will be to changes in current market conditions. The fact that ARMs are not continuously adjusted prevents ARM coupon rates from perfectly responding to changes in thrifts' cost of funds.

9.2.4 Teaser Rate

At origination the ARM coupon rate is frequently set below its fully indexed level, index plus margin, so as to provide an initial inducement to the borrower. This initial coupon rate is referred to as the ARM's teaser rate. Typically the teaser rate is in effect for the initial adjustment period. The last few years have seen thrifts more often utilizing teaser rates, offering increasingly larger discounts from the fully indexed loan rate. For example, the size of this discount on ARMS based on a 1-year Treasury index rose sharply from an average of 0.3 percent in late 1986 to an average of 3 percent in late 1988, further increasing to an average of 3.5 percent in early 1989 (see Gordon, Luytjes, and Feid 1989). It has been suggested that the size of this discount has now grown to where new ARM originations are no longer profitable, thereby contributing to the ongoing thrift crisis.

9.2.5 Lifetime Cap

An ARM's lifetime cap contractually stipulates an upper bound which its coupon rate cannot exceed. In other words, if at adjustment the fully indexed loan rate exceeds the lifetime cap, then the ARM's coupon rate remains at the lifetime cap. The ARM's coupon rate is fixed at the lifetime cap until the fully indexed loan rate falls below the lifetime cap at a subsequent adjustment. Section 3806 of the Alternative Mortgage Transaction Parity Act of 1982 requires that all ARMs be subject to a lifetime cap provision. Typically a 5 or 6 percent maximum change in an ARM's coupon rate relative to its teaser rate is permitted over the life of a loan based on a 1-year Treasury index. Lifetime caps subject the ARM originator to potentially significant interest rate risk as the ARM coupon rate is contractually prevented from fully responding to significant increases in the thrift's cost of funds.

9.2.6 Lifetime Floor

An ARM's lifetime floor contractually stipulates a lower bound below which the ARM's coupon rate cannot fall. That is, the ARM coupon remains at the floor if the fully indexed loan rate falls below the floor. As opposed to the lifetime cap, which is beneficial to the borrower, the inclusion of a lifetime floor is generally viewed as being advantageous to the originator. However, it should be noted that the lifetime floor will typically not be binding since most interest-sensitive borrowers will prepay at sufficiently low interest rates in order to lock in low fixed refinancing rates.

9.2.7 Periodic Cap

The periodic cap limits the amount by which the ARM coupon rate can change, in either direction, over any adjustment period. In other words, if the underlying index increases or decreases by more than the periodic cap, the ARM coupon rate changes only by the magnitude of the periodic cap.[2] Typically, ARMs based on a 1-year Treasury index feature periodic caps of 2 percent per year. Periodic caps effect lags in adjustments of the ARM coupon rate to changes in a thrift's cost of funds, though in the case of falling interest rates the consequence would be beneficial to the originator.

While the above discussion has concentrated on each contractual feature of an ARM in isolation, it should be emphasized that these various features may potentially interact with one another. For example, the fact that the teaser rate is usually set well below the fully indexed loan rate implies that the periodic cap will almost certainly be binding at the ARM's first adjustment. It is important to jointly model all of these institutional features to fully capture these interactions and to therefore properly value ARMs.

9.3 A Two-Factor ARM Valuation Model

In this section we develop a two-factor model to value ARMs which takes into account their previously described institutional features. The model allows us to examine the pricing of lifetime cap insurance, other options embedded in ARMs, and the dynamic hedging of these mortgage instruments. Our analysis is couched in perfect frictionless markets and, therefore, we ignore transaction costs, such as points charged at the ARM's origination.

The point of departure of our ARM valuation model is Brennan and Schwartz's (1982) two-factor model of the term structure of default-free interest rates. This model assumes that all relevant information about the term structure can be summarized by the instantaneous riskless rate of interest (the "short rate") and the continuously compounded yield on a default-free consol bond (the "long rate"). Given the assumed dynamics of the short and long rates, an absence of arbitrage opportunities yields the fundamental ARM valuation equation which must be solved subject to appropriate boundary and terminal conditions.

To properly value ARMs it is important to model borrowers' prepayment behavior. Despite the fact that ARM coupon rates tend to vary with market interest rate conditions, the empirical analysis of Bartholomew, Berk, and

Roll (1988) documents that ARM borrowers tend to prepay when refinancing rates are low in order to lock in what they believe are low fixed rates. Clearly a failure to properly model this prepayment behavior will result in the systematic mispricing of ARMs. We incorporate prepayment behavior by specifying the borrower's prepayment function, which gives the conditional probability of a borrower prepaying an ARM, as a proportional hazards model (Green and Shoven 1986). The baseline hazard function measures the effect of seasoning, or mortgage age, on prepayment behavior. However, the conditional probability of prepayment does not depend solely upon the ARM's age. Our prepayment function recognizes that prevailing interest rate conditions also influence the prepayment decision of the ARM borrower.

9.3.1 ARM Cash Flows

We consider a fully amortizing mortgage having an original principal of $P(0)$ and an original term to maturity of T years with a continuously compounded teaser rate of $c(0)$. As a result, the ARM's continuous payout rate over the initial adjustment period is $C(0)$ where

$$C(0) = c(0)P(0)/(1 - \exp(-c(0)T)).$$

The loan's principal outstanding, $P(t)$, during the initial adjustment period is given by

$$P(t) = P(0)(1 - \exp(-c(0)(T - t)))/(1 - \exp(-c(0)T)).$$

At the ARM's ith adjustment, at time t_i, given a coupon rate of $c(t_i)$, the ARM's payout rate, $C(t_i)$, is now given by

$$C(t_i) = c(t_i)P(t_i)/(1 - \exp(-c(t_i)(T - t_i))),$$

while during the ith adjustment period the loan's principal outstanding is given by

$$P(t) = P(t_i)(1 - \exp(-c(t_i)(T - t)))/(1 - \exp(-c(t_i)(T - t_i))).$$

The ARM's coupon rate at adjustment is determined by adding the contractually specified margin, m, to the prevailing level of the underlying index, $x(t)$, subject to the ARM's lifetime and periodic cap constraints. Let $c^*(t_i)$ represent the fully indexed loan rate in the absence of any cap constraints:

$$c^*(t_i) = x(t_i) + m.$$

If $c^*(t_i) > c(t_{i-1})$, then the ARM's coupon rate is given by

$$c(t_i) = \min[\, c^*(t_i), c_L, c(t_{i-1}) + p],$$

where c_L denotes the ARM's lifetime cap and p the ARM's periodic cap. Conversely, if $c^*(t_i) < c(t_{i-1})$, then the ARM's coupon rate is given by

$$c(t_i) = \max[\, c^*(t_i), c_F, c(t_{i-1}) - p],$$

where c_F denotes the ARM's lifetime floor.

These ARM cash flows represent the mortgagor's contractual interest and repayment of principal, and typically include a servicing fee to the originator. However, since we are interested in the market valuation of the ARM, we must explicitly take into account any included servicing fee. We do so by subtracting an exogenously specified servicing fee, s, from these cash flows:

$$C(t) - sP(t).$$

The ARM's value reflects the investor's receipt of these cash flows, subject to the loan's prepayment.

9.3.2 Prepayment Function

We assume that the mortgagor's annualized conditional probability of prepayment depends upon the mortgage's age as well as prevailing interest rate conditions, and is given by the following proportional hazards model:

$$\pi(x, t) = \pi_0(t)\exp(\beta(x(0) - x(t))). \tag{1}$$

The baseline hazard function, $\pi_0(t)$, measures the effect of seasoning on prepayment behavior. We assume that the baseline hazard function is given by 100 percent of Public Securities Association (PSA) experience:

$$\pi_0(t) = \min(0.024t, 0.06).$$

That is, the annualized baseline probability of prepayment is zero at the ARM's origination, increases by 0.002 per month for the first thirty months of the ARM's life, and then remains constant at an annualized rate of 0.06 from the thirtieth month until maturity.

Prevailing interest rate conditions also influence the mortgagor's prepayment decision. To model interest-sensitive ARM prepayments, we include a single covariate measuring the difference between the underlying index's level at origination, $x(0)$, and its prevailing level, $x(t)$. The higher the prevailing level of the index relative to its level at the ARM's origination, the lower the probability of prepayment, conditional on the ARM not having been previously prepaid. We can interpret β as measuring the speed of prepayment. The larger is β, ceteris paribus, the more sensitive are ARM prepayments to prevailing interest rate conditions.

9.3.3 Valuation Equation

The dynamics of the state variables, the short rate r and the long rate l, are assumed to be given by

$$dr = (a_1 + b_1(l - r))dt + \sigma_1 r dz_1 \tag{2}$$

and

$$dl = l(a_2 + b_2 r + c_2 l)dt + \sigma_2 l dz_2, \tag{3}$$

where z_1 and z_2 are standardized Wiener processes. Increments to z_1 and z_2 are assumed instantaneously correlated:

$$dz_1 dz_2 = \rho dt. \tag{4}$$

In the absence of arbitrage opportunities the value of the ARM, $V(r,l,t)$, must satisfy the following second-order partial differential equation:

$$\begin{aligned} &\tfrac{1}{2}r^2\sigma_1^2 V_{rr} + rl\rho\sigma_1\sigma_2 V_{rl} + \tfrac{1}{2}l^2\sigma_2^2 V_{ll} + (a_1 + b_1(l - r) - \lambda\sigma_1 r)V_r \\ &+ l(\sigma_2^2 + l - r)V_l + V_t - (r + \pi)V \\ &+ \pi P(t) + (C(t) - sP(t)) = 0, \end{aligned} \tag{5}$$

where λ is the market price of short-term interest rate risk. Since the ARM is fully amortizing, the following terminal condition must be satisfied:

$$V(r,l,T) = 0. \tag{6}$$

9.3.4 Monte Carlo Simulation Solution Technique

When cash flows are path dependent, the most efficient numerical method for solving the partial differential equation (eq. [5]), subject to the corresponding terminal condition (eq. [6]), is provided by Monte Carlo solution techniques (see Boyle 1977, and Schwartz and Torous 1989). This is particularly so in our valuation framework where the cash flows depend upon past coupon rates.

Monte Carlo simulation methods require that r and l are generated by the following correlated risk-adjusted stochastic processes:

$$dr = (a_1 + b_1(l - r) - \lambda\sigma_1 r)dt + \sigma_1 r dz_1 \tag{2'}$$

and

$$dl = l(\sigma_2^2 + l - r)dt + \sigma_2 l dz_2. \tag{3'}$$

To value an ARM, we generate correlated normal random variables corresponding to r and l at every month during the ARM's life. At each adjustment we set the ARM's coupon rate as previously discussed in section 9.3.1, and consequently each month determine the ARM's cash flows—contractually obligated plus prepayments. The present value of these cash flows provides a realization of the ARM's value. By repeating this procedure, the average of these realizations gives the required solution of the partial differential equation.

9.3.5 Equilibrium Valuation of Cap Options and the Fair Lifetime Cap Insurance Fee

We can use our ARM valuation procedures to determine the equilibrium values of lifetime and periodic cap options embedded in ARMs as well as the fair fee to charge for lifetime cap insurance.

For example, subtracting the value of an ARM with both lifetime and periodic caps from the value of an otherwise identical ARM without the lifetime cap gives the value of the lifetime cap option. Similarly, by subtracting the value of an ARM without the lifetime cap from the value of an otherwise identical ARM without both lifetime and periodic caps gives the value of the periodic cap option.

Lifetime cap insurance insures against the ARM's coupon rate exceeding its lifetime cap. The fair lifetime cap insurance fee is simply that premium which will make an ARM without a lifetime cap have the same value as an otherwise identical ARM with a lifetime cap. The larger the fair lifetime cap insurance fee, the greater the probability that the ARM's lifetime cap will be binding, and therefore the greater the interest rate risk.

9.4 Valuation Results

This section documents the magnitudes as well as sensitivities of periodic cap options, lifetime cap options, and the fair lifetime cap insurance fee to systematic changes in ARM features. These results will provide insights into the determinants of an ARM originator's interest rate risk exposure. Clearly the greater the interest rate risk exposure of an ARM originator, the greater the possibility of the thrift's financial distress.

Since we are interested in systematically varying the features of an ARM, we require a base case against which to compare these results. For this purpose we consider the following 30-year ARM offered by a southern California thrift in December 1989 which was representative of available ARMs:

index = 1-year Treasury index
lifetime cap = 14 percent
lifetime floor = 8 percent
periodic cap = 1 percent
teaser rate = 8 percent
adjustment period = 1 year
margin = 2.75 percent.

Our valuation analysis assumes that the originating thrift requires a fee of 1 percent to service this ARM. Also, interest rate conditions prevailing in December 1989 are summarized by a short rate of $r = 8$ percent and a long rate of $l = 9$ percent.

Notice that our base case ARM is indexed to a short-term riskless rate of interest. While our valuation framework can accommodate a variety of index specifications, we assume that the ARM's coupon rate is perfectly indexed to the short rate r in order to simplify the subsequent analysis. This assumption is consistent with ARMs being indexed to relatively short-term, as opposed to relatively long-term, rates of interest. However, as a result of this simplifying assumption, our subsequent analysis does not investigate the interest rate risk exposure of an ARM originator owing to changes in the ARM's index not being perfectly correlated with changes in market interest rate conditions.

The risk-adjusted interest rate processes (eqs. [2′] and [3′]) characterize the interest rate environment in which we value ARMs. The parameters of the risk-adjusted interest rate processes used here are taken from Schwartz and Torous (1989). There the short rate is approximated by the annualized one-month CD rate, while the long rate is approximated by the annualized running coupon yield on long-term treasury bonds. Given these data over the sample period December 1982 through April 1987, together with an estimate of the market price of short-term interest rate risk of −0.01, the corresponding maximum-likelihood parameter estimates of the risk-adjusted interest rate processes are summarized as follows:

$$\Delta r = (-0.0416 + 1.987(l - r) - (-0.01)(0.189)r)\Delta t + 0.189r\Delta z_1,$$
$$\Delta l = l(0.125^2 + l - r)\Delta t + 0.125l\Delta z_2,$$

with an estimated correlation coefficient of 0.373.

To complete the characterization of our ARM valuation framework, we must explicitly specify the parameters of the prepayment function. As mentioned earlier, we assume that the baseline hazard function is given by 100 percent of PSA experience. Rather than estimate the speed of prepayment parameter β from ARM prepayment data, we determine that particular value of β which results in our model valuing the base-case ARM at par at origination. As a result, we imply an ex ante β estimate of 41.4. Assuming the appropriateness of our valuation framework, the advantage of implying the speed of prepayment parameter is that it provides a forward-looking estimate which reflects anticipated prepayment behavior.

Given that the base-case ARM is valued at par or $100 at origination,[3] the corresponding value of the base-case ARM's lifetime cap option is $1.87, which translates into an annualized fair lifetime cap insurance fee of 31 basis points. The corresponding value of the base-case ARM's periodic cap option is $5.58. The relatively large value of the periodic cap option reflects the fact that with a teaser rate of 8 percent and an initial fully indexed loan rate of 10.75 percent, the periodic cap of 1 percent will most likely be binding at future adjustments of the base-case ARM's coupon rate. By contrast, for a more typical periodic cap of 2 percent and holding all other features fixed, the value of the ARM's lifetime cap option increases to $3.74, which translates into a fair lifetime cap insurance fee of 61 basis points, while the value of the ARM's periodic cap option decreases to $1.81. These changes reflect the fact that the periodic cap is now less likely to be binding at future coupon rate adjustments.

Our subsequent analysis, summarized in table 9.1 and figures 9.1–9.6, examines the sensitivities of cap option values and fair lifetime cap insurance fees of the base-case ARM to systematic changes in the ARMs' contractual features.[4]

9.4.1 Lifetime Cap

Panel A of table 9.1 documents the sensitivities of ARM cap option values to changes in the level of the ARM's lifetime cap. We consider lifetime caps

Table 9.1 **Value of Cap Options as a Function of ARM's Features**

Panel A

Lifetime cap (%)	10	11	12	13	14	15	16	17	18	19	20
Value of lifetime cap option ($)	7.63	5.41	3.82	2.68	1.87	1.28	0.87	0.57	0.37	0.24	0.14
Fair lifetime cap insurance (basis points)	126	89	63	44	31	21	14	9	6	4	2
Value of periodic cap option ($)	5.46	5.50	5.54	5.56	5.58	5.60	5.60	5.61	5.61	5.61	5.62

Panel B

Lifetime floor (%)	5	6	7	8	9
Value of lifetime cap option ($)	1.89	1.89	1.87	1.74	1.25
Fair lifetime cap insurance (basic points)	31	31	31	29	21
Value of periodic cap option ($)	5.58	5.58	5.58	5.58	5.59

Panel C

Periodic cap (%)	.25	.50	.75	1.00	1.25	1.50	1.75	2.00
Value of lifetime cap option ($)	0.00	0.34	1.10	1.87	2.54	3.06	3.46	3.74
Fair lifetime cap insurance (basis points)	0	6	18	31	42	50	57	61
Value of periodic cap option ($)	14.81	10.59	7.63	5.58	4.12	3.09	2.34	1.81

Panel D

Adjustment period (months)	3	6	9	12	15	18	21	24	27	30
Value of lifetime cap option ($)	4.89	3.80	2.72	1.87	1.23	.81	.50	.31	.18	.10
Fair lifetime cap insurance (basis points)	80	62	45	31	20	13	8	5	3	2
Value of periodic cap option ($)	1.09	2.59	4.15	5.58	6.79	7.59	8.36	8.93	9.28	9.56

Panel E

Teaser rate (%)	6	7	8	9	10	11
Value of lifetime cap option($)	1.51	1.70	1.87	2.00	2.08	2.14
Fair lifetime cap insurance (basis points)	25	28	31	33	34	35
Value of periodic cap option ($)	10.16	7.54	5.58	4.37	3.72	3.03

(continued)

Table 9.1 (continued)

Panel F						
Margin (%)	1.25	1.75	2.25	2.75	3.25	3.75
Value of lifetime cap option ($)	0.84	1.22	1.56	1.87	2.19	2.52
Fair lifetime cap insurance (basis points)	14	20	26	31	36	41
Value of periodic cap option ($)	0.33	1.92	3.55	5.21	6.92	8.67

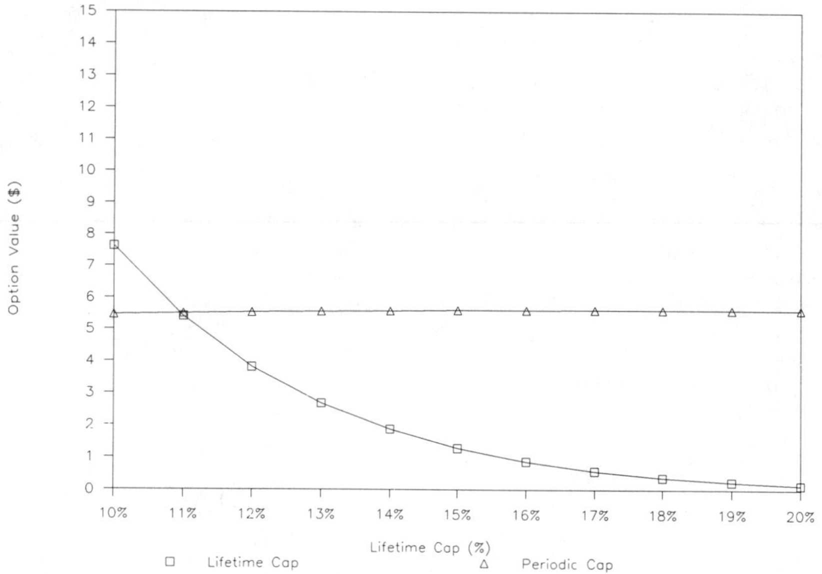

Fig. 9.1 Value of cap options for different lifetime caps

ranging from 10 to 20 percent in increments of 1 percent. These results are graphically presented in figure 9.1.

Notice that the value of the lifetime cap option and the corresponding fair lifetime cap insurance fee decrease with increases in the lifetime cap. For example, when the lifetime cap is 12 percent the fair lifetime cap insurance fee is 63 basis points, while for a lifetime cap of 20 percent the fair lifetime cap insurance fee is reduced to only 2 basis points. This result follows simply from the fact that the higher the level of the lifetime cap, the lower the probability of this cap becoming binding.

By contrast, the value of the periodic cap option increases slightly as the level of the lifetime cap increases. When the lifetime cap is 12 percent the periodic cap option is valued at $5.54, while for a lifetime cap of 20 percent the periodic cap option increases in value to $5.62. Intuitively, as the level of the lifetime cap increases and, as such, the lifetime cap becomes less binding, the probability that the periodic cap will become binding increases.

9.4.2 Lifetime Floor

ARM cap option values are extremely insensitive to changes in the level of the ARM's lifetime floor. We consider lifetime floors ranging from 5 to 9 percent in increments of 1 percent and tabulate the resultant ARM cap option values in panel B of table 9.1. These results are graphically summarized in figure 9.2. The reason for the insensitivity of ARM cap option values to changes in the lifetime floor is that the states of the world in which the lifetime floor becomes binding are precisely those states of the world in which there exists a financial incentive for borrowers to prepay. These results indicate that the lifetime floor option, which is viewed as being beneficial to the ARM originator, is practically worthless. As a result, the lifetime cap option embedded in ARMs typically derives value only from its upper cap.

9.4.3 Periodic Cap

We tabulate the sensitivities of ARM cap option values to changes in the level of the periodic cap in panel C of table 9.1. The periodic cap ranges from 0.25 to 2.00 percent in increments of 0.25 percent, while maintaining a 12-month adjustment period. These results are graphically depicted in figure 9.3.

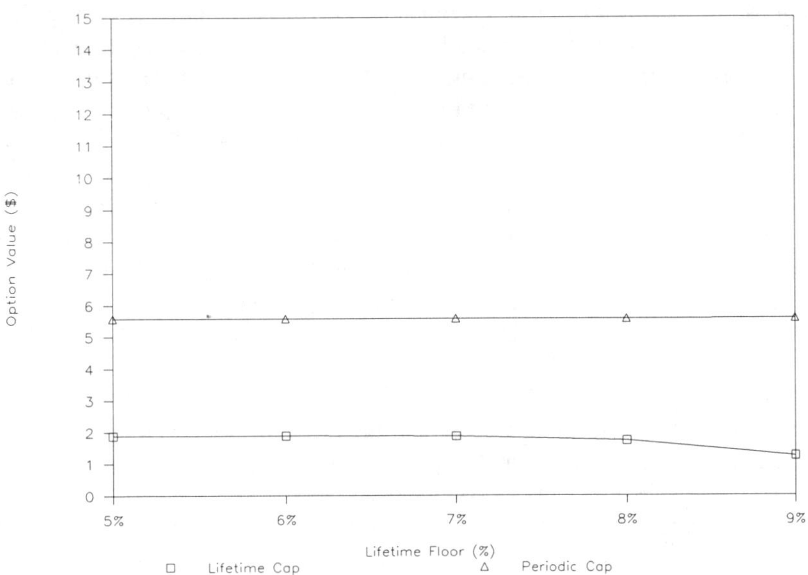

Fig. 9.2 Value of cap options for different lifetime floors

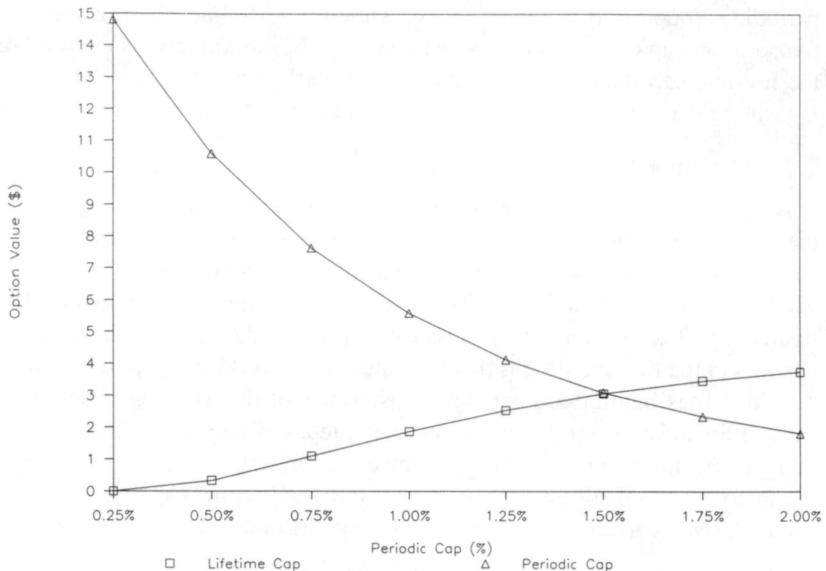

Fig. 9.3 Value of cap options for different periodic caps

The value of the lifetime cap option and the corresponding fair lifetime cap insurance fee increase with increases in the level of the periodic cap. For a periodic cap of 0.25 percent the fair lifetime cap insurance fee is negligible, but the fee increases to 71 basis points for a periodic cap of 2.00 percent. The smaller the periodic cap, the less binding a given lifetime cap. For example, for a periodic cap of 0.25 percent, it would take a minimum of 24 years for a lifetime cap of 14 percent to be reached from a teaser rate of 8 percent, and hence the value of the lifetime cap option is negligible.

Conversely, the value of the periodic cap option decreases with increases in the ARM's periodic cap. For a periodic cap of 0.25 percent, the periodic cap option is valued at $14.81, while for a periodic cap of 2.00 percent the periodic cap option is valued at $1.81. The smaller the periodic cap, the more likely it will be binding, and hence the more valuable the periodic cap option.

9.4.4 Adjustment Period

We vary the ARM's adjustment period from 3 months to 30 months, in increments of 3 months, and document the resultant ARM cap option values in panel D of table 9.1. Figure 9.4 graphically summarizes these results.

The value of the lifetime cap option and the corresponding fair lifetime cap insurance fee decrease with the lengthening of the ARM's adjustment period. For example, for an adjustment period of 3 months the fair lifetime cap insurance fee is 80 basis points, while for an adjustment period of 30 months the fair insurance fee is only 2 basis points. For a fixed periodic cap, the longer

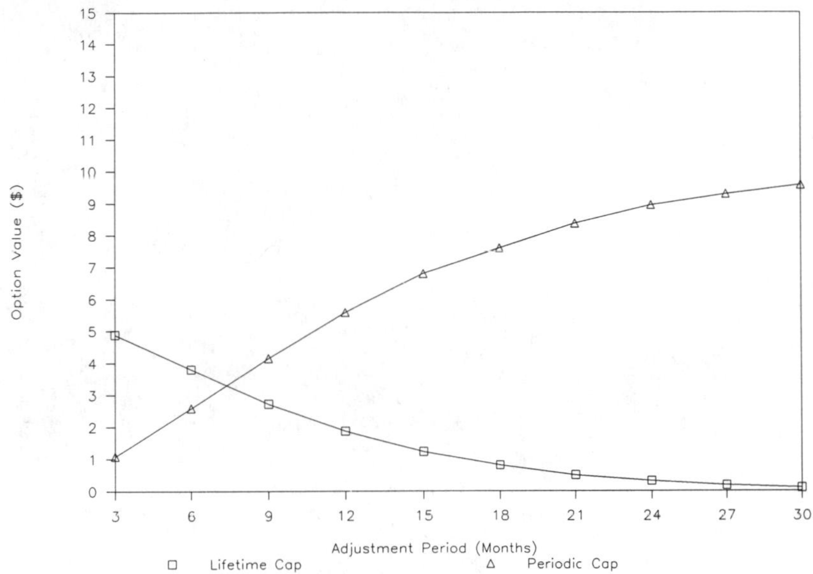

Fig. 9.4 Value of cap options for different adjustment periods

the adjustment period, the longer, on average, the time required to reach the ARM's lifetime cap, and hence the less valuable the lifetime cap option. If the adjustment period is 30 months, it would take a minimum of 15 years to reach a lifetime cap of 14 percent starting from a teaser rate of 8 percent. In the limit, as the adjustment period approaches the ARM's original term to maturity, the ARM becomes a fixed rate mortgage and the lifetime cap option becomes worthless.

By contrast, the value of the periodic cap option increases with the lengthening of the ARM's adjustment period. For an adjustment period of 3 months the periodic cap option is valued at $1.09, while for an adjustment period of 30 months the periodic cap option is valued at $9.56. Intuitively, the longer the adjustment period, the more likely the periodic cap will be binding.

9.4.5 Teaser Rate

Panel E of table 9.1 reports ARM cap option values as the teaser rate is varied from 6 to 11 percent in increments of 1 percent. These results are graphically presented in figure 9.5.

Increases in the teaser rate result in increases in the value of the lifetime cap option and the corresponding fair lifetime cap insurance fee. For example, for a teaser rate of 6 percent the fair lifetime cap insurance fee is 25 basis points, and the fee increases to 35 basis points for a teaser rate of 11 percent. The higher the teaser rate, the closer the ARM's initial fully indexed loan rate is to the lifetime cap and, as such, the more valuable the lifetime cap option.

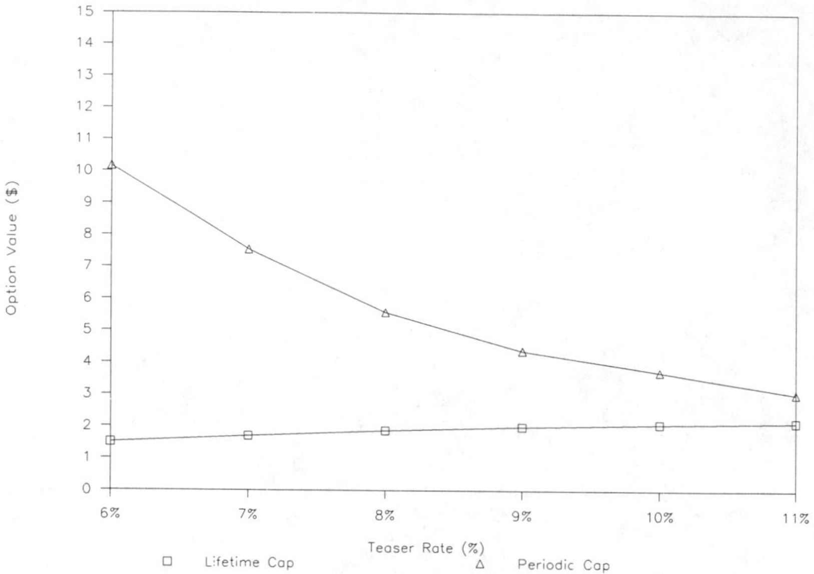

Fig. 9.5 Value of cap options for different teaser rates

However, the value of the periodic cap option decreases with increases in the teaser rate. For a teaser rate of 6 percent the periodic cap option is valued at $10.16, while for a teaser rate of 11 percent the periodic cap option is valued at $3.03. The lower the teaser rate the more valuable is the periodic cap option, since the initial adjustment in the ARM's coupon to the corresponding fully indexed loan rate will be larger and hence the periodic cap will be more likely to be binding.

9.4.6 Margin

Finally, panel F of table 9.1 examines the sensitivities of ARM cap option values to the level of the ARM's margin. The margin is varied from 1.25 to 3.75 percent in increments of 0.25 percent. The results are graphically depicted in figure 9.6.

As expected, the value of the lifetime cap option and the corresponding fair lifetime cap insurance fee increase with increases in the margin. For a margin of 1.25 percent the fair lifetime cap insurance fee is 14 basis points, while for a margin of 3.75 percent the fair fee is 41 basis points. The larger the margin, the greater the possibility that a given lifetime cap will be binding.

Similarly, the value of the periodic cap option increases with increases in the ARM's margin. For a margin of 1.25 percent the periodic cap option is valued at $3.94, while for a margin of 3.75 percent the periodic cap option is valued at $7.60. This result follows from the fact that the larger the margin, the larger will be the initial adjustment in the ARM's coupon rate to the corresponding fully indexed loan rate.

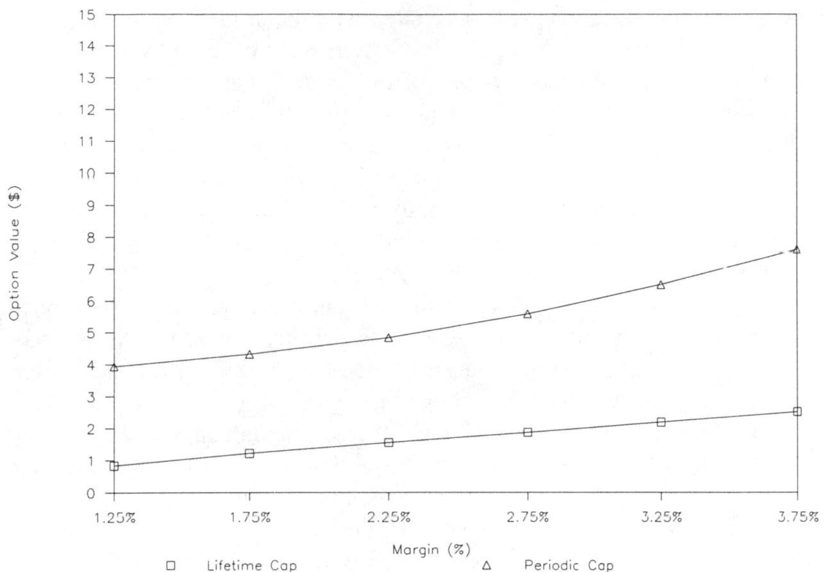

Fig. 9.6 Value of cap options for different margins

9.5 Hedging ARM Interest Rate Risk

Our preceding analysis has established that the various contractual features of ARMs subject originating thrifts to potentially substantial interest rate risk exposure. For example, the presence of a lifetime cap provision contractually prevents an ARM's coupon rate from fully responding to significant increases in a thrift's cost of funds. The thrift's resultant interest rate exposure, as measured by the corresponding fair lifetime cap insurance fee, can be considerable. We now turn our attention to dynamic hedging strategies which will allow the originating thrift to minimize the interest rate risk exposure arising from the various contractual features of ARMs. Alternatively, these dynamic hedging strategies can be implemented by lifetime cap insurers to hedge their resultant interest rate risk.

Our ARM valuation equation (eq. [5]) is based on dynamic hedging arguments. In other words, assuming that the two factors, r and l, determine the value of all default-free interest-rate-dependent claims, it is always possible to form a portfolio of three interest-rate-dependent claims that is insensitive to instantaneous changes in these factors. Therefore, in the absence of arbitrage opportunities, the instantaneous return to this hedge portfolio must equal the prevailing instantaneous riskless rate of interest. These arbitrage arguments yield the partial differential equation (eq. [5]) and also form the basis for hedging interest rate risk inherent in all interest-rate-contingent claims.

We note at the outset that we are able to use our valuation framework to fully hedge the interest rate risk associated with the origination of ARMs because of the following two simplifying assumptions of the model. First, we assume that the ARM's index is one of the model's state variables. Second, we assume a prepayment function which depends only on the prevailing value of the state variable and the mortgage's age, and neglect other demographic and socioeconomic factors which influence borrowers' prepayment decisions. Both of these assumptions do not strictly hold in practice, and therefore will adversely affect our ARM hedging performance. To fully assess these implications would require further empirical analysis.

To dynamically hedge an ARM's interest rate risk requires offsetting positions in other interest-rate-sensitive securities. In particular, the ARM's sensitivities to changes in interest rates must be offset by the corresponding sensitivities of these other securities. For illustrative purposes, we assume these interest-rate-sensitive securities are default-free coupon bonds of varying maturities, although in practice, to minimize transaction costs, this dynamic hedging strategy would most likely be implemented with interest rate futures.

Table 9.2 documents the sensitivities of the base-case ARM to changes in r and l,[5] as well as the corresponding sensitivities of 9% continuously compounded coupon, non-amortizing, non-callable, default-free bonds of various maturities. For example, the base-case ARM's value decreases by 0.30 percent for a 1 percent increase in r from 8 to 9 percent, while a 1 percent increase in l from 9 to 10 percent will decrease its value by 3.66 percent. By contrast, the sensitivities of a 1-year 9% coupon bond with respect to these changes in r and l are -0.42 percent and -0.54 percent, respectively.

As expected, lengthening the maturity of the default-free bond decreases its sensitivity to the short rate and increases its sensitivity to the long rate. Comparing these sensitivities, notice that the interest rate sensitivities of the base-case ARM are similar to the corresponding sensitivities of the 5-year coupon bond. Despite the fact that the ARM's coupon rate is indexed to the short rate of interest, its numerous institutional features together with the posited prepayment behavior make the ARM's interest rate sensitivities more similar to a 5-year default-free bond as opposed to a default-free bond of shorter term to maturity.

These sensitivities allow us to formulate a dynamic portfolio strategy in the

Table 9.2 **Sensitivies of ARM and Various Default-free Coupon Bonds to Changes in Short and Long Rates**

	Sensitivity to r	Sensitivity to l
ARM	−.30	−3.66
1-year 9% bond	−.42	−.54
5-year 9% bond	−.32	−3.99
10-year 9% bond	−.18	−7.18
20-year 9% bond	−.05	−10.01
30-year 9% bond	−.02	−10.63

coupon bonds to hedge the interest rate risk incurred by the originator of the base-case ARM. Since the ARM represents an asset to the originating thrift, the structure of its liability portfolio should be such that its sensitivities to the two factors exactly offset the ARM's corresponding sensitivities.

To be more precise, let

$$\beta_r^j = V_r^j \,/\, V^j$$

and

$$\beta_l^j = V_l^j \,/\, V^j$$

be the sensitivities of asset j with respect to r and l, respectively. Assume that we want to hedge perfectly an investment of X_3 dollars in asset 3 (for example, ARMs) using two other interest-rate-dependent assets, X_1 dollars in asset 1 and X_2 dollars in asset 2 (for example, default-free coupon bonds of differing maturities), then X_1 and X_2 satisfy the following system of equations:

$$X_1\beta_r^1 + X_2\beta_r^2 = X_3\beta_r^3$$

and

$$X_1\beta_l^1 + X_2\beta_l^2 = X_3\beta_l^3.$$

To complete the perfect hedge, the difference $X_3 - (X_1 + X_2)$ must be invested in the instantaneously risk-free asset.

For example, the base-case ARM can be hedged initially by borrowing 51 percent of its value in a 9% 1-year default-free bond, 47 percent in a 9% 10-year default-free bond, and the remaining 2 percent at the prevailing instantaneous risk-free rate. Alternatively, the base-case ARM can be hedged initially by borrowing 91 percent of its value in a 9% 5-year default-free bond, 2 percent in a 9% 1-year default-free bond, and the remaining 7 percent at the prevailing instantaneous risk free rate. Finally, we can initially hedge the base-case ARM by borrowing 95 percent of its value in a 9% 5-year default-free bond, 7 percent at the prevailing instantaneous risk-free rate, and lending 2 percent of its value in a 9% 10-year default-free bond. Of course, as time evolves and the levels of the state variables change, the sensitivities of the base-case ARM and the default-free coupon bonds also change. This implies that the hedge portfolio in the liabilities must be dynamically adjusted according to these revised sensitivities in order to continue to offset the ARM's interest rate sensitivities.

9.6 Conclusions and Policy Implications

This paper develops a two-factor model to value adjustable rate mortgages which integrates their essential contractual features with borrowers' prepayment behavior into a partial equilibrium framework. We value the periodic and lifetime cap options embedded in ARMs, and determine the fair fee to charge for insuring the lifetime cap. We investigate the sensitivities of these

ARM cap option values and the fair lifetime cap insurance fee to systematic changes in the ARM's contractual features. Also, we discuss dynamic hedging strategies which can be used to minimize the interest rate risk exposure associated with the origination of ARMs.

An important characteristic of ARMs currently available is the great diversity in their contractual features. ARMs differ in their underlying index, margin, adjustment period, and teaser rate, as well as their lifetime and periodic cap provisions. Our analysis indicates that all these contractual features must be jointly modeled to take into account properly their interaction in determining the value of ARMs.

ARM originators are subject to potentially considerable interest rate risk exposure. Clearly, the greater the interest rate risk exposure of an ARM originator, the greater the possibility of the thrift's financial distress. Two ways of dealing with this interest rate risk are presented. First, the ARM originator can use dynamic hedging techniques to reduce this risk. Second, the ARM originator can purchase lifetime cap insurance. To be properly valued, this lifetime cap insurance should vary with the contractual features of the ARM, as the originator's corresponding interest rate risk exposure and the possibility of financial distress also varies with these contractual features.

Notes

1. See Wallace and Wang (1989).

2. In this paper we consider periodic rate caps as opposed to periodic payment caps. A periodic payment cap imposes a limit on the changes in an ARM's monthly payment; its effects are similar to those of a periodic rate cap, but can lead to negative amortization. For more details, see Bartholomew, Berk, and Roll (1986).

3. To obtain the estimate of a security's value, we replicate our Monte Carlo procedure one thousand times. Standard deviations of all values reported in this paper are on the order of 0.25 percent.

4. Our sensitivity analysis assumes that prepayment behavior does not vary with the contractual features of the ARM. A more general analysis would allow for interaction between prepayments and these contractual features.

5. To numerically compute partial derivatives, we perturbate the initial values of the state variables and use Monte Carlo simulation methods to compute the resultant security value. The difference in security values divided by the magnitude of the perturbation in the respective state variable approximates the partial derivative or dollar sensitivity.

References

Bartholomew, L., J. Berk, and R. Roll. 1986. Adjustable Rate Mortgages: An Introduction. Goldman, Sachs and Co., November. Typescript.

———. 1988. Adjustable Rate Mortgages: Prepayment Behavior. *Housing Finance Review* 7 (Spring):31–46.

Boyle, P. 1977. Options: A Monte Carlo Approach. *Journal of Financial Economics* 4:323–38.

Brennan, M., and E. Schwartz. 1982. An Equilibrium Model of Bond Pricing and a Test of Market Efficiency. *Journal of Financial and Quantitative Analysis* 17:201–29.

Buser, S., P. Hendershott, and A. Sanders. 1985. Pricing Life-of-Loan Rate Caps on Default-Free Adjustable Rate Mortgages. *AREUEA Journal* 13:248–60.

Gordon, J., J. Luytjes, and J. Feid. 1989. Economic Analysis of Thrifts' Pricing of Adjustable-Rate Mortgages. Office of Thrift Supervision, November. Typescript.

Green, J., and J. Shoven. 1986. The Effects of Interest Rates on Mortgage Prepayments. *Journal of Money, Credit and Banking* 18:41–59.

Kau, J., D. Keenan, W. Muller, and J. Epperson. 1985. Rational Pricing of Adjustable Rate Mortgages. *AREUEA Journal* 13:117–28.

Roll, R. 1987. Adjustable Rate Mortgages: The Indexes. *Housing Finance Review* 6:137–52.

Schwartz, E., and W. Torous. 1989. Prepayment and the Valuation of Mortgage-Backed Securities. *Journal of Finance* 44:375–29.

———. 1990. Prepayment, Default and the Valuation of Mortgage Pass-Through Securities. Anderson Graduate School of Management, UCLA. Typescript.

Wallace, N., and A. Wang. 1989. The Pricing of Adjustable Rate Mortgages with a No-Arbitrage Binomial Pricing Model. University of California, Berkeley. Typescript.

10 The Failure and Survival of Thrifts: Evidence from the Southeast

George J. Benston, Mike Carhill, and Brian Olasov

10.1 Conditions Leading to the Debacle

The cost of the failures of thrifts (savings and loan associations and savings banks previously insured by the Federal Savings and Loan Insurance Corporation [FSLIC]) in the 1980s and 1990s, and probably beyond, is enormous. Present-value estimates range from $150 billion to $300 billion. Some of this cost will be borne directly by owners of thrifts and banks in the form of higher deposit insurance premiums to the Federal Deposit Insurance Corporation (FDIC).[1] Some will be borne by the customers of these insured depositories, depending on their elasticities of demand for deposits and bank loans. The bulk of the cost probably will be paid by U.S. taxpayers.

The initial cause of the debacle should be well known. Prior to 1982, most thrifts invested primarily in long-term fixed-interest mortgages that were funded by deposits and other liabilities with much shorter durations. Consequently, thrifts faced considerable interest rate risk. When interest rates increased sharply in 1979–81 to a peak of about 15 percent on long-term U.S. Treasury obligations and over 18 percent for thirty-year mortgages, the present value of their assets declined much more than the present value of their short-term liabilities, and a large number of thrifts became economically insolvent. The number of insolvent thrifts and the extent of their insolvency is not known with much precision because thrifts and most other enterprises do not record unrealized capital gains and losses. Carron (1982, 19) estimates that the savings and loan industry had an aggregate economic (market value)

George J. Benston is the John H. Harland Professor of Finance, Accounting, and Economics at Emory University. Mike Carhill is an economist at the Federal Home Loan Bank of Atlanta. Brian Olasov is the Financial Institutions Specialist at Long Aldridge & Norman in Atlanta, Georgia.

The views expressed here do not necessarily reflect the views of either the Federal Home Loan Bank or Long Aldridge & Norman.

negative net worth of $17.5 billion at year-end 1980 and negative $44.1 billion on 30 June 1981. Kane (1985, table 4.6) estimates that, by year-end 1982, some two-thirds of the nation's thrifts were economically insolvent, with aggregate negative net worth of perhaps $109 billion.[2] Some 85 percent of all institutions were unprofitable in accounting terms in 1982.

Relatively few economically insolvent thrifts were liquidated or merged by the Federal Home Loan Bank Board (FHLBB) through 1984. From 1981 through 1984, 180 thrifts were officially announced as having failed. An additional 295 are identified by FHLBB economists as having been forced to merge by the FHLBB to avoid failure (a total of 475). But, as many as 71 other thrifts had negative net worth according to regulatory accounting principles (RAP). With net worth measured according to generally accepted accounting principles (GAAP), as many as 434 operating thrifts had negative net worth.[3] Annual numbers are given in table 10.1, as measured by economists at the FHLBB and at the General Accounting Office (GAO). Although none of these metrics measure economic insolvency, the numbers indicate that the FHLBB permitted many probably insolvent thrifts to continue operations.

Furthermore, the FHLBB reduced the legal net worth (RAP) requirement over the period. RAP was adopted to increase the measure of net worth. In 1979 the FHLBB permitted thrifts to take up to 250 basis points of fees on loans into income (and, hence, into net worth), even though GAAP requires taking fees into income over the life of the institution's ownership of the loans, with the exception of fees that reimburse currently charged expenses. In 1981 the FHLBB permitted thrifts to defer losses on the sale of assets with below-market yields over the lives of the loans sold rather than reduce net worth immediately. Also in 1981 the FHLBB permitted capital-deficient thrifts to issue qualifying mutual capital certificates and income capital certificates that were purchased by the FSLIC and included in the thrifts' net worth. In 1980

Table 10.1 **Failures and Accounting Insolvencies of Savings and Loans, 1981–1984**

Year	Official Failures per B	FHLBB Failures per BR	RAP Insolvent per BR	GAAP Insolvent per BR	GAAP Insolvent per GAO
1981	28	81	41	65	53
1982	72	251	80	201	222
1983	53	101	54	287	281
1984	27	42	71	434	434
Totals	180	475			

Sources: Official failures: Benston (1985, table 1). FHLBB failures per BR: Barth and Regalia (1988, table 6). RAP (regulatory accounting principles) insolvent per BR: Barth and Regalia (1988, table 6). GAAP (generally accepted accounting principles) Insolvent per BR: Barth and Regalia (1988, table 6). GAAP (generally accepted accounting principles) Insolvent per GAO (General Accounting Office): Garcia (1988, table 2).

the FHLBB reduced the net worth requirement from 5 to 4 percent of liabilities and, in January 1982, the net worth requirement was reduced to 3 percent. In July 1982, liability accounts, such as loans in process, unearned discounts, and deferred fees and credits, were reclassified as contra-assets, which reduced liabilities and increased the ratio of RAP net worth to liabilities. In that same month the FHLBB approved an accounting change that allowed goodwill from an acquisition (including goodwill resulting from an exchange of stock rather than only from a purchase) to be expensed over forty years, while gains from the write-up to market of assets acquired would be taken into income (and, hence, into net worth) over a five- to ten-year period. In November 1982, in an effort to prevent sale and lease backs of thrifts' fixed assets, the FHLBB permitted the use of appraised equity capital to increase regulatory net worth.[4] The net effect of these and other differences increased RAP over GAAP by 17, 16, and 20 percent on average in 1982, 1983, and 1984.[5] The results of these regulatory changes and accounting gimmicks are reflected in the considerably greater number of GAAP-insolvent compared to RAP-insolvent thrifts presented in table 10.1.

Congress sought to alleviate the deposit outflow with the Depository Institutions Deregulation and Monetary Control Act (DIDMCA), enacted on 31 March 1980. To permit chartered depository institutions to compete with unregulated alternative investments, particularly money market mutual funds (MMMFs) and brokers' cash management accounts, Regulation Q ceilings on time and savings deposits were phased out over a six-year period and deposit insurance coverage was raised from $40,000 to $100,000 per account. These changes had the effect of shifting risk, as well as risk-monitoring, away from thrift depositors and to the FHLBB and FSLIC.

DIDMCA also permitted federally chartered thrifts to diversify their assets somewhat by allowing them to invest up to 20 percent of their assets in a combination of nonresidential real estate, commercial and consumer loans, commercial paper, and corporate debt securities. They also were permitted to invest up to 3 percent of assets in service corporations, as long as one-half of the investment over 1 percent of assets was devoted to community or inner-city developments. Ceilings on the amounts that could be loaned on mortgages and geographical restrictions on loans were removed. Nationwide lending was permitted by the FHLBB in 1983.

Further liberalization was permitted by the Garn–St Germain Depository Institutions Act, enacted on 15 October 1982. The deregulation of deposit interest rates was hastened by permitting institutions to offer interest-bearing checking (NOW) accounts and money market deposit accounts that were competitive with MMMFs. The act authorized thrifts to make commercial real estate loans up to 40 percent of assets, make consumer loans up to 30 percent of assets, make commercial and agricultural loans up to 10 percent of assets, invest in personal property for rent or sale up to 10 percent of assets, and invest in commercial paper and corporate debt securities up to 100 percent of assets. Until Garn–St Germain, federal charters could be obtained only for mutual associations; the act permitted federal stock charters and allowed the conversion of mutuals to stockholder ownership.

Several states permitted the thrifts they chartered more extensive asset powers. The permissible limits varied considerably. Equity securities could not be held by thrifts in thirty states. Fourteen of these also prohibited thrifts from having an equity interest in non-business-premise real estate.[6] The states experiencing substantial numbers of failures are of special interest. In 1980, Florida was first to allow its thrifts to invest 20 percent of their assets in service corporations and 10 percent in real estate. In 1982, Texas permitted thrifts to invest up to 10 percent of assets in service corporations and amounts up to their equity in real estate. California eliminated all real estate asset restrictions in 1983 (subject to specific supervision by state authorities). Arizona allowed its thrifts to invest 10 percent of assets in real estate and equity securities and 6 percent in service corporations. Among states with relatively few failures, Nebraska and Wisconsin imposed no dollar limitations on direct investments in real estate.

As the 1980s progressed, it became increasingly clear that the number and cost of thrift failures was far greater than the officially recognized figures, and that the decline in interest rates by 1984 to levels somewhat above the pre-1978 level but much below the prior peak would not "bail out" the sickest institutions. The number of official and internally recognized failures was 70 in 1985. The chairman of the FHLBB, Edwin Gray, strongly (and almost single-mindedly) urged thrifts to make adjustable-rate mortgages, which were federally authorized in April 1981, as the primary means of reducing their exposure to interest rate risk. He concentrated on three sources of what he believed was excessive risk-taking by thrifts: brokered deposits, direct investments, and growth. In January 1984 the FHLBB and the FDIC jointly announced a proposed regulation that, if enacted, would have virtually denied deposit insurance to depositors who used the services of brokers to place their funds. The regulation was not enforced because it was found to be illegal by the Federal District Court (District of Columbia) in June 1984, a decision upheld by the United States Court of Appeals for the District of Columbia in January 1985. In March 1985 the FHLBB limited direct investments by state-chartered FSLIC-insured thrifts to the lower of 10 percent of assets or twice RAP-measured equity without the prior approval of the FHLBB. In June 1987, direct investments were further limited, and land loans and nonresidential construction were subjected to limitations.[7] In March 1985, the growth of savings and loan associations was limited by a regulation imposing higher capital requirements on institutions that increased their total liabilities by more than 15 percent a year, measured quarterly. In addition, growth at an annual rate of 25 percent of liabilities was prohibited without prior approval by the FHLBB.

10.2 Hypotheses on the Causes of the Debacle

Several, somewhat overlapping, hypotheses have been suggested and asserted to explain the factors responsible for the thrift debacle. Each is discussed briefly.[8] Because none of the explanations appears sufficient to explain the collapse of the industry, we later model them operationally and subject them to empirical test.

1. Unbalanced Durations of Assets and Liabilities—Interest-Rate Risk

Thrifts generally have made and held long-term fixed-interest mortgages funded with liabilities that are repriced at much shorter intervals, and thus are subject to interest-rate risk. Before the Great Depression, savings and loan associations (S&Ls) financed their mortgage holdings with share capital that, allegedly, could not be readily withdrawn. As Barth and Regalia (1988, 117) point out, "it was not until the advent of federal deposit insurance for savings and loan associations in the 1930s that the taking of deposits as such became widespread." Furthermore, because the average maturity of their mortgage holdings was about eleven years, the durations of the two sides of their balance sheets were probably not as greatly mismatched, nor were they subjected to the amount of interest-rate volatility recently experienced (Benston and Kaufman 1990).

In the subsequent years, the duration of mortgages increased, following the lead of FHA-insured mortgages. FSLIC insurance guaranteed the par value of the shares (initially up to $5,000 per shareholder), effectively transforming S&L shares into deposits with short durations. This mismatch strategy works well as long as the yield curve is positively sloped. The duration "bomb" did not go off before 1979–81 because previous interest rate increases were insufficient to use up the economic capital S&Ls had amassed as a result of favorable tax treatment and restraints on entry into their markets.

As we stated earlier, the sharp increase in rates in 1979–81 caused economic insolvencies amounting to perhaps $100 billion. The actual amount is not well established. The published estimates may be overstated because thrift managers and owners and the FHLBB expected interest rates to decline. If this were the situation, the expected cash flows from mortgages and other fixed-interest obligations should be discounted by the interest rates expected rather than by the rates recorded for mortgages made in 1981, 1982, and so forth. These "actual" rates include the value of the mortgagors' option to refinance when interest rates decline.

2. Excessive Risk-Taking by Economically Insolvent and Weak Thrifts

Economic theory (or even simple common sense) suggests that the owners and managers of economically, though not regulatorily, insolvent institutions have very great incentives to take very high risks promising large returns (which they retain) and large losses (which the FSLIC and other uninsured creditors, if any, absorb). The effect of the FHLBB's permitting insolvent institutions to continue operations has not been well established. As discussed below, most of the research uses data from thrifts with stock traded on exchanges. While such data are preferable to accounting numbers, the observations exclude most thrifts and may include biases endemic to these thrifts. Other research uses traditional accounting data, from which RAP, GAAP, and TAP (tangible accounting principles)[9] net worth is derived. None of these measures reports the economic market value of a thrift. Consequently, we devoted a large part of our effort to measuring the market value of thrifts' assets and liabilities to determine the market value of their net worths. We use these market-value data to test the hypothesis that losses in post interest-rate-increase periods were a function of the economic value of thrifts rather than deregulation and other factors.

3. Overspecialization in Mortgage Loans—Insufficient Diversification and Declines in Economic Conditions

Tradition, government subsidies, and regulatory constraints have caused thrifts to concentrate on home mortgages and other real estate lending and investing. Prior to the Great Depression, most S&Ls (at that time called building and loans) were societal organizations established to help their members buy homes. They tended to be small: the average S&L had only $750,000 in assets. Their rate of failure during the Great Depression reflected their specialization and size. Of the 11,777 S&Ls operating in 1930, 526 failed (4.5 percent). These failed associations held $410.6 million of the industries' $8,828.6 million total assets (4.7 percent) and had an average asset size of $781,000 (Benston and Kaufman 1990). This failure rate exceeded that of the now similar mutual savings banks (MSBs). Only eight (1.3 percent) MSBs failed during the Great Depression, in large part because they held much more diversified portfolios: 55 percent of their assets were mortgages, 14 percent government obligations, and 22 percent in other securities (Welfling 1968, 73–74). However, S&Ls did much better than commercial banks, which experienced a 38.5 percent drop in numbers, from 24,970 in 1929 to 15,348 in 1934. The S&Ls' better experience appears due to the close relationship of shareholders (there were no depositors) and mortgagors, which provided strong incentives and opportunities for monitoring loans.[10]

Legislation enacted during and following the Great Depression, particularly deposit insurance and favorable tax treatment tied to home mortgage investments, allowed and encouraged specialization by S&Ls in mortgages and real-estate-related consumer loans. Until 1983, S&Ls could write mortgages only within 100 miles of their offices or within their state. Although the Garn–St Germain Act of 1982 authorized S&Ls to invest up to 10 percent of its assets in commercial loans and 100 percent in state or local government securities, it permitted them to branch only if they met the Internal Revenue Code's qualified thrift lender (QTL) test. To be a QTL, a thrift had to hold 60 percent of its assets in home mortgages, mortgage-backed securities, cash, student and passbook loans, or certain government securities. The QTL threshold was changed to a more restrictive 70 percent in 1989 by the Financial Institutions Reform, Recovery, and Enforcement Act (FIRREA).[11]

As a result of specialization in real estate loans concentrated geographically, thrifts tended to be vulnerable to local economic depressions. This concentration may account for the large number and cost of failures in such states as Texas, Louisiana, Oklahoma, and Colorado, which were particularly hard hit by the collapse of petroleum prices in the 1980s.[12] Local overbuilding and overoptimistic pricing followed by a collapse of real estate prices in such states as Arizona and perhaps Massachusetts similarly may account for thrift failures. However, it should be noted that not all thrifts failed in these areas, and many thrifts failed in states that did not experience severe reductions in real estate values.[13]

An additional factor contributing to thrift losses is the 1986 change in the income tax statute which disallowed fast write-offs of commercial real estate. This reduced the expected net cash flows from new and purchased commercial real estate investments and projects, rendering negative the present values of many of these ventures. The owners then had incentives to default on their mortgage obligations.

4. Deposit Insurance and the Removal of Interest-Rate Ceilings on Savings Deposits

Federal deposit insurance, instituted in 1934 with the establishment of the FSLIC, relieved most depositors in thrifts from concern about the risks taken by those institutions. The increase in 1980 from $40,000 to $100,000 per account, together with lower computing costs that permitted investors to divide large sums efficiently into many thrift and bank accounts and the "too-large-to-fail doctrine," is thought to have resulted in de facto 100 percent deposit insurance for savings placed with insured depositories. Consequently, when ceilings on savings deposits (including certificates of deposit, or CDs) were removed beginning in April 1980 and accelerated in December 1982, thrifts could attract funds from outside their market areas through the services of brokers or directly from their own efforts.

Kane (1985, 1989), among others, emphasizes the moral hazard costs of deposit insurance as the primary cause of the thrift (and bank) losses. He points out that severely unbalanced duration portfolios would not be feasible if depositors (and, consequently, depository institutions) had to bear the cost of interest-rate risk.[14] The federal deposit insurance agencies do not charge a direct risk-related premium, which gives thrift owners and managers incentives to take on high-risk projects promising high returns but negative expected present values. However, the insurance agencies can impose indirect risk-related costs on thrifts in the form of intrusive examinations and strict supervision.[15] If it is measured in terms of economic market values, capital also can serve as a means of imposing deductible or coinsurance. The effectiveness of these means of reducing moral hazard is examined below.

5. *Deregulation of Asset Investments and Brokered Deposits*

Deregulation of asset investments exacerbated by growth made possible by brokered deposits appears to be the most often charged cause of the thrift disaster, at least among legislators, regulators, the thrifts' principal trade association (the United States League of Savings Institutions), and the press. The former chairman of the FHLBB, Edwin Gray, was particularly concerned about direct investments and brokered deposits. His concern resulted in regulations enacted in 1985 and extended in 1987, limiting the amount of such investments by insured thrifts.[16] As noted above, he unsuccessfully tried to eliminate brokered deposits, but he was able to put on growth restrictions in 1985. Mr. Gray's belief was echoed by the United States League of Savings Institutions (Strunk and Case 1988). It also is reflected in the provisions of FIRREA. Thrifts' investments in commercial real estate loans now are restricted to four times capital rather than the Garn–St Germain limit of 40 percent of assets. The powers of state-chartered savings and loan associations are restricted generally to those permitted federally chartered associations, and investments in real estate equity and non-investment-grade (junk) bonds by all thrifts must generally be phased out by mid 1994. The legislation also restricts troubled institutions from accepting brokered deposits. As mentioned above, the act further emphasizes residential mortgages by increasing the QTL test to 70 percent from 60 percent of assets. In large measure then, FIRREA has re-regulated the thrift industry to its position before the Garn–St Germain Act of 1982 with respect to asset powers.[17]

Evidence in support of the FIRREA asset and brokered deposits restrictions has not been published, to our knowledge. As summarized later, some studies report findings that are inconsistent with the assumptions underlying reregulation. Additional evidence on the relationship between the assets restricted by FIRREA and the insolvency of thrifts is presented below.

6. *Risk Aversion and Risk Preference of Mutual Compared to Stock Thrifts*

Prior to enactment of the Garn–St Germain Depository Institutions Act of 1982, only state-chartered S&Ls could issue equity claims. Encouraged by the Reagan administration, the act permitted federally chartered S&Ls and mutual savings banks to convert to stock ownership. Both the ownership status and the conversion itself may have affected the propensity of thrifts to take risks that, on average, led to considerable losses.

Economic theory provides reason to expect managers of mutual institutions to be more risk-averse than owners and managers of stockholder-owned institutions. Managers of mutuals in effect are the owners of those institutions, subject to the constraint that they can be removed by the supervisory authorities and are subject to control by a board of directors whom they essentially appoint but may not control completely. Importantly, mutual managers cannot directly garner large gains from successful operations, because they do not own stock that can be sold to realize those gains. Instead, their rewards come in the form of higher salaries and perquisites, the magnitudes of which are restricted by the supervisory authorities. Furthermore, they cannot transfer the wealth embodied in the positions to their heirs or others, except indirectly by providing jobs for favored persons and arranging for their positions to be "inherited" by their sons or daughters. All of these constraints and limitations should lead them to be risk-averse, as their income and wealth is concentrated in their job positions and can continue only so long as their associations are, at a minimum, allowed to stay open.

The managers who are not owners of stock thrifts are in a similar situation. Should their decisions turn out badly, they are likely to lose their jobs. Should these decisions turn out well, they will reap rewards, but these are not likely to be symmetrical with their expected costs. Hence, they should tend to be risk-averse, unless they are controlled effectively by the owners of their firms, *cet. par.*

In the absence of punitive supervision, owners of thrifts should tend to prefer risk, which increases inversely with the firm's capital cushion, given the presence of deposit insurance that is not priced to reflect completely the cost of risk, *cet. par.* Their preference for risk, though, may be restrained by the diversification they can achieve in their personal portfolios. As is the situation for the managers of mutuals, a very large portion of some owners' wealth may be firm-specific. Given decreasing marginal utility of wealth, these owners may not perceive benefits from greater risk-taking.

7. *Fraud, Self-Dealing, Incompetence, and Inadequate Supervision*

Allegations of fraud and self-dealing by managers and owners of failed thrifts abound. Several books and newspaper exposes have been published describing how the "bad guys" looted specific thrifts.[18] There seems to be little doubt that such illegal behavior occurred. Although FIRREA provided funds to enhance the Department of Justice's prosecution of miscreants, the extent to which wrongdoers will be successfully prosecuted and the stolen or misapplied resources recovered is in doubt. The extent to which the losses incurred are due to the illegal behavior also is not known and may never be known.

Incompetence of thrift managers also is alleged as an important cause of losses. This hypothesis is related to the issues of specialization and deregulation. Before high and variable interest rates characterized the market, thrift management did not require sophisticated financial knowledge. But unsettled conditions and the new asset and activity powers granted to thrifts in the early 1980s required considerable financial expertise. As a result, thrift managers may have invested poorly because of inexperience rather than dishonesty. (This hypothesis leads to predictions about losses that are contrary to the prediction expected from the risk-aversion hypotheses previously discussed.)

Another explanation of why poor performance occurred in the 1980s to a greater extent than in earlier periods (assuming that such is the case) is a breakdown of effective examination and/or supervision. The possibility of fraud and self-dealing always is present in depository institutions. Indeed, earlier investigations found fraud and mismanagement to be the principal cause of bank and thrift failures.[19] A major purpose of field examinations is (or should be) to uncover and discourage such problems, and a major function of supervision is to use examiners' reports and other sources of information to stop and mitigate these problems. Institutions with negative or low economic capital should be closely monitored and supervised, as their managers and owners have considerable incentives to "steal or bet the bank." Evidence on the effectiveness of the FHLBB in these regards, and the effect of managerial incentives and deregulation on examination and supervision is considered below.

10.3 Previous Evidence on Failures and FSLIC Losses

10.3.1 Causes of Failures and Insolvencies

Benston (1985) and Barth, Brumbaugh, Sauerhaft, and Wang (1985)

Benston matched each of the 202 thrifts that officially failed between 1 January 1980 and 31 August 1985 with four nonfailures, two just larger and two just smaller, in each of five regions. Various balance sheet ratios of these thrifts were compared for each year. Barth, Brumbaugh, Sauerhaft, and Wang (hereafter BBSW) similarly analyzed 318 official and unofficial (unannounced FSLIC-assisted mergers) failures in 1982 and 1983. Benston also analyzed separately failed and nonfailed thrifts in California, Texas, Florida, Ohio, and Louisiana; the findings are similar to those reported for the total sample. Both studies used accounting rather than market values.

Benston found that negative (book value) net worth in the year prior to failure was not a necessary condition for failure. However, compared to their nonfailed peers, the failed thrifts' net worth to total asset ratios are significantly lower in each year prior to failure. The failed thrifts' return on total assets also are significantly lower than their peers' by an average of 2.2 percentage points, due primarily to lower net interest margins. (BBSW report similar results.) The lower margins are the result of higher cost of funds, apparently arising from significantly greater reliance on jumbo CDs, Federal Home Loan Bank advances, and brokered deposits. Yields on earning assets are not significantly different, which is inconsistent with the hypothesis that the failed thrifts took greater risks than their nonfailed peers, assuming that the accounting numbers reflect correctly the economic values of the thrifts' assets, liabilities, and expected loan losses.

Foreclosed mortgages to total loans in the Benston study is significantly greater for the failed thrifts in both studies. Nonresidential mortgages to total loans also is significantly greater, although this variable exhibits considerable variance among institutions (BBSW do not use this variable). Both studies find that nontraditional assets (nonmortgage commercial and consumer loans, and direct investments) are unrelated to failures. Perhaps surprisingly, growth in assets at the failed and nonfailed thrifts is not much different for Benston's data (BBSW do not report this variable).

The relationship of the financial ratios and other variables to failure also was analyzed by Benston and BBSW with a multinomial logit model. Benston and BBSW find significant inverse relationships between failure and net worth to total assets and return on total assets. With net worth to total assets excluded, significant inverse relationships to failure were found for the yield on earnings assets and for state rather than federal charter, and significant positive relationships for the change in the cost of funds and change in total assets (BBSW did not use these variables). Among the variables not related to failure, even at the 0.10 level, are large liabilities (CDs over $1 million plus Federal Home Loan Bank advances and other debt) to earnings assets, deposits to earnings assets, and direct investments to total assets. BBSW report a similar finding for direct investments.

Benston additionally analyzed the financial statements of the twenty-one failures that held direct investment of more than 5 percent of total assets. The reasons for their failures appeared to be quite diverse. High growth was found at only 52 percent of the thrifts, 43 percent experienced high interest expenses relative to revenue, 24 percent recorded large non-operating expenses, and 43 percent incurred large loan losses. Direct investments do not appear related to failure of any of the thrifts.

Benston's monograph also includes chapters devoted to an analysis of returns and risk from direct investments over the three years ending 30 June 1984. He finds that direct investments yielded considerably higher returns than other assets and appeared to reduce portfolio risk slightly. Another chapter analyzes growth, return, and risk over the years 1981 through 1984 for thrifts disaggregated into small (less than $100 million in assets) and large. About half of the growth at fast-growing (over 15 percent a year) thrifts was funded from jumbo CDs and brokered deposits, with the remaining funding coming from ordinary deposits. Faster growing thrifts tended to increase regulatory net worth in about the same proportion as slower growing thrifts. The funds generated by smaller, faster-growing thrifts were invested more in nonresidential mortgages, while the large, faster-growing thrifts invested more in acquisition, development, and construction loans, and somewhat more in direct investments. Regressions of the change in regulatory net worth over the three years ending 30 June 1984 found growth significantly positively related to higher net worth. Thus, growth, as such, does not appear to be due to financial weakness, which is inconsistent with the deposit-insurance hypothesis.

Benston (1989)

Benston analyzed the change in tangible net worth (ΔTNW) over the two-and-a-half years between 31 December 1983 and 30 June 1986 of all California thrifts operating since 31 December 1981, as functions of the amounts of various types of assets on 31 December 1983 and on their change through 30 June 1986. Separate regressions also were computed for weak and stronger thrifts (tangible net worth to total assets less or greater than 0.01 on 31 December 1983). ΔTNW is significantly positively related to the change in multifamily mortgages and beginning TNW, and to asset growth when residential mortgage loans are omitted. Among the weak thrifts, only the change in multifamily mortgages is significantly (positively) associated with ΔTNW when residential mortgage loans are omitted. Among the stronger thrifts, ΔTNW is significantly positively associated with residential mortgage loans and asset growth, and inversely with change in other real estate loans and change in consumer loans, whether or not residential mortgage loans are excluded.

ΔTNW also was regressed on various income-statement flows over the two-and-a-half-year period, with TNW on 31 December 1983 included and excluded. The only statistically significant positive relationships found are between ΔTNW and direct investments net income and net interest margin for all samples, and also for income from foreclosed real estate operations, sale of other assets, and adjustments to prior periods for the stronger thrifts and the total sample. Thus, there is but weak support for the asset-deregulation hypothesis.

Benston also analyzed 73 of the 82 thrifts that failed in 1986 (data on the others could not be obtained) with respect to their TNW, direct investments (DI), and nonresidential real estate loans (NREL), relative to total assets on 31 December 1985. Fifteen (21%) of the failed thrifts had DI in excess of 10 percent of their assets, while 66 (90%) had NREL in excess of 10 percent of assets. Negative TNW was reported by 58 (79%) of the failed thrifts at the year-end before failure; while this is not surprising, 48 of the 58 (83%) were not closed until at least three months after their year-end balance sheet showed negative TNW. Furthermore, 42 of the 73 failures in 1986 (58%) had negative TNW on 31 December 1984.

Barth and Bradley (1989)

Barth and Bradley (hereafter BB) compare the performance of thrifts that were solvent or insolvent (as defined by GAAP) at year-end, over the years 1979 though 1988 (second quarter). Through year-end 1984, the annual after-tax net income of both groups moved similarly, with the insolvents' net income lower. After 1984 the insolvent thrifts' losses as a percentage of assets increase dramatically: −1.2 in 1985, −5.2 in 1986, −7.7 in 1987, and

− 12.0 in 1988, due primarily to net non-operating losses. A detailed analysis of June 1988 balance sheets reveals that insolvent thrifts held considerably more commercial mortgages, somewhat more equity-risk investments and brokered deposits, and slightly more commercial loans than solvent thrifts.[20] BB also show that more than two years before June 1988, 71 percent of the GAAP insolvent thrifts reported negative tangible capital, 61 percent reported negative GAAP capital, and 53 percent reported negative RAP capital.

Carhill and Mauldin (1989) and Rudolf and Topping (1988)

These studies find that, from 1984 through 1988, thrifts with relatively high percentages of assets in residential mortgages or mortgage-backed securities were the most successful with respect to reported GAAP net profits, while those that responded to deregulation by diversifying their portfolios and adopting unconventional strategies were unsuccessful. The authors could not determine whether unprofitable operations caused thrifts to adopt unconventional strategies, unconventional strategies caused thrifts to become unprofitable, or the causation runs both ways.

The effect of competition and local market conditions on thrifts' profitability and investment strategy was examined in Florida. This state's economy has been stable through the 1980s (Fritz 1989), while competitive pressure increased substantially and the financial health of financial intermediaries declined dramatically (Hasan 1989). At the same time, Florida thrifts which followed more nontraditional strategies did about as well as other thrifts. Hence, both the poor financial condition of Florida thrifts and their adoption of nontraditional strategies appear due primarily to the effects of increased competition (Hasan 1989; Carhill 1989).

Risk as Indicated by Stock Market Data

Benston and Koehn (1990) used weekly rates of return of forty publicly traded California thrifts from July 1978 through April 1985 to examine the systematic risk of twenty-nine institutions that operated successfully throughout the period compared to eleven that failed during the period. The failed group tended to have higher institution-specific risk, which was shifted to FSLIC. Risk-shifting did not appear to have been affected by the increase in deposit ceilings, deregulation of interest rates, and expansion of asset powers. Positive associations with overall risk were found only for low thrift net worth, brokered deposits and direct investments at low-capital thrifts, and for state-chartered rather than federally chartered thrifts.

10.3.2 FSLIC Losses

Barth, Brumbaugh, Sauerhaft, and Wang (1985) and Brumbaugh (1986)

BBSW examine the FSLIC's losses for 31 thrifts that failed during 1982–83. They find a statistically significant relationship only for foreclosed real estate (positive); direct investments (positive); and log of total assets (negative). (All variables except log total assets are divided by total assets.) Unfortunately, each of these variables was included without the other two in the same regression. Hence, any one can stand for the other one or two.

Brumbaugh essentially replicates BBSW with an expanded sample of 88 thrifts that failed from 1982 through 1984. Various combinations of different forms of the net worth variable together with two forms of the direct investments variable were tried in twelve regressions. Seven variables had significant coefficients, as noted: net worth (negative for the tangible and market-value forms, positive for the regulatory and GAAP forms); commercial loans (often negative); slow loans and scheduled items (positive); foreclosed real estate (often negative); direct investments (sometimes positive and sometimes negative); jumbo CDs (positive); and brokered deposits (positive).

Barth, Brumbaugh, and Sauerhaft (1986)

This study analyzed 324 thrift failures from December 1981 through October 1985. It is notable because it includes a variable measuring the number of months between insolvency and closure. The following variables are significantly positively related to FSLIC losses: tangible net worth, cost of FHLBB advances, delinquent loans, acquisition and development loans, direct investments, and months between insolvency and closure ("growth" is not included as a variable). Total assets and the constant have negative significant coefficients. (All dollar variables are divided by total assets.)

Benston (1985, 1989)

The 1985 study regressed the FSLIC's losses at the 95 failed thrifts during the period 1 January 1980 through 31 August 1985 for which the loss amounts were made publicly available. Statistically significant positive coefficients were found only for total assets, yield on total assets, brokered deposits to earning assets, and change in nonresidential real estate loans to total loans. Negative significant coefficients were found for change in total assets and change in brokered deposits to earning assets (somewhat surprising results). Direct investments to total assets were significantly and positively related to FSLIC losses only for small thrifts, and this only when the change in direct investments to total assets was excluded.

The 1990 study used all publicly available FSLIC loss data (28 thrifts) for failures between 1 September 1985 through 31 December 1986. Significant negative coefficients were found for adjustable-rate mortgages, residential mortgages, and foreclosed real estate. The strongest relationship found was for nonresidential mortgage loans, which are significantly positively related to FSLIC losses.

10.3.3 Summary and Limitations[21]

The studies reviewed reveal several reasonably consistent findings. For thrifts failing before 1986, the major variable distinguishing failed from operating thrifts is negative book-value (GAAP) net worth prior to failure. This is hardly surprising, as this variable defines failure in an accounting sense. However, negative net worth often precedes failure by several years. The failed thrifts compared to nonfailed peers experienced lower return on total assets, determined primarily by lower net interest margins resulting from a higher cost of funds and larger proportions of interest-bearing liabilities to earning assets. Among the asset holdings, foreclosed mortgages are higher at failed thrifts. Nonresidential mortgages also are higher, although the relative amounts vary considerably. Nonmortgage loans, direct investments, rapid growth, brokered deposits, and large CDs are not significantly related to failure. The 1986 failures are characterized by negative tangible net worth and relatively high proportions of nonresidential mortgages. Direct investments appear to have played a minor role.

Failure, however, is not the same as insolvency, as many book-value insolvent institutions were permitted to continue operations. A comparison of GAAP-solvent and – insolvent institutions shows that after 1984 the insolvent institutions had considerable increases in non-operating losses. The 1988 GAAP-insolvent institutions held relatively more commercial mortgages, equity-risk investments, and brokered deposits than solvent institutions. A high proportion of these insolvent thrifts reported negative tangible capital at least two years before 1988.

Studies of changes in tangible net worth at California thrifts over the two-and-a-half years ending 30 June 1986 find a positive association with direct investments, multifamily mortgages, residential mortgages, and higher growth rates. A negative association is found for other real estate loans.

Evidence of risk-shifting to the FSLIC by California publicly traded thrifts is reported. Higher risks appear to have been taken by thrifts with low capital and those with state rather than federal charters, and are associated with direct investments and brokered deposits only at low-capital institutions.

Losses reported by the FSLIC are associated with higher levels of commercial real estate loans, foreclosed real estate, acquisition and development loans, time between insolvency and closure, change in total assets and brokered deposits, and possibly with direct investments, jumbo CDs, and brokered deposits.

A major shortcoming of most of these studies is that they are based on accounting book values. Neither GAAP nor regulatory accounting permits thrifts to record losses or gains on assets unless these assets are sold. (Regulatory accounting even permits institutions to defer recording losses on mortgage sales.) Hence, the effect of changes in interest rates is not recorded when they occur, but rather over time in the form of lower- or higher-than-market interest earnings. Furthermore, there is reason to believe that many thrifts did not record credit losses until after they clearly were insolvent. For these reasons, it is essential that the net worth of thrifts be restated at market values before an analysis of their performance is undertaken.

An additional shortcoming is the use of cross-sections rather than time-series of thrifts. Changes in thrifts' performance need not have taken place within a year or two. Consequently, we sought to examine a sample of thrifts over time.

10.4 Market-value Estimates

Accounting values reflect the market value of assets and liabilities at the time they are acquired. In accordance with generally accepted accounting principles (GAAP), subsequent changes in market conditions and price levels are ignored, except for physical assets and marketable securities that suffer "permanent" price declines. In particular, changes in interest rates are ignored, even when the consequence is a substantial reduction in the present value of a financial asset or liability. Under GAAP, changes in the probability that cash flows on financial assets, such as loans, will be less than previously expected normally should be accounted for by reductions in asset amounts through increases in a contra-asset account, "allowance for loan losses." However, these valuations often are not reliable, and reporting has been at the discretion of the thrift managers. GAAP-determined numbers, therefore, do not provide valid measures of economic market values, particularly during periods of changing interest rates and credit risk, such as the 1980s. If one is to describe the incentives facing thrift owners, one should improve on accounting values as measurements of the economic value of the owners' investments in their enterprises.

The Federal Home Loan Bank of Atlanta Market-Value Model (MVM) is designed to provide this improvement. (For a complete documentation, see Benston, Carhill, and Olasov 1991.) The data base comes from the *Thrift Financial Report* (*TFR*), in which each thrift reports quarterly detailed financial information. Contract maturities and rates of interest for each thrift's financial assets and liabilities have been reported in the *TFR* Section H, beginning with the first quarter of 1984. This section of the *TFR* was unchanged through 1988; it was revised substantially in June 1989. We supplemented these data with our model's prepayment projections, the FHLBB's estimated decay rates for passbook liabilities, and thrift-specific credit experience. The result is a detailed cash-flow projection for each thrift, which lends itself to discounted-cash-flow analysis.

Concurrent market interest rates and standard present-value equations are used to discount the expected cash flows. On the liability side, we discount the thrifts' payout cash flows by the concurrent certificate of deposit (CD) rates, which we assume are the marginal cost of attracting funds. Because passbook deposits carry rates below current CD rates, the discounting results in a lower-than-book-value number; the reduction often is considered an asset, the "core deposit intangible." On the asset side, we use secondary market rates. For example, the Federal Home Loan Mortgage Corporation's commitment rate (which includes a factor for credit risk) is used to discount cash flows from mortgage loans. Commercial loan rates from Federal Reserve survey information are used to discount cash flows from commercial loans. Agency rates are used to discount cash flows from securities portfolios. The available interest rates generally do not include all maturities. We constructed a full term structure for each interest rate from the U.S. Treasury bill and note series.

Mortgage-servicing rights are estimated by multiplying "mortgages serviced for others less mortgages serviced by others" by 1.75 percent, which a review of the literature and interviews with market participants revealed to be reasonably accurate in the absence of more detailed information. Recorded intangible assets, such as goodwill and various deferrals, are assumed to have zero values. All remaining assets and noninterest-bearing liabilities are valued at GAAP book values.

While some commentators have expressed the reservation that present-value mathematics and the choice of discount rates is too complicated to provide valid value estimates, our experience does not confirm this objection. We found the selection and justification of discount rates and the mathematics, although quite tedious, to be workable and noncontroversial. However, there are three aspects of the MVM which create considerable difficulties or are potentially controversial: the lack of thrift-specific information, which necessitates generic assumptions; the use of standard present-valuation methodology, which implicitly assumes a random walk of the term structure of interest rates in place of a "normal-rate" assumption; and the treatment of credit quality.

We use generic assumptions because thrift-specific assumptions would be feasible only in a small-sample study. For example, the *TFR* does not provide information on the composition of thrifts' security portfolios, so the MVM discounts all security portfolios at the interest rate on federal agency debt. This procedure can result in a material misstatement of high-gross-yield, high-risk assets, such as "junk" bonds and some commercial and nonresidential real estate loans.[22] These and other generic assumptions are the primary disadvantage of using the MVM in place of RAP, GAAP, or GAAP-tangible book values, which give the balances of more specific assets and liabilities. We emphasize that this disadvantage does not apply to market-value accounting, per se, which could use all the information provided by current accounting methodologies plus those data gathered from on-site inspections, but only to large-scale estimation of market values from generic financial reports.

While standard present-value methodology and the efficient-market hypothesis are generally accepted, their assumption that current market and term structure of interest rates provide the best estimate of future rates of interest may not reflect the perceptions of market participants. For example, a current version of the "conventional wisdom" alleges that rates of interest on mortgage loans will fluctuate around a 10 percent long-run normal. This is Keynes's "normal-rate hypothesis" à la Wall Street. If the normal-rate hypothesis were correct, our method would understate market values when rates are above their norm, and overstate market values when rates are below their norm.

Commercial, construction, and development mortgage loans present a special problem. Much like zero-coupon bonds, these loans often do not require interim payments, and thus do not become delinquent for many years. Yet, they are usually high risk, and so carry high rates of interest. Thus, our delinquency-based approach to market valuation of risky loans might overstate the market values of thrifts with a high proportion of such risky loans. To check for this problem, we examined a number of thrifts. Surprisingly, this inspection revealed that, for thrifts with risky but stable portfolio strategies, delinquencies generally had time to "catch up" to the high yields, resulting in little overestimation of market values. However, for those few thrifts that radically and suddenly shift their portfolios, our delinquency-based approach appears to yield overstated net worth. In addition, because we discount all mortgage loans by the same (Federal Home Loan Mortgage Corporation commitment) rate, we tend to overstate the present value of loans with lagged delinquencies. This measurement problem appears important for explaining the failure of apparently initially solvent thrifts (see later discussion of tables 10.8 and 10.9).

The ultimate test of the MVM is its ability to predict, relative to the alternative measures provided by RAP, GAAP, and tangible book values. As detailed in Benston, Carhill, and Olasov (1991), despite its generic nature, the MVM outperforms these alternative estimates, particularly in predicting thrift failures. However, we were not able to reject the hypothesis that the market follows the normal-rate hypothesis; values from the MVM perform well in predicting the direction of stock-price movements, but appear to overstate volatility.

10.5 Empirical Analysis of Southeastern Thrifts

The Southeast refers to the area supervised and served by the Federal Home Loan Bank of Atlanta (district 4). It includes Alabama, the District of Columbia, Florida, Georgia, Maryland, North Carolina, South Carolina, and Virginia. The area is quite diverse in that it encompasses rural and urban communities and states with stable, growing, and declining economies. As such, it represents a good cross-section of the United States, with the notable exception of the boom and bust southwestern states of Texas, Louisiana, Colorado, and Arizona, where a very large part of the losses imposed on the FSLIC (and later on its successors, the FDIC and taxpayers) occurred. Hence, although the findings reported likely are not representative of the southwestern states, they probably provide a good picture of the rest of the nation. In this study, we analyze data from the 517 FSLIC-insured thrifts in operation at year-end

1984. These are 16.5 percent of the 3,136 U.S. total. In terms of total assets at book value, the southeastern thrifts represent 15.6 percent of the U.S. total.

Thrifts "fail" when the FHLBB (now the Office of Thrift Supervision, or OTS) decides to close them, place them in conservatorship, or force their merger with another institution, often with resources provided by the FSLIC (now the FDIC). Clearly, this is an insufficient definition of failure or measure of the cost of the S&L debacle to solvent thrifts and banks and to the taxpayers. Consequently, we measure the cost in terms of economic market value of equity—assets less liabilities that were not insured, de facto or de jure, by the FSLIC. A thrift's losses, then, are measured by the decline in its market-value equity adjusted for dividends and equity issues or distributions.

10.5.1 Losses Through Year-End 1984 at Thrifts Then Operating

It would have been interesting to have measured the effect of interest rate changes on the present values of thrifts' assets and liabilities year by year from, say, 1977, when the rise in interest rates began. Interest rates on 10-year U.S. Treasury notes, the duration of which is roughly comparable to mortgages with 30-year contracted maturities (the average for thrift mortgages is about 25 years), were relatively stable in the years before 1977. This rate then rose from 7.8 percent at year-end 1977 to a peak of 15.8 percent in September 1981, declined to 10.5 percent at year-end 1982, and was 11.6 percent at year-end 1984. Unfortunately, the data which we require to estimate present values were not reported by thrifts until 1984. However, if one assumes that the administration and/or the Congress did not act to close economically insolvent thrifts because they expected interest rates to decline, it is reasonable to expect that the benefits from lower interest rates should have been fully accomplished by 1984. The FHLBB, as well as the managers and owners of operating thrifts, should have had little reason to expect further benefits from still lower interest rates, particularly considering that interest rates had increased again (by about 90 basis points) between 1982 and 1984.

We should measure the losses incurred from interest rate changes as the present value of affected assets and liabilities at year-end 1984 less the present value of those mortgages at year-end 1977, both in amounts and as percentages of the asset and liability values and net worth at year-end 1977. For these measures to be meaningful, we must adjust the beginning balances for payments made over the period and new mortgages put on the books during the period. Fortunately, this apparently formidable task can be accomplished rather easily for financial assets.

Because of the relative stability of interest rates before 1977, we can assume that the book values of mortgages still outstanding at year-end 1984 provide valid measures of their present values at year-end 1977. Mortgages booked over the period 1977 through 1984 should have been recorded at their market values when the mortgages were made. Reductions in mortgages as a result of payments, payoffs, and write-offs are reflected in the year-end 1984 book values. Hence, these year-end figures accurately reflect the original market values of mortgages made before year-end 1984 and still outstanding at that time. Similarly, the book values of other assets and liabilities measure their present values at the beginning and during the years prior to year-end 1984. Hence, we measure the change in present value for financial asset *i* from 1977 through 1984 as

$$(1) \qquad CAV_{i\Delta t} = AM_{it} - AB_{it},$$

where $CAV_{i\Delta t}$ is the change in asset *i*'s value over time $t-1$ through $t(\Delta t)$, and AM_{it} and AB_{it} are the asset's market and book values at time *t*.

These changes in value also are presented as percentages of total assets at book value, the book values of the individual assets at year-end 1984 (time *t*), and as percentages of the book value of net worth at year-end 1984 to show the relative change in values. These later ratios are measured as

$$(2) \qquad CAV_{i\Delta t} / AB_t = CAVA_{i\Delta t}$$

where $CAV_{i\Delta t}$ is the change in asset value to the book value of the asset.[23]

We calculate a similar measure for liabilities. The difference between the book and market values of the liabilities on 31 December 1984, however, does not measure fully the impact of interest rate changes between 1977 and 1984. In 1977, thrifts undoubtedly had a "core deposit intangible" asset (the difference between the market and book value of deposits) because Regulation Q constrained the amounts that could be paid directly to depositors and thrifts had unrecorded goodwill. Hence, the book value of deposit and other liabilities on 31 December 1984 does not measure their market values at year-end 1977 or in the intervening years. We should note, though, that the lower level of market interest rates in 1977 (the January three-month Treasury bill rate is 4.62 percent) gave rise to smaller core deposit intangible amounts.

The amount of the loss, as calculated with equation (1), provides a measure of the amount lost primarily as a result of the 1979–82 increase in interest rates and their subsequent decline through year-end 1984. The 517 southeastern thrifts operating on 31 December 1984 had aggregate RAP net worth of \$5,814 million. The net worth of these thrifts at market values totaled −\$2,264 million (−1.5 percent of their total assets at book value). Thus, they suffered an aggregate loss of \$8,078 million (5.3 percent of their total assets). It should be recalled that our measure of present values includes the effect of expected credit losses as well as interest rate losses and gains. Hence, the asset losses measured tend to overstate the losses due to interest rate changes. In 1984 the overstatement decreases market values by about 12 percent, on average.

Table 10.2 presents the numbers derived from equations (1) and (2) for net worth, assets, and liabilities at the 517 FSLIC-insured thrifts operating in the

Table 10.2 Interest-Rate-Induced Changes in Asset and Liability Values at 517 Thrifts Operating at Year-end 1984

	Mean	Std. Error of Mean	Percentiles 5	25	50	75	95
(A) Market less Book Values as Percentages of Total Assets (at Book Value)							
Net worth	−3.6	3.2	−9.0	−5.2	−3.5	−1.6	1.1
Total mortgages	−3.7	0.2	−7.3	−5.2	−3.8	−2.4	0.5
Fixed rate	−3.6	0.2	−6.7	−4.8	−3.7	−2.4	0.0
Adjustable rate	0.2	0.6	−0.2	0.0	0.2	0.5	1.0
Other	−0.4	0.5	−1.4	−0.6	−0.3	0.0	0.3
Second	0.0	0.1	0.0	0.0	0.0	0.0	0.0
Commercial loans	0.0	0.0	0.0	0.0	0.0	0.0	0.0
Securities	0.1	0.3	−0.3	0.0	0.1	0.2	0.4
Mortgage servicing, net	0.1	0.0	0.0	0.0	0.0	0.2	0.7
Total assets	−4.6	0.1	−9.5	−6.2	−4.6	−2.8	0.8
Passbook deposits[a]	−1.9	1.5	−4.9	−2.5	−1.7	−1.1	−0.2
Other deposits and liabilities[a]	0.8	0.5	0.4	0.7	0.9	1.1	1.7
Total liabilities	−1.1	0.1	4.3	−1.8	−0.9	−0.1	1.0
(B) Market less Book Values as Percentages of Book Values							
Net worth	−71.5	33.1	−1,035.4	−173.2	−84.3	−36.9	6.7
Total mortgages	−4.7	3.1	−9.5	−6.7	−5.0	−3.1	1.3
Fixed rate	−7.2	3.3	−11.9	−9.3	−7.5	−5.5	−0.9
Adjustable rate	1.6	2.5	−1.9	0.8	1.8	2.7	4.6
Other	−5.1	5.3	−14.2	−8.8	−5.1	−1.5	3.2
Second	−0.5	3.7	−7.7	−1.9	0.3	1.4	4.1
Commercial loans	−0.9	5.3	−9.5	−1.2	0.2	1.0	4.0
Securities	0.4	2.6	−2.6	0.2	0.7	1.3	2.5
Passbook deposits[a]	−25.1	4.0	−25.7	−25.6	−25.6	−25.1	−24.8
Other deposits and liabilities[a]	1.1	0.5	0.5	0.8	1.0	1.3	1.9

[a]Difference as of 1984 only; 1977 amount not deducted (see text for details).

Southeast as of year-end 1984. Panel A shows the change in value (market less book) as percentages of total assets at book value at each thrift. The mean reduction in net worth is 3.6 percent (the median reduction is 3.5). At least three-quarters of the 517 thrifts suffered reductions in net worth that were not recorded according to RAP. Mortgages in total are responsible for reducing assets by a mean of 3.7 percent. Almost all of this reduction is due to 1–4 family fixed-interest mortgages; adjustable-rate mortgages, other mortgages, second mortgages, and securities contributed but slightly to the change in net worth, on average, and at the extremes.[24] Revaluations of commercial loans (of which there were hardly any at southeastern thrifts) and securities were of small importance.[25] We valued the intangible asset for mortgaging servicing as 1.75 percent of mortgages serviced for others,[26] and removed the asset "purchased mortgage servicing"; as a result, total assets increased on average by 0.1 percent. The removal of other book-value intangibles, primarily goodwill and deferred losses on mortgage sales, resulted in an additional decrease in net worth of about 0.8 percentage points, on average. In total, the revaluation of financial assets to market decreased book net worth as a percentage of total assets by 4.6 percent, at the average (mean) thrift. Passbook accounts have considerably lower market than book values, giving rise to the core-deposit intangible asset (recorded in table 10.2 as a decrease in the liability). At the average thrift, this intangible increased the book value of net worth by 1.9 percent of total assets. As noted above, an unknown proportion of the core-deposit intangible asset existed in earlier years, although the differential between market and passbook rates was considerably smaller in 1977 than in subsequent years. Increases in the market value over book of other liabilities decreased net worth by 0.8 percentage points.

Panel B of table 10.2 shows the percentage change in value of net worth, assets, and liabilities to their book values at year-end 1984. Net worth decreased by 71.5 percent on average. The range of this change is considerable because some thrifts had low RAP net worth.[27] Total mortgages at market value are lower by an average of 4.7 percent of their book values. The greatest decrease (relative to the balances outstanding) is in fixed-rate 1–4 family mortgages (7.2 percent) and other mortgages (5.1 percent). The market values of adjustable-rate mortgages are higher than their book values, by an average of 1.6 percent. As shown in panel A, fixed-rate 1–4 family mortgages dominate the mortgages held by the southeastern thrifts. Passbook deposits' market value is 25.1 percent lower than book value, on average. The effect of this large reduction in the value of this liability on net worth is mitigated considerably because passbook deposits are a relatively small percentage of most thrifts' liabilities. The market and book values of other deposits and liabilities were similar because these liabilities tend to be more exposed to competitive pricing pressures.

Several factors may be responsible for one or another thrift absorbing larger or smaller market-value losses or (in a few cases) gains. As discussed above in section 10.2 with respect to hypotheses 3 and 6, these factors include the thrifts' initial net worth position, economic conditions in an area, opportunities for diversification, and type of thrift ownership. To test these hypotheses, as well as to gain a greater understanding of the phenomenon, we examined the following relationship:

$$(3) \quad CNW_{\Delta 84} = b_0 + b_1 TA_{84} + b_2 TA_{84}^2 + b_3 M * TA_{84} + b_j S_j * TA_{84},$$

where

$CNW_{\Delta 84}$ = change in net worth (market less book value) through year-end 1984;

TA_{84} = total assets at book value at time t = year-end 1984 (book value is used as the "size" variable because this measures the amount originally invested by each thrift);

M = 1 if a mutual thrift, 0 if a stock, multiplied by TA_{84} to account for the expectation that the effect of ownership form is proportional to the size of an institution; and

S_j = state dummy, equals 1 for each state j with the exception of North Carolina or Florida (the states with the most thrifts), one of which is omitted to avoid overidentification, multiplied by TA to account for the expectation that the effect of state location is proportional to the size of an institution.

The square to total assets is included to test the hypothesis that the change in net worth is not related linearly to size. To reduce the effect of collinearity, the variables are divided by *TA* and equation (3′) was calculated:

$$(3') \qquad CNW_{\Delta 84} / TA_{84} = 1 / TA_{84} + 1 + b_2 \, TA_{84} + b_3 \, M + b_j \, S_j.$$

The coefficients estimated are presented in table 10.3, with the dummy variables for Florida and North Carolina included or omitted. The intercept (which measures the effect of *TA*) is significantly negative, indicating that larger thrifts experienced greater amounts of net worth losses than smaller thrifts (which is not surprising, as the larger thrifts had more to lose). The coefficient of *TA* (which measures TA^2) also is significantly negative, indicating that the loss at larger thrifts is proportionately greater than at smaller thrifts. Mutuals also had greater net worth losses than stocks, *cet. par.* The only statistically significant state dummy variable is for Virginia, which appears to have experienced greater reductions in equity, *cet. par.*

We examined further the reasons for the thrifts' change in net worth and the level of market-value net worth at year-end 1984 by regressing these variables on the thrifts' June 1982 amounts of book-value net worth, passbook deposit accounts, and 1–4 family mortgages, and the growth in their assets from June 1982 through December 1984. We used June 1982 as the beginning date because this preceded passage of the Garn–St Germain Act of 1982 which "deregulated" thrift assets and was coincident with the gradual removal of Regulation Q ceilings on deposit interest rates, and preceded the introduction (in December 1982) of money market deposit accounts that allowed thrifts to compete with money market mutual funds. The available data are deficient in two important regards. First, the number of observations are smaller because 485 of the 517 thrifts operating at year-end 1984 were operating in June 1982 (the balance were chartered in the interim). Nevertheless, the mean net worth change for this subset of −3.82 percent is similar to the mean change for the full data set of −3.56 percent. Second, we are unable to identify and separate

Table 10.3 Change in Market-Value Net Worth through Year-end 1984 Related to Size, Ownership Form, and State Location (equation [3′]), Coefficients and [Probability Coefficient > 0]

Mean of Dependent Variable (in percentage):
Market less Book Value of Net Worth ÷ Total Assets = −3.56%

Independent Variables	Coefficients [prob > 0] Excluding: Florida	North Carolina
1/Total assets ($ thousands)	379	379
[intercept]	[<.01]	[<.01]
Intercept	−4.30	−4.04
[total assets]	[<.01]	[<.01]
Total assets	−1.2 E−6	−1.2 E−6
[total assets squared]	[<.01]	[<.01]
Mutual = 1	−1.80	−1.82
Stock = 0	[<.01]	[<.01]
North Carolina = 1	0.30	
	[.46]	
Florida = 1		−0.30
		[.46]
District of Columbia = 1	−1.51	−1.82
	[.19]	[.12]
Alabama = 1	−0.30	−0.63
	[.57]	[.25]
Georgia = 1	0.00	−0.30
	[.95]	[.45]
South Carolina = 1	−0.52	−0.80
	[.38]	[.13]
Virginia = 1	−1.01	−1.33
	[.03]	[.06]
Maryland = 1	0.53	0.24
	[.26]	[.60]
Adjusted R^2	0.22	0.22
Number of observations[a]	509	509

[a]Eight observations omitted because states were not known.

asset growth due to mergers from growth from deposits and borrowings. (As shown in table 10.6, growth through mergers skews the mean rate).

We ran the following regressions:

$$(4a) CNW_{\Delta 84} / TA_{84} = 1 / TA_{84} + 1 + c_2 TA_{84} + c_3 M + c_4 NWB_{82} / TA_{84} + c_5 PD_{82} / TA_{84} + c_6 \mathit{1\text{–}4M}_{82} / TA_{84} + c_7 \Delta TA / TA_{84},$$

where

NWB_{82} = book-value net worth on 30 June 1982;
PD_{82} = passbook deposits on 30 June 1982;

$1\text{–}4M_{82}$ = 1 to 4 family mortgages (including second mortgages and construction loans on 1–4 family dwellings);[28] and

ΔTA = change in total assets from 30 June 1982 through 31 December 1984;

and the other variables are as described for equation (3).

$$(4b) NWM_{84} / TA_{84} = 1 / TA_{84} + 1 + c_2 TA_{84} + c_3 M + c_4 NWB_{82} / TA_{84} + c_5 PD_{82} / TA_{84} + c_6 1\text{–}4M_{82} / TA_{84} + c_7 \Delta TA / TA_{84},$$

where

NWM_{84} = net worth at market value at year-end 1984.

The state dummy variables were not included in the regressions because they are generally insignificant and their inclusion would reduce the sample by eight observations (see table 10.3).

The coefficients, presented in table 10.4, show (as in table 10.3) that total asset size (measured by the intercept in equations [4a] and [4b]) is significantly inversely related to the change in net worth and to the year-end 1984 amount of market-value net worth; both total assets and total assets squared

Table 10.4 **Change in Market-Value Net Worth through Year-end 1984 Related to Size, Ownership Form, and Mid-year 1982 Values (equation [4]), Coefficients and [Probability Coefficient > 0]**

	Mean of Dependent Variables (in percentages)			
	Market less Book Value of Net Worth ÷ Total Assets = −3.82%		Market Value of Net Worth at Year-end 1984 ÷ Total Assets = 0.47%	
Independent Variables	Coefficients	[prob > 0]	Coefficients	[prob >0]
1/Total assets ($ thousands) [intercept]	240	[<.01]	161	[<.01]
Intercept [total assets]	−7.31	[<.01]	−8.22	[<.01]
Total assets ($ thousands) [total assets squared]	−1.13 E−6	[<.01]	−8.18 E−7	[.01]
Mutual = 1, Stock = 0	−1.05	[<.01]	−1.37	[<.01]
Book value net worth 6/82 ÷ total assets, in percentages	0.40	[<.01]	1.65	[<.01]
Passbook deposits 6/82 ÷ total assets, in percentages	0.18	[<.01]	0.18	[<.01]
1–4 Family mortgages 6/82 ÷ total assets, in percentages	−0.03	[.14]	−0.04	[.15]
Asset growth, 6/82–12/84 ÷ total assets, in percentages	0.06	[<.01]	0.10	[<.01]
Adjusted R^2	0.34		0.54	
Number of observations	485		485	

Note: Total assets as of year-end 1984.

have negative significant coefficients. Mutual thrifts experienced a greater reduction in net worth by one percentage point, on average. The June 1982 amounts of book-value net worth and passbook deposits are significantly positively related and mortgages on 1–4 family dwellings are inversely related (at the 0.15 level) to the change in net worth and amount of market-value net worth. Asset growth is significantly positively related to the dependent variables, a finding that is inconsistent with the belief that growth, as such, was detrimental to thrifts, at least through year-end 1984.

Assuming that the June 1982 book values reflect the thrifts' pre-1979 market values, these results indicate that the thrifts that experienced reductions in net worth (many of which became economically insolvent, as shown in table 10.6) were those with low initial percentages to total assets of net worth and of passbook deposits (see tables 10.4 and 10.6). Low relative amounts of passbook deposits are consistent with thrifts having obtained deposits from outside their local market areas, perhaps because they faced strong local competition. These results, together with the inverse relationship between asset size and the change and level of year-end 1984 market-value net worth, are consistent with the hypothesis that the thrifts that became insolvent when interest rates increased in 1979–81 were those that had expanded beyond their passbook-deposit base without proportionately having increased their net worth. The negative sign of the coefficient of the 1–4 family mortgages variable indicates that these mortgages (which, in 1982, were largely fixed-rate, longer-term obligations) also are responsible for reductions in and lower amounts of market-value net worth.

10.5.2 The Behavior of Continuing and Failed Thrifts Classified by Market-Value Solvency

It is likely that financial institutions take actions with consequences that occur over a period longer than a year. Consequently, we first examine the investments and changes in net worth of thrifts classified according to their economic (market-value) net worth at the end of 1984 over the years through 1988. The observations are divided into two groups: thrifts that operated throughout the period and those that ceased operations as a result of failure. Those that ceased being independent institutions because of voluntary mergers are not included in this group and are not analyzed at this point. This separation was made so that the changes over time would not be subjected to sample-composition bias, at least for those thrifts that continued operating.

Continuously Operating Thrifts

The continuously operating thrifts also are classified according to whether their net worth to total assets in market values at year-end 1984 is $< -3\%$, $-3\% < 0\%$, $0\% < 3\%$, $3\% < 6\%$, and 6% and over. The assets, net worths, and liabilities as percentages of total assets (at book values) of these thrifts then are given for each year.[29] Table 10.5 presents the data for the 455 thrifts

Table 10.5 **455 Thrifts in Continuous Operation from 1984 through 1988 (asset and liability amounts as percentage of book-value total assets except where noted; grouped by market-value net worth to total assets as of 31 December 1984)**

	Market Value of Net Worth/Total Assets (in percentages)									
	< −3%		−3% < 0%		0% < 3%		3% < 6%		> 6%	
	Mean	Std. Error of Mean	Mean	Std. Error of Mean	Mean	Std. Error of Mean	Mean	Std. Error of Mean	Mean	Std. Error of Mean
Total assets ($ millions)										
1984	**579**	78	**355**	55	**292**	66	**126**	21	**59**	11
1985	**633**	91	**378**	60	**305**	66	**150**	25	**80**	15
1986	**664**	103	**410**	63	**334**	71	**171**	30	**107**	26
1987	**700**	122	**439**	68	**371**	77	**190**	34	**122**	28
1988	**779**	148	**500**	81	**423**	91	**205**	36	**133**	29
Market value of net worth to total assets at market value										
1984	**−6.0**	0.3	**−1.3**	0.7	**1.3**	0.1	**4.2**	0.1	**12.5**	1.1
1985	**−1.0**	0.6	**3.1**	0.2	**4.9**	0.4	**7.0**	0.3	**10.5**	0.4
1986	**0.3**	0.7	**4.4**	0.3	**6.3**	0.5	**7.7**	0.4	**9.8**	0.5
1987	**−1.2**	0.7	**3.8**	0.4	**5.8**	0.7	**7.4**	0.5	**8.7**	0.6
1988	**−0.1**	1.5	**3.4**	0.5	**5.5**	0.9	**7.0**	0.7	**7.8**	0.7
Book-value net worth										
1984	**1.9**	0.2	**3.2**	0.1	**4.5**	0.1	**5.7**	0.2	**12.3**	1.1
1985	**2.9**	0.5	**3.9**	0.1	**4.9**	0.3	**6.0**	0.2	**8.4**	0.3
1986	**3.3**	0.6	**4.7**	0.2	**5.5**	0.4	**6.4**	0.3	**7.9**	0.3
1987	**2.8**	0.7	**5.2**	0.3	**6.1**	0.6	**7.0**	0.4	**8.2**	0.4
1988	**3.6**	1.5	**5.3**	0.4	**5.9**	0.9	**6.8**	0.6	**8.1**	0.4
Annual growth in total assets										
1985	**6.6**	1.6	**5.7**	0.8	**8.3**	0.9	**11.7**	1.3	**25.6**	2.8
1986	**3.8**	1.3	**6.7**	0.8	**7.6**	0.6	**10.5**	1.0	**18.9**	1.6
1987	**2.4**	1.4	**4.8**	0.7	**5.9**	0.8	**6.4**	1.0	**11.0**	1.4
1988	**6.2**	1.7	**7.0**	1.0	**7.4**	0.8	**6.9**	1.2	**8.4**	1.2
Passbook deposits to total assets										
1984	**6.9**	0.4	**7.0**	0.3	**7.8**	0.3	**9.5**	0.7	**12.3**	1.3
1985	**6.1**	0.4	**6.6**	0.3	**7.1**	0.3	**8.6**	0.7	**11.3**	1.2
1986	**4.0**	0.5	**7.2**	0.3	**7.7**	0.3	**9.5**	0.8	**11.3**	1.1
1987	**7.6**	0.5	**7.5**	0.3	**8.1**	0.3	**10.5**	0.8	**11.0**	1.0
1988	**8.1**	1.1	**6.9**	0.3	**7.6**	0.3	**9.8**	0.8	**10.5**	1.0
Traditional (1–4 family first) mortgages										
1984	**64.9**	1.3	**70.2**	1.1	**68.3**	1.2	**68.0**	1.6	**64.4**	2.5
1985	**60.0**	1.4	**66.6**	1.2	**63.7**	1.3	**65.3**	1.5	**64.1**	2.2
1986	**57.4**	1.3	**64.4**	1.2	**61.4**	1.3	**62.1**	1.4	**63.1**	2.0
1987	**59.3**	1.4	**66.2**	1.1	**64.3**	1.3	**64.8**	1.5	**65.5**	2.1
1988	**61.2**	1.5	**66.4**	1.2	**64.9**	1.2	**66.3**	1.4	**65.7**	2.1
Fixed-interest rate (1–4 family first) mortgages										
1984	**46.0**	1.7	**52.6**	1.4	**50.6**	1.4	**47.7**	2.0	**41.4**	3.3
1985	**38.4**	1.5	**44.0**	1.5	**42.1**	1.5	**40.2**	2.0	**37.2**	3.2
1986	**34.5**	1.4	**39.7**	1.4	**36.8**	1.4	**36.0**	1.9	**37.4**	2.9
1987	**33.2**	1.4	**37.4**	1.6	**35.7**	1.6	**35.4**	2.0	**38.1**	3.0
1988	**29.4**	1.4	**33.6**	1.5	**32.4**	1.6	**32.4**	2.0	**36.8**	3.0

(continued)

Table 10.5 (continued)

	Market Value of Net Worth/Total Assets (in percentages)									
	< −3%		−3% < 0%		0% < 3%		3% < 6%		> 6%	
	Mean	Std. Error of Mean	Mean	Std. Error of Mean	Mean	Std. Error of Mean	Mean	Std. Error of Mean	Mean	Std. Error of Mean
Adjustable-interest-rate mortgages										
1984	**17.8**	1.1	**17.1**	1.0	**17.9**	1.2	**20.1**	1.4	**18.1**	2.4
1985	**24.7**	1.3	**24.3**	1.2	**26.0**	1.4	**28.2**	1.9	**28.9**	3.0
1986	**27.5**	1.4	**28.6**	1.3	**29.9**	1.5	**30.0**	1.8	**29.3**	2.9
1987	**31.5**	1.6	**33.2**	1.5	**34.9**	1.7	**34.6**	2.0	**31.0**	2.9
1988	**36.4**	1.7	**37.3**	1.5	**39.1**	1.8	**39.4**	2.1	**33.3**	2.8
Multifamily and nonresidential mortgages										
1984	**13.4**	1	**11.8**	0.7	**12.2**	1.0	**11.7**	1.2	**12.8**	1.4
1985	**14.1**	1	**13.1**	0.7	**14.3**	1.1	**12.0**	1.2	**15.7**	1.9
1986	**15.5**	1.1	**13.1**	0.7	**14.4**	1.1	**11.9**	1.1	**15.1**	1.8
1987	**12.3**	0.9	**9.8**	0.6	**11.5**	0.9	**9.5**	0.9	**11.3**	1.3
1988	**11.9**	0.9	**9.5**	0.6	**11.0**	0.8	**9.4**	0.8	**10.9**	1.2
Second mortgages										
1984	**0.8**	0.2	**0.7**	0.2	**0.6**	0.1	**0.5**	0.1	**1.3**	0.4
1985	**1.0**	0.3	**0.8**	0.1	**0.6**	0.1	**0.5**	0.7	**1.3**	0.3
1986	**1.4**	0.4	**0.6**	0.1	**0.6**	0.1	**0.4**	0.1	**0.9**	0.2
1987	**1.6**	0.4	**0.6**	0.7	**0.5**	0.1	**0.4**	0.1	**0.9**	0.2
1988	**1.7**	0.4	**0.7**	0.1	**0.5**	0.1	**0.5**	0.1	**0.8**	0.2
Consumer loans										
1984	**4.7**	0.5	**3.8**	0.4	**3.3**	0.3	**3.9**	0.4	**2.7**	0.4
1985	**5.5**	0.6	**4.7**	0.4	**4.0**	0.4	**4.7**	0.6	**3.6**	0.5
1986	**5.5**	0.6	**4.8**	0.4	**4.3**	0.4	**4.6**	0.6	**3.1**	0.5
1987	**5.6**	0.6	**5.1**	0.5	**4.7**	0.4	**4.6**	0.5	**3.1**	0.6
1988	**6.1**	0.6	**5.5**	0.4	**5.2**	0.4	**5.0**	0.6	**3.4**	0.6
Commercial loans										
1984	**0.8**	0.2	**0.4**	0.1	**0.5**	0.1	**0.6**	0.2	**1.7**	0.6
1985	**1.3**	0.2	**0.7**	0.1	**0.8**	0.2	**0.9**	0.2	**1.6**	0.4
1986	**1.6**	0.3	**0.9**	0.2	**1.1**	0.2	**1.2**	0.3	**1.8**	0.4
1987	**1.7**	0.3	**1.1**	0.2	**1.1**	0.2	**1.3**	0.3	**1.5**	0.3
1988	**1.7**	0.3	**1.2**	0.2	**1.2**	0.2	**1.4**	0.3	**1.5**	0.3
Investment securities										
1984	**10.5**	0.9	**10.1**	0.7	**12.7**	0.8	**14.1**	1.3	**20.0**	2.2
1985	**11.1**	1.0	**9.9**	0.7	**13.8**	0.9	**13.3**	1.1	**14.9**	1.3
1986	**12.0**	0.9	**11.8**	0.7	**14.8**	0.9	**15.3**	1.1	**15.3**	1.1
1987	**10.4**	0.9	**10.1**	0.7	**11.7**	0.7	**12.6**	1.2	**14.0**	1.3
1988	**9.6**	0.9	**9.9**	0.8	**10.5**	0.7	**11.2**	1.2	**12.4**	1.1
Delinquency on (all) mortgages, percentages of total mortgages										
1984	**2.8**	0.4	**1.7**	0.1	**1.7**	0.1	**1.5**	0.1	**1.3**	0.1
1985	**2.8**	0.4	**2.4**	0.4	**2.5**	0.3	**2.0**	0.2	**2.0**	0.2
1986	**3.2**	0.4	**2.5**	0.3	**3.1**	0.4	**3.1**	0.8	**2.2**	0.3
1987	**3.4**	0.4	**2.5**	0.3	**3.0**	0.4	**2.5**	0.4	**3.4**	0.7
1988	**3.2**	0.4	**2.2**	0.2	**2.4**	0.3	**2.2**	0.3	**3.1**	0.5

Table 10.5 (continued)

	Market Value of Net Worth/Total Assets (in percentages)									
	< −3%		−3% < 0%		0% < 3%		3% < 6%		> 6%	
	Mean	Std. Error of Mean	Mean	Std. Error of Mean	Mean	Std. Error of Mean	Mean	Std. Error of Mean	Mean	Std. Error of Mean
Delinquency on nonmortgages, percentages of nonmortgages										
1984	**1.9**	0.3	**1.7**	0.4	**9.8**	0.3	**0.9**	0.2	**0.9**	0.5
1985	**2.7**	0.5	**2.8**	0.7	**1.7**	0.6	**1.2**	0.3	**0.9**	0.3
1986	**3.6**	0.7	**2.8**	0.6	**2.2**	0.5	**2.2**	0.7	**1.8**	0.6
1987	**3.1**	0.5	**2.4**	0.4	**2.5**	0.7	**1.5**	0.4	**1.7**	0.3
1988	**4.0**	0.7	**2.6**	0.4	**2.4**	0.6	**1.8**	0.4	**1.7**	0.4
Number of observations	77		106		112		82		78	
Percentage of total	17%		23%		25%		18%		17%	

that operated continuously through year-end 1988.[30] Data on the 31 thrifts that were terminated during this period are presented in table 10.7. (The remaining 31 thrifts that ceased independent operations for other reasons are not included in this portion of the analysis.)

Considering first the 455 continuously operating thrifts, as of year-end 1984, 77 (17% of the sample) had market-value equity to asset ratios of less than −3 percent, 106 (23%) had ratios between −3 and 0 percent, 112 (25%) between 0 and 3 percent, 82 (18%) between 3 and 6 percent, and 78 (17%) 6 percent and over. Table 10.5 shows an inverse relationship between market-value solvency and total asset size, which also is revealed by the statistically significant negative coefficient of total assets estimated for equations 3′ and 4b (see tables 10.3 and 10.4). This relationship continues throughout the five-year period and probably back at least to mid 1982. Table 10.6 presents data on the book-value net worth to total assets and passbook deposits to total assets as of 30 June 1982 and the percentage growth in total assets through 31 December 1984 of the 485 thrifts operating on 30 June 1982. While this group is not directly comparable to the 455 continuously operating thrifts because of merger and new charters before year-end 1984 and cessation of operations after year-end 1984, it provides a valuable (and the only available) benchmark.

One reason for the solvency of southeastern thrifts at year-end 1984 appears to be a higher relative ratio of passbook deposits to total assets. Solvency and the percentage of passbook deposits are directly related, and smaller thrifts tend to have relatively more of these deposits, both at mid-year 1982 and year-end 1984. While the percentage of passbook deposits over the period declined by 54 to 61 percent (which is not surprising, considering the large increase in market interest rates and much smaller rise in the Regulation Q ceiling), the solvent thrifts still held larger percentages at year-end 1984 than the insolvent thrifts. As noted above, higher proportions of passbook deposits also may proxy for the competitiveness of the thrifts' marketplace. (Had we the data, we would have related the solvency of thrifts to their Herfindahl index or other measure of competition.) Thus, the solvent thrifts appear to have benefited from a slower run-off of their below-market-rate liabilities and possibly from less competition in their markets. This conclusion is supported by the regression reported in table 10.3, which shows a significant positive relationship between market-value net worth and passbook deposits.

Another hypothesis for the inverse relationship between size and solvency is that thrifts rendered insolvent by the 1979–81 sharp increase in interest rates may have grown relatively more rapidly before 1984, in an attempt to "grow" out of their old balance sheets, than those that were still solvent in 1982. The data presented in tables 10.4 and 10.6, though, are inconsistent with this hypothesis. The regression coefficients given in table 10.4 show a significant positive relationship between asset growth and market-value net worth. The magnitude of the relationship, though, is small: a \$100 million increase in assets is associated with a \$100,000 increase in market-value net worth. The univariate relationship shown in table 10.6 indicates that most of the measured multivariate positive relationship is due to the group with market-value net worth above 6 percent. This group has a relatively large number of newly chartered thrifts, as indicated by the small assets size and the greater number at year-end 1984 than at mid-year 1982 (at least 78 compared to 61).[31] Hence, it is not surprising that the group experienced higher mean growth rates. (Newly chartered thrifts also are less likely to have suffered from interest-rate-increase induced losses, as they have more currently priced fixed-rate mortgages.) Table 10.6 gives mean growth rates over the entire period and over the eighteen months ending 31 December 1983. Over both periods the rate of growth of the solvent thrifts exceed that of the insolvent thrifts. The table also shows the median, quartile, and five and ninety-five percentile growth rates. These data reveal that the mean growth rates are considerably affected by some large values, probably the result of mergers. We consider the median rates, therefore, more meaningful indicators of growth due to the acquisition of deposits and debt. These rates for the entire period and the period through year-end 1983 show only slightly higher growth for the more solvent thrifts. This finding is inconsistent with the hypothesis that insolvent and weak thrifts took advantage of deposit insurance to grow excessively. This contention also is inconsistent with the positive relationship found between growth and solvency for the June 1982 through December 1984 period, as shown in table 10.4.

A third hypothesis is that thrifts' year-end 1984 insolvency is due to their prior net worth position. This hypothesis is supported by the "market value of net worth at year-end 1984" regression given in table 10.4 and the book-value net worth reported in table 10.6. The coefficient of "book-value net worth

Table 10.6 **485 Thrifts' Characteristics from June 1982 (grouped by market-value net worth to total assets as of 31 December 1984)**

	Market Value of Net Worth/Total Assets (in percentages)									
	< − 3%		− 3% < 0%		0% < 3%		3% < 6%		≥ 6%	
	Mean	Std. Error of Mean	Mean	Std. Error of Mean	Mean	Std. Error of Mean	Mean	Std. Error of Mean	Mean	Std. Error of Mean
Book-value net worth to total assets, in percentages										
	2.7	0.2	**3.7**	0.1	**5.5**	0.4	**5.9**	0.3	**6.5**	0.8
Passbook deposits to total assets, in percentages										
	12.5	0.5	**12.6**	0.4	**13.5**	0.5	**15.5**	0.7	**22.8**	1.5
Growth in total assets from 6/82 to 12/84, in percentages										
	62.6	17.1	**64.0**	14.5	**97.7**	28.9	**63.2**	12.8	**102.0**	31.1
Percentile										
95%		220.5		244.3		555.7		297.4		495.8
75%		47.4		51.5		45.7		44.8		54.5
50%		24.1		24.5		25.3		27.6		24.3
25%		10.0		14.5		15.7		17.0		16.8
5%		0.3		4.1		2.4		3.2		3.7
Growth in total assets from 6/83 to 12/84, in percentages										
	24.3	4.6	**27.4**	3.6	**40.9**	9.2	**43.0**	13.5	**38.2**	6.0
Percentile										
95%		64.8		105.0		146.0		177.3		175.7
75%		25.7		31.1		31.1		29.1		42.4
50%		15.6		15.8		17.4		18.0		19.5
25%		8.4		8.8		11.3		10.4		11.1
5%		−2.2		−0.5		1.9		0.4		4.5
Number of observations	93		123		125		83		61	
Percentage of total	19%		25%		26%		17%		13%	

6/82" of 1.65 in table 10.4 indicates a greater than proportional relationship between book value on 30 June 1982 and market-value net worth on 31 December 1984. Table 10.6 shows that the very insolvent thrifts (< 3% market-value net worth to total assets) had mean book-value net worth of 2.7 percent and the −3% < 0% thrifts had mean book-value net worth of 3.7 percent of total assets at mid-year 1982. In comparison, the solvent thrifts had mean book-value net worth of at least 5.5 percent of total assets (the differences are statistically significant).

Returning now to table 10.5, the second group of figures, market-value net worth to total assets at market value, indicates that the average relative solvency position of the continuously operating thrifts improved dramatically in 1985 when interest rates declined, for all except the strongest group (≥ 6%), but did not change much thereafter. The continuous decline in the strongest groups' average market-value net worth appears to be due to rapid expansion by strong, small, often newly chartered thrifts, as shown by the increase in the average amounts of total assets. After 1985 the average market-value ratios remain fairly constant. These data are not consistent with the hypothesis that insolvent and weak thrifts engaged in excessive risk-taking resulting in net losses, on average. (Note that these data do not include thrifts that failed during the period.) However, the regulatory book-value net worth ratios for the insolvent groups tend to increase more than for the solvent thrifts. This may reflect their strong incentive to use RAP modifications to bolster reported capital, thereby preventing takeover by the authorities. As is shown later, the increase in RAP net worth of insolvent thrifts is not simply a function of their having taken and benefited from additional interest-rate risk.

Surprisingly, perhaps, growth in assets does not appear to be a function of the market-value solvency of the thrifts in the post-1984 years, nor (as we report above) in the mid 1982 through year-end 1984 period. Indeed, the 1984 insolvent thrifts grew at a slower rate than the solvent thrifts, particularly the strongest thrifts. This finding is inconsistent with the "deposit-insurance" hypothesis.

All groups tended to decrease their investment in fixed-interest-rate 1–4 family first mortgages and increase their holdings of adjustable-rate mortgages (relative to total assets). Investment in traditional (1–4 family first) mortgages relative to total assets is not very different among the solvent groups, with the exception of the $< -3\%$ net worth group, where the percentage is significantly lower by about five percentage points. The percentages of fixed- and adjustable-interest-rate mortgages to total assets is insignificantly different among the groups. Multifamily and nonresidential mortgages relative to total assets decreased significantly over the period and are about the same for all groups. Second mortgages are a significantly higher percentage of total assets at the most insolvent thrifts after 1985, although the average percentage only reaches 1.7 (in 1988). This may, however, signal a willingness among these thrifts to accept higher loan-to-value loans—the most important indicator of credit losses on mortgages. On the whole, though, the data are inconsistent with the hypothesis that insolvency encouraged thrifts to take advantage of expanded mortgage loan powers.

Commercial loans are also small proportions of total assets for all groups, but are similar among the groups. Consumer loans, though, are a relatively greater percentage of total assets, on average, at the most insolvent thrifts; however, the difference is greatest for the most insolvent group, which has significantly higher percentages than the most solvent group (e.g., in 1986, 5.5 vs. 3.1 percent). Investment securities are higher percentages of total assets at the most solvent thrifts. Given that consumer loans are not considered to be inherently risky and were permitted prior to the Garn–St Germain Act of 1982, this evidence either is inconsistent with the "insolvency-driven, excessive risk-taking" and "asset-deregulation" hypotheses, indicates that asset type is an inadequate measure of risk (which is contrary to the basic consumption of the "asset-deregulation" hypothesis), or supports the view that the fourth district supervisors were effective in restraining excessive risk-taking.

The delinquency percentages (to mortgages outstanding) are available only for portfolios of mortgages and nonmortgages. All groups experienced significant increases in delinquencies (which our model assumes are total losses). The delinquency rates are not significantly different among the groups with respect to solvency, which is inconsistent with the "insolvency-driven, excessive risk-taking" hypothesis. However, the delinquency rate on nonmortgages is significantly higher and escalates quickly for the very insolvent thrifts after 1985, particularly as compared to the strongest thrifts. These data are consistent with the hypothesis and perhaps with the "asset-deregulation" hypothesis, although with commercial mortgages included in the mortgage delinquency rate, the hypothesis cannot really be tested with these data. Furthermore, as noted above, nonmortgage (commercial and consumer) loans are relatively small percentages of total assets at most thrifts, although relatively high delinquencies on small amounts of loans could be sufficient to drive weakly capitalized thrifts into insolvency.

On the whole, the data appear inconsistent with the hypothesis that insolvency and low capital ratios, measured in market-value terms, encouraged surviving thrifts to take excessively high risks, nor did their operations tend to result in large losses. Alternatively, the supervisory authorities may have constrained excessive risk-taking. However, the sample is biased in that the institutions that were closed (failed) are not included. We turn to those now.

Failed Thrifts

Table 10.7 shows the assets and liabilities of the 35 thrifts that were operating at year-end 1984 and closed by year-end 1988. The table presents financial ratios for these thrifts in the year-ends preceding failure. The failed thrifts are smaller, on average, than the most insolvent operating thrifts (although the large standard errors of the means among the 1986 and 1987 failures indicates a wide variance) and about the same size as the weak operating thrifts.[32] The market-value net-worth-to-total-assets-at-market percentages indicate they were insolvent, on average, in the years before they were closed. Examination of the individual data indicates that most of these thrifts were insolvent in those years. However, on average and individually, they rarely were book-value insolvent except in the year just preceding their being closed.

High rates of growth did not precede failure, on average and (with a few exceptions) individually, which again is inconsistent with the "deposit-insurance" hypothesis. The small average amounts of brokered deposits as a percentage of total liabilities also is inconsistent with this hypothesis. (Indeed, only two thrifts in each failure year had more than trivial amounts of brokered deposits.) Deposits over $100,000 as a percentage of total liabilities are relatively larger at the failed thrifts (compare with tables 10.8 and 10.9),[33]

Table 10.7 **35 Thrifts That Were Closed in 1985 through 1988 (balance sheet amounts and ratios in the years before closure)**

			Total Assets (TA) (book value in $ millions)		Market-Value Net Worth as % of TA		RAP Net Worth as % of TA		Annual Growth in TA in percentages		Nontraditional Assets[a] as % of TA	
	Year-End	Number of Thrifts	Mean	Std. Error of Mean	Mean	Std. Error of Mean	Mean	Std. Error of Mean	Mean	Std. Error of Mean	Mean	Std. Error of Mean
Closed in 1985	1984	3	232	94	−27.0	4.6	−11.4	7.4	not calculated		7.0	3.3
Closed in 1986	1984	8	460	225	−4.3	2.0	1.9	1.2	not calculated		35.3	11.6
	1985	8	490	247	−7.2	2.7	−2.0	1.7	0.5	7.4	35.8	7.5
Closed in 1987	1984	11	489	216	−3.4	2.2	1.3	1.1	not calculated		37.3	6.2
	1985	11	510	231	−4.1	3.9	−0.3	1.7	0.6	6.0	38.5	7.5
	1986	11	460	198	−15.5	7.2	−7.2	3.8	−12.8	4.8	36.5	5.0
Closed in 1988	1984	13	353	85	−1.2	1.5	2.8	0.7	not calculated		22.5	4.8
	1985	13	355	81	0.0	1.1	2.8	0.4	3.0	3.9	31.0	6.8
	1986	13	354	87	−3.8	1.4	1.3	0.8	−1.5	5.1	31.1	6.0
	1987	13	344	92	−13.0	2.7	−5.7	2.3	−8.6	4.7	26.9	5.3

[a]Mortgages other than first mortgage 1–4 family loans, commercial and consumer loans, and real estate held for investment.

	Year-End	Number of Thrifts	Traditional Mortgages[b] as % of TA		Fixed-Interest Mortgages as % of TA		Adjustable-Rate Mortgages as % of TA		Delinquency Rate on Mortgages		Delinquency Rate – on Nonmortgages	
			Mean	Std. Error of Mean	Mean	Std. Error of Mean	Mean	Std. Error of Mean	Mean	Std. Error of Mean	Mean	Std. Error of Mean
Closed in 1985	1984	3	73.8	6.3	66.8	8.1	6.2	3.1	2.0	1.0	1.0	1.0
Closed in 1986	1984	8	47.2	9.3	29.1	7.6	31.2	9.0	5.5	1.9	4.3	2.3
	1985	8	48.4	8.6	22.8	5.8	43.9	6.7	12.2	4.9	14.2	7.7
Closed in 1987	1984	11	42.8	6.6	34.4	6.3	19.2	3.9	4.1	1.2	1.2	0.5
	1985	11	45.8	5.1	28.5	5.5	35.1	6.5	8.6	2.5	3.7	2.0
	1986	11	42.5	4.7	25.9	4.7	32.1	5.6	18.1	5.0	7.2	4.5
Closed in 1988	1984	13	66.6	4.6	36.3	6.1	26.2	6.9	2.1	0.4	0.8	0.5
	1985	13	53.6	4.0	28.9	4.2	35.6	7.1	4.0	2.6	1.4	0.7
	1986	13	49.7	4.6	26.6	5.8	34.5	6.3	7.7	1.6	4.9	2.7
	1987	13	52.4	4.2	30.4	4.7	33.1	6.3	12.4	3.4	1.5	0.6

[b]1–4 family first mortgages.

(continued)

Table 10.7 (continued)

	Year-End	Number of Thrifts	Passbook Deposits as % of Total Liabilities (TL)		Deposits Under \$100,000 as % of TL		Deposits Over \$100,000 as % of TL		Brokered Deposits as % of TL	
			Mean	Std. Error of Mean	Mean	Std. Error of Mean	Mean	Std. Error of Mean	Mean	Std. Error of Mean
Closed in 1985	1984	3	4.7	0.4	76.3	10.6	8.1	4.9	0.0	0.0
Closed in 1986	1984	8	2.9	0.8	80.7	2.1	10.8	2.4	5.9	3.8
	1985	8	2.8	0.9	87.3	2.9	6.9	2.6	3.5	2.4
Closed in 1987	1984	11	7.5	3.8	70.0	5.8	15.5	4.1	1.1	0.6
	1985	11	7.6	4.0	73.4	4.9	14.7	4.3	2.7	1.5
	1986	11	8.4	3.9	77.8	4.5	8.7	2.0	2.1	1.5
Closed in 1988	1984	13	4.2	0.9	73.4	4.1	10.8	1.8	2.5	1.3
	1985	13	4.0	0.9	72.3	3.7	11.7	2.5	3.6	2.6
	1986	13	5.7	1.1	77.7	3.4	9.6	1.9	2.6	2.0
	1987	13	5.5	1.0	78.5	4.2	7.3	2.0	3.9	2.0

which indicates that they had local funding problems but were able to obtain partially insured funds. This conclusion is supported by the failed thrifts' relatively lower amount of deposits under $100,000 as compared to the stronger operating thrifts. However, in the year before their failure, the percentage of deposits over $100,000 decreased substantially (indicating that holders of these deposits correctly predicted failure) and the percentage of fully insured deposits increased, but not sufficiently to offset the decrease in partially insured funds. The shortfall was made up with advances from the Federal Home Loan Bank.

Nontraditional assets (first mortgages other than 1–4 family loans, commercial and consumer loans, and real estate held for investment) are considerably higher at the failed thrifts, although there is little evidence of increase over the time before they were closed. Traditional mortgages as a percentage of total assets are about two-thirds of the percentages at operating thrifts, particularly for thrifts that failed before 1988. The percentages of fixed- and adjustable-interest-rate mortgages to total assets are not significantly different from the operating groups, with the exception of the three thrifts that failed in 1985. These thrifts concentrated on traditional mortgages and held almost no adjustable-interest-rate mortgages, which appears to account for their early failure.

After 1985, delinquencies play a large role in the failure of southeastern thrifts. The delinquency rates (to mortgages and to nonmortgage loans outstanding) are significantly higher among the failed thrifts compared to all except the most insolvent operating thrifts. However, unlike these institutions, the failed thrifts' delinquency rates tend to be higher for mortgage than for nonmortgage loans. This may be due to their capitalizing unpaid interest on restructured commercial loans. In all cases, delinquencies rapidly escalated from year to year as weak credits emerged or supervisors forced recognition.

10.5.3 The Behavior of Thrifts that Were Market-Value Insolvent or Solvent at Year-End 1984 and That Subsequently Were Closed or Open through 31 March 1990

The analysis of operating and failed thrifts just presented does not speak directly to the question of why some thrifts failed while others survived. To answer this question, we put the data together and constructed table 10.8, which presents data on the 517 thrifts operating at year-end 1984 for the subsequent four years. These thrifts are classified into four major groups (solvency is as of year-end 1984, according to our measure of market values; closure is through 31 March 1990, the latest data available at the time this table was constructed): insolvent and subsequently closed (50 thrifts, 10% of the 517 in operation at year-end 1984); insolvent and subsequently open (still operating) (170 thrifts, or 33%); solvent and subsequently closed (22 thrifts, or 4%); and solvent and subsequently open (275 thrifts, or 53%). To test further the hypothesis that economically insolvent thrifts with RAP net worth

Table 10.8 **The Condition of the 517 Thrifts That Were Insolvent or Solvent at Year-end 1984 And That Subsequently Were Closed or Open through 31 March 1990**

		Number of Observations		Total Assets (TA) (book value in $ millions)		Annual Growth in TA (percentages)		Market-Value Net Worth as % of TA		RAP Net Worth as % of TA	
	Year-end	Number	% in Year	Mean	Std. Error of Mean	Mean	Std. Error of Mean	Mean	Std. Error of Mean	Mean	Std. Error of Mean
Insolvent and Closed	1984	50	10	579	102	not calculated		−7.3	1.0	0.9	0.9
	1985	47	9	632	124	−0.9	2.2	−4.2	1.1	0.8	0.6
	1986	40	8	665	164	−3.4	2.2	−5.2	1.5	−0.6	1.2
	1987	34	7	718	238	−2.5	2.4	−8.6	1.2	−2.6	1.3
	1988	29	6	883	343	−1.8	2.0	−9.3	1.5	−4.1	1.8
Insolvent/RAP NW > 3% and Closed	1984	12	24	1,061	307	not calculated		−4.1	1.1	3.8	0.2
	1985	12	26	1,195	372	6.3	3.9	−3.1	1.9	3.0	0.4
	1986	10	25	1,261	568	2.9	2.7	−3.7	1.6	2.3	1.1
	1987	7	21	1,826	1,061	3.4	4.3	−8.0	2.0	−0.2	1.8
	1988	7	24	2,080	1,355	−1.4	3.9	−10.7	2.3	−2.8	2.4
Insolvent and Open	1984	170	33	407	45	not calculated		−3.0	0.2	2.8	0.1
	1985	164	32	656	51	6.6	0.7	2.0	2.9	3.8	1.9
	1986	161	32	475	54	6.9	0.7	3.6	0.3	5.2	0.2
	1987	158	33	484	55	4.2	0.8	3.2	0.3	13.5	0.5
	1988	153	34	557	66	8.1	1.0	4.1	0.7	14.3	0.6

Insolvent/RAP NW > 3% and Open	1984	69	41	504	88	not calculated		−2.2	0.3	4.1	0.1
	1985	68	41	564	100	7.8	1.1	3.2	0.5	5.0	0.4
	1986	66	41	599	104	7.2	0.9	5.1	0.6	6.2	0.5
	1987	65	41	584	103	4.0	0.9	4.7	0.5	6.5	0.3
	1988	62	41	667	126	8.2	1.3	4.8	0.5	6.6	0.3
Solvent and Closed	1984	22	4	160	40	not calculated		4.2	1.3	4.7	1.3
	1985	22	4	191	46	14.0	4.5	1.6	1.9	1.8	1.5
	1986	21	4	212	56	3.8	4.3	−6.8	4.0	−1.6	2.5
	1987	16	3	261	93	5.1	3.5	−11.6	4.9	−4.0	4.2
	1988	12	3	285	138	−2.2	4.4	−14.8	6.9	−10.2	7.5
Solvent and Open	1984	275	53	189	30	not calculated		5.4	0.4	7.1	0.4
	1985	275	54	207	30	13.7	1.0	7.3	0.2	2.4	0.1
	1986	274	55	231	33	11.4	0.6	7.9	0.2	6.8	0.2
	1987	265	56	251	37	7.4	0.6	7.8	0.2	7.5	0.2
	1988	260	57	279	43	8.0	0.6	7.6	0.3	7.5	0.2

Note: Except for market-value worth and total assets, all numbers are based on book values.

(continued)

Table 10.8 (continued)

		Nontraditional Assets[a] as % of TA		Traditional Mortgages as % of TA		Fixed-Interest Mortgages as % of TA		Adjustable-Rate Mortgages as % of TA		Delinquency Rate on All Mortgages, in percentages	
	Year-end	Mean	Std. Error of Mean	Mean	Std. Error of Mean	Mean	Std. Error of Mean	Mean	Std. Error of Mean	Mean	Std. Error of Mean
Insolvent and Closed	1984	24.5	2.5	60.4	2.1	43.0	2.2	20.0	2.2	3.7	0.6
	1985	25.2	1.7	55.4	1.9	34.3	1.8	27.2	2.2	5.2	1.1
	1986	25.7	1.5	52.4	2.0	33.8	2.1	25.8	1.9	6.0	0.9
	1987	23.2	1.6	56.2	1.8	34.7	2.1	26.7	2.2	5.6	0.9
	1988	21.8	1.6	59.5	2.1	32.8	2.3	31.9	2.4	4.7	0.8
Insolvent/RAP NW >3% and Closed	1984	27.1	7.8	57.0	5.7	37.0	5.3	28.5	5.3	3.5	1.0
	1985	22.0	3.7	56.4	4.4	32.2	4.1	29.6	5.1	6.3	0.3
	1986	24.4	3.5	50.6	4.4	32.7	2.5	24.6	3.9	6.0	0.1
	1987	24.4	4.0	53.4	3.9	36.2	4.0	23.8	4.1	6.7	0.3
	1988	23.9	3.6	53.0	5.6	32.9	4.5	30.0	4.8	7.2	0.3
Insolvent and Open	1984	16.3	0.6	68.9	0.9	51.1	1.1	17.1	0.8	1.7	0.1
	1985	18.7	0.8	64.9	1.0	42.9	1.2	24.5	0.9	1.8	0.1
	1986	19.3	0.9	62.7	1.0	38.2	1.2	28.2	1.0	2.0	0.1
	1987	20.0	0.9	64.6	1.0	35.9	1.2	33.3	1.2	2.2	0.2
	1988	20.2	0.9	65.2	1.0	31.8	1.2	37.8	1.3	2.2	0.2

Insolvent/RAP NW >3% and Open	1984	14.4	0.9	70.3	1.3	53.3	1.8	16.5	1.2	1.6	0.2
	1985	17.0	1.1	66.4	1.5	43.9	1.9	24.7	1.6	1.8	0.2
	1986	17.7	1.2	64.7	1.7	39.6	1.9	27.8	1.7	1.7	0.2
	1987	18.2	1.3	66.4	1.6	37.5	1.9	33.3	1.9	1.8	0.2
	1988	18.3	1.4	66.0	1.7	33.6	2.0	36.4	2.0	1.6	0.2
Solvent and Closed	1984	32.1	4.4	48.4	5.6	20.2	4.0	30.1	4.4	2.6	0.5
	1985	47.5	4.9	45.3	4.1	16.7	1.6	51.2	5.1	6.7	1.6
	1986	45.5	4.2	42.9	3.1	15.9	2.9	47.4	5.0	13.7	3.0
	1987	39.5	4.8	48.7	3.5	16.1	2.7	49.0	5.4	14.9	2.9
	1988	34.2	4.6	52.2	3.2	16.9	3.9	49.1	6.4	11.1	1.6
Solvent and Closed	1984	16.1	0.7	67.6	0.9	47.8	1.2	18.2	9.1	1.5	0.1
	1985	18.2	0.8	64.4	0.9	40.9	1.1	26.2	1.1	1.9	0.1
	1986	18.3	0.8	62.2	0.9	37.3	1.1	28.7	1.1	2.0	0.1
	1987	18.9	0.9	65.1	0.9	36.9	1.2	33.0	1.2	2.2	0.2
	1988	18.8	0.8	66.2	0.9	34.4	1.3	37.1	1.3	2.2	0.2

[a]Mortgages other than first 1–4 family loans, commercial and consumer loans, and real estate held for investment.

(continued)

Table 10.8 (continued)

		Delinquency Rate on Nonmortgages, in percentages		Passbook Deposits as % of Total Liabilities (TL)		Deposits Under $100,000 as % of TL		Deposits Over $100,000 as % of TL		Brokered Deposits as % of TL	
	Year-end	Mean	Std. Error of Mean	Mean	Std. Error of Mean	Mean	Std. Error of Mean	Mean	Std. Error of Mean	Mean	Std. Error of Mean
Insolvent and Closed	1984	3.3	0.2	5.6	0.4	74.2	1.8	11.3	1.3	2.2	0.8
	1985	4.2	0.4	5.2	0.4	75.4	1.7	10.2	1.1	1.8	0.6
	1986	5.0	0.3	6.2	0.5	73.7	2.0	9.7	1.3	1.5	0.5
	1987	5.3	0.2	6.2	0.5	75.0	2.5	6.8	1.1	2.1	0.8
	1988	6.2	0.2	5.7	0.5	73.5	2.7	6.4	1.3	2.7	1.2
Insolvent/RAP NW >3% and Closed	1984	1.2	0.5	5.4	0.7	77.5	3.5	10.8	2.5	1.5	1.3
	1985	6.6	0.5	4.9	0.7	73.2	3.8	12.4	2.8	3.1	1.6
	1986	2.1	0.8	6.4	1.0	70.6	4.2	12.1	3.9	3.2	1.5
	1987	6.9	0.3	6.2	1.0	73.2	7.7	8.3	3.6	4.9	3.3
	1988	6.5	0.2	5.7	0.9	71.7	7.7	8.9	4.5	5.3	4.4

Insolvent and Open	1984	1.4	0.2	7.3	0.3	81.9	1.0	8.5	0.7	0.5	0.2
	1985	2.3	0.2	6.8	0.2	83.0	0.8	7.9	0.4	0.3	0.1
	1986	2.6	0.3	7.4	0.3	81.1	0.9	8.7	0.5	0.2	0.1
	1987	2.1	0.3	7.9	0.3	79.6	0.9	8.1	0.4	0.5	0.1
	1988	2.6	0.2	7.7	0.6	83.5	5.5	10.0	2.2	0.6	0.1
Insolvent/RAP NW > 3% and Open	1984	1.7	0.5	7.8	0.4	84.8	1.2	7.3	0.7	0.4	0.2
	1985	1.6	0.4	7.3	0.4	84.7	1.1	6.9	0.5	0.3	0.2
	1986	2.5	0.9	7.7	0.4	82.9	1.2	7.4	0.5	0.2	0.2
	1987	1.6	0.4	8.4	0.5	80.7	1.4	7.4	0.5	0.5	0.2
	1988	2.4	0.7	7.5	0.5	77.8	1.6	7.5	0.5	0.5	0.3
Solvent and Closed	1984	1.8	0.4	5.3	2.1	71.2	3.4	19.1	2.9	4.3	0.1
	1985	6.2	1.1	5.3	2.2	75.6	3.5	16.1	3.0	4.2	0.2
	1986	10.0	1.1	6.8	2.3	79.6	3.1	11.9	2.3	3.1	0.2
	1987	5.8	0.7	5.4	1.5	80.8	3.5	7.7	0.1	3.3	0.2
	1988	12.0	0.8	5.9	1.7	81.8	3.5	6.2	0.4	4.3	0.2
Solvent and Open	1984	0.9	0.2	9.6	4.4	85.6	7.8	9.4	0.6	0.7	0.1
	1985	0.9	0.2	8.8	0.4	85.4	7.1	9.2	0.5	0.5	0.1
	1986	1.5	0.3	9.2	3.9	84.4	7.0	9.9	0.4	0.5	0.1
	1987	1.8	0.3	9.7	4.2	83.8	6.8	8.8	0.4	0.5	0.1
	1988	1.6	0.2	10.0	4.1	83.5	6.7	8.8	0.4	0.3	0.2

that met the FHLBB's informal definition of adequate solvency had a stronger incentive to take excessive risks, we subclassified the insolvent thrifts into those with RAP net worth of over 3 percent (RAP NW > 3%). The twelve insolvent/RAP>3% thrifts that subsequently closed constitute 24 percent of the total insolvent and closed group. The 69 open insolvent/RAP>3% thrifts are 41 percent of the insolvent and open group.[34]

Table 10.8 shows that the insolvent thrifts are significantly larger than the solvent thrifts, consistent with table 10.5. However, a striking finding revealed by table 10.8 is that the closed insolvent/RAP>3% group is over twice as large, on average, than the other insolvent thrifts. The 1987 and 1988 standard errors of the means are quite large because the data include one small thrift (total assets of about $35 million) and one very large thrift (with total assets of $4 billion in 1984 and $10 billion in 1988; the next largest thrift had $1.6 billion in assets). While this group had few members, they imposed large cost on the FSLIC.

The costs to the FSLIC (and, largely, to the taxpayers) are indicated by the negative market-value-to-total-asset percentages. All of the 50 insolvent and closed thrifts had negative market-value net worth in each year they were operating. However, about half of these thrifts had positive book-value net worth ratios in 1984, 1985, and 1986. These positive RAP net worth values appear to explain why the insolvent thrifts were allowed to continue operating. Most of the 22 solvent thrifts that were closed started their downward slide in 1986. Five of the 21 institutions still operating in 1986 were closed in 1987, and 4 were closed in 1988.[35] Most (over 75 percent) of the year-end 1984 insolvents that remained open (including those with RAP NW > 3%) became market-value solvent after 1984, and almost all had positive book-value net worth.

On average, the insolvent thrifts that closed had negative growth rates in all five years. Although the closed insolvent/RAP>3% groups grew, on average, in 1985, 1986, and 1987, the maximum annual rate at any of these thrifts did not exceed 24 percent. Thus, high growth does not appear to have been a strategy followed by or permitted to insolvent thrifts that were closed. Year-end 1984 insolvent thrifts that remained open grew, on average, in each year studied, as did the year-end 1984 solvent thrifts, with one exception. Average negative growth rates were experienced by the solvent and closed thrifts in 1988. Although this group of thrifts grew at an average rate of 14.0 percent in 1985, this rate is not significantly different from the 13.7 percent rate experienced by the solvent thrifts that were not closed. Thus, growth, as such, does not appear to be related to initial solvency or closure.

Investment in nontraditional assets (other than first mortgages secured by 1–4 family residential property, commercial and consumer loans, and real estate held for investment) is significantly higher at thrifts that closed than at thrifts that survived. The closed thrifts also experienced significantly higher delinquency rates, possibly in association with their high level of nontraditional investment. However, the insolvents did not noticeably increase their nontraditional investments between 1984 and closure, in contrast to the 22 solvents that closed. These institutions not only began with high levels of nontraditional assets, but dramatically increased these investments through 1986. The overwhelming type of nontraditional asset held by the 1984 solvent-and-closed group is commercial mortgages, which constitute from one-half to almost all of the nontraditional assets. Mortgages on multifamily residential property is the next most popular nontraditional asset. Commercial loans of between 10 and 15 percent of total assets were held by only five thrifts; the percentage is less than 4 percent at the rest. Consumer loans are less than 10 percent of assets at all except four thrifts (one of which had a quarter of its assets in consumer loans). Few of these thrifts had real estate held for investment; as a percentage of total assets, only two had as much as 9 percent, one had 7 percent, three had between 1 and 3 percent, and fifteen had none. The delinquency rates on both mortgage and nonmortgage loans experienced by the 1984 solvent-and-closed thrifts are higher than those experienced by the other thrifts, substantially so for 1986, 1987, and 1988. Thus, reasons for the failure or survival of 1984 solvent southeastern thrifts appears to be poor loan underwriting and possibly regional downturns, and may be related to deregulation that allowed higher investment in commercial mortgages.

Two other factors also appear important. First, 14 of the 22 thrifts (64 percent) were chartered after 1979; six of these (27 percent) were chartered after 1982. Two of these post-1982 thrifts were heavily (over 70 percent) invested in nontraditional assets. Second, the mean market-value net worth to assets ratios in 1984 and 1985 for the solvents that closed are 4.2 and 1.3 percent, compared to the ratios for open solvents of 5.4 and 7.3 percent in those years. One of the solvent and closed thrifts has a 30.0 percent ratio in 1984, which declined to 12.6 percent in 1985 and 5.4 percent in 1987, as it grew. With this newly chartered thrift omitted, the mean ratio for the group at year-end 1984 is 3.0 percent and 1.1 percent at year-end 1985. Thus, although it seems clear that rapid movement into nontraditional assets was the proximate cause of the solvent thrifts' failure, these thrifts' newness and net worth weakness may have been the proximate cause of their undertaking this strategy. It also should be noted that this group of thrifts are only 4 percent of the total number in the Southeast operating at year-end 1984.

All of the groups tended to decrease their holdings of fixed-interest-rate 1–4 family mortgages as percentages of total assets over the period, while increasing their holdings of adjustable-interest-rate mortgages (ARMs). The largest holdings of ARMs relative to total assets is by the solvent and closed group. These thrifts may have experienced relatively large delinquency rates and operating losses because they underwrote large amounts of ARMs with below-market "teaser" rates without qualifying mortgagors at the higher post-teaser rates. Unfortunately, the data required to test this hypothesis are not available.

Passbook deposits, which give rise to the core deposit intangible asset, are somewhat higher percentages of total liabilities at open than at the closed thrifts, on average. However, these average only from 5 to 10 percent of total liabilities. Deposits under $100,000, which average above 70 percent of total liabilities, are significantly greater at the open compared to the closed thrifts. These fully insured deposits did not increase as a percentage of total liabilities at the insolvent thrifts, and decreased at the insolvent/RAP>3% thrifts, which is inconsistent with the insolvency-incentive, deposit-insurance hypothesis. Indeed, fully insured deposits on average are highest at the solvent and open thrifts. Deposits over $100,000 tended to decrease as a percentage of total liabilities at the closed thrifts (both insolvent and solvent). They were replaced largely with advances from the Federal Home Loan banks. Finally, brokered deposits were under 5 percent, on average, for all groups in all years. However, they were highest among the insolvent/RAP>3%, and solvent and closed thrifts.

10.5.4 The Behavior of Thrifts that Were Market-Value Insolvent or Solvent at Year-End 1986 and That Subsequently Were Closed or Open through 31 March 1990

Many of the thrifts recovered substantially by year-end 1986, as interest rates declined. Consequently, we calculated the percentages of net worth, assets, and liabilities (presented in table 10.9) for the 496 thrifts still operating as of year-end 1986. In contrast with the earlier period, 81 percent of the thrifts were solvent and open (compared to 53 percent at year-end 1984), while the insolvent and open group decreased from 33 percent to 6 percent. About the same percentages of thrifts were insolvent and closed (8 compared to 10 percent in 1984) and solvent and closed (4 percent in both years).

The distribution of total assets among the groups is similar to that found for the 1984 insolvents: the solvent thrifts are smaller and the largest thrifts are those that are insolvent/RAP>3%. The total asset growth rates are negative, on average, for the insolvent and closed thrifts, but are significantly positive and roughly similar for the other groups. All of the closed insolvent thrifts remained insolvent until they were closed, while the open insolvents improved their solvency over the years: half are solvent by year-end 1988. A similar pattern is found for the open and closed insolvent/RAP>3% groups. On the other hand, three-quarters of the solvents that were closed became insolvent in 1987 and all but two are insolvent in 1988. However, most of these thrifts show positive RAP net worth through year-end 1988.

The average percentages of nontraditional assets to total assets are similar for the 1986 and the 1984 insolvents. The mortgage and nonmortgage delinquency rates similarly are significantly higher for the closed than for the open thrifts. But these rates are not higher for the insolvent/RAP>3% groups or for the insolvent and open groups compared to the solvent and open groups. Thus, while credit losses appear to have been a cause of thrifts' losses and

Table 10.9 **The Condition of the 496 Thrifts That Were Insolvent or Solvent at Year-end 1986 And That Subsequently Were Closed or Open through 31 March 1990**

		Number of Thrifts		Total Assets (TA) (book value in $ millions)		Annual Growth in TA (percentages)		Market-Value Net Worth as % of TA		RAP Net Worth as % of TA	
	Year-end	Number	% in Year	Mean	Std. Error of Mean	Mean	Std. Error of Mean	Mean	Std. Error of Mean	Mean	Std. Error of Mean
Insolvent and Closed	1986	42	8	573	157	−5.7	2.2	−10.0	2.1	−2.9	1.5
	1987	34	7	635	239	−4.6	2.4	−11.8	2.1	−5.5	2.2
	1988	26	6	839	384	−5.6	2.8	−14.4	3.3	−9.6	3.8
Insolvent/RAP NW > 3% and Closed	1986	10	24	994	579	3.2	4.1	−6.3	1.8	3.7	0.2
	1987	8	24	1,334	959	7.9	3.4	−7.7	1.7	1.0	1.8
	1988	5	19	2,434	1,918	7.1	4.3	−4.6	1.8	3.2	0.8
Insolvent and Open	1986	31	6	564	128	6.9	2.4	−2.4	0.4	2.9	0.5
	1987	30	6	510	116	2.5	1.6	−2.1	0.6	3.2	0.4
	1988	27	6	583	135	9.1	3.2	−1.3	0.7	3.7	0.4
Insolvent/RAP NW > 3% and Open	1986	21	68	559	162	8.0	2.9	−2.1	1.0	3.9	0.2
	1987	20	67	458	128	1.5	1.7	−2.0	0.8	4.1	0.4
	1988	17	63	537	155	9.1	4.4	−1.3	1.0	4.1	0.4
Solvent and Closed	1986	19	4	367	90	9.7	3.5	3.4	0.7	3.4	0.7
	1987	16	3	437	124	9.5	2.3	−5.0	2.8	2.2	0.9
	1988	15	3	481	139	4.4	2.7	−4.9	1.7	0.5	0.7
Solvent and Open	1986	404	81	303	30	10.0	0.5	6.9	0.2	6.3	0.1
	1987	393	83	325	32	6.5	0.5	6.6	0.2	6.9	0.1
	1988	386	85	368	39	7.9	0.5	6.8	0.3	7.0	0.2

(continued)

Table 10.9 (continued)

		Nontraditional Assets[a] as % of TA		Traditional Mortgages as % of TA		Fixed-Interest Mortgages as % of TA		Adjustable-Rate Mortgages as % of TA		Delinquency Rate on All Mortgages, in percentages	
	Year-end	Mean	Std. Error of Mean	Mean	Std. Error of Mean	Mean	Std. Error of Mean	Mean	Std. Error of Mean	Mean	Std. Error of Mean
Insolvent and Closed	1986	29.2	2.1	50.9	2.2	30.1	2.5	31.2	2.9	10.1	1.8
	1987	23.9	1.7	55.8	2.0	32.1	2.5	30.3	3.2	7.8	1.2
	1988	21.5	1.6	60.0	2.3	32.1	2.9	33.9	3.8	5.5	1.0
Insolvent/RAP NW > 3% and Closed	1986	22.7	4.1	50.1	5.1	30.4	6.0	25.6	6.8	6.8	2.1
	1987	17.7	2.9	56.7	4.3	38.2	6.4	25.3	7.7	5.5	2.2
	1988	16.4	3.7	57.4	3.4	34.9	5.9	26.3	7.8	1.0	0.4
Insolvent and Open	1986	22.8	1.8	53.8	2.0	26.8	2.3	31.1	2.4	2.9	0.4
	1987	22.9	1.5	59.4	2.1	28.7	2.6	35.3	2.8	3.0	0.6
	1988	24.7	1.6	56.2	2.2	24.3	2.2	38.1	3.0	2.8	0.4
Insolvent/RAP NW > 3% and Open	1986	21.4	2.3	53.0	2.6	25.9	2.9	30.6	2.9	2.8	0.5
	1987	21.2	2.0	57.9	2.7	25.7	2.7	36.2	3.5	3.3	0.9
	1988	22.8	2.2	55.0	3.2	22.9	3.0	38.2	4.3	3.0	0.5
Solvent and Closed	1986	39.9	4.5	45.4	2.9	22.1	3.1	38.0	4.7	5.5	1.0
	1987	38.0	4.9	49.9	3.2	21.6	3.0	41.2	4.5	9.9	2.8
	1988	32.9	4.1	52.6	2.6	22.1	2.9	42.0	3.6	8.1	1.5
Solvent and Open	1986	18.4	0.6	63.1	0.7	38.5	0.9	28.3	0.8	1.9	0.1
	1987	19.1	0.7	65.3	0.7	37.2	0.9	33.0	0.9	2.2	0.1
	1988	19.0	0.6	66.5	0.7	34.1	1.0	37.3	1.0	2.1	0.1

	Year-	Delinquency Rate on Nonmortgages, in percentages		Passbook Deposits as % of Total Liabilities (TL)		Deposits Under $100,000 as % of TL		Deposits Over $100,000 as % of TL		Brokered Deposits as % of TL	
		Mean	Std. Error of Mean	Mean	Std. Error of Mean	Mean	Std. Error of Mean	Mean	Std. Error of Mean	Mean	Std. Error of Mean
Insolvent and Closed	1986	7.5	1.2	6.0	0.5	75.2	2.1	10.0	1.5	2.2	0.8
	1987	6.2	1.1	6.4	0.6	76.5	2.7	6.7	1.1	3.1	1.0
	1988	8.4	1.7	6.4	0.6	74.0	3.1	6.0	1.4	3.2	1.4
Insolvent/RAP NW > 3% and Closed	1986	3.6	2.3	5.8	1.5	69.7	2.8	9.2	1.5	8.6	2.7
	1987	2.2	1.0	5.6	1.8	65.6	5.1	8.9	3.0	7.8	3.8
	1988	2.4	1.0	5.0	2.2	55.5	6.3	10.5	6.2	7.0	6.0
Insolvent and Open	1986	2.7	0.8	6.6	0.6	78.2	2.0	8.4	1.2	0.6	0.6
	1987	2.7	1.2	6.9	0.7	78.6	1.9	7.0	0.7	1.1	0.5
	1988	2.0	0.4	6.1	0.6	76.3	2.1	6.9	0.8	1.2	0.6
Insolvent/RAP NW > 3% and Open	1986	1.8	0.5	7.6	0.7	76.8	2.5	8.9	1.6	0.7	0.4
	1987	1.7	0.4	8.0	0.9	77.6	2.3	7.4	1.0	1.0	0.6
	1988	1.9	0.5	7.2	0.8	76.0	2.4	7.4	1.0	1.1	0.8
Solvent and Closed	1986	3.5	1.5	7.2	2.4	76.9	3.0	11.7	2.0	1.6	1.3
	1987	3.8	1.1	4.9	1.3	77.7	3.3	8.1	2.0	1.1	0.4
	1988	6.9	1.7	4.8	1.3	79.3	2.9	6.9	1.4	3.7	1.5
Solvent and Open	1986	1.9	0.3	8.6	0.3	83.6	0.6	9.5	0.4	0.4	0.1
	1987	1.8	0.2	9.2	0.3	82.5	0.6	8.7	0.3	0.5	0.1
	1988	2.0	0.2	8.8	0.4	84.0	2.2	9.4	0.9	0.7	0.1

Note: Except for market-value net worth and total assets, all numbers are based on book values.

[a]Mortgages other than first 1–4 family loans, commercial and consumer loans, and real estate held for investment.

failure, these data do not provide support for the insolvency-incentive hypothesis. However, of the 19 thrifts that were solvent at year-end 1986 but subsequently were closed, 7 (37 percent) were insolvent at year-end 1984, and the mean market-value net worth to assets of the group at year-end 1986 is 3.4 percent, compared to 6.9 percent for the solvent and open thrifts. Thus, net worth weakness may have played a role in the investment strategy of the 1986 solvent thrifts that closed.

Over the years 1986 through 1988, the percentage of fixed-interest-rate 1–4 family mortgages to total assets remained fairly stable, on average, with the exception of a significant decrease in the solvent and open group (which still has about the highest percentages). ARMs percentages are similar to those found for the 1984 insolvencies: lowest for the insolvent/RAP>3% and closed group, but the differences among the groups are not statistically significant.

Among the liabilities, passbook deposits as a percentage of total liabilities is significantly higher at the solvent and open groups and insolvent/RAP>3% and open groups, and somewhat higher at the insolvent and open group, which may explain, in part, why they were able to survive. As with the year-end 1984 insolvents, deposits under \$100,000 as a percentage of total liabilities is significantly higher at the solvent and open group, which is inconsistent with the deposit-insurance hypothesis. Deposits over \$100,000 as a percentage of total liabilities are somewhat higher, on average, at the thrifts that were closed. However, as table 10.7 shows, these partially insured deposits decreased considerably as the thrifts neared closure. Finally, brokered deposits are a very small percentage of total liabilities (most thrifts had none). The average percentages are highest for the insolvent/RAP>3% that closed, but this mean is due to three of the ten in 1986, two in 1987, and one in 1988 (which funded 31 percent of its liabilities with brokered deposits).

10.5.5 Excessive Risk-Taking, Solvency, Type of Ownership, and Change in Ownership

Risk-taking may take the form of holding a duration-unbalanced portfolio of financial assets and liabilities, investing in assets with highly variable net cash flows not offset by cash flows from other assets, or taking excessive credit risk (as discussed below). These behaviors are hypothesized to be a function of the market-value solvency of a thrift, an insolvent thrift appearing to be solvent as measured by its RAP net worth being at least 3 percent of its assets, whether the thrift is a mutual or stockholder owned, and whether ownership or management changed in the recent past.

Interest-Rate Risk

The year-end Freddie Mac commitment rate on thirty-year fixed-interest first mortgages is 13.4 percent in 1983, 13.1 percent in 1984, 10.8 percent in 1985, 9.3 percent in 1986, 10.6 percent in 1987, and 10.8 percent in 1988. Thus, the improvement in the solvency of the least-solvent thrifts from 1984 to 1985 shown in table 10.5 may have been the result of these thrifts taking interest-rate risk from which they benefited when interest rates declined. Although we would have preferred using the duration of the thrifts' portfolios, these data are not available. Instead, we used the one-year-repricing gap between assets and liabilities to measure thrifts' propensity toward interest-rate-risk taking, and assume that this gap is representative of the entire portfolio. The gap and the independent variables are measured as of the end of a year to measure ex ante propensity toward taking interest-rate risk. The following relationship is examined (all variables are taken from year-end financial reports: consequently, the year subscript is omitted):

$$(5) \qquad GAP1 = b_1\, TA + b_2\, NTA + b_3\, NWM + b_4\, IN\text{-}RAP3\%{*}TA + b_5\, CC{*}TA + b_6\, M{*}TA,$$

where

*GAP*1 = gap (difference) between the amount of assets and liabilities that are repriced within one year;

TA = total assets at book value, included as a measure of size;

NTA = nontraditional assets (mortgages other than first 1–4 family loans, commercial and consumer loans, and real estate held for investment), included to account for relevant assets differences, because these assets tend to be interest-rate repriced within a year;

NWM = net worth at market value;

IN-RAP3% = (RAP net worth ÷ total assets at book value = *NWR*) less (net worth ÷ total assets [multiplied by *TA* to account for scale], both at market value = *NWM*) if $NWR > 3\%$ and $NWM < 0\%$; 0 otherwise;

CC = 1 if there was a change in control in the current year or in any past year beginning in 1983, the earliest year for which we have data (multiplied by *TA* to account for scale); 0 otherwise; and

M = 1 if a mutual (multiplied by *TA* to account for scale); 0 if stockholder owned.

The variables in equation (5) were divided by *TA* to reduce heteroscedasticity, and the following regression was computed for each of the five years, 1984 through 1988:

$$(5') \qquad GAP1 / TA = b_1 + b_2\, NTA / TA + b_3\, NWM / TA + b_4\, IN\text{-}RAP3\% + b_5\, CC + b_6\, M.$$

The observations include all thrifts operating during the year, including those that failed or merged in the following year.

Table 10.10 presents the mean of the dependent variable and the coefficients estimated, together with the probability that the coefficients are greater than

Table 10.10 One-Year Interest-Rate Gap: One-Year-Maturity Assets less Liabilities ÷ Total Assets (in percentages), Coefficients [Probability Coefficient > 0]

Year-end	1984	1985	1986	1987	1988
Dependent variable mean	−36.4	−23.9	−18.1	−24.1	−20.2
Intercept	−43.0	−31.5	−25.1	−36.9	−33.8
[total assets]	[<.01]	[<.01]	[<.01]	[<.01]	[<.01]
Nontraditional ÷ total assets at	0.29	0.23	0.19	0.42	0.44
book values, in percentages	[<.01]	[<.01]	[<.01]	[<.01]	[<.01]
Net worth ÷ total assets at mar-	1.10	0.50	0.43	0.82	0.87
ket values, in percentage	[<.01]	[<.01]	[<.01]	[<.01]	[<.01]
RAP NW if > 3% less MV NW	0.17	0.11	−0.18	0.14	0.91
if < 0, percentage of TA; or 0	[.46]	[.82]	[.58]	[.68]	[.04]
Change in control, current and	−4.30	5.35	1.09	2.13	−0.21
years through 1983	[.34]	[.11]	[.67]	[.36]	[.92]
Mutual rather than stock	−1.80	−2.15	−2.70	−1.19	−1.09
	[.18]	[.16]	[.06]	[.42]	[.47]
Adjusted R^2	0.26	0.09	0.08	0.21	0.22
	[<.01]	[<.01]	[<.01]	[<.01]	[<.01]
Number of observations	507	499	487	464	442

Note: All variables measured at year-ends.

zero (in square brackets).[36] As expected, the average one-year gap is negative, indicating that the southeastern thrifts would tend to gain if interest rates declined. The average gap is greatest at year-end 1984—36.4 percent of total assets. It declined by about one-third in 1985 and then by one-quarter in 1986, after which it increased to the 1985 level and then declined again in 1988. The intercept (which is the coefficient of *TA*) indicates that *GAP* is approximately proportionate to the size of the institution, but is not completely due to size alone. The thrifts' holding of nontraditional assets is significantly related to their gap throughout the period, indicating that higher levels of these assets enabled thrifts to reduce their negative gap, and hence their exposure to interest-rate risk.

Market-value net worth is very significantly positively related to *GAP.* The coefficient is largest, by far, in 1984. Thus, it appears that the most insolvent thrifts tended to take the most interest-rate risk, particularly in 1984. This finding is consistent with the solvency improvement reported in table 10.5. However, the insignificant coefficient for *IN-RAP3%* indicates that this subset of the insolvent thrifts did not take advantage of their appearance of solvency, perhaps because the supervisory authorities were not fooled or because the thrifts' managers expected a rise in rates.[37]

Perhaps surprisingly, change in control is not reflected in greater interest-rate-risk taking. The coefficient of mutual-rather-than-stock ("mutual") also is insignificant in the regression. However, as shown in table 10.11, mutual is significantly negatively related to nontraditional assets. Furthermore, the means of *GAP1* are significantly more negative at mutuals than at stocks, for

Table 10.11 **Nontraditional Assets as a percentage of Total Assets, Coefficients [Probability Coefficient > 0][a]**

Year-end	1985	1986	1987	1988
Dependent variable mean	20.3	20.4	20.3	19.9
Intercept	17.8	20.5	20.7	18.7
[total assets]	[.<.01]	[.<.01]	[.<.01]	[.<.01]
Net worth ÷ total assets at market values, in percentages	−0.28	−0.68	−0.65	−0.36
	[.01]	[.<.01]	[.<.01]	[.<.01]
RAP NW if > 3% less MV NW if < 0, percentage of TA; or 0	−0.73	−0.80	−1.11	−0.19
	[.<.01]	[.06]	[.<.01]	[.53]
Change in control, current and years through 1983	3.3	−1.5	3.8	0.2
	[.48]	[.62]	[.13]	[.94]
Mutual rather than stock	−12.8	−11.5	−10.0	−8.2
	[.<.01]	[.<.01]	[.<.01]	[.<.01]
Adjusted R^2	0.16	0.19	0.20	0.14
	[.<.01]	[.<.01]	[.<.01]	[.<.01]
Number of observations	500	488	465	444

[a]Nontraditional assets include mortgages other than first 1–4 family loans, commercial and consumer loans, and real estate held for investment. Nontraditional and total assets at book values. Independent variables measured as of the beginning of the year.

each year 1984 through 1988. The medians (which is a preferable measure, as *GAP1* at some thrifts is positive) also are more negative. These findings are consistent with the coefficient for mutual reported in tables 10.3 and 10.4, which indicated that mutuals had significantly greater market-value losses through 1984 and conforms with conventional wisdom that mutuals tend to be "portfolio" lenders as opposed to selling off their mortgage production. Despite the collinearity between nontraditional and mutual, we included both variables in equation (5) to estimate the relative importance of each variable with respect to *GAP1*. From this equation, it appears that mutuals' taking greater interest-rate risk is related primarily to their holding relatively lesser amounts of nontraditional assets, as is shown next.

Investment in Nontraditional Assets

The Garn–St Germain Act of 1982 permitted federally chartered thrifts to invest in much higher proportions of nontraditional assets—mortgage loans other than first 1–4 family loans, commercial and consumer loans, and real estate held for development—than they previously could hold. We seek to explain the southeastern thrifts' investment in these assets with a regression similar to equation (5′):

$$(6)\quad NTA\,/\,TA = c_1 + c_2\,NWM\,/\,TA + c_3\,IN\text{-}RAP3\% + c_4\,CC + c_5\,M;$$

where the variables are defined as for equations (5) and (5′).

The observations include all thrifts operating during the year, including those that failed or merged in the following year. The mean of the dependent variable, the coefficients calculated, and the probability that the coefficients are greater than zero for each year, 1985 through 1988, are presented in table 10.11.

The solvency of a thrift (*NWM/TA*) is significantly negative related to its holdings of nontraditional assets, on average. Furthermore, the magnitude of the relationship in 1986 is more than twice that in 1985. However, the magnitudes are small. The coefficients of *NWM/TA* indicate that a $100 decrease in net worth is associated with a $28 increase in nontraditional assets in the beginning of 1985, $68 in 1986, $65 in 1987, and $36 in 1988. The coefficient of *IN-RAP3%* is significantly negative except in 1988, indicating that these institutions tended to invest less in nontraditional assets as the difference between market and RAP net worth widened, *cet. par.*

Change of control does not appear related to investment in nontraditional assets. Mutuals, though, tended to invest significantly less in nontraditional assets than stocks. This finding is consistent with mutuals taking more interest-rate risk through traditional mortgage lending, as we report above.

Excessive Credit Risk

In the absence of federal deposit insurance, the risk-neutral managers and owners of a wealth-maximizing thrift would lend funds such that the present value of the expected net cash flows was positive. For such decision makers, risk taken ex ante is not excessive. However, deposit insurance, unless priced to reflect the insurance agency's risk, gives thrifts an incentive to make loans and investments with greater variances of expected cash flows. The owners of stocks and managers of mutuals have a put option to the FSLIC that increases in value as market-value net worth approaches zero and as the variance of cash flows increases. In particular, thrifts with zero or negative net worth have nothing to lose from taking risks. Consequently, they can gain from investing in high-variance assets that have negative expected present values. Alternatively, thrifts could hold assets on which credit losses are expected, but be compensated in the form of up-front fees and higher interest rates.[38] We consider this possibility in the following section.

We do not have data on the ex ante expected cash flows from loans made by thrifts. We indirectly test the hypothesis that thrifts tended to take excessive risks by regressing the year-end delinquency rate on mortgages (and, separately, on nonmortgages—commercial and consumer loans) on variables measuring their solvency, change in control, stock versus mutual ownership, and variables designed to account for relevant exogenous and endogenous factors, all measured at the beginning of the year:

$$(7) \quad DELM_t = d_0 + d_1\, MT_{t-1} + d_2\, MT^2_{t-1} + d_3\, 1\text{–}4FM_{t-1} + d_4\, \Delta REP_{st} * MT_{t-1} + d_5\, NWM_{t-1} + d_6\, IN\text{-}RAP3\%_{t-1} * MT_{t-1} + d_7\, CC_{t-1} * MT_{t-1} + d_8\, M_{t-1} * MT_{t-1},$$

where

$DELM_t$ = delinquencies on mortgages in total at time *t;*
MT_{t-1} = mortgages in total at time $t-1$;
$1\text{–}4FM_{t-1}$ = 1 to 4 family residential mortgages at time $t-1$;
ΔREP_{st} = change in an index of real estate prices in state *s* during time *t*, in percentages; and the other variables are defined as for equations (5) and (5′).

Total mortgages (*MT*) is included as a variable to account for the expected positive relationship between loans and the delinquencies on those loans. The square of *MT* is included to test the hypothesis that the relationship is not linear, perhaps because of economies of scale in originating and monitoring mortgages. The *1–4FM* variable is included to test the hypothesis that traditional mortgages are less risky than other types of mortgages. Alternatively, *1–4FM* includes ARMs, on which greater delinquencies may have been experienced if thrifts wrote mortgages with low "teaser" rates that became delinquent when, subsequently, interest rates increased. *ΔREP* is included in the regression to account for exogenous changes in real estate prices, as these could affect delinquencies. We had to use statewide indexes that were assigned to thrifts according to the location of their home office, even though thrifts often hold mortgages on out-of-state property.[39] *ΔREP, IN-RAP3%, CC,* and *M* are multiplied by *MT* because their effect on delinquencies should be proportional to the amount of mortgages held by a thrift. The independent variables are taken as of the beginning of the period, because they are designed to predict the delinquencies that occur by the end of the period. This procedure does not capture delinquencies on loans made as a result of, say, low market-value net worth in one year that become delinquent in a subsequent year. However, the data presented in tables 10.7, 10.8, and 10.9 indicate that delinquencies tend to increase in the year after a thrift becomes very insolvent. Furthermore, a thrift that is insolvent in one year usually is insolvent or very weak in preceding years; hence, a thrift's solvency in one year is a proxy for its solvency in previous years.

As is done similarly for other relationships, the variables are divided by TM_t to reduce heteroscedasticity. Consequently, equation (7′) was estimated:

$$(7') \quad DELM_t / TM_{t-1} = d_0 / TM_{t-1} + d_1 + d_2\, MT_{t-1} + d_3\, 1\text{–}4FM_{t-1} / TM_{t-1} + d_4\, \Delta REP_{st} + d_5\, NWM_{t-1} / TM_{t-1} + d_6\, IN\text{-}RAP3\%_{t-1} + d_7\, CC_{t-1} + d_8\, M_{t-1}.$$

The mean of the dependent variable, the coefficients calculated, and the probability that the coefficients are greater than zero for each year, 1985 through 1988, are presented in table 10.12. Before discussing the findings, we should note that delinquencies at year-end are not a complete measure of loan losses,

Table 10.12 **Mortgage Delinquencies as Percentage of Total Mortgages Regressed On Market-Value Net Worth and Other Variables, Coefficients [Probability Coefficient > 0][a]**

Year-end	1985	1986	1987	1988
Dependent variable (mortgage delinquencies as percentage of total mortgages) mean	2.38	2.84	2.88	2.52
Intercept ($ thousands)	9.60	12.00	13.74	8.78
[total mortgages]	[<.01]	[<.01]	[<.01]	[<.01]
Total mortgages	−2.1 E−7	−5.3 E−7	−7.8 E−7	−5.8 E−7
[total mortgages squared]	[.59]	[.27]	[.07]	[.04]
1–4 Family mortgages as	−0.07	−0.09	−0.10	−0.06
percentage of total mortgages	[<.01]	[<.01]	[<.01]	[<.01]
Real estate price index (statewide),	−0.19	−0.09	−0.19	−0.14
percentage change	[.01]	[<.01]	[<.01]	[<.01]
Market-value net worth as	−0.10	−0.19	−0.16	−0.13
percentage of total mortgages	[<.01]	[<.01]	[<.01]	[<.01]
RAP NW if > 3% less MV NW if	−0.04	−0.05	−0.09	0.00
< 0, percentage of TA; or 0	[.34]	[.58]	[.13]	[.96]
Change in control, current and	−0.30	−0.02	2.18	0.76
years through 1983	[.79]	[.99]	[<.01]	[.11]
Mutual rather than stock	−0.68	−1.06	−0.64	−0.66
	[.06]	[.02]	[.10]	[.03]
1 ÷ Total mortgages	15,331	19,929	16,008	10,935
($ thousands) [intercept]	[<.01]	[<.01]	[.01]	[.01]
Adjusted R^2	0.15	0.22	0.29	0.29
	[<.01]	[<.01]	[<.01]	[<.01]
Number of observations	499	487	464	442

[a]Independent variables measured as of the beginning of the year.

even if delinquencies equal expected loan losses, as we assume. Not included in this measure are loans written off as uncollectible during the year. In addition, as we note above, offsetting income and operating expenses, which are trade-offs for loan losses, are not included in the dependent variable.

As expected, mortgage delinquencies are significantly positively related to mortgages. However, the greater magnitude of the coefficients compared to the mean of the dependent variable indicates that other factors mitigate this relationship. In 1987 and 1988, one mitigating factor is the amount of mortgages; the negative sign on d_2 (the coefficient of total mortgages, TM, in equation [7′], which is the square of TM in the basic equation [7]) indicates economies of scale with respect to delinquencies, at least for those years. One-to-four family residential mortgages appear to have significantly lower delinquencies, *cet. par.* The change in the index of real estate prices (ΔREP) has significant negative coefficients in all years. Thus, it appears that exogenous factors played a role in a thrift's absorbing credit losses (which we measure with delinquencies).

The coefficients of market-value net worth are significantly negative, indicating that the greater a thrift's solvency, the less likely it was to have credit losses. However, the magnitude of the coefficients are small; a 1 percent decrease in net worth is associated, on the average, with at most a 0.22 percentage point increase in mortgage delinquencies, which is less than 10 percent of the mean amount of delinquencies. The variable designed to measure a particular propensity toward excessive risk taking, *IN RAP3%,* has very insignificant coefficients in all years except 1987, when it has an unexpected negative sign.

Prior change in control is not significantly related to mortgage delinquencies, except for 1987, when there is a strong positive significant relationship. Mutuals have significantly lower delinquencies than stockholder-owned thrifts, on average.

We computed a similar set of regressions for delinquencies on nonmortgage (commercial and consumer) loans. The adjusted *R* squares ranged from zero to two percent. None of the variables was consistently statistically significant, with the exception of the amount of nonmortgage loans, where the coefficients are very close in magnitude to the means of the dependent variable. (The means of nonmortgage delinquencies as a percentage of delinquencies are 1.92 in 1985, 2.48 in 1986, 2.25 in 1987, and 2.48 in 1988.) The only other variable with a statistically significant coefficient is stock versus mutual ownership, where mutuals had significantly lower delinquencies than stocks in 1985 and 1986 (1.00 and 1.90 percentage points lower, on average), and lower delinquencies on consumer than on commercial loans in all years except 1988.

As noted above, delinquencies are not a sufficient measure of excessive risk-taking. Thrifts that experience high delinquency ratios could have been compensated with commensurately higher fees and interest payments. They also could have incurred lesser amounts of operating expenses and accepted greater amounts of delinquencies. In addition, loans written off during the year were not considered. Consequently, we turn now to an analysis of thrifts' net profits, which should summarize the joint effects of credit losses, income, and operating expenses.

10.5.6 The Determinants of Market-Value Net Profits

The ultimate measure of whether investment in deregulated assets, deposits acquired through brokers, change of control, and type of ownership strengthened or weakened thrifts is the net gain or loss in their market-value net worth. We measure this gain or loss by the change in the market value of net worth adjusted for dividends and additional capital investments. This measure is superior to accounting net profits, which do not include gains and losses from changes in market values. However, it suffers (as does GAAP) from being an ex post measure. Unexpected changes in interest rates are reflected in changes in market-value net profit, and thus this variable can have more to do with whether thrifts took interest-rate risk and won or lost the gamble than with whether they were well or badly operated. We deal with this problem by computing market-value net profit over years in which interest rates were relatively stable.

Investment in Deregulated Assets and Other Factors

We consider first the effect on market-value net profit of thrifts' investment in traditional residential mortgages (*TM*, which includes mortgage-backed securities) and nontraditional assets (*NTA*, which includes mortgages other than 1–4 family loans, commercial and consumer loans, and real estate held for investment). Variables representing the source of funds, such as brokered and over $100,000 (jumbo) deposits, are not included in this analysis (they are considered below). To the extent that funding sources are associated with traditional or nontraditional mortgages, the net profit advantage or disadvantage should accrue to that investment. In addition, we consider the effect on net profits of ownership type and change in control, as well as propensity toward risk-taking, as measured by *IN-RAP3%*. Net profits also are affected by exogenous factors, particularly unexpected changes in real estate prices, which we measure as the percentage change of an index of real estate prices by state (ΔREP_s).

We examine the following relationship:

$$(8) \quad MVNP_t = b_0 + b_1\, TM_{t-1} + b_2\, NTA_{t-1}, + b_3\, \Delta REP_{st} * TA_{t-1} + b_4\, IN\text{-}RAP3\% * TA_{t-1} + b_5\, CC_t * TA_{t-1}, b_6\, M_t * TA_{t-1},$$

where

$MVNP_t$ = market-value net profit, the change in the market value of equity adjusted for dividends and additional capital investments through time *t;*

TM_{t-1} = traditional residential mortgages (including mortgage-backed securities) at market value at the beginning of period *t;* and the other variables are as defined for equations (5) and (7).

Total assets is not included in the regression because traditional mortgages and nontraditional assets constitute almost all of most thrifts' total assets. Consequently, the coefficients estimated for these variables include the effects on net profits of other, nonspecified assets (as well as liabilities) that are correlated with traditional mortgages and nontraditional assets. To reduce heteroscedasticity, the variables are divided by total assets at book value (*TA*) at the beginning of the period (time $t-1$), and the following regression was run for years 1985 through 1988, individually:

$$(8') \quad MVNP_t / TA_{t-1} = b_0 / TA_{t-1} + b_1\, TM_{t-1} / TA_{t-1} + b_2\, NTA_{t-1} / TA_{t-1} + b_3\, \Delta REP_t / TA_{t-1} + b_4\, IN\text{-}RAP3\% + b_5\, CC_t + b_6\, M_t.$$

The observations include all thrifts operating during a year, including those that failed or merged in the following year, with the exception of eight thrifts not identified by location. Because market-value net profit is measured over a year, we can include only 1985 through 1988. To account for the possibility that a single year's net profit is subject to noise, we also measure market-value net profit averaged over two-year periods, 1985–86 and 1987–88.[40] The means of the dependent variable, the coefficients calculated, and the probability that the coefficients are greater than zero are presented in table 10.13.

The average market-value net profit per dollar of book-value assets, shown by the mean of the dependent variable, exhibits considerable change over the years studied. In 1985 the average profit rate is 3.24 percent. It then declines to 0.17 percent in 1986, −1.16 percent in 1987, and −0.77 percent in 1988. The large profits in 1985 are due to that year's decrease in interest rates.

Table 10.13 Market-Value Net Profit as a Percentage of Total Assets Regressed On Traditional Mortgages, Nontraditional Assets, and Other Variables, Coefficients [Probability Coefficient >0][a]

Year-end	1985	1986	1987	1988	1985–86	1987–88
Dependent variable (market-value net profit ÷ total assets): mean	3.24	0.17	−1.16	−0.77	1.74	−0.88
Traditional mortgages ÷ total assets, in percentages	0.06	0.02	−0.01	−0.01	0.04	−0.02
	[<.01]	[<.01]	[.15]	[.01]	[<.01]	[<.01]
Nontraditional assets ÷ total assets, in percentages	−0.07	−0.05	−0.07	−0.04	−0.06	−0.05
	[<.01]	[<.01]	[<.01]	[<.01]	[<.01]	[<.01]
Net worth ÷ total assets in market value, in percentages	−0.29	0.00	0.09	0.09	−0.22	0.09
	[<.01]	[.89]	[<.01]	[<.01]	[<.01]	[<.01]
RAP NW if > 3% less MV NW if < 0, percentages of TA; or 0	0.16	0.12	0.20	0.22	0.08	0.22
	[.02]	[.34]	[.02]	[<.01]	[.14]	[<.01]
Change in control, current and years through 1983	−0.13	0.16	−2.52	−0.45	−0.56	−1.05
	[.91]	[.85]	[<.01]	[.36]	[.57]	[.01]
Mutual rather than stock	1.27	1.47	0.64	0.66	1.31	0.69
	[<.01]	[<.01]	[.07]	[.03]	[<.01]	[<.01]
Real estate price index (statewide), percentage change	0.15	0.06	0.09	0.08	0.05	0.06
	[.06]	[.01]	[.07]	[.02]	[<.01]	[<.01]
1 ÷ Total assets[b] [intercept]	−12,654	−15,501	−4,702	−10,160	−4,888	−7,777
	[.07]	[.04]	[.55]	[.14]	[.41]	[.10]
Adjusted R^2	0.29	0.13	0.26	0.16	0.50	0.34
	[<.01]	[<.01]	[<.01]	[<.01]	[<.01]	[<.01]
Number of observations	499	487	464	442	487	442

[a]Market-value net profit = change in market-value net worth plus dividends less additional investments. Traditional mortgages = 1–4 family first mortgages and mortgage-backed securities, at book value. Nontraditional mortgages = other mortgages, commercial, and consumer loans, and real estate held for investment, at book value. Independent variables measured as of the beginning of the year.

[b]In thousands of dollars.

The regressions indicate that traditional mortgages are significantly positively related to market-value net profit in 1985 and 1986, negatively and significantly in 1988, and insignificantly negatively in 1987. This finding is verified by the two-year regressions (1985–86 and 1987–88). It also is consistent with the one-year *GAP*s reported in table 10.10, which show a greater negative gap at year-end 1984 than at the other year-ends, and with the observation that interest rates decreased through the first quarter of 1987. Thus, there is reason to believe that the greater profitability of traditional mortgages in 1985 and, to a lesser extent, in 1986 is due to thrifts with traditional mortgages (that tend to be fixed interest in 1984 and 1985, see tables 10.5, 10.8, and 10.9) winning an interest-rate-change gamble in those years, and losing it in 1987 and 1988.

Nontraditional assets are significantly negatively associated with annual market-value net profit in all years. On average, southeastern thrifts annually lost 4 to 7 percent of their investment in nontraditional assets. Over the two-year periods studied, the loss averages 6 and 5 percent.

A positive relationship between market-value net worth and market-value net profit is expected because the factor cost of capital is not recorded as an expense. The coefficients' market-value net worth is positive and statistically significant for 1987 and 1988, indicating that additional net worth yielded 9 percent, on average. However, the coefficient is negative and statistically significant for 1985. This finding appears due to the weaker thrifts having won their interest-rate-risk gamble in that year. The coefficients of the *IN-RAP3%* variable are positive and significant for all years except 1986. This finding is inconsistent with the hypothesis that these thrifts tended to make negative-value investments.

Change in control has a significant negative coefficient for 1987 and the two-year 1987–88 period; for the other years, the coefficients are very insignificant. Thus, there is only some evidence supporting the hypothesis that a change in control is detrimental to the deposit insurance fund. Mutuals had significantly higher net profits than stocks, particularly in 1985 and 1986. This finding is consistent with their taking greater interest-rate risk (as reported in table 10.10) and holding relatively less nontraditional assets (as reported in table 10.11). The mutuals also may obtain higher market-value net profits because they tend to be located in less competitive markets, as reported by Carhill and Hasan (1990). Finally, the change in real estate prices (ΔREP) is significantly positively related to market-value net profits in all years.

Insured-Deposit Growth and Brokered Deposits and Other Factors

It is alleged that thrifts took advantage of the increase in deposit insurance coverage from $40,000 to $100,000 per account in 1980 and removal of interest-rate ceilings on deposits in the following years to acquire interest-rate-sensitive funds that were invested in risky projects. An alternative to growth with fully insured deposits is growth with deposits over $100,000. These deposits often carry a premium because they are only partially insured by the FSLIC, and hence should result in lower net profits, *cet. par.* Another alternative considered particularly pernicious by the supervisory authorities is growth by means of brokered deposits.

We related the growth of thrifts' assets between mid-year 1982 and year-end 1984 to their market-value net worths at year-end 1984 (see tables 10.4 and 10.6). The regression coefficients and summary statistics reported are inconsistent with the hypothesis that insolvent thrifts grew more rapidly than solvent thrifts. If anything, the contrary appears to have occurred.

We now examine the relationship between the change in insured, partially insured, and brokered deposits and the thrifts' market-value net profits since 1984. For this purpose, we specified the following relationship:

$$(9)\quad \begin{aligned} MVNP_t = {} & b_0 + b_1\,\Delta ID_{t-1} + b_2\,\Delta PID_{t-1} \\ & + b_3\,\Delta BD_t + b_4\,NWM_{t-1} * TA_{t-1} \\ & + b_5\,IN\text{-}RAP3\% * TA_{t-1} \\ & + b_6\,M_t * TA_{t-1} + b_7\,CC_t * TA_{t-1}, \end{aligned}$$

where

ΔID = change in insured (under \$100,000) deposits;
ΔPID = change in partially insured (over \$100,000) deposits;
ΔBD = change in brokered deposits; and the other variables are defined as for equation (5).

Total assets (*TA*) is not included in this relationship because the sum of the deposits almost equals total assets. As is done earlier, all the variables are divided by *TA*, and we calculated the following regression for each year and for two-year average net profits:

$$(9')\quad \begin{aligned} MVNP_t / TA_{t-1} = {} & b_0\,1 / TA_{t-1} + b_1\,\Delta ID_{t-1} / TA_{t-1} \\ & + b_2\,\Delta PID_{t-1} / TA_{t-1} + b_3\,\Delta BD_t / TA_{t-1} \\ & + b_4\,NWM_{t-1} + b_5\,IN\text{-}RAP3\% + b_6\,M_t + b_7\,CC_t. \end{aligned}$$

Table 10.14 gives the coefficients and other statistics estimated from equation (9′). The coefficients for the change in fully insured deposits (deposits under \$100,000) are significantly positive for 1988 and the two-year period 1987–88, and not significant for the other years. The coefficients estimated also are very small. This finding indicates that thrifts that increased their funding through fully insured deposits experienced trivial market-value net gains. The coefficients for the change in partially insured deposits (over \$100,000) are positive and statistically significant for all years. This source of deposits is associated with market-value net profits. It may be that partially insured depositors sought out better-managed thrifts or that better-managed thrifts were able to attract partially insured deposits.

The coefficients on the change in brokered deposits are negative and significant only for 1988 and for the two-year period 1987–88; in the other years the coefficients are insignificant. On balance, the change in brokered deposits

Table 10.14 Market-Value Net Profit as a Percentage of Total Assets Regressed On Deposits and Other Variables, Coefficients (Probability Coefficient > 0][a]

Year-end	1985	1986	1987	1988	1985–86	1987–88
Dependent variable (net profit as a percentage of total assets): mean	3.24	0.17	−1.16	−0.77	1.74	−0.89
Change in deposits of < $100,000 as a percentage of assets	0.00 [.96]	−0.06 [.13]	0.05 [.12]	0.06 [.01]	0.04 [.46]	0.04 [.03]
Change in deposits of > $100,000 as a percentage of assets	0.16 [.01]	0.17 [<.01]	0.12 [.01]	0.18 [<.01]	0.39 [<.01]	0.15 [<.01]
Change in brokered deposits as a percentage of assets	0.02 [.83]	−0.11 [.24]	−0.12 [.13]	−0.15 [.03]	−0.09 [.34]	−0.25 [<.01]
Net worth ÷ total assets at market value, in percentages	−0.29 [<.01]	0.07 [.02]	0.06 [.02]	0.05 [.01]	−0.20 [<.01]	0.04 [.01]
RAP NW if > 3% less MV NW if < 0, percentage of TA; or 0	0.58 [<.01]	0.18 [.13]	0.13 [.14]	0.17 [.02]	0.33 [<.01]	0.12 [.08]
Change in control, current and years through 1983	−1.10 [.52]	−0.26 [.77]	−2.66 [<.01]	−0.62 [.21]	−0.14 [.33]	−1.23 [.01]
Mutual rather than stock	−0.32 [.49]	1.61 [<.01]	1.87 [<.01]	1.13 [<.01]	0.01 [.97]	1.41 [<.01]
1 ÷ Total assets[b] [intercept]	59,105 [<.01]	−4,006 [.56]	−1,312 [.09]	−17,355 [.01]	4,401 [<.01]	−1,436 [<.01]
Adjusted R^2	0.26 [<.01]	0.11 [<.01]	0.19 [<.01]	0.14 [<.01]	0.30 [<.01]	0.27 [<.01]
Number of observations	499	487	464	444	487	444

[a]Market-value net profit = change in market-value net worth plus dividends less additional investments. Independent variables measured as of the beginning of the period.
[b]In thousands of dollars.

seems to be weakly associated with lower market-value net profits and may reflect a reduced capacity to fund through local deposits.

The coefficients of market-value net worth, *IN-RAP3%*, change in control, and mutual rather than stock variables are similar in this regression as in the regression with asset values rather than deposits (equation [8′]), with one exception. The mutual-rather-than-stock dummy variable has an insignificant coefficient in 1985 when deposits are the other independent variables, but a significantly positive coefficient when assets are the other independent variables.

10.5.7 Deposit Growth and Solvency

We further test the "deposit-insurance" hypothesis by examining the relationship between the change in thrifts' deposits over a year and their market-

value net worth at the beginning of a year. The following relationships are specified:

(10a) $$\Delta ID_t = b_1\, NWM_{t-1} + b_2\, IN\text{-}RAP3\% * TA_{t-1} + b_5\, CC_t * TA_{t-1} + b_6\, M_t * TA_{t-1},$$

and

(10b) $$\Delta PID_t = b_1\, NWM_{t-1} + b_2\, IN\text{-}RAP3\% * TA_{t-1} + b_5\, CC_t * TA_{t-1} + b_6\, M_t * TA_{t-1},$$

where the variables are as defined for equation (9) above.

All variables were divided by TA_{t-1} before calculations were made, and the following regressions were calculated:

(10a′) $$\Delta ID_t\, /\, TA_{t-1} = b_1\, NWM_{t-1}\, /\, TA_{t-1} + b_2\, IN\text{-}RAP3\%_{t-1} + b_5\, CC_t + b_6\, M_t,$$

and

(10b′) $$\Delta PID_t\, /\, TA_{t-1} = b_1\, NWM_{t-1} + b_2\, IN\text{-}RAP3\% * TA_{t-1} + b_5\, CC + b_6\, M_t.$$

The means of the dependent variables, the coefficients estimated, and the probability that the coefficients are greater than zero are given in table 10.15.

The change in fully insured deposits averages 10.2 percent in 1985, but then drops to 3.0 percent in 1986, and becomes so small as to be insignificant in 1987 and 1988. The coefficient estimated for market-value net worth in 1985 is positive, significant, and large, indicating that growth in insured deposits was greatest at the more solvent thrifts. The coefficients are significant but much smaller and positive in 1986, and negative in 1987 and 1988. With respect to partially insured deposits, the coefficient for 1985 indicates that the more solvent thrifts tended not to grow with deposits over $100,000 in 1985, but did use these deposits in the other years. However, the coefficients are small in magnitude, though statistically significant. The coefficients in *IN-RAP3%* are insignificant for both kinds of deposits, except for 1985 fully insured deposits. The significant positive coefficient and large magnitude gives some evidence that these thrifts took advantage of deposit insurance to grow in that year. Thereafter, their growth may have been restrained by the supervisory authorities.

Change in control is positively associated with deposit growth, but the relationship is statistically significant only in 1988 for fully insured deposits and in 1986 for partially insured deposits. Mutuals had a significantly lesser propensity than stocks to grow with fully insured deposits in all years, and a positive (though lesser) propensity to grow with partially insured deposits than stocks in all years. This finding is consistent with stocks offering more risk to depositors.

Table 10.15 **Change in Deposits as a Percentage of Total Assets Regressed On Market-Value Net Worth and Other Variables, Coefficients [Probability Coefficient > 0][a]**

Year-end	1985	1986	1987	1988
A. Fully Insured Deposits (under $100,000)				
Dependent variable (percentage change in deposits to total assets): mean	10.2	3.0	−0.3	1.1
Net worth ÷ total assets at market value, in percentages	3.55 [<.01]	0.21 [<.01]	−0.46 [<.01]	−0.37 [<.01]
RAP NW if > 3% less MV NW if < 0, percentage of TA; or 0	1.13 [.02]	−0.28 [.45]	−0.12 [.27]	−0.30 [.22]
Change in control, current and years through 1983	6.30 [.55]	−3.80 [.19]	1.00 [.66]	7.70 [<.01]
Mutual rather than stock	−12.6 [<.01]	−8.5 [<.01]	−8.0 [<.01]	6.2 [<.01]
Adjusted R^2	0.46 [<.01]	0.16 [<.01]	0.14 [<.01]	0.14 [<.01]
B. Partially Insured Deposits (over $100,000)				
Dependent variable (percentage change in deposits to total assets): mean	−0.4	0.3	−1.1	−2.2
Net worth ÷ total assets at market value, in percentages	−0.14 [<.01]	0.13 [<.01]	0.06 [.04]	0.03 [.04]
RAP NW if > 3% less MV NW if < 0, percentage of TA; or 0	−0.08 [.41]	−0.07 [.63]	−0.03 [.57]	0.01 [.92]
Change in control, current and years through 1983	1.50 [.45]	3.70 [<.01]	−1.10 [.27]	0.70 [.14]
Mutual rather than stock	1.4 [.01]	1.9 [<.01]	2.6 [<.01]	0.7 [<.01]
Adjusted R^2	0.05 [<.01]	0.07 [<.01]	0.14 [<.01]	0.02 [<.01]
Number of observations	507	496	473	453

[a]Independent variables measured as of the beginning of the period.

10.6 Implications of the Analysis for the Hypotheses

1. Unbalanced Durations of Assets and Liabilities—Interest-Rate Risk

The losses measured for thrifts operating at year-end 1984 indicate that the increase in interest rates in the preceding years was responsible for a large portion of their losses. Over this period, we estimate that the southeastern thrifts lost 5.3 percent of their assets, or $8,078 million. Over three-quarter of the institutions suffered reductions in net worth that were not recorded according to RAP. Not surprisingly, most of the decline was due to mortgages, predominantly on 1–4 family homes. These losses were offset, somewhat, by increases in the value of the thrifts' core-deposit intangible asset related to their passbook-deposit liabilities. (See table 10.2 for details.) We regressed the change in net worth on total assets, total assets squared, state location

of the thrifts, and on their mutual or stock form of ownership (see table 10.3). The net worth change and amount of market-value net worth also was regressed on these variables (except state), on the mid-year 1982 amounts of book-value net worth, passbook deposits, and 1–4 family mortgages, and on growth in assets over the period (see tables 10.4 and 10.6). The larger thrifts suffered the greatest losses. Mutuals had significantly greater losses than stocks. Losses in net worth and lower amounts of market-value net worth are significantly associated with low initial book-value net worth and low passbook deposits. Perhaps surprisingly, asset growth is slightly associated with lesser losses and higher levels of market-value net worth.

As we show in section 10.7, interest-rate-induced losses dominate the losses through 1984 taken by southeastern thrifts. Despite these losses, only 31 of the 517 thrifts operating at year-end 1984 were closed (another 31 voluntarily merged with other institutions).

Additional interest-rate declines in 1985 and 1986 reduced the thrifts' insolvency considerably. On average, the 1984 insolvent thrifts that were operating through year-end 1988 became solvent in 1985 and 1986 (see table 10.5). However, not included in these numbers are 31 thrifts that failed through year-end 1988. All but one of these that failed in 1985 and 1986 were market-value insolvent at year-end 1984, as were slightly over half of those that failed in 1987 and 1988 (see table 10.7).

2. *Excessive Risk-Taking By Economically Insolvent and Weak Thrifts*

The data support the hypothesis that many thrifts' pre-1984 insolvency and later solvency are related to interest-rate risk-taking, particularly in 1985 (see table 10.10). Indeed, as we discuss above, this appears to be the principal reason that insolvent operating thrifts became solvent, on average, in 1985 and 1986.

However, the data strongly reject the hypothesis that insolvent thrifts grew more than solvent thrifts between mid-year 1982 (just before passage of the Garn–St Germain Act) and year-end 1984. Nor is growth in assets after 1984 a function of the market-value net worth of the thrifts. To the contrary, the most insolvent thrifts, including those that failed, grew at a slower rate than the solvent ones.

Most of the data studied also do not support the hypothesis that insolvent thrifts increased their investment in nontraditional assets (mortgages other than 1–4 family first mortgages, commercial and consumer loans, and real estate held for investment) in an effort to gamble their way to solvency. At year-end 1984, the insolvent thrifts held somewhat higher percentages of multifamily and nonresidential mortgages to total assets than did solvent thrifts. Very low percentages of commercial loans and trivial amounts of real estate held for investment were on the books of any southeastern thrifts. Consumer loans were slightly higher at the most insolvent thrifts. The growth in these nontraditional assets, though, is similar at thrifts grouped according to the ratios of net worth to assets, measured as market values (see tables 10.5 and 10.8). This conclusion also holds when insolvency is measured at year-end 1986 (see table 10.9). Regressions of nontraditional assets on market-value net worth (and other variables) using data from all thrifts operating in a particular year reveals significant negative coefficients, but the magnitudes are small.

Regressions of the annual change in fully insured deposits on market-value net worth shows a large, significant positive relationship (see table 10.15). No such relationship is found for the change in partially insured deposits (over $100,000). Nor are brokered deposits related to thrifts' market-value net worth or subsequent failure.

Delinquency rates on mortgages are not higher at the 1984 continuously operating insolvent thrifts over the years studied than at the solvent ones; delinquencies on other loans, though, are somewhat higher for the most insolvent group (see table 10.5). The failed thrifts, most of which were insolvent at year-end 1984, had considerably greater delinquencies after 1985, particularly on mortgage loans. Regressions of mortgage delinquencies on market-value net worth using data from all thrifts operating in a particular year also find a significant negative relationship (see table 10.12), which supports the tabular data showing higher delinquencies at the insolvent thrifts that were closed. Thus, although the insolvent thrifts did not hold higher amounts of nontraditional assets, those assets they held appear to have been riskier (as measured by delinquencies) than those held by more solvent thrifts.

The net effect of the actions taken by and the impact of events on thrifts is their net profit or loss. We measured this change in wealth as the change in the market-value of net worth adjusted for dividends and new investments. Regressions of this variable on market-value net worth at the beginning of a year or two-year period show significant though small positive relationships for 1986, 1987, and 1988 (see tables 10.13 and 10.14). Thus, it appears that insolvent thrifts did not, on average, take actions that resulted in net losses. This finding is inconsistent with the hypothesis.

3. Overspecialization in Mortgage Loans—Insufficient Diversification and Declines in Economic Conditions

We were able to test this hypothesis only with a statewide index of real estate prices. Changes in the index are significantly negatively related to delinquencies in 1986, 1987, and 1988 (see table 10.12). The real estate index change is not significantly related to market-value net profit, though. Assuming that this latter result is not due to the crude nature of the variable, the experience of the southeastern thrifts in the period studied does not support this hypothesis.

We were not able to relate directly the 1986 change in the income tax statute to losses incurred by thrifts. Delinquencies on mortgages increased substantially in 1987 and 1988 among the continuously operating thrifts (see table

10.5) and at the thrifts that failed in 1988. However, delinquencies also were high at the failed thrifts in 1986 and 1985, and increased on nonmortgage loans in 1987 and 1988 (see table 10.7). Thus, the data only support the need for further study.

4. Deposit Insurance and the Removal of Interest-Rate Ceilings on Savings Deposits

As we note above, growth in assets both before and since 1984 is not related to the solvency of the thrifts studied. We examined the data more closely by regressing the change in fully and partially insured deposits on market-value net worth and other variables. A large significant positive relationship was found for fully insured deposits in 1985 and a small positive significant relationship in 1986 (see table 10.15). But small negative significant relationships between the change in insured deposits and solvency were found for 1987 and 1988. A small significant negative relationship between partially insured deposits (over $100,000) and solvency was found for 1985, and small significant positive relationships for the other years. The change in partially insured deposits is significantly positively related to market-value net worth, which indicates that the more-solvent thrifts were able to attract such funds and put them to good use.

On the whole, the data do not support the hypothesis, at least for the period studied. By mid-year 1982, at least, the supervisory authorities may have constrained opportunistic behavior by insolvent thrifts or the thrifts' managers may not have attempted such behavior, on average. However, it is clear that without deposit insurance the thrifts rendered insolvent by interest-rate increases would not have been able to remain open and to obtain additional deposits. Indeed, absent deposit insurance, thrifts may not have been structured so as to be exposed to interest-rate risk.

5. Deregulation of Asset Investments and Brokered Deposits

The findings discussed above for the "excessive risk-taking by insolvent thrifts" hypothesis do not indicate an inverse relationship between thrifts' solvency and growth in their investment in deregulated assets, which also is inconsistent with the "deregulation of assets" hypothesis. However, a negative relationship is revealed between holdings of nontraditional assets and market-value net profits annually averaging 5 to 6 percent of nontraditional assets. Thrifts that were solvent at year-end 1984 and that subsequently were closed (4 percent of the sample) had substantially higher investments in nontraditional assets than other thrifts in 1984 that increased considerably in 1985, although those that were insolvent and closed or remained open did not (see tables 10.8 and 10.9). Thus, the evidence is mixed. Delinquencies are importantly related to a thrifts' solvency (particularly among those that were closed), and differences in thrifts' asset choices appear sufficient to explain variations in delinquency rates. It should be noted, though, that thrifts rendered insolvent by interest-rate increases did not grow more since mid-year 1982 than solvent thrifts (see tables 10.4 and 10.6). Thus, on average, insolvent thrifts did not or were not permitted to use the deregulation of interest rates for deposit growth to fund excessively risky assets.

Brokered deposits are a somewhat larger percentage of total liabilities at closed thrifts (see tables 10.8 and 10.9). However, a detailed analysis of these thrifts reveals that this average is due to a few institutions only (see table 10.7). A significant inverse relationship between the change in brokered deposits and market-value net profits was found only for 1988. Thus, it does not appear that brokered deposits played much of a role at southeastern thrifts.

On the whole, we conclude that the southeastern thrifts' failures are primarily due to the damage done by the high interest rates of the early 1980s; most of the failures in the late 1980s were thrifts that became insolvent during the early 1980s. At most, 30 percent of the Southeast's 1985-through-first-quarter-1989 failures (22 of 72) survived the sharp interest-rate increases with their solvency intact, but then lost heavily by investing in deregulated assets. We have reason to suspect that many of these 22 may have actually been insolvent prior to 1984, but gained the appearance of solvency because our market-value model overstates the present value of high interest-rate loans when delinquencies are delayed or underreported. Furthermore, 64 percent of the 22 thrifts were newly chartered, which may have contributed to their failure. Thus, while we can estimate an upper limit on the percentage of the Southeast's failures caused by deregulated-asset investments, we cannot preclude the possibility that almost all failures in fact were caused by the 1979–81 interest-rate run up or the difficulties faced by newly chartered thrifts in the following years.

6. *Risk Aversion and Preference of Mutual Compared to Stock Thrifts*

Mutual thrifts incurred significantly larger interest-rate-increase-induced losses through 1984 than did stocks (see tables 10.3 and 10.4) and had larger negative one-year maturity gaps at year-end 1984, which subjected them to additional interest risk. When interest rates decreased in 1985 and 1986, mutual thrifts benefited. Mutuals tended to hold lower proportions of nontraditional assets to total assets (see table 10.11) and had lower delinquencies (see table 10.12). They also obtained lower amounts of fully insured deposits and slightly higher amounts of partially insured deposits than did stock thrifts, *cet. par.* (see table 10.15). On balance, in the period studied, this strategy apparently resulted in their having higher market-value net profits in 1986, 1987, and 1988, and possibly in 1985 (see tables 10.13 and 10.14).

The data studied are consistent with the conclusion that mutuals tend to hold traditional assets and are more conservative than stocks, a strategy that benefits them when interest rates do not increase unexpectedly, as they did before 1982, or decrease unexpectedly, as they did in 1985 and 1986.

7. Fraud, Self-Dealing, Incompetence, and Inadequate Supervision

Change in control is alleged as a source of thrift failures, particularly ones that impose considerable costs on the deposit insurance fund. We tested this hypothesis by including in relevant regressions a dummy variable measuring a change in ownership or senior management in 1983 and subsequent years. The coefficient of this variable is insignificant with respect to interest-rate risk as measured by the one-year gap (see table 10.10), holdings of nontraditional assets (see table 10.11), mortgage delinquencies (see table 10.12), market-value net profit (see tables 10.13 and 10.14), and change in deposits (see table 10.15), with a few exceptions. The exceptions are a significant positive relationship with delinquencies in 1987, the change in fully insured deposits in 1988, and the change in partially insured deposits in 1986, and a significant negative relationship to market-value net profit in 1987.

We could not test the inadequate supervision hypothesis directly. However, insolvent thrifts tended to grow less than the solvent thrifts and did not invest excessively in nontraditional assets. These findings are consistent with the conclusion that the supervisory authorities in District 4 were diligent in preventing market-value insolvent thrifts, on average, from taking excessively large risks, thereby imposing higher costs on the FSLIC.

10.7 Failure and Survival

Failure for thrifts may be defined in two ways. One is economic insolvency, the other is closure or involuntary merger by the supervisory authorities. We used both definitions. A comparison of the 455 thrifts that were not closed from year-end 1984 through year-end 1988 with those that were closed during this period (see tables 10.5 and 10.7) reveals that, on average, the closed thrifts were significantly insolvent at the beginning of the period and in every year until closure. The thrifts that were insolvent at year-end 1984 had significantly lower book-value net worths and lower amounts of passbook deposits and somewhat higher amounts of 1–4 family mortgages (all relative to assets) as of mid-year 1982 than did solvent thrifts (see tables 10.4 and 10.6). The 1987 and 1988 closed thrifts also incurred or recognized large losses from delinquencies in the year before they were closed, which no doubt increased the FSLIC's costs. They had higher levels of adjustable-interest-rate mortgages and were larger than the operating thrifts. They held about the same proportions of traditional mortgages. Thus, their principal distinction was initial insolvency and subsequent large credit losses.

We studied the thrifts additionally by examining financial ratios for those that were solvent or insolvent at year-end 1984 and that were closed or open through 31 March 1990, the latest date we could use (see table 10.8). We also studied a subset of the insolvent thrifts—those with RAP net worth above 3 percent—to determine if thrifts that met the FHLBB's informal definition of financial strength behaved differently from other insolvent thrifts. All the thrifts operating at year-end 1984 are included in this analysis, even though some ceased independent operations because of closure or voluntary mergers. The insolvent thrifts with RAP net worth above 3 percent (*IN-RAP3%*) that were closed are substantially larger than the other thrifts. As noted above, they did not appear to engage in opportunistic behavior; they did not grow more or invest more heavily in nontraditional assets, although they did obtain funds through brokers somewhat more than did the other thrifts.

The principal differences between the insolvent thrifts that were closed compared to insolvents that survived is substantially lower rates of growth (the failure thrifts declined in size, on average), higher proportions of nontraditional to total assets, lower initial (1984–85) fixed-interest-rate mortgages to total assets, lower later (1986–88) adjustable-rate mortgages to total assets, higher delinquency rates, slightly lower proportions of passbook deposits and fully insured deposits, and higher (though still small) relative amounts of brokered deposits. A comparison of 1984 solvent thrifts that were closed with those that survived reveals considerably larger proportions of nontraditional assets and adjustable-rate mortgages, much higher delinquency rates, about half the proportion of passbook deposits, substantially more brokered deposits, and much heavier reliance on deposits over $100,000 (at least in the years before they were closed).

Because the thrifts' solvency improved dramatically in 1985 and 1986 (see table 10.5), we examined the 1986, 1987, and 1988 financial ratios of those that still were insolvent at year-end 1986 (see table 10.9). The picture found for the 1984 insolvents is very similar, except that the insolvent thrifts that were not closed were, on average, still insolvent through year-end 1988. These probably represent losses to the deposit insurance fund (now the taxpayers). The relatively few thrifts that were solvent at year-end 1986 but subsequently closed (19, or 4 percent of the total number) had much higher proportions of nontraditional assets and delinquencies than the thrifts that remained open.

Hence, we conclude that the principal determinants of survival or failure among southeastern thrifts are, first, their year-end 1984 insolvency resulting from the increase in interest rates in 1979–81 and initial relatively low levels of net worth and passbook deposits and, second, credit losses. The interest-rate-induced losses were disproportionately borne by larger thrifts that appear to have grown before 1982 by expanding beyond their local market areas, perhaps due to the competitive conditions they faced. We do not know whether this expansion was induced by or resulted in low levels of net worth relative to assets, but these relatively low capital ratios provided them with an insufficient buffer to absorb the interest-rate-induced losses. Following 1984, interest-rate decreases resulted in gains to many insolvent thrifts. But investment in both traditional and nontraditional assets (primarily commercial and multifamily mortgage loans) on which credit losses were incurred by insolvent and solvent thrifts exacerbated the insolvencies and resulted in additional insolvencies. That credit losses were incurred on both types of assets suggests that generally poor lending, perhaps exacerbated by unexpected regional downturns, rather than deregulation of assets granted by the Garn–St Germain Act of 1982, is responsible for thrift failures. Growth permitted by the deregulation of interest rates or the increase in deposit insurance from $40,000 to $100,000 per account, does not appear to be responsible for the southeastern thrifts' insolvency.

10.8 The Annual Cost of Insolvency

To close the paper, we estimate the annual costs that the FSLIC (and, hence, taxpayers and solvent depositories and their customers) would have incurred had the 517 southeastern thrifts in operation at year-end 1984 been closed when they became market-value insolvent. For this exercise, we assume that our measure of market values provides a sufficient estimate of the costs the FSLIC would have had to assume. We should point out that this measure is deficient in several important respects. First, we measure market values in terms of present values of cash flows for financial assets and liabilities and book values for other assets and liabilities, as reported in the *Thrift Financial Reports*. If these numbers were misreported, intentionally or not, our estimates would be incorrect. The book values of fixed assets (such as buildings and equipment) probably do not equal their market values; however, these amounts are relatively small and are likely to understate market values because they are not adjusted for inflation. Second, our reduction in loan values to account for expected nonrepayment losses—the amount of delinquencies—is a crude metric. It is not clear, though, whether this over- or understates expected losses. Third, the costs do not include losses due to the deterioration of assets that are taken from the private sector into a government agency. These costs are higher for losses due to defaulted mortgages than to interest-rate increases because property acquired from defaulted mortgages often deteriorates in value when it is managed by government agents rather than property owners. Outstanding and current commercial real estate loans also tend to lose value after a thrift is taken over by a conservator or government agency because of their practice of calling the loans and refusing to extend additional credit. Finally, we do not include loss due to fraud that was not discovered until after a thrift was closed. Hence, the costs incurred by the FSLIC (now the FDIC and RTC [Resolution Trust Corporation]) are likely to exceed the numbers generated by our market-value model.

Table 10.16 and figure 10.1 show the losses the FSLIC would have incurred had market-value insolvent thrifts been closed plus the negative market values of the thrifts that were closed in each year 1984 through 1988. These amounts then are put on comparable basis for each year. We calculated these costs first

Table 10.16 Ex Post Annual Closure Costs (in $ millions), 1984–1988 (based on negative market-value net worth (NW) at year-end before closure)[a]

	1984	1985	1986	1987	1988
1984:					
Insolvents in operation at year-end	3,920	4,250	4,524		
1986 closures not 1984 insolvent[b]			3		
Total through 1986			4,527	4,833	
1987 closures not 1984 insolvent[b]				150	
Total through 1987				4,983	5,365
1988 closures not 1984 insolvent[b]					155
Total through 1988					5,520
1985:					
Closed in 1985 (NW 1984)[b]	150				
Insolvents in operation at year-end	2,109				
Total 1985		2,259	2,405	2,568	
1987 closures not 1985 insolvent[b]				15	
Total through 1987				2,583	2,780
1988 closures not 1985 insolvent[b]					155
Total through 1988					2,935
1986:					
Closed in 1986 (NW 1985)[b]	588				
1985 closures plus interest of 6.45%	160				
Total closures through 1986	748				
Insolvents in operation at year-end	1,841				
Total 1986			2,589	2,764	2,976
1988 closures not 1986 insolvent[b]					62
Total through 1988					3,038
1987:					
Closed in 1987 (NW 1986)[b]	518				
Prior closures plus interest of 6.77%	799				
Total closures through 1987	1,317				
Insolvents in operation at year-end	2,047				
Total 1987				3,364	3,621
1988:					
Closed in 1988 (NW 1987)[b]	265				
Prior closures plus interest of 7.65%	1,417				
Total closures through 1988	1,682				
Insolvents in operation at year-end	2,110				
Total 1988					3,792

[a] Previous year's cost compounded (earned forward) at one-year Treasury bill rate.

[b] Including interest for one-half year at one-year Treasury bill rate.

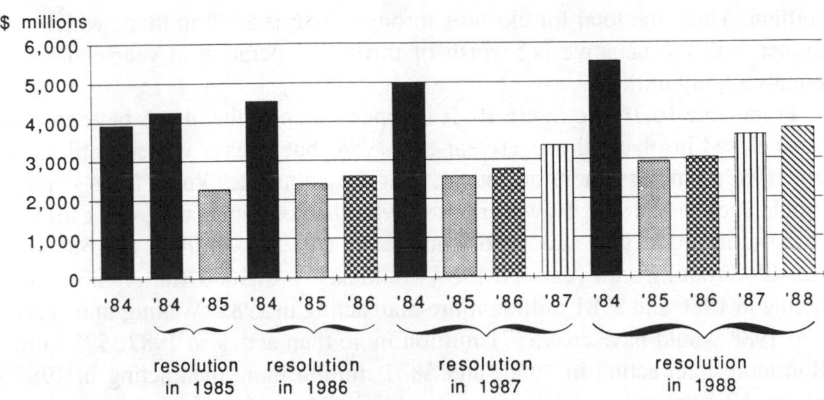

Fig. 10.1 Cost of resolution – current year and carryforward amounts had resolution been accomplished in previous year

by summing the negative market-value net worth of thrifts operating at year-end. For 1984 this is $3,920 million.[41] By year-end 1985, this amount (had it been incurred) would be equal to $4,250 million ($3,920 million plus interest at the Treasury bill rate of 8.42 percent). In fact, the 1984 insolvents that were not closed partially recovered and had market-value net worth of −$2,109 million. To this amount we add $150 million, the negative net worth of the 1984 insolvents that failed in 1985 (and hence were not operating at year-end) plus interest. (On the assumption that these thrifts failed at mid-year, on average, we added interest for six months at the U.S. Treasury bill rate.) Thus, the amount that the FSLIC would have incurred by year-end 1985 had it closed all insolvent thrifts is $2,259 million. The amount is less than the comparable 1984 amount of $4,250 million because of the decline in interest rates.

A walk through the 1986 calculations is necessary to illustrate an additional adjustment required to make the numbers comparable at a point in time. As we did before, the 1984 carryforward to 1985 of $4,250 million is increased by interest of 6.45 percent to $4,524 million. An additional $3 million is added to this figure to account for thrifts closed in 1986 that were not insolvent in 1984, and hence are not included in 1984 amounts but are included in the 1986 amounts to which the 1984 amounts are compared. The 1985 amount of $2,259 million is carried forward similarly, but there is no additional amount because all of the thrifts that closed in 1986 were insolvent at year-end 1985. The negative net worth of insolvents in operation at year-end 1986 is $1,841 million. The thrifts that failed in 1986 had negative net worth at year-end 1985 (plus a half-year's interest) of $588 million. For comparability with the data from 1984 and 1985, we carried forward the negative net worth of 1985 failures of $150 million plus interest for a full year of $10 million, a total of $160 million. Thus, the total for closures through 1986 is $748 million, which together with the negative net worth of thrifts in operation at year-end 1986 equals $2,589 million.

From table 10.16 and figure 10.1, it appears ex post that it was better not to have closed insolvent thrifts at year-end 1984, but to have waited until year-end 1985. This assumes, of course, that the authorities knew interest rates would decline in 1985. However, after 1985 the costs increased. We estimate that waiting until year-end 1986 would have cost $184 million ($2,589 less $2,405). Waiting until year-end 1987 would have cost $600 million more than acting in 1986 and $781 million more than acting in 1985. Waiting until year-end 1988 would have cost $171 million more than acting in 1987, $735 million more than acting in 1986, and $831 million more than acting in 1985. Figure 10.1 presents the data given in table 10.16 graphically.

An indication of the extent to which the losses presented in table 10.16 are due to pre-1985 factors (primarily interest-rate risk) is the amount of costs to the FSLIC (or the taxpayers) of closed and insolvent though still operating thrifts that are due to thrifts that were insolvent at year-end 1984. These figures are given in table 10.17 for each year, 1984 through 1988. In 1985 and 1986 almost all the losses (99 and 91 percent) are attributable to thrifts that were insolvent at year-end 1984. In 1987 the 1984 insolvents are responsible for 87 percent of the total, and in 1988 for 83 percent of the total. These percentages understate the effect of the pre-1985 interest-rate-induced losses,

Table 10.17 **Amount of Insolvency Cost (in $ millions) of Closed and Operating Thrifts Due to Thrifts that Were Insolvent at Year-End 1984**

	Total Amount	1984 Insolvents	Percentage of Total
1984:			
Insolvents in operation at year-end	3,920	3,920	100
1985:			
Closed in 1985	150	150	100
Insolvents in operation at year-end	2,109	2,097	99
Total	2,259	2,247	99
1986:			
Closures through 1986	748	745	100
Insolvents in operation at year-end	1,841	1,621	88
Total	2,589	2,366	91
1986			
Closures through 1987	1,317	1,164	88
Insolvents in operation at year-end	2,047	1,754	86
Total	3,364	2,918	87
1988:			
Closures through 1988	1,682	1,362	81
Insolvents in operation at year-end	2,110	1,777	84
Total	3,792	3,139	83

because this exercise considers thrifts that were brought close to insolvency by these losses to have become insolvent later from other causes.

10.9 Conclusions

In this paper we examine data on southeastern thrifts. From reports in other studies and from impressionistic press reports, we must conclude that our findings are somewhat at odds with the general perception of the causes and extent of the thrift debacle. It is reported that most of the losses incurred by the southwestern thrifts (particularly those in Texas) are due to defaulted commercial real estate loans for which the value of the collateral is much less than the amounts owed. Allegations of massive fraud also have been made, particularly with respect to some very large thrifts.

We were unable to determine whether the reports made to the Federal Home Loan Bank of Atlanta, on which we based our study, were fraudulently prepared. However, we examined opportunistic behavior, defined as thrifts taking advantage of expanded investment powers and funding risky assets with federally insured money. In the aggregate, we conclude that insolvent thrifts did not expand more rapidly than did solvent thrifts and, in general, did not take greater risks. At the margins, we found some examples that the thrift charter was taken advantage of and that several of these extreme cases proved to be the most costly in terms of resolution. But the fact that this behavior was not characteristic of southeastern thrifts indicates that, in this region at least, existing controls generally were effective. The principal reason that many thrifts ultimately were closed, we found, is that they were initially weak and could not absorb the losses they incurred in the early 1980s due to high interest rates. Later decreases in interest rates offset some of the losses, but were insufficient in part because they occurred after thrifts had reduced the duration of their portfolios, principally by shifting into adjustable-rate mortgages. The remaining deficits could not subsequently be overcome by normally profitable operations.

In short, we draw the following conclusions:

- The most important cause of the thrift debacle, at least in the Southeast, is losses incurred as a result of the increase in interest rates in 1979–81.
- Deposit insurance is not a proximate cause of insolvencies and losses, except in that it allowed the thrift industry to subject itself to interest-rate risk while holding low levels of capital. Absent deposit insurance, it is doubtful that thrifts would so heavily invest funds derived from short-term liabilities in long-term fixed-interest mortgages.
- Insolvent thrifts did not take advantage of the deregulation of interest rates and brokered deposits to grow excessively.
- Deregulation of assets (primarily commercial real estate and multifamily mortgage loans) played a role in the losses incurred by some thrifts, particularly newly chartered thrifts and those with low (though positive) levels of

net worth at year-end 1984, but this was generally subsumed under portfolio-wide credit problems. Furthermore, investment in nontraditional assets tends to reduce exposure to interest-rate risk. Had interest rates gone up instead of down during the period studied, losses incurred by thrifts with lower proportions of nontraditional assets might have exceeded the credit losses experienced by those with relatively more of these assets.

- Change in control of thrifts after 1982 had some negative effect on their net profits (measured on a market-value basis) in only one year (1987). (We do not have data on change in control before 1983.)
- Changes in real estate prices and perhaps in the tax law are inversely associated with higher delinquency rates and directly associated with market-value net profits.
- Credit losses (measured by delinquencies) during a year are directly associated with failures after 1986, and inversely related to thrifts' market-value net worth and 1–4 family mortgages at the beginning of the year.
- Most of the losses incurred by southeastern thrifts through 1988 are the result of interest-rate-risk losses and the insolvent but operating thrifts' cost of funding their negative net worth.

Notes

1. The Financial Institutions Reform, Recovery, and Enforcement Act (FIRREA) of 1989 transformed the Federal Savings and Loan Insurance Fund (FSLIC) into the Savings Association Insurance Fund (SAIF), and transferred the assets of the Federal Deposit Insurance Corporation (FDIC) to the Bank Insurance Fund (BIF). Both funds and insolvent S&Ls and banks now are administered by the FDIC. Premiums on deposits for S&Ls increased from 20.8 basis points to 23 basis points in 1991–93. Premiums for banks increased from 8.3 basis points to 12 basis points in 1990 and to 15 basis points in 1991.

2. Kane overstates the negative net worth, as he deducts his estimate of the interest-rate-caused decrease in mortgage values from book net worth, which does not include unbooked intangible assets, such as charter value, mortgage-servicing rights, and the value of core deposits. (The measurement of these assets is described below.) Kane's estimate of 1983 aggregate net worth is negative $73 billion.

3. As is explained next, RAP net worth is greater than GAAP net worth.

4. See Barth and Bradley (1989, table 3) for details.

5. See Benston (1985, 14) for details.

6. See Benston (1985, 84–85) for details.

7. Thrifts with tangible capital of at least 6 percent could hold direct investments and "equity risk investments" (land loans and nonresidential construction loans with loan-to-value ratios over 80 percent) equal to three times tangible capital. Thrifts that met regulatory capital requirements but with less than 6 percent tangible capital could hold these assets in amounts not exceeding the greater of 3 percent of assets or two-and-one-half times the thrift's tangible capital. Thrifts not meeting regulatory capital requirements were prohibited from holding such assets without approval from federal regulators. Also, additional capital equal to 10 percent of the assets must be held.

8. The description of the hypotheses should be read with the caveat, *ceteris paribus,* assumed.

9. There actually are not tangible accounting *principles*. This commonly used term refers to GAAP net worth less intangible assets, primarily goodwill, whether purchased in an arm's length market transaction or recorded as a result of a supervisory merger.

10. See Benston and Kaufman (1990) for citations to works on which this conclusion is based.

11. The IRS application of the QTL should not be confused with the regulatory application of the Competitive Equality and Banking Act (CEBA) of 1985, which required regulators to enforce a QTL but which had not been implemented before it was superceded by the FIRREA QTL.

12. See Horvitz (1989) for a very good descriptive account of the failures of Texas banks and S&Ls.

13. It is possible, though, that the solvent S&Ls held much more diversified portfolios, and hence avoided losses resulting from local economic declines.

14. Casual observers claim that the removal of interest-rate ceilings increased costs to depository institutions which resulted in their incurring losses that led to failures. It is true that deposit interest-rate ceilings can, in the short run, result in transfers of wealth from savers with relatively interest-rate-inelastic savings supply functions to S&Ls and banks with locational advantages. However, the ceilings induced the development and promotion of alternatives (most notably MMMFs), which also benefited from computer developments that lowered costs. Consequently, had deposit-ceiling rates not been removed, S&Ls would have suffered greater losses from disintermediation or increased borrowing from unregulated sources (such as jumbo CDs, which were exempt from the Regulation Q ceiling).

15. See Flannery (1989) for a model that explicitly includes these costs.

16. "Regulation of Direct Investments by Insured Institutions," 51 *Fed. Reg.* 32925.

17. See Barth, Benston, and Wiest (1990) for an explication and critique of FIRREA.

18. See, for example, Pizzo, Fricker, and Muolo (1989), Pilzer (1989), and a series of articles in the *Houston Post* claiming that the CIA and the Mafia were involved in S&L failures.

19. An FDIC summary of bank failures between 1934 and 1958 concluded: "In approximately one-fourth of the banks, defalcation or losses attributable to other financial irregularities by officers or employees appear to have been the primary cause of failure. Such irregularities have been responsible for most of the cases since World War II" (FDIC 1958, 29). Benston (1973) analyzed the 56 bank failures that occurred from January 1958 through April 1971. He reports that "most of the reasons for bank failures were fraud, defalcation and similar irregularities on the part of bank officers and, occasionally, lesser employees. Inept or poor management, which was adjudged responsible for from a quarter to a half of bank failures before the Great Depression, . . . has been a very small cause of bank failures in recent years" (pp. 39–40). The Comptroller of the Currency (1988) published an evaluation of 171 national bank failures from 1979 through 1987, and compared these to 38 healthy and 51 rehabilitated banks. This study found that "insider abuse . . . was a significant factor leading to failure in 35 percent of the failed banks. About a quarter of the banks with significant insider abuse also had significant problems involving material fraud" (p. 9). However, the principal problems identified were overly aggressive, incompetent management and weak boards of directors.

20. Also see Garcia (1988, table 4) for a comparison of GAAP-solvent and -insolvent thrifts as of 30 September 1986.

21. The preceding brief review of studies necessarily obscures some possibly im-

portant anomalies revealed in those studies, and this summary suffers even more from compression. Hence, it should be read with caution.

22. As of year-end 1988, only seven of the thrifts in our study held more than 1.0 percent of their assets in junk bonds, and none held more than 1.6 percent. We do not know whether these junk bonds were held in subsidiaries (in which event they would be valued at market) or as investment securities (in which event we would discount their cash flows at the agency rate). Discounting at the agency rate results in an overstatement of about 28 percent for a 10-year security, which would overstate assets at the thrift with 1.6 percent in junk bonds by no more than 45 basis points.

23. The ratio of the change in asset value to net worth is not a useful measure because many of the net worth balances are very small and negative, giving rise to very large ratios and ambiguous signs.

24. Delinquencies (which are available only for aggregate mortgage and nonmortgage loan portfolios) were allocated among the four kinds of mortgages in proportion to their market values. Because delinquencies in 1984 are relatively small, this crude allocation method probably makes little difference, particularly for the averages, although it might have a significant effect on individual thrifts.

25. Consumer loans' book values were assumed to equal their market values due to their heterogeneity and short duration.

26. The servicing spread on a thrift's own mortgages is already included in the net cash flow attributed to those mortgages.

27. Further reductions in negative RAP net worth are recorded as negative percentages.

28. Data separating first and second mortgages, construction and other loans, fixed- and adjustable-rate mortgages were not reported in 1982.

29. Real estate held for investment is not included because it amounted to less than one-half of 1 percent of the assets at almost all southeastern thrifts. We inadvertently did not include brokered deposits and other than passbook deposits in this table; these liabilities are included in the other tables.

30. The approximately 150 thrifts that joined the fourth district either as de novos or the Maryland thrifts that joined the FSLIC are not included.

31. The year-end 1984 number excludes thrifts that ceased independent operations after 1984. One of these thrifts failed; we did not record the market values of thrifts that ceased operations for other reasons.

32. Congressional testimony by former FHLBB Chairman Danny Wall indicates that the targeting of smaller thrifts for closure was a consequence of the FSLIC's inability to resolve large institutions.

33. We failed to record brokered deposits and some other data for table 10.5, which was created early in the project.

34. The numbers decline over time as some thrifts failed or voluntarily merged.

35. The median market value percentages in 1987 and 1988 are −7.5 and −6.8. The large mean values are due primarily to two thrifts.

36. Because *GAP1* is an incomplete measure of duration, the coefficients estimated do not provide a sufficient measure of the magnitudes of the relationship between interest-rate risk and the independent variables specified.

37. The regulators calculated this gap number and, after March 1987, encouraged thrifts to minimize interest-rate risk through the use of capital credits.

38. The Financial Accounting Standards Board's Statement 91, which became effective after 15 December 1987, limits lenders' ability to record up-front fees in excess of associated expenses as current income.

39. Eight thrifts had to be dropped from the regressions because their locations were not on the data tapes.

40. The change in sample size as thrifts are closed or merge may affect the comparison of the annual coefficients estimated.

41. This is less than the $8,078 million in losses incurred by the southeastern thrifts; the balance was absorbed by net worth.

References

Barth, James R., George J. Benston, and Phillip R. Wiest. 1990. The Financial Institutions Reform, Recovery, and Enforcement Act of 1989: Description, Effects and Implications. *Issues in Bank Regulation* 13 (Winter):3–11.

Barth, James R., and Michael G. Bradley. 1989. Thrift Deregulation and Federal Deposit Insurance. *Journal of Financial Services Research* (September):231–60.

Barth, James R., R. Dan Brumbaugh, Jr., and Daniel Sauerhaft. 1986. Failure Costs of Government-Regulated Financial Firms: The Case of Thrift Institutions, Research Working Paper no. 123. Office of Policy and Economic Research, Federal Home Loan Bank Board, Washington, D.C.

Barth, James R., R. Dan Brumbaugh, Jr., Daniel Sauerhaft, and George H. K. Wang. 1985. Thrift Institution Failures: Causes and Policy Issues. *Proceedings of the Conference on Bank Structure and Performance,* Federal Reserve Bank of Chicago, 184–216.

Barth, James R., and Martin A. Regalia. 1988. The Evolving Role of Regulation in the Savings and Loan Industry. In *The Financial Services Revolution: Policy Directions for the Future,* ed. Catherine England and Thomas Huertas, 113–61. Boston and Washington, DC: Kluwer Academic Publishers and the Cato Institute.

Benston, George J. 1973. *Bank Examination.* New York University Graduate School of Business Administration, Institute of Finance (*The Bulletin*), nos. 89–90, May.

———. 1985. *An Analysis of the Causes of Savings and Loan Association Failures.* New York University Graduate School of Business Administration, Salomon Brothers Center for the Study of Financial Institutions (*Monograph Series in Finance and Economics*), Monograph 1985–4/5.

———. 1989. Direct Investments and FSLIC Losses. In *Research in Financial Services,* vol. 1, ed. George J. Kaufman. Greenwich, CT: JAI Press.

Benston, George J., Mike Carhill, and Brian Olasov. 1991. Market-Value vs. Historical Cost Accounting: Evidence from Southeastern Thrifts. In *Reform of Deposit Insurance and the Regulation of Depository Institutions in the 1990s: Setting the Agenda,* ed. James R. Barth and R. Dan Brumbaugh, Jr. New York: Harper Collins.

Benston, George J., and George G. Kaufman, 1990. Understanding the savings-and-loan debacle. *The Public Interest* 99 (April):79–95.

Benston, George J., and Michael F. Koehn. 1990. Capital Dissipation, Deregulation, and the Insolvency of Thrifts. Emory University, typescript.

Brumbaugh, R. Dan, Jr. 1986. Empirical Evaluation of the Determinants of Losses for the Federal Savings and Loan Insurance Corporation (FSLIC), 1982–1984. Washington, D.C.: Federal Home Loan Bank Board, February 28.

Carhill, Mike. 1989. Fourth District Thrift Profitability in 1988. *Federal Home Loan Bank of Atlanta Review* 38 (June):1–6.

Carhill, Mike, and Iftekhar Hasan. 1990. Mutual vs. Stock Behavior at Southeastern Thrifts. Federal Home Loan Bank of Atlanta, typescript.

Carhill, Mike, and Patrick D. Mauldin. 1989. A Critical Comparison of Alternative Thrift Management Strategies. *Federal Home Loan Bank of Atlanta Review* 38 (March):1–11.

Carron, Andrew S. 1982. *The Plight of the Thrift Institutions.* Washington, DC: The Brookings Institution.

Comptroller of the Currency. 1988. *Bank Failure: An Evaluation of the Factors Contributing to the Failure of National Banks*. Washington, DC: Government Printing Office.

FDIC (Federal Deposit Insurance Corporation). 1958. Operations of the Federal Deposit Insurance Corporation to Protect Depositors in Failing Banks, 1934–1958. *Annual Report,* 27–127.

Flannery, Mark J. 1989. Capital Regulation and Insured Banks' Choice of Individual Loan Default Risks. *Journal of Monetary Economics* 24 (September):235–58.

Fritz, Richard G. 1989. Florida's Housing Market: Prospects for the 1990s. *Federal Home Loan Bank of Atlanta Review* 38 (December):4–13.

Garcia, Gillian. 1988. The FSLIC is "Broke" in More Ways Than One. In *The Financial Services Revolution: Policy Directions for the Future,* ed. Catherine England and Thomas Huertas, 235–49. Boston and Washington, DC: Kluwer Academic Publishers and the Cato Institute.

Hasan, Iftekhar. 1989. More Branching is Increasing Competition for the Florida Thrift Industry. *Federal Home Loan Bank of Atlanta Review* 38 (December):14–24.

Horvitz, Paul. 1989. The Causes of Texas Bank and Thrift Failures. CBA Working Paper Series, no. 222. University of Houston, College of Business Administration.

Kane, Edward J. 1985. *The Gathering Crisis in Federal Deposit Insurance*. Boston, MA: MIT Press.

———. 1989. *The S&L Insurance Mess: How Did It Happen?* Washington, DC: Urban Institute Press.

Pilzer, Paul Zane, with Robert Dietz. 1989. *Other People's Money: The Inside Story of the S&L Mess*. New York: Simon and Schuster.

Pizzo, Stephen, Mary Fricker, and Paul Muolo. 1989. *Inside Job: The Looting of America's Savings and Loans*. New York: McGraw-Hill.

Rudolf, Patricia M., and Sharon Topping. 1988. Which Thrift Strategies Have Worked? *Federal Home Loan Bank Board Journal* 18 (December):16–20.

Strunk, Norman, and Fred Case. 1988. *Where Deregulation Went Wrong: A Look at the Causes Behind Savings and Loan Failures in the 1980s*. Washington, DC: U.S. League of Savings Institutions.

Welfling, Weldon. 1968. *Mutual Savings Banks: The Evolution of a Financial Intermediary.* Cleveland, OH: The Press of Case Western Reserve University.

Contributors

George J. Benston
Business School
Emory University
Atlanta, GA 30322

Ben S. Bernanke
Woodrow Wilson School of Public and International Affairs
Princeton University
Princeton, NJ 08544

Charles W. Calomiris
Department of Economics
Northwestern University
Evanston, IL 60208

Mike Carhill
Research Department
Federal Home Loan Bank of Atlanta
P.O. Box 105565
Atlanta, GA 30348

Bankim Chadha
External Adjustment Division
Research Department, Rm 9–518
International Monetary Fund
700 19th Street, NW
Washington, DC 20431

Barry Eichengreen
Department of Economics
787 Evans Hall
University of California
Berkeley, CA 94720

Peter M. Garber
Department of Economics
Box B
Brown University
Providence, RI 02912

Mark Gertler
Department of Economics
New York University
269 Mercer Street, 7th floor
New York, NY 10003

Gary Gorton
The Wharton School
University of Pennsylvania
Philadelphia, PA 19104

Patric H. Hendershott
Department of Finance
Hagerty Hall
Ohio State University
1775 South College Road
Columbus, OH 43210

R. Glenn Hubbard
Graduate School of Business
609 Uris Hall
Columbia University
New York, NY 10027

Harold James
Department of History
Princeton University
Princeton, NJ 08544

Anil Kashyap
Graduate School of Business
University of Chicago
1101 E. 58th Street
Chicago, IL 60637

Frederic S. Mishkin
Graduate School of Business
Uris Hall 619
Columbia University
New York, NY 10027

Brian Olasov
Long Aldridge & Norman
Marquis Two Tower, Suite 1500
285 Peachtree Center Avenue
Atlanta, GA 30303

Eduardo S. Schwartz
Anderson Graduate School of Management
University of California
405 Hilgard Avenue
Los Angeles, CA 90024

James D. Shilling
School of Business
322 Commerce Building
University of Wisconsin
1155 Observatory Drive
Madison, WI 53706

Steven Symansky
External Adjustment Division
Research Department, Rm 9–518
International Monetary Fund
100 19th Street, NW
Washington, DC 20431

Walter N. Torous
Anderson Graduate School of Management
University of California
405 Hilgard Avenue
Los Angeles, CA 90024

Mark J. Warshawsky
Mail Stop 89
Division of Research and Statistics
Board of Governors of the Federal Reserve System
Washington, DC 20551

Author Index

Subject Index

20. Malcolm W. Browne, "Signal Travels Farther and Faster Than Light," Thomas Jefferson National Accelerator Facility (Newport News, VA) online newsletter (July 22, 1997). Website: **www.cebaf.gov/news/internet/1997/spooky.html**.

21. This quotation from the project leader, professor Nicholas Gisin, is drawn from an article describing the experiment. "Geneva University Development in Photon Entanglement for Enhanced Encryption Security and Quantum Computers" (2000). Website: **www.geneva.ch/Entanglement.htm**.

22. Malcolm W. Browne, "Signal Travels Farther and Faster Than Light."

Chapter 2

1. *The Illuminated Rumi,* Coleman Barks, trans. (New York: Broadway Books, 1997): p. 13.

2. Quoted by Carl Seelig, *Albert Einstein* (Barcelona, Spain: Espasa-Calpe, 2005).

3. John Wheeler, from an interview with Mirjana R. Gearhart of *Cosmic Search,* vol. 1, no. 4 (1979). Website: **www.bigear.org/vol1no4/wheeler.htm**.

4. Ibid.

5. Joel R. Primack, a cosmologist at the University of California at Santa Cruz, "According to the big bang, space itself is expanding. I don't understand: If space is expanding, into what is it expanding?" an online article from the "Ask the Experts" section of the *Scientific American* Website: **www.sciam.com** (posted October 21, 1999). "According to modern cosmological theory, based on Einstein's General Relativity (our modern theory of gravity), the big bang did not occur somewhere in space; it occupied the whole of space. Indeed, it created space."

6. The Rig Veda, as cited in "Hinduism—Hindu Religion: Discussion of Metaphysics & Philosophy of Hinduism Beliefs & Hindu Gods." Website: **www.spaceandmotion.com/Philosophy-Hinduism-Hindu.htm**.

7. Ibid.

8. This effect was first reported in Russia: P.P.Gariaev, K.V. Grigor'ev, A.A. Vasil'ev, V.P. Poponin, and V.A. Shcheglov, "Investigation of the Fluctuation Dynamics of DNA Solutions by Laser Correlation Spectroscopy," *Bulletin of the Lebedev Physics Institute,* no. 11–12 (1992): pp. 23–30, as cited by Vladimir Poponin in an online article "The DNA Phantom Effect: Direct Measurement of a New Field in the Vacuum Substructure" (Update on DNA Phantom Effect: March 19, 2002). The Weather Master Website: **www.twm.co.nz/DNAPhantom.htm**.

9. Ibid.

10. Vladimir Poponin, "The DNA Phantom Effect: Direct Measurement of a New Field in the Vacuum Substructure," performed the Russian study again in 1995 under the auspices of the Institute of HeartMath, Research Division, Boulder Creek, CA.

11. Ibid.

12. Glen Rein, Ph.D., Mike Atkinson, and Rollin McCraty, M.A., "The Physiological and Psychological Effects of Compassion and Anger," *Journal of Advancement in Medicine,* vol. 8, no. 2 (Summer 1995): pp. 87–103.

13. Julie Motz, "Everyone an Energy Healer: The Treat V Conference" Santa Fe, NM, *Advances: The Journal of Mind-Body Health,* vol. 9 (1993).

14. Jeffrey D. Thompson, D.C., B.F.A., online article, "The Secret Life of Your Cells," Center for Neuroacoustic Research (2000). This article references the work of Thompson's colleague Dr. Cleve Backster and a book about

Backster's research of the same title. Website: **www.neuroacoustic.org/articles/articlecells.htm**.

15. The Institute of HeartMath was founded in 1991 as a nonprofit research organization "providing a range of unique services, products, and technologies to boost performance, productivity, health and well-being while dramatically reducing stress." For more information, please visit the Website: **www.HeartMath.com/company/index.html**.

16. Glen Rein, Ph.D., "Effect of Conscious Intention on Human DNA," Proceedings of the International Forum on New Science (Denver, CO: 1996).

17. Glen Rein, Ph.D., and Rollin McCraty, Ph.D., "Structural Changes in Water and DNA Associated with New Physiologically Measurable States," *Journal of Scientific Exploration,* vol. 8, no. 3 (1994): pp. 438–439.

18. Rein, "Effect of Conscious Intention on Human DNA."

19. Elaine Pagels, *The Gnostic Gospels* (New York: Random House, 1979): pp. 50–51.

20. Planck, "Das Wesen der Materie."

PART II

Chapter 3

1. Chief Seattle, "A Message to Washington from Chief Seattle." Website: **www.chiefseattle.com**.

2. From an interview with John Wheeler by Tim Folger, "Does the Universe Exist if We're Not Looking?" *Discover,* vol. 23, no. 6 (June 2002): p. 44.

3. Neville, *The Power of Awareness* (Marina del Rey, CA: DeVorss, 1961): p. 9.

4. Neville, *The Law and the Promise,* p. 57.

5. Neville, *The Power of Awareness,* pp. 103–105.

6. Ibid., p. 10.

7. Ibid.

8. Seelig, *Albert Einstein.*

9. Michio Kaku, *Hyperspace: A Scientific Odyssey Through Parallel Universes, Time Warps, and the 10th Dimension* (New York: Oxford University Press, 1994): p. 263.

10. C. D. Sharma, *A Critical Survey of Indian Philosophy* (Delhi, India: Motilal Banarsidass Publishers, 1992): p. 109.

11. Neville, *The Law and the Promise,* p. 13.

12. "The Gospel of Thomas," translated and introduced by members of the Coptic Gnostic Library Project of the Institute for Antiquity and Christianity (Claremont, CA). From *The Nag Hammadi Library,* James M. Robinson, ed. (San Francisco, CA: HarperSanFrancisco, 1990): p. 137.

13. "John 16:23–24," *Holy Bible: Authorized King James Version* (Grand Rapids, MI: World Publishing, 1989): p. 80.

14. *Prayers of the Cosmos: Meditations on the Aramaic Words of Jesus,* Neil Douglas-Klotz, trans. (San Francisco, CA: HarperSanFrancisco, 1994): pp. 86–87.

15. Amit Goswami, "The Scientific Evidence for God Is Already Here," *Light of Consciousness,* vol. 16, no. 3 (Winter 2004): p. 32.

16. *The Illuminated Rumi,* p. 98.

17. *The Expanded Quotable Einstein,* p. 205.

18. Jack Cohen and Ian Stewart, *The Collapse of Chaos: Discovering Simplicity in a Complex World* (New York: Penguin Books, 1994): p. 191.

19. One of the clearest sources for the mind-body connection was documented in a landmark study by James Blumenthal at Duke University. "Chill Out: It Does the Heart Good," Duke University news release (July 31, 1999) citing the technical study of the relationship between emotional response

and heart health, originally published in the *Journal of Consulting and Clinical Psychology*. Website: **www.dukemednews.org**.

20. A beautiful example of applying what we know about inner peace to a wartime situation is found in the pioneering study done by David W. Orme-Johnson, Charles N. Alexander, John L. Davies, Howard M. Chandler, and Wallace E. Larimore, "International Peace Project in the Middle East," *The Journal of Conflict Resolution,* vol. 32, no. 4, (December 1988): p. 778.

21. "The Gospel of Thomas," *The Nag Hammadi Library,* p. 134.

22. Joan Carroll Cruz, *Mysteries, Marvels, Miracles in the Lives of the Saints* (Rockford, IL: TAN Books and Publishers, 1997).

23. There are a number of accounts of the miraculous life of Padre Pio that include prophecy, miraculous scents, stigmata, and bilocation. The best source that I could find for this particular account during World War II is the Eternal Word Television Network Website: **www.ewtn.com/padrepio/mystic/bilocation.htm**.

Chapter 4

1. Holographic technology was invented in 1948 by Hungarian scientist Dennis Gabor. In 1971, Gabor was awarded the Nobel Prize in physics for the discovery that he made 23 years earlier.

2. Russell Targ in a special-features commentary with the producers of the 2004 motion picture *Suspect Zero,* directed by E. Elias Merhige (Paramount Studios, DVD release April 2005).

3. Ibid.

4. Ervin Laszlo, "New Concepts of Matter, Life and Mind," a paper published with permission by Physlink at the Website: **www.physlink.com/Education/essay_laszlo.cfm**.

5. Francis Harold Cook, *Hua-yen Buddhism,* p. 2.

6. Ibid.

7. Laszlo, "New Concepts of Matter, Life and Mind."

8. Karl Pribram, as quoted in an interview by Daniel Goleman, "Pribram: The Magellan of Brain Science," on the SyberVision Website: **www.sybervision.com/Golf/hologram.htm**.

9. Ibid.

10. "International Peace Project in the Middle East," *The Journal of Conflict Resolution,* p. 778.

11. "Matthew 17:20," *The New Jerusalem Bible: The Complete Text of the Ancient Canon of the Scriptures,* Standard Edition, Henry Wansbrough, ed. (New York: Doubleday, 1998): p. 1129.

12. Neville, *The Power of Awareness,* p. 118.

13. *101 Miracles of Natural Healing,* an instructional video in the step-by-step methods of the Chi-Lel™ method of healing created by founder Dr. Pang Ming. Website: **www.chilel-qigong.com**.

14. Neville, *The Power of Awareness,* p. 10.

Chapter 5

1. *The Expanded Quotable Einstein,* p. 75.

2. Yitta Halberstam and Judith Leventhal, *Small Miracles: Extraordinary Coincidences From Everyday Life* (Avon, MA: Adams Media Corporation, 1997).

3. Jim Schnabel, *Remote Viewers: The Secret History of America's Psychic Spies* (New York: Bantam Doubleday Dell, 1997): pp. 12–13.

4. Russell Targ, from *Suspect Zero* DVD.

5. Jim Schnabel, *Remote Viewers,* p. 380.

6. Benjamin Lee Whorf, *Language, Thought, and Reality,* John B. Carroll, ed.

(Cambridge, MA: MIT Press, 1964): pp. 58–59.

7. Ibid., p. 262.

8. Ibid.

9. Ibid., p. 59.

10. "Mathematical Foundations of Quantum Theory: Proceedings of the New Orleans Conference on the Mathematical Foundations of Quantum Theory," *Quantum Theory and Measurement,* J. A. Wheeler and W. H. Zurek, eds. (Princeton, NJ: Princeton University Press, 1983): pp. 182–213.

11. Yoon-Ho Kim, R. Yu, S.P. Kulik, Y.H. Shih, and Marlan O. Scully, "Delayed 'Choice' Quantum Eraser," *Physical Review Letters,* vol. 84, no. 1 (2000): pp. 1–5.

PART III

Chapter 6

1. Carlos Castaneda, *Journey to Ixtlan: The Lessons of Don Juan* (New York: Washington Square Press, 1972): p. 61.

2. Douglas-Klotz, *Prayers of the Cosmos,* p. 12.

3. Gregg Braden, *The God Code: The Secret of Our Past, the Promise of Our Future* (Carlsbad, CA: Hay House, 2005), p. xv.

Chapter 7

1. Ernest Holmes, *The Science of Mind* (from the original 1926 version, Part IID, Lesson Four: Recapitulation). Website: **ernestholmes.wwwhubs.com/sompart2d.htm**.

2. "The Gospel of Thomas," *The Nag Hammadi Library,* p. 136.

3. Ibid., p. 126.

4. Ibid., p. 136.

5. Ibid., p. 134.

6. Ibid.

Chapter 8

1. *Meetings with Remarkable Men: Gurdjieff's Search for Hidden Knowledge* (Corinth Video, 1987). This motion picture is based on the life of Gurdjieff and his relentless search to know the secret teachings of the past. His travels led him throughout the world and ultimately to a secret monastery believed to be located in the remote wilderness of mountainous Pakistan. These are the words that his teacher offered to him as he attained the mastership that he had searched for for so long.

2. Ten Years After, from their album *A Space In Time* (Capitol Records, 1971).

3. Daniel Dennett, *Consciousness Explained* (Boston: Back Bay Books, 1991): p. 433.

4. "The Thunder: Perfect Mind," *The Nag Hammadi Library,* pp. 297–303.

5. *Sefer Yetzirah: The Book of Creation,* Aryeh Kaplan, ed. (York Beach, ME: Samuel Weiser, 1997): p. 165.

INDEX

The letters *b* and *f* following a page number refer to a box or figure on that page.

ABOUT THE AUTHOR

New York Times best-selling author **Gregg Braden** has been a featured guest for international conferences and media specials, exploring the role of spirituality in technology. A former senior computer systems designer (Martin Marietta Aerospace), computer geologist (Phillips Petroleum), and technical operations manager (Cisco Systems), Gregg is considered a leading authority on bridging the wisdom of our past with the science, healing, and peace of our future.

For more than 20 years, Gregg has searched high mountain villages, remote monasteries, ancient temples, and forgotten texts to uncover their timeless secrets. His search led to the 2004 release of his paradigm-shattering book *The God Code,* revealing the actual words of an ancient message coded into the DNA of all life.

Between 1998 and 2005, Gregg's journeys into the monasteries of central Tibet revealed a forgotten form of prayer that was lost during the biblical edits of the early Christian church. In his 2006 release, *Secrets of the Lost Mode of Prayer,* he documents this mode of prayer that has no words or outward expression, yet gives us direct access to the quantum force that connects all things.

From his groundbreaking book *Awakening to Zero Point,* to the intimacy of *Walking Between the Worlds* and the controversy of *The Isaiah Effect,* Gregg's work awakens the best in each of us, inspiring our deepest passions with the tools to build a better world.

For further information, please contact Gregg's office at:

Wisdom Traditions
P.O. Box 5182
Santa Fe, New Mexico 87502
(505) 424-6892
Website: **www.greggbraden.com**
E-mail: ssawbraden@aol.com

NOTES

NOTES